LITERARY DEBATE

ALSO IN THE NEW PRESS POSTWAR FRENCH
THOUGHT SERIES

RAMONA NADDAFF
SERIES EDITOR

Histories: French Constructions of the Past
Postwar French Thought, Volume I
Edited by Jacques Revel and Lynn Hunt

Literary Debate

TEXTS AND CONTEXTS

DENIS HOLLIER
AND
JEFFREY MEHLMAN

TRANSLATED BY
ARTHUR GOLDHAMMER AND OTHERS
POSTWAR FRENCH THOUGHT, VOLUME II
RAMONA NADDAFF, SERIES EDITOR

NEW YORK

Published in the United States by The New Press, New York
Distributed by W. W. Norton & Company, Inc., New York

Library of Congress Cataloging-in-Publication Data

Literary debate : texts and contexts / edited by Denis Hollier and
Jeffrey Mehlman ; translated by Arthur Goldhammer and others.
      p.   cm. — (The New Press postwar French thought series ;
v. 2)
    Includes bibliographical references (p.   ).
    1. French literature—History and criticism.   2. French prose
literature—20th century.   3. Mallarmé, Stéphane, 1842–1898—
Criticism and interpretation.   I. Hollier, Denis.   II. Mehlman,
Jeffrey.   III. Goldhammer, Arthur.   IV. Series.
PQ116.L48   1999
840.9—dc21   99-19036
                                         CIP

The New Press was established in 1990 as a not-for-profit alternative
to the large, commercial publishing houses currently dominating the
book publishing industry. The New Press operates in the public interest rather than for private gain, and is committed to publishing, in
innovative ways, works of educational, cultural, and community value
that are often deemed insufficiently profitable.

www.thenewpress.com

Printed in the United States of America

9 8 7 6 5 4 3 2 1

To Guillaume de Lorris and Jean de Meung
In Memoriam

Contents

PART III
THE CENTRAL CASE OF MALLARMÉ

PART IV
NOVELTIES

PART V
PSYCHOANALYSIS AND LITERATURE

LITERARY DEBATE

Series Preface

In 1995 The New Press inaugurated its Postwar French Thought Series with the publication of *Histories: French Constructions of the Past,* edited by Jacques Revel and Lynn Hunt. Denis Hollier and Jeffrey Mehlman's *Literary Debate: Texts and Contexts* marks the second volume in this series. Forthcoming volumes include *Antiquities* (Nicole Loraux, Gregory Nagy and Laura Slatkin) and Philosophy (Etienne Balibar and John Rachjman). The aim of The New Press Postwar French Thought Series is to produce a multivolume anthology of seminal writings since 1945 that reflects the theoretical innovations and richness of French thought. Rather than reproduce excerpts of the canon of French authors, articles, and books already known to an English-speaking audience, the editors intend to generate, from the unique perspective of the Franco-American teams selecting texts, a new history of ideas proper to each discipline. Moreover, the collaboration of French and American editors has set in motion a productive dialectic which engaged them in the rethinking of their own disciplines. The resulting history will necessarily include texts and authors with whom specialists and non-specialists alike are familiar. But the context and problematics within which editors situate them will allow for the inclusion of other forgotten and unknown writings and thinkers whose dynamic influence has been ignored by previous critics.

RAMONA NADDAFF

Permissions

DENIS HOLLIER,
JEFFREY MEHLMAN, RAMONA NADDAFF

Preface

Philippe Sollers, in a moment of apparent Anglophobia rare for a native of
Bordeaux, once wrote of his disdain for those readers (or critics) who choose to
divide an author in order better to rule over him. The comment calls for two
remarks. First, the Sollers who made that observation in 1962 was plainly not
the Sollers (or at least *Tel Quel*, the journal he edited, was not yet the *Tel Quel*)
whose model of the self-divided text would make so resounding a difference in
the years that followed. Second, in the present case, for the most obvious reasons, the reader, in any event, will not have a choice.

The editors of this specific volume found themselves impelled to embrace
the series editor's wager of assigning a French and an American editor to col-
laborate. Given French fears of an inexorable Americanization of France, a
tradition whose seeds are at least as old as Tocqueville, and American anxieties
(or jubilation) at the utter Gallicization of literary studies, it might have been
possible, after all, to expect these concerns to coincide and bring about a more
or less seamless web of a book. Yet if the inspiration behind the project meant
anything, the editors, a Frenchman long resident in the United States, and an
American long a student of France, would of necessity be working at cross
purposes. (Chiasmus, as Paul de Man used to say, is a particularly strong figure.) And such, to the surprise of both editors—who have been friends for a
quarter of a century—proved to be the case. Out of modesty, the French editor
was drawn most often to the pungently (or drolly) characteristic. The American editor, on the other hand, tended more often than not—also out of
modesty—to the authors he had found most enduringly insightful. Each re-
viewed the selections of the other, argued, cajoled, and was finally won over by
the case made by the other's interpretation of the project. For this reason, we
have included two orienting essays along with this prefatory note: the first,
"Literature After Silence," introduces the volume; the second, "*Ad Centrum?*",
precedes the central sections and speaks to what is in telling ways the volume's
core.

A word on the book's organization. Beyond its nine chapters, it may be regarded as divided into three main sections. The first (Parts I and II) and the last
(Parts VII–IX) offer, in more or less chronological order, programmatic statements about the nature and future of literature as an institution. The first sec-

tion spans the Liberation and the Cold War years, the last the period that followed decolonization and May '68 (to mention two symbolically charged references). This historical perspective, revealing a literature destabilized by its historical context, is framed by discussions of the question of commitment, which was raised at the beginning of the half-century and raised anew as that period came to an end.

In between, close to the volume's center, an argument is made for the odd centrality of the case of Mallarmé. Our intention in Part III, however, has been less to offer an anthology of recent approaches to the poet than to show the extent to which the reading of Mallarmé over the last fifty years has served as a prism within which the most luminous tendencies of recent French thought as a whole may be captured and understood. Indeed, it has been our sense that much of what has thrived in this country under what is probably the misnomer of "literary theory"—and particularly the fertile field of psychoanalytic and para-psychoanalytic commentary on literature represented in our Part V— may be meaningfully construed as nothing so much as a series of lessons culled from the ever-more attentive reading of Mallarmé.

Throughout the composition of the volume, an amused reference to *Le Roman de la rose,* the jointly authored masterpiece of the thirteenth century, served as consolation and warning. The good news, regarding *Le Roman de la rose*, was that the incompatibility between the two authors' perspectives has long been seen as a principal source of the work's distinction, the bad that it took several centuries for that truth to sink convincingly in. In an era of ever shorter publishing cycles, it is our hope that to whatever extent the first part of that proposition—the good news—is applicable to the present case, the applicability of the second, at least, will be minimal.

From beginning to end and in between, many colleagues and friends have contributed to the making of *Literary Debate*. Timothy Hampton, Martin Jay, Lawrence Kritzman and Susan Suleiman provided invaluable comments and suggestions on the selection of texts and the volume's overall conception. Grace Farrell and Ted Byfield assured the careful preparation and production of the manuscript. Jessica Blatt's editorial assistance and advice were crucial at every stage of our work. André Schiffrin was an influential participant in our dialogues, providing necessary and important moments for reflection and revisions. Finally, we would like to thank Arthur Goldhammer for his eloquent and intelligent translations, his irreplaceable contribution to *Literary Debate*.

DENIS HOLLIER

The Pure and the Impure: Literature After Silence

The change that the concept of literature has undergone—a change
made manifest in France by movements associated with the labels
"new novel," "new criticism," and "structuralism"—did not stem
directly from World War II, since it began long before. Nevertheless, the war did hasten recognition of a fundamental crisis, a turning point whose significance we still cannot fathom for want of a
language.

— Maurice Blanchot, *"Guerre et littérature," L'Amitié,* p. 128

A STRANGE VICTORY

1945: The date is not ill chosen as a starting point for an anthology of recent
French literary thought, for it was the year of literature's enthusiastic and unconditional surrender to history. Never before had literature followed so
closely on the heels of events. Never before had it pondered its (historical) *premises* in the hope that they might reveal its essence, duties, destiny.

The aftermath of one victory is never like that of another. Among the
French intelligentsia, the armistice of 1918 had triggered an almost unanimous
farewell to ideological arms. In 1919, when *La Nouvelle revue française* resumed publication after a four-year hiatus, its first issue opened with an editorial by Jacques Rivière calling for a "demobilization of intelligence." France,
Rivière continued, "no longer wants its prestige to be the sole reason behind the
ideas that we [writers] formulate."[1]

In 1945 things were completely different. To begin with, as the reader will
see in the excerpt from Simone de Beauvoir's *The Mandarins* included in this
volume, France had a hard time dealing with this new victory, which was even
harder to think of as a French triumph than that of 1918 had been. Indeed, the
French were tempted at times to see the victory, paradoxically, as an irrevocable judgment that would henceforth relegate their country to a minor role on
the world stage. The period that began in 1940 with what Marc Bloch called "a
strange defeat" ended in 1945 with a no less strange victory.

In free France (Paris was liberated in August 1944, the rest of the country in the months that followed), the year 1945 marked the advent of a politics of reconstruction whose two main facets were purges (of wartime collaborators) and nationalizations. How did this affect literature? In at least one respect: Jean-Paul Sartre drew on this bipolarity to define his program for *littérature engagée* or "committed literature" in the editorials he wrote for the first issues of *Les Temps modernes* (developed and published two years later in his book *What Is Literature?*)

In his "Presentation," reproduced below, and in countless contributions to the political and literary debates of the postwar period, Sartre, true to the spirit of the purges, denounced the myth of the writer who claims to be unfettered by responsibility. He argued that a writer must know that writing entails a commitment, and he must also know what it commits him to. Literature thus marched in step with the purges. But this was just the beginning. One month later, Sartre's second editorial corrected certain mistaken impressions that his first had given rise to. It was at this point that he raised the issue of nationalization. The writer, he insisted, assumes his responsibilities *alone*. The literary function bestowed responsibility, but that responsibility must not be interpreted too pragmatically: the writer's commitment must not be mistaken for a form of national service.

This second editorial was entitled "The Nationalization of Literature." In it, Sartre painted a portrait of a France gripped by self-doubt after the war and clinging to its last prized possession—literature. At stake, however, was no longer the essence of France, as in 1919, but her very existence. No longer was the claim that literature—like the idea of infinite substance in a finite soul, according to Descartes—had always and forever been inscribed in the concept *France*. Now the concern was not with eternity but with history. Writers were being summoned to assume their responsibilities because, from now on, the existence of France would depend on them and them alone.

Sartre, just back from the United States, was plainly irritated by this existential blackmail and by his having been sent on what he perceived as a propaganda mission. He had recently given up his teaching career. If he spoke of assuming responsibility, it was not in order to secure himself a position in another ministry. The affirmation of the writer's responsibility, a crucial plank in the platform of literary commitment, was thus closely linked to a refusal to identify with the territorially defined nation. In this respect, one might view Sartre's position as an early act of resistance to what Marc Fumaroli, in a very different spirit, would denounce forty years later as *l'Etat culturel*.

FROM THE REPUBLIC OF SILENCE
TO THE REPUBLIC OF LETTERS

The physical *purge* would not in itself matter so much if the will to *purification* were greater.

—Vladimir Jankélévitch, "Dans l'Honneur et la dignité,"
Les Temps modernes, 1948, p. 2259

Purges and nationalizations, the defining features of postwar French politics, were thus re-inscribed with opposite signs in the platform of committed literature. Nationalization was banished from literary space; purges were admitted. Sartre's "Presentation" was written against the backdrop of the purge trials, most notably that of Robert Brasillach, who was executed for his crimes. Sartre had nothing but ironic scorn for the false naïveté of those who defended collaborationist writers such as Brasillach: "Does the stuff a man writes actually commit him?" If literature, discredited by the irresponsible anarchism of the interwar years, was again to become respectable, writers must learn, and be seen to have learned, that they were responsible for their words—on pain of death by firing squad. *Les Temps modernes* hailed the purge trials for ushering in a society that would ask more of its writers than to be entertainers: a society in which writers would knowingly risk death for what they wrote. Writing is meaningful, in other words, only in a context in which the writer inscribes his death on the horizon of his utterances (or at the very least inscribes his utterances on the horizon of his death).

The vast majority of literary professionals subscribed to this program. Among the few exceptions was Georges Duhamel, who worried about bestowing on writers "the redoubtable honor of being dealt with harshly."[2] With the lesson of recent events fresh in mind, nearly all declared themselves ready to enter into a Faustian bargain, to sign their texts in their own blood, to run risks, to assume responsibilities. As to those responsibilities, Sartre wrote that "the Occupation has taught us ours."

Words are commitments. They are followed by effects. Hence they can incriminate. The extent of the writer's responsibility was to start with a matter for the penal code. Yet the purge trials should not be allowed to serve as a smokescreen. To indict individuals for what they had said, written, or printed was but a first step, a legal matter; literature was something else, something greater. A writer is not simply responsible for and through his words; he is also responsible for and through his silences. To be sure, he is as accountable as anyone else for what he says—but as a writer he is also accountable for what he does not say. Brasillach and others of his ilk had been condemned for incitement to murder. Yet one could be innocent of that charge and still be guilty of failing to assist a person in danger—also a crime. For Sartre, in fact, this was the literary crime par excellence. Silence itself could be incriminated in the name of responsibility: not legal responsibility in the narrow sense but moral, historical, if not humanitarian responsibility. Take Flaubert: his silences, the blanks in his texts, are significant. Thus Sartre could write, "I hold Flaubert and the Goncourts responsible for the repression that followed the Commune because they didn't write a line to prevent it."

Not all silences are alike, however. Flaubert refused to utter a saving word. He was in a position to speak, but instead he held his peace. This supportive silence had nothing in common with the silence of protest practiced by writers either active in or sympathetic to the Resistance who refused to publish during the Occupation. Despite the differences, however, both were still writerly silences, literary strategies. But there was also a third type of silence: the literal silence of the resistant who, when tortured, chose to die rather than speak. There was nothing literary about it. That is why it fascinated Sartre the writer: between the martyr to good and the martyr to evil, between the sublime heroism of the rank-and-file *résistant* who paid with his life for the words he refused to utter and the abject heroism of the collaborator who paid with his life for the filth he had written, the committed writer's service was comparatively modest. Whether it took the form of dignified silence or courageous pronouncement, that service entitled him to respect. But it was never a matter of life and death.

The "resistantialist" myth thrived on a certain romanticism of silence. Whenever Sartre mentions the Resistance, the word silence follows with the predictability of a leitmotif. For example, an article he published in *Les Lettres françaises* just after the Liberation, describes the years of occupation as "The Republic of Silence." And there are the descriptions of those dark years scattered throughout *What Is Literature?*. "Beaten, burned, blinded, shattered, most resistants nevertheless refused to talk," Sartre wrote. "They bit their tongues, and man was born of their silence."[3]

They bit their tongues, wrote Sartre. They were silenced, wrote Jean Paulhan.[4] They were doubly silent: they did not talk, and they would never again speak. They chose the unwitnessed heroism of a silence from which they would never return, from which no witness would ever emerge—an unattestable silence, forever "out of print," which would leave no trace because their refusal to speak marked an irrevocable withdrawal from any possibility of exchange.

More than anything else, literary commitment expressed a (contradictory) wish to keep faith with this silence. How could any writer survive the republic of silence? How could any writer survive without betraying it? How could he keep faith with it after the republic of letters was restored? How could he keep faith with it in writing? How could he bear witness to a silence that had no witnesses? It was awareness of this same double bind that impelled Francis Ponge, the poet of *Le Parti pris des choses*, to write, "The mute world is our sole fatherland."

It was not just a matter of "exercises in silence" (to borrow the title of a clandestine journal published briefly during the Occupation). Silence—literal, not literary silence—was the wellspring of the Sartrian theory of committed literature, a theory whose first goal was to recover for literature the capital of authenticity that a nonliterary Resistance had accumulated in silence, *through* its silence.[5]

AUTHENTICITY IN EVERYDAY LIFE

What is striking in many retrospective accounts of everyday life in occupied France is the tinge of bitterness and disillusion—a note of something close to regret. Why this nostalgia?

In reading memoirs of the Occupation one often has the impression that the emergency laws of the time suspended the Heideggerian opposition between the authentic and the everyday. With language itself subject to restriction, everyday life, reduced to near silence, escaped the tyranny of the trivial to become a realm of existential authenticity. Because every speech act was a de facto infraction, even the simplest, most routine exercise of language bore the stamp of authenticity, that hallmark of decisions taken in the face of death. "We had lost all our rights," Sartre wrote, "beginning with the right to speak." Thus "each and every individual choice was authentic because it was made in the presence of death."[6] Here, there is nothing corporatist about Sartre's "we." In these sentences, literature clearly is not at issue; or, rather, it has forfeited its privileges. Sartre is talking about each and every individual. The Occupation, he says, raised everyday speech to a level of authenticity traditionally associated with the literary use of language. It allowed everyone to achieve an authenticity through language which, in more normal circumstances, remained a monopoly of literature.

At the Liberation, however, authenticity and everyday life went their separate ways. The restoration of free speech deprived speech acts of the capital of authenticity that had been accumulated in the silence of the dark years. Literature itself felt ill at ease in the tolerant postwar publishing climate, as if it had grown too small for its breeches. If language achieved authenticity by daring to violate a taboo, how was that authenticity to be preserved once the rights of language had been restored? The advancement of an aesthetic of formal transgression, an insistence on the essentially transgressive character of literary language (the definition of literariness as infraction, as deviant linguistic behavior) opened up a niche of illegality that allowed the conjunction of literature with authenticity to survive the Occupation.

For literature, then, freedom of speech became the most pernicious of the dangers to which it was subjected. Literature rejected its rightful status and defined itself as a discourse that, in the deepest sense, claims no rights other than, in the case of Maurice Blanchot's "terrorist," the "right to death."[7] Literature needed to be fundamentally taboo, illegitimate in its very essence. A literary utterance was first and foremost an unauthorized utterance. What authentic writer would agree to speak on command? In order to survive in the postwar climate, therefore, literature was obliged to re-invent itself along the lines of a secret society, or at any rate a secession, an internal exile. And now that circumstances no longer required it to remain underground, it had to accomplish this without a historical excuse.

Shortly after the Liberation, Raymond Queneau noted a change in the behavior of subway riders. During the Occupation they had read books—Plato, Montaigne, *Gone with the Wind* ("in early 1941 one still saw an innocent soul or two lost in a German grammar, but their kind soon disappeared"). Now, however, they read newspapers.[8] The press was the first and primary beneficiary of the simultaneous restoration of newsprint and freedom of speech. Did this success come at the expense of books and literature? There is no denying the fact that for a literature that, under the dual patronage of Mallarmé and Heidegger, had only yesterday linked its fate to the possibility of authentic speech, the liberalism of the media represented the threat of a fall from *la parole parlante* into *la parole parlée*, to borrow a distinction first made by Maurice Merleau-Ponty and widely repeated: a fall, in other words, into the one-dimensionality of everyday speech, which threatened to erase the difference between the literary and the nonliterary to the profit of the latter.

Nostalgia for the prohibitions of the Occupation was sustained by a widespread fear that the media somehow threatened to deprive literature of what Pierre Bourdieu would later call its "distinction." This fear lent a distinct anti-liberal cast to the various attempts to defend literature. Sacralized as rarely before, literature marched in the vanguard of a crusade against media barbarism. It was enlisted in a battle against faceless information and the routinization of daily existence (*la sérialisation de la quotidienneté*), in which the main targets were mass culture in both its American and Soviet forms—market and party, advertising and propaganda.

Several of the texts included in the present volume relate to this Cold War aesthetic, whose French version was best formulated by André Malraux. Indeed, Malraux would make it the linchpin of his cultural policy, invoking the aesthetic deterrence of what he called *haute culture* to repel both adversaries. "How can we keep psychological techniques from destroying the quality of human intelligence?" Francis Ponge, for his part, linked poetry (*donner un sens plus pur aux mots de la tribu*, in Mallarmé's phrase) to a project of linguistic purification, or semantic cleansing, as we see in his brief diatribe against the idolators of radio, the new cultural garbage can. Louis Aragon's embarrassed response to attacks by working-class readers upset by his decision to publish Picasso's portrait of Stalin in the communist literary magazine he edited sheds a similar light on the kinds of difficulties that literature encountered when it braved the eddies that swirl around the dividing line between high and low.

LITERATURE AND THE EXPERIENCE OF DEATH

Language, if it was to be authentic, had to be raised to the level of death. At times this requirement could be taken almost literally, as in the bullfighting aesthetic that Michel Leiris elaborated before the war: to achieve authenticity, Leiris had argued, the writer would have to face the same risk that a bullfighter faced in the arena. This literalism would not survive the war, however, and Leiris would modify his aesthetic in "The Autobiographer as Torero" (published in *Les Temps modernes* in 1947 and included below). The writer, he conceded, was not exposed to any actual threat of death, "other than in a manner external to his art." Sartre expressed similar reservations about the inflated resistantialist rhetoric of risk. True, the Occupation had taught us our responsibilities. Nevertheless, quite apart from the fact that the responsibility of the resistance writer was not measured by the same yardstick as that of the collaborator, the risks that resistance writers ran were minimal compared with those involved in less symbolic acts. "When we wrote in clandestinity, our risks were small compared to the printer's," he recalled. "I have often felt ashamed of this."

Yet the renunciation of literalism did not lead to a corresponding renunciation of the thematics of death. True, the writing desk was no torture chamber. The writer did not literally place his life in danger simply by writing, nor was writing strictly speaking a choice of self in the face of death. And yet the exaltation of literature in the existential discourse of the period was associated with the project of extending the values of authenticity beyond literal risk, whether in the bull ring or elsewhere. Language could be raised to the level of death in nonliteral ways, as we see with Maurice Blanchot.

What mattered was not whether literature as a type of speech act did or did not imply an actual risk of death but whether, through literature, language itself could achieve—as Blanchot, citing Rilke, put it—a proper relation to death. The relation between death and language was in a sense reversed: instead of death bestowing authenticity on language, it was language that bestowed authenticity on death. (Blanchot linked Rilke's distinction between "inessential" and "authentic" death to Mallarmé's distinction between "inessential" and "authentic" language.) Previously the question was how to prevent the rituals of the republic of letters (the animal kingdom of the spirit) from tarnishing the authenticity of those who had chosen to die in silence. Blanchot stood this problem on its head: it is precisely language, he argued, that allows death to realize itself as my most intimate possibility. Outside of language, man has no hope of realizing his being toward death. It is only in and through language that he can achieve a just, authentic relation to death.[9]

In these meditations of Blanchot's, the silence of the torture chambers in which the martyrs of the Resistance had suffered—a primal scene common to many postwar reflections on literature—had begun to fade into an already-legendary past. One more step and it would become possible for literature to achieve authenticity without even thematizing its relation to death in any way, whether literal or literary: literature could now dispense with death.

According to Heidegger's celebrated formula, dying, my most intimate possibility (or "ownmost" possibility, as Heidegger's translators put it), is the one thing that no one can do for me, the one thing that I cannot do for anyone else. In the new stylistics of authenticity, the exclusion of vicariousness, the ban on substitution implied by Heidegger's proposition, was applied to language. Literature exists whenever a writer speaks a language that is his alone, whenever his language becomes his signature. What he says, he says alone: he is not just the only one *to* say it but the only one who *can* say it. Hence a work interrupted by the death of its author must remain forever unfinished. Writing is the one thing that no one else can do for me.

Earlier I alluded to Merleau-Ponty's distinction between *la parole parlante* and *la parole parlée*, which is taken from one of the most celebrated chapters of *The Phenomenology of Perception*. As we have seen, *la parole parlante*, the "authentic act of expression," is to be found according to Merleau-Ponty in "the child's first words and the words of the writer."[10] In other words, utterance becomes expressive by forging a language for which there is no model. It is like primitive art, art created in the absence of museums. Nothing is said here about death, only birth. The words of literature are not last words but always first. The stylistics of authenticity allow literature to dispense with death.

THE DEATH OF THE AUTHOR (VERSION ONE)

To reduce is to "drop" something, or, rather, to "eliminate" an unnecessary element for the sake of something else buried or hidden by such excess. Hence it is to *purge* or *purify*.

—Jean Beaufret, "Note sur Husserl et Heidegger,"
in *Introduction aux philosophies de l'existence*
(Paris: Denoël, 1971), p. 170

The sarcophagi of Roman "intellectuals" were frequently decorated with bas reliefs depicting the deceased among the Muses, listening to music, or reading. This motif was not simply a reminder of the dead man's tastes (and of his class, for frequenting the Muses was already a sign of social distinction). Future-oriented, the scene was more performative than representative. The very walls of the tomb in which a man's mortal remains were laid to rest were meant to offer to those he left behind a preview of the precincts for which his liberated soul had departed. To frequent the Muses during one's lifetime was to purify the soul, which thereby earned a kind of guarantee of immortality.[11] A soul became immortal by not waiting until the body had breathed its last to cleanse itself of the sin of existence. To frequent the Muses was an ascetic activity whose cathartic effect (here a phenomenologist might speak of *épochè*, or reduction) would be to sever the soul from its empirical substrate. Unless one abandons the notion of author entirely, it would be difficult to avoid some such ascetic model in which the soul is purified by music (or letters); and Merleau-Ponty himself, despite his eudemonism, allowed it to shape his descriptions of literary creation. If a writer's life is to become the basis of his oeuvre, he wrote, the writer must first, "in order *to become true,* prepare himself in a way that cuts him off from the fellowship of the living."[12]

This is what might be called the existential version of the death of the author. Implicit in it is a testamentary conception of the work. The work is not considered for itself but, rather, for its cathartic effects. Here, the crucial division is not between the man and the work, as in traditional criticism, but between the man and the author, separated one from the other by the work. In this view, the work is first and foremost a device for converting a man into an author. Thus, Blanchot can place a crisis at the center of his study of Lautréamont—a crisis, he remarks, "whose disturbing, uncanny quality will be familiar to anyone who writes."[13] In other words, the literary field is no longer centered on works without authors but, rather, on authors who owe their existence to their works.

But what is this creature, Lautréamont the author, which the actual writer Isidore Ducasse must become? In speaking of the author of the *Chants de Maldoror*, Blanchot uses a strange formula: "He had only the remotest inkling of the person he would have to become within a creation that would create him so that he might create it." Elsewhere he observes how remarkable it was that it was possible for words to "emanate from this as yet non-existent Lautréamont, who thereby came into being."[14] The temporal configuration implicit in the syntax of this sentence (with its discordant tenses) points to a genetic scheme beyond the narrative competence of biography. The chronological succession of what (linear) literary history calls *life* is disrupted, as if, in order to approach the origin of an oeuvre, one must abandon the vulgar "linear" conception of time. The experience in which the work originates suspends empirical chronology. The work originates in a self that has freed itself from its origins— from its life, its biography. In other words, an *origin* is never empirical. The central concept of Sartre's existential psychoanalysis, that of the original choice, also points toward a concept of origin beyond any chronological inscription, since it refers to the choice that man makes of himself in the presence of death.

The rejection of biography implicit in these propositions would be the major premise of what was referred to in the 1950s as "the new criticism." One of the great merits of thematic criticism was to have developed a model of reading in terms of which an oeuvre could be seen to possess a coherence that owes nothing to the narrative structure of a "life." Jean Starobinski, for example, began his study of Rousseau, *Transparency and Obstruction*, with the statement "this is not a biography." Roland Barthes followed suit: his goal in *Michelet par lui-même* was "to discover the structure of an existence (I do not say a life)."[15] The work is not yet enclosed within its own self-referential structure; Barthes was not yet proposing an immanent textual criticism. For him, the referent of the work was what he called "existence" (German: *Dasein*), in order to make it clear that it was not "biographable" empirical reality he had in mind. Existentialism (from which thematic criticism drew its inspiration) was most definitely not "biographism." Yet this repudiation of biography could lead to strange, ephemeral alliances. For example, it enabled Barthes, in the sentence just quoted, to associate with seeming innocence the two words *existence* and *structure*, which would soon become the rallying cries of two antagonistic version of the death of the author. For Barthes in 1954, however, they could still be joined in common cause against biography.

THE DEATH OF THE AUTHOR (VERSION TWO)

The heyday of French structuralism can be dated from the publication of Claude Lévi-Strauss's *Structural Anthropology* in 1958. In the previous year, Lévi-Strauss had chosen to devote his seminar at the Collège de France to the burial rituals of Indians in southern California, rituals intended, "if one can put it this way, to liquidate the soul and all notions associated with it."[16] In other words, these rituals sought a symbolic efficacy opposed to that of the Roman sarcophagi mentioned earlier, which offered a guarantee against just such a liquidation of the soul. This choice of subject, which Lévi-Strauss approached with evident sympathy and even enthusiasm, is a good example of structuralism's scathing hostility to the pathos of the existentialist SOS.[17] Among his targets, direct and indirect, were any number of unanalyzed religious survivals in the soul-searching existentialist notion of "person."

In the course of a memorable debate with Paul Ricoeur, Lévi-Strauss offered a pithy response to the philosopher's objection: "You seem to me to be linking the notion of discourse to the notion of person."[18] Unlinking them turned out, in retrospect, to have been the first structuralist act: in every field in which it intervened (literature included), structuralism sought to develop protocols for analyzing discourse without reference to any personalizing agency whatsoever. The extraordinary promotion of myth to the status of exemplary structuralist discourse came about precisely because the enunciation of myth is independent of any personal premise. Indeed, Lévi-Strauss defined myth as a narrative "for which there is no personal transmitter."[19]

This voiding of the authorial function suggested a new version of the death of the author. It differed from the previous version as the *nihil privativum* differs from the *nihil negativum* in Kant's essay on negative quantities. As we have seen, the first (existentialist) version of the death of the author conformed to the logic of cathartic sacrifice, a sort of tragic purification by fire. The second (structuralist) version was essentially secular and hygienic. It was rather like what anthropologists call a second burial. "The author," Gérard Genette writes, "becomes an author only when he ceases to be a man and becomes a literary *machine*."[20] Both versions agree that the author has turned his back on life (in the biographical sense). In one case, however, he does so in order to become soul (a purified self, a transcendental ego), in the other to become a (soulless) device. While the author may not yet have vanished altogether, he had been reduced to little more than an accessory in what Louis Althusser would call a "process without a subject."

In this respect, structuralism was a vast effort to "desensitize" the notion of person. If that notion survived, plucked out of its "personalist" context, it did so only after being divested of its ontological connotations: the individual, transcendent, substantial, even immortal soul, and so on. No longer did it refer to an independent subjective substance (a psyche).[21] The shift from psychology to linguistics plunged the notion of person into a spartan minimalism (*minima personalia*), shrinking it to what Emile Benveniste called an "empty sign": the subject of the verb, a mere linguistic access code (password, user ID) to speech without referential anchorage.[22] There is no one (no person, no longer a person) outside the text—*pas de je qui soit hors jeu*, which one might translate "no play, no say." What remained, then, were discourses (rather than oeuvres) with no personal ties: selfless, orphaned discourses, on the edge of anonymity.

Structuralism, far from being repelled by anonymous discourse, actually had a predilection for unauthenticatable texts. Indeed, the fact that myths have no single authentic version was for Lévi-Strauss a strong argument in their favor.[23] Structuralists displayed a decided taste for texts that could be studied apart from any personal reference such as popular literature and the products of mass culture, which, like myth, are not rooted in what Leo Spitzer called a "these texts having psychological etymology." For even if a popular novel has an author (as in the case of the James Bond novel on which Roland Barthes based his landmark "Structural Analysis of Narrative"), it would be pointless and absurd to read it as one would read a canonical work, looking to the author for a "creative personality." The author of such a novel is personally responsible for very few things in the production of his own book. Thus, structuralism's hostility to the hermeneutic coupling of author and authenticity encouraged the rehabilitation of a whole range of texts belonging to what Genette called appropriately, since it was in the context of an *hommage* to Lévi-Strauss, the "so to speak ethnographic area of literature,"[24] these texts having the same decentered marginality vis-à-vis the core curriculum of the European tradition as do non-Western civilizations. Once the literariness of a text ceased to be defined by its "personalizing" vocation and to be centered on some sort of "psychological etymology," functionalism could be extended to literary works themselves, where it could continue its work of dissolution. Once the literariness of a text ceased to be defined by its "psychological etymology," its "personological" vocation, the functionalist desubstantialization, which had

previously depersonalized the self, could be extended to the works themselves. Thus Genette could write: "There is, strictly speaking, no literary object
but only a *literary function,* which can devolve upon or flee from any object of
writing."

HIROSHIMA, IN FRANCE

HE: "What was Hiroshima to you, in France?"
SHE: "The end of the war."[25]

For Sartre, when a writer became committed, he assumed responsibility for the
historicity of the present. Practically nothing of this sensitivity to the historical
present remains in structuralism. Lévi-Strauss took antihistoricism to the extreme of suggesting that history might not be anything more than a Western
prejudice, and although his work was, deeply and in more than one way, contemporary with and attuned to the demise of empire, it never addressed the
post-colonial context as such.

Yet, apart from this historical context, the sudden proliferation of ethnological references in French thought and, more surprising still, in French literary
criticism is difficult to account for. Why did the entire culture suddenly seize
upon ethnology? Ethnology studies so-called ahistorical peoples: the new interest in ethnology has been seen as a way of turning one's back on history at the
very moment when history was calling into question the very existence of ahistorical peoples. Like the fabled fox that judged unripe those grapes it could not
reach, structural anthropology might be, for the European mind, what Sartre
called a magical solution—a way of thumbing one's nose at a history that was
moving beyond Europe's grasp. In some respects, this is not an inaccurate diag-
nosis, but it is incomplete and one-sided. Structuralism's antihistoricist bias
must itself be situated in historical perspective.

Furthermore, the structuralist wariness of traditional historicist constructs
was not wholly unfounded, for those constructs were ill-adapted to understanding the history that was in the process of unfolding. Perhaps one can put it
this way: the structuralist moratorium was a time-out necessary to take account
of the way in which the concept of history had itself been changed by several
factors. Notable among them was the disappearance of ahistorical peoples. Notable, too, was the fact that history was no longer the exclusive "intimate possibility" of what Husserl called the European consciousness (at any rate in its
empirical, geographical version).

Hiroshima, mon amour, the film by Alain Resnais and Marguerite Duras,
was released in 1958, the same year as Lévi-Strauss's *Structural Anthropology*. It
is a film based on a dual system of historical and geographical references and, as
such, a particularly eloquent testimonial to the postcolonial decentering of the
geopolitical narrative. The story is set in Hiroshima in 1957. There, a man and

a woman meet. In 1944–45 each of them experienced, in different ways and at opposite ends of the earth, the end of the war in a manner that made it difficult for either of them to share the general sense of that moment as a triumph—he because he is Japanese, she because, as a girl of eighteen on the day Nevers was liberated, she witnessed the murder of her lover, a German soldier, and fell victim herself to a postwar purge when she was subjected, as the penalty for her liaison, to the public humiliation of having her head shaved.

This encounter, which takes us back to the events surrounding the first issue of *Les Temps modernes*, allows us to measure the shift that had taken place since 1945. It was in October of that year that Sartre's journal commenced publication. The inaugural issue began with the "Presentation," which, as we have seen, seized on the purges as an opportunity to teach literature a lesson in responsibility. But this was not Sartre's only contribution; his topical article on "The End of the War," written just after the dropping of the two atomic bombs and Japan's subsequent surrender, portrays the French as disoriented, wary, and worried about their future in this "vast world Peace in which France is left with a very small place."[26] The war had ended far away, on the opposite side of the globe, leaving the French under the impression that this strange, remote victory had inaugurated a history that would no longer speak French. Of Sartre's two articles, then, one addressed the purges, the other the nuclear peace. But they did so separately. In 1945, Sartre was not (yet) able to collect his thoughts about Nevers and Hiroshima, the purges and the atomic bomb, under a single heading—and he was certainly not alone.

If the Resnais–Duras film had such a symbolic impact, it was in part because it offered a postcolonial version of what one might call, borrowing a phrase from a title of André Breton's, "communicating vessels." It attests to the emergence of a narrative space in which communication was initiated between voices, languages, places, and histories that had not previously spoken to one another.

French as a Second Language

> What is an event, for us? Something that happened elsewhere, without us, which nevertheless has an impact here and on us. So what is happening in the world, to the same extent as what is not happening here, cuts us off from the world.
>
> —Edouard Glissant, *Le Discours antillais*, p. 100

Surveys of French literature always take special pride in what has been achieved in the language outside France. Gustave Lanson and his heirs invariably paid due homage to the small European elite who saw to it that "our" language resounded in the corridors of Sans-Souci and Saint-Petersburg in the eighteenth century.

Since then, things have changed a great deal. In simple quantitative terms, it is an unavoidable fact that French today is spoken by more people outside France than inside. But the qualitative change is even more spectacular: simply put, French is spoken *en masse*. The "embassy French" that could once be heard throughout Europe has given way to a less "proper," more plebeian, more exotic, and phonetically more accented French. It is also no longer exclusively a language of the international elite of crowned and mitered heads: Frantz Fanon's French has replaced Frederick II's. The name *"francophonie"* has been bestowed on what might seem, if one were to judge according to the values once espoused by the Alliance Française, like a downscale version of the old aristocratic myth of the universality of the French tongue.

Accordingly, *Caliban parle*, the title that Jean Guéhenno gave to his 1928 book on the proletariat's then-recent emergence into humanist culture, might seem apt as well for the chapter on Francophone literatures that every up-to-the-minute history of French literature is now obliged to include. There is a problem, however: Guéhenno's Calibans were engaged in the class struggle. The history of their assertion of a right to self-expression could be cast as a national epic à la Michelet. With political emancipation came a right to symbolic self-government and a revival of ancient cultural rights (and riches): the people regained possession of a culture that had always been theirs, a culture in which they were, in a sense, already at home.

The postcolonial situation is quite different. To be sure, Caliban speaks—but he does so in a language upon whose shores he happens to have fetched up in the aftermath of a series of world-historical storms as traumatic as the tempest which, in Shakespeare's play, brought Prospero to Caliban's island.[27] In France, nobility used to be measured in quarters. With *francophonie* came a generation of writers without patents of linguistic nobility. The language in which they write is not irrigated by the sap of their genealogical tree. Their French is a graft, or, to borrow the botanical metaphor that Gilles Deleuze and Félix Guattari use in what could be called their "minority linguistics," a rhizome.[28] The Calibans of postcolonial literature do not come from the inner circles; they have plucked French from its etymological orbit. Their impact has been one not of decentralization, as with traditional regionalisms, but of a far more radical decentering: these foreign Frenchmen point toward a future in which the center of gravity of the French language might no longer be situated within the continental "hexagon."

Is a language cut from another (*un langage d'emprunt*) necessarily badly cut (*un langage "emprunté"*), a wordy suit that doesn't suit? "Their borrowed language," Edouard Glissant, somehow defiantly, writes of his fellow Creole writers, "forces them into a derisive use of the other's language."[29] To which Abdelkebir Khatibi echoes: "I write in French, a language that is not part of my heritage but in which I am a professional foreigner."[30] While Assia Djebar asks, in the introduction to her *Women from Algiers*, "I could say: 'stories translated from. . . ,' but from which language?"[31] Hélène Cixous thanks her mother: "It is she who makes the French language always seem foreign to me."[32] And even Jacques Derrida: "I have but one language, and it is not my own."[33] Abdelwahab Medded, for his part, has described the strangeness of seeing his own name transcribed into Roman characters on the covers of his books: it seemed somehow expropriated, his real name yet at the same time an assumed name, almost a pseudonym.[34] Each of these authors might subscribe in one way or another to Glissant's ironic comment: "They would rather I be more 'authentic,' indeed." For the writer whose only instrument is a language whose etymology is not inscribed in his memory, and who must write from a place not inscribed in the memory of his language, access to authorial status frequently offers nothing more than a parody of "authenticity."[35]

Merleau-Ponty, it will be recalled, offered two examples of "authentic acts of expression": "the child's first words and the words of the writer." But if, according to the philosopher of language acquisition, literature was for the speaking subject primarily a gift of eternal linguistic virginity, a gift with the power to restore to every speech act the tentativeness and solemnity of a first time, this Rousseauist myth has perished in a postcolonial situation where all literary practice must begin with the unavoidable experience of linguistic secondariness—French as a second language.

Instead of *parole parlante* and *parole parlée*, Merleau-Ponty sometimes opposes "authentic or transcendental language" and "empirical language." Postcolonial language emphasizes the empirical parameters of its own production. It is establishing a legitimating process that ignores transcendental ascesis, that is, the death (or disembodiment) of the author, in favor of verbalizing specific contingent, empirical traits of identity. Here, the literary self increasingly cleaves to its casual attributes, birthplace paramount among them, along with the birthmarks imprinted by events on bodies thus brought into the world.

What can be said about the re-inscription of such worldly geographical coordinates in the topography of what Blanchot called "literary space"? The emergence of Francophone literature has been associated with the return of a direct, literal referentiality. It coincides with the rearrangement of the ideological landscape that followed the collapse of the structuralist concordat between avant-garde literature and literary theory, between highbrow literature and literary science—contemporary, in other words, with what Pascal Quignard ten years ago hoped might prove to be a salutary "deprogramming of literature."[36]

Is it correct, however, to reduce this development to a form of resistance to theory, or antitheoretical backlash? Literary production, liberated from its theoretical superego (in a period that also witnessed a strong revival of literary biography), is once again prospering, undisciplined and unpunished, in the blind spots of yesterday's theory. Francophone literature, currently the site of the most promising explorations, fully identifies with this post-theoretical inspiration: "The difficulty of conceptualizing the literary," wrote Glissant, "may have been among the prerequisites of our emerging 'literature.'"[37] Thus, Fredric Jameson's characterization of the 1960s—"a prodigious release of untheorized new forces"[38]—paradoxically applies all the more to the uncharted "empiricities" (*empiricités*) to which the literature of the 1980s proved to be particularly receptive.

EGOGRAPHIES

> A few weeks after the trial in Rennes and the pardon, Félix Valloton published a cartoon that I remember quite vividly to this day. Captain Dreyfus, serious and somber, is sitting on a chair bouncing two joyful children on his lap. But when the younger one says, "Daddy, tell us a story," he turns away. A story? Captain Dreyfus was probably incapable of telling his own.
>
> —Léon Blum, *Souvenirs sur l'Affaire* (1935)

A fictional hero, writes René Girard, is someone whose tragic fate *"makes him capable of writing the novel"* in which he appears.[39] According to Léon Blum, this was an ability that Captain Dreyfus lacked. Strangely enough, the hero of the affair never became a Dreyfusard—he never succumbed to the "mystique" that surrounded him. At no time did he join his voice to the chorus of his supporters. Whence the narrative bifocality that played a part in the sense of incompleteness and lack of closure that many of Dreyfus's defenders felt at the conclusion of the affair. That conclusion—or absence of a conclusion—disappointed almost everyone.

In "The Storyteller," Walter Benjamin treats death, in a similar vein, as the crucial moment in narrative transmission. A man's real life, he writes, "and this is the stuff that stories are made of—first assumes transmissible form at the moment of his death."[40] Yet even if Dreyfus's actual death in 1935 served as the pretext for Léon Blum to write his memoir, he did not write it as the captain's heir; his story did not give voice to a dying man. Dreyfus died narratologically intestate. Some people bequeath their bodies to science, but Dreyfus refused to bequeath his voice to a narrator. He did nothing to lay the groundwork for his narrative afterlife.

To be sure, the fictional hero does not write his own story. Nevertheless, it is his death that gives birth to the voice that will assure his narrative survival. "The hero," Girard continues, "succumbs upon attaining the truth and bequeaths his lucidity to his creator." One could hardly put better the idea that the death of the hero is merely the metaphorical inscription, within the fictional narrative, of the preconditions of its narration. Death reduces the hero to a scapegoat whose sacrifice cleanses the author of the "sin of existing" and thereby transforms him into a fictional narrator. The hero's death is necessary to separate the narrative voice of the novel from the body of its author. Girard himself uses Edmund Husserl's terminology to describe this separation: "The art of the novelist," he writes, "is a phenomenological *époché*."[41]

The new empiricities are taking root in the literary realm by resisting these mechanisms of purification (of which the novel is one of the most effective). For instance, Philippe Lejeune, a poetician of the second generation, has re-shaped narratology by turning his attention to a new genre, away from the traditional concern with fictional narration (the novel) and toward what he calls "life stories." The poeticians of the first generation, Genette and Tzvetan Todorov, excluded autobiography from the scope of narratological investigation (in fact if not in principle), no doubt because of the inescapable impurity of its narrative devices. The reader of an autobiography is continually interrupted by an author who is always knocking at the door as if he had something to say. The author does not want to allow himself to be converted into a narrative voice or to be bracketed or purified out of existence.

The author of an autobiographical narrative—in other words, the individual who answers "in real life" to the name printed on the cover of the book—is all three persons of the narrative trinity rolled into one: author, narrator, and protagonist, one and triune. The "autobiographical pact," to borrow the title of Lejeune's first book, supplants the fictional pact of the novel, whose twofold distinction between author/narrator and hero/narrator, was the very basis of narratology.[42] But this resistance to the narrative *époché* is even more apparent when we shift our focus, as Lejeune has since done, from autobiography to the private diary, where the distinction between author and narrator ceases to make sense. As inconclusive as any genre of writing can be, the private diary has no other purpose than to allow an unconverted and perhaps unconvertible self to record its daily experience of inauthenticity.

Was Lejeune's intention to extend narratology to an unduly neglected area? Or to rehabilitate the first person, to defend its right to narratological respect by loosening the monopoly of the third person? Lejeune denies any such ambitions. For him, the goal is not so much to expand the scope of narratology as to distance himself from theory. "Despite the fact that I am sometimes labeled a 'theorist' of autobiography," he confesses in his last book, "I have read very little theory, and that was a long time ago. I am increasingly empirical."[43] Interestingly enough, moreover, Lejeune is coy enough to have written his study of the diary in the form of a diary.

When Dreyfus returned to Paris after his years of confinement on Devil's Island, he did not say to himself the sentence that, according to Las Cases's recollections in *Mémorial de Sainte-Hélène*, in diametrically opposed circumstances, inspired Napoleon at the moment of sailing away into exile, and that in Stendhal's *Le Rouge et le Noir* Julien Sorel, that inveterate reader of the *Mémorial de Sainte-Hélène*, borrows from him as he sits in prison in Besançon awaiting execution: "What a novel my life has been!" Instead, in keeping with the antinovelistic logic that was to make him a prototype of what no one yet called the antihero, he wrote down, in real time—all too real time—his experience of a hell that was, in every sense, of this earth. He wrote a diary.[44]

Writing Out of Print

Perversion is a term applied to a passion that has been diverted from its natural object. Foremost among the perversions to which literature is subject is bibliophilia, the fetishism of the letter detached from its meaning, isolated from the process of reading, frozen in the opacity of its plastic materiality. As we shall see in Roger Caillois's essay "The Ultimate Bibliophilia," included in this volume, it can achieve a degree of sophistication worthy of J.-K. Huysmans's creation, Des Esseintes. Books diverted from their intended purpose: Caillois speaks of "books that exist for the express purpose of not being read" but, rather, being touched, smelled, looked at, and so on. Paradoxically, however, even with all its sensual refinement, this celebration of the "body" of the text actually serves as a springboard for a more austere purpose: the radical separation of the two substances, soul and body, spirit and letter, and the subsequent liberation of a spiritual content totally independent of the factuality of the signifying graphic—an "out of print" spirit (or "pure potentiality," as Caillois puts it). "The existence of ideas," Merleau-Ponty wrote—and Caillois would surely have agreed with his premise—"is not to be confused with the empirical existence of means of expression."[45]

This distinction between ideas and their means of expression is not easy to maintain in one of the most recent approaches to the study of the literary text, genetic criticism, which proposes to examine "idealities" which have not yet matured to the point where they can be detached from their empirical underpinnings. The genetic critic studies not books but the manuscripts or drafts that precede publication, in other words, that exist prior to the "emergence" of literature (to borrow Glissant's description of postcolonial literature): his or her object is writing that has not yet grasped its own premises, not yet thrust its object across the dividing line between the empirical and the transcendental, the empirical and the authentic. The iterability inherent in the mark as such has yet to be realized in the form of actual iteration. A manuscript is an expanse of graphical marks that have stopped short of their destination, mechanical reproduction. It has the same status as letters that, as Derrida might say, have not even been posted, which have broken down at the start and therefore been condemned to a sort of site-specificity, frozen in the empirical materiality of their archive. What there is of a work (of the spirit, of ideality) exists, as the saying goes, "only on paper."

Structural poetics, according to Todorov, is concerned with "the general laws governing the inception of each individual work."[46] Genetic criticism takes the opposite tack: instead of working from the general to the particular, it delves into the archival record of some specific work for the purpose of tracing its inception in all its singularity and contingency. Rather than seek a pure origin, rather than search for what Sartre called an "original choice," genetic criticism catalogs the vestiges of an actual inception, the physical evidence of writing, the graphical marks produced by the movement of the writer's hand, the physical act that precedes the work's typographical idealization and mechanical reproduction. In *A Remembrance of Things Past*, for example, the genetic critic will look not for the narrative voice of a disembodied Marcel but for indications of the hand of Proust: the manuscript is treated as one vast fingerprint.

As it happens, Jean Paulhan has suggested—as did Jean Dubuffet in "Pilot Céline" (p. 88ff.)—that "genuine" literature is ontologically (or, as Paulhan puts it, "by nature") unpublishable: genuine literature, like Eurydice, does not appear. Nevertheless, one may form an approximate idea of what it is like by reading what does not appear, what publishers reject rather than what they publish. Genetic criticism to some extent embraces this paradox, for in its approach to literature it too emphasizes what did not appear, what was abandoned along the path to creation: the victims of editorial purges. Contributing in its way to the myth of an essentially unpublished literature, an "anecdotal" (in the etymological sense) literature, it explores the vast continents of the "out of print."

Some geneticians refer to these masses of manuscripts, above which the work, like an iceberg in proximity to the Gulf Stream, appears only with the greatest of difficulty, as the "diary" of the work. The choice of this particular word is of some interest. The diary and the manuscript are intersecting spaces: for instance, both refer to writing in real time. So it is not merely coincidental that the two are often studied concurrently. For example, Lejeune, in his book on Georges Perec, is interested in both genetic criticism of the work and the author's diaries. Indeed, a diary is often a text not written for publication. As Lejeune points out, some diaries have everything to lose if they are taken out of manuscript form: "The same text, if printed, would become abstract and retrospective."[47] Publication may well pervert the purpose of a diary; indeed, a diary is a text whose purpose may well be perverted by publication.

Critique of Pure Criticism

Es heisst jede Erkenntniss rein *die mit nichts Fremdartiges vermischt ist.*[48]

At the height of the structuralist purge, Genette reclaimed the label "poetics" from classical rhetoric to define a discipline he characterized, in the title of an article that was tantamount to a manifesto, as "pure criticism," giving the expression its full Kantian sense: a criticism that would deal "not with individuals or works but with essences." Tzvetan Todorov, the co-founder of a journal that took the word *Poétique* as its title, offered a similar definition: poetics, he said, is the science whose object is "not real literature but possible literature." Elsewhere he elaborated on this: the object of poetics is not "a set of empirical facts (literary works) but an abstract structure (literature)."[49]

In this way, structuralism returned to the question that Blanchot and Paulhan had raised in the early 1940s: How is literature possible? In any case, it demonstrated a predilection, if not for "potential literature" in the sense of Oulipo (*Ouvroir de littérature potentielle*), then at least for what was still only a possibility. Thus literary theory always emphatically differentiated itself from literary history, an irretrievably empirical discipline concerned not with essence but with existence, not with possible works but with actual ones. Structuralism represented the ideal of a reduced literature—reduced, for starters, to pure possibility, literature in the state of "pure potentiality," to borrow Caillois's phrase—literariness without literature.

Gaëtan Picon, in a text included in this volume, expresses his surprise at the coexistence of two diametrically opposed literary extremisms in the France of the 1960s and 1970s. Literature was simultaneously invoked by two contradictory fanaticisms: that of purity and that of impurity. On the one hand was a literature reduced to its possibility, its concept (by way of structural modeling); on the other was a literature at once irreducible and impure, irreducibly impure. One invoked the name structuralism, while the other invoked writers like Antonin Artaud and Georges Bataille, examples in spite of themselves, for whom literature (if the word still has any meaning) would sustain itself primarily by resisting possibility, and especially its own possibility: a language that would do everything possible to undermine its own possibility, to avoid being reduced to an example, a possibility. Thus, as Blanchot writes, literature represents "a kind of power that is not predicated upon possibility."[50]

Is this invocation of impurity enough to justify talk of empiricism? Is irreducibility condemned to be reduced to the empirical? Might there be such a thing as pure impurity? What might a nonempirical impurity be? Empiricism does not have a good reputation. It evokes a laziness of thought which detests risk, believes only in what is clear and certain, sticks to the facts, and cultivates its garden—a garden reserved, like that of Tarbes, for homegrown flowers: a stay-at-home empiricism, an empiricism of decency.[51]

There are, however, flowers that do not come from Tarbes—heterogeneous flowers (in the literal sense). One sees them (like the head of Medusa) only severed from their origins. There is an empiricism of what is clear but also an empiricism of what is obscure. Besides dogmatic empiricism, which is suspicious of theory and constantly repeats that the intelligible must be rooted in the perceptible, there is also another empiricism, the true empiricism, which is above all, in Deleuze's phrase, "unprincipled" thought, thought that obliges itself to confront what it is incapable of confronting, that which does not come from thought, including that which is repulsive to thought: the external, the nondeducible, the event.[52] (Deleuze saw empiricism as the novel's revenge on theory.) This empiricism points toward a kind of thought (or, rather, writing) that is adventurous and playful, willing to venture beyond the limits of what it knows, into uncharted territory, and to pursue an experience of which it has no idea of the limits of possibility. It was to this kind of empiricism—a grammatological empiricism—that Derrida was referring when he wrote: "The *way out* is radically empiricist."[53]

NOTES

[1] Jacques Rivière, *Une Conscience européenne (1916–24)* (Paris: Gallimard, 1992), pp. 126–27.

[2] Quoted in Pierre Assouline, *L'Epuration des intellectuels* (Brussels: Complexe, 1990), p. 91. Stendhal had earlier portrayed Mathilde de La Môle scrutinizing the features of Count Altamira for "those eminent qualities that can earn a man the honor of being sentenced to death." See *Le Rouge et le Noir* II, p. ix.

[3] Sartre, *Qu'est-ce que la littérature?* (Paris: Gallimard, 1948), pp. 219–20.

[4] What is the source, Paulhan asked in December 1944 in what amounts to his own "Republic of Silence," of the tranquil calm we feel when we think about the dead: "It comes from the fact that they represent for us our share of silence, which we all too readily forget. They are silent because they were silenced." (Jean Paulhan, "Les Morts," *Oeuvres* 5 (Paris: Cercle du Livre Précieux, 1970), p. 302.

[5] In this Sartrean view of the period, what is most striking today is probably the way in which the isolated, individual acts of heroism, whose secrets perished in the torture chamber confrontation between torturer and victim, obscured a far less Hegelian, far less "anthropogenic" scene, to borrow Alexandre Kojève's neologism for the dialectic of master and slave: the unheroic anonymity of genocide, of mass arrests and deportations and gassings.

[6] Sartre, "La République du silence" (September 1944), *Situations, III: Lendemains de guerre* (Paris: Gallimard, 1949), pp. 11, 12. These pages, written at the time of the Liberation, reveal a Sartre more Heideggerian than he ever was before, more Heideggerian in particular than he was during the war, when he wrote *L'Etre et le Néant*.

[7] Maurice Blanchot, "La littérature et le droit à la mort," *La Part du feu* (Paris: Gallimard, 1949), pp. 309–311.

[8] Raymond Queneau, "Lectures pour un front," in *Bâtons, chiffres et lettres* (rev. ed. Paris: Gallimard, 1965), p. 159.

[9] In an essay on Rilke, Blanchot wrote that a work of poetry is a response to the need for a "dying faithful to death." See *L'Espace littéraire* (Paris: Gallimard, 1955), p. 163.

[10] Maurice Merleau-Ponty, *Phénoménologie de la perception* (Paris: Gallimard, 1945), p. 229. And Sartre, in *Qu'est-ce que la littérature?*, says that the writer is "the man who names what has not yet been named" (p. 29).

[11] Henri-Irénée Marrou, *Mousicos Aner: Etude sur les scènes de la vie intellectuelle figurant sur les monuments funéraires romains* (Grenoble: Didier and Richard, 1938); Franz Cumont, *Recherches sur le symbolisme funéraire des Romains* (Paris: Librairie Orientaliste Paul Geuthner, 1942); Henri-Irénée Marrou, "La Symbolique funéraire des Romains," *Journal des savants* (April–June 1944). See also Maurice Blanchot, "Le Chant des sirènes," in *Le Livre à venir* (Paris: Gallimard, 1959).

[12] Maurice Merleau-Ponty, "Recherches sur l'usage littéraire du langage," *Résumés de cours: Collège de France (1952–60)* (Paris: Gallimard, 1968), p. 23.

[13] Maurice Blanchot, *Lautréamont et Sade* [1949] (repr. Paris: Minuit, 1963), p. 290.

[14] Ibid., pp. 190, 287.

[15] Blanchot, too, substituted the distinction between life and existence for that between life and work. "What *Les Pensées* postulate or require," he wrote in his article on Pascal, "is not factual incidents concerning his life or his beliefs but his existence as a whole, which of course does not mean his entire existence or the entire history of that existence, but existence as such." See "La Main de Pascal," in *La Part du feu*, p. 257. After Georges Bataille's death, he wrote similarly, "I know, we have the books." But, he added, "books themselves point to an existence." See Blanchot, "L'Amitié" in *L'Amitié* (Paris: Gallimard, 1971), p. 327.

[16] Claude Lévi-Strauss, "Recherches récentes sur la notion d'âme," *Paroles données* (Paris: Plon, 1984), p. 261.

[17] "Save Our Souls," according to one of the interpretations suggested by Michel Leiris of this morse code signal of maritime distress (Michel Leiris, *Langage tangage* [Paris: Gallimard, 1985], p. 77).

[18] Lévi-Strauss, "Réponses à quelques questions," *Esprit* (Nov. 1963), p. 640.

[19] Ibid., p. 641.

[20] Gérard Genette, "La Littérature comme telle," *Figures* (Paris: Seuil, 1966), p. 259.

[21] As Sartre still does in *L'Etre et le Néant*: "By Psyche we mean Ego, [which] . . . in the double grammatical form of I and Me represents our *person* as a transcendent psychic unity" (Paris: Gallimard, 1943), p. 200.

[22] Cf. Francis Ponge on Giacometti's erect figures, which he called "J-shaped specters" ("J" standing, in French, for the English "I"): "Giacometti is the plastic poet of the personal pronoun, the J"; "That slender, ambiguous entity that stands at the head of most of our sentences, that 'I.' " See "Joca Seria: Notes sur les sculptures d'Alberto Giacometti," *Nouveau recueil* (Paris: Gallimard, 1967), pp. 93–94.

[23] Lévi-Strauss: "There is no correct version or authentic or primitive form." See Claude Lévi-Strauss and Didier Eribon, *De Près et de loin* (Paris: Odile Jacob, 1990), p. 196.

[24] Gérard Genette, "Structuralisme et critique littéraire," *Figures* (Paris: Seuil, 1966), p. 159. (This essay was written for the special issue *L'Arc* devoted to Lévi-Strauss.)

[25] Marguerite Duras, *Hiroshima, mon amour* (Paris: Gallimard, 1960), p. 48.

[26] Reprinted in Sartre, "La Fin de la guerre," *Situations III,* p. 64. In the first issue of *Les Temps modernes*, this article was followed by "V.J. Day in New York," signed "D," the initial of Dolores to whom the "Presentation" of the journal was dedicated. In this letter to Sartre, Dolores quotes what an acquaintance of theirs has said about the redrawing of the geopolitical map of the planet in the wake of the war: "I asked X . . . what he thought about the two countries [the United States and the Soviet Union] which, after being dragged belatedly into the war, had emerged from it as the rulers of the world. He said, 'It's as if the capitals had gone to war with their suburbs and the suburbs had won' " (p. 169).

[27] In 1968, Aimé Césaire wrote *Une tempête* (*A Tempest,* based on Shakespeare's *The Tempest*, adaptation for a black theater, translated by Richard Miller. New York: Borchardt, 1986).

[28] Gilles Deleuze and Félix Guattari, *Kafka: Pour une littérature mineure* (Paris: Minuit, 1975).

[29] Edouard Glissant, *L'Intention poétique: Poétique II* [1969] (Paris: Gallimard, 1977), pp. 42, 49.

[30] Abedelkebir Khatibi, "La Loi du partage," *L'Interculturel*, Etudes littéraires maghrébines 6 (Paris: L'Harmattan, 1995), p. 12.

[31] Assia Djebar, *Women from Algiers in their Apartment*, translated by Marjolijn de Jager (Charlottesville: University of Virginia, 1992), p. 1.

[32] Hélène Cixous, *Coming to Writing and Other Essays*, ed. Deborah Johnson (Cambridge, Mass.: Harvard University Press, 1991), p. 22.

[33] Jacques Derrida, *Le Monolinguisme de l'autre* (Paris: Galilée, 1996), p. 13.

[34] Abdelwahab Medded, *Talismano* (Paris: Sindbad, 1987), pp. 194–96.

[35] The prototype of such parodic utterance is Jean Genet's "clownerie," *Les Nègres* (Décines: Barbezat, 1958). As for the embedding of French *lieux de mémoire* in French soil, one has only to consult the table of contents of the volumes published under that title by Pierre Nora: it is clear that, despite France's imperial past, her memory does not extend beyond her continental boundaries.

[36] "The decline in the status of the university and of teaching and the devaluation of academic judgment was a positive thing for the creative writer. Theory went totally to pot. It was reduced to a religion of quaking fanaticism and became almost moribund. Paradoxically, the discrediting of criticism for all sorts of reasons further reduced the constraints on writers. Criticism no longer had the power to intimidate. Another favorable factor was the fact that French lost its purity and influence." Pascal Quignard, "La Déprogrammation de la littérature," *Le Débat* (March–April 1989), p. 87.

[37] Glissant, *L'Intention poétique*, vol. 2, p. 189.

[38] Fredric Jameson, "Periodizing the 60's" in *The Ideologies of Theory*, vol. 2 (Minneapolis: University of Minnesota Press, 1988), p. 208.

[39] René Girard, *Mensonge romantique et vérité romanesque* (Paris: Grasset, 1961), p. 332.

[40] Walter Benjamin, "The Storyteller," in *Illuminations*, translated by Harry Zohn (New York: Schocken Books, 1969), p. 95.

[41] Ibid., p. 336. Cf. Paul Ricoeur: "For us it suffices that the author, external to his work and now dead, has transformed himself into a narrative voice still audible in his work." See Ricoeur, *Temps et roman* (Paris: Seuil, 1984), vol. 2, p. 215. On the disappointment of Dreyfus's supporters, Charles Péguy's 1910 *Notre jeunesse*: "We would have died for Dreyfus. Dreyfus didn't die for Dreyfus. It is right and proper that the victim should be impervious to the mystique of his own affair" (Paris: Gallimard, 1993, p. 151). Right and proper? Not according to the laws of narrative transmission, which requires the victim to assent to the logic of his own sacrifice.

[42] Philippe Lejeune, *Le Pacte autobiographique* (Paris: Seuil, 1975).

[43] Philippe Lejeune, *Le Moi des demoiselles* (Paris: Seuil, 1993), p. 91. A similar empiricism can be found in the countless sociological inquiries stimulated by the growing interest in writing modes impervious to literature. See, for example, Daniel Fabre, ed., *Ecritures ordinaires* (Paris: P.O.L./Centre Georges-Pompidou, 1993).

[44] See Jean-Louis Lévy, "Alfred Dreyfus, anti-héros et témoin capital," afterword to Dreyfus' diary, *Cinq années de ma vie (1894–1899)*, published with a preface by Pierre Vidal-Naquet, "Dreyfus dans l'Affaire et dans l'histoire" (Paris: Découverte, 1994).

[45] Merleau-Ponty, *Phénoménologie de la perception*, p. 447. Here as earlier (when Merleau-Ponty opposed authentic language and empirical language), the word "empirical" marks the negative pole of the opposition.

[46] Todorov, *Poétique* (Paris: Seuil, 1968), p. 19.

[47] Lejeune, *Le Moi des demoiselles*, p. 41.

[48] Kant quoted in André Lalande, *Vocabulaire technique et critique de la philosophie* (Paris: Alcan, 1928), s.v. "Pur".

[49] Gérard Genette, "Raisons de la critique pure," in *Figures II* (Paris: Seuil, 1965); Todorov, *Poétique*, pp. 19–20, 25.

[50] See my "Must Literature Be Possible?" in *Absent Without Leave: French Literature under the Threat of War*, trans. Catherine Porter (Cambridge, Mass.: Harvard University Press, 1997).

[51] Cf. Jean Paulhan, *Les Fleurs de Tarbes* (Paris: Gallimard, 1941).

⁵² Gilles Deleuze and Claire Parnet, *Dialogues* (Paris: Flammarion, 1977), p. 69: "Empiricists are neither theorists nor experimentalists, they never interpret, they have no principles."

⁵³ Derrida, *De la grammatologie* (Paris: Minuit, 1967), p. 232. Elsewhere Derrida writes: "the true name of this bowing of thought before the Other, of this resolute acceptance of the incoherent incoherence inspired by a truth deeper than the 'logic' of philosophical discourse, the true name of this *resignation* of the concept, of the *a prioris* and transcendental horizons of language, is *empiricism*" ("Violence et métaphysique," in *L'Ecriture et la différence* [Paris: Seuil, 1967], p. 224). See also his *Marges* (Paris: Minuit, 1972), pp. 7, 227–30.

PART I
Postwar Positions

From Resistance
to Commitment
(A Time for Timeliness)

———

JEAN-PAUL SARTRE

Presentation
1945

French literature has always demonstrated a weakness for manifestos, a genre midway between theorization and happening. Sartre's inaugural piece for Les Temps modernes, *an event in itself, was moreover the promotion of the very category of the event as such, forcing the postwar Parisian intelligentsia to reset its clock according to the standards of commitment and timeliness. Sartre had just discovered the beauty of the actuality effect. He had just discovered that literature knows only one, both political and aesthetic, imperative—writing "on time." Punctuality (a word in which already resonates what Roland Barthes will later call* punctum*) has become the politeness no longer of kings but of committed writers.*

Commitment can be viewed as a hard-core, militant version of Horatius's carpe diem: *the aesthete's rule—seize the day—is appropriated by his enemy, the activist. A writer, Sartre claims, is a man who has a date with his own time. But his relationship to the here and now is no longer that of a detached, passive consumer or spectator; for him it is no longer a matter of savoring the sensuous uniqueness of the ephemeral but of making sense of the present by giving it a future that would endow it with meaning.*

Ever since Mallarmé, literature had defined itself in contradistinction to the media; but this aesthetic of timeliness puts literature in competition

Jean-Paul Sartre, "Presentation," trans. Jeffrey Mehlman, in *What Is Literature? and Other Essays* (Cambridge, Mass.: Harvard University Press, 1988), pp. 249–67, from "Présentation des *Temps modernes*," in *Situations II* (Paris: Gallimard, 1948), pp. 9–30.

with journalism. The world of media is no longer perceived as a threat but as a challenge, the opportunity for literature to re-invent itself in a context of mass culture and under the pressures of journalistic temporality. Infatuated with his own recent experiments in journalism (he reported on the street fights of the Liberation of Paris in August 1944, and on his American tour for two major Parisian dailies in early 1945), Sartre anticipates that reportage will become the major literary genre of the twentieth century (the equivalent, somehow, of what the sonnet was for the sixteenth, the classical, five-act verse tragedy for the seventeenth, the epistolary form for the eighteenth, and the novel for the nineteenth). Les Temps modernes is conceived as a platform for the launching of journalism into literature.

All writers of middle-class origin have known the temptation of irresponsibility. For a century now, it has been a traditional part of the literary career. An author rarely establishes a link between his works and the income they bring. On the one hand, he writes, sings, or sighs; on the other, he is given money. The two facts have no apparent relation: the best he can do is tell himself that he's being paid in order to sigh. As a consequence, he is apt to regard himself more as a student enjoying a scholarship than as a worker receiving wages for his efforts. The theoreticians of Art for Art's Sake and of Realism have confirmed him in that opinion. Has it been noted that they share the same purpose and the same origin? According to the former, the author's principal concern is to produce works that serve no end; if they are quite gratuitous, thoroughly bereft of roots, they are not far from seeming beautiful to him. He thus situates himself at the margins of society; or rather, he consents to appear there only in his role as pure consumer—precisely as the scholarship holder. The Realist, for his part, is also a willing consumer. As for producing, that is a different matter: he has been told that science is not concerned with utility and he aspires to the sterile impartiality of the scholar. Have we not been told often enough that he "pores over" the social groups he is intent on describing? He pores *over*! Where was he, in that case? In the air? The truth is that unsure of his social position, too fearful to stand up to the bourgeoisie from whom he draws his pay, and too lucid to accept it without reservations, he has chosen to pass judgment on his century and has thereby convinced himself that he remains outside it, just as an experimenter remains outside the system of his experiment. Thus does the disinterestedness of pure science join with the gratuitousness of Art for Art's Sake. It is not by chance that Flaubert should be simultaneously a pure stylist, a purist in his love of forms, and the father of Naturalism; it is not by chance that the Goncourt brothers should flatter themselves for simultaneously knowing how to observe and having a highly aestheticized prose style.

That legacy of irresponsibility has troubled a number of minds. They suffer from a literary bad conscience and are no longer sure whether it is admirable or grotesque to write. In former times, the poet took himself for a prophet, which was honorable. Subsequently, he became a pariah and an accused figure, which was still feasible. But today he has fallen to the rank of specialist, and it is not without a certain malaise that he lists his profession on hotel registers as "man of letters." Man of letters: that association of words is in itself sufficient to disgust one with writing. One thinks of an Ariel, a vestal virgin, an enfant terrible, and also of a fanatic similar in type to a numismatist or body-builder. The whole business is rather ridiculous. The man of letters writes while others fight. One day he's quite proud of it, he feels himself to be a cleric and guardian of ideal values; the following day he's ashamed of it, and finds that literature appears quite markedly to be a special form of affectation. In relation to the middle-class people who read him, he is aware of his dignity; but confronted with workers, who don't, he suffers from an inferiority complex, as was seen in 1936 at the Maison de la Culture. It is certainly that complex which is the source of what Paulhan calls *terrorism*; it is what led the Surrealists to despise literature, on which they lived. After the other war, it was the occasion of a particular mode of lyricism: the best and purest writers confessed publicly to what might humiliate them the most and expressed their satisfaction whenever they succeeded in eliciting the disapproval of the bourgeoisie: they had produced a text that, through its consequences, bore a slight resemblance to an act. Those isolated attempts could not prevent words from undergoing a devaluation that increased by the day. There was a crisis of rhetoric, then one of language. On the eve of this war, most practitioners of literature were resigned to being no more than nightingales. Finally came a few authors who pressed their disgust with writing to an extreme. Outdoing their elders, they declared that publishing a book which was merely useless was not enough: they maintained that the secret aim of all literature was the destruction of language, and that it was sufficient, in order to attain this end, to speak so as not to say anything. Such voluble silence was quite in fashion for a while, and Hachette used to distribute capsules of silence, in the form of voluminous novels, to many a railroad station bookstore. Today things have gone sufficiently far that we have seen writers who once were blamed or punished for renting their pens to the Germans who express a pained astonishment. "What do you mean?" they ask. "Does the stuff someone writes actually commit him?"

We do not want to be ashamed of writing, and we don't feel like writing so as not to say anything. Moreover, even if we wanted to we would not be able to: no one can. Every text possesses a meaning, even if that meaning is far removed from the one the author dreamed of inserting into it. For us, an author is indeed neither a vestal virgin nor Ariel: he is "implicated," whatever he does— tainted, compromised, even in his most distant retreat. If, at certain periods, he uses his art to forge what Mallarmé called "trinkets of sonorous inanity" (*bibe-lots d'inanité sonore*) this in itself is a sign—that there is a crisis of Letters and, no doubt, of Society, or even that the dominant classes have channeled him without his realizing it toward an activity that seems pure luxury, for fear that he might take off and swell the ranks of the revolutionaries. What is Flaubert—who so raged against the bourgeoisie and believed he had withdrawn outside the social machine—for us if not a talented man living off his investments? And does not his meticulous art presuppose the comfort of Croisset, the solicitude of a mother or a niece, an orderly regimen, a prosperous commercial endeavor, dividends received on schedule? Few years are needed for a book to become a social datum, to be questioned like an institution or recorded as a statistical reality; not much distance is needed for it to merge with the furnishings of an era, its habits, headgear, means of transport, and nourishment. A historian will say to us, "They ate this, read that, and dressed thus." The first railroads, cholera, the revolt of the Lyons silk-workers, Balzac's novels, and the rise of industry all contribute equally to characterizing the July Monarchy. All this has been said and repeated since Hegel; what we want to do is draw the practical consequences. Since the writer has no way of escaping, we want him to embrace his era—tightly. It is his only chance; it was made for him and he was made for it. We regret Balzac's indifference toward the revolutionary days of 1848; we regret Flaubert's panicky incomprehension when confronted with the Commune. We regret them *for them:* those events are something they missed out on forever. We don't want to miss out on anything of our time. There may be better ones, but this one is ours: we have only *this* life to live, and *this* war, and perhaps *this* revolution. Let it not be concluded from this that we are preaching a variety of populism; quite the contrary. Populism is an offspring of the very old, the sad scion of the last Realists; it is yet another attempt to remove one's stakes from the board. We are convinced, on the contrary, that one *cannot* remove one's stakes from the board. Even if we were as deaf and dumb as pebbles, our very passivity would be an action. The abstention of whoever wanted to devote his life to writing novels about the Hittites would in itself constitute taking a position. The writer is *situated* in his time; every word he utters has reverberations. As does his silence. I hold Flaubert and the Goncourts responsible for the repression that followed the Commune because they didn't write a line to prevent it. Some will object that this wasn't their business. But was the Calas trial Voltaire's business? Was Dreyfus's sentence Zola's business? Was the administration of the Congo Gide's business? Each of those authors, at a particular time in his life, took stock of his responsibility as a writer. The Occupation taught us ours. Since we act upon our time by virtue of our very existence, we decide that our action will be voluntary. Even then, it must be specified: it is not uncommon for a writer to be concerned, in his modest way, with preparing the future. But there is a vague, conceptual future which concerns humanity in its entirety and on which we have no particular light to shed: Will history have an end? Will the sun be extinguished? What will be the condition of man in the socialist regime of the year 3000? We leave such reveries to futurist novelists. It is the future of *our* time that must be the object of our concern: a limited future barely distinguishable from it—for an era, like a man, is first of all a future. It is composed of its ongoing efforts, its enterprises, its more or less long-term projects, its revolts, its struggles, its hopes: When will the war end? How will the country be rebuilt? How will international relations be organized? What social reforms will take place? Will the forces of reaction triumph? Will there be a revolution, and, if so, what will it be? That future we make our own; we don't want any other. No doubt, some authors have concerns that are less contemporary, and visions that are less shortsighted. They move through our midst as though they were not there. Where indeed are they? With their grandnephews, they turn around to judge that bygone age which was ours and whose sole survivors they are. But they have miscalculated: posthumous glory is always based on a misunderstanding. What do they know of those nephews who will come fish them out of our midst! Immortality is a terrible alibi: it is not easy to live with one foot in the grave and another beyond it. How might one expedite current business if one saw it from such a distance? How might one grow excited over a battle, or enjoy a victory? Everything is equivalent. They look at us without seeing us: in their eyes, we are already dead, and they return to the novel they are writing for men they will never see. They have allowed their lives to be stolen from them by immortality. We write for our contemporaries; we want to behold our world not with future eyes—which would be the surest means of killing it—but with our eyes of flesh, our real, perishable eyes. We don't want to win our case on appeal, and we will have nothing to do with any posthumous rehabilitation. Right here in our own lifetime is when and where our cases will be won or lost.

We are not, however, thinking of instituting a literary relativism. We have little taste for the purely historical. Besides, does the purely historical exist anywhere but in the manuals of Monsieur Seignobos? Each age discovers an aspect of the human condition; in every era man chooses himself in confrontation with other individuals, love, death, the world; and when adversaries clash on the subject of disarming the FFI [Forces Françaises de l'Intérieur, the combined underground paramilitary forces of the Resistance—Trans.] or the help to be given the Spanish Republicans, it is that metaphysical choice, that singular and absolute project which is at stake. Thus, by taking part in the singularity of our era, we ultimately make contact with the eternal, and it is our task as writers to allow the eternal values implicit in such social or political debates to be perceived. But we don't care to seek them out in some intelligible heaven: they are of interest only in their contemporary guise. Far from being relativists, we proclaim that man is an absolute. But he is such in his time, in his surroundings, on his parcel of earth. What is absolute, what a thousand years of history cannot destroy is *that* irreplaceable, incomparable decision which he makes at this moment concerning these circumstances. What is absolute is Descartes, the man who escapes us because he is dead, who lived in his time, who thought it through day by day with the means available to him, who formed his doctrine on the basis of a certain state of the sciences, who knew Gassendi, Caterus, and Mersenne, who in his childhood loved a girl who was cross-eyed, who waged war and impregnated a servant girl, who attacked not the principle of authority in general but precisely the authority of Aristotle, and who emerges in his time, unarmed but unvanquished, like a milestone. What is relative is Cartesianism, that errant philosophy which is trotted out from century to century and in which everyone finds what he puts into it. It is not by running after immortality that we will make ourselves eternal; we will become absolutes not because we have allowed our writings to reflect a few emaciated principles (which are sufficiently empty and null to make the transition from one century to the next), but because we will have loved it passionately and accepted that we would perish entirely along with it.

In summary, our intention is to help effect certain changes in the Society that surrounds us. By which we do not mean changes within people's souls: we are happy to leave the direction of souls to those authors catering to a rather specialized clientele. As for us, who without being materialists have never distinguished soul from body and who know only one indivisible reality — human reality — we align ourselves on the side of those who want to change simultaneously the social condition of man and the concept he has of himself. Consequently, concerning the political and social events to come, our journal will take a position in each case. It will not do so *politically* — that is, in the service of a particular party — but it will attempt to sort out the conception of man which inspires each one of the conflicting theses, and will give its opinion in conformity with the conception it maintains. If we are able to live up to what we promise, if we succeed in persuading a few readers to share our views, we will not indulge in any exaggerated pride; we will simply congratulate ourselves for having rediscovered a good professional conscience, and for literature's having become again — at least for us — what it should never have stopped being: a social function.

Yet, some will ask, what is that conception of man you pretend to reveal to us? We respond that it can be found on every street corner, and that we claim not to have discovered it but only to have brought it into better focus. I shall call this conception "totalitarian." But since the word may seem unfortunate, since it has been used to designate not the human individual but an oppressive and antidemocratic type of state, a few explanations are called for.

The bourgeoisie, it seems to me, may be defined intellectually by the use it makes of the analytic mode, whose initial postulate is that composite realities must necessarily be reducible to an arrangement of simple elements. In its hands, that postulate was once an offensive weapon allowing it to dismantle the bastions of the Old Regime. Everything was analyzed; in a single gesture, air and water were reduced to their elements, mind to the sum of impressions composing it, society to the sum total of individuals it comprised. Groups disappeared; they were no more than abstract agglomerations due to random combinations. Reality withdrew to the ultimate terms of the decomposition. The latter indeed—and such is the second postulate of analysis—retain unalterably their essential properties, whether they enter into a compound or exist in a free state. There was an immutable nature of oxygen, of hydrogen, or nitrogen, and of the elementary impressions composing our mind; there was an immutable human nature. Man was man the way a circle is a circle—once and for all. The individual, be he transported to the throne or plunged into misery, remained fundamentally identical to himself because he was conceived on the model of the oxygen atom, which can combine with hydrogen to produce water, or with nitrogen to produce air, without its internal structure being changed. Those principles presided over the Declaration of the Rights of Man. In society, as conceived by the analytic cast of mind, the individual, a solid and indivisible particle, the vehicle of human nature, resides like a pea in a can of peas: he is round, closed in on himself, uncommunicative. All men are *equal*, by which it should be understood that they all participate equally in the essence of man. All men are *brothers*: fraternity is a passive bond among distinct molecules, which takes the place of an active or class-bound solidarity that the analytic cast of mind cannot even imagine. It is an entirely extrinsic and purely sentimental relation that masks the simple juxtaposition of individuals in analytic society. All men are *free*—free *to be men*, it goes without saying. Which means that political action ought to be strictly negative. A politically active individual has no need to forge human nature; it is enough for him to eliminate the obstacles that might prevent him from blossoming. Thus it was that, intent on destroying divine right, the rights of birth and blood, the right of primogeniture, all those rights based on the notion that there are differences in men's natures, the bourgeoisie confused its own cause with that of analysis and constructed for its use the myth of the universal. Unlike today's revolutionaries, they were able to achieve their goals only by abdicating their class consciousness: the members of the Third Estate at the Constituent Assembly were bourgeois precisely to the extent that they considered themselves to be simply men.

A hundred and fifty years later, the analytic cast of mind remains the official doctrine of bourgeois democracies, with the difference that it has now become a defensive weapon. It is entirely in the interest of the bourgeoisie to blind itself to the existence of classes even as it formerly failed to perceive the synthetic reality of the institutions of the Old Regime. It persists in seeing no more than men, in proclaiming the identity of human nature in every diverse situation; but it is against the proletariat that it makes that proclamation. A worker, for the bourgeoisie, is first of all a man—a man like any other. If the Constitution grants that man the right to vote and freedom of expression, he displays his human nature as fully as does a bourgeois. A certain polemical tradition has too often presented the bourgeois as a calculating drone whose sole concern is to defend his privileges. In fact, though, one *constitutes* oneself as a bourgeois by choosing, once and for all, a certain analytic perspective on the world which one attempts to foist on all men and which excludes the perception of collective realities. To that extent, the bourgeois defense is in a sense permanent, and is indistinguishable from the bourgeoisie itself. But it is not revealed in sordid calculations; within the world that the bourgeoisie has constructed, there is room for carefreeness, altruism, and even generosity—except that the good deeds of the bourgeois are individual acts addressed to universal human nature insofar as it is incarnated in an individual. In this sense, they are about as effective as a skillful piece of propaganda, since the beneficiary of the good deeds is obliged to receive them on the terms on which they are offered—that is, by thinking of himself as an isolated human being confronting another human being. Bourgeois charity sustains the myth of fraternity.

But there is another form of propaganda of more specific interest to us, since we are writers, and writers have turned themselves into its unwitting agents. The legend of the irresponsibility of the poet, which we were criticizing a while ago, derives its origin from the analytic cast of mind. Since bourgeois authors themselves think of themselves as peas in a can, the solidarity binding them to other men seems strictly *mechanical* to them—a matter, that is, of mere juxtaposition. Even if they have an exalted sense of their literary mission, they think they have done enough once they have described their own nature or that of their friends: since all men are made the same, they will have rendered a service to all by teaching each man about himself. And since the initial postulate from which they speak is the primacy of analysis, it seems quite simple to make use of the analytic method in order to attain self-knowledge. Such is the origin of intellectualist psychology, whose most polished exemplar we find in the works of Proust. As a pederast, Proust thought he could make use of his homosexual experience in depicting Swann's love for Odette; as a bourgeois, he presents the sentiments of a rich and idle bourgeois for a kept woman as the prototype of love, the reason being that he believes in the existence of universal passions whose mechanism does not vary substantially when there is a change in the sexual characteristics, social condition, nation, or era of the individuals experiencing them. Having thus "isolated" those immutable emotions, he can attempt to reduce them, in turn, to elementary particles. Faithful to the postulates of the analytic cast of mind, he does not even imagine that there might be a dialectic of feelings—he imagines only a mechanics. Thus does social atomism, the entrenched outpost of the contemporary bourgeoisie, entail psychological atomism. Proust *chose himself* to be a bourgeois. He made himself into an accomplice of bourgeois propaganda, since his work contributes to the dissemination of the myth of human nature.

We are convinced that the analytic spirit has had its day, and that its sole function at present is to confuse revolutionary consciousness and to isolate men for the benefit of the privileged classes. We no longer believe in Proust's intellectualist psychology, and we regard it as nefarious. Since we have chosen as an example his analysis of the passion of love, we shall no doubt contribute to the reader's enlightenment by mentioning the essential points on which we are totally at odds with him.

First of all, we do not accept a priori the idea that romantic love is a constitutive affect of the human mind. It may well be the case, as Denis de Rougemont has suggested, that it originated historically as a correlate of Christian ideology. More generally, we are of the opinion that a feeling always expresses a specific way of life and a specific conception of the world which are shared by an entire class or an entire era, and that its evolution is not the effect of some unspecified internal mechanism but of those historical and social factors.

Second, we cannot accept the idea that a human emotion is composed of molecular elements that may be juxtaposed without modifying each other. We regard it not as a well-constructed machine but as an organized form. The possibility of undertaking an *analysis* of love seems inconceivable to us, because the development of that feeling, like that of all others, is *dialectical*.

Third, we refuse to believe that the love felt by a homosexual offers the same characteristics as that felt by a heterosexual. The secretive and forbidden character of the former, its Black Mass side, the existence of a homosexual freemasonry, and that damnation toward which the homosexual is aware of dragging his partner are all elements that seem to us to exercise an influence on the feeling in its entirety and even in the very details of its evolution. We maintain that the various sentiments of an individual are not juxtaposed but, rather, that there is a synthetic unity of one's affectivity, and that every individual moves within an affective world specifically his own.

Fourth, we deny that the origin, class, environment, and nation of an individual are simple accessories of his emotional life. It seems to us, on the contrary, that every affect—like, for that matter, every other form of physical life—*manifests* his social situation. A worker who receives a salary, who does not own the instruments of his craft, whose work isolates him from material reality, and who defends himself from oppression by becoming aware of his class can in no way *feel* the same way as does a bourgeois of analytic propensities, whose profession puts him into relations of *politesse* with other members of his class.

Thus do we have recourse, against the spirit of analysis, to a synthetic conception of reality whose principle is that a whole, whatever it may be, is different in nature from the sum of its parts. For us, what men have in common is not a nature but a metaphysical condition—by which we mean the totality of constraints that limit them a priori, the necessity of being born and dying, that of being *finite* and of existing in the world among other men. In addition, they constitute indivisible totalities whose ideas, moods, and acts are secondary, dependent structures and whose essential characteristic lies in being *situated*, and they differ from each other even as their situations differ in relation to each other. The unity of those signifying wholes is the meaning which they mani-

fest. Whether writing or working on an assembly line, whether choosing a wife
or a tie, a man constantly manifests . . . He manifests his professional surroundings, his family, his class, and ultimately (since he is situated in relation to
the world in its entirety) the world itself. A man is the whole earth. He is everywhere present, everywhere active. He is responsible for all, and his destiny is
played out everywhere—Paris, Potsdam, Vladivostok. We adhere to these
views because to us they seem true, because to us they seem socially useful at the
present time, and because to us a majority of people seem to intuit them in their
thinking and indeed to call them forth. We would like our journal to contribute in a modest way to the elaboration of a synthetic anthropology. But, we
repeat, it is not simply a question of effecting an advance in the domain of pure
knowledge: the more distant goal we are aiming at is a *liberation*. Since man is a
totality, it is indeed not enough to grant him the right to vote without dealing
with the other factors that constitute him. He must free himself totally—that
is, make himself *other*, by acting on his biological constitution as well as on his
economic condition, on his sexual complexes as well as on the political terms of
his situation.

This synthetic perspective, however, presents some grave dangers. If the individual is the result of an arbitrary selection effected by the analytic cast of
mind, doesn't one run the risk, in breaking with analytic conceptions, of substi-
tuting the domination of collective consciousness for the domination of the person? The spirit of synthesis cannot be apportioned its mere share: no sooner is
man as a totality glimpsed than he would be submerged by his class. Only the
class exists, and it alone must be delivered. But, it will be objected, in liberating
a class is one necessarily freeing the men it comprises? Not necessarily. Would
the triumph of Hitler's Germany have been the triumph of every German?
Where, moreover, would the synthesis stop? Tomorrow we may be told that
the class is a secondary structure dependent on a larger totality, say, the nation.
The great attraction that Nazism exercised on certain minds of the left undoubtedly came from the fact that it pressed the totalitarian conception to the
absolute. Its theoreticians also denounced the ill effects of analysis, the abstract
character of democratic freedoms; its propaganda also promised to forge a new
man and retained the words "revolution" and "liberation." Except that for a
class-proletariat a proletariat of nations was substituted. Individuals were reduced to mere dependent functions of their class, classes to mere functions of
their nation, nations to mere functions of the European continent. If, in occupied countries, the entire working class rose up against the invader, it was undoubtedly because it felt wounded in its revolutionary aspirations, but also
because it felt an invincible repugnance to allowing the individual to be dissolved in the collectivity.

Thus does the contemporary mind appear divided by an antinomy. Those
who value above all the dignity of the human being, his freedom, his inalienable rights, are as a result inclined to think in accordance with that analytic cast

of mind which conceives of individuals outside their actual conditions of existence, which endows them with an unchanging, abstract nature, and which isolates them and blinds itself to their solidarity. Those who have profoundly
understood that man is rooted in the collectivity, and who want to affirm the
importance of historical, technical, and economic factors, are inclined toward
the synthetic mode, which, blind to individuals, has eyes only for groups. This
antinomy may be perceived, for example, in the widely held belief that socialism is diametrically opposed to individual freedom. Thus, those holding fast to
the autonomy of the individual would be trapped in a capitalist liberalism
whose nefarious consequences are clear; those calling for a socialist organization of the economy would be requesting it of an unspecified totalitarian authoritarianism. The current malaise springs from the fact that no one can
accept the extreme consequences of these principles: there is a "synthetic" component to be found in democrats of good will, and there is an "analytic" component in socialists. Recall, for instance, what the Radical Party was in France.
One of its theoreticians wrote a book entitled *The Citizen Versus the Powers that
Be* [Emile Chartier (who signed Alain) published *Le Citoyen contre les pouvoirs*
(1926)—TRANS.]. The title sufficiently indicates how he envisaged politics:
everything would be better if the isolated citizen, the molecular representative
of human nature, controlled those he elected and, if need be, exercised his own
judgment against them. But the Radicals, precisely, could not avoid acknowledging their own failure. In 1939 the great party had no will, no program, no
ideology; it was sinking into the depths of opportunism, because it was intent
on solving politically problems that were not amenable to a political solution.
The best minds were astonished. If man was a political animal, how could it be
that in granting him political freedom his fate had not been settled once and for
all? How could it be that the unhampered interaction of parliamentary institutions had not succeeded in eliminating poverty, unemployment, and oppression by monopolies? How could it be that a class struggle had emerged on the
far side of the fraternal competition between parties? One would not have to
push things much further to perceive the limits of the analytic cast of mind.
The fact that the Radicals consistently sought an alliance of leftist parties
clearly indicates the direction in which their sympathies and confused aspirations were taking them, but they lacked the intellectual technique that would
have allowed them not only to solve but even to formulate the problems they
intuited obscurely.

   In the other camp, there is no less perplexity. The working class has made
itself heir to the traditions of democracy. It is in the name of democracy that it
demands its liberation. Now the democratic ideal, as we have seen, has manifested itself historically in the form of a social contract among free individuals.
Thus do the analytic demands of Rousseau frequently interfere in many minds
with the synthetic demands of Marxism. Moreover, the worker's technical
training develops his analytic propensities. Similar in that regard to the scien-

tist, he would resolve the problems of matter by way of analysis. Should he turn toward human realities, he will tend, in order to understand them, to appeal to the same reasoning that has served him in his work. He thus applies to human behavior an analytic psychology related to that of the French seventeenth century.

The simultaneous existence of those two modes of explanation reveals a certain uncertainty. The perpetual recourse to the phrase "as though . . ." indicates sufficiently that Marxism does not yet have at its disposal a synthetic psychology adequate to its totalitarian conception of classes.

As far as we are concerned, we refuse to let ourselves be torn between thesis and antithesis. We can easily conceive that a man, although totally conditioned by his situation, can be a center of irreducible indeterminacy. The window of unpredictability that stands out within the social domain is what we call freedom, and a person is nothing other than his freedom. This freedom ought not to be envisaged as a metaphysical endowment of human "nature." Neither is it a license to do whatever one wants, or some unspecified internal refuge that would remain to us even in our chains. One does not do whatever one wants, and yet one is responsible for what one is—such are the facts. Man, who may be explained simultaneously by so many causes, is nevertheless alone in bearing the burden of himself. In this sense, freedom might appear to be a curse; it *is* a curse. But it is also the sole source of human greatness. On this score, the Marxists will agree with us in spirit, if not in letter, since as far as I know they are not reluctant to issue moral condemnations. What remains is to explain it—but this is the philosophers' business, not ours. We would merely observe that if society constitutes the individual, the individual, through a reversal analogous to the one Auguste Comte termed "the transition of subjectivity," constitutes society. Without its future, society is no more than an accumulation of raw data, but its future is nothing other than the self-projection beyond the status quo of the millions of men composing it. Man is no more than a situation; a worker is not *free* to think and feel like a bourgeois. But for that situation *to be a man*, an integral man, it must be lived and transcended toward a specific aim. In itself, it remains a matter of indifference insofar as a human freedom does not charge it with a specific sense. It is neither tolerable nor unbearable, to the extent that a human freedom neither resigns itself to it nor rebels against it— that is, to the extent that a man does not choose himself within it, by choosing its meaning. And it is only then, within this free choice, that the freedom becomes a determinant, because it is overdetermined. No, a worker cannot live like a bourgeois. In today's social organization, he is forced to undergo to the limit his condition as an employee. No escape is possible; there is no recourse against it. But a man does not exist in the same way that a tree or a pebble does: he must *make himself* a worker. Though he is completely conditioned by his class, his salary, the nature of his work, conditioned even in his feelings and his thoughts, it is nevertheless up to him to decide on the meaning of his condition and that of his comrades. It is up to him, freely, to give the proletariat a future of constant humiliation or one of conquest and triumph, depending on whether he chooses to be resigned or a revolutionary. And this is the choice for which he is responsible. He is not at all free to choose: he is implicated, forced to wager; abstention is also a choice. But he is free to choose at the same time his destiny, the destiny of all men, and the value to be attributed to humanity. Thus does he choose himself simultaneously as a worker and as a man, while at the same time conferring a meaning upon the proletariat. Such is man as we conceive him—integral man. Totally committed and totally free. And yet it is the free man who must be *delivered*, by enlarging his possibilities of choice. In certain situations there is room for only two alternatives, one of which is death. It is necessary to proceed in such a way that man, in every circumstance, can choose life.

Our journal will be devoted to defending that autonomy and the rights of the person. We consider it to be above all an instrument of inquiry. The ideas I have just presented will serve as our guiding theme in the study of concrete contemporary problems. All of us approach the study of those problems in a common spirit, but we have no political or social program; each article will commit its author alone. We hope only to set forth, in the long run, a general line. At the same time, we will draw from every literary genre in order to familiarize the reader with our conceptions; a poem or a novel, if inspired by them, may well create a more favorable climate for their development than a theoretical text. But that ideological content and those new intentions may also influence the very form and techniques of novelistic production; our critical essays will attempt to define in their broad lines the—new or ancient—literary techniques best suited to our designs. We will attempt to support our examination of contemporary issues by publishing as often as we can historical studies, when (as in the efforts of Marc Bloch or Henri Pirenne on the Middle Ages) they spontaneously apply those principles and the method they entail to past centuries; that is, when they forsake an arbitrary division of history into histories—whether political, economic, ideological, the history of institutions, the history of individuals—in order to attempt to restore a vanished age as a totality, one that they will consider as the age expresses itself in and through individuals and as individuals choose themselves in and through their age. Our chronicles will strive to consider our own era as a meaningful synthesis and, consequently, will envisage in a synthetic spirit the diverse manifestations of our contemporaneity—styles and criminal trials as well as political events and works of the mind—always seeking to discover in them a common meaning far more than to appreciate them individually. Which is why, contrary to custom, we will no more hesitate to pass over in silence an excellent book that, from our point of view, teaches us nothing new about our era, than to linger, on the contrary, over a mediocre book that, in its very mediocrity, may strike us as revealing. Each month we will assemble, in addition to such studies, raw documents; they will be selected in as various a manner as possible, simply requiring of them that they clearly demonstrate the interrelation of the collective and the person. We will supplement those documents with polls and news reports. It strikes us, in fact, that journalism is one of the literary genres, and that it can become one of the most important of them. The ability to grasp meanings instantly and intuitively, and a talent for regrouping them in order to offer the reader immediately comprehensible synthetic wholes, are the qualities most crucial to a reporter; they are the ones we ask of all our collaborators. We are aware, moreover, that among the rare works of our age destined to endure are several works of journalism, such as John Reed's *Ten Days That Shook the World* and, above all, Arthur Koestler's admirable *Spanish Testament* . . . Finally, in our chronicles we will devote a good deal of space to psychiatric studies, when they are written in the perspective that interests us. Our project is obviously ambitious; we cannot implement it by ourselves. At the start, we are a small crew, who will have failed if, in a year, we have not increased our numbers considerably. We appeal to all men of good will; all manuscripts will be accepted, whatever their source, provided they be inspired by preoccupations related to our own and provided they possess, in addition, literary merit. I recall, in fact, that in "committed literature," *commitment* must in no way lead to a forgetting of *literature*, and that our concern must be to serve literature by infusing it with new blood, even as we serve the collectivity by attempting to give it the literature it deserves.

TRANSLATED BY JEFFREY MEHLMAN

SIMONE DE BEAUVOIR

The Mandarins
1954

Published in 1954, Simone de Beauvoir's novel The Mandarins *(winner of the Goncourt prize of that year) is a fictional account of the years following the Liberation. In her memoirs* (La Force des choses, *1963), Beauvoir adamantly denied that the protagonists were modeled on real people: Dubreuilh is not Sartre, Scriassine is not Koestler, and neither is the novel's swarm of characters the group of leftist existentialists who teamed up with Sartre at the beginning of* Les Temps modernes. *She also claimed that, even though the novel uses the Liberation as its backdrop, it is imbued with the more somber atmosphere of the Cold War.*

The scene included here takes place, early in the novel, at a party on the Left Bank, where the editorial team of a new journal, L'Espoir, *celebrates the first postwar Christmas (1945). Their conversations reflect the mood of a France that doesn't find much to rejoice about in her supposed victory; but the feeling of being suspended at the threshold of a catastrophic world-historical change derives not so much from France's new marginality in postwar geopolitics as from the double bind in which French intellectuals find themselves caught, between literary commitment and mass culture. Literature must enter the political arena, but, in so doing, it runs the risk of being swept up into the mass media. It is as if the 1945 victory of the Allies, having irreversibly brought obsolescence to literary values, had inaugurated a world of unidimensional mass culture, with its two competing versions, Capitalist America and Communist USSR.*

The first victim of the victory (and of the Cold War it launched) is understood to have been high culture. Hence the intellectual's pervasive feeling of being on the brink of cultural extinction.

"You don't seem to be having a very good time," he said.

"Well, I'm doing the best I can."

"Too many young people here. Young people are never gay. And far too many writers." He pointed his chin toward Lenoir, Pelletier, and Cange. "They're all writers, aren't they?"

Simone de Beauvoir, *The Mandarins*, trans. Leonard M. Friedman (New York: World Publishing, 1956), pp. 37–42, from *Les Mandarins* (Paris: Gallimard, 1954), vol. 1, pp. 50–55.

"Every last one of them."

"And you, do you write, too?"

"God, no!" I said, laughing.

I liked his brusque manner. Like everyone else, I had read his famous book, *The Red Paradise*. But I had been especially moved by his book on Austria under the Nazis. It was something much more than a mere journalistic account; it was an impassioned testimony. He had fled Austria after having fled Russia and finally became a naturalized French citizen. But he had spent the last four years in America and we had met him for the first time only this fall. Almost immediately he began calling Robert and Henri by their first names, but he never seemed to notice that I existed.

"I wonder what's going to become of them," he said, turning his eyes from me.

"Who?"

"The French in general and these people here in particular."

I studied his triangular face with its prominent cheekbones, its hard, fiery eyes, its thin, almost feminine mouth. It wasn't at all the face of a Frenchman. To him Russia was an enemy nation, and he did not have any great love for the United States. There wasn't a place on earth where he really felt at home.

"I returned from New York on an English boat," he said with a slight smile. "One day the steward said to me, 'The poor French! They don't know if they won the war or lost it.' It seems to me that that sums up the situation rather well."

There was an irritating complacency in his voice. "I don't think it matters much what kind of tag you put on things that happened in the past." I said. "What does matter is the future."

"That's just it," he said spiritedly. "To make something good of the future, you have to look the present in the face. And I get the distinct impression that these people here aren't doing that at all. Dubreuilh talks to me of a literary review, Perron of a pleasure trip. They all seem to feel they'll be able to go on living just like before the war."

"And of course, you were sent from heaven to open their eyes," I said dryly.

Scriassine smiled. "Do you know how to play chess?"

"Very poorly."

He continued to smile and all trace of pedantry vanished from his face—we were intimate friends, accomplices, had known each other since childhood. "He's working his Slavic charm on me," I thought. And as a matter of fact, the charm worked; I smiled back at him.

"When I'm just watching chess, I can spot good moves more clearly than the players themselves, even if I'm not as good at the game as they are. Well, that's the way it is here; I'm an outsider, an onlooker, so I can pretty well see what's in store for you people."

"What?"

"An impasse."

"An impasse? What do you mean by that?"

Suddenly, I found myself anxiously awaiting his reply. We had all been living together in such a tightly sealed circle for so long a time, with no intrusions by any outsiders, any witnesses, that this man from without troubled me.

"French intellectuals are facing an impasse. It's their turn now," he added with a kind of satisfaction. "Their art, their philosophies can continue to have meaning only within the framework of a certain kind of civilization. And if they want to save that civilization, they'll have no time or energy left over to give to art or philosophy."

"This isn't the first time Robert's been active in politics," I said. "And it never before stopped him from writing."

"Yes, in '34 Dubreuilh gave a great deal of his time to the struggle against fascism," Scriassine said in his suave voice. "But to him, that struggle seemed morally reconcilable with literary preoccupations." With a slight trace of anger, he added, "In France, the pressure of history has never been felt in all its urgency. But in Russia, in Austria, in Germany, it was impossible to escape it. That's why I, for example, was never able to write."

"But you have written."

"Don't you think I dreamed of writing other kinds of books, too? But it was out of the question." He shrugged his shoulders. "To be able to continue taking an interest in things cultural in the face of Stalin and Hitler, you have to have one hell of a humanistic tradition behind you. But, of course," he went on, "in the country of Diderot, Victor Hugo, Jaurès, it's easy to believe that culture and politics go hand in hand. Paris has thought of itself as Athens. But Athens no longer exists; it's dead."

"As far as feeling the pressure of history is concerned," I said, "I think Robert could give you a few pointers."

"I'm not attacking your husband," Scriassine said, with a little smile that reduced my heated words to nothing more than an expression of conjugal loyalty. "As a matter of fact," he continued, "I consider Robert Dubreuilh and Thomas Mann to be the two greatest minds of this age. But that's precisely it: if I predict that he'll give up literature, it's only because I have confidence in his lucidity."

I shrugged my shoulders. If he was trying to soften me up, he was certainly going about it the wrong way. I detest Thomas Mann.

"Robert will never give up writing," I said.

"The remarkable thing in all of Dubreuilh's works," said Scriassine, "is that he was able to reconcile high aesthetic standards with revolutionary inspiration. And in his own life, he attained an analogous equilibrium: he was organizing vigilance committees at the same time he was writing novels. But it's precisely that beautiful equilibrium that's now becoming impossible."

"You can count on Robert to devise some new kind of equilibrium," I said.

"He's bound to sacrifice his aesthetic standards," Scriassine said. Suddenly his face lit up and he asked in a triumphant voice, "Do you know anything about prehistoric times?"

"Not much more than I do about chess."

"But perhaps you know this: that for a vast period of time the wall paintings and objects found in caves and excavations bear witness to a continuous artistic progress. Abruptly, both drawings and sculpture disappear; there's an eclipse lasting several centuries which coincides with the development of new techniques. Well, right now we're at the edge of a new era in which, for different reasons, humanity will have to grapple with all sorts of difficult problems, leaving us no time for the luxury of expressing ourselves artistically."

"Reasoning by analogy doesn't prove very much," I said.

"All right then, let's forget that comparison," Scriassine said patiently. "You've probably been too close to this war we've gone through to properly understand it. Actually, it was something entirely different from a war—the liquidation of a society, and even of a world, or rather the beginning of their liquidation. The progress that science and engineering have made, the economic changes that have come about, will convulse the earth to such an extent that even our ways of thinking and feeling will be revolutionized. We'll even have difficulty remembering just who and what we had once been. And, among other things, art and literature will become nothing more than peripheral divertissements."

I shook my head and Scriassine resumed heatedly: "Don't you see? What weight will the message of French writers have when the earth is ruled by either Russia or the United States? No one will understand them any more; very few will even speak their language."

"From the way you talk, it would seem you're rather enjoying the prospect," I said.

He shrugged his shoulders. "Now isn't it just like a woman to say a thing like that! They're simply incapable of being objective."

"Well, let's be objective then," I said. "Objectively, it's never been proven that the world *must* become either American or Russian."

"In the long run, give or take a few years, it's bound to happen." With a gesture of his hand, he stopped me from interrupting him and then gave me one of his charming Slavic smiles. "I think I understand you. The liberation is still fresh in your mind. All of you are wading shoulder deep in euphoria. For four years you suffered a great deal and now you think you've paid enough. Well, you can never pay enough," he said with a sudden harshness. He looked me squarely in the eyes. "Do you know there's a very powerful faction in Washington that would like to see the German campaign continued right up to Moscow? And from their point of view, they're right. American imperialism, like Russian totalitarianism, requires unlimited expansion. In the end, one or the other has to win out." A note of sadness entered his voice. "You think you're celebrating the German defeat, but what you're actually witnessing is the beginning of World War Three."

"Those are *your* prognostications," I said.

"I know Dubreuilh believes in peace and in the possibility of maintaining a free and independent Europe," Scriassine said. "But even brilliant minds can sometimes be mistaken," he added with an indulgent smile. "We'll be annexed by Stalin or colonized by America, of that you can be sure."

"Well, if that's the case, then there's no impasse," I said gaily. "If it's inevitable, what's the sense of worrying about it? Those who enjoy writing will just go right on writing."

"What an idiotic game that would be! To write when there's no one to read what you've written."

"When everything has gone to hell, there's nothing to do but to play idiotic games."

Scriassine remained silent for a moment and then a half-smile crossed his face. "Nevertheless, certain conditions would be less unfavorable than others," he said confidently. "If Russia wins, there's no problem: it's the end of civilization and the end of all of us. But if America should win out, the disaster wouldn't be quite so bad. If we were able to give her certain values while maintaining some of our own ideas, there'd be some hope that future generations would one day re-establish the ties with our own culture and traditions. But to succeed in that would require the total mobilization of all our potential."

"Don't tell me that in case of a war you'd hope for an American victory!" I said.

"No matter what happens, history must inevitably lead to a classless society," Scriassine said in reply. "It's a matter of two or three centuries. But for the happiness of those men who'll be living during the interval, I ardently hope that the revolution takes place in a world dominated by America and not by Russia."

"In a world dominated by America," I said, "I have a sneaking suspicion that the revolution will cool its heels a good long time."

"And you think that it should be a Stalinist revolution? The idea of revolution had quite an appeal in France, around 1930. But let me tell you, in Russia it wasn't quite so appealing." He shrugged his shoulders. "You're preparing a big surprise for yourselves! The day the Russians occupy France you'll begin to realize what I mean. Unfortunately, it'll be too late then."

"You yourself don't believe in a Russian occupation," I said.

Scriassine sighed. "Too bad," he said. "Let's be optimists. Let's admit that Europe has a chance of remaining independent. But we can't keep her that way except by waging a constant, interminable battle. Working for oneself will be entirely out of the question."

I did not attempt to answer him. All that Scriassine wanted was to reduce

French writers to silence, and I clearly understood why. There was nothing really convincing in his prophecies, and yet his tragic voice awakened an echo in me. "How shall we live?" The question had been painfully pricking me all evening and for God knows how many days and weeks.

TRANSLATED BY LEONARD M. FRIEDMAN

Resistance to Commitment (A Space for Timelessness)

JEAN PAULHAN

Three Cheers for Uncommitted Literature Presenting the "Cahiers de la Pléiade" 1946

After the Liberation, Jean Paulhan, one of the early organizers of the literary Resistance, participated as both editor and contributor in the first issues of Sartre's Les Temps modernes. *He used this position as an opportunity to publish pages from manuscripts that commercial presses had rejected; a periodical, he thought, was the right place to bring out types of writing too original to be published in book form by an industry all too respectful of the economic realities of the literary market.*

Paulhan kept the same editorial practice in the Cahiers de la Pléiade, *the journal he founded in 1946 when the shift from post-Resistance unanimism to Cold War factionalism prompted the disbanding of* Les temps modernes's *editorial committee, leaving the journal under Sartre's single-handed directorship. Yet with a slight difference: the manuscripts he now rescued from editorial censorship were no longer the victims of the market's aesthetic conformism. Conformism had become ideological. To be publishable now, a text, regardless of its literary originality, had to be formatted according to either a recognizable and receivable political line or the agenda of the news.*

Hence Paulhan's own paradoxical What Is Literature?. *Considering*

Jean Paulhan, "Three Cheers for Uncommitted Literature," from "Présentation des 'Cahiers de la Pléiade'," *Oeuvres complètes* (Paris: Cercle du Livre Précieux, 1969), vol. 4, pp. 367–68.

the cultural priorities imposed by today's agenda of commitment, he sug-
gests, we may have entered a period where the only remaining reliable test
for the literary quality of a text is its "negative selection" by editorial com-
mittees. It is literature itself, literature as such, that is on the verge of going
underground, of becoming clandestine.

Every day we are apt to run into fine (or not so fine) folks who will say to
us, "So, I guess recent events have taught you a thing or two."
      "I hope so."
"No one today can possibly believe that art is an end unto itself—"
"I certainly don't."
"—or that a work's formal perfection is enough to justify its existence."
"It's rather the opposite that's true."
"Admit that the writer is part of the world such as it is—"
"He is."
"—and that he must therefore take cognizance of the great issues of the
day."
"Of course."
Well, here is one such issue, an issue of such importance that it may well
overshadow all the rest.
It so happens that in 1939 a well-known government official, Mr. Molotov,
made an astonishing statement. This concerned certain actions by another
well-known official, Mr. Hitler. Mr. Molotov said, "Let's wait a bit before making up our minds, the meaning of the word 'aggression' is just now changing."
With thoroughly official seriousness he even added that "events have recently
infused this word with a new historical content, opposed to the old." Subsequently, as we know, the meaning of various other words such as "peace" and
"fascism," to say nothing of "beauty," "art," and "literature," was also transformed.
So much for government officials: they do what they can. Simply put, it is (in
my view) right, proper, and necessary that there remain a place—however
narrow, and however modest—where men and words can be cleansed of the
filth accumulated through years of war, occupation, and deliverance. Where
"peace" still means peace. Where by "literature" and even "poetry" people
mean what decent people have always meant: not necessarily arguments in
support of an ethical position or thesis (however attractive) but works capable
of affording us a certain revelation, a certain pleasure, whose nature is unique
in the following two respects:
First, it is enormously vast, and shared. Nothing about life (as it is called)
can be understood by anyone who has not experienced it, if only once—
nothing about that dancing folly (sometimes more dance, sometimes more
folly) which whirls around us and catches us up. There is no point in even

trying. Without this experience we are simply stupid, we have no clue. We can of course try to imitate the people around us, but after a while this becomes tiring if we're not really involved.

And second, it remains all but unpredictable. It never repeats itself and is never where one expects to find it. In short, it is not like cooking (for which one relies on professionals) but rather like love (in which professionals are always to some extent suspect).

Of course, one can try to get close to it by promulgating rules and laws and frequenting famous people who have triumphed in the genre, attempting to duplicate their success. (This is the function of the *Pléiade*.) But this doesn't always work. Anyway, it seems that something undefinable always needs to be added to the rules, thereby weakening them—and ridding us of them.

As for the *Cahiers*: it can easily happen that children or madmen or totally naïve or uneducated people will hit the bullseye with their first shot or arrive straightaway at the sort of visionary work that we find so enchanting. (The danger then is that they will naïvely persist in their naïveté and make a system of it. Unfortunately, there is no easy way out of this.)

As will be apparent, the *Cahiers de la Pléiade* deal, as unobtrusively as possible, with issues far more serious than the great social and national conflicts that people have lately tended to bore us with. They deal with these issues in the rigorous yet modest way required by their seriousness. They are not even concerned with publishing thoroughly admirable texts by the great writers of the moment. They take the view that a less than perfect text is not always without merit, and that even the great writers of the moment occasionally nod. Their modest hope is simply to bring together certain curious and apparently useless texts, which other journals, busy with their great and noble projects, may be prone to neglect.

TRANSLATED BY ARTHUR GOLDHAMMER

MAURICE MERLEAU-PONTY

Review: *Les Cahiers de la Pléiade* April 1947

Reviewing the first issue of Paulhan's Les Cahiers de la Pléiade *for* Les Temps modernes, *Maurice Merleau-Ponty disputes Paulhan's disingenuously reductive interpretation of what literary commitment means: it is unfair, he argues, to reduce it to partisan writing. "Committed" does not mean "political," rather, it means "authentic." The term qualifies any type of authentic existential choice implemented by linguistic means. In other words, literature, whether or not it deals with politics or with current events, is in essence committed: writing, when literary, is a total—or as Sartre put it, "totalitarian"—mode of being in the world which engages a speaking subject unreservedly. The truly uncommitted writer would be the barely imaginable one who managed to remain disengaged from what he writes—someone who, as Sartre put it in the "Presentation," would write "so as not to say anything."*

This argument is an elegant way of avoiding the thorny issue of politics in literature in the very name of commitment; it provides Merleau-Ponty with an easy way out. But it misses Paulhan's point, which was less literary than editorial, less about writing than about publishing. For Paulhan, the question was not about Jean Giono's (or Albert Camus's or André Malraux's) being committed in their writing; rather, it was about the texts of Louis-Ferdinand Céline and other former collaborationists being committed to the metaphorical flames of nonpublication by politically committed editorial boards.

"Three cheers for uncommitted literature!" says the wrapper of this issue of the *Cahiers*. But we at *Les Temps modernes* are too much under the influence of Jean Paulhan to look only at the surface. So we searched for a secret here, and we found one. In fact, for the careful reader, this

Maurice Merleau-Ponty, "*Les Cahiers de la Pléiade*, avril 1947: Gallimard, éditeur" (*Les Temps modernes*, Dec. 1947), pp. 1151–52.

issue of the *Cahiers* is nothing less than a manifesto in favor of the writer's commitment.

Of course, I am well aware that the table of contents includes such apolitical figures as Malraux and Camus. But the least frivolous of our noted authors, Jean Giono, is not a man to write about such matters as civil war in Spain or China or an imaginary epidemic in Oran. Indeed, he has written quite forcefully about the war that was fought in France. In September 1939, in a village in Meurthe-et-Moselle in which our military qualifications had landed us, we went to a small bookstore and purchased the *Carnets de Moleskine* by Lucien Jacques, which contains a long and admirable preface by Giono. Close on our heels followed two gendarmes, who confiscated the remaining copies of the work. To date, no such fate has befallen any of Sartre's works. This is because Giono wrote about the Second World War which was then just about to begin, more frankly than Sartre has ever written about the Third. Consider what Giono had to say about the man of peace:

> Purity was all he wanted. And when he found it, he clung to it tenaciously. He is where he is because he is still holding fast, in spite of everything. He knows that he must stand alone. His enterprise is essentially individual. In what he does, there can be no troops because there can be no commanders. The commander is never pure; command defiles. Whatever purity a man may possess he loses the minute he commands other men. Troops comfort other troops. Their strength is always based on numbers. They always represent the resort to force. They are always the solution of impotence. For the person who refuses to fight, the logical thing is not to seek battle but to seek purity, for his fight begins after death. Thousands of peace-lovers add up to thousands of individual deaths, nothing more. In death there are neither troops nor commanders. Death is the loneliest thing in the world. Here it is a common destiny, a mark. I know: this is a death, and I detest death. But contempt pleases me; I like to make use of contempt. "Let me finish him off," screams the professional military mind. Up at dawn, hands tied behind his back, tied to the stake and forced to kneel, his eyes blindfolded, the peace-lover faces the firing squad. The time left to him is infinitesimal. He is alone. But he stands in opposition.

This is provocatively dated June 1939, Manosque. (And three cheers for uncommitted literature.)

Someone may object that, once the *Voyage en calèche* ran afoul of the censors, we had, from 1940 to 1944, no further statement from Giono concerning that other military machine with which we were so burdened during those years. But if one holds a low opinion of one military machine, that opinion also applies to others, even foreign ones. The implication is clear: Giono's prewar writings in a sense spoke for him, so that in the end, if we take a broad view of things, we must forthrightly admit that Giono was the first of our resistance writers. If Jean Paulhan now publishes a fine text of his, full of clouds, trees, and mountains, make no mistake: this is nothing but litotes, irony, a sophisticated way of making the point—which is the very point of *Les Temps modernes*—that a truly great writer accedes to the eternal by living in his own time.

As for Jean Paulhan's article, seven-sixteenths of it is devoted to politics, or should I say polemic? He pretends to have been forced to make this choice against his will: "Try, difficult though it may be, to accept the fact that for the moment history has decided to leave you in peace. Perhaps this might not be a bad time to look into . . . matters you know something about." Again, however, we need to read more carefully: "When I look at how things are going, I have the sense that we're not yet there, that man's destiny has not yet been fulfilled, that things may have been decided a little too quickly, and with loaded dice, and what we need to do is start over from the beginning." So Paulhan has his own ideas about man's destiny. He has his own opinions about the way things are going. If he meditates about "meetings" and "jockeys" and "football" and asks us to think about it, it isn't because he has nothing else on his mind but because everything else disgusts him. Here we have an opinion, a position, almost a political platform. But he doesn't tell us enough about it. Perhaps in the next issue of the *Cahiers*.

In the meantime, the true conclusion of this issue is one that pleases us. It is this: In the broad sense, all literature is committed the moment it says something, because it always defines our relations, poetic or profane, to the world and to other men. Since, moreover, it proposes to change these relations solely through the virtues of expression and truth, it is in conflict with propaganda and with other profane pragmatics; it is, if you will, uncommitted. In the narrow and sectarian sense, committed literature is presumably literature that forgets about being literature, and uncommitted literature is literature that says nothing about anything.

TRANSLATED BY ARTHUR GOLDHAMMER

JULIEN GRACQ

Literature in Your Face
1950

*One could not overemphasize how central the issue of the media was for
French literature's self-definition after World War II. Sartre, for one, re-
acted in the most positive way to the post-Liberation boom of the press,
urging writers not to withdraw but to assert their presence in the expanding
field and turn the threat of the media to literature's advantage.*

Julien Gracq (a Surrealist-inspired novelist who wrote The Distant
Shore *and other works) took the opposite stand—in many ways he did so
with Sartre's negative example in mind. Gracq's 1950 Swiftian pamphlet,*
La Littérature à l'estomac, *advocates uncompromising secession as the
only way for literature to survive in the age of media culture. The surprising vogue for existentialism, promoted by the media, the wide and blind
acceptance of what should have been the least marketable literary product,
was the result of the most unlikely cultural short-circuit: metaphysics as
news item. To the two types of literature Roland Barthes would distinguish: one writable and the other legible, Gracq suggests adding a third: the
chattable, a literature that is neither what a writer writes nor what a reader
reads, but what people talk about. Preserved in its* bouillon de culture,
*embalmed and encrypted like the deities of forgotten religions, literature
reaches an increasingly simulacral stage where the best-sellers of the day
have a remoteness, an indirect existence akin to, for example, Sophocles' lost
tragedies or Plato's lost dialogues.* Timeo Danaos et dona ferentes: *Gracq
follows Laocöon's advice, fear the media. And especially when, no longer
the anticultural Beotians of the heroic ages, they've decided to be* à la page,
*intent on demonstrating that there is no type of obscurity, no level of diffi-
culty, no degree of transgressiveness that can't become marketable. For with
Sartrian commitment, the real danger isn't politics itself but rather one of
literature being led to surrender to the market by the Sirens of politics.*

From Julien Gracq, *La Littérature à l'estomac* (Paris: Corti, 1950), pp. 47–57.

Only a small percentage of the people who talk about literature nowadays really know anything about it. It is impossible to account for this bizarre fact without seeking a more general explanation of the extraordinary changes that have, over the past few decades, affected public perception and behavior in all its forms. It will be useful here to review a number of ideas that are no less important for being familiar. Over, say, the past half century, the sum total of human knowledge has grown almost beyond comprehension in nearly all fields. For some time now it has been impossible for any normally constituted brain to keep track of all this knowledge or to form even the remotest conception of it without relying on popular accounts, on vulgarizations that are no longer even second- but third- or fourthhand. As the individual has lost his grip on mankind's collective knowledge, human beings have become ever-more acutely aware of the unrelenting pressure of the whole. It is as if each individual has become the needle of a seismograph, which every second records tremors from alarming if largely indecipherable events: from flights over the polar caps to railway strikes in Chicago, from the discovery of a new form of nuclear technology in Siberia to that of a new insecticide in Texas. So long as man refuses to take refuge in the ultimate if infinitesimal individual paradise of indifference, a thousand technological, political, scientific, and economic developments of the utmost topical interest continually vie for his attention. Intuitively, he senses that none of this is innocuous. In a confused way he feels that no branch of human activity—including such traditionally anodyne fields as history, genetics, and statistics—is today without *teeth and claws*, teeth and claws that *threaten him*. Hence, to ignore them entirely is out of the question. Yet the amount of time and attention reserved for each has been drastically curtailed, so that each gets no more attention than a radio chat and no more time than it takes to read an article on page two of the evening paper. With the result that, now, in 1950, there is—speaking numerically—virtually no *firsthand* audience of any kind (the few specialists who follow the latest developments in their own field constituting third- or fourthhand audiences for everything else). Some time ago, out of force of habit, a short battle was waged against the unconscionable conditions under which the mind must now operate: pride in *individual scrutiny* briefly outlived the possibility of exercising it. Twenty years ago such pride still manifested itself in grotesque if touching fashion: like someone caught in quicksand and waving frantically before sinking into darkness, a few men of the world still railed passionately, angrily, at the idea that space was curved as Einstein insisted, while a few lighthouse-keepers sneered at the notion of continental drift. In the Hiroshima affair, even more egregious than the devastation of one city among a hundred was the elimination of the last champions of a *common measure;* even more than it opened the way to outright worldwide tyranny, it seems to have inaugurated an era of voluntary intellectual servitude. Something gave way, and it wasn't wooden walls or paper partitions: the public, its last-ditch defenses overwhelmed, suddenly capitulated to the blinding idea of an astronomical, unbreachable distance between what its eye could see and the *how* of phenomena. All at once it abdicated its last remaining powers of verification and control. It *resigned itself* from then on to inhabit, like a house pet, a colorless, quotidian world of fantasy and to accept humbly what it was given without searching for reasons. Privately, a sense of foolishness and even guilt insidiously colored the increasingly fearful reactions of each individual, and even in areas such as literature, where taste had no reason to allow its right of judgment to be summarily abrogated, a sort of contamination occurred. Given the extremely prudent and cautious, inhibition-ridden reaction of the average reader today when asked to offer a judgment in the absence of any critical guidance, one has the impression that, here, the sanction of the *specialists* to whom he is instinctively prone to appeal on all subjects is sorely lacking, that the individual reader feels that he is being asked to venture into a minefield for which he is *ill-equipped*. Nothing is more revealing in this respect than the startlingly passive, indeed pusillanimous attitude of much of the educated public and many critics in the debate that erupted over a now-celebrated literary counterfeit.[1] When some people dared to voice opinions based on the text alone, thereby burning their bridges, the ensuing astonishment gave considerable food for thought, as did the admiring sense that those bold individuals were truly *not afraid* to speak their minds. In a flash, one caught a glimpse of the depths of indifferent docility, of nonresistance, upon which literature nowadays blindly sails. The vast majority of people of course just "waited to see what the newspaper would say," taking the easy way out and abdicating any opinion of their own, as if the matter involved some thorny question of nuclear physics. The sad truth must be told: a large, a very large part of the *cultivated* reading public "keeps up" with the latest progress in literature in much the same way that it "keeps up" with the latest progress in nuclear physics: both are beyond direct perception, subjects about which one reads in the newspapers. The same readers feel the same patriotic and wisely unquestioning thrill when they read that a new reactor has been put into operation as when they read that a new "avant-garde" poet has arrived. If the years after 1945 seem to me to mark a major turning point in our literary history, not so much for the value of the works produced as for the shift in the relation between the work and its audience, it is because for the first time a literary school has gained the recognition and *approval* of the majority without that majority's insisting on being able to enjoy that school's works or understand its theories. Twenty-five years ago, the vast majority of the same audience probably took just a little pleasure in the works of the Surrealists and just as little interest in their theories, but then the audience did not capitulate: it saved its honor by having, if nothing else, the courage of its incomprehension. In twenty-five years we have thus gone from an era in which revolutions sprang from mass passions to an era in which outcomes are decided, over the heads of the people yet with their consent, by inaccessible "ruling circles." The fantastic, mythological fear of being left on the sands of history, of failing "to be of one's own time"—as one might miss the last subway (Lautréamont once described the great nightmare that haunts the modern intellectual as that of a child *running after a bus*)—has added fewer self-professed converts to the ranks of "existentialism" than has the skillful exploitation of the staggering inferiority complex that people have come to feel with respect to everything they now admit (convinced as they are by tangible proof) to be "beyond them." In this respect, existentialism has gambled and won across the board: it has benefitted from the belated remorse of a public that has sworn, in a fit of zeal, that it would never again be blamed for allowing an *écrivain maudit* to die of hunger (hence that in case of doubt, it would opt systematically for admiration), and it has benefitted even more from the unexamined prestige automatically accorded nowadays to anyone who claims to be a *specialist* in any abstruse science whatsoever. (After five thousand years, the world has come to grant anyone who deals in *hieroglyphics* a right to unquestioning veneration: in *Les Temps modernes*, for example, we find, alongside the stars who operate primarily in the realm of metaphysics, a neophyte who, having learned his lesson, seeks to secure his position as a literary critic by flaunting his knowledge of Chinese.) The truth is that literature has in the past few years been the victim of a formidable campaign of intimidation by the nonliterary—the nonliterary of the most aggressive sort: I became aware of this, to my great astonishment, while perusing recent issues of *Les Temps modernes*, which, in a laudable "progressive" spirit, has decided to teach us the rudiments of sex. I do not know Mme de Beauvoir. What one gleans of her character inspires respect, and I have not forgotten that she has given us, with *L'Invitée*, what is undoubtedly, and by a rather wide margin, the best existentialist novel to date. In any case, it was courageous of her—a woman—to broach this hopeless subject, almost in the manner of a Christian venturing forth to face the lions. She would invariably, as she must have known, have to contend with the nastiness of the French, and no matter what she did, people would inevitably respond with boisterous laughter. In the event, however, one felt—alas—no urge to laugh. One was transfixed, scandalized—not, unfortunately, as when one reads an "erotic" novel but rather as when the unflappable Raymond Poincaré used to speechify in the cemeteries—by a startling, suffocating impropriety of tone. Astounding! A certain superficial crudeness, which makes the skin crawl, today garners glory for a literary work much as a thick accumulation of dust distinguishes a fine old bottle of wine: it is *proof of origin*. One divines that these people, who *are busy with other things,* occupied with great works, don't have time to wash their faces. We live in an age when in literature, at long last, Caliban has found his voice—and this is no laughing matter. The invasion of metaphysics began with that rumble of boots that is always so impressive at first: people looked on as these strange occupiers, these *tall, white barbarians,* marched past, and naturally the silent spectators wondered about the incomprehensible secret of the invaders' strength, which of course signifies nothing so much as the ephemeral inanity of their opposite numbers. A friend who used to edit a literary journal confessed to me one day his fear of the rising tide of grotesque "papers"—Jaspersian, Husserlian, Kierkegaardian—piling up on his doorstep. A hungry tribe, long confined to the outer reaches, had seized the opportunity to settle, as in conquered territory, on public land far more fertile than its forsaken moors. It came—this tribe of *doctors,* a species unknown to the natives—fully armed and victualed, prepared with customs, recreations, and even a language of its own. The breach in the walls was in fact closed fairly quickly, for the land could absorb no more settlers, but not before a small nation with curious customs had colonized literature. A secret passageway seems to have been created between the watercloset and the *Revue de métaphysique et de morale*, reminding one at times of a remark of Sainte-Beuve's: "What is needed is a door between the stable and the library, so that when *Francisque Michel* has finished in one place he can be pushed into the other—but such people can never be allowed into the salon." When one sees the public whispering in hushed tones about novels that make one think the late Charles Renouvier's *Uchronie* would be a best-seller if it were published today, one wonders if we have not returned to the time when people revered certain *sacred texts* precisely because they believed that the obscene symbols they contained gave proof of the forever elusive esoteric meaning within. There is a kind of provocative scatology which, contrary to common belief, cannot be eliminated from the modern metaphysical novel with impunity: for the public this is the mark of *mystery* itself. It is a fetish, a grigri, which transfixes like Père Ubu's broom. The literary public's reaction to the meager pittance it has been offered is a comedy worthy of the ample gallery of collective insanity that our century has given us: it might be called the *monkey's dance before the organ grinder.*

TRANSLATED BY ARTHUR GOLDHAMMER

NOTE

[1] In 1947, a fake Rimbaud was published under the title: *La chasse spirituelle*. Almost alone, André Breton exposed the hoax in *Flagrant délit* (1947).

ROGER CAILLOIS

The Ultimate Bibliophilia
1963

Literature, Sartre claims, must first answer the question for whom does one write? Who is the reader in the text? In this piece, written as a preface for a rare books catalogue, Roger Caillois answers (or avoids) Sartre's summons by perversely emphasizing pleasures that are less those of the text than those of the page: the pleasures of texts that seem to have been written not so much to be read as to be printed—to end up existing, as Mallarmé would have said, in the guise of a book. A bibliophile's love for books precludes their use value for a reader.

There is a passage in Saint-John Perse that has always aroused a curious resonance in me. It held my memory in such thrall that I used to go around repeating it in spite of myself, and despite the fact that I could not remember what poem I had taken it from. Finally, I found it in *"Amitié du prince."* Here it is: *"Qu'on m'apporte—je veille et je n'ai point sommeil—qu'on m'apporte ce livre des plus vieilles Chroniques. . . . Sinon l'histoire, j'aime l'odeur de ces grands livres en peau de chèvre (et je n'ai point sommeil)."* [Bring me— I'm awake and not sleepy—bring me that book of the most ancient chronicles. . . . If not history, what I like is the smell of those big books bound in kidskin (and I'm not sleepy)].

Today these lines remind me of a passage in the Book of Esther, in which the following is reported of King Ahasuerus: "That night the king, unable to sleep, commanded that the annals be brought to him." But Ahasuerus also orders that the annals be read to him, thus initiating a series of events that leads to Mordechai's return to favor and Haman's disgrace, whereas the insomniac prince in Perse's poem is content simply to sniff the bindings of his volumes. In his way, he is a bibliophile, not a reader. He loves books not for their content, but, strange to say, for their smell.

Dare I admit it? I understand him better than I understand today's biblio-

Roger Caillois, "L'Ultime bibliophilie," [1963] in *Cases d'un échiquier* (Paris: Gallimard, 1970), pp. 165–69.

philes, whose attraction to books is rather impure for my taste. What is a bibliophile if not a person who values the book as object more than the quality of the
text within? While people tend to think of these two tastes as complementary,
to my mind they are in fact incompatible. Indeed, what must be done in order
to scrutinize a book's printed pages is a threat to its integrity as a physical object. The more attentive or impatient the reading, the more precious and less
sturdy the volume, the greater the risk. Open a book too wide and its spine will
break; cut or turn a page too quickly and irreparable disaster will follow. Any
use of a book is a potential violation. Hence the book lover will keep his precious volume safe behind glass and take it out only on rare occasions: when he
cannot sleep, or when the scent of ink and paper draws him to it, or when he
longs to admire the perfection of the typography, the layout of the pages, or the
use of some novel font. Of course I am well aware of how outrageous it is that
books exist for the express purpose of not being read, and that people acquire
books for the express purpose of not reading them. This is a paradoxical or
contradictory state of affairs. If everyone used books in this way, it might be
better to abolish literature and even printing. Bibliophilia is thus fundamentally idolatrous and sacrilegious, in some ways related, and not just etymologically, to necrophilia.

Here, as is often the case, perversion is coupled with sanctimony. A kind of
fetishism supplants the interest that should be bestowed upon rigorous
thought, artful writing, and purely intellectual accomplishment, from which
the sumptuousness of the container is presumably a mere distraction. The bibliophile, however, wants to experience sensual as well as intellectual pleasure;
he wants beauty of another order for his eyes and hands to contemplate and
caress. His misplaced homage to the text at once exalts it and annihilates it,
erects barriers around it, hedges it about with such sophisticated refinements
that it becomes almost untouchable. Flawless type, impressive bindings, sumptuous papers, masterful illustrations, and a thousand other perfections are essential to the bibliophile. At once expensive and difficult to achieve, these can
be seen as so many tributes to an elemental power that ultimately deserves
homage of a very different kind, namely, the honor of entering memory free of
material intervention and without a trace. At this extreme, the written word
itself is already a sign of decadence, not to say an affront to honor. And yet there
is no form of mental excellence that one does not wish to see durably enshrined,
consigned to vellum or inscribed in stone.

Let me return to the sleepless prince who, unlike Ahasuerus, is reluctant, at
whatever hour of the day or night, to turn his mind to the story within. He
handles the physical object without opening it, explores it with his touch, in-
hales its peculiar smell. He allows his sensitive fingers and languorous gaze to
wander over a binding that once might have been made of kidskin but today is
more likely to come from the skin of an ostrich or a penguin. He lingers plea-
surably over the tiny craters which prove that on this surface feathers once

grew. I know these feelings. I have experienced such pleasures. Who would claim to be immune from such desires?

I can even recall once having had a book bound in a thin skin, dusty gray in color and pleasantly uneven in texture, like a dried-out mucous membrane with a raised polygonal pattern reminiscent of the trenches of a fortification or the geometry of the beehive and so coarsely wrinkled that it seemed mineral, though it still bore the stigmata of the stuff of life. Purchased at the base of the Andes and preserved by drying, the swatches from which this cover was made came from the hideous pouches that dangle beneath the throats of condors. I derived additional pleasure from the fact that these strange skins were put to use to cover not a small box or jewel case but a book. In this I sinned, for I knew what I was thereby condemning the book to silence, and took perverse delight in doing so.

One may as well admit that, while any number of arts have helped to draw literature and bibliophilia together, a fundamental hostility remains. Literature predated printing and can survive without it. In fact, it survived without the printing press, and even without writing, for thousands of years.

But that is not the real reason for the latent hostility between the two. It comes, rather, from the fact that there is no necessary relationship between the content of the book and the book itself, the material substrate of the printed text. Indeed, there is less of a relationship between the two than between the taste of a mollusk's flesh and the shell in which it is housed. A lover of seafood, who savors oysters, clams, and abalone, may well evince no interest whatsoever in the splendid spirals, cones, and spines that festoon their shells; he may be ignorant of Haliotidae and Spondylidae and never have heard of *Argonauta argo*, *Thatcheria mirabilis*, and *Ocenebra eurypteron*. Conversely, a shell collector may detest crustaceans, just as the bibliophile may feel not even hatred but simply indifference toward a work and yet carefully preserve a coveted edition of it in his library. The writer and the lover of literature thrive on art and ideas. They may pay no attention to the shell, may not recognize paper by its batch or watermark, and may never have heard the names Garamond, Baskerville, and Bodoni. Such differences are by no means astonishing. It is nothing but a felicitous coincidence when a gourmet also happens to be a collector of shells, or when a writer or passionate reader also takes an avid interest in fine typography.

So fortuitous is such a coincidence that it embarrasses me. For the sake of an innocent bibliophilia, I wish there were a meaningless set of type, whose characters would convey no message, like the whorls of shells, the patterns on butterfly wings, or effigies within stone, like all the abandoned literature enshrouded in the history of the planet and slowly accumulating in its archives.

I suppose that bibliophilic pleasure is also the goal of the person who searches for striking or rare samples. Books defended by their covers, slipcases, glassed-in shelves, and locked cabinets hold in mute captivity a message whose vocation was neither silence nor prison, while each remarkable parcel of the universe derives glory from its simple presence, its taciturn yet eloquent existence.

One of Alejo Carpentier's heroes wonders "whether the higher forms of aesthetic emotion might not simply consist in supreme knowledge of the world. Perhaps men will someday discover an alphabet in flecks of quartz or in the velvety brown of a moth's wing. Then we will learn, to our astonishment, that every spotted shell was always a poem." The visible world continually provides us with an infinite lexicon, composed not of words but of figures that express nothing but themselves, and that it is pointless to try to decipher. Here, no appearance or substance, no illustration or type face threatens to get in the way of the message. The figures themselves constitute the totality of that message, if there is one. Anyone who takes pleasure in collecting these strange tokens of a secret splendor exhibits them in a new light by setting them in isolation. He compels them if not to speak then at least to resonate. Whereupon they become the instigators of dreams, passions, and meditations. And so there is born what one might call an absolute bibliophilia, which, rather than collect precious volumes draws on the vast panoply of the world's riches. Behind this lies neither art nor literature but, unmediated, the inexhaustible universe. And when this happens, it is as if textual value were being granted even to signs that belong to no written language and previously had refused to break their silence.

TRANSLATED BY ARTHUR GOLDHAMMER

PART II
Cold War Aesthetics

Politics and Mass Culture

FRANCIS PONGE

Radio
1946

Even though Francis Ponge's Le Parti pris des choses *(1942) was rendered into English as* The Voice of Things, *the poet's real aesthetic—and even ethical—*parti pris *or "commitment" puts him infallibly on the side of voiceless things. Hence his repulsion for the radio receiver, a thing with a voice. A slightly less physical sister of the garbage can, this "speaking can" brings home the latest ideological and linguistic litter. Poetry takes charge of the ensuing cleaning cycle. For this literary purge Ponge chose, as a lyre, if not the washboard, at least an archaic form of the washing machine— the boiler ("La Lessiveuse" [1943])—not to mention the soap ("Le Savon" [1942–46], pub 1967) he celebrated, after the war, on the waves of a German radio station, in a bubbly text that tries to cleanse itself of the grime of being broadcast.*

Nothing protrudes from the polished box but a small knob, which, when turned slightly until it clicks, soon causes several small, aluminum skyscrapers within to glow feebly, whereupon harsh voices simultaneously emanate from within and vie for our attention.

What marvelous "selectivity" this little appliance has! How clever to have added so dramatically to the power of our ears! Why? To subject oneself constantly to the crudest insults.

The stinking effluvia of the world's melody.

Francis Ponge, "La Radio" [1946], in *Pièces* (*Le grand recueil*, vol. 3) (Paris: Gallimard, 1961), p. 100.

What an excellent idea! Manure needs to be collected and spread out in the sun to dry. Sometimes it proves to be good fertilizer.

Still, we'd better get back to the box quickly and shut it off.

Occupying a place of honor in every home in recent years, right in the middle of the living room, with the windows wide open—yet another garbage can, small in size, buzzing and glowing.

TRANSLATED BY ARTHUR GOLDHAMMER

ANDRÉ MALRAUX

The Conquerors
1949

*In 1947, Malraux had become the leading ideologue of the Gaullist move-
ment he had joined during the Resistance, a long way from the front-line
Communist fellow traveller he had been during the 1930s. In order to help
his readers adjust to this change, he added the transcript of one of his legendary public improvisations at a political rally as an afterword to his first
novel,* The Conquerors *(1927).*

    *This text is another illustration of how, in French Cold War culture, the
political polarities (left versus right, communism versus capitalism,
America versus Soviet Union) were overdetermined by the cultural ones
(high versus low). Thus, in Malraux's anticommunism one can often perceive the political rationalization of a resistance to mass culture: high culture, here, has become the cultural wing of NATO, so to speak.*

    *Malraux's geopolitics were organized around the defense of an Atlantic
civilization that both includes America and excludes Russia. For him, Russia simply wasn't part of Europe. As for his America, it might have become
the military, even the economic powerhouse of the Western Alliance, but
one shouldn't lose sight of the fact that the real historical purpose of such an
alliance was and remains to ensure that European culture remains the cultural standard of the West.*

    *However, this Eurocentric model, with both political and cultural fronts
matching each other, faces a growing challenge—not so much from the all
too obvious military ambitions of the Eastern bloc, but, unexpectedly, from
the expanding appeal of a specifically American culture. For Malraux, the
very concept of mass culture is contradictory. And if it is America he sides
with, this is at least in part because capitalist advertising never claimed to
constitute a culture. True, American-type advertising and Soviet propaganda are equally contemptible versions of psychological manipulation
("Whether it's selling soap or winning votes, there's no psychological tech-*

André Malraux, "1949," in *The Conquerors*, trans. Stephen Becker (New York: Holt,
Rinehart, and Winston, 1976), pp. 179–98, from *Les Conquérants* (Paris: Grasset, 1948), pp.
228–252.

nique that doesn't start with contempt for the buyer or the voter"); but no
American, according to Malraux, ever cared to present this consumerist ver-
sion of "dehumanization by means of psychological techniques" as the
ground of a new culture, the way Soviet propaganda did. The Soviet Union
is the sole place where mass culture has been associated with a cultural
claim. At least until America started marketing its homegrown nonculture
as a positive, specifically American culture.

The real catastrophe that haunts Malraux's culture world politics, less
political than cultural, is the collapse of the wall separating the twin mass
barbarisms of capitalism and communism. Hence his view of the museum
as Europe's last recourse against the world expansion of the henceforth-
indisguishable logic of the party and the market.

O ver twenty years have passed since the publication of this young man's
novel, and much water has flowed under how many broken bridges!
Twenty years after the capture of Peking by Chiang Kai-shek's revolutionary army, we await the capture of Chiang Kai-shek's Canton by Mao
Tse-tung's revolutionary army. In twenty years will another revolutionary
army drive out the "facist" Mao? What does the shade of Borodin think of all
this, Borodin who when last heard of, before the war, was petitioning the
Kremlin for "a lodging with a fireplace"? And the shade of Galen, a suicide?

And yet, despite the complicated interplay that has perhaps—perhaps—
cast China on Russia's side, Mao's troops have plucked their victories from
the revolt that inspired other troops in 1925. It is not the old passion for liberation that has altered. What has altered most is not China and not Russia, but
Europe: out there, Europe has ceased to matter.

But this book bears only superficially on history. If it has survived, it's not because it depicted certain episodes of the Chinese revolution but because it portrayed a certain type of hero who combined culture, logic, and a talent for
action. Those values were indirectly linked to the values of Europe at the time.
And as I am now asked, "What has become of intellectual values in today's
Europe?" I prefer to answer with the appeal I made to intellectuals on 5 March
1948 at the Salle Pleyel in Paris, on behalf of my Gaullist colleagues.

Its form—the transcript of a speech improvised from notes—shows only
too well that this is no carefully tooled essay. Certain of the ideas expressed here
have been developed on another level in *The Voices of Silence*. But the element
of breathless preaching inevitable in a prepared speech seemed better reserved
to the novel's passions (and the novel's limits), and not superimposed on a pretended objectivity. The decay of European consciousness is only summarily
analyzed here. The problem was to focus on the most immediate, and at the
same time the most insidious, threat: dehumanization by means of psychologi-

cal techniques (propaganda has come a long way since Garine); and to specify what, in our opinion, must be *preserved*.

The European spirit is the object of a double metamorphosis. As we see it, the drama of the twentieth century is this: simultaneously the political myth of the International is dying and an unprecedented internationalization of culture is proceeding inexorably.

Throughout the last century, from Jules Michelet's mighty voice to Jean Jaurès's mighty voice, there seemed to be serious evidence that in shattering the bonds of nationality we became more human. That was neither baseness nor error: it was the shape of hope. Victor Hugo thought that the United States of Europe would develop effortlessly and would foreshadow the United States of the World. But the United States of Europe will be born in travail, and the United States of the World is a long way off. . . .

What we have learned is that Russia's grand, scornful gesture in discarding its anthem, the "Internationale" (which will always be linked to Russia, whether she likes it or not, in mankind's eternal dream of justice), sweeps away the dreams of the nineteenth century at one stroke. We know now that in becoming less French we do not become more human, only more Russian. For better or for worse, we are tied to the nation. And we know that we shall not create the European without her; that willy-nilly we must create the European upon her.

As that immense hope died, as each man was flung back upon his homeland a flood of new works burst upon civilization: music and the plastic arts had invented their printing press. Translations crossed borders freely; Colonel Lawrence sat side by side with Benjamin Constant; the Payot series with the Garnier Foreign Classics.

And finally the cinema was born. At this very moment a Hindu woman watching *Anna Karenina* may burst into tears seeing a Swedish actress and an American director express the Russian Tolstoy's idea of love.

If we haven't reconciled the dreams of the living, at least we've bound the dead closer!

And in this hall tonight we can say without embarrassment, "You gathered here are the first generation of mankind to inherit the entire earth."

How is such a legacy possible? We note carefully that every vanished civilization appealed to only a part of man. That of the Middle Ages was primarily a culture of the soul; that of the eighteenth century, a culture of the mind. From age to age successive civilizations, appealing to successive elements in man, were superimposed; they were probably fused only for their inheritors. Inheritance is always metamorphosis. The true heir to Chartres is of course not the art of Saint Sulpice, but Rembrandt. Michelangelo, striving to remake Antiquity, made Michelangelo.

What would our civilization's ancestors have had to say to one another? It combines a Greek element, a Roman, a Biblical, we all know that; but what would have passed between Caesar and the prophet Elijah? Insults. For the true birth of a dialogue between Christ and Plato, Montaigne had to be born.

Only in the inheritor comes the metamorphosis from which life springs.

And who lays claim to that metamorphosis today? The United States, the Soviet Union, Europe. Let's clear the ground a bit before we go on to the essential problem, and let's discard the foolish notion that cultures are in constant conflict, as countries are. Latin America alone proves how silly that is. In our own time she is in the process of reconciling—without a pitched battle—what she wants to take from the Anglo-Saxon world and what she wants to take from the Latin world. There are irreducible political differences; but it is absolutely not true that cultural conflicts are by definition irreducible. They may be, and most dangerously; or they may not be at all.

Let's also spare ourselves that ridiculous Manichaeism, that distinction between the speaker's friends, angels, and the speaker's enemies, devils, which has come into fashion when America and Russia are the topic. What we think of Russian policy toward our own country is obvious: we think that the same forces that made her France's ally at the Liberation have made her France's implacable adversary since; and we intend to do something about that. But Stalin doesn't diminish Dostoyevsky, any more than Mussorgsky's genius guarantees Stalin's politics.

Let's look first at the American claim to the world's cultural heritage. First point: There is no culture in America which defines itself as specifically American. That's a European invention. In America one feels that there is a characteristic context to life. One feels that America is a rootless country, an urban country, a country unaware of the ancient and profound connection with trees and stones common to the most ancient spirits of China and the most ancient spirits of the Occident. A country with the great advantage over us of being able to, and wanting to, welcome all the world's heritages with equal fervor; and a country in which any major museum displays, in the same hall, Romanesque statues gazing off at our Occident, and T'ang statues gazing off at Chinese civilization.

But a superior antiquarian's warehouse, even on an epic scale, is not a great culture. And the moment we set aside Europe's influence, American culture is a realm of acquired knowledge infinitely more than a realm of organic culture.

Furthermore, the mass arts—radio, films, the press—are now picking up an American accent everywhere.

Its art seems specifically American to us when it's an art of the masses. And there's not really that much difference between the spirit of *Life* magazine and the spirit of *Samedi soir*; it's just that there are more Americans than there are Frenchmen.

And finally, America possesses a characteristic romanticism. But again, is it specifically American? Incontestably there is an American way of looking at the world which eternally reduces that world to its romantic version. But must I remind you that in *The Three Musketeers* Richelieu is important not for his influence on France but because he warns that Anne of Austria's diamond studs, gift of the king, are missing? For the moment, America represents the romantic more than any country, but probably because she is a country of masses. And culture ranges far beyond such questions. What do cultivated Americans think? They think that American culture is one of the national cultures of the Western world, that there is no more difference between high American culture and high French culture than between the latter and high English culture, or what high German culture used to be. We Europeans aren't all that much alike! And believe me, the distance from Bergsonism to behaviorism is of the same order as the distance from Hegel to Bergson. In short, relative to us America has never seen herself, on the cultural plane, as a discrete part of the world; *she has always seen herself as part of* our *world*. There's not so much an American art as American artists. We live by the same value systems; they don't reflect everything essential from Europe's past but, rather, everything in them that's essential is linked to Europe. I repeat: an American culture, as distinct from our own as Chinese culture, is purely and simply a European invention.

And there are no specifically American cultural assumptions in conflict with our own except precisely insofar as Europe has abdicated its beliefs and responsibilities.

It's hard to be altogether comfortable with the idea of Russia as a European country.

St. Petersburg used to give us (and Leningrad still does) the impression of a European "settlement," a vast imperial branch of the Occident—shops, barracks, and cupolas—a New Delhi of the north.

But to take the Russians for Asiatics, and therefore for a kind of Chinese or Hindus, as their enemies always have, is ridiculous. The truth may be that we ought not to take maps too seriously, and that Russia is neither in Europe nor in Asia (it's in Russia), as Japan, where love and the army are so important, is neither in China nor in America.

The other countries of Europe share its culture on many levels and by way of exchanges. In one century or another Italy, Spain, France, and England have predominated. Those countries have much in common: the cultural myth of Greece and Rome, and the heritage of fifteen countries of a common Christianity. That last heritage, which itself separates the Slavs of Bohemia from the Slavs of Russia, is surely an important influence; and the heritage of Byzantium is so influential in Russia that Russian painting has never worked free of it, and Stalin invokes Basil II at least as often as Peter the Great.

Russia entered Western culture in the nineteenth century, with her composers and novelists. And at that, Dostoyevsky is probably the only one of their novelists to consider himself distinctly Russian.

Ilya Ehrenburg commented indirectly on an interview I gave about Atlantic civilization, by asking, "Which is European, the atomic bomb or Tolstoy?"

If it's all right with you, we won't bother with the atomic bomb tonight. If the Russians had none then, it wasn't for lack of trying. And to urge Stalin on us as a man of Gandhi's sort doesn't make much sense.

There remains Tolstoy. Which Tolstoy? The author of *Anna Karenina* and *War and Peace* isn't simply a European but one of the giants of the Western spirit. The old warning goes, "Don't spit where you drink." When he wrote his novels, he willed himself European and felt that he was Balzac's rival in particular. But if we're talking about the Count Lev Nikolaevich who tried to live like a Gandhian Christian, who died in the snow like an old epic hero, who wrote that he "preferred a good pair of boots to Shakespeare," then I think of the great Byzantine visionaries—and if I absolutely had to compare him to another genius, it would be Tagore, inseparable from India and writing, in *The Home and the World*, one of the great universal novels; it would not be Stendhal.

What most separates him from us is doubtless what also separates us from Russia—his Oriental dogmatism. Stalin believes in his own truth, and there is no free play in that truth; but Tolstoy, when he divorced himself from the West, believed no less in his own truth; and Dostoyevski's genius was at the service of his implacable preaching all his life. Russia never had a Renaissance, nor an Athens; nor a Bacon, nor a Montaigne.

In Russia there's always been an urge toward Sparta and an urge toward Byzantium. Sparta integrates itself smoothly with the Occident; Byzantium, no. In the frenzied industrialization of that immense country, under way for thirty years now, we can see the most furious drive to westernize since Peter the Great. "Catch up with America! Pass her!" But the greater that effort, the harder the Russian spirit resists.

It's no accident that the Russian communists are attacking Picasso. His painting throws doubt on the fundamentals of their system; it is willy-nilly a most intensely European presence.

In the realm of the intellect everything that Russia calls formalism, that she has deported or tirelessly liquidated for the past ten years, is Europe. Suspected painters, writers, filmmakers, philosophers are above all suspected of submitting to the influence of a "degenerate Europe." Europeans, Eisenstein, Babel, Prokofiev! The spirit of Europe is a danger to a Pharaonic industry. Moscow's rebuke to Picasso is no accident: it represents a defense of the five-year plans. . . .

Depending on whether an artist dies in time, or a little too late, he's buried with honors in the Kremlin wall or without honor at the foot of a wall in a Siberian prison camp.

The real reason why Russia is not European has nothing to do with geography. It's the Russian will.

I'm not giving a course here in the history of culture. I'm talking about Europe only in relation to the Soviet Union and the United States. Europe shows two characteristics at the moment:

The first is the link between art and culture. Those two realms are kept separate in Russia by a general dogmatism of thought. They are no less irreducibly separated in the United States, because in the United States the man of culture is not the artist, he is a university man. An American writer— Hemingway, Faulkner—isn't at all the equivalent of Gide or Valéry, but the equivalent of Rouault or Braque. They are dazzling specialists within a systematic culture of systematic knowledge; they are neither men of history nor ideologues.

The second point, important in another way: the will to transcend, to survive. Careful! Europe is the part of the world where Chartres, Michelangelo, Shakespeare, and Rembrandt lived in succession. Do we repudiate them, yes or no? No! Then we have to know what we're talking about.

We seem to think of ourselves as poor unfortunates, facing one immense culture called American novelists and another immense culture called I'm not too sure what—at best, Russian composers (which is incidentally not bad).

Yet the whole world still looks to Europe ultimately, and Europe alone can answer its most profound questions. Then who took Michelangelo's place? The glow they seek in Europe is the last glow of Rembrandt's light; and Europe's grand, tremulous gesture in what she thinks is her death agony is still the heroic gesture of Michelangelo. . . .

They've just reproached us: "Those are bourgeois values." But why this definition of art by its context?

Understand me well. I see justice in a Russian philosopher—shipped to Siberia since, by the way—saying that "Plato's thought is inseparable from slavery." It's true that there's a historical setting to thought, a social conditioning of thought. But the problem doesn't end there; it begins there. You, for example, you've read Plato! But neither as slaves nor as slaveholders!

No one in this hall—myself no more than any other—knows what feelings inspired an Egyptian sculpting a statue in the Old Kingdom; nevertheless our admiration for that statue is hardly derived from any exaltation of bourgeois values. And there's the problem exactly: to discover what it is that ensures the transcendence, the partial survival, of dead cultures.

I'm not talking about eternity; I'm talking about metamorphosis. Egypt has reappeared for us, after a disappearance of over fifteen hundred years. The metamorphosis is unforeseeable? Then we're up against a basic fact of civilization, namely the unpredictability of renaissances. But I prefer an unpredictable world to a world pretending to be what it isn't.

Europe's current drama is the death of man. With the atom bomb, and even before, we came to realize that what the nineteenth century called "progress" had extorted a heavy ransom. We realized that the world had become dualistic again, and that man's immense, unmortgaged hope for the future was no longer valid.

But it isn't because nineteenth-century optimism has disappeared that there's no more human thought! Since when has striving depended on immediate optimism? If that were true, there would have been no French Resistance before 1944. More than one old adage tells us to begin even without hope.

Man must be created again, yes, but not from sentimental cartoons. Europe is still defending the world's highest intellectual values. To know that, you need only imagine Europe dead. If, on the spot that was Florence, on the spot that was Paris, we'd come to the time when "the swaying and murmurous rushes shall bow," do you really think it would be very long before they became holy places in man's memory?

Only we Europeans have ceased to believe in Europe: in apprehensive and distant veneration the world still gazes upon these old hands groping in shadow. . . .

If Europe is thinking not in terms of liberty but in terms of destiny, it's not for the first time. Things were going pretty badly about the time of the Battle of Mohács. Things were going pretty badly when Michelangelo carved on the pedestal of "Night," "If it be to open thine eyes upon tyranny, mayest thou never waken."

So there's no question of Europe going under. I wish they'd stop that nonsense! On the one hand, there's a hypothesis: Europe is becoming a principal element of the Atlantic civilization. And, on the other hand, there's a question: What is Europe becoming in the Soviet view of the world? The Atlantic civilization invokes and, deep down, respects Europe as a culture; the Soviet view scorns its past, hates its present, and accepts only a European future empty of all that Europe was.

Europe's values are threatened from within by techniques developed in media that appeal to collective passions: press, movies, radio, advertising—in a word, propaganda. In a more elegant style, "psychological manipulation."

Those techniques are most highly developed in the countries we've just been talking about. In America they are primarily in the service of an economic system and tend to force the individual to buy things. In Russia they're in the service of a political system and tend to force the citizen into unquestioning loyalty to his leaders' ideology; for that, they involve the whole person.

Let's not confuse the application of such techniques in their countries of origin with their effect on Europe, especially France. The effect of American psychotechniques on our culture is secondary; that of Russia's psychotechniques means to be decisive.

And, above all, let's not talk tonight about some future culture, which Russian psychotechniques always refer to. Let's talk about what is: the totality of Soviet techniques in France today amounts practically to a systematic organization of lies selected for their effectiveness.

To condemn Georges Bernanos peremptorily in the name of a mythical proletariat might be defensible if we were not also compelled to admire Garaudy's edifying novels.[1] Ah, all those hopes betrayed, all those outrages, all those dead, only to substitute one shelf of childish sentiment for another!

And then there's the famous hoax of revolutionary continuity. As everybody knows, the gold-braided marshals are the legitimate heirs of Lenin's leather-jacketed colleagues. This has to be explained. André Gide and I were asked to go to Hitler with the petitions protesting the conviction of Dimitrov, innocent of the Reichstag fire. It was a great honor for us (not everybody was rushing to join us). And now, when Dimitrov in power has the innocent Petkov hanged, who's changed? Gide and I, or Dimitrov?

In the beginning Marxism redrew the world for the sake of liberty. The emotional freedom of the individual played a huge role in Lenin's Russia. Lenin had Chagall paint frescoes for the Jewish theater in Moscow. Today Stalin heaps shame on Chagall; who's changed?

One of my books, *Man's Fate*, made an impression on quite a few Russians in its day. Eisenstein would make a movie of it, with music by Shostakovich; Meyerhold a play, with music by Prokofiev—is that a long enough honors list of death and recantation for one book? It will be explained to me that I am ignorant of the dialectic. So are prisoners at forced labor. So are the dead.

Innumerable writers have broken away: Victor Serge, Gide, Hemingway, Dos Passos, Mauriac, so many others. And the social problem had nothing whatever to do with it. It was never understood that our "tomorrows that sing" would be that long howl rising from the Caspian to the White Sea, and that their song would be the song of convicts.

We're here on this platform tonight and we do not repudiate Spain. Let a Stalinist stand here someday and defend Trotsky!

In Russia the problem is different. It's a closed country, and by that alone cut off from the mainstream of modern culture. Now it's the country where everything has to have happened first. I quote from the young people's manual of history:

> It is a Russian schoolteacher, Sholkovsky, who developed the theory of jet propulsion. It is a Russian electrotechnician, Popov, who first invented the radio. (*Simlia Russkaia*, p. 55.)

> In capitalist countries education is a private matter and very expensive. For a very large number of young men and women it is an unattainable desire and dream. (Ibid., p. 277.)

Enough.

On the positive side, there is a mode of thought that tends to exalt solidarity, work, and a certain noble messianism, though with a note of scorn always present in liberators. But then there are psychotechniques intended to create both an image of the world and an attitude toward it that reflect most favorably on the party line. "Writers are the engineers of the soul." And how!

But for all that, they claim to have truth on their side. Let's not forget that the largest Russian newspaper is called *Pravda*—the Truth. But there are those who know better, and that raises an interesting question: In today's Russia, beginning at what rank does a man have the right to lie? Stalin knows as well as I do that public education exists in France. There are those who are in on the game and those who aren't. And I believe that's worth thinking about; so is the contempt implied by psychological techniques. Whether it's selling soap or winning votes, there's no psychological technique that doesn't start with contempt for the buyer or the voter—otherwise it would be useless. Here the whole man is at stake; the system is a totality. The technique can exist without totalitarianism; but it follows upon totalitarianism as ineluctably as the GPU, because without police it's a vulnerable monster. For some years it was hard to deny that Trotsky built the red army: for *L'Humanité* to be fully effective, readers must be denied an opposition newspaper.

There's no free play, no give and take, and that's why even a small disagreement with the system leads any artist to *a recantation*.

So we come to the essential question: How can we keep psychological techniques from destroying the quality of human intelligence? There's no totalitarian art in the world anymore, if there ever was any. Christianity has no more cathedrals, but builds Sainte Clotilde, and with its portraits of Stalin, Russia scales the heights of the most conventional bourgeois art. I said "if there ever was" because the masses have never been sensitive to art as such. (On this point aristocracy and bourgeoisie are masses too.) I call artists those who are sensitive to the specific disciplines of an art; the others are sensitive to its emotional values. There is no "man who knows nothing about music"; there are those who love Mozart and those who love marches. There is no "man who knows nothing about painting"; there are those who love painting and those who love Detaille's *The Dream* or cats in baskets.[2] There is no "man who knows nothing about poetry"; there are those who enjoy Shakespeare and those who enjoy romantic stories. The difference between the two is that for the second group art is a means of emotional expression.

At certain periods it happens that this emotional expression blends with a very great art. That's what happened in Gothic art. The union of the deepest sentiments—love, the frailty of the human condition—and an appropriate plastic power produces an art of genius that reaches everybody. (There's something similar in the great romantic individualists: Beethoven, Wagner a little, Michelangelo surely, Rembrandt, and even Victor Hugo.)

Whether or not a certain sentimental work is artistic, it exists, it's a fact and not a theory or a principle. So the urgent problem before us is to replace the illusory appeal of whatever totalitarian culture with the genuine creation of a democratic culture. It's a question not of rubbing the masses' noses in an art they're indifferent to but to opening the realm of culture to anyone who wants admission. In other words, the right to culture is purely and simply the desire for access to it.

[Here followed our proposed cultural program.]

So we don't make the foolish claim to be establishing a pattern for culture; we want to bring to culture some means of maintaining—in its next metamorphosis—the highest levels it has achieved for us.

We believe that the fundamental value of the European artist in our greatest ages, from the sculptors of Chartres on up to the great individualists, from Rembrandt to Victor Hugo, lies in the desire to use art and culture as objects of conquest, of mastery. More precisely, I say that genius is a difference overcome; that genius begins—whether it's Renoir's or a Theban sculptor's—in this: a man who from his earliest years sees and studies admirable works of art that seriously distract him from the world's practicalities one day finds himself rebelling against those forms, either because they're not serene enough for him or because they're too much so. And his need to subordinate the world, and the very works of art that have shaped him, to a truth mysterious and incommunicable except through his own work, is what determines his genius. Put another way, there is no imitative genius, there is no slavish genius. And never mind all the twaddle about the great artisans of the Middle Ages! Even in a civilization where all the artists were slaves, the imitator of forms would still be different from the slave who discovered unknown forms. In art, as in other realms, there is a kind of signature of genius in discovery, and that signature has been consistent throughout the five millennia of recorded history.

If there is one eternal datum of mankind, it is unquestionably the tragic ambiguity of the man who will be called, for centuries afterward, an artist—an ambiguity before a work of art that he feels more deeply than anyone, that he admires more than anyone, and that, alone of all mankind, he wants to go underground to destroy.

But if genius consists of discovery, we must also remember that the resurrection of the past is based on that discovery. At the beginning of this talk I spoke of what a renaissance might be, what a cultural heritage might be. A culture is reborn when men of genius, seeking their own truth, wrench from the depths of centuries everything that once resembled that truth, even if they aren't sure what that truth is.

The Renaissance created the ancient world at least as much as the ancient world created the Renaissance. Negro fetishes created the Fauves no more than the Fauves created Negro fetishes. And after all, the true inheritor of the art reborn in these fifty years is neither America, which collects its masterpieces, nor Russia, whose once-great aspirations are now satisfied by bargain-basement icons; it's that "formalist" school of Paris, whose revivals of so many centuries seem to compose one immense family. It was our adversary Picasso who would reply to *Pravda*: "I may be decadent and rotten as you say, but if you knew how to look at my painting instead of admiring all those musta-chioed icons, you might notice that your pseudo-history is a small thing in the surge and swell of generations; and that my ephemeral painting happens to revive, with the Sumerian statues, a language forgotten for four thousand years."

Now, this conquest is possible only when the mind is free to roam and search. Whatever opposes the dogged impulse to discover leads, if not to the death of art (for in art there is no death; surely Egyptian art lives), then to paralysis of the artist's most fruitful faculties. We therefore proclaim the need to protect that freedom to roam and search from every tendency to determine its direction in advance. And most of all from methods of psychological ma-nipulation based on appeals to the collective unconscious for political purposes.

First and foremost we proclaim the values not of the unconscious but of the conscious mind; not resignation but purpose, not propaganda but truth. (I know that a famous personage once asked, "What is truth?" In the area we're discussing, truth is what is verifiable.) And finally the freedom to explore. And all that not "toward what?" because we have no idea—but, rather, "starting where?" like modern science. Whether we like it or not, "The European will light his way by his own torch, even if it scorches his hand."

And we want to base these values on the present. All reactionary thought is oriented to the past, as we've long known; all Stalinist thought centers on a Hegelianism oriented to a future impossible to verify. What we need first of all is to discover the present.

What we're defending here tonight will be defended by every great nation of the West before the end of the century. We want to recast France in the role she's played so many times, during the Romanesque and Gothic as in the nine-teenth century, a role that set Europe's tone when that tone was of daring and liberty all compounded.

Intellectually speaking, you are almost all liberals. For us, the guarantee of political and intellectual freedom is not political liberalism, doomed in any con-frontation with Stalinism; the guarantee of freedom is the strength of the na-tion at the service of *all* its citizens.

When was France great? When she did not take refuge in France. She is uni-versalist. To the rest of the world the greatness of France is much more the cathedrals or the Revolution than Louis XIV. Some countries, like Britain— and it may be to their honor—are the greater the more alone. France has never been greater than when she spoke for all mankind, and that is why her silence is heard so poignantly today.

What will become of the human spirit? It will be what you make of it.

TRANSLATED BY STEPHEN BECKER

NOTES

[1] Georges Bernanos was a conservative Catholic novelist, playwright, and essayist. Roger Garaudy was a left-wing novelist; he was later repudiated by the Communist Party. — TRANS.

[2] Edouard Detaille (1848–1912), realistic French military painter. — TRANS.

LOUIS ARAGON

On a Portrait of Stalin
1953

When Stalin died in 1953, Aragon, now a member of the Central Commit-
tee of the Communist Party, had just been promoted to director of Les
Lettres françaises, *the former underground journal that the party wanted*
to transform into its highbrow cultural showcase.

Accordingly, Aragon asked Picasso (himself a communist at the time)
for a portrait of the dead leader to publish on the journal's front cover. The
response was an immediate, massive, and vehement uproar: the portrait
lacked realism.

This crisis was another manifestation of turbulence at the intersection
between culture and the masses, between high culture (regardless of the
political positioning of its proponent) and the media, between what Aragon
calls the people of culture and the culture of the people. In the cultural
subfield, class struggle presents peculiarities that are not automatically in
line with the political master narrative.

Aragon, who for years had been relentlessly advocating a content-
oriented socialist-realism, was caught off-guard by this condemnation. Far
from intending to use Stalin's death as an opportunity for launching, with a
"modernist" statement, his editorship, he made sure that a photo of Stalin
would be sent to Picasso. But good will is not enough: his failure to antici-
pate the reaction of unrefined proletarian readers show how deeply his per-
sonal culture had remained that of a bourgeois intellectual. He saw a
particularly "realistic" Picasso, whereas the working-class readers of Les
Lettres françaises *saw an "unlikely" Stalin. He didn't focus on the fact*
that the communist worker, whose cultural capital didn't provide him with
the same familiarity with forty years of Picasso's production, could only
compare it with photographic portraits of the dead comrade, not with other
Picassos. Aragon thus pleads guilty: his bourgeois attachment to the creative
individual prevented him from anticipating the masses' attachment to the
icon of their dead leader.

Louis Aragon, "Sur un Portrait de Staline" [9 avril 1953], *Oeuvres poétiques* (Paris: Club
du Livre Diderot, 1980), vol. 12, pp. 487–94.

SPEAKING OUT, 9 APRIL 1953

"If you hurt someone, and he cries out in pain and says unfair things about you, you mustn't say that he has no right to complain. He has that right because he is in pain, and it isn't easy for a person in pain to weigh his words properly. Because you have hurt him, and know that you have, and own up to it, you should accept the unfairness of his accusation out of deference to the sincerity of his suffering."

I said as much to myself more than once as I read through the deluge of mail set off by my mistake: publishing a drawing without anticipating how readers—the majority of the readers—would respond. But I'm not the sort of person to turn the other cheek to an insult, and my correspondents' vehement invective often went beyond mere complaint. When their words sprang from their suffering (which was not always the case), I knew that if I acknowledged my part in causing that suffering, I would no longer feel the insult or the unfairness of their words. I would feel only the regret that everybody feels at causing pain unintentionally.

Most of the letter-writers who were truly hurt wanted to know one thing: How could you, Louis Aragon, have published that drawing, how could you have done such a thing? This is a question that deserves an answer: How did it happen?

HOW DID IT HAPPEN?

Some comrades wrote: "Obviously you published the drawing because you didn't have the heart to turn down a drawing by Picasso." I replied that they were mistaken. Anyone who says such a thing can't know me very well, and can't know much about my relationship with that great man, whom I respect, but with whom I am not always in agreement, as he well knows. Sometimes we argue. If I had thought that this drawing would affect so many people as it has, I wouldn't have published it, and I would have told Picasso my reasons why. But I did publish it. I asked my comrades: "To begin with, do you think Picasso did this deliberately to cause harm?" In no uncertain terms they replied, "Don't be silly!" Then I asked, "And as for me, do you think I published it deliberately to cause harm?" This, they said, was ridiculous. All right. But the fact remains that I did publish the drawing. It has to be granted, then, that I published it because I saw nothing wrong with it, nothing that could hurt anyone, nothing incompatible with the great sadness that Picasso, I, and our readers all felt at that moment, our profound sadness at the death of Stalin.

And this, precisely, is what stuns my correspondents. This is why they ask: "How was this possible?"

The answer is quite simple. It hardly matters that I first saw the drawing only at the last minute, at the printing plant, an hour and a quarter before the magazine was to be put to bed, and it still had to be sent out for electrotyping, which meant that I had it in front of me for no more than a minute. This makes no difference. When I first laid eyes on the picture, I did not react as it turned out readers did later on. This is the simple truth. I saw a young Stalin, with very marked characteristics of his Georgian national origin, drawn by Picasso. I was touched by the fact that Picasso, because Stalin's death must have affected him deeply, had wanted to do the portrait that the bourgeois press had been hounding him to do for years, while Stalin was still alive. The image I saw contained none of the distortions that Picasso often applies to the human figure. What is more, every touch was characteristic of Picasso, like a signature: the way of indicating the hair, the line at the bottom as in the portrait of Paul Eluard, and so on. So in the brief moment that I had the drawing in front of me, I saw forty Picasso signatures, and to me this was the essential thing, the proof that Picasso had drawn on the full range of his technique and on his experience in all its sincerity to create this image of Stalin.

That is what I saw, and that is all I saw. So I said, "Print it." The next time I saw the portrait was in the printed edition of the magazine. I say these things not to excuse myself but to explain myself. That is how it happened.

The problem, of course, is that being accustomed all my life to looking at a Picasso drawing in relation to all of Picasso's work, I lost sight of the reader, who would look at the image without thinking about touch and technique. That was my mistake. I have paid for it dearly. I have owned up to it. I own up to it here and now. And that is why I want to offer these words by way of explanation to those who have suffered.

WHAT IS AT ISSUE?

So these words are for them, and for anyone else who may benefit from a clear understanding of the roots of this error, which was perhaps not mine alone because many people think as I do: I have in mind people of culture, who judge art more by its manner than by what it represents. The odd thing is that this should have happened to me, when for years I have been in the forefront of the battle against this deviation of the critical intelligence. Perhaps the reason I was able to identify this error was that I still shared it. If any useful discussion is to emerge from all this, it seems to me that this is the central issue.

I tried to explain this in an articled that appeared in *L'Humanité* on the day after the Statement by the Secretariat of the French Communist Party. The fact that I wrote this article before that statement was formulated, and that the Party Secretary had my article in hand at the meeting during which the statement was drafted, is worth mentioning only to make it perfectly clear that I did of course fully and sincerely subscribe to that statement, hard though it was on me, because the sentiments it contained were already my own.

In that article ("Reread, Study Stalin") I looked at the youthful work of Stalin's ("Anarchism or Socialism?") and tried to examine, in my own area of expertise, some of the thoughts that Stalin's text inspired in me. I pointed out that, in the minds of men like me (to whom I referred as *us*), men of culture, precisely because we are men of culture, certain basic traits of bourgeois culture persist because this was the culture we were inescapably brought up with. I referred specifically to vestiges, perhaps unconscious, of individualism, which comes under the head of anarchism rather than socialism, and which places us in contradiction with ourselves insofar as we see ourselves as socialists and Marxists.

The fact that I gave priority to the creative individual over the feelings of the masses concerning the thing represented was to me the sign that, despite my efforts to combat the old individualism, vestiges remain. In the youthful text of Stalin's that I just mentioned, where the anarchist slogan "everything for the individual" is contrasted with the socialist and Marxist slogan "everything for the masses," I discovered the roots of an error which I was not alone in committing and to which I shall remain steadfastly opposed, despite having succumbed to it once in judging a drawing by Picasso. It was with a heavy heart that I made this discovery about myself, as many people remarked. Especially the bourgeois press, which raised a ruckus, and certain radio programs (*La Vie en rouge*), which took the view that owning up to one's errors is not the done thing, a view that these critics justified, not surprisingly, by invoking the individual against the masses.

I am bound to say, however, that roughly half of the people who wrote me after this article appeared seem to have missed this point or failed to understand it. Indeed, I'm afraid that it wasn't my article that they read carelessly but rather the newspaper of their class, because the vast majority of these correspondents were readers of *L'Humanité*.

WHAT IS NOT AT ISSUE

I'm not sure that what I've said will be understood by the people to whom it is addressed. Nevertheless, I set them entirely apart from those correspondents who were slow to feel the pain that caused others to cry out involuntarily. Time, moreover, is not the only issue. It is one thing to feel sorrow because Stalin has just died and another to use that sorrow as a pretext for settling various scores that have nothing to do with him, or to score a victory in a realm in which one has always claimed to be right, even against the leadership of one's own party.

I confess that a number of letters shocked me *precisely* because the publication, on the occasion of Stalin's death, of a picture that did not correspond to many people's idea of him caused those people pain. I, too, was sad at that time, overwhelmed by an immeasurable loss. Because of that loss I was distressed by the disrespectful tone of certain statements. The people who made those statements, whether in writing or elsewhere, will have to content themselves with my silence. I do not ask them to thank me for it.

I have to say that many people nowadays like to deal in low blows. I see no reason why the people to whom I'm addressing myself should have any notion of the kind of mail I've been subjected to morning and night for the past three weeks. Being people for whom emotion outweighs calculation, they cannot possibly imagine it for themselves. I won't reveal the vengeful pettiness of certain correspondents or the familiar way in which others allowed themselves to address me. But one letter, deliberately selected from among the most naive and innocent, may serve to show that appropriate limits were not always respected during those weeks. So by way of example, here is a letter from a reader who lives in the Thirteenth Arrondissement of Paris.[1] It needs no commentary:

Paris, March 18, 1953

To Les Lettres françaises

Astonishment and anger leave me speechless before the "portrait" of Stalin by Picasso for whose publication Aragon is to blame.

Astonishment: this is not a picture of HIM, and try as I might I can find nothing in it that reminds me of our FRIEND.

Rage because of the damage done to a prestigious name and the affront to the purest of emotions.

Look, Picasso, it's not Madame X . . . you're dealing with here!!! Stick to your business and don't make fun of the people who look at your work. You have a lot to learn, especially about respecting both your model and the person who tries to understand the meaning of your work. Don't be so pretentious: your talent is no match for a man like Stalin.

And you, Aragon? A little modesty and humility would be nice. You bear just as much responsibility in this affair as Picasso, because you set yourself up as an art critic. Unfortunately for you, this mishmash could have been signed by anybody. You, too, need to learn some simple lessons from simple people. Stick to writing and stay away from flackery and art criticism. . . .

I hope that both you and Picasso will profit from this confrontation, and remember that I wouldn't write in these harsh terms if I didn't hold you both in the highest esteem.

[signed] C.M.B., a subscriber to the Lettres.

P. S. I apologize for the delay in sending this letter of protest, which was written in the grip of emotion, but my work kept me away from Paris. Sincerely yours, C.M.B., March 27, 1953.

A VAST HUE AND CRY

If, convinced that Marxism is correct, we wish to understand what Stalin's contrast between the individualist, anarchist slogan "everything for the individual" and the socialist, Marxist slogan "everything for the masses" requires of us, we must acknowledge, not only in art but in other areas as well, the consequences of our actions. We call ourselves socialists, Marxists, and materialists, and yet in our work as artists, writers, or scholars we sometimes fail to recognize the idealist counteroffensive in our own conduct. The materialist believes that the world exists outside of his personal existence. What does this belief entail for, say, the representation of the world in art? The answer would be obvious were it not for the fact that art has a long history, a series of traditions perpetuated or contested, which constitute the baggage of the artist and reflect not only the history of art but history itself. This is what truly calls for honest self-examination at the present time, not just a drawing, which is much less at issue than the error of judgment I was capable of making in regard to it. And it is not just Picasso and myself who need to re-examine our positions. Idealism, which the young Marx called *the enemy,* is an enemy far more clever than certain artists, writers, and scholars believe. I know people in no doubt whatsoever that this is a sin they never commit and yet who might benefit if only they could admit that self-criticism is required of everyone, not just Picasso and Aragon.

I, for one, look forward to this debate. There is much to be learned, I think, if the tone can be kept calm and civilized, for otherwise it is all too easy to lose sight, once again, of the *masses* and focus entirely on *individuals*.

TRANSLATED BY ARTHUR GOLDHAMMER

NOTE

[1] The publication of Picasso's drawing, in the March 12 issue of *Les Lettres françaises*, a weekly, was condemned by the Secretariat of the Party on the 17th. Anticipating this condemnation, Aragon had already pleaded guilty once, in the article published by *L'Humanité*. This is thus his second apology.

JEAN DUBUFFET

Pilot Céline
1964

According to the painter Jean Dubuffet, the founder of Art Brut aesthetics, the purported political reasons for the postwar censoring of Louis-Ferdinand Céline—his antisemitic writing and his collaborationist activities—were merely a way for French high culture to cover up its panicked reaction to Céline's creative nonconformism, his scathing disregard for the cultural codes of social and aesthetic distinction. Political propriety is merely an after-the-fact pretext for aesthetic allergies.

The fallen hero of a war of popular linguistic subversion, Céline is thus the victim of a cultural backlash; according to Dubuffet, he has to expiate for his fight against modernist aesthetocracy and its cultural piety, for his disrespect for the ritualistic conventionality of high, official art.

One can only wonder, of course, how genuinely candid Dubuffet was in invoking "the honest, blameless Céline."

The revolting treatment that Céline has received of late at the hands of the French intelligentsia, though logical and predictable in the current literary and journalistic climate, has nevertheless been one of the most depressing spectacles I have ever witnessed. I consider Céline to be an innovator of genius and a poet of considerable magnitude (even if the overused word "poet" scarcely does him justice). In fact, to my mind, he is the most important poet not only of our time but of the modern era, a period among the most crucial in the history of writing. It is almost incredible that his importance was not immediately apparent to my intellectual contemporaries, or at any rate not apparent enough to silence their grumbling and halt their chicanery, or to prevent their banding together in such remarkable unanimity to denounce his monumental creation and transplant it to the wretched terrain of politics. In order for such a broad consensus to become possible, a notable shift in the status of writing had to take place: people had to forget entirely what literature could

Jean Dubuffet, "Céline pilote" [1964] in Hubert Damisch, ed. *Prospectus et tous écrits suivants* (Paris: Gallimard, 1967), vol. 2, pp. 46–53.

and should be expected to provide. They had to lose sight of the distinctive nature of art, that noble dance; their mental fevers had to subside; they had to allow a taste for (the illusions of) analytic and discursive thinking to obscure the incandescence of poetic creation; and they had to begin looking to literature for nothing more than hair-splitting discussions of topics as elementary, insipid, and pointless as sociology and civics. It is truly astonishing to find poets, including some who trumpet their supposed liberation from conventional morality, singing the same inane, tired tune as the sociologists and patriots, all warbling together in one overweening chorus. It takes us right back to the good old days of the Wars of Religion.

What is more, those who would pick a fight with Céline on grounds of patriotic feeling and civic spirit are entirely unjustified. No patriot had a warmer, more fraternal heart than he: the man is exemplary. But there are two kinds of patriotism—doctrine and the patriotism of action and immediacy. Céline was a patriot of the second kind.

It is worth noting that hostility toward Céline reared its head long before he expressed his views on any political matter, probably owing to the zeal for demystification so apparent in his earliest writing. The intelligentsia sensed that this was a man bent on clearing literature of every gimmick, as one might clear a minefield of mines. The whole status of the intelligentsia rests on an occult system of influence and machinations so complex and far-flung that any one of its outposts can be blown to kingdom-come without endangering the system as a whole. But when a great debunker comes along, a man who strikes at the very heart of the system, a saboteur of genius, alarm bells sound and insiders of every rank and station rush to the ramparts with vats of boiling oil. By general agreement, the social function of the intelligentsia is to engage in harmless criticism of institutions and *assume* the role of defending the public against abuse (lest someone take up that role for real). When it comes to talking a good line, intellectuals can't be beat. Their role is to play the rebel, but of course their rebellion is *fake*. So when a real rebel comes along, somebody not in cahoots with the others, everybody panics.

Céline detested mystification and shunned it in every way. He rejected it in his own work and tried to show that it was not useful for producing art, or at any rate not genuine art. He hoped that his work would have impact without it, indeed, that it would have far more impact because he rejected it. This made people angry. Mystification is something to which writers and artists cling tenaciously. In this they are not alone. Contrary to what one might think, and contrary to the demystifier's belief that people will thank him for his trouble, the public likes to be deceived. It connives in its own deception and erupts in anger the minute anyone dares to expose the truth. The public is fearful. Its attitude—not a little absurd—is that while mystification may be counterfeit currency, it's better than having no money at all. The public doesn't much believe in the intrinsic value of poetry, which it regards as an ephemeral (not to say illusory) murmur that cannot exist unless surrounded by suitable ritual. So when poetry suddenly appears not as a murmur but as a thunderclap, not on a prepared stage but on crowded streets, not clad in cheap finery and masks but barefaced, cantankerous, and full of rage, the public, not surprisingly, fails to see any resemblance to what it has been taught poetry looks like.

I trust that people will know what I mean when I say that literature has been riding on mystification of late. Literature is a hundred years behind painting. For several centuries now it has been living not on direct knowledge of life but on prior works of literature, like bees feeding on honey rather than on flowers. It is irresistibly drawn to earlier works, to whose guidance it submits. So great is the prestige of these works of the past that no writer, try as he might, can shake it off and return to the state of innocence that creation requires. Painting has long since completed its revolution. Literature, with the sole exception of Céline, has not. Despite superficial changes (new stuffing for the liver, as it were, in the form of changes in theme rather than technique, in setting rather than depth), literature is frozen, bogged down. Anyone but an expert could easily mistake a page in a contemporary work for a page by Voltaire or Descartes. Just compare the difference between a contemporary painting and a Raphael with the difference between a page of Sartre and a page of Diderot and you'll see what I'm talking about. Painting has totally changed its form, while writing has all but remained the same. But in art, form determines the whole effect of the work. If the form is the same, so is the content. It is changes in form that lead to changes in content. Literature imagines that what matters is its mind, not its body. It accepts the Christian mind–body view of things. It believes that it can innovate intellectually without touching its body, which it takes to be nothing more than an inert vessel, a container. This is a mistake! The result is no innovation at all. Only when literature makes up its mind to invent new bodies for itself (as painting has done) will it discover what new intellectual positions are truly possible; only then will its flame be rekindled.

It is impossible to repeat often enough that art is a matter of form and not content. Writers who fill their works with hard-to-find information and subtle analyses are wasting their effort. Analytic thinking is one thing and art is another, quite different thing. Art's resources are both more abundant and more efficient. In the blink of an eye, in half a sentence (as in Céline), art can do what a whole volume of heavy-handed analysis cannot. Painters, too, long believed that their mission was to find ways to paint the same old Christs and Virgins with ingeniously novel expressions. When at last they decided to turn their attention to apples, glasses of absinthe, and packets of tobacco instead, they made a revolution. This happened when they focused their inventiveness not on the object represented but on the medium and materials, the manner of transcription, and the syntax. At that point they really took off! And how high they have continued to soar ever since!

Painting may have been given a boost by the development of photography.

This stripped it of a function that perpetually created confusion about the nature of the painter's art. Like painting, writing also serves a variety of purposes, and some clarity about the differences among them would be useful. Just as painting and drawing are sometimes used for purposes of art and sometimes for purposes of information or documentation (as in industrial drawings, geographical sketches, and the like, or in portraits of loved ones and reproductions of admired sites), writing, too, serves not only the poet but also the lawyer, the journalist, and the notary. These two functions are not always differentiated as carefully as they ought to be. It is a truly remarkable fact that texts written for creative purposes are so similar in form, indeed almost identical, to police reports, political speeches, and users' manuals. My sense is that people are not sufficiently aware of the incongruity. So it comes as no surprise to discover that the intellectual mannerisms of the lawyer, journalist, and politician have insinuated themselves into the forms of writing and supplanted artistic creativity so thoroughly that people have forgotten what literature can and should be.

Creative writing begins only when words are used not literally (in this impoverished register they are capable of stating only the most simplistic ideas) but *artfully*, as jugglers use hats, eggs, and handkerchiefs for purposes quite unrelated to covering the head, stuffing the gullet, or blowing the nose. When used in this way, words become the keyboard of an instrument capable of expressing ideas with blunt, searing force. Céline showed the way, and in his work he followed the same path as contemporary painting, which has made similar use of signs, marks, and colors not just to represent figures (and therefore in ways that beg to be "taken literally") but, on the contrary, to break down the all too immediate association with direct, objective representation. Painting thus introduces a gap, a rift, between the signs of a transcription and the objects transcribed. By opening the way to a flood of new ideas and echoes, this hiatus becomes a source of fecundity.

It may seen paradoxical that supposedly negative characteristics such as impropriety and unsuitability may, if shrewdly turned to advantage, considerably enhance the power of a transcription. This happens when the painter (or the writer, if he happens to be Céline) makes sure that facts and description *are linked in such a loose, flexible way* that the user of the work is forced to make frequent interpolations, so that he is forced to read not the lines themselves but between the lines. The work thereby takes on a new dimension, a kind of relief or resonance, like the timbre of a voice, which is similarly the result of two vibrations that are simultaneous but not quite identical.

Céline uses words in such a masterful way that, in addition to conveying their intrinsic meaning, they also operate as markers *between* which he excels at making his meanings appear without stating them (as in a photographic negative, or the hollow of a mold). In this respect, the style of writing that he so miraculously perfected (not only invented but immediately developed to a pitch of perfection that seems hard to rival) resembles the most pungent speech. In speech—and of course I have in mind real communication, direct, spontaneous expression—the thought is conveyed not by the choice of words but by tone, intonation, and mimicry, in such a way that the essential point, the fruit, is clear without being formulated, and clear in an instantaneous, comprehensive, forceful way that no explicit formulation, no matter how long-winded, can possibly match. The recourse to the implicit may indeed be characteristic of art. To my mind, no one has ever used the implicit as powerfully as Céline. The power of implication was the force that drove his writing.

Céline's life, career, and destiny were in every respect disruptive and extraordinary. His first two books, *Journey to the End of the Night* (*Voyage au bout de la nuit*) and *Death on the Installment Plan* (*Mort à crédit*), scored a resounding success with readers, owing in part, no doubt, to a misunderstanding. Both books are certainly admirable, but by comparison with those which followed they remain, it seems to me, still somewhat mired in, and deferential toward, the classical tradition of the novel. No doubt, that is why they were so successful. People thought they were reading Zola, *verismo*, a documentary, a slice of life. The age is infatuated with *verismo*, which does duty for art. But Céline goes far beyond mere photographic realism. He is an artist, a true artist. He extrapolates and transmutes. He can seize on a moment in everyday life and, with an alchemy all his own, whip the pettiest of facts, the most banal of thoughts and attitudes, into a maelstrom of ideas, a whirl of subtle touches, as in the dervishlike *Féerie pour une autre fois* and its successors. Strangely enough, these books, the works that Céline wrote in full mastery of his craft, remain virtually unknown. They sold few copies, were little read, and are rarely mentioned. Did the writer overestimate his audience? Perhaps. In any case, the public today knows little beyond his first two books, apart from the specious image of him as an alleged racist and Nazi sympathizer, an image established by distortions of his views and false accusations publicized by a press bent on defeating racism and Nazism and without compunctions about hurling the honest, blameless Céline and his demiurgic epics into the flames for the good of the cause.

But were Céline's political views the true and only reason for this relentless persecution? It seems likely. I spoke earlier of the mystification on which literature, the academy and the cultural myth rest. In this they are not alone. In the "aesthetocracy" that is France (it may be the same elsewhere for all I know, but probably not to the same degree), anyone who claims membership in the dominant caste also prides himself on good taste, aesthetic discrimination, elegant speech, and stylish writing. Fine arts, fine manners, and fine literature go with everything else that is fine. The ruling caste proclaims itself a patron of the arts and stakes its legitimacy on that claim. Culture is its last line of defense, its protective armor. When Madame Snob, Madame High Fashion, or Madame Classy Apartment uses the subjunctive as it should be used, she knows that the plumber who has just repaired her faucet will stand frozen with awe even if madam can't afford to pay him for his work. It's not money that allows people to move up in the world, it's the proper use of the subjunctive. Has this been sufficiently remarked? I doubt it. The myth of fine writing is a crucial element in the defense of the bourgeoisie. If you want to strike at the heart of the ruthless class, go for the subjunctive, go for the ritual invocation of elegant but hollow language, go for the mincing ways of the aesthete. Whoever knocks down the holy relics they brandish as a Negro witchdoctor might brandish a fetish—their great writers, their Mona Lisas, their Louis XV chairs, their correct grammar, their sterile, dead language, and that whole heap of dry bones they try to pass off as art and culture—whoever alerts the folks at the back of the train to the fact that the only genuine, living art, the only true, creative innovation, lies with them and not with the crap subsidized by the government, will have signaled that the time has come for that ruthless class to exit the scene. Meanwhile, however, you can count on that class to defend itself. It defends its myth with its style: in this game, anything goes. Still, I do not believe that it can hold out for long against what Céline accomplished.

TRANSLATED BY ARTHUR GOLDHAMMER

ROLAND BARTHES

On Popular Theater
1954

Theater is one of the most critical points of the dialectical tension between quality and quantity that is almost automatically set in motion by any attempt to merge high culture and mass audiences. For these reasons, during the 1950s, it was on the frontline of the debates concerning popular culture. The magazine Théâtre populaire, *founded in 1953, was associated with a generation of stage directors who followed the lead of Jean Vilar, the charismatic renovator of Paris's* T.N.P. *(Théâtre national populaire); it was also the first outspokenly Brechtian journal in France. Roland Barthes was one of its founding editors and, for years, together with Bernard Dort and Lucien Goldmann, a regular contributor. The journal's program was defined by a double-edged militant utopia: opening a connection between theater and popular audiences that would terminate the century-old cultural monopoly of bourgeois censorship over the medium, and promoting a form of popular high culture that would save the masses from the tidal wave of home entertainment recently unleashed by television.*

It has become increasingly common of late to speak in the name of the people. The people, "who produce everything and presumably could constitute a formidable force merely by refusing to work" (Mirabeau), are surrounded by a swarm of clever advocates generously ready to lend them words, purposes, and capabilities of their own in exchange for a moral seal of approval. Regimes, parties, newspapers, literatures, aesthetics—what doesn't claim to be "popular" nowadays? The winds have shifted over the past century, and clearly the conscience now rests easy on the people's side.

We at the *Revue du théâtre populaire* aim to be less profligate with our good offices, even if this puts our moral well-being at somewhat greater risk. We have no intention of using our title as a respectable alibi to hide behind. Our goal is to sharpen our idea of "popular theater" by looking at actual recent

Roland Barthes (anon.), "Editorial" for *Théâtre populaire* (Jan.–Feb. 1954), in *Oeuvres complètes* (Paris: Seuil, 1993), vol. 1, pp. 381–82.

experiments, and we are more than willing to relinquish the hope of coming up with an impressive-sounding general definition in favor of a more limited but also more pragmatic understanding.

The first step is to decide what is not possible. To be perfectly frank, it is not within our power to determine in advance the character of a community theater tailored to the needs of a community that does not yet exist. We no longer think of the people, as many in the nineteenth century did, as an eternal category, an immutable essence unaffected by historical choices. On the contrary, we refuse to endorse the myth of the people as a panacea or totem capable of curing every aesthetic deficiency merely by bestowing its name. The people always exist in History, and it is always History that makes the people, that fills the word with different content in different periods, creating now a people of the city-state, now a bourgeois people, and now again a proletarian people.

How could we claim to know what form collective theater in France should take when French society is all too obviously torn apart, condemned by its economic structure to a distressing secession of the social classes? We cannot move more rapidly than History itself (although we would of course like it to move faster than it does). We cannot draw checks on the future and say to the theater, in a society that needs economic reconciliation more than cultural reconciliation, "Thou shalt be this or that, thou shalt speak in such and such a manner, in such and such a place, about such and such ideas."

We believe that the social order is antecedent to, and coextensive with, the cultural order. We believe that our struggle can and should be exclusively to lay the groundwork for a free theater subject to a free society. And we believe that while we cannot anticipate what form either will take, we must at least clear a space, dispel the shadows that prejudice, fraud, and mediocrity perpetually recreate, and cleanse the theater of those who would sell it to the highest bidder.

To be sure, we live in a divided society, in thrall to economic necessity and the tyranny of myth, and our present alienation makes it impossible for us to imagine in any concrete way what form an authentic popular theater might take. Yet these very flaws of our society have taught us what fraudulent theater is. From the depths of our social imperfection, what we can say, forthrightly and repeatedly, is what kind of theater we *don't* want.

The theater that we despise is the theater of Money; the theater of high admission prices, whose audience is determined solely by wealth; in which poverty (labor) is banished as far as possible from the stage; in which the pretentious sumptuousness of scenery and costume hypocritically passed off as "French good taste" in fact reflects a whole sordid economy of fool's gold and visual trumpery, paid for by thousand-franc orchestra seats; and in which the standard repertory consists exclusively of plays in which man is a petty creature defined by the trappings of fortune and endowed with a psychology utterly divorced from the tragic in History.

This theater of Money has a name: it is the bourgeois theater. Further subtlety is futile; there is no point in attempting a byzantine analysis of the present state of the French bourgeoisie simply to say that it is no longer what it was a hundred years ago. Economically that may be true, but culturally it is false: apart from a few avant-garde experiments—the Théâtre National Populaire, a few provincial centers, and a few intellectual theaters—we have no contemporary theater. What we have on the vast majority of our stages is an aging, unrepresentative, anachronistic theater shaped through and through by traditional bourgeois ideology. Its audience, no longer defined, perhaps, by inherited wealth but just as surely circumscribed by the sources of its income, comes in search of soothing or escapist myths that can calm its fears and ease its remorse. And because money insists on it, what this audience finds when it goes to plays is apt to be a close, stuffy hall with cushy upholstery, unsuitable for tragic productions and fit only for mysterious intrigues and discreet flirtations, a place where the self-satisfied spectator can sit impassively while paid performers painlessly relieve him of his trivial anxieties.

This bourgeois theater, established and maintained to perpetuate the clear conscience of the privileged, obviously does not want for state support. The only new theater that receives so much as a penny of state funding, the TNP, gets about 3.5 percent of what goes to the temples of bourgeois theatricality (the Comédie-Française and the Réunion des Théâtres Lyriques). And even that small amount is not given without ominous warnings (in the form of strict limits on the use of state funds, negative propaganda in the press, and threatened budget cuts): clearly, it is an accident that any money is given at all.

The indulgence currently accorded to the bourgeois theater is so universal that our task can only be destructive. We can define the popular theater only as a theater purged of its bourgeois armature and rescued from the alienation of money and its masks. What we have to focus on first, therefore, is our opposition. That opposition is broad-gauged; it does not trouble itself with subtleties. But is it our fault if the era, in the grip of a variety of regressive forces, is not a very heroic one? When myth reigns triumphant, demystification is the only possible response.

TRANSLATED BY ARTHUR GOLDHAMMER

GEORGES BATAILLE

The Dispossessed
1976

In its way of taking for granted the coming of the kingdom of undifferentiated mankind, this section of Georges Bataille's posthumous work Sovereignty *owes much to Alexandre Kojève's interpretation of Hegel's concept of the end of history. Originally titled "Equivalence and Distinction," it develops a kind of sociopolitical science fiction in which, in the wake of the universal triumph of the working-class worldview, mankind is on the verge of being leveled under the materialist law of a proletarian ethics of work and needs.*

Among the effects of this entropic apocalypse, Bataille focuses on the cultural dispossession to which Western intellectuals find themselves drawn. Following the example of the French aristocrats who voted for the abolition of feudal privileges on 4 August 1789, he saw contemporary intellectuals as having actively contributed to the legitimization of a social system that, by its own logic, would deny them legitimacy; they had committed themselves to the birth of a society that, ruled only according to the laws of need, would have no need for them. In the name of needs, communism is the radical contestation of all values that, according to Bataille, "don't have their place close to mineshafts"—quite closely related to what Aragon experienced with the proletarian rejection of Picasso's portrait of Stalin.

Here again, Bataille doesn't discuss the positive implications—political or economic—of this Kojévian version of the communist ideal type; he discusses the negative, exclusionary effects of its cultural radicalism, namely the waning of a culture that valued distinction. "The man of the society 'without class' has 'no class'," Bataille writes later on, in the same work *("La Souveraineté", Oeuvres complètes, vol. 8. p. 654). His view of such an outcome, however, is far from simply negative; on the contrary, in fact. For this very impossibility for distinction ever to be lawfully registered on*

Georges Bataille, "Equivalence and Distinction" in *The Accursed Share*, trans. Robert Hurley (New York: Zone Books, 1991), pp. 329–31, from "La Souveraineté," *Oeuvres complètes* (Paris: Gallimard, 1976), vol. 8, pp. 365–69.

the social map opens up the space of a clandestine aesthetics, an aesthetic of
subversive uncanniness or Unheimlichkeit. *Literature realizes its essence*
by becoming interdit de séjour.

1. THE CONTESTING OF VALUES
THAT DON'T CONCERN WORKING-CLASS MILITANTS

Whatever its effects, the sovereignty that is won and at the same time renounced could doubtless be offered as the best solution to a problem that,
moreover, is of another age. In any case, this solution answers necessity, to the
extent (questionable, it is true) that accumulation forces itself upon us.

Further on I will say from what perspective and in what way the present, in
spite of everything, in spite of itself, transcends it. But the situation of communism raises, from the point of view of sovereignty, a new problem, as fundamental as the first one.

One of the least apparent results of communism is the rift it brings about, in
the consciousness of the most sensitive men, between what they love and what
they affirm: on the one hand, what secretly sustains them, on the other, what
they openly say that they care about. A kind of timidity, of bad conscience, of
shame, takes hold of minds at the idea of the lack of value, the lack of weight—
compared with the concerns of communist politics—of what engages them
personally. In itself, the individual feeling of a worker does not necessarily appear to them to be preferable, but the general importance of the proletariat give
it preference: the only true value is the one that concerns a worker. What capti-
vates only men who are relatively rich and cultivated does not count.

In these circumstances, a kind of dispossessed man has formed, a man who
no longer grants himself the right of life except to deny what he deeply is,
effacing himself at the least alarm. Often it's a question of persons who are well
off, enjoying possessions that make life worth living in their eyes, but which, on
the first occasion, they are sincerely prepared to declare of no account.

Such an attitude is capable of displaying various aspects, according to the
circumstances or values involved, but in any case communism is there, contesting the value of that which moves the most sensitive men.

The problem always comes down to the interest presented by such-and-such
product of a civilization whose generally human character is overlooked: this
civilization's system deprives it of meaning—it has become the symbol of a
defect, which is bourgeois life. Sometimes this object is a poem, a painting, a
personage endowed with prestige; sometimes it is a strong feeling, a passion, an
excessive joy: for men of bad conscience, these goods have a secondary importance, *working-class humanity* counts before *humanity* (before the forms of life
that are common to men, but unevenly developed in the different classes).

2. JUSTIFICATION AND FLIMSINESS OF THE PROTESTS AGAINST WORKING-CLASS COARSENESS

Far from this bad conscience, minds given to anxiety—and to avarice—claim that civilization is fragile; that, perhaps even reluctantly, a social revolution would destroy the most precious assets of the civilized world. What is worthy of being loved requires oases in the midst of a society controlled by an awful necessity, refuges protected from what the theoreticians of communism regard as a fundamental reality. For communism, and perhaps with good reason, reality is manifested above all in the set of human relations connected, for example, with the activity of a mining center. Those who see civilization as fragile, who worry about it, think on the contrary that the values that don't have their place close to mine shafts deserve to be defended. Dissatisfied with their living conditions, the miners struggle to obtain other conditions, which answer their requirements, not the desires of certain idle profiteers of the "established order." In this way, they reduce civilization to the standard of basic needs. In principle, a pure and simple reduction, in the practice that is inherent in communism, is considered a bad thing by the communists themselves. On the whole, it nonetheless explains—and no doubt justifies—the "directives" concerning Soviet literature and art. I don't really see why a working-class world, exhausted by labor, would concern itself with the possibilities accessible to the minority that doesn't work. Actually, the bourgeois pessimists are right to take account of a radical difference between their value judgments and those of the workers. But the question goes beyond the narrow purview to which they deliberately confine themselves.

Here I will set out the primary terms of that question: *Isn't the generosity of the communist intellectuals—and bourgeois—preferable to the avarice of the conservatives? Do those goods which make life worth living for both these groups deserve to be defended? When the voice of a throng condemned to the labor of the mines makes itself heard, what importance does the protest of a negligible refinement and a morbid sensitivity have?*

3. CLASSLESS "HUMANITY" AND THE MORE OR LESS "HUMAN" CHARACTER THAT FOUNDS THE DIVISION INTO CLASSES

Under the present conditions, this protest remains in the throats of most people. Even those who accuse communism of an error have received as their share that "bad conscience" which communism imposes on most of those whom it alarms. In our time, the moral effect of communism predominates. Refinement and morbid sensitivity are not openly defended (they are defended only from the angle of comfort).

*   *   *

The attitude of the communists is in fact the major position, to which anticommunism opposes only a line of insignificant positions, of contradictory positions. But this primary character of communism usually goes unrecognized because of a determination not to talk about it. Assuming one were to ask communists to state the *principles underlying* their morals, they would probably refuse. Everything is clear in their eyes; they have no need for discussion. The *consequences* of their moral stance are explicit. I will nevertheless attempt to bring to light the principles that justify it.

With respect to the various principles of living to which men have adhered, communism, by affirming nothing, and indeed "by the fact that it affirms nothing," implies a system of values that it is possible to define *after the event*.

The very silence of the doctrine places this first point beyond doubt: that the value principle is *man*, and man alone, *irrespective of any meaning or specific attribute* that we give him. It is not the attainment of a civilization, represented by those who benefit from it, it is any man, black or white, skilled or unskilled, coarse, brutal or absurd, educated or illiterate. . . . The apparently sacred value thus implied in man must not be tied to any definition that would establish this sacredness. For communism there is not, and there cannot be, any other definition of man than that of the *natural* sciences, which sees no clear-cut difference between us and the animals: man is that primate, anatomically different from the (vanished) hominids and the apes, who are definitively characterized by the use and fabrication of tools.

If I introduced, beyond this rudimentary definition, any notion of the value that man has and that animals, plants, or stones don't have (such as religiosity, consciousness), I would have to envisage a gradation whereby some men, more than others, would have this value as their share. The decision to assign in this way a *particular*, definable if not actually defined, value seems to us to be one of the attributes of the human race. For humanity as a whole—and even, in the end, for the communists—the human quality is not distributed equally among all men. Leaving aside religion properly speaking and consciousness, certain basic behaviors, our way of eating for example, or of evacuating, or sexual activity subject to rules, distinguish man from animals. From this point of view, each man is certainly superior to animals, but *more or less so:* the way in which he satisfies his *animal* needs is *more or less human.* Doubtless, the introduction of these particulars will surprise some people. Be that as it may, these kinds of distinctions are found in everyday life, at all levels of society. There are few men who have not on occasion been disgusted by the relative animality of another: this *more or less* humanity involves primary value judgments—based on repugnance and sympathy—which stand in contrast with the communist principle of equal value, and which don't depend on a calculation of interest.

TRANSLATED BY ROBERT HURLEY

Testimony and Narration

JEAN PAULHAN

The Damsel with the Mirrors
1938

"The human condition," wrote Jean Paulhan, "is such *that I am unable to understand, or even approach it except by means of an interposed person. In the very center of our lives events [are] taking place such that I am unable to apprehend them directly."[1] Rhetoric, in Paulhan's view, is a device similar to Freud's psychoanalytical method in that it gives one access to what is structurally blocked from the field of one's consciousness. In many regards, Paulhan is one of the very first French writers whose early scrutiny of language was prompted by what Shoshana Felman has recently termed a "crisis of witnessing."*

Objectivity, to start with, has ceased to be an absolute. Modern epistemology focuses more and more on the distortions induced in the field by the presence of the observer; like Friday's footsteps on the sand of Robinson Crusoe's island, the shadow of the observer is always, somehow, imprinted on phenomena.

Paulhan's "The Damsel with the Mirrors" points, however, toward a deeper and more radical crisis of witnessing, toward a traumatic realism that poses as real those very "referents" that do not allow for a witness: Eurydice cannot be reached by Orpheus's gaze, and Medusa turns whoever meets hers into blind stone.

How to describe what we are—or at least would be—dying to see? How to approach events whose program includes the elimination of their witnesses? Imagining them is not the solution (would Orpheus care about imagining Eurydice?). In Greek legend, Perseus used a mirror to deflect Medusa's gaze and approach her obliquely and safely. The tropes of rheto-

Jean Paulhan, "La Demoiselle aux miroirs" [1938] in *Oeuvres complètes* (Paris: Cercle du Livre précieux, 1966), vol. 2, pp. 171–83.

ric, according to Paulhan, are similar devices of indirection. After a century of Romantic rejection, he claims, rhetoric should be rehabilitated—no longer on aesthetic, decorative grounds however, but on epistemological ones: to allow for the indirect approach of what cannot be reported upon live.

S ome solutions are stranger than the problems they purport to solve. The problem, at least, was *just one* question, but the solution may raise a thousand new ones. Clearly, we have located the source of the literary paradox. It is that the terrorist himself is the pure spirit, infinitely free in language, that the rhetorician called forth. Hence Terror and Rhetoric are both justified, the one in saying what it says, the other is being what it is. A curious difficulty remains.

I can readily accept, as conventional wisdom urges, the idea that to hesitate between one word and another, to waver in one's choice, to change one's mind, to weigh one's words endlessly, reflects thought more purged of language than usual because it is thought that has not yet found but is still seeking its expression: thought *prior to words*, if such a thing exists. With equal certainty, I *know* what a man is thinking when he stands at a crossroads and first starts down the path to the left, then reverses himself and takes the path to the right. Or another man, when he begins to slide down a cliff and hesitates between two clumps of grass that might arrest his fall. But this clear truth has another side, a face of darkness and paradox.

The point is that we had to *assume* what the terrorist was thinking. We deduced it from his own words. We did not *witness* it. Even worse, the terrorist himself seems incapable of pinning down his own thought with any precision, incapable of knowing what he thinks (because he stubbornly insists that he is right). And what, in the end, is a thought of which we remain unconscious? A mere wisp. Thus, we seem bound to substitute a new paradox for the old one and to shift the ground of the difficulty rather than resolve it.

THE MACHIAVELLIANISM OF RHETORIC

It was said of Mme Camoin that her prestige derived from the fact that she plunged enemies and friends alike into a state of contradiction in which they complained now about her excessive gentleness and now about her ferociousness, now about her tenacity and now again about her indifference, so that in the end all were forced to acknowledge that she possessed some secret beyond mildness or vehemence, nonchalance or will. And in the same vein, G. K. Chesterton once said of Christianity that its enemies, having denounced it for being not only too optimistic but also too utterly forlorn of hope, not only too tender but also too brutal, and not only too unworldly but also too pragmatic, were ultimately obliged to admit that it was rather a goad to gentleness as well as violence, to optimism as well as pessimism, and, indeed, that it cast each of these alternatives in its proper light.

So, too, might one say of Rhetoric that it derives its virtue from the welter of objections to which it gives rise. "I write without discipline," one man says, "and in the order in which things occur to me. To impose discipline on emotion is to lose hold of it." But another says, "*I take pains* to write without discipline. The first draft is merely conventional." In other words, one rejects Rhetoric because it is artificial, the other because it is natural. "It is pure contortion, which distorts the mind." Or, "it is pure naiveté, in which the mind follows its well-worn rut."

But if Rhetoric provokes objections, it also elicits praise. One person says, "I subject my forever-fleeting thoughts to fixed rules and thereby impose on them a beginning and an end—an existence." But another says, "I use rules in order to free my mind and thus allow it to revert to its natural measure and rhythm." In other words, Rhetoric is praised now, as it was blamed a moment earlier, for being natural as well as for being artificial, for serving the spirit as well as for opposing it.

Yet if one takes account *simultaneously* of *both* types of compliment and *both* types of criticism, it might seem more accurate to say that Rhetoric possesses a secret that surpasses both artifice and nature, both the chiseled sentence and the spontaneous one. In short, there is nothing one can say about it that does not *enter into its plan*.

Before tackling the rhetorical problem head-on, I simply want to restate it in more *familiar* terms. We sometimes say that a particular feeling became true because we believed it. About Rhetoric, however, one must say that it becomes true to the extent that one doesn't believe it—by dint of its groping search and of its *various* rejections. What is more, one cannot say that it defends falsehood in order to know truth. Rather, it pretends to defend falsehood in order to provoke truth. "She reproached me," Rousseau said, "for being too bold, in order to let me know that I could be bolder still." Rhetoric thus follows the example of the courtesan—as if there were no combination of words to which the mind had any choice but to respond with new inventions.

Everyone knows that conflicts and wars can never be prevented simply by forging new laws. Indeed, the more extensive the commentaries on the law, the greater the obscurities, and the more one tries to anticipate difficulties, the faster they multiply. Every commentary and every anticipation engenders new disputes on top of the old ones. And so it is with Rhetoric, whose every rule gives rise to contrary thoughts. If a tyrant were interested in court cases *for their own sake,* he would have every reason to promulgate new laws. But who is not interested in Letters *for their own sake?* Hence, there is every reason to multiply precepts, conventions, and unities. Some subjects may be prohibited. The novelist (for example) may be permitted to deal with love but not money. The playwright may be permitted to deal with friendship and family feeling but never with reveries or matters of health. Some traits of style and rhetorical figures may be allowed, while others may be forbidden. The subtlest rhythmic combinations may be accepted. When two people use the same language, they do not sacrifice their individuality but, rather, reveal it and in a sense give birth to it, and so it is when two authors deal with the same set subjects or themes: *Phèdre* distinguishes Racine from Pradon, and *Amphitryon* distinguishes Molière from Plautus. If Rhetoric was ever invented, it was no doubt in order to focus attention on the personality of the writer. If its (ever so gentle) recommendation was not to *seek* to be personal, it was to make the point that one *could not help being so*. Ultimately, Rhetoric insisted on urging every writer to dance, as they say, in chains.

Do not be misled by this image. It may well be stimulating to dance in chains, but I have never actually *seen* anyone manage it (unless the chains were fake). And while I must admit that rules may serve and stimulate the writer, I have a hard time imagining just how. So long as I remain uncertain about this, Rhetoric will remain incomprehensible to me—at the mercy of the first argument I stumble across. To take the crudest of these, Pascal complains that poets invented certain phrases to which they applied the label "poetic beauty": *golden age,* for example, or *modern-day miracle*, or *lips of rose*. But, he adds, "anyone who tries to imagine a woman in this way, which amounts to saying little things with big words, will be a pretty village lass buried beneath the weight of a hundred mirrors." To this it was all too easy for a Voltaire or a Dacier to respond that "lips of pink" and "golden age" are not "big words" or stiff phrases but naive expressions of surprise and delight. And to this we in turn may respond that "lips of pink" ought ultimately to correspond, at the point where two forms of language intersect, to the purest of thoughts, indeed, to a thought pure enough to accommodate both Pascal's opinion and Voltaire's. But I would like to have a clearer picture of that thought.

This brings us back to the first difficulty mentioned above. I will not tackle it head-on. Rather, I will try, through a series of related examples, to measure its extent.

Who knows exactly what he thinks? Phédon thinks he hates Junie, but his hatred is really the beginning of a great love. Hermas considers himself indifferent to Lélie but is in fact only too susceptible to her charms. Claude had thought he owed a debt of gratitude to Celse, who saved his life, yet he rejoices when death claims both Celse and his gratitude. Moralists readily recognize that feelings can be learned, like a language.

This type of error takes an acute form. We constantly deal with feelings that we cannot observe in ourselves or can observe only with difficulty. It is easy to make fun of the preacher who said, "When it comes to modesty, no one outdoes me." But one has to recognize the paradox that such mockery conceals: it is contradictory both to *be* modest and to *know* that one is modest. For to be modest is to diminish oneself, but if one knows that one is modest, one also knows that one is in fact grander than one appears to be, and one thereby ceases to be modest. Conversely, the same can be said of pride. Broadly speaking, pride can be defined as making oneself out to be important. But if one *sees* that one is exaggerating one's importance, one thereby ceases to exaggerate it. To see oneself as proud is a trait of modesty, to see oneself as modest is a trait of pride.

And so it is with many other attitudes and ideas. To be good or dutiful is to behave in certain ways, *not to know* that one is good or dutiful. If a hero recognizes his courage and the gravity of his situation, he immediately ceases to be a hero and becomes a suicide. Space, time, and civilization are clear ideas for us as long as we don't look at them too closely, yet the moment they are explicitly named, they become murky and confused. The minute we try to say what they mean, their meaning becomes inexpressible; the minute we try to grasp hold of them, they slip through our fingers. In this the *rhetorical condition* is hardly an exception; it is, rather, subject to the same fate as all thought.

In this case, however, the fate in question is rather more bizarre, and we are less resigned to it. The difference is that courage, time, and modesty are simple, *unpretentious* ideas or feelings, and it is only too natural to think of them as disturbed by our attention. But Rhetoric made us a promise that it did not keep. It claimed to reveal the authentic spirit, pure thought itself, yet stumbled at its first step over a familiar obstacle.

We Cannot Observe Our Thinking Without Changing It

It is curious that the unconscious, as described by psychologists and psychoanalysts, is ordinarily just a *circumstantial* unconscious. It consists of thoughts, worries, and obsessions that might just as easily be conscious if some social taboo—law, propriety, or scruple—did not prevent it.

The unconscious whose existence we now find ourselves forced to assume, however, is unconscious *by nature*. In fact, a simple but obvious observation should have led us immediately to this conclusion: our only means of knowing thought is thought itself. To be conscious of an idea, concern, or feeling is first of all to *deduct* that portion of the thought required in order for us to become aware of it. We never see our thoughts in their pure state; we reflect—and reflection is *also* thought—only on thought already diminished by that reflection. Man can no more see his mind *intact* than he can see his own neck. But for looking at the neck there are mirrors; for the mind there are none. Inchoate thought may have its unknown powers, its mysterious associations, its extreme freedom. But we know nothing of all this—and I am speaking not only of psychologists and philosophers (who seem to have taken it upon themselves to reassure us on this score) but of all of us, of the man in the street, of you and me. Perhaps no anxiety is more acute than that which stems from this blind spot of ours, to judge by the stories and myths to which it has given rise. When Elsa tries to find out who Lohengrin is, Lohengrin disappears. The moment Psyche catches a glimpse of Amor, Amor vanishes. When Lot's wife turns around, she turns into a pillar of salt. Orpheus looks at Eurydice, and Eurydice returns to the underworld. No manner of precaution can help us in the matter: no matter how brief the glance, how slight the nod, the damage is already done. Or consider what hardly needs mentioning, those amusing vignettes that have supplanted myth in our thinking: the dog chasing its own tail, the cat stalking its own shadow, the person obsessed with the desire to see himself, if only just once, as others see him. Legends, some naive, others subtle, warn us that what is closest to us is best hidden. As long as we live, each of us carries hidden within the invisible lover who was given to Psyche.

Yet legend also tells us that we are not resigned to this. As proverbs indicate, we continue to be surprised that the torch does not illuminate its own base, that the gaze cannot see itself, and that man "knows everything but himself." We find it unbearable that Orpheus cannot see Eurydice. I grant, moreover, that our obsession with another *country,* an unknown country, is in its way an expression of our preoccupation with *our* unknown country and only taboo. What we cannot accept, however, is that it should be taboo forever.

Here it is possible to imagine more than one method, more than one avenue of inquiry. Of these, the most natural, those which occur to us first, fail: neither haste and extreme abruptness, nor negligence, absence, or self-effacement can ultimately teach us anything that rises above the banal. And sooner or later it will be recognized that dream and reverie, automatic writing, *le chant profond* and *le cri* only accentuate the ordinary workings of our consciousness: more reflective than reason, more calculated than our calculations, more literary than literature, and always attuned to the day's fashion. This should come as no surprise: there is no reason why the observing thought should necessarily be quicker than the observed thought, or why the occult thought should become apparent when the familiar is pushed aside. As I said earlier, there is just one kind of thought, to which our desire for a solution ascribes various qualities according to the circumstances: the dog is no more likely to catch its tail simply because it runs more quickly.

When the direct approach fails, one can always try the indirect approach. Some say that man can know himself by patiently observing his conduct and actions. Perhaps, but I fail to see what such observation could possibly teach us. Even if I grant (though the point is not proven and seems to me implausible) that my behavior is a more exact *likeness* of my deepest thoughts than my reflections are, it is still the case that I become conscious of my behavior by way of reflection. Hence the very distortion I fear may occur here, and all the more readily in that a prior *expression* is likely to have left a thought whose integrity is already threatened if not forever compromised. One might hope to find a more effective method.

One point has to be granted: since our reflection is *aware* of our real thought, and of the same nature, it cannot be altogether mistaken. This is because it grasps a part of the original thought, a part deprived, to be sure, of its subtlety and essential quality and distorted as much as you like, but still a part, and such that, from it, if only we could discover the nature of the distortion and identify the feature of which reflection deprives it, we could reconstitute the original thought. It would suffice to observe, *in another place,* how reflection works and what kind of distortion it introduces. By "in another place" I mean in connection with another thought that we are somehow allowed to grasp both *before* and *after* reflection, so that the distortion in question is magnified. No sooner is the problem stated than the outlines of a solution begin to emerge.

There is a feature of all translation that has not in my view received suffi-cient attention, namely, the fact that, to put the point in its simplest form, a translation expresses a thought or feeling that has *already* received expression elsewhere. No matter how much the translator tries to forget the words of the original text so as to retain only their spirit, and no matter how passionately he desires this spirit to enter into him, he cannot neglect the letter entirely, and the careful reader remains free to compare the two texts at any time. And for our purposes, as it happens, that comparison takes on singular importance.

For if there is a distinctive characteristic of expression *as such*—for example, a certain *alteration* that it induces in thought—then this alteration will be *in-creased* in the second text. I leave aside the possibility of error that may come into play. I have in mind the strictest, most faithful translation possible. If my hypothesis is correct, the translation should, to the very extent that it is faithful, *differ consistently* from the original, such difference being intrinsic to expression itself. Hence, in order to work our way back from the original to the pure thought that it expresses, we should have *only to discover in it, and reduce, a difference of the same nature.*

Care would of course have to be taken to choose translations of a sort where this difference would be likely to emerge clearly: either two languages of very different structure, perhaps a civilized tongue and a primitive one, or else a single language at two different moments in time or two different levels of usage, such that the slightest variation will stand out, as for example modern French contrasted with either argot or sixteenth-century French.

Merely stating the question suggests a possible answer: Translation, whether from Kikuyu or Cherokee into contemporary French (or English or German, for that matter), or from the argot of butchers and bandits into liter-ary French, or from sixteenth-century French into twentieth-century French, inevitably points up a difference in the *nature* of the source and target languages, a difference so clear and striking that more than one quite serious tome has been written about it. Specifically, the language to be translated, whether argot, Cherokee, or the poetry of François Villon, seems both richer in *imagery* and more *concrete* than the language into which we translate it.

ON ONE AVENUE TO AUTHENTIC THOUGHT

Victor Hugo said that ordinary French limits itself to naming things while argot shows them. As one of several examples he offered *lancequiner* (slang for "to rain"), a word with the felicitous property of suggesting a comparison between raindrops and the lances carried by *lansquenets* (footsoldiers). *Eye* is an abstract word, but words like *peepers*, *lights*, and *windows* conjure up images. *Chatterbox* is more expressive than *garrulous person*, and *sweet-talk* is more expressive than *persuade*.

The issue goes beyond the difference between formal and colloquial language, however. Owing to the authority of Diderot and Rousseau, it was long accepted that the language of savages and children was truly poetic. Some people still believe this. When little Jacqueline says that the swans are *plowing up* the water and her brother *gropes* for words, the whole family gapes with admiration. But *ripples*, *eyes*, and acts of *persuasion* would seem no less images to us if familiarity did not deprive these words of vividness. And the same familiarity conceals from the child and the thief the fact that they are speaking in metaphors: to them, *peepers* and *lights* are no less abstract than our *eyes*, and *chatterbox* is no less abstract than our *talkative individual*. As for *lancequiner*, it was Hugo, carried away by a translator's delusion, who turned it into a metaphor: the word is in fact a regular derivative of *ance* (water). This delusion can also take another form, namely, the belief that primitive languages are more concrete than modern ones. People have always been quick to speak about the naiveté of the old authors, their respect for the smallest details, and their inability to use abstraction. Explorers have admired the fact that in Lapp there is no general word for *reindeer* but specific words for the reindeer at age one, age two, age three, and so on. Or that in Luganda there is no general word for *arm* but specific words for right arm and left arm.

It is easy to respond that English has words for chicken, pullet, chick, and rooster but, like Lapp, no word for the species to which these various animals belong (which does not imply that English-speakers have no abstract idea of that species). English speakers distinguish between *loving* God and *liking* potatoes but (unlike Malagasy and French) have no word that serves for both feelings. Hence the Ugandan and the Lapp, misled by the opposite illusion, will tend to see French and English as excessively concrete tongues. But the error is less important to us than the illusion.

It is strange that the mind is slower than the hand or eye to free itself from its natural illusions. The black spot that we perceive from a distance is not a speck of dust or a midget but a man like us. We know this: we think we *see* a man. But we continue to believe (and there are plenty of serious books with no other subject) that argot and exotic languages are concrete and rich in images while our own language is highly abstract. When I try to discover the reason for this persistent illusion, this is what I come up with: namely, that the first effect of any translation, especially the most faithful, is to *free the stereotypes* in a text. Translation restores independence to elements of meaning that were associated in the original language. Consider these lines of François Villon:

> *Beaux enfants vous perdez la plus*
> *Belle rose de vos chapeaux*
>
> [Beautiful children, you are losing the most
> beautiful rose in your hats.]

If I read these lines carelessly, I can easily come away with a vague feeling of loss or decline and leave it at that. If I am a translator or close reader, I may recall first that flowered hats were once fashionable even in the most serious society. Then I may note that here the most beautiful rose in the hat metaphorically denotes the wearer's most precious possession. This translation is careful enough to give me the sense of a language both figurative and concrete. But where is the image? Where is the concreteness? Only in the translation, and in the operation whereby I restore specific meaning to a partially obscure sentence. A contemporary of Villon would have heard nothing but a simple cliché, not unlike what we hear in a phrase like "the finest flower of our youth." In the same way, *chatterbox*, *peepers*, *plowing the water*, *yearling reindeer*, and *right arm* give a feeling of concreteness or imagery *only in the process of translation*. To the savage, child, or thief, our *head*, *ripple*, *rooster*, and *hen* will seem like concrete details or images because they have to begin by filling in the details and images, building around them an entire sentence, almost a small fable.

Nothing I say here is foreign to the current practice of translators. When André Gide observes of the *Thousand and One Nights* that J.-C. Madrus's translation, while surely unfaithful to the storyteller's idea, goes a long way toward restoring the spirit and imaginativeness of the Arabic tongue, or when Paul Mazon remarks on the insurmountable difficulty of translating the *Iliad*—that by translating the concrete detail of the Homeric formulas one distorts the natural movement of the text—both are simply remarking on the distortion inherent in all translation, a distortion for which the time has come to seek a remedy.

As for the truth of the contention that all reflection affects our original thought in the same way that translation alters a text, I seek no proof other than common consent. It is widely taken for granted that analysis disintegrates and petrifies our passions and emotions. Thus Lot's wife turns to salt, and the Gorgon's visitor to stone. Not a single myth shows us the soul, *once attended to*, in any wise other than dispersed or frozen. And Mazon speaks of the *Iliad* translated as the old mythologies describe Amor once glimpsed by Psyche. Except perhaps we *now* know how it might be possible to avoid this glaciation or deformation.

It would suffice to restore to translation—as well as to the mind—the stereotypes and places, the *abstract disposition*, of which our gaze has deprived it. The problem faced by translators is susceptible to but a *single* solution. Of course, this is not to substitute simple abstract words for the clichés of the original text (for then the freedom and peculiar nuance of the formulation may be lost). Nor is it to translate the cliché word for word (for one then adds to the text a metaphor not originally present). Rather, the reader must be induced to *hear* the translation *as a cliché*, just as the original reader or listener must have heard it. He must, rather than dwell on the image or concrete detail, continually *turn away* from it.

This, of course, requires a certain education of the reader and even of the author. If, by dint of such effort, one can *also* work one's way back from the immediate thought to the authentic thought, it may not be too much to ask— if, that is, it will give us exact information not just about the *Iliad* but also about that more secret text that each of us carries within. In passing, we note the rhetorical *treatment*.

We sometimes say offhandedly that the rules of rhetoric and grammar are purely arbitrary and that there is no obvious necessity of thought to which rhyme or meter corresponds. But if, on the contrary, owing precisely to this *gift* and to our regard, a perceptible thought bears all the hallmarks of the arbitrary and false, then rhythm, rhyme, and meter must be recognized as possessing a singular value and merit: namely, that by restoring to the mind the stereotypes and commonplaces of which our attention deprived it, they restore it to its primordial state.

Something extraordinary has happened: it is as if the problem that we stated at the outset, far from being resolved in what followed, had in a sense been stood on its head. At first it seemed an affront to reason that the value of rhetoric depended on reference to an unconscious mind—real, I grant, and observable in its effects yet ultimately beyond our grasp.

The unconscious continues to elude us. Our discovery lay elsewhere—in the idea that it is not because rhetoric is abnormal and artificial that we have such a difficult time conceiving of it but, rather, because it is a little too normal and natural—by which I mean too close to nature and to those primary thoughts of which our ideas and feelings, once we begin to *distinguish* them, are merely a distorted echo.

I do not claim that this is a rare or unexpected discovery. All in all, it does little but justify the impression that has long tormented us. What else might be signified by the concern, common among rhetoricians, with a spirit *just a bit more* spiritual than usual? Indeed, it was in connection with Rhetoric that the paradox of reflection seemed *particularly* intolerable to us. Finally, who does not know from experience that there exists more than one poem, more than one verse, in which the eternal, the immediate, the intimate, and *that which is everyman's* like the day and the night, or space and time, are reflected as in a mirror—one of those mirrors with which we adorn the pretty country lass.

TRANSLATED BY ARTHUR GOLDHAMMER

NOTE

[1] See Jean Paulhan, "La Rhétorique renaît de ses cendres" (1930), in *Oeurves complètes*, vol. 2, pp. 157–167.

MAURICE BLANCHOT

The Novel, Work of Bad Faith
1947

Maurice Blanchot's review of Jean Pouillon's Temps et roman, *though published under the auspices of Sartre's journal, is a strong rebuttal of the premises of Sartre's aesthetics of commitment.*

Commitment presupposes that life and books are continuous; that they happen in the same world; that words, both literary and not, are always part of the same existential surrounding. There might be different ways of using them, but they are always the same words. To Sartre's common-law aesthetics and his program for a literature without privileges, Blanchot opposes literature's ontological exception: literature is incommensurable with common life, its words, incommensurable with ordinary words, its creatures with ordinary beings.

Pouillon's theory of the novel rests on the postulate that "the attitude of author and reader to the character is analogous to any individual's attitude toward himself and others": author, reader, and heroes are, with respect to one another, "what actual, living human beings are with respect to other actual, living human beings." The fact that characters in a novel need to be named in order to exist, that they don't exist prior to being named, doesn't afford them dispensation from obeying the fundamental requirements of psychological empathy.

This is where, according to Blanchot, the concept of bad faith comes into play. As developed by Sartre in Being and Nothingness, *it refers to structures of consciousness that allow for a subject not to know, not to mean, not to be aware of, or not to feel responsible for what he or she is doing or thinking. In a similar fashion, the narrative efficacy of the novel requires the denial of its linguistic medium (its linguistic mediation). Hence the novel's ingrained realist delusion, which is an expanded version of the linguistic sign's own bad faith: namely, the false modesty by means of which a sign—all the more efficient in that it remains unnoticed, transparent— deflects its user's attention toward its referent.*

Maurice Blanchot, "Le Roman, oeuvre de mauvaise foi," *Les Temps modernes* (April 1947), pp. 1304–17.

J ean Pouillon's views on the novel avoid the usual vagueness of literary judgment.[1] They are based on clearly stated principles. For this he deserves credit. When one begins to think about literary works, it is surprising to discover how far one can go with extremely imprecise ideas and no notion of how those ideas might be justified or what they might imply. Indeed, it seems that such ignorance is required not only of literature but of any consideration of literature. Apparently, the critic is not entitled to ask too many questions about literary works or to explore fundamental issues, as if the sine qua non of all criticism were a certain essential ignorance, intrinsic to art, or, more precisely, a concealment of that ignorance by seeming to dispel it with a parade of commentary that explains nothing while excusing in advance the peremptory exclusion of certain matters from critical consideration. In this respect, criticism can be compared to theology; but theology is admirably elaborate and precise, even if that precision sometimes serves as a defense against illegitimate questions. Apparently, the critic has no right to precision or rigor; on the contrary, he must make what he is talking about comprehensible by professing ignorance of his own theoretical domain and adopting the same blind approach as literature itself, an approach whose felicitous results literature has presumably demonstrated in advance. Criticism reproduces this ignorance, but it must not study or recognize it, much less formulate it as a problem. It thereby raises vagueness to a pitch of perfection, which of course negates its value. But criticism is not disappointed by this, because it thereby pays a final homage to its object, which can now be seen in its true light as capable of contradicting or nullifying any attempt to study it theoretically.

Not that this critical aversion to rigor is nonsensical. Nor is it easy to overcome in order to explore rigorously an area that, being a realm of deception, transforms rigor into yet another form of bad faith. Pouillon's work on time and the novel lays the groundwork for rigorous investigation by refusing to avoid clarity and precision of thought and refusing to accord certain privileges to literature. In pursuit of these goals, Pouillon encounters more obstacles than he acknowledges; but while I shall try to describe these, my aim is not to discredit the principles on which his research is based, without which it would have been impossible to note the difficulties that remain.

How can one achieve a degree of rigor in the study of the novel while avoiding the vague and approximate categories of traditional criticism? Pouillon's method is to focus exclusively on features of the novel about which clear ideas can be borrowed from more mature disciplines. He shows, for example, that the novel involves various forms of knowledge of self and others; that everything we know about such knowledge, and the conditions that govern it, should be applied to the study of literary fiction; that a novel is valuable only if it respects those conditions; and that one can therefore, in theory at any rate, arrive at a definition of what a good novel is, namely, a text that, in the special realm of written language, has no purpose other than to reconstitute the various ways in which individuals take cognizance of themselves and others.

Pouillon insists on denying any special privilege to the novel. A novel is a work of fiction couched in written form; it is associated with a unique, real individual, the novelist, whose work is supplemented by the activity of one or more other real individuals, the reader or readers. Ultimately, Pouillon discounts the significance of these singular facts. For him, the problem of expression is unimportant. To be sure, the novel places invented characters in a fictitious plot, but there is nothing about this recourse to the unreal that is specific to the novel form. In reality, every conscious being makes use of fiction. Such a being is conscious of and understands itself and other such beings only in the fictionalizing act through which it imputes meaning to its own existence and that of others. To understand, grasp, see—all these are acts of imagination. To imagine, as the novel requires, is therefore not to ignore the real but to put oneself in a situation where the only aspect of reality that one retains is the signifying act.

Pouillon insists that the author must not enjoy any privilege over the reader. For the author who creates characters and events by describing them, these must be exactly what they will be later on for the reader who recreates those same characters and events by reading the author's descriptions. This is equivalent to saying that the author's knowledge is identical to the knowledge he would have of those characters and events if they were real. Author, hero, and reader are in no sense in a unique situation. With respect to one another, they must be what actual, living human beings are with respect to other actual, living human beings. They can know one another only as human beings know one another. More precisely, the characters of a novel are likely to have fictional value only if they understand one another, and behave with respect to one another, in such a way that neither author nor reader appears to rely on any special comprehension in creating or recreating them; the attitude of author and reader to the characters is analogous to any individual's attitude toward himself and others.

One of the ways in which Pouillon's study is flawed, however, is that it fails to disclose its own intrinsically paradoxical nature, though the paradoxes are obvious. It may well be right to condemn the author's privilege with respect to the reader and the novelist's privilege with respect to the hero, and to assert that the writer of a fictional story should place himself on an equal footing with the person who will read that story; and it may also be true that, when the novelist describes fictional characters in words, he should adopt toward them the same attitude he would adopt toward real individuals who exist without his intervention. Surely this much is correct. But how can this be done? This, too, is an important question.

Pouillon distinguishes between novels of two types, which he calls "peer-narrated" [*le roman-avec*] and "narrated from above" [*le roman par derrière*]. In novels of the first type, the writer accompanies his heroes, stands beside them, is what they are, and knows about them only what they know about themselves in every situation and twist of his plot. In novels of the second type, the writer stands at a certain distance from his characters, which allows him to judge them and to seek all possible motives for their actions—in short, to analyze them. But he stands aloof in order to contemplate his characters, not to urge them on or to animate them from without. He ponders their actions and tries to understand them through reflection. But what he understands about them always depends on an existence independent of his intervention. In both cases, the novelist is to some extent ignorant of his characters: either because, in identifying with them, he knows only what can be known by a consciousness that cannot contemplate itself from outside, or because, in contemplating them from outside as they reflect inwardly, he must at least respect the distance without which such knowledge is impossible, and which at the same time inevitably renders it conjectural and incomplete.

Pouillon apparently finds such ignorance normal and in any case does not regard it as raising very serious issues. He concedes that when a character describes himself as living a life of unreflective spontaneity (for example, Benjy in William Faulkner's *The Sound and the Fury*), a small problem arises. "To be sure, I, the writer, do not live this way, so there is an element of bad faith here, as always in literature: if I want to be an 'unreflective consciousness,' I cannot possibly be unreflective, because in order to want this I must know what an unreflective consciousness is, and to know this I must reflect." Nevertheless, he adds that "this is not important provided that the reflection does not appear in person in the work." To my mind, however, it is very important indeed. I mention Faulkner's Benjy because the example seems well chosen for illustrating certain anomalies of the novelist's art. First problem: How can the unreflective consciousness of an idiot present itself as such and describe itself in a more or less objective style? Second problem: How can the reflective act that is to some extent required by the writing of a novel coincide with an unreflective existence of this sort? Third problem: How can the reader receive a direct impression of the life of a mute idiot through language imputed to him by a reflective author? This last problem is the most important of the three, assuming that Pouillon is correct in asserting that the reader's point of view is paramount in the comprehension of the novel. The goal is clear: the reader, in reading Benjy's monologue, should feel trapped in the worldview of an unreflective, illogical consciousness incapable of speech or comprehension and must not feel the author's reflective consciousness behind the character. But when is that goal attained? When the author, by restricting himself to language of utter incoherence, attempts to immerse himself in the stupor he intends to describe? Or when, with the skill and tact of reflective art, he employs a style calculated to cover its tracks and thus to evoke the inarticulateness and absence of reason that he wishes to suggest? There is no proof that the author's unreflectiveness, or recourse to a form in which unreflectiveness is omnipresent, is the best way of convincing the reader or persuading him to feel what the author wants him to feel. No matter how hard the novelist tries to approximate an unseeing consciousness, it is highly likely that the reader will see only unnaturalness of style, arbitrariness, and manipulation. In the case of Benjy's monologue, the artifice is obvious: interior though it may be, the language of an idiot deprived of language can exist in written form only by dispensation of the writer, who lends the character his own voice. Merely calling this an interior monologue does not eliminate the anomaly. What is more, no one can possibly believe that an idiot's inner speech is anything like the disciplined and essentially objective language that Benjy uses. Faulkner's method is thus eminently conventional. Yet the reader forgets the conventions and little by little, as he takes in Benjy's very artificial words, confronts the mute presence presented to him by the text.

The novelist writes, the reader reads. It is easy to forget this difference of function, but it is a difference that makes Pouillon's rule about illegitimate privileges very difficult to apply. What, ultimately, does that rule imply? Does it mean that the writer, rather than renounce his rights, should hide or camouflage them from the reader? Perhaps. Such precautions are the capital of all premeditated art. They take account of the difference in perspective between writer and reader, which no theoretical requirement can eliminate. But their result is this: not only are the privileges of the writer left intact, but the very act of camouflaging them lays claim to the additional privilege of appearing not to have any. The writer, in an act of consummate bad faith, claims to renounce all conventions while inventing yet another.

Such deception does not appear to be what is desired by Pouillon, who writes in the clearest possible manner: "Someone may object, of course, that it is absurd to criticize the novelist for knowing the end of the story he is telling and for organizing his narrative with that end in view. To be sure, the writer has finished his work before one reads it, but what he is being asked to do is either to write it as the reader must read it or else to cause it to be read as he wrote it. Surely, nothing could be clearer than this, or more contradictory. For if I want the reader to see my book as a work in which rhetoric is reduced to a minimum, I may be forced to pile trope upon trope. If I adopt the automatic writing of the spontaneous consciousness, the reader may discover a reflection in disguise, which reveals itself by pretending to hide. In order to be read as I write, I must write in a way different from that in which I will be read. In order for Benjy to appear as a dumb consciousness in the throes of disintegration, Faulkner must grant him, through language, knowledge of his behavior and the power to locate himself in a world shared with others. Furthermore, in asking the novelist to force the reader to read as he writes, Pouillon twists his rule by adding an intention of intellectual honesty not contained in the rule itself. For Pouillon, a novel is valuable insofar as the novelist's vision corresponds to an authentic psychological attitude in the reader. The goal is therefore to connect with a potential for genuine comprehension on the reader's part. But such comprehension can be achieved in a variety of ways, including deception, trickery, and fraud on the one hand and fantasy, unreality, and implausibility on the other. If the reader is to be our law, then his consciousness must be our warrant, and if the reader is deceived, then that deception takes on the full value of a truth.

The novelist bestows reality upon unreal events and people by means of the written word. The reader bestows reality upon these same events and people by means of the read word. As Pouillon rightly remarks, "in reading, the reader bestows reality." For that reason he believes that the novel must express reality. Let us take a closer look, however. Pouillon treats the role of expression in the novel rather superficially, and he is content to make the usual distinctions, noting that in poetry expression governs content but that in the novel expression depends on content. On these grounds he feels justified in relegating questions of novelistic form to the background. He neglects one problem, however: specifically, there is a considerable difference between a sentence read in a novel and the same sentence uttered in real life—why? Here I can do no more than recall observations that I develop more fully elsewhere. In the ordinary course of life, the words that I read vanish behind their meaning; indeed, no definite image need correspond to that meaning at all. It is not a real object that emerges behind the word as the support of its meaning, nor even an image of such an object, but an empty set of relations and intentions, an opening onto an ambiguous complexity. It is as if, in real life, the countless people and things that solicit our attention acquired meaning only through language—but language that is not only empty of things because it consists of signs but also intrinsically blank (*vide de langage*) because always beyond words. This nullity of a language sustained solely by the void of a possible intention underlies our everyday powers of comprehension.

In the novel, however, even a novel written in the most prosaic prose and with the most everyday diction, a radical transformation occurs, a change that comes from a change in the attitude toward words of the person who is writing or reading. In a narrative, neither the writer nor the reader starts from a preexisting reality, given with his own existence. Both begin with a world that has yet to reveal itself, either because it does not yet exist, having yet to enter the world of the written text, or because it exists only in the form of a book as yet unread. Furthermore, both are dealing with an imagined creation that will always remain unreal, but upon which reality is to be bestowed by the actions of writer and reader alike. How? In and through words. Hence, a sentence in a narrative cannot be content simply to serve as a sign or to disappear behind the meaning of words that vanish the moment they are read. No matter how little the language of fiction matters, it has a specific role to play: rather than refer to the real world, it brings us into contact with a fictional world. Hence, it is indispensable not as a sign for already-absent people and things but, rather, as a means of making those people and things present, of making us feel and experience them through words. Now, insofar as the language of the novel allows both reader and writer to give reality to this otherwise unreal world by means of words, it takes on importance as verbal paraphernalia and aspires to establish itself as a materially and formally valid linguistic system. This is not to say that style is more important than anything else in the novel but, rather, that the events, characters, and dialogues of the fictional world necessarily bear the impress of the words that render them real, hence they require a style "thick" enough not just to signify but to make present, visible, and comprehensible.

To this Pouillon would respond that the world of fiction cannot be said to be unreal: it is a part of reality, obviously not of physical reality but of psychological reality. This, he would say, is self-evident, for otherwise it would elude consciousness and be impervious to formulation of any kind. Finally, the imagination that produces the fictional world is precisely the same as the imagination at work in the apprehending consciousness, and this role of the imagination shows that various psychological attitudes from real life can be related to the fictional situations of the novel which inevitably give embodiment to their meaning. On this point, however, it seems to me that Pouillon is taking the easy way out. Even if we assume that the imagination is shaped by the structure of consciousness and can exist only because consciousness always stands at some distance from itself, it does not follow that all acts of consciousness in which this distance manifests itself are equivalent and identical in meaning. Imagination, as the ability to make what is absent present and to present it both in its absence and as absent, remains a distinct kind of activity. Furthermore, "fictitiousness" is not eliminated by the fact that imagined experience is indeed real, for it is a real experience whose distinctive feature is to give us what is unreal, to connect up with something nonexistent which we see as nonexistent. When, moreover, Pouillon looks at the classical definition of imagination—"to make something that does not exist exist for us"—he remarks that nonexistence is the mode of all that is conscious, of all that is psychological, and from this he concludes that the imagination is concerned with "psychological existence" rather than with "nonexistence." But this is a strange argument, for it neglects to ask whether one of the ways in which "psychological reality" (in itself an equivocal term) appears to us—namely, through positing a thing as nothingness and conjuring it up in that very nothingness—is in fact consciousness of nonexistence, for in this case I am not simply conscious of something that exists in consciousness but of something I am conscious of as being nonexistent, unreal.

A novel is a work in which fictitious events and characters achieve reality in words through the double act of writing and reading, the one perpetually off-kilter with respect to the other. The fact that the fiction needs words in order to achieve reality and that, apart from words, it has no way of manifesting itself shows that fiction is the distinctive reality of the novel. Furthermore, although the writer bestows reality by writing and the reader by reading, it would be inaccurate to say that because of these actions there is no essential difference between real existence and the existence evoked by the novel. In fact, the opposite is true. No matter how vivid the fiction, the reader and perhaps also the writer of that fiction relate to the events and characters in it differently from the way in which they relate to the events and characters of real life. In fact, the more vivid the fiction, the more different the relationship and the greater the tendency to live in the unreal world, to delay as long as possible the return to real life. To be sure, the reader's immediate reaction, like that of the writer, who is often even more naive, leads him to credit his enchantment with characters he cannot get out of his mind to an extraordinary reality quotient: they are alive, he tends to say, they are real. But this reaction is easily explained. Not even in the truest of novels are the characters true or alive or real. Being fictitious, rather, they draw the reader into the fiction so powerfully that he allows himself to slip momentarily out of the real world: that world is lost to him and he to it as he loses his bearings and throws himself wholeheartedly into the fiction, from that moment on accepting the fictional world as a substitute for the real world, regarding it as real, and in his readerly existence taking it not only as his life but as life itself. This proves not that the fiction has ceased to be imaginary but that a real person, a writer or reader, fascinated by a certain form of absence he finds in words, which words derive from a fundamental power of consciousness, frees himself from all real presence and seeks to live in the absence of life, to unreify himself in the absence of reality, and to establish the world's absence as the only genuine world.

These remarks do not pretend to resolve any problems. On the contrary, they raise very difficult ones. I simply want to say that if we are to form an idea of the novel, we must first try to conceive of what fiction is, what makes it possible, and what attitudes it presupposes in those who create it by writing or produce it by reading. It may be that an essential tendency of the novel is to be a fiction that contests itself qua fiction, an imaginative narrative that desperately seeks to re-establish contact with the world, and with the responsibility and seriousness of the world, in the most diverse ways. But if this tendency is, as I believe, constitutive of the novel in the sense that the novel cannot renounce it with impunity, it only makes sense within and in relation to fiction, against which it engages in unrelenting if hopeless struggle.

In the novel, the imaginary asks to be taken as real by the writer as well as by the reader (and it is primarily in this sense that Pouillon's remark on illegitimate privileges is useful). But "taken as real" can be understood in two ways. It can mean that the imaginary world entirely takes the place of the real world, stands in its place, elides it. This is, of course, the ideal of reading that aims to *grip* the reader, to enchant him, to reduce him to being nothing but a reader — that aims, in short, to be so enthralling that it puts the person committed to it to sleep, indeed a sleep from which no awakening is possible. But it can also mean that fiction has value insofar as it can be taken for real, hence that it derives its value from its equivalence with existing things, and that in return it is also what is valuable in reality, that it is the meaning of reality, is itself what it longs for when it is not the goal of our confused striving to be present to real people and things. This brings us back to Pouillon's view of the matter.

A novel, even if it is not symbolic, claims to depict the true relations of people in the world, for it claims to embody the meaning of those relations. This claim to express the meaning of reality rests, paradoxically, on the unreality that is the mode of being of fictional objects: being imaginary, such objects are by nature destined to remain always at a distance, apart from what they are, from what they would be if they truly existed. Furthermore, it is this separation from reality that constitutes their intrinsic reality and allows them to represent the movement from which the things of the world derive their meaning, a movement that is possible only when those things are kept at a distance, by virtue of their being held at arm's length. Indeed, because the things of fiction are always at a distance from themselves and must maintain this essential character, the only reality they can achieve is equivocal, and the role of language is to give them that reality in an ambiguous, questioning manner.

It is the fate of the successful novel to merit praise (or blame) on two simultaneous, and contradictory, counts: for being true and for not being true, for being a good (because fantastic) likeness, and for being an unfaithful (because too exact) portrait. We are now in a position to divine the origins of the endless debates about certain novelists, who for some are models of realism and for others models of creative imagination. In a recent study, Albert Béguin reopened this debate apropos of Balzac by pointing to the surreal nature of the Balzacian world, the product of a powerful vision having little in common with precise, objective observation.[2] His comments are not easily refuted. Concerning Balzac, Pouillon makes the rather specious argument that the writer constructs analytically characters who are petrified by that analytic process, yet despite their lack of individual vitality they emerge as powerful types that help us to understand real individuals. In the real world, in other words, these characters are animated by the very vitality they lack or are denied in the novel. This is a strange observation, for it contradicts the experience of any reader of Balzac for whom an oeuvre such as his is, as Béguin points out, first of all an autonomous world, a closed empire, with its own laws, perspectives, and proportions. Once we have crossed the borders into that empire, it impresses us with such authority that we forfeit all right to contest it in the name of life "as it really is." Perhaps Pouillon is right to say that Balzac's characters are not alive, but if they impress the reader as being so it is not because they explain living individuals but, rather, because they make real people useless and beside the point, because they enclose us in the hermetic universe of reading in which they reign supreme. And if Balzac remains the supreme genius of the novel, it is because he dared to conceive and create this universe of reading on such a grand scale, and with such enthralling power, that the novel truly seems to vie with the world, to "compete" with it in richness and fecundity, and to afford the reader who ventures into it the illusion of being able to remain there for close to an entire lifetime.

Balzac's world can be "taken for real" because it stands apart from the real. Of course it wants to be regarded not as fictitious but as deep as life—as the meaning which animates the real and which we have so much difficulty recognizing in real life that, when a novelist reveals it, he seems to bring it into being. But the signifying power that the novel claims does not exist outside the novel, and it cannot even be separated from the fictional universe taken as a whole: the novel's fragmentary power is not carried by each individual character, nor is it carried by any plot element assigned the task of signifying a particular idea. The characters of a novel may well be inconsistent or too consistent, too simple or too obvious, and yet the novel may for all that be no less rich or significant or close to the reality that it simplifies. For Pouillon, the novel consists of characters, and the truth of the novel is proportional to their vital depth. Why? Because human experience begins with consciousness, and if we fail to recognize this fundamental fact, we forfeit any possibility of connecting with human existence. This is a very just and very important reminder. But it does not follow that subjectivity can reveal itself only in the "I" of the characters, in the way in which the writer who imagines his characters' lives respects the actual conditions of conscious existence and the relations between one consciousness and another. If that were true, the genre of the novel would be of no importance whatsoever. Recall the definition of the "peer-narrated novel," the genre of novel that comes closest to the attitudes of real life: to be someone's peer, to be "with" that person, Pouillon tells us, "is not to be conscious of him in a reflective way; it is not to know him but to have, 'along with' him, the same unreflective self-consciousness that he has. How, then, could we distinguish between that person and ourselves?" In reality, though, the problem is how we can avoid distinguishing between that person and ourselves. If the peer-narrated novel would have us live "with" another person exactly as that person lives "with" himself, some fundamental deception must be involved, for life offers us no such opportunity. Even if our relations with others are unmediated, we never encounter another individual except as other, that is, as forever different from ourselves. Only in the novel can we put ourselves "in someone else's skin." Only a reader can allow himself to slip into a life that is not his own and, thanks to the fascinating void that reading creates, acquiesce in living the life of another as if he had ceased to be himself in order to become purely other.

The only possible term for this is deception—a deception essential to art in general and to the art of the novel in particular. But there is no reason to despair over this if such deception marks the beginning of the truth of art. When Pouillon, in a passage quoted earlier, remarks that in literature there is always an element of bad faith, he is tactfully reminding literature of its inherent deceptiveness. Literature cannot eliminate this deceptiveness or hide it or evade it. Because of it, literature entertains perpetual doubts about its value, so much so that these doubts are incorporated into whatever it does, becoming the source of its works and the measure of their authenticity.

The novel is a work of bad faith—bad faith on the part of the novelist, who believes in his characters and yet sees himself as standing above them, ignoring them, creating them as strangers and finding in the words of which he is master the means to arrange their fate while continuing to think of them as beyond his control. And bad faith on the part of the reader, who toys with the imaginary, plays at being the hero he is not, pretends to take fiction for real, and ultimately becomes caught up in it; who, while holding existence at arm's length, discovers in his enchantment a possibility of finding meaning in that existence. Such bad faith is not specific to the novel or to literature in general. But it is inherent in the novel and in literature to welcome it as such, to take it as an object, and to succeed not so much in transcending it as in organizing it as a special kind of experience in which the meaning of the human world as a whole can be recovered.

That experience needs to be studied in itself and for itself. To be sure, this is not easy. One of the first questions to be asked has to do with the enchantment of the reader (and writer), which is no less active in novels in which man finds himself than in novels in which he loses himself, in works that claim to be means of discovery than in works without depth. True, for both the writer and the reader, the novel claims to be an instrument of knowledge. But it is a knowledge that begins with the emptiness of fascination, a discovery that assumes the authority of luminous ignorance. It is an apprehension of being whose condition is the reign of the absence of being, an absence that wants to be everything and to realize itself in the paradoxical double form of particular absence *and* total absence. In this world of enchantment and fascination, what becomes of individuals and of their ways of living with and understanding each other? To what extent does the notion of character remain predominant, and to what extent do the enchanting thickness of fiction and the existence of a fictional *world* succeed in making the novel more than a dream? And finally, what about characters who need to enchant us in order to play their game with us? Must they in turn fall prey to this very fascination? Are they capable of fascinating us because they are themselves fascinated, incapable of governing their own behavior no matter how masterful or lucid they appear to be, as we see in the case of the classic heroes of Mme de La Fayette, Benjamin Constant, and Stendhal, as well as in the heroes of Faulkner to whom Pouillon devotes some extremely interesting pages? This would make sense of Malraux's remark: "In literature, the domination of the novel is significant, because of all the arts (including music), the novel is the least disciplined, the one in which the realm of the will is most limited. . . . And the essential thing is not that the artist is dominated but that for the past fifty years he has been increasingly able to choose that which dominates him and to organize the resources of his art with that domination in mind. Some great novels were for their authors initially the creation of the one thing that could overwhelm them."[3] The novel might thus be the most striking result of the bad faith of language, if that bad faith were capable of constituting a world of illusion so worthy of faith that its own author would be reduced to nothingness by the power of his belief in it, and if the illusory nature of that world could be transformed into a void in which the truest of meanings might finally appear.

TRANSLATED BY ARTHUR GOLDHAMMER

NOTES

[1] Jean Pouillon, *Temps et roman* (Paris: Gallimard, 1946).

[2] Albert Béguin, *Balzac visionnaire* (Geneva: Skira, 1946)

[3] See, in particular, Maurice Blanchot, "Kafka et la littérature," and "Le langage de la fiction" in *La part du feu* (Paris: Gallimard, 1949), pp. 21–34 and pp. 79–98.

RENÉ GIRARD

The Mimetic Desire
of Paolo and Francesca
1976

The novel, according to René Girard—and, in his view, one must consider all novelistic masterpieces as one homogeneous corpus—has been developed as the narrative tool best suited to perform the practical criticism of yet another form of realism: not primarily that of referential description but, rather, that of desire.

According to Girard, there are two laws of desire. First: A desire always imitates another desire. One only desires by proxy. There is one and only one condition for anything to become an object of desire; that it be already marked by someone else's desire. (Poor little Oedipus, who believes he is in love with his mother—he is only imitating his father's desire.) Second: The structure of desire is such that it always and necessarily represses its cause. Mimicry is unconscious; infatuated with what it takes to be its objective cause (its object and its source), desire is blind to its mimetic, mediated, intersubjective structure. It is the task of the novel to expose its workings and liberate the protagonist from its tyranny.

Essential to the definition of the novel is thus a conclusion that, Girard claims, stages not the victory of desire but the victory over desire, not the possession but the relinquishing of the object of worldly desire. The novel's form of happy ending thus is never the reunion of a desire and its matching object but, rather, the subject's ultimate untying of the bonds of desire, his disentanglement from the plots of desire, and the fetishistic attachment to the object it commands.

The task of the novel is thus to counter the Romantic infatuation with desire understood as the mark of a strong, nonconformist personality, desire as the ultimate signature of originality; there is nothing less "personal," less original, nothing more socially constructed, hence more commercially ma-

René Girard, "The Mimetic Desire of Paolo and Francesca," in *To Double Business Bound: Essays on Literature, Mimesis, and Anthropology*, translated by Petra Morrison (Baltimore: Johns Hopkins University Press, 1978), pp. 1–8, from "De 'La Divine comédie' à la sociologie du roman," in *Critique dans un souterrain* (Paris: Grasset, 1976), pp. 143–50.

nipulable, than desire. As Girard hints briefly at the end of this piece, this approach suggests a possible sociohistorical link between the development of the novel in the nineteenth century and the contemporary expansion of a liberal market defined as the economic space for the mass production of serialized desires.

Paolo and Francesca, the adulterous lovers of *The Divine Comedy*, enjoyed a very special popularity at the beginning of the nineteenth century. The two young people defy human and divine laws and appear to bring about the triumph of passion, even in the realm of eternity. What does Hell matter to them, since they are there together? In the minds of innumerable readers, in modern times as well as in the Romantic era, the infernal setting, however artistically remarkable it may be, is no more than a deferential nod in the direction of the moral and theological conventions of the time.

Far from unsettling faith in individualism, romantic passion is regarded as being its fulfillment. The lovers give themselves to each other in an act that is utterly spontaneous and involves only themselves, though it involves them totally. Thus, we have a kind of lovers' *cogito ergo sum* on which existence is founded for the couple—the only real existence in their eyes—and which engenders a new being, at once unified and double, absolutely autonomous with regard to God and to men.

It is this image of love that emerges from the commentaries on Dante, just as it emerges from a thousand other literary works of the time. Yet this romantic reading is obviously contrary to the spirit of *The Divine Comedy*. For Dante, Hell is a reality. No true union is possible between the disembodied "doubles" that Paolo and Francesca represent for each other. The lovers' undertaking does indeed have a Promethean aspect, but its defeat is total; it is this defeat that the romantic reader does not perceive. To reveal the contradiction in its entirety one need only read of the origin of the passion, as described by Francesca herself at Dante's request.

One day, Paolo and Francesca were quite innocently reading the story of Lancelot together. When they reached the love scene between the knight and Queen Guinevere, Arthur's wife, they became embarrassed and blushed. Then came the first kiss of the legendary lovers. Paolo and Francesca turned toward each other and kissed likewise. Love advances in their souls in step with their own progress through the book. The written word exercises a veritable fascination. It impels the two young lovers to act as if determined by fate; it is a mirror in which they gaze, discovering in themselves the semblances of their brilliant models.

Thus, Paolo and Francesca never achieve, even on earth, the coupled solipsism that is the definition of absolute passion; the Other, the book, the model, is present from the beginning. It is the model that originates their future self-absorption. The romantic and individualist reader fails to perceive the role played by bookish imitation precisely because he too believes in absolute passion. Draw the attention of such a reader to the fact of the book and he will reply that it is an unimportant detail; reading it, for him, does no more than uncover desire that existed beforehand. But Dante gives this "detail" an emphasis that renders even more striking the silence of modern commentators on this point. Interpretations that minimize the role of the model are all belied by the conclusion of Francesca's narrative:

> *Galeotto fu il libro e chi lo scrisse.*
> (Galeotto was both the book and its author.)

Galleot (or Gallahad) is the treacherous knight, Arthur's enemy, who sows the seeds of passion in the hearts of Lancelot and Guinevere. It is the book itself, Francesca maintains, that plays the role of the diabolical go-between, the pander, in her life. The young woman curses the romance and its author. There is no question of drawing our attention to any particular writer. Dante is not writing literary history; he is stressing that, whether written or oral, it has to be some person's word that suggests desire. The book occupies in Francesca's fate the place of the Word in the Fourth Gospel: the Word of man becomes the Word of the devil if it usurps the place of the divine Word in our souls.

Paolo and Francesca are the dupes of Lancelot and the queen, who are themselves the dupes of Galleot. And the romantic readers, in their turn, are dupes of Paolo and Francesca. The malignant prompting is a process perpetually renewed without its victims' being aware of it. An identical internal censorship erases any cognizance of the mediator, suppresses all information contrary to the romantic solipsistic *Weltanschauung*. George Sand and Alfred de Musset, leaving for Italy, took themselves for Paolo and Francesca but never questioned their own spontaneity. Romanticism turns *The Divine Comedy* into a new novel of chivalry. It is an extremity of blindness that forces into the role of pander the very work that expressly denounces it.

The Francesca who speaks in the poem is no longer a dupe, but she owes her clear-sightedness to death. An imitator of imitators, she knows that the resemblance between her and her model is real (because one always obtains what one desires strongly). However, this resemblance does not consist in the triumph of an absolute passion, as the lovers at first imagined and as the readers imagine still, but, rather, in defeat—a defeat already accomplished at that moment when, in the shadow of the Lancelot story, the first kiss was exchanged.

Don Quixote, in his imitation of a chivalric model, courts the same quasi-divinity as Paolo and Francesca. Like them, he spreads the evil of which he is a victim. He has his imitators, and the novel of which he is the hero had its plagiarists. This fact allowed Cervantes, in the second part, to make his ironic prophecy about the insensate criticism that would rage around it once more with the Romantic period—Unamuno, for instance, would insult Cervantes, the novelist himself, for exhibiting a "lack of understanding" of his sublimely inspired hero. The individualist is not unaware that there exists a second, and derivative, form of passion, but it is never, for him, "true passion," that is to say, his own or his model's. The genius of Dante, like that of Cervantes, is bound up with the abandonment of the preconceptions of individualism. That is why the very essence of their genius has been misunderstood by the Romantics and their successors of today.[1]

Cervantes and Dante discover within the world of literature a whole territory of awareness that includes Shakespeare's "play within a play" and Gide's *mise en abime*. In connection with modern novels, the same writers also afford us a rendering of unhappy consciousness that differs significantly from that of Hegel.

The hero in the grip of some secondhand desire seeks to conquer the *being*, the essence, of his model by as faithful an imitation as possible. If the hero lived in the same world as the model instead of being forever distanced from him by myth or history, as in the examples above, he would necessarily come to desire the same object. The nearer the mediator, the more does the veneration that he inspires give way to hate and rivalry. Passion is no longer eternal. A Paolo who encountered Lancelot every day would no doubt prefer Queen Guinevere to Francesca unless he managed to link Francesca and his rival, making the rival desire her, so as to desire her the more himself—to desire her *through* him or, rather, against him, in short, to tear her from a desire that transfigures her. It is this second possibility that is illustrated in *Don Quixote* by the story of "the inquisitive, impertinent man," and in Dostoyevsky by the short story, "The Eternal Husband." For novelists who write of *internal* mediation, it is envy and morbid jealousy that triumph. Stendhal speaks of "vanity," Flaubert and his critics of Bovaryism; Proust reveals the workings of snobbery and of *l'amour-jalousie*.

The model in these instances is still an obstacle. At a lower level of "degradation," every obstacle will serve as a model. Masochism and sadism are thus degraded forms of mediated desire. When the erotic attachment is displaced from the object onto the intermediary-rival, one has the type of homosexuality demonstrated by Marcel Proust. The divisions and agonies produced by mediation find their climax in the hallucination of the double, present in the work of numerous Romantic and modern writers but comprehended only by the greatest as a conflictual structure.

One must treat the great works of fiction as a single entity, a totality. The individual and collective history of secondhand desire always moves toward nothingness and death. A faithful description would elucidate a dynamic structure in the form of a descending spiral.

How is it possible for the novelist to see the structures of desire? The vision of the totality is simultaneously a vision of the whole and of the parts, of the detail and of the ensemble. It demands detachment and anything but detachment at one and the same time. The true novelist is neither the Olympian, inactive god whom Sartre describes in *What Is Literature?* nor the committed man whom Sartre would like to substitute for the false God. The novelist must be at once committed and uncommitted. He is the man who has been caught in the structure of desire and has escaped from it. The Flaubert of the first *Sentimental Education*, the Proust of *Jean Santeuil*, and Dostoyevsky before *Notes from Underground* present us with all the ambivalences engendered by mediation as objective outcomes of the world. Their vision remains shot through with Manichaeism. All of them were "Romantics" before writing "novels."[2]

This initial captivity of the writer in illusion corresponds, in his major work, to the illusion, finally revealed as such, of the hero himself. The hero never frees himself until the end of the novel, through a conversion in which he rejects mediated desire, that is, death of the romantic self, and a resurrection in the true world of the novel. This is why death and disease are always physically present in the conclusion and why they always have the nature of a happy deliverance. The final conversion of the hero is a transposition of the novelist's fundamental experience, of his renunciation of his own idols, of his own spiritual metamorphosis. In *Time Regained*, Marcel Proust makes plain this reasoning, which is always present but veiled in the work of previous novelists.

The ending that is death for the world is birth for the creative world of the novel. We can verify this fact in quite concrete form in the chapter entitled "Conclusion" in *On Art and Literature* (*Contre Sainte-Beuve*) and in other writings left by Proust. The preliminary drafts of *Time Regained* boil down to a generalized testament of defeat, to an actual and literary despair that existed just before Proust began work on *The Remembrance of Things Past*.

We must use the same method for endings as for the worlds of the novel: we must envisage them as a single significant totality. What we find this time is not a continuous historical development but a dynamic form always virtually identical, though realized more or less perfectly in the work of individual novelists. The final revelation illuminates, retrospectively, the path traversed. The work is itself retrospective; it is at the same time the narrative of and the recompense for spiritual metamorphosis. In the light of this metamorphosis, worldly existence, the spiral descent, appears as a *descent into Hell*, that is, as a necessary ordeal on the way to final revelation. The descending movement finishes by transforming itself into an ascending movement, without there being any going back. It is obvious, I believe, that this forms the structure of *The Divine Comedy*. And doubtless we must look back further still to define the archetype of the novel form—back to the *Confessions* of saint Augustine, the first work whose genesis is truly inscribed in its form.

These observations emerge not only from theology but from the phenomenology of the novel. I am not making any superficial attempt to "Christianize" novelists; and I am saying virtually the same thing as Lucien Goldmann when he writes:

> The final conversion of Don Quixote or Julien Sorel is not . . . the attainment
> of authenticity or transcendence to a higher plane, but simply the recognition of
> the vanity and degraded character of not only the previous quest, but also of any
> hope, of any possible quest.[3]

This sentence is even more true of Flaubert than of Stendhal and Cervantes.
These novelists mark a "minimal" conversion in contrast with the "maximal"
conversion of Dostoyevsky; but the Dantean and Augustinian archetype remains inscribed in the form of their work. The resort to Christian symbolism
in the work of Stendhal or Proust is all the more striking in that it has no
religious significance; and their work deliberately excludes all overt imitation
of any recognizably Christian form.

The problem that presents itself here is not that of the ultimate meaning of
reality but that of the "view of world views." In the *Confessions*, there is this
overview of a pagan view that is the Christian view; it is in the transition from
one view to the other that the two views become visible. Dante's *Vita Nuova*
carries somewhat analogous implications; so does the transition from Romanticism to the novel, which may certainly be defined as "self-realization" but can
hardly be something simple and easy, something that occurs of its own accord,
as Lucien Goldmann suggests in the quotation given above. In this regard, his
interpretation seems to me to be incompatible with his concept of worldview
and with the stability, the resistance to change, that characterizes social and
spiritual structures.

It may be argued that the Dantean archetype seems to reappear in works
whose contents reflect widely different philosophies. Without wishing to minimize these divergences, we may note that there are close analogies as well, and
that these analogies are not confined to novelists. One finds them, for example,
in the work of Georg Lukács, whose theory of worldviews necessarily rests on
a view of these worldviews, that is, on an experience somewhat similar to that
of the novelist. There is something Dantean in Lukács's approach. When he
describes the degraded quests of fictional heroes as "demonic," is he not giving
us the metaphorical equivalent of that Hell where Dante immersed his own
heroes? In *The Meaning of Contemporary Realism*, the following expressions
often recur to describe the literature of the Western avant-garde: "infernal,"
"diabolic," "phantasmal," "monstrous," "grimacing," "subterranean powers,"
and "demonic principle." One can, of course, accuse Lukács of being a little too
severe on contemporary literature; but this reproach, however legitimate, and
the somewhat facile irony evoked by his theological language must not distract
us from the profound intuition that language expresses. Freud, too, uses the
term "demonic" to describe the morbidly repetitive nature of neurosis.

True religious thought, the great novels, psychoanalysis, and Marxism have
this in common, that they are all opposed to any "idolatry" or "fetishism." We
hear on all sides that Marxism is a "religion," but Judaism and primitive Chris-

tianity, equally fiercely iconoclastic, appeared to the pagan world to be forms of atheism at first. The accusation of fetishism is turned today against a Christianity that has often deserved it and deserves it still; but it is this Christianity, it must not be forgotten, that has handed on to us horror of fetishism in all its forms.

The irreplaceable quality of religious language forces us to ask whether the kind of thinking that first animated that language may not be more appropriate for dealing with actuality than is sometimes imagined. No mode of this thought strikes us as more antiquated and meaningless than patristic and medieval allegory. Perhaps the progress of modern thought will oblige us to revise this judgment. It seems that nothing could be further removed from allegorical thought than the connection that Goldmann establishes between the world of desire in the novel and the market economy:

> In economic life, which constitutes the most important aspect of life in modern society, every genuine relationship with the qualitative aspect of things and of beings tends to disappear—both relationships between men and things as well as between human beings—to be replaced by a mediated and degraded relationship: the purely quantitative relationship of exchange values.[4]

All particular idols are caught up together and engulfed by the supreme idol of the capitalist world: money. There is a "rigorous homology" between every condition of our existence. Our emotional life and even our spiritual life have the same structure as our economic life. The idea seems outrageous to a religious attitude that affirms the autonomy of "spiritual values" merely to provide better cover for mediation and degradation. But the Fathers of the Church— they who made money symbolically analogues to the Holy Ghost and the spiritual life—would have welcomed the Marxist insight. If money is becoming the center of human life, it is also becoming the heart of an analogous system that replicates the structure of Christian redemption in reverse; that, in fact, plunges us again into the Hell of Dante and the "demonic" of Lukács and Freud. Allegorical thought may perhaps be something more than a literary game. To recognize the bonds that unite patristic mediation to the most advanced elements of contemporary thought is to discover a paradoxical unity of Western thought beyond the superficial divergences of beliefs and ideologies.

TRANSLATED BY PETRA MORRISON

NOTES

[1] In the general indifference to mimetic desire, there are some exceptions. In his *Nuovi Studii Danteschi* (Milan: Hoepli, 1907), p. 531, Francesco d'Ovidio writes that the line *"Galeotto fu il libro e chi lo scrisse"* expresses the fear of the poet at the thought that he too might become a Galehalt. More remarkable still is the analysis of the whole episode by Renato Poggioli, in an essay entitled "Tragedy or Romance? A Reading of the Paolo and

Francesca Episode in Dante's *Inferno*" (*Proceedings of the Modern Language Association* 72 [June 1957], pp. 315–58). The author ascribes to Dante's "imagination" the idea of rooting the passion and destruction of the two lovers in the example provided by the romance of Lancelot. Then, he goes on to say:

> The real kiss of Paolo and Francesca follows the imaginary kiss of Lancelot and Guinevere, as an imaging reflecting its object in a perspective similar and different at the same time. In brief, the seduction scene fulfills within the entire episode the function of a play within a play, more properly, of a romance within a romance. This creates an effect of parody, or, if we prefer to use a less negative term, something akin to what, in modern times, has been called "romantic irony," which in this case operates in an antiromantic sense.

I thank John Freccero for drawing my attention to this important essay.

[2] This is an untranslatable allusion to *Mensonge romantique et vérité romanesque*, the French title of Girard's *Deceit, Desire, and the Novel*.

[3] Lucien Goldmann, *Pour une sociologie du roman* (Paris: Gallimard, 1964), p. 22.

[4] Ibid., p. 25.

MICHEL LEIRIS

The Autobiographer as Torero
1947

"In a narrative, neither the writer nor the reader starts from a pre-existing reality, given with his own existence." Taken literally, this statement by Maurice Blanchot should lead to the exclusion of autobiography from the field of literature: since, as a narrative, it relies on a reality that, by definition, pre-exists it, a reality that is given with the existence of the author. What Philippe Lejeune called the "autobiographical pact" takes exception to Blanchot's ontological dissidence. Autobiography ignores Blanchot's claim that characters in a narrative cannot be the object of the same type of knowledge as people in real life. Both edges—internal and external—of the volume are continuous; the same individual appears both inside and outside of the book; the author, whose name appears on the cover, is at once, the protagonist and the narrative voice. In that sense, Leiris is fully justified to present his autobiography as "the negation of a novel."

*However, beyond this referential, almost documentary realism Leiris's autobiographical project (*Manhood *will be followed by the four-volume* Rules of the Game*) is integrated in a performative project. It is rooted in the search for an authenticity defined in terms not so much of truth as of risks, not so much through forms of representation as in marks of present-ness, not so much in the guise of iconic resemblance between portrait and model as in the signals of feedback, of indexical, retroactive effects of a performance that doesn't leave the model untouched or disturbs its resemblance.*

Reaching some truth about oneself by means of self-analysis is a first and necessary step for the autobiographer; but it remains for this truth to be authenticated in the real arena of the autobiographical performance, which isn't the reflexive privacy of the self meditating on the self, but the interactive and possibly confrontational space of communication. Precisely be-

Michel Leiris, preface to *Manhood: A Journey from Childhood into the Fierce Order of Virility*, trans. Richard Howard (San Francisco: North Point, 1984), pp. 153–64, "De la littérature considérée comme une tauromachie,"in *L'Age d'homme* (Paris: Gallimard, 1947), pp. 9–25.

*cause, in an autobiography, writer and reader start from a pre-existing
reality, given with their own empirical existence, the publication of an often masochistically unflattering autobiography shouldn't remain without
effects on the social status of its "model." Hence the promotion of risk as an
aesthetic category to which Leiris refers by means of the metaphor of the
bullfight.*

"According to the boundary that French law traces across the lifetime of
every man under its jurisdiction—to which his birth has made him
subject—it was in 1922 that the author of *Manhood* reached the cli-
macteric which inspired the title of his book. In 1922: four years after the war
which, like so many other boys of his generation, he had experienced as
scarcely more than a long vacation, as one of them called it.

"In 1922, the author entertained few illusions as to the reality of the link
that, theoretically, united an actual maturity with his legal majority. By 1935,
when he completed this book, he no doubt supposed his existence had already
sustained enough vicissitudes for him to pride himself on having attained the
age of virility at last. Now in 1939, when the young men of the postwar period
see the utter collapse of that structure of facility which they despaired of trying
to invest with not only an authentic fervor but a terrible distinction as well, the
author freely acknowledges that his true 'manhood' still remains to be written,
when he will have suffered, in one form or another, the same bitter ordeal his
elders faced.

"However unjustified his book's title may appear today, the author has decided to retain it, convinced that, all things considered, it does not belie his
ultimate intent: the search for a vital fulfillment that cannot be realized without a catharsis, a liquidation for which literary activity—and particularly the
so-called literature of confession—appears to be one of the most suitable instruments.

"Among the many autobiographical novels, private journals, memoirs, and
confessions that in recent years have enjoyed so extraordinary a vogue (as if the
creative aspect of a literary work were subordinate to the problem of *expression*,
the object produced merely accessory to the man who conceals—or parades—
himself behind it). *Manhood* is therefore offered without any claim on its author's part to more than having tried to talk about himself with the maximum
of lucidity and sincerity.

"One problem troubled his conscience and kept him from writing: is not
what occurs in the domain of style valueless if it remains 'aesthetic,' anodyne,
insignificant, if there is nothing in the fact of writing a work that is equivalent
(and here supervenes one of the images closest to the author's heart) to the
bull's keen horn, which alone—by reason of the physical danger it repre-

sents—affords the torero's art a human reality, prevents it from being no more than the vain grace of a ballerina?

"To expose certain obsessions of an emotional or sexual nature, to admit publicly to certain shameful deficiencies or dismays was, for the author, the means—crude, no doubt, but which he entrusts to others, hoping to see it improved—of introducing even the shadow of a bull's horn into a literary work."

This was the preface I was writing for *Manhood* on the eve of the "phony war." I am rereading it today in Le Havre, a city I have so often visited for a few days' vacation and to which I am bound by many old ties (my friends Limbour, Queneau, and Salacrou, who were born here; Sartre, who taught here and with whom I became associated in 1941 when most of the writers remaining in occupied France united against the Nazi oppression). Le Havre is now largely destroyed, as I can see from my balcony, which overlooks the harbor from a sufficient height and distance to give a true picture of the terrible tabula rasa the bombs made in the center of the city, as if there has been an attempt to repeat in the real world, on a terrain populated by living beings, the famous Cartesian operation. On this scale, the personal problems with which *Manhood* is concerned are obviously insignificant: whatever might have been, in the best of cases, its strength and its sincerity, the poet's inner agony, weighed against the horrors of war, counts for no more than a toothache over which it would be graceless to groan; what is the use, in the world's excruciating uproar, of this faint moan over such narrowly limited and individual problems?

Yet even in Le Havre, things continue, urban life persists. Above the still-intact houses as above the site of the ruins there shines intermittently, despite the rainy weather, a bright, beautiful sun. Boat basins and gleaming roofs, a whitecapped sea in the distance, and the gigantic wasteland of the razed neighborhoods (long since abandoned, as for some astounding "crop rotation") submit—when the climate allows—to the influence of the aerial humidity perforated by the sun's rays. Motors hum; trolleys and bicycles pass; people stroll by or are busy at work; and many chimneys send up their columns of smoke. I contemplate all this, a spectator who has not taken the plunge (or who has only dipped in his toe) and who shamelessly claims the right to admire this half-devastated landscape as he might a beautiful painting, gauging in light and shade, in pathetic nakedness and picturesque bustle, the place still inhabited today where a tragedy, hardly more than a year ago, was enacted.

I was dreaming, then, of a bull's horn. I found it hard to resign myself to being nothing more than a *littérateur*. The matador who transforms danger into an occasion to be more brilliant than ever, who reveals the whole quality of his style just when he is most threatened: that is what enthralled me, that is what I wanted to be. By means of an autobiography dealing with a realm in which discretion is de rigueur—a confession whose publication would be dangerous to the degree that it would be compromising and likely to make more difficult, by making more explicit, my private life—I intended to rid myself for good of certain agonizing images, at the same time that I revealed my features with the maximum of clarity and as much for my own use as to dissipate any erroneous sense of myself which others might have. To effect a catharsis, to achieve my definitive liberation, this autobiography would have to take the form most capable of rousing my own enthusiasm and of being understood by other people as well. For this I counted on the strictest care taken in the actual writing and on the tragic light shed on the whole of my narrative by the very symbols I would employ: Biblical and classical figures, heroes of the stage or else the torero—psychological myths that affected me by their revelatory power and constituted, for the literary aspect of the operation, not only motifs but intermediaries suggesting an apparent greatness where I knew only too well there was no such thing.

To paint the clearest and closest portrait of the person I was (as some artists brilliantly render sordid landscapes or everyday utensils), to let artistic preoccupations intervene only with regard to style and composition: this is what I undertook to do, as if I had anticipated that my talent as a painter and whatever exemplary lucidity I might manifest would compensate for my mediocrity as a model, and as if, in narticular, an extension of the moral order would result for me from the difficulties of such an undertaking, since—even without eliminating some of my weaknesses—I should at least have proved myself capable of that objective gaze turned upon myself.

What I did not realize was that at the source of all introspection is a predilection for self-contemplation, and that every confession contains a desire to be absolved. To consider myself objectively was still to consider myself—to keep my eyes fixed on myself instead of turning them beyond and transcending myself in the direction of something more broadly human. To expose myself to others, but to do so in a narrative I hoped would be well written and well constructed, perceptive and moving was an attempt to seduce my public into being indulgent, to limit, in any case, the scandal by giving it an aesthetic form. I believe, then, that if there has been a risk, a bull's horn, it is not without a certain duplicity that I have ventured to accept it: yielding, on the one hand, once again to my narcissistic tendency; trying, on the other, to find in my neighbor less a judge than an accomplice. Similarly, the matador who seems to risk everything is concerned about his "line" and relies, in order to overcome the danger, on his technical sagacity.

Still, for the torero there is a real danger of death, which never exists for the artist except outside his art (for instance, during the German Occupation, there was a clandestine literature that involved genuine danger, but insofar as it was part of a much more general struggle and, after all, independent of the writing itself). Am I therefore justified in maintaining the comparison and in regarding as valid my attempt to introduce "even the shadow of a bull's horn into a literary work"? Can the fact of writing ever involve, for the man who makes it his profession, a danger that, if not mortal, is at least positive?

To write a book that is an act: such is, broadly, the goal that seemed to be the one I must pursue when I wrote *Manhood*. An act in relation to myself, since I meant, in writing it, to elucidate by this very formulation certain still-obscure things to which my psychoanalysis, without making them entirely clear, had drawn my attention. An act in relation to others, since it was apparent that despite my oratorical precautions, the way I would be regarded by others would no longer be what it had been before publication of this confession. An act, finally, on the literary level, consisting of a backstage revelation that would expose, in all their unenthralling nakedness, the realities that formed the more or less disguised warp, beneath surfaces I had tried to make alluring, of my other writings. This was less a matter of what is known as "committed literature" than of a literature in which I was trying to engage myself completely. Within as without: expecting it to change me, to enlarge my consciousness, and to introduce, too, a new element into my relations with other people, beginning with my relations with those close to me, who could no longer be quite the same once I had exposed what may have been already suspected, but only in a vague and uncertain way. This was no desire for a brutal cynicism but actually a longing to confess everything in order to be able to start afresh, maintaining with those whose affection or respect I valued relations henceforth without dissimulation.

From the strictly aesthetic point of view, it was a question of condensing, in the almost raw state, a group of facts and images which I refused to exploit by letting my imagination work upon them; in other words, the negation of a novel. To reject all fable, to admit as materials only actual facts (and not only probable facts, as in the classical novel), nothing but these facts and all these facts, was the rule I imposed upon myself. Already a trail had been blazed for me in this direction by André Breton's *Nadja*, but I dreamed above all of making my own that project Baudelaire was inspired to undertake after reading a passage in Poe's *Marginalia*: to lay bare one's heart, to write that book about oneself in which the concern for sincerity would be carried to such lengths that, under the author's sentences, "the paper would shrivel and flare at each touch of his fiery pen."

For various reasons—divergences of ideas, as well as personal differences it would take too long to discuss here—I had broken with surrealism. Yet it was nonetheless true that I remained steeped in it. Receptivity to what appears to be *given* without our having sought it (automatic writing, *objet trouvé*); poetic value attached to dreams (considered also as rich in insight); broad faith in Freudian psychology (which has mined an alluring ore of images and, moreover, affords every man a convenient means of achieving the tragic level by seeing himself as a new Oedipus); repugnance for everything that is a transposition or arrangement, in other words, a fallacious compromise between real facts and the pure products of the imagination; insistence on speaking frankly (particularly about love, which bourgeois hypocrisy all too readily treats as the subject for entertainment when it does not relegate it to the domain of the forbidden): these are some of the great lines of force—encumbered by much dross and not without some contradictions—that continued to pass through me when I had the idea of this work in which are confronted childhood memories, accounts of real events, dreams, and actually experienced impressions, in a kind of surrealist collage or, rather, photomontage, since no element is used which is not of strict veracity or of documentary value. This predilection for realism—not feigned, as in most novels, but positive (since it was exclusively a matter of things experienced and presented without the least disguise)—was not only imposed upon me by the nature of what I wanted to do (take my bearings and publicly reveal myself), but also corresponded to an aesthetic requirement: to speak only of what I knew from experience and what touched me most closely, so that each of my sentences would possess a special density, an affecting plenitude, in other words, the quality proper to what we call "authenticity." To tell the truth, in order to achieve this resonance so difficult to define, which the word "authentic" (applicable to such diverse things, and among others to purely poetic creations) is a far cry from having explained—that is what I was tending toward, my conception of the art of writing here converging with my moral notion of my "engagement" in writing.

Turning to the torero, I observe that for him, too, there is a code he cannot infringe and an authenticity, since the tragedy he acts out is a real tragedy, one in which he sheds blood and risks his own skin. The point is to discover if, under such conditions, the relation I establish between his authenticity and my own is not based on a mere play on words.

Let us grant once and for all that to write and publish an autobiography does not involve, for the man who undertakes such a thing (unless he has committed an offense whose admission makes him liable to capital punishment) any danger of death, except under exceptional circumstances. Undoubtedly, he risks suffering in his relations with those close to him, and risks social opprobrium if his avowals run too counter to accepted ideas; but it is possible, even if he is not a pure cynic, that such punishments may be of little enough consequence for him (may even please him, should he regard as salubrious the atmosphere thus created around him), so that he is dealing with an entirely fictional risk. Whatever the case, a moral risk of this kind cannot be compared with the bodily risk the torero faces. Even conceding a common measure between them on the level of *quantity* (if the attachment of some people and the opinions of others count as much or more for me than my life itself, though in this realm it is easy to be mistaken), the danger to which I expose myself by publishing my confession differs radically, on the level of *quality*, from that which the matador constantly assumes in performing his role. Similarly, what may be aggressive in one's intention of proclaiming the truth about oneself (since those one loves might suffer thereby) remains quite different from a killing, whatever the havoc one provokes. Should I therefore regard as misleading the analogy I had sketched between two spectacular means of acting and of incurring danger?

I have already spoken of the fundamental rule (to tell the whole truth and nothing but the truth) to which the writer of confessions is bound, and I have also alluded to the precise ceremony to which, in his combat, the torero must conform. For the latter, it is evident that the code, far from being a protection, contributes to his danger: to deliver the thrust under the requisite conditions demands, for instance, that he put his body, during an appreciable length of time, within reach of the horns; hence there is an immediate connection between obedience to the rule and the danger incurred. Now, all things considered, is it not to a danger directly proportional to the rigor of the rule he has imposed on himself that the confessional writer is exposed? For to tell the whole truth and nothing but the truth is not all: he must also confront it directly and tell it without artifice, without those great arias intended to make it acceptable, tremolos or catches in the voice, grace notes and gildings that would have no other result than to disguise it to whatever degree, even by merely attentuating its crudity, by making less noticeable what might be shocking about it. This fact that the danger incurred depends on a more or less close observance of the rule therefore represents what I can, without too much presumption, retain of the comparison I chose to establish between my activity as a writer of confessions and that of the torero.

If it seemed to me, originally, that to set down an account of my life from an erotic point of view (a preferential one, since sexuality then seemed to me the cornerstone in the structure of the personality), if it seemed to me that a confession bearing on what Christianity calls "the works of the flesh" was enough to make me, by the act this represents, a kind of torero, I must still consider whether the rule I had imposed upon myself—a rule whose rigor, I was satisfied to note, endangered me—is actually comparable, relation to danger aside, to that which dictates the terero's movements.

In a general way, one might say that the bullfighting code pursues one essential goal: aside from the fact that it obliges a man to incur serious danger (while arming him with an indispensable technique), and not to dispatch his adversary just anyhow, it prevents the combat from being a mere slaughter; as punctilious as a ritual, it presents a tactical aspect (put the bull in a state to receive the final thrust though without having exhausted the animal more than was necessary), but also an aesthetic aspect: to the degree that the man is "exposed in profile," as he must be when giving his sword thrust, there is an arrogance in his posture; to the degree that his feet remain motionless throughout a series of close and fluid passes, the cape moving slowly, he forms with the beast that glamorous amalgamation in which man, material, and the huge horned mass seem united by a play of reciprocal influences; everything combines, in short, to imprint upon the confrontation of bull and torero a *sculptural* character.

Looking on my enterprise as a sort of photomontage and choosing for my expression a tone as objective as possible, trying to gather my life into a single solid block (an object I can touch, as though to insure myself against death, even when, paradoxically, I am claiming to risk everything), even if I opened my door to dreams (a psychologically justified element but tinged with romanticism, just as the torero's cape work, technically useful, is also a series of lyrical flights), I was imposing on myself a rule quite as severe as if I had intended to compose a classical work. And it is ultimately this very severity, this "classicism"—not excluding such excess as one finds in even our most formalized tragedies and relying not only on considerations of form but on the notion of thereby achieving a maximum of veracity—which seems to me to have afforded my undertaking (if I have managed to succeed at all) something analogous to what constitutes for me the exemplary value of the *corrida* and which the imaginary bull's horn could not have contributed by itself.

To use materials of which I was not the master and which I had to take as I found them (since my life was what it was and I could not alter, by so much as a comma, my past, a primary *datum* representing for me a fate as unchallengeable as for the torero the beast that runs into the ring), to say everything and say it without "doctoring," without leaving anything to the imagination and as though obeying a necessity—such was the risk I accepted and the law I had fixed for myself, such the ceremony with which I could make no compromise. Though the desire to *expose myself* (in every sense of the term) has constituted the first impulse, the fact remained that this *necessary* condition was not a *sufficient* condition, and that, further, it was from this original goal that the form to be adopted had to be deduced, with the almost automatic force of an obligation. These images I gathered together, this tone I employed—at the same time that they deepened and sharpened my self-awareness—had to be (unless I failed) what would accord my emotion a better chance of being shared. Similarly, the order of the *corrida* (a rigid framework imposed on an action in which, theatrically, chance must appear to be dominated) is a technique of combat and at the same time a ritual. It was therefore necessary that this method I had imposed upon myself—dictated by the desire to see into myself as clearly as possible—function simultaneously and effectively as a rule of composition. Identity, so to speak, of form and content, but, more precisely, a unique procedure revealing the content to me as I gave it form, a form that could be of interest to others and (at its extreme) allow them to discover in themselves something homophonous to this content I had discovered in myself.

Obviously I am formulating this quite a *posteriori*, in order to define as well as I can the procedure I used, and without being qualified, of course, to decide if this "tauromachic" code, a guide for action and a guarantee against complacency, has turned out to be capable of such effectiveness as a means of style, or even (as to certain details) if what I claimed to see as a necessity of method did not actually correspond to an ulterior motive concerning composition.

I distinguish in literature a genre of major significance to me, which would include those works where the horn is present in one form or another, where the author assumes the direct risk either of a confession or of a subversive work, a work in which the human condition is confronted directly or "taken by the horns" and which presents a conception of life "engaging" its partisan—or its victim; works showing an attitude of something like humor or madness toward things, and the intent to make oneself the mouthpiece of the great themes of human tragedy. I can suggest in any case—but no doubt this is battering down an open door?—that it is precisely to the degree that one cannot see in a work any other rule of composition than the Ariadne's thread the author followed throughout the explanation he was making (by successive approaches or at point-blank range) to himself that works of this genre can be regarded, in literary terms, as "authentic." This by definition, from the moment one admits that literary activity, in its specific aspect as a mental discipline, cannot have any other justification than to *illuminate certain matters for oneself at the same time as one makes them communicable to others,* and that one of the highest goals that can be assigned to literature's pure form, by which I mean poetry, is to restore by means of words certain intense states, concretely experienced and become significant, to be thus put into words.

At this point I am far from utterly immediate and dismaying events such as the destruction of a great part of Le Havre, so different today from the city I knew, and despoiled of those places to which, subjectively, I was attached by memories: the Hôtel de l'Amirauté, for instance, and the hot streets with their buildings now flattened or gutted, like the one on whose wall still remains the inscription LA LUNE THE MOON, with a drawing of a smiling face within the lunar disc. There is the beach, too, strewn with a strange foliage of scrap iron and laboriously piled stones, facing the sea where the other day a freighter was blown up by a mine, adding its wreck to so many others. I am far, indeed, from that authentic horn of the war of which I see, in the ruined houses, only the least sinister effects. Were I more "engaged" physically, more active, and thereby more threatened, perhaps I should consider the literary phenomenon more lightly. Perhaps I should be less obsessed by my desire to make literature into an *act*, a drama by which I insist on incurring, positively, a risk—as if this risk were the necessary condition for my self-realization as a whole man. There would nonetheless remain that essential "engagement" one has the right to demand of the writer, the engagement that derives from the very nature of his art: not to misuse the language and therefore to make his words, however he is able to set them down on paper, always tell the truth. And on the intellectual or emotional level, he must contribute evidence to the trial of our present system of values and tip the scales, with all the weight by which he is so often burdened, toward the liberation of *all* men, without which none can achieve his own.

TRANSLATED BY RICHARD HOWARD

ANDRÉ BAZIN

Death Every Afternoon
1951

This is André Bazin's review, written for the Cahiers du cinéma, *of Pierre Braunberger's feature-length documentary movie* The Bullfight (La Course de taureau), *for which Michel Leiris wrote the voice-over commentary.*

At the core of Bazin's concept of photographic realism and of the documentary inflection it gives to his film aesthetics, there is a tension between the event and its representation: real presence is unrepresentable. The real doesn't lend itself to representation. Hence the focus on the indexical dimension of the photographic image from which Bazin derives his law of authenticity: "the nature of the event [must] not be contradictory with its reconstitution." How can such a requirement be fulfilled? Antonin Artaud condemned theater for its rehearsals and repetitions. Why shouldn't a film incur the same blame?

How is it, for example, that the bullfighting event is preserved, on film, in its authenticity, in its obtuse condition as event? How does its here and now *manage to be preserved, as if nothing essential were lost in the change of medium, in the transfer from bullring to screen? This exception is grounded in cinema's commitment to the documentary specificity of its medium, the indexical nature of an image that allows each filmic event to celebrate again and again, as in Raymond Roussel's novels, the mystery of what Bazin calls the "repetition of what occurs only once." Less an image than a sample—almost a biopsy—of the event, it keeps it, forever suspended, forever stilled in its happening.*

In many regards, thus, the bullfight is ontologically akin to the documentary ideal of the filmic image. In both cases, acting is excluded: only shots from actual bullfights, with real toreros, real blood, real events, real time. Nothing is reconstituted. If they die, they die "live." For that reason,

André Bazin, "Mort tous les après-midi," *Cahiers du cinéma* (Dec. 1951), repr. in Jean Narboni, *Le Cinéma français de la Libération à la nouvelle vague (1945–58)* (Paris: l'Etoile, 1983), pp. 251–52.

Braunberger's film about bullfighting is something more than a mere documentary. The medium is somehow allegorized by the subject.

Pierre Braunberger nursed the idea for this film for a long time, and it is easy to see why. The result proves that it was worth the wait. But perhaps Braunberger, a well-known aficionado, saw the project as simply a tribute to bullfighting and a film that its producer would not regret. In the latter regard, he will surely prove to have been correct (and I hasten to add that any profits the film earns will have been well deserved), because bullfighting fans will rush to see it while the uninitiated will go out of curiosity. And aficionados will not be disappointed, because the bullfight scenes are quite beautiful. Fans of the corrida will be delighted by the astonishingly effective sequences that Braunberger and Myriam have put together of the most famous matadors in action. To have assembled such a full picture of what goes on in the bullring, the filmmakers must have shot plenty of footage on many different occasions. Countless passes and kills involving major stars in important events are filmed in sequences of medium to close-medium shots which continue for minutes at a time without a cut. And when a bull's head appears in close-up, it is not stuffed; the rest follows.

Perhaps my astonishment at Myriam's talent is evidence of my naiveté. Her editing of this documentary footage is remarkably skillful, and one has to be paying very close attention indeed to notice that the bull returning to the field on the left is not always the same one that exited to the right. One would have to examine the film on an editing machine to say for sure how many separate shots went into composing some of its sequences, because the movements are so perfectly matched. A "veronica" begun with one matador and bull ends with another man and another animal, yet the viewer does not notice the substitution. Since *Le Roman d'un tricheur* and *Paris 1900*, there has been no doubt about Myriam's great talent as an editor of film. *The Bullfight* confirms this judgment once again. At this degree of art, the editor's contribution is far greater than usual: it is a major ingredient in the creation of the film. There is a great deal to be said, moreover, about the use of montage in this film. In no sense does it represent a return to the primacy of montage over découpage (scripting) advocated by the early Soviet filmmakers. *Paris 1900* and *The Bullfight* are not films in the *ciné-oeil*, or camera-as-eye, style but "modern" works aesthetically contemporary with such scripted films as *Citizen Kane, The Rules of the Game, La Vipère*, and *Bicycle Thief*. Here, the purpose of montage is not to suggest abstract, symbolic relations among images as in Kulechov's famous experiment with Moszhukin's close-up. If the phenomenon revealed by this experiment plays a role in Myriam's latter-day montage, it is for an entirely different purpose: to achieve the physical plausibility as well as the logical malleability of the scripted sequence. The intercutting of the image of the naked woman with Moszhukin's ambiguous smile signified lubricity or desire. Indeed, the moral significance of the sequence was in a sense prior to the physical significance: image of naked woman + image of smile = desire. To be sure, the existence of desire logically implies that the man looks at the woman, but this geometry is nowhere to be found in the images. The deduction is almost superfluous—for Kulechov, it was secondary; what counted was the meaning imparted to the smile by the clash of images. In Myriam's editing, the relation between images is of a quite different sort: the primary goal is physical realism. The illusion of montage is pushed toward the plausibility of découpage. The linking of two bulls in motion is not meant to symbolize the strength of the bull; rather, it provides a seamless substitute for the nonexistent image of a bull that we think we see despite its absence. Realism is thus the sole basis upon which the editor constructs the meaning of her montage, just as it is the sole basis upon which the director constructs the meaning of his découpage. Thus, what we have here is not the camera-as-eye but the adaptation of the technique of montage to the aesthetic of the camera-as-pen.

For that reason, viewers like myself, ignorant of bullfighting, will find here as clear and complete an introduction to the subject as possible. The editing of this documentary material does not obey random visual affinities but a clear and rigorous order. The history of bullfighting (and of fighting bulls), as well as the evolution of toreador style up to and, since Belmonte, is set forth with all the didactic resources of the cinema. In describing each figure, the image is frozen at the critical moment and the commentator explains the relative positions of man and animal. Probably because he lacked slow-motion sequences, Braunberger uses freeze-frames, but the procedure is just as effective. No doubt the film's didactic qualities are also its limitation, or so it might seem at first sight. The work is less ambitious and less expansive than Hemingway's in *Death in the Afternoon*. *The Bullfight* can be viewed as a feature-length documentary, an exciting documentary to be sure, but still a documentary. But it would be unjust and, in my view, mistaken to see it that way. Unjust because the pedagogical modesty of the execution is not so much a limitation as a deliberate choice. Given the grandeur of the subject and the richness of the material, Braunberger opted for humility. The commentary is limited to explanation. It avoids the kind of facile verbal lyricism that the objective lyricism of the image would overwhelm. And to dismiss his effort as a mere documentary would also be mistaken, I believe, because the film's subject in a sense transcends itself: in this respect, Braunberger's cinematographic achievement is perhaps even greater than he may think.

Our experience with filmed theater—and its virtually total failure and recent successful attempts changed the parameters of the problem—has made us aware of the role of real presence. We know that photographing a play gives us only a performance drained of psychological reality, a body without a soul. The reciprocal presence, the flesh-and-blood confrontation of actor and spectator, is no mere physical accident but an ontological fact that makes the theatrical performance what it is. Based on this theoretical notion, as well as on experience, one might well conclude that bullfighting is even less a cinematic subject than theater. If the reality of the theater cannot be captured on film, then what can one say about the tragedy of the corrida, with its accompanying liturgy and almost religious feeling? Recording it photographically might have a documentary or didactic value, but how could this possibly restore the essence of the drama: the mystical triangle consisting of the animal, the man, and the crowd?

I have never attended a bullfight, and I am not foolish enough to pretend that the film makes me feel all the attendant emotions, but I do contend that it gives me the essential, metaphysical core of the phenomenon, which is death. The tragic ballet of the bullfight is constructed around the presence, the permanent threat, of death (of both man and animal). Death turns the bullring into something more than a theatrical stage: on the stage one mimics death, but in the arena the torero, like the trapeze artist who works without a net, gambles with his life. Now, death is one of the rare events worthy of a phrase that Claude Mauriac is fond of using, "inherently cinematic." An art whose essence is time, cinema enjoys the signal privilege of reliving a moment again and again. This is a privilege shared by all the mechanical arts, but one that cinema can use far more powerfully than can a phonograph recording or radio broadcast. Let me be even more specific, since there are other temporal arts, such as music. In music, however, time is immediately, and by definition, aesthetic time, whereas cinema achieves or constructs its aesthetic time only in terms of lived time—the Bergsonian *durée*—which is in essence irreversible and qualitative. The reality that cinema can reproduce at will, and structure, is the reality of the world of which we are a part, the sensory continuum of which the film takes a spatial as well as temporal mold. I cannot repeat a single moment of my life, but cinema can indefinitely repeat any of life's moments before my eyes. Now, if it is true that for consciousness no instant is identical to any other instant, there is one instant toward which this fundamental differentiation of the moments of time converges, namely, the moment of death. For any living being, death is the unique moment par excellence. Time as qualitatively experienced in life is defined retroactively in relation to death. Death marks the boundary between conscious duration and the objective time of physical reality. Death is but one moment that follows others, but it is the last. To be sure, no lived moment is identical to any other, but any number of such moments may resemble one another as the leaves of a tree resemble one another. Hence the repetition of such moments in film is more paradoxical in theory than in practice: despite the inherent ontological contradiction, we allow such repetition as a sort of objective replica of memory. Nevertheless, two moments in life are radically excluded from this concession of consciousness: the sexual act and death. Each is in its own way an absolute negation of objective time: the qualitative instant in its purest form. Like death, the act of love can be experienced but not represented: there is a reason why it is sometimes referred to as *la petite mort*. Or at any rate it cannot be represented without doing violence to its nature. That violence goes by the name obscenity. The representation of actual death is also a form of obscenity—not a moral obscenity, as in the case of the sexual act, but a metaphysical obscenity. One cannot die twice. In this respect, photography lacks the power of film: a photograph can depict a person in the throes of death or a corpse, but not the elusive transition from one to the other. In the spring of 1949, a newsreel featured haunting footage of the execution of alleged communist "spies" in Shanghai, men publicly put to death by a pistol shot to the head. At each new showing the victims were brought back to life as if on command, only to flinch yet again as the same bullet entered the backs of their necks at the same spot as before. Viewers were not even spared the sight of the policeman whose pistol jammed, forcing him to pull the trigger a second time. This was intolerable to watch, not so much for its objective horror as for its ontological obscenity. Before film, we knew only desecrated corpses and violated graves. Thanks to film, we can now violate, and expose at will, our only inalienable temporal possession. Those who are condemned to die eternally on film are truly without rest.

The ultimate cinematic perversion, as I imagine it, would be an execution filmed and shown in reverse, as in those comic shorts in which a diver shoots upward out of the water and lands back on his diving board.

This digression has not taken me as far as might seem from *The Bullfight*. Perhaps the reader will understand what I mean if I say that a filmed performance of *Le Malade imaginaire* (*The Imaginary Invalid*) would have no value, whether theatrical or cinematic, but that if there had been a camera at Molière's last performance, the resulting film would have been of inestimable value.

That is why the representation on the screen of the killing of a bull (with the implied risk of the matador's death) is in principle as moving as the spectacle of the real moment that it reproduces—more moving in a sense, because it magnifies the quality of the original moment through the contrast of repetition. It thereby bestows on that moment an additional solemnity. Film has given Manolette's death a material eternity.

TRANSLATED BY ARTHUR GOLDHAMMER

Poetry After Rhyme

BENJAMIN PÉRET

The Dishonour of the Poets
1945

Written in Mexico City, where Benjamin Péret spent World War II as an expatriate, this pamphlet provides a dire assessment, measured according to the surrealist scale of values, of the damages incurred by French poetry as a result of the war. Its title is a sarcastic rephrasing of The Honor of Poets *(L'Honneur des poètes), the title given to a much-circulated anthology celebrating what was then called "Resistance poetry." According to Péret, there was nothing to celebrate there: it amounted to the selling out of fifty years of poetic invention and transgression for the sake of the most retrograde form of militant poetry.*

The first regression was thematic: poetry, shamelessly instrumentalized, was invaded by patriotic motifs. But Péret, confirming Jean Giraudoux's suggestion in La Guerre de Troie n'aura pas lieu *of the affinity of rhyme and marching drums, notes a second, formal, regression: the return to the old national meters advocated by Louis Aragon in "La Rime en 1940," his manifesto to accompany the powerful tearjerkers (mixing alexandrine and patriotic communism) inspired by the phony war and the military debacle of 1940.*

For a Surrealist like Péret, this repulsive patriotic exploitation of poetry represented a French equivalent of what Stalin did to communism— poetry in a single country. Poetry, in Péret's view, is allergic to claims of national identity: together with dreams and myths, it taps into the "collective treasure" of mankind. And if, as Breton never stopped claiming, Surrealism's foremost ambition is "to speak internationally," this program

---

Benjamin Péret, "The Dishonour of the Poets," trans. Anthony Melville, in *Death to the Pigs, and Other Writings*, trans. Rachel Stella et al. (Lincoln: University of Nebraska Press, 1988), pp. 200–206, from "Le Déshonneur des poètes," in Benjamin Péret, *Oeuvres complètes* (Paris: Corti, 1995), pp. 7–12.

entails, together with the de-emphasizing of its linguistic dimension, a revo-
lutionary de-versification of poetry:[1] poetry should no longer be subjected
to formal constraints such as the "totally external combinations of meter,
rhythm and even rhyme" any longer.[2] In support of this view, Breton quotes
Hegel, according to whom "poetry can be translated, even shift from verse
to prose, without undergoing any significant alteration."[3]

If one looks for the original significance of poetry, today concealed by the thousand flashy rags of society, one ascertains that poetry is the true inspiration of humanity, the source of all knowledge and knowledge itself in its most immaculate aspect. The entire spiritual life of humanity since it began to be aware of itself is condensed in poetry; in it quivers humanity's highest creations and, land ever fertile, it keeps perpetually in reserve the colorless crystals and harvests of tomorrow. Tutelary god with a thousand faces, it is here called love, there freedom, elsewhere science. It remains omnipotent, bubbling up in the eskimo's mythic tale; bursting forth in the love letter; machine-gunning the firing squad that shoots the worker exhaling his last breath of revolution and thus of freedom; gleaming in the scientist's discovery; faltering, bloodless, as even the stupidest productions draw on it; while its memory, a eulogy that wishes to be funereal, still penetrates the mummified words of the priest, poetry's assassin, listened to by the faithful as they blindly and dumbly look for it in the tomb of dogma where poetry is no more than delusive dust.

Poetry's innumerable detractors, true and false priests, more hypocritical than the priesthood of any church, false witnesses of every epoch, accuse it of being a means of escape, a flight from reality, as if it were not reality itself, reality's essence and exaltation. But incapable of conceiving of reality as a whole and in its complex relations, they wish to see it only under its most immediate, most sordid aspect. They see only adultery without ever experiencing love, the bomber plane without recalling Icarus, the adventure novel without understanding the permanent, elementary, and profound poetic inspiration that it has the ambition of satisfying. They scorn the dream in favor of their reality, as if the dream were not one of the most deeply moving aspects of reality; they exalt action at the expense of meditation, as if the former without the latter were not a sport as meaningless as any other. Formerly, they opposed the mind to matter, their god to man; now they defend matter against the mind. In point of fact, they have brought intuition to the aid of reason without remembering from whence this reason sprang.

The enemies of poetry have always been obsessed with subjecting it to their immediate ends, with crushing it under their god or, as now, with constraining it under orders of the new brown or "red" divinity—the reddish brown of dried blood—even bloodier than the old one. For them, life and culture are summed up in the useful and the useless, it being understood that the useful takes the form of a pickaxe wielded for their benefit. For them, poetry is only a luxury for the rich — the aristocrat and the banker — and if it wants to become "useful" to the masses, it should become resigned to the lot of the "applied," "decorative," and "domestic" arts.

Instinctively they sense, however, that poetry is the fulcrum Archimedes required, and they fear that the world, once raised up, might fall back on their heads. Hence the ambition to debase poetry, to deny it all efficacity, all value as an exaltation, to give it the hypocritical, consolatory role of a sister of charity.

But the poet does not have to perpetuate for others an illusory hope, whether human or celestial, nor disarm minds while filling them with boundless confidence in a father or a leader against whom any criticism becomes a sacrilege. Quite the contrary, it is up to the poet to give voice to words always sacrilegious, to permanent blasphemies. The poet should first become aware of his nature and place in the world. An inventor for whom a discovery is only the means of reaching new discoveries, he must relentlessly combat the paralyzing gods eager to keep humanity in servitude with respect to social powers and the divinity, which complement one another. Thus, he will be a revolutionary but not one of those who oppose today's tyrant, whom they see as baneful because he has betrayed their interests, only to praise tomorrow's oppressor, whose servants they already are. No, the poet struggles against all oppression: first of all, that of man by man and the oppression of thought by religious, philosophical, or social dogmas. He fights so that humanity can attain an ever-more perfect knowledge of itself and the universe. It does not follow that he wants to put poetry at the service of political, even revolutionary action. But his being a poet has made him a revolutionary who must fight on all terrains: on the terrain of poetry by appropriate means and on the terrain of social action, without ever confusing the two fields of action under penalty of re-establishing the confusion that is to be dissipated and consequently ceasing to be a poet, that is to say, a revolutionary.

Wars like the one we are undergoing are possible thanks only to a conjunction of *all* forces of regression, and they signify, among other things, an arrest of cultural expansion, checked by the forces of regression that culture threatens. This is too obvious to be gone into. From this momentary defeat of culture fatally ensues a triumph of the spirit of reaction and, above all, religious obscurantism, the necessary crown of every reactionary movement. One must go back very far in history to find a period when God, the Almighty, Providence, and so on, were so frequently invoked by heads of state or for their benefit. Churchill hardly makes a speech without assuring himself of the Lord's protection; Roosevelt much the same; de Gaulle puts himself under the aegis of the Cross of Lorraine; Hitler daily invokes Providence; and, from the morning to night, metropolitans of all kinds thank the Lord for the blessing of Stalinism. Far from being an unusual demonstration on their part, their attitude consecrates a general movement of regression at the same time that it reveals their panic. During the preceding war, the clerics of France solemnly declared that God was not German, while on the other side of the Rhine their counterparts proclaimed his German nationality. And never have the churches of France known so many faithful as since the commencement of German hostilities.

Where does this renaissance of fideism come from? First, from the despair engendered by the war and general misery: people no longer see a terrestrial solution for their horrible situation—or they do not yet see it—and they look to a fabulous heaven for consolation of their material ills, which the war has magnified to unheard-of proportions. For all that, during the unstable period called peace, humanity's material conditions, which gave rise to the consoling religious illusion, subsisted, though attenuated, and imperiously demanded satisfaction. Society was presiding over the slow dissolution of the religious myth without being able to find a substitute except for civic saccharin— fatherland or leader.

Faced with this ersatz, some people, thanks to the war and the conditions of its development, remain bewildered, without any recourse but a return to religious faith pure and simple. Others, finding these substitutes insufficient and old-fashioned, have tired either to replace them with new mythical products or to regenerate the old myths. Hence the great apotheosis in the world—on the one hand, Christianity; on the other, fatherland and leader. But fatherland and leader, like religion—which is at the same time their brother and rival—can nowadays dominate minds only by coercion. Their current triumph, fruit of an ostrichlike reflex, far from signifying their brilliant renaissance, presages their imminent demise.

This resurrection of God, fatherland, and leader has also been the result of people's extreme confusion, engendered by the war and its beneficiaries. Therefore, the intellectual ferment created by this situation, to the extent that one is carried away by it, remains entirely regressive, affected by a negative coefficient. Its products remain reactionary, whether they are the propaganda "poetry" of fascism or antifascism, or religious exaltation. An old man's aphrodisiacs, they restore a fleeting vigor to society only to better strike it down. These "poets" in no way participate in the creative thought of the revolutionaries of Year II or Russia 1917, for example, or in the thought of the mystics or heretics of the Middle Ages; for they are destined to provoke a factitious exaltation in the masses, while revolutionaries and mystics were the products of a real and collective exaltation that their words translated. They expressed, then, the thoughts and hopes of an entire people imbued with the same myth or animated by the same spirit, while propaganda "poetry" aims to restore a little life to a myth in its death throes. Civic hymns, they have the same soporific power as their religious patrons, from whom they directly inherit the conservative function; for if mythical then mystical poetry creates the divinity, the hymn exploits this divinity. Just as the revolutionary of Year II or 1917 created a new society while the patriot and the Stalinist of today take advantage of it.

To compare the revolutionaries of Year II and 1917 with the mystics of the

Middle Ages does not in any way amount to situating them on the same plane; but in trying to bring the illusory religious paradise down to earth, revolutionaries do not fail to exhibit psychological processes similar to those of mystics. Still, one must distinguish between mystics, who, despite themselves, tend to consolidate myth and involuntarily prepare the conditions that will lead to its reduction to religious dogma, and heretics, whose intellectual and social role is always revolutionary because it brings into question the principle on which myth relies to mummify itself in dogma. Indeed, if the orthodox mystic (but can one speak of an orthodox mystic?) conveys a certain relative conformism, the heretic, on the other hand, expresses opposition to the society in which he lives. Only priests, then, are to be considered in the same light as the current supporters of fatherland and leader, for they have the same parasitic function in regard to myth.

I could want no better example of the preceding than a small pamphlet that recently appeared in Rio de Janeiro: *The Honor of the Poets*, which contains a selection of poems published clandestinely in Paris during the Nazi occupation. Not one of these "poems" surpasses the poetic level of pharmaceutical advertising, and it is not by chance that the great majority of their authors has believed it necessary to return to classical rhyme and alexandrines. Form and content necessarily maintain a very strict relation to each other, and in these "verses" they react on each other in a mad dash to the worst reaction. It is rather significant that most of these texts strictly associate Christianity and nationalism as if they wished to demonstrate that religious dogma and nationalist dogma have a common origin and an identical social function. The pamphlet's very title, *The Honor of the Poets*, considered in regard to its content, takes on a sense foreign to all poetry. All said, the honor of these "poets" consists of ceasing to be poets in order to become advertising agents.

In the case of Loys Masson the nationalism–religion alloy contains a greater share of fideism than patriotism. In fact, he limits himself to embroidering on the catechism:

> *Christ, grant my prayer to draw strength from deep roots*
> *Let me deserve the light of my wife at my side*
> *That I might go without weakening to the people in jail*
> *Whom she washes with her hair like Mary.*
> *I know that behind the hills you are striding closer.*
> *I hear Joseph of Arimathea crumbling the ecstatic wheat over the Tomb*
> *and the vine singing in the broken arms of the thief on the cross.*
> *I see you: As it touched the willow and the periwinkle*
> *spring settles on the thorns of the crown.*
> *They blaze:*
> *Firebrands of deliverance, traveling firebrands*
> *oh! may they pass through us and consume us*
> *if that is their road to the prisons.*

The dosage is more equal in Pierre Emmanuel:

> *O France seamless gown of faith*
> *soiled by traitorous feet and spit*
> *O gown of soft breath ferociously ripped*
> *by the tender voice of revilers*
> *O gown of the purest linen of hope*
> *who know the price of being naked before God* . . .

Accustomed to the Stalinist censer and amens, Aragon nonetheless does not succeed as well as the preceding "poets" in alloying God and country. He meets the first, if I may say so, only at a tangent and obtains a text that would make the author of the French radio jingle "Levitan's furniture is going to endure" turn pale with envy:

> *There is a time for suffering*
> *When Joan came to Vaucouleurs*
> *Oh! cut France to pieces*
> *The light had that pallor*
> *I remain king of my sorrows*

But it is to Paul Eluard, the only contributor to this pamphlet who was ever a poet, that one owes the most finished civil litany:

> *On my gourmand and tender dog*
> *On its pricked-up ears*
> *On its clumsy paw*
> *I write your name.*

> *On the springboard of my door*
> *On familiar objects*
> *On the tide of holy fire*
> *I write your name* . . .

It should be noted, incidentally, that the litany form appears in the majority of these "poems" doubtless because of the idea of poetry and lamentation it implies and the perverse taste for evil that the Christian litany aims to exalt with a view to deserving heavenly bliss. Even Aragon and Eluard, formerly atheists, feel obliged, the one to evoke in his productions the "saints and prophets" and "Lazarus' tomb," and the other to return to the litany, no doubt in obedience to the famous slogan: "The priests are with us."

In reality, all the authors of this pamphlet proceed, without admitting it even to themselves, from an error of Guillaume Apollinaire's, which they further aggravate. Apollinaire had tried to treat war as a poetic subject. But if war, considered as combat and separate from any nationalist spirit, can at a pinch remain a poetic subject, the same cannot be said for a nationalist slogan, even if the nation in question is, like France, oppressed by the Nazis. The expulsion of the oppressor and the propaganda to this end falls within the realm of political, social, or military action, depending on how one envisages this expulsion. In any case, poetry does not have to intervene in their debate by other than its own means, by its own cultural significance, leaving poets free to participate as revolutionaries in routing the Nazi adversary by revolutionary means—without ever forgetting that this oppression corresponded to the wish, whether avowed or not, of all the enemies—first the national, then the foreign—of poetry understood as the total liberation of the human spirit. For, to paraphrase Marx, poetry has no homeland because it belongs to all times and all places.

Much more could be said about the freedom so often involved in these pages. First, which freedom are we talking about? Freedom for a small number to squeeze the entire population, or freedom for this population to bring this small number of privileged people to their senses? Freedom for the believers to impose their God and their mortality on the whole of society, or freedom for this society to reject God, his philosophy, and his morality? Freedom is like "a breath of air" said André Breton; and to fulfill its role this breeze must first sweep away all the miasmas of the past that infest this pamphlet. As long as the malevolent phantoms of religion and fatherland, in whatever disguise they borrow, buffet the intellectual and social air, no freedom is conceivable. Every "poem" that exalts a "freedom" wilfully left undefined, even when not adorned with religious or national attributes, first ceases to be a poem and then constitutes an obstacle to the total liberation of humanity, for it deceives in presenting a "freedom" that dissimulates new chains. From every authentic poem, on the other hand, issues a breath of absolute and active freedom, even if this freedom is not evoked in its political or social aspect: in this way the poem contributes to the real liberation of humanity.

TRANSLATED BY ANTHONY MELVILLE

NOTES

[1] André Breton, *Position politique du surréalisme* (1935), in *Oeuvres complètes* (Paris, Gallimard, 1992) vol. 2, p. 473.

[2] André Breton, *Ibid.*, p. 481.

[3] André Breton, *Ibid.*, p. 480.

ANDRÉ BRETON

Ascendant Sign
1947

Breton always considered, as a fundamental premise of Surrealism, that
poetry was once and for all liberated from the constraints of versification.
Thus, the "poetry effect" could no longer be associated with form or meter;
its only guiding light was the semantic spark generated by the surrealist
"image."

Breton's theory of the image—which he credits to Pierre Reverdy—is
as old as Surrealism itself; it was first formulated in the 1924 Manifesto.
What's new here is the fact that Breton presents it, in a primitivist perspec-
tive, as a way of re-accessing the heart of what he calls "early mankind."
What was initially envisioned as a modernist device has thus become a
way to reconnect with the archaic, with the world's "more enduring
aspects"—a means to escape the tyranny of the present moment. This
primitivist reference isn't new in itself, but it has become central. Breton's
years of exile in the United States were the occasion of the most substantive
exchange between Surrealism and anthropology: in the wake of, among
other things, the collapse of the Bolshevik reference, myth has replaced
revolution as the movement's key word.

The desire that the female feels for the male resembles the mists
rising from the earth toward the sky. Once they have gathered into
clouds, it is the sky that waters the earth.

—*Zohar*

Only on the level of analogy have I ever experienced intellectual pleasure. For me the only *manifest truth* in the world is governed by the
spontaneous, clairvoyant, insolent connection established under certain conditions between two things whose conjunction would not be permitted

André Breton, "Ascendant Sign," in *Free Rein*, trans. Michel Parmentier and
Jacqueline d'Amboise (Lincoln: University of Nebraska Press, 1995), pp. 104–107,
from "Signe ascendant," in *La Clé des champs* (Paris: Sagittaire, 1953), pp. 133–137.

by common sense. As much as I abhor, more than any other, the word *therefore*, replete with vanity and sullen delectation, so do I love passionately anything that flares up suddenly out of nowhere and thus breaks the thread of discursive thinking. What comes to light at the moment is an infinitely richer network of relations whose secret, as everything suggests, was known to early mankind. It is true that flare quickly dies out, but its glimmer is enough to help measure on their dismal scale the exchange values currently available that provide no answer except to basic questions of a utilitarian nature. Our contemporaries, indifferent to whatever does not concern them directly, are ever-less sensitive to anything that could present them with an in-depth investigation into nature: drifting on the surface of things seems enough of a task. There is an age-old conviction that nothing exists gratuitously, that, quite to the contrary, there is not a single being or natural phenomenon that does not carry a message to be deciphered by us. This conviction, which was at the heart of most cosmogonies, has been replaced by a numb and stupefied apathy: we have thrown in the towel. We hide in order to ask ourselves: "Where do I come from? Why do I exist? Where am I going?" But it is not absurd or even impudent to aim at "transforming" the world when one no longer cares to make sense of its more enduring aspects. The primordial links are broken. It is my contention that those links can only be restored, albeit fleetingly, through the force of analogy. Hence the importance taken on at long intervals by those brief flashes from the lost mirror.

> The diamond and the pig are hieroglyphs of the thirteenth passion (harmonism), which civilized people do not experience. — Charles Fourier.

> The white of the eye is a bedframe. The iris is a base for the mattress of the pupil on which a ghost of ourselves rests while we are dreaming.
> — Malcolm de Chazal

Poetic analogy has this in common with mystical analogy: it transgresses the rules of deduction to let the mind apprehend the interdependence of two objects of thought located on different planes. Logical thinking is incapable of establishing such a connection, which it deems a priori impossible. Poetic analogy is fundamentally different from mystical analogy in that it in no way presupposes the existence of an invisible universe that, from beyond the veil of the visible world, is trying to reveal itself. The process of poetic analogy is entirely empirical, since only empiricism can provide the complete freedom of motion required by the leap it must perform. When we consider the impression it creates, it is true that poetic analogy seems, like mystical analogy, to argue for an idea of a world branching out toward infinity and entirely permeated with the same sap. However, it remains without any effort within the sensible (even the sensual) realm, and it shows no propensity to lapse into the supernatural. Poetic analogy lets us catch a glimpse of what Rimbaud named "true life" and points toward its "absence," but it does not draw its substance from metaphysics nor does it ever consider surrendering its treasures on the altar of any kind of "beyond."

> *The dream is a heavy ham*
> *Hanging from the ceiling.*
> *—Pierre Reverdy*

> *I arrive as a hawk and come out a phoenix.*
> *—Voice of the third soul, Egypt*

At the present stage of poetic research, the purely formal distinction once established between metaphor and comparison should not receive much emphasis. The fact remains that they both serve as interchangeable vehicles of analogical thinking. Metaphor does have the ability to dazzle the mind, but comparison (think of Lautréamont's series of "as beautiful as") has the considerable advantage of *deferring*. Naturally, compared to these two, the other "figures" that rhetoric persists in enumerating are totally devoid of interest. The trigger of analogy is what fascinates us: nothing else will give us access to the motor of the world. Whether it is stated or implied, "as" is the most exhilarating word at our command. It gives free rein to human imagination, and the supreme destiny of the mind depends on it. That is why we choose to dismiss rather scornfully the ignorant indictment of the poetry of our time, accused of making excessive use of the "image." On the contrary, what we expect from it in this respect is an ever-growing luxuriance.

> *Your aggressive breast straining against the silk.*
> *Your triumphant breast is a splendid armoire.*
> *—Charles Baudelaire*

The analogical method was held in high regard throughout Antiquity and the Middle Ages. Since then, it has been summarily supplanted by the "logical" method, which has led us to our familiar impasse. The primary duty of poets and artists is to restore to it all its prerogatives. To this end, analogy must be rescued from the parasitic undercurrent of spiritualism, which weakens or even cripples its potentialities.

> *Your teeth are like a flock of sheep even-shorn, coming back up from the washpen.*
> *—Song of Songs*

Pierre Reverdy, who, thirty years ago, looked into the wellspring of the image, was led to formulate this cardinal law: "The more remote and accurate the connections between two realities that are brought together, the stronger the image—the stronger its emotional potential and its poetic reality." This condition, while absolutely necessary, cannot be deemed sufficient. It must make room for another requirement that, in the final analysis, could well be an ethical one. Let us beware! The analogical image, to the extent that it brings under the strongest light what are merely *partial similarities*, cannot be translated into an equation. It moves between the two confronting realities in a single direction *that can never be reversed*. From the first of these realities to the second one, it creates a vital tension straining toward health, pleasure, tranquillity, thankfulness, respect for customs. Disparagement and depressiveness are its mortal enemies. In this regard, to make up for the disappearance of noble words, some so-called poets cannot help but call attention to their sham by using vile metaphors such as the archetypal "Guitar singing bidet" from the pen of an author who is fairly prolific when it comes to such strokes of inspiration.

I saw a gathering of spirits. They wore hats on their heads. —*Swedenborg*

> *Your tongue*
> *A goldfish swimming in the bowl*
> *Of your voice*
> *— Guillaume Apollinaire*

We went along that avenue lined with blue breasts where a comma is all that distinguishes night from day and a smear of itching powder a sardine from a may-bug.
—Benjamin Péret

The finest light illuminating the general, compelling direction that any image worthy of its name must take is found in this apologue from the Zen tradition: "As an act of Buddhist kindness, Basho once ingeniously reversed a cruel haiku made up by his witty discipline. Kikaku had said: 'A red firefly / Tear off its wings / A pepper.' Basho substituted: 'A pepper / Give it wings / A red firefly.'"

TRANSLATED BY MICHEL PARMENTIER AND JACQUELINE D'AMBOISE

JEAN BEAUFRET

Conversation Under the Chestnut Tree
1963

During the summer of 1955, the philosopher Jean Beaufret invited Martin Heidegger and René Char to Ménilmontant, the neighborhood in Paris where he lived. This anecdotal "encounter" becomes the allegorical back-ground for a meditation on the conditions of possibility of a true, reciprocal recognition, by poetry and by thought, of each other's specificity. Beaufret's approach is colored by the nostalgic light of an almost-mythical pre-Socratic world whose unity predated the split between the poetic and the noetic, the early fall of thought into philosophy and of poetry into verbal craftsmanship. Char's re-invention of a poetics of aphorism as well as Heidegger's deconstruction of metaphysics are presented as signs that the founding schism of the West, separating a poetry reduced to "stale game" and a philosophy shrunk to the dimensions of an academic discipline, might be on the verge of being overcome.

Under the branches of a chestnut tree in Ménilmontant, a philosopher and a poet discuss what they know and what they are. As they speak, Martin Heidegger and René Char are learning the language of their dialogue. Paris is on vacation. The year is 1955. "During my time in France," Heidegger had written, "I would be pleased to make the acquaintance of Georges Braque and René Char."

Impromptu meetings are always chancy. But here, at the beginning of a summer's night,

> The bread and the wine gleam
> On the table in pure light.[1]

Despite the differences of experience and language that separate the two men, a meeting of the minds has taken place. The result is a dialogue between poetry and philosophy.

Jean Beaufret, "L'Entretien sous le marronnier," from René Char, *Oeuvres complètes*, 1983, pp. 1138–1143. *L'Arc* 22 (1963), pp. 1–7.

Thought, in its innermost depth, is dialogue. Thought seeks, through dialogue, to situate itself: from the very beginning, thinkers have sought a space for themselves. All of Aristotle is a dialogue with Plato. Hegelian dialogue is an attempt to open itself up to the totality of language. But language is not just the language of thought. Before the noetic thought of the thinker reverberated the poetic thought of the poet. Homer's language touched the essence of things before Heraclitus. It created a place, situated a world, the Greek world, in which philosophy would be born. Long before philosophy, it opened up the space within which, as Hesiod put it, "the gods confronted man." But why does language serve for thought as well as for poetry? From what does this intrinsic duality derive? "Whatever blossoms forth delights in pulling back." With these words Heraclitus tells us that the question must remain unanswered. At best we can try to relate to the duality in language.

To relate to the duality in language is to enter the dimension of dialogue. Dialogue never seeks to reduce the other, as haughty philosophy does in its claim to complete its other reductions by elaborating an aesthetic that would ultimately reduce poetry to a theme of philosophical explanation. Dialogue, by contrast, seeks to let the other be. "This is truly the first time," Char said of Heidegger, "that a man of this sort did not try to explain to me what I am and what I do." Heidegger listens more than he explains. From this listening to the point of silence comes the possibility of relating without responding, without offering a response that has already transformed what is to be thought about into a problem, that is, in Leibniz's terms, into a proposition, part of which is "left blank . . . as when we are asked to find a mirror that will focus all the sun's rays on a single point."[2] The poet is such a mirror, of course, but he is never to be "found." Because the poet cannot be grasped, he represents a danger for thought, but perhaps a salutary danger.

Three dangers threaten thought.

The miraculous and therefore salutary danger is the proximity of the poet, the closeness of his song.

The malicious danger, keenest of all, is thought itself: it must think uphill, which it is seldom able to do.

The pernicious danger, which confesses everything, is philosophizing.

In such terms did Heidegger speak to himself "when the wind suddenly shifted, causing the beams of the cabin to groan, and the weather began to turn sour."[3]

If poetry and thought are two proximate modes of speech, the poet nevertheless remains for the thinker the other in a perilous dialogue, a dialogue that therefore demands extraordinary forbearance on the part of thought. "If," Heidegggger once said, "the dialogue with poetry begins with thought, . . . [it] is in constant danger of disturbing the language of the poem rather than allowing it the miracle of its voice."[4] Less uncertain is the dialogue of poet with poet. Thus Hölderlin, in his translations of *Oedipus* and *Antigone* and in the remarks that follow these translations, was in dialogue with Sophocles. So, too, did Ronsard enter into dialogue with the Greek poets, and Racine with Euripides, and Victor Hugo with Vergil. And dialogue is equally what Char attempts, for example, in his *Recherche de la base et du sommet* and elsewhere, when, in texts that are in no sense essays in aesthetics, criticism, or exegesis, he sets before us Hugo, Baudelaire, Rimbaud, and "the infallible foil of the most benevolent Mallarmé," "*le fleuret infaillible du très bienveillant Mallarmé*," without intending to exhaust with these quick sketches a deeper relationship that his poetry has consistently elaborated and wrapped in enigma—the poet's relationship with poetry itself. Such brilliant fragments nevertheless attest to an uninterrupted dialogue, and if, as Hölderlin said, the poem is a gift that requires no explanation, it is nevertheless "best grasped in profound study."[5]

Heidegger thus mentions two possibilities for dialogue—that of poet with poet and that of thought with poetry. But is there not a third possibility, the dialogue of poetry with thought? Heidegger does not discuss this. Char, however, without explaining himself, takes the risk of such a dialogue. At times in its history poetry has, seemingly of its own accord, allied itself with the métier of thought. Without ceasing to be poetry, it has found a way to become thinking. Despite what Proclus would say centuries later, Parmenides' poem is not "more correctly versified than truly poetic." This was, of course, a very different kind of poetry from that of Homer or Sappho. Yet the noetic content did not stanch the flow of rhythm, did not, in other words, cut the poem off from the source that feeds it just as surely as the spring feeds the river. In a very different sense, and in a manner all its own, Pindar's poetry searched for and found thought. And what of Heraclitus? Heraclitean language, like Zeus' thunderbolt in Aeschylus, "neither falls short of its target nor sails off beyond the stars," but strikes the heart dead center, causing the *noema* to blossom in the exact image of the poem it carries within. The crucial separation of the poetic from the noetic would not occur until later, with the debasement of the noematic to the didactic, with the founding of the schools and the subsequent scholastic exploitation of that to which thought, in an earlier stage, had been able to relate, long before language became expression and speech became proposition—in an era, in other words, when speech was still speech, that is, a call, and the poetic was not yet the enemy of the noetic but its friend and neighbor, even if neighborly relations are not always the best. Later, however, after language, now understood as expression and meaning, had formulated itself canonically as proposition, the philosopher could hardly fail to see the poet as anything but a parasite on language. What chance was there then for dialogue between poetry and thought?

Nowadays the language of thought is a sad affair, only occasionally revived by polemic. When poetry tries to engage with thought, it finds nothing in present-day philosophy, which gravitates, theologically or otherwise, toward science in general and ever-greater confusion with the "human sciences" in particular. Surrealism committed a memorable error in believing that the possibility of progress lay in this direction. The wedding of poetic talent with scientific hubris yielded a few impressive monsters, nothing more. As Heidegger says, there is no bridge from science to thought: One has to jump."[6] And philosophy is no more thought than science is. Hegel taught that philosophy is just "thought in a particular guise, whereby thought becomes knowledge, and, more specifically, knowledge through concepts."[7] This is what thought is for philosophy, and for Hegel philosophy was obviously the highest form of thought. But is it really? Might there not be a form of deep thought that is not philosophy, in the sense that Heraclitus was not yet philosophic, or, as Heidegger says in his *Letter on Humanism*, in the sense that "the tragedies of Sophocles and their language contain ethos in a form prior to that of Aristotle's teachings on ethics."?[8] If so, then thought might become thinking not by philosophizing more but, rather, by freeing itself from philosophy. It might become thinking through what Heidegger dares to call the "destruction of philosophy," where the word *destruction* is to be understood in Char's sense: "If in the end you destroy, let it be with nuptial implements."[9]

"Nuptial destruction" might also describe what could happen to the poet's craft if it renounced its stale game and instead sought to join the elements of language together in a new way. Rimbaud was gone in a flash, like a meteor, yet he had time to say that "poetry will no longer set action to rhythm" but will *precede*. All of Char's poetry is in that final word. But will poetry's forward march drive far enough to mow down the barricades that currently divide poetry devoid of thought from thought specialized as philosophy, thereby making way for language unified at a higher level? "This would be soul for soul's sake . . . thought hooking thought and pulling." If the poet heeds Rimbaud's words, he is perhaps bound to come upon those *matinaux*,[10] or early risers in the world of thought, the first Greek thinkers, who were present at the inception of thought, before the schism in the heart of language occurred. They precede us only in appearance. In the maelstrom of changing times, their past is also a future. With the thought of Heraclitus, Char says, "at the tip and in the wake of the arrow, poetry races directly to the summit."[11] Perhaps poetry and thought both have to risk a new morning. This, of course, does not mean imitating the Greek morning, in which poetic and noetic language were not yet enemies. The morning to come assumes endless centuries of braving the trials of day, evening, and night, ordeals of which we are the survivors. Char's extraordinary statement is addressed to the survivors of a lengthy history. It says that no history can stanch the true wellspring. It says this frequently, in the rigorous language of aphorism. To speak in aphorisms is to refrain from saying too much; avoiding philosophy, it provides that much more food for thought. In a stroke, it creates space to breathe. It restores breath. No one who has not had his breath taken away can learn of it. Aphorism is not always in season. Only at the height of crisis does it deliver its boon. Without pessimism or optimism, without owing anything to man, without avoiding anxiety in any way, "it wishes us well, exhorts us."[12] The ancients knew the aphorisms of Hippocrates and passed them on to us. If, in Char's work, the modern piecing-together of poetry and thought is aphoristic, it is because "we have reached the time, the indescribable time, of supreme despair and hope for nothingness."[13]

The major difference between poetry and thought is perhaps that poetry already exists, whereas thought does not yet think. Or, rather, thought arose only to decline at once into philosophy, that is, into metaphysics. The dialogue with poetry could begin only by appealing to thought that was barely possible, to thought at last unencumbered by metaphysics and its conceptual retinue. Only with such thought was poetry ready to converse. Always conceived by Heidegger as a dialogue with poetry, thought, if it has yet to come, is nevertheless in its advent less the novice for having dared to listen to poets. But when, for its part, poetry embraces thought, this does not, as some have erroneously believed, imply any metaphysical vocation or inflation of its language. Rather, poetry in its own way demolishes metaphysical representation. At a single bound it leaps ahead of thought without needing first to overtake it. "The fate of the world," Heidegger has written, "is heralded in the work of poets without already being manifest as history of being."[14] And Char: "To each collapse of proof, the poet responds with a salvo of future."[15] If a salvo salutes, it also saves. Heraclitus is a savior in this sense. If thought must resort to lengthy meditation to join him in his pre-Socratic remoteness, the poet has already acknowledged him as a kindred spirit. Thus, the contrast between the meditative slowness that "thinks uphill" and the speedy poem that "races directly to the summit" conceals a secret closeness. That closeness occurs in a common site: speech, and the language that is spoken. Only within the illuminated enclosure of language does man find a home by losing himself. Without such an enclosure nothing opens up. "In the swallow's loop a storm takes shape, a garden is made."[16] From the first, thought responded to the finiteness of poetry by transcribing its message. The initiators of thought, from the dawn of Greek civilization, thought with the Greek tongue, thereby opening up a space for themselves, a territory in which everyone thinks as much as his neighbor, but each in his own way.

"The poem," Char said underneath the chestnut tree, "has no memory. I am urged to move ahead." And as we know, he also said, "of all clear waters, poetry is that which lingers least over the reflections of its bridges."[17] Heidegger admired this speed, whose law is to burn its bridges. If the poet never exists but in passing, if he leaves only traces of his presence, he nevertheless sets out for the future from the most distant past. Only the arrow's vital if elusive trajectory bestows depth on the drawing back from which it emanates. "Behind modern poetry lies a vast territory that is dark only at its edges. Over this frozen expanse no banner flies for long: it gives itself to us when it wishes and reclaims itself at will. Yet it makes us see the Lightning, and its untapped resources."[18]

When thought has become more thinking than philosophy, it, too, will have to contend with this frozen expanse, and to this task it will have to bring a patience quite different from that of history, which can at best construct landmarks in the tundra. But little by little, as the thawing wind begins to blow, the immobile has begun to move. What existed no more has begun to stir once again. The language of being has begun to speak, responding in its way to the declaration of the poet, who went ahead in search of his own echo.

And so on a summer night it came to pass that two individuals, different from each other yet of the same race and both distinguished by the sparkle of solitude, came together, for they differed only within their shared concern to shun words so that speech might exist.

TRANSLATED BY ARTHUR GOLDHAMMER

NOTES

[1] Georg Trakl, "Winter Night."

[2] *New Essays*, IV, 2.7.

[3] *Aus der Erfahrung des Denkens.*

[4] Heidegger, *Unterwegs zur Sprache*, p. 39.

[5] Friedrich Hölderlin, *Friedensfeier*.

[6] Heidegger, *Essais et conférences* (Paris: Gallimard), p. 157.

[7] G. W. F. Hegel, *Encyclopedia*, § 2.

[8] Heidegger, *Lettre sur l'humanisme* (Paris: Aubier), p. 139.

[9] Char, *Les Matinaux* (Paris: Gallimard), p. 110.

[10] Beaufret is punning on the title of Char's collections of poems cited in note 9, above. — TRANS.

[11] Char, Foreword to Heraclitus, trans. Yves Battistini (Cahiers d' Art).

[12] Char, *Les Matinaux* (Paris: Gallimard), p. 105.

[13] Char, *A une sérénité crispée* (Paris: Gallimard), p. 45.

[14] Heidegger, *Lettre sur l'humanisme*, p. 97.

[15] Char, "Partage formel," in *Fureur et mystère* (Paris: Gallimard), p. 90.

[16] Char, "A la santé du serpent," in *Fureur et mystère* (Paris: Gallimard), p. 228.

[17] Char, Ibid., p. 231.

[18] Char, Introduction to *Arthur Rimbaud* (Paris: Club Français du Livre), p. xvi.

MICHEL DEGUY

&—as in Po&try
1977

"The outright, outspoken, explicit refusal of philosophy," writes Michel Deguy, "will always look naive in the eyes of philosophy."[1] For Deguy, poet & philosopher, poetry is the name of a non-naive resistance to philosophy, a resistance that would have all the cunning required to engage philosophy itself. Typographically, with its ampersand grafted at the center of the word (like an inaudible typo, or like a leaking caesura in the middle of a verse), the title of the journal he founded in 1977 embodies a poetry that would lose its philosophical naiveté and its purity at one and the same time. Always already broached by one of its many others (philosophy is one of them), poetry is a definitively mixed media.

"In the middle of the word '*poésie*,' a man scratches himself and grumbles" (Paul Eluard, 1920). The sign *Po&sie* is intended to express the *et* (and) in *poésie*, an "and" of diversity, of plurality. &: not an abbreviation (rather, the opposite) but an ideogram symbolizing instability, novelty, and space for connection and interaction. *Po&sie* is also a reminder of the one-in-two of translation, of the disjunction and conjunction that are part of the work of poetic writing, of poetry's anxiety about its essence, of the danger of poetry's modern dismemberment, and of a sense of an impending reconstitution.

We impose no restriction on our collaborators other than that they be willing to publish under the heading "poem," even though they may not believe in the "purity of the genre."

The Committee, June 1977.

TRANSLATED BY ARTHUR GOLDHAMMER

NOTE

[1] Deguy, "Certitude et fiction", *Poétique* 21 (1975), p. 5.

Michel Deguy, *Po&sie* 1 (1977), p. 1.

JACQUES ROUBAUD

A Brief Note
1988

Mallarmé and the Symbolists, it is generally accepted, liberated French poetry from verse. Since that time, poetry identifies more and more with the often straying search for its essence: the question "What is?" has replaced the more traditionally craft-oriented "How to?" Having less and less to do with constraints, formal or other, poetry became the ultimate form of free speech.

However, once the excitement of formal transgression had subsided and time had come for assessing the outcome, a surprise was waiting in the wings: poetry, though officially de-versified, had unwittingly remained haunted by the ghost of what it claimed to have liquidated. It had rid itself of verse, but not of its memory. Its obsolescence was equaled by its resilience. Some form of verse, it appeared (limping, playing hide and seek, vaguely clandestine), still lurked under the surface of a poetry that, for decades, had vociferously claimed to be done with it. Verse may have died, but like the original Marathon runner, it is still in motion (underground, like the old mole).

The poet, novelist, and mathematician, Jacques Roubaud, a member of Oulipo—Ouvroir de littérature potentielle—*that, against the grain of the antirhetorical inspiration of most modernist poetic trends, emphasizes the playful potential of formal constraints, reported on the encouraging prognosis for the future of this precipitously buried line in a book he named, after the canonical verse of French poetry,* Aging Alexander.

1. The question of verse still arises because
2. Poetry has not disappeared.
3. To be sure, it has all but disappeared from what is called the "media" (diverse and ephemeral variants of what Mallarmé called "newspapers") but

Jacques Roubaud, *La Vieillesse d'Alexandre: Essai sur quelques états récents du vers français* (2d ed., Paris: Ramsay, 1988), pp. 203–205.

not from publishers' catalogues (there are even some publishers—small, to be sure, but still publishers—who devote most of their effort to it).

4. Nor has poetry entirely disappeared among those who call themselves poets (there are some).

5. Finally, it can be verified that verse still exists in poetry, which still exists.

6. This also means that the sometimes considerable effort expended to conceal its existence by giving it other names (the text of the novel, for example) have not really borne fruit.

7. The question of designation is not without interest. There is no poetry in the novel, in sunsets, in nuclear physics, or in the Dow Jones Index.

8. It follows that if there is no poetry proclaimed as poetry, there is no poetry. This is the implicit or explicit working hypothesis of poets, that is, people who write, compose, and propose poetry.

9. This being the case, the *question of verse* remains central to the question of the existence of poetry. The fact is that the modes of existence of verse are undergoing a profound mutation. In what follows, I will succinctly indicate a few of these modes.

10. In one mode of poetry, which once again exists, to an ever-greater degree, in oral form, the verse unit tends to be defined primarily in the mouth. In this mode, sonic parameters become increasingly autonomous, and inscription on the page becomes secondary—a notation, a score.

11. In one mode of poetry, which once again exists, to an ever-greater degree, in written form (as in part of the medieval tradition, defeated and never really replaced or transformed by printing, which was the first "historical" defeat of poetry in the "modern" era), the verse unit tends to be defined in space (usually in more than two dimensions). In this mode, visual parameters become increasingly autonomous, and the transition to voice, although still possible in some cases, becomes primarily an illustration, an accompaniment, a performance.

12. By virtue of their very direction, these two modes are the most "aggressive" and seem "newest," because they define themselves in terms of a "breakdown" of the eye–ear equilibrium, which has been the compromise accepted by almost all poets since the Renaissance.

13. The line of verse, as examined and partially described in this book, can increasingly be seen as the heir to poetry's traditional mode of existence.

14. As far as this type of verse is concerned (and this has been the primary focus of the previous chapters), the situation seems to have settled down and stabilized in one of three modes.

15. The first, which is dominant (more or less throughout the world), is what I will call *international free verse*: invented by the great "modern" American poets and generalized by a generation of "readers" (who have made "readings" a universal phenomenon), it is characterized by smoothness in the relation, whether oral or written, between verse and language: line breaks,

whether sonic or typographical, do not necessarily coincide with "natural" breaks in the syntax of the language but set up more or less complex (but generally quite basic) rhythmic relationships with the articulations of the phrase or discourse. The resulting interplay is not "shocking" to either eye or ear, is quite supple, and obviously has no formal implications.

16. *International free verse* "passes" readily from one language to another. It is eminently translatable. It is verse designed for "free trade," which no metrical customs officer will stop at any border. No matter what words are used, it can be identified instantly from Toronto to Helsinki, from San Francisco to Milan, from Budapest to Tokyo.

17. A second, relatively minor mode involves a return to traditional verse, and generally to relatively recent forms of traditional verse. For some poets, it is a sign of propriety, dandyism, more or less deliberate postmodernism, insolence, or amusement.

18. In a third mode, also minor, prose, in which Mallarmé saw "broken" verse, is called upon as a means of trying out a still undefined verse, a verse fragment, in which bits of language are isolated and assigned the status of constituent elements of a yet to be established meter.

19. Relatively independent of each of these modes, and potentially compatible with all, in a relatively abstract branch of poetry (for instance, in the line stemming from OULIPO, which has very ancient roots), the unit of verse tends to be defined within a possible world of language (differing from one world to the next). In this mode, combinatorial parameters become increasingly autonomous, and the manner in which they are used, the visible or invisible system of "axioms," becomes an integral and essential part of the poem's meaning.

TRANSLATED BY ARTHUR GOLDHAMMER

JEFFREY MEHLMAN

Ad Centrum?

Our effort in this volume has been to convey something of the range of literary debate in France over the last half century by presenting a series of interpretive clusters, groupings of texts around specific issues that have preoccupied the reading—and writing—communities in France since World War II. Not a linear history, then, but a series of configurations, each with its own temporality, its own polemical energies, its own pattern of illumination, and, on occasion, its own way of intersecting with the concerns or achievements around which other clusters have been assembled.

There is, nonetheless, a hidden center of sorts to our richly dispersed field, a constellation (or sequence) of such sustained significance that it at times feels like a microcosm of the book itself. For the ongoing interpretation (and re-interpretation) of Mallarmé, the subject of Chapter III, has functioned as a uniquely luminous test case, a "radioactive tracer," as it were, wending its way through the tissue of French thought over the last half century.[1] From Jean-Paul Sartre to Maurice Blanchot, Michel Foucault to Jacques Derrida, Jean Hyppolite to Gilles Deleuze and Jacques Rancière—not to mention the spe-cifically literary exegeses of critics such as Georges Poulet and Charles Mauron, Jean-Pierre Richard and Gérard Genette, Julia Kristeva and Philippe Sollers—one is hard put to find a significant French thinker since the war who has not at some point felt obliged to come to terms with the evanescent poetry of the fin-de-siècle Symbolist.

Why, then, Mallarmé? After all, of the heirs of Baudelaire, it might have been thought that the future lay with the ultraromantic lineage of Rimbaud (and the Surrealists) far more than with the diminutive English teacher and self-styled martyr to poetry whose centenary France celebrated in 1998. On the way to an answer, the remarkable experience of Charles Mauron, the doyen of the Mallarmé readers we have assembled and the author of four books devoted to the poet, offers some guidance.[2] Mauron was a pioneer of the heroic days of Mallarmé exegesis, a period when the principal urgency lay in deciphering the meaning (if any) of the extraordinarily oblique and formally polished poems whose subject, more often than not, appeared to be the disappearance of what-ever the poet, in his indirection, made bold (or shy) to evoke. Mauron, and others, succeeded in this pioneering task.[3] As early as 1941, *Mallarmé l'obscur*, for example, offered a series of eminently convincing glosses. Take the two poems referred to in the selection included in this chapter: "*Sainte*" evokes with due serenity shifting perceptions of a stained-glass Saint Cecilia midst the changing light of a northern church. *"Don du poème"* has the poet, depressed at his sterility, handing over his all but stillborn child, figure of the poem, to a nurse perhaps capable of reviving it.

Now, Mauron's surprise was to discover that both poems, eminently different in subject, seemed to be structured by (a transformation of) the same network of images. Moreover, the phenomenon is present throughout Mallarmé's oeuvre. To the extent that Mallarmé himself sensed it, he called it a shimmering beneath the surface, " *un miroitement en-dessous.*" It was a stunning breakthrough; for it is one thing to make one's way through the poet's genially oblique formulations to a recognition of the twin versions of Saint Cecilia in the northern church glass, or to an intuition of the erotic fiasco at the heart of *"L'Après-midi d'un faune"*—at high noon under a sweltering Sicilian sky, a mythological Faun loses (or dreams he loses) the two delectable nymphs he believes he is about to ravish. But it is an altogether different one to realize that at the level of textual structure, the twin versions of Saint Cecilia and the two nymphs can be compellingly characterized as versions or metaphors of each other. For if such be the case, the hard-won subject of each poem would appear, at some level, to be secondary to the insistence of a structure invisible in individual poems but perceptible in the resonance between the two.

Mallarmé, in sum, was pursuing his oeuvre within a space fully as kaleidoscopic as the "savage thought" Claude Lévi-Strauss had begun to explore during the postwar years.[4] Reference, however precise, was strictly contingent, subordinate to the arch syntax of a repetitive structure. That circumstance was sufficient to mark Mallarmé as bête noire of Sartrean existentialism.[5] For if language were essentially prose, as Sartre would have it, and prose were at bottom *instrumental*, utilitarian, in its *engagement* of the world, what might one make of the hand afloat between the Saint Cecilia figure of *"Sainte,"* her finger plucking a harp (-shaped wing of a passing angel), and the crazed Faun, his finger pressing the "feathery whiteness" (*"candeur de plume"*) of the more glacial of the nymphs for whatever erotic titillation it might elicit? The purposeful hand of a would-be activist writer—Sartre's enduring ideal—finds itself subject to a strangely rigorous passivity in the poetry of Mallarmé.[6] Thus, the poet is cast as a Sartrean antihero: a terrorist fearful of sullying . . . his hands, a suicide artist, "sad mystifier," and brilliant casualty of the "death of God."[7] The wings (of angel, then—feathery whiteness of a—nymph) we have been charting make a brief appearance toward the end of the Sartre essay we have included here: little remains of Mallarmé's dying swan caught in the ice save the frenzied but slowing beat of his white wings against the white landscape of the wintry scene. The poet, according to Sartre, sings of his own death: he is a nihilist, a "last man" of the sort Alexandre Kojève would read from Nietzsche into Hegel.[8] And yet does not the white-on-white of Mallarmé's poem, a sonnet all but reduced to the sheer rhythm of a beating wing, convey even more compellingly an intuition of the virtual effacement of reference by structure which was the horizon, if never fully acknowledged, of Mauron's reading of Mallarmé?

To have been alive to that dimension and accorded it centrality remains the signal achievement of Maurice Blanchot.[9] In terms that at times ring late-Heideggerian, Blanchot perfected an idiom attuned to the extraordinary negativity of Mallarmé's poetry—though without providing the critical readings on which that extreme sense of "literary space" rests. Blanchot's Mallarmé sets out in search of the very origin or being of poetry, sees existence itself "gnawed" away in the process, only to confront a single "residue" sustaining language: "the word *c'est.*"[10] Being itself is affected by a fundamental negativity, what Blanchot calls the *"désoeuvrement de l'être,"* a listlessness or "undoing" of the work (of being) profoundly related to the effacement of reference figured by the dying swan fading white into white. It would remain for Derrida to witness or effect the implosion of being (*c'est*) within Mallarmé's poetry—at which point the deconstruction of being might be properly read as a protracted appendix to a reading of Mallarmé. It is a development to which we shall return.

Mallarmé proposed an "Orphic explanation of the Earth." Blanchot, in his fidelity to the most extreme possibilities opened up by Mallarmé, remained convinced that the strong moment of the Orpheus myth was neither his enchanted descent into the underworld nor his near retrieval of the dead Eurydice but, rather, his subsequent dismemberment. The reader of this volume will encounter the critical counterpart of just such an experience of dismemberment; for Mauron observes the dispersion of the "angelic musician" of *"Sainte"* through the interior depicted in *"Don du poème"*: the wing is now that of dawn crashing through the window, the lamp is termed "angelic," the raised finger might press a milk-white breast to nurse the poem-child. Such are the perspectives opened by the category of (Orphic) dismemberment in Mallarmé. And yet a central dimension of Mauron's work constitutes something of a retreat from precisely that limit. It is a development rich with implications for French critical history and is worth evoking, however schematically, at this juncture.

The network of metaphors Mauron had detected *between* the poems of Mallarmé soon evolved into a mobile play of forces and a structured conflict. It was a conflict, then, which was visible not in individual poems but in the resonance—*"deux à deux rongeur"*—established between them. Moreover, the ramifications and intricacies of the network were such that one was hard put to attribute them to any intentionality on the poet's part. It was at this point that Mauron had the surprise of recognizing in an adolescent narrative, composed by the poet shortly after the trauma of his sister's death, the precise contours of the structured conflict he had noted within the intertextuality of the poems. The critic was confronted with an invisible and pervasive conflict, of a complexity and obliqueness that defied intentionality, and that appeared to be intimately bound to a childhood trauma. Almost in spite of himself, Mauron found himself backing into a Freudian interpretation; the result was his 1950 *Introduction to the Psychoanalysis of Mallarmé*, from which our selection has been taken. The astonishing network of images was now tethered to a ready-made Oedipal scheme out of Freud. The poet was Orpheus, allowed to tap the riches of his own unconscious (underworld) on the sole condition that they remain unconscious. The dismemberment of Orpheus was somehow left behind in a rush to eulogize the unique poetic gift of "reversible regression."[11]

That term was a coinage of the tradition of Freudian interpretation that had thrived in the United States under the name of "psychoanalytic ego psychology."[12] It may serve to remind us of a fundamental irony of critical history in France: while Mauron, in Provence, was tethering his stunning readings of literary texts to fairly predictable schemata out of psychoanalysis, in Paris, around Lacan, the texts of Freud were being scrutinized with an eye to unsuspected modes of coherence and an implicit poetics whose upshot was a major reinterpretation of Freud. That reinterpretation is in many ways a separate (and central) chapter in the history of reading in France (and is treated below as such). Yet the nexus between Freud and Mallarmé—who also advocated "yielding the initiative to words"—is peculiarly apposite. The Faun's question at the beginning of Mallarmé's famous poem (*Aimai je un rêve? Was I enamored of a dream?*) was, after all, Freud's own question, in 1897, when he claimed to realize that his entire theory was founded on sexual assaults that may have been mere fantasies.[13] The Freud reference, that is, once established by Mauron, would continue to shadow Mallarmé interpretation in many of its principal manifestations.

Such would be the case for what is undoubtedly the most ambitious exercise of Mallarmé criticism, a *locus classicus* of thematic reading, Jean-Pierre Richard's *L'Univers imaginaire de Mallarmé*.[14] Richard set out to weave the entirety of Mallarmé's corpus into a thematic whole in an exercise he termed "*totalitaire*."[15] Now for all the skill Richard brought to the task, one is nevertheless struck by the dissonance between the critic's "totalizing" gesture, on the one hand, and the fundamentally minimalist and negativizing bias of the poet's oeuvre on the other. Precisely where erosion and evanescence seemed the hallmark of the Mallarméan, Richard subordinated the negative to the active fullness of a corporeal existence, "*la plénitude active d'une chair*," a dimension that his "concrete phenomenology" was particularly well suited to capture.[16]

His reference to "phenomenology" was a discrete borrowing from the philosopher of science Gaston Bachelard (see Chapter VI). Bachelard maintained a lifelong fascination with "epistemological obstacles," the gratifying but misguided investment of pre-scientific investigators in seemingly unmediated perceptions of almost literary intensity—hence the title, midway between literary criticism and scientific prophylaxis, of one of his most famous books, *The Psy-*

choanalysis of Fire.[17] Whereas Freudian psychoanalysis had been dominated by the categories of repression and discontinuity (above all in its encounter with Mallarmé), Bachelard's adaptation of psychoanalysis cast its lot with the fundamentally continualist notion of sublimation. In Richard, this perspective took the form of such continualist propositions as "The idea thus does not become detached from the dream subtending it. . . ."[18] Whence Gérard Genette's attack on Richard for his "sensualist" and "eudaemonist" propensities: the claim that even *this* poetry would be rooted in an experience of the flesh and its ultimately *felicitous* expression.[19] Or Mauron's critique of Richard's jimmied-up version—via Bachelard—of psychoanalysis.[20] Moreover, it was during the years of Richard's publication that Lacan gave prominence to the term *"imaginaire"* as a designation for the fundamentally deluded register of narcissism.[21] Things could not have looked less auspicious for Richard's monumental endeavor.

A glance at *"Hérodiade,"* Mallarmé's central (and unfinished) poem, and the readings it has elicited may clarify matters. The poem, a dramatic fragment, is a bizarre recasting of the myth of Salome, in which not only does the heroine (inexplicably renamed Hérodiade) fail to perform her notorious dance before her stepfather Herod, but Herod himself disappears from the poem even as Hérodiade–Salome, countering the tradition that runs from Heine to Wilde, waxes hysterical at the idea of being so much as *seen* by John the Baptist. It is no surprise, then, that Mauron, for all his admiration for Mallarmé, should call the poem one of the most *"gauche"* in the French language. Now the agonizing composition of *"Hérodiade"* was associated with a deep depression the poet went through in 1867. What do our critics make of the poem? For Richard, the self-regarding heroine, caught up in a "specular obsession," is a figure of "reflexive consciousness" or "narcissism." For Mauron, the *Hérodiade* scenario is so much a recasting of the plot of the celebrated adolescent narrative (titled *"Ce que disaient les trois cigognes"*) that it is less a manifestation of a repressively narcissistic ego than of the repressed itself. However, the differences between the adolescent narrative and the hysterical scenario of *"Hérodiade"* are instructive. In the juvenile text, a mourning father watches his dead daughter emerge from the grave one wintry evening and dance for him: in other words, it has the missing elements from the Salome scenario, father and dance, although we find neither reference to the myth proper (Salome) nor to any sensuality in the dance—the daughter is virginally pure. Might it be that the crucial interest of the adolescent narrative lies less in its allusion to a traumatic event (a sister's death) than in the play of distortion between the narrative and its celebrated aftertext? Consider that during the entirety of his daughter's dance, the father, in a state of "transport," caresses the "huge languorous tail" (*"grande queue pleine de nonchaloir"*) of his cat Puss. It is a remarkably amplified detail that Mauron, in his rush to tie the text to the death of the poet's sister, fails to note. But here we approach that re-interpretation or strong reading of Freud we

have already alluded to. For in his etiology of symptoms, Freud initially referred to *two* scenes: A "sexual–presexual" episode in which an adult, perhaps
unwittingly, intrudes his sexuality into the existence of a child too young ("presexual") to do anything more than store it in some psychical limbo for future
reference; and a later postpuberty episode in which an innocuous event triggers
a reminiscence of the first episode, which the now-comprehending psyche, attacked *from within*, cannot defend against. The symptom is generated, in sum,
through "deferred action" (*"Nachträglichkeit"*). Return to Mallarmé: for between the initial "sexual–presexual" narrative (innocent dance/masturbatory
cat's tail) and the *"Hérodiade"* fragment, with its frenzied but repressed
eroticism and hysterical distortions, might Mallarmé be serving us up a configuration—*Nachträglichkeit*—precisely congruent to Freud's at his most provocative? Such is a perspective leading once again from Mallarmé to the most
liberating perspectives in Freud interpretation, a subject to which we will return.

If Mauron, reading *"Hérodiade,"* appears to have elided the full complexity
of "the repressed," Richard, on the same poem, appears to have been constrained by his own presuppositions to cast the poem on the (glaringly narcissistic) side of repression. As though his book were a monument to a perspective
doomed by its own anachronism. It is precisely in the context of Genette's and
Mauron's attacks on Richard's book that Michel Foucault's ringing defense
comes into full relief.[22] Foucault, eager to stake out a ground that was neither
psychoanalytic nor linguistic-structuralist, discusses Richard's Mallarmé at
length on his way to the constitution of his notion of an archive. What appealed
to him most in Richard was the will to delineate a corpus mid-way between
"life" and "work," a domain of "stagnating language" or discourse. At a time
when Foucault was being cast (by Sartre among others) as a structuralist ideologue, Foucault, in formulations often as eloquent as they are elusive, took his
distance from Genette, a classical structuralist, as much as from Mauron.[23]
Foucault's investment in the continuities of what he called Richard's "tertiary"
domain are clearest in one of his footnotes, where he compares the situation in
Mallarmé studies to that in

> the field known as the history of ideas. The preservation of documents has given
> rise, in the sciences, philosophy, and literature, to a mass of ancillary texts that
> are wrongly regarded as false sciences or quasi-philosophies . . . or even as
> foreshadowings or subsequent reflections of what would later become . . .
> philosophy or science.[24]

What attracted Foucault was the prospect of doing away with the Bachelardian
distinction between pre-science (or what Althusser, drawing on Bachelard,
would call "ideology") and science. For if the target of one's genealogy is nothing less than the will to truth, then the very distinction between (politically
tainted) ideology and (wholly disinterested) science would have to be relin-

quished in favor of a composite *savoir-pouvoir* resistant to every prospect of separating the two.[25] Richard's continualism, that is, in so far as it is discursively incompatible with a notion such as *"coupure épistémologique"* and the central discontinuity it would introduce, emerges, in its very anachronism, as congenial to the perspective Foucault sought to introduce.

Were one—following Mauron's lead, but steering clear of Freud—to superimpose those poems in which Mallarmé aspired to "vanquish chance word by word," an almost abstract tableau would soon emerge: the slimmest of partitions separating a mass of white from a waning red (frequently against a ground of azure). But it is a tableau pulsating with conflictual energy: white is the color of ennui, reality at its most intolerable; the declining red-on-azure is the color of an apparently taboo dream or aspiration, unbearable in its intensity. At which point the only sustainable locus for the poem becomes the partition or dividing line itself. Or rather the urgency would be for the poem to make its way toward the taboo dream even as it takes its distance from it: the line begins to vibrate, the wings we observed earlier begin to beat.

It was the achievement of Jacques Derrida to perceive all that was at stake in the aspiration of the Mallarmean poem to coincide with the differential vibration of that partition or line, and to affirm its inability to coincide with what one hesitates to call *itself*. An "undecidable" line, then: like the Mallarmean "hymen," meaning both marriage or consummation and membrane or barrier to consummation. As though there were always already *"trop d'hymen,"* an excess of hymen, in the charged expression of Mallarmé's Faun. On one side, the lily-white ingenuousness to which the Faun would be cast back by being awakened from what may have been no more than an erotic dream; on the other the combustion of *"tout brûle"* against a sky of Sicilian blue; and, in between, the vibrating locus of the poem—*"trop d'hymen."*

It is as though the nucleus of Derrida's Mallarmé lay in an elaboration of Heidegger's pun on an Ernst Jünger title in the very essay (*"Zur Seinsfrage"*) in which the German philosopher gave us the term "deconstruction" (*Abbau*): no longer *"Über die Linie"* in Jünger's transgressive sense of *trans lineam*, over the line, but rather *"Über 'die Linie'"* in the sense of *de linea*, on (the subject of) the line.[26] Later, in a longer essay for which the shorter one included in this volume appears to have been something of a dry run, Derrida used a Mallarméan text (*"Mimique"*) as the lever with which to "overturn Platonism" (in the consecrated Nietzschean phrase).[27] Mallarmé, then, or the deconstruction of being, the implosion already heralded by Blanchot.

Or was it always already an explosion? In a brief Mallarmé poem, unmentioned by Derrida (*"Indomptablement a dû"*), a bird (perhaps) literally explodes in song at an unseen height. Will it lie scattered on some path (ah! the wings beating in the window)? Or might that wrenching sob have been not the hypothetical bird's but my own? Might it have emerged from *"mon sein pas du sien*," (my breast and not his)? The resonance with "*L'Après-midi d'un faune*" is palpable. But Mallarmé, for all his notoriety as an English teacher, was married to a German. *Sein*, anagrammatized as *sien*, means not only "breast," but, in German (the language in which, according to Julien Gracq, he perhaps *should* have been writing in the first place), Being.[28] Mallarmé, in sum, or the deconstruction of Being.

A demonstration by counterexample. In 1994, the journal *Le Débat* made a second attempt to restage the celebrated controversy over New Criticism that had erupted in 1965 around Raymond Picard's polemic over the Racine criticism of Mauron, Roland Barthes, and several others.[29] The first rematch pitted the eminent literary historian Marc Fumaroli against the structuralist critic and co-founder of the review *Poétique* Gérard Genette.[30] It came to something of an impasse nicely captured by Antoine Compagnon, when he suggested that in the age-old confrontation between Benedictine scholarship obsessed with minutia, and Jesuit rhetoric, entranced with generalities, Fumaroli, the author of *L'Age de l'éloquence,* a genealogy of literature out of a rhetorical culture with which it was rapidly losing touch, was to a significant extent the "Benedictine of Jesuitism."[31] Whence the falsity of the proposed confrontation between the neo-Jesuit (Genette) and his alleged other (Fumaroli) . . . *Le Débat*, not to be deprived of its debate, subsequently staged a second confrontation, between Fumaroli and Philippe Sollers, the co-founder of the avant-garde journal *Tel Quel*.[32] Fumaroli is represented in this volume by a section of his incisive history of "Conversation," an essay in praise of that "oral literary *atelier*" in which "the delights of listening" take priority over what Barthes called "the pleasure of the text."[33] In his attack against a concept of literature "too exclusively tied to print," Fumaroli represents an unabashed "logocentrism."[34] Sollers had been the publisher of Derrida's long essay on Mallarmé, "*La Double Séance*," as well as the author of an article, "*Littérature et Totalité*" (1966), intent on inscribing the poet of *dis*possession in the not yet discredited camp of Revolution.[35] The clash was bound to be intense, particularly on the subject of Mallarmé. Fumaroli:

> Concerning Mallarmé, since his name has again been mentioned, allow me to recall a point that is not unrelated to these disasters. The renascence of 1910–1912, which provided such great impetus to French letters up until 1940, was pursued *against* rather than with Mallarmé. Fortunately, Mallarmé was an act of defiance, not a program. In Claudel, Valéry, and the first *Nouvelle revue française*, one finds a fecundity and a reappropriation of the tradition which Mallarmé's *gnosis* did not portend. French literature succeeded in being modern without being modernist. The same holds for French painting between 1909 and 1940. It is the modernism whose herald you [Sollers] have been which found with Blanchot that nihilistic disembodiment of speech, that blank, absent, and abstract mode of writing which was justified in laying claim to Mallarmé.[36]

Fumaroli or the re-emergence of logocentrism in a polemic against a literary and philosophical culture centered in Mallarmé.

Return to the configuration subtending the poems of Mallarmé: the slimmest of partitions—glass, tombstone, window, meridian, line of music or paint or whatever—separating white from red. It is as though the poetry of Mallarmé were a perpetual-motion machine eradicating chance, endlessly regenerating, as different from itself, a partition establishing a difference. It should be noted that the configuration of an agent sorting out molecules spectrally (red or white) on either side of a partition is the very model invented by James Maxwell in *his* scientific fantasy of what came to be known as "Maxwell's demon."[37] By endlessly re-instituting difference "without expenditure of work," the demon eradicates chance, the random mingling of, say, reds and whites; thwarts entropy, the universal tendency toward disorder, noise, or randomness; and lays the conditions for a "perpetual motion machine." That observation takes on interest when one observes that Jean Hyppolite, the dean of French historians of philosophy, would pen an essay reading Mallarmé's *"Un Coup de dés"* cybernetically—with Norbert Wiener—as an allegory of Maxwell's demon . . . going under.[38] In his last years Mallarmé issued a stereographic palinode: a throw of the dice (even should it result in the *right* number) would never abolish chance. The old man of Mallarmé's poem, his fist clenched around the dice he would perhaps never throw, goes down into the chaos of the sea. With entropy (or noise) in the ascendant, no message can be transmitted entire. The eternal return of the perpetual-motion machine gives way to the downward spiral of a cycle, the demon's, increasingly unable to right itself. It is a perspective that would eventually be amplified at book length in Michel Serres's extrapolations on literature and thermodynamics.[39]

Hyppolite was not alone in implying a dissonance between Mallarmé and Nietzsche. Gilles Deleuze, whose *Nietzsche and Philosophy* served as a generation's guide to the German philosopher, felt impelled to include a chapter on "Nietzsche and Mallarmé."[40] Just as the Mallarmé of an eternal return (the perpetual-motion machine) appears to give way to a poet who has reversed his position in Hyppolite, so a Mallarmé fundamentally attuned to Nietzsche's articulation of play, chance, tragic thought, and the cosmos is revealed by Deleuze to be, in the last analysis, a nihilistic parody of Nietzsche. "Hérodiade is not Ariadne, but the icy creature of resentment and bad conscience, a spirit denying life. . . ."[41] For Deleuze, Mallarmé, despite his apparent affinities with Nietzsche, despite the ambivalent but tutelary presence of Wagner, represents a triumph of the negative, a throw of the dice, but under the auspices of nihilism, as far from Derrida's quite Nietzschean subverter of Platonic seriousness as may be imagined.

The most recent of French philosophers to have engaged Mallarmé is Jacques Rancière, whose unexpected *Mallarmé: la politique de la sirène* was published in 1996.[42] Rancière had been among the most brilliant members of Althusser's seminar on Marx at the Ecole Normale Supérieure, and the author of the third volume of the collective endeavor *Lire le 'Capital'*.[43] The mature Marx emerged in that reading as a structuralizing critic of the "young" (humanist) Marx, who was said to have been mystified by Ludwig Feuerbach's vision of man's dialectical reappropriation of an essence he had alienated in a God of his own invention. Mature Marx, that is, was above all a theorist of *reading* (the residual presence of "ideological" illusions that might continue to contaminate the new "science" into which Marx had emerged after what Althusser, borrowing from Gaston Bachelard, called his "epistemological break"). Rarely had the Althusserian case been substantiated as compellingly as in Rancière's reading of Marx.

Shortly after May '68, however, Rancière came to the conclusion that Althusser's entire problematic of a young "ideological" Marx separated by an "epistemological break" from a mature "scientific" one had functioned as a politically motivated mystification.[44] That model, generalized into the politics of a clear-cut distinction between "scientific truth" and "ideological error," was seen to have been a justification for subordination on the part of those deemed from above to be ideologically tainted and for inactivity on the part of the "scientifically" or "theoretically" engaged, who, to be sure, would forestall any political action until its concomitant theory had been completed. Whence, in part, the political fiasco of May '68. "Theory" (that is, science) had been revealed to be not the pristine *other* of politically tainted ideology, but a formation shot through with political implications.[45]

Rancière's Mallarmé, like Sartre's, is emphatically and self-consciously post-Christian; but unlike Sartre's, Rancière's is not a victim of that circumstance. For his is the project of a new communitarian cult, poetry, characterized by its rejection of every mode of *incarnation*. The poet's task is to "consecrate" the human "sojourn" through an elevation of its evanescent aspects, its "virtuality." As a reader of Mallarmé, Rancière is finely attuned to the poet's repeated preference for the minimalist glint over the central presence: not the lumbering nonexistence of *le néant* but the quasi-nothing of *rien*; not the raised chalice of the mass but the quintessential Mallarméan gesture of the toast; not the shipwreck at sea but (perhaps!) the barely perceptible plunge of the siren. (At times, in fact, Rancière's Mallarmé reads like a series of addenda to the La Fontaine fable of the—impressive but vulnerable—oak and the—preferable because supple—reed.)

Now, curiously enough, in Rancière's reading, Mallarmé's rival in the effort to elaborate a post-Christian cult is none other than the very Feuerbach whom Althusser's "mature" Marx had held at bay. The repatriation of man's alienated essence à la Feuerbach was to be opposed by Mallarmé's "religion" of artifice. Moreover, there were grounds for viewing the major shipwreck to which the poet preferred the evanescence of the siren as a metaphor for revolution itself. Such would be the moral of Mallarmé's maritime fable: "the time is not yet come for the glorious shipwreck."[46] Ours is the time of the siren trying out virtualities with the virtuosity of a musician tuning up for a concert. In the interim, the "restrained action" through which the poet separates himself from the "crowd" would best be understood in terms of Marx's notion of the "necessary maturation of revolutionary conditions."[47]

All of which makes Rancière's celebration of Mallarmé—in its implicit critique of Feuerbach, its will to a *provisional* separation from the laboring masses, and its central insistence that the time for revolution has not yet come—read like an implicit retraction of his post-'68 polemic against Althusser.

Our volume begins with Sartre's postwar "Presentation" of his journal *Les Temps modernes* and all but ends with a fragment of Derrida's contribution to a celebration of the fiftieth anniversary of that same journal. Somewhere in between, we have included remarkably different "introductions," by both Sartre and Derrida, to Mallarmé. Mallarmé as central reference, then . . . All of which implies that, at some level, the imperative might be to "Mallarméize" literature itself. Such indeed might be one interpretation of deconstruction, the effort to open up thought itself to a stratum construable as Mallarméan. (From the Heidegger–Jünger confrontation *über die Linie* to the Derrida-Mallarmé nexus at the self-transgressing *hymen*, an entire history of one strain of twentieth-century thought might be sketched.)

Yet before Derrida's extrapolation of the Mallarméan to the tenuous ground of thought itself, Mauron, in the 1950s, had made a first effort to open up a stratum comparable to the one he had all but stumbled upon in Mallarmé in texts other than those of the fin-de-siècle master. Mauron, that is, has been widely hailed (or attacked) as a pioneer of psychoanalytic criticism, but it may be claimed with equal justification that his success lay more in choosing Mallarmé as paradigm than Freud, or, rather, that he was successful in his Freudianization only to the extent that it was also a "Mallarméization."

How then might one open up the Mallarméan stratum, attain the equivalent of those free associations without which "psychoanalytic criticism" will tend to what an inspired typist, in a telling slip, called applied SPYCHOANALYSIS? Mauron's answer, derived from the nineteenth-century polymath Francis Galton, was the "superimposition" of texts. Just as Galton had superimposed the negatives of photos of members of the same family, blurring out individual features and allowing a composite portrait to emerge, so might one proceed with the texts of a single author. The result would again (as in the case of Mallarmé) issue in a proto-poem invisible in individual texts but insistent in the resonances between them. It was an early instance of interest in what would later flourish under the rubric "intertextuality," and the first author on whom Mauron tried it out at full length was Racine.[48] The impressive result was the constitution of the entirety of the dramatist's oeuvre as something approaching a musical score—elaborate in its architectonic effects, its characters marked by a porousness of identity (and a persecutory bent) that made them full-fledged contemporaries of the novels of Nathalie Sarraute.[49]

The transition from Mallarmé to Racine, from, say, Hérodiade's rejection of her imploring nurse back to Phèdre's rejection of *hers* (surely one of Mallarmé's sources) had worked, and one of the aftereffects was the so-called Controversy over New Criticism, which was launched, as noted, by Raymond Picard's *Nouvelle critique ou nouvelle imposture* in 1965. Roland Barthes, whose *Sur Racine* was the principal target of the Sorbonne professor, significantly began that book with an acknowledgment of the extent of his debt to Mauron.[50] Picard himself was obsessed with the psychoanalytic damage the new criticism had done to literature as he understood it. He reproached his adversaries with wanting to "surrealize," in the name of the unconscious, the entirety of French literature.[51] This reference to Breton and company was, however, wrong precisely to the extent that it was a reading not of the Surrealists but of the *counter-tradition* exemplified by Mallarmé that had been the source. It is little wonder then that Barthes, responding to Picard, saw the prime interest of the controversy to lie in the extent to which the persistent French allergy to psychoanalysis should continue to pass for literary taste.[52]

A more probing insight into what was at stake in the psychoanalytic interpretation of Racine might be gleaned by confronting two texts. The first is Gérard Genette's saluting of the "typically structuralist" tactic of Mauron; Genette insists that if the Racine book was the best of Mauron's endeavors, it was because Oedipus was, after all, a tragic myth before being a psychoanalytic complex—and that Mauron, in reading Racine "oedipally," was perhaps doing no more than reclaiming for literature what was rightfully and originally its own.[53] The second is a recent essay by Jean Laplanche that posits a fundamental discontinuity at the inception of Freud's thought between the "associative-analytic" and the "mytho-symbolic" modes of interpretation.[54] The first of these methods would run counter to repression and the second—including the entire Oedipal array, and in particular Little Hans's invention of the "castration complex"—would actually *espouse* the cultural pathology of the society and flourish in harmony with it: "What could be less sexual, in the last analysis, than Sophocles' tragedy?"[55] The Oedipal, in sum, would partake not of the repressed but of the repressive . . .

That last observation and the gesture through which it is affirmed is part of a general perspective that had profound implications for the history of interpretation in France. It held that Freud's most potent insights (specifically concerning the irreducible nature of repression) were of necessity perpetually escaping him, undergoing repression. Consequently, the task of analytic theory was less to come up with new empirical data than to elaborate the perverse rigor with which the discovery of repression itself was being repressed in the very course of its consolidation. That insight forms the horizon informing our section on literature and psychoanalysis. It begins with Mauron's early methodological statement on the superimposition of texts[56] and then moves on to the effort by Jean Starobinski, a master of thematic criticism, to "phenomenologize," in the wake of Merleau-Ponty, the subject of literature and psychoanalysis: "the latent is best defined as the implicit, what is manifest *within* what is said and not behind it."[57] We touch here on that *continualist* prejudice which was one target of Genette's critique of Richard's reading of Mallarmé.

The critique of the notion that psychoanalysis and phenomenology were convergent (and not conflicting) endeavors, a notion Starobinski develops in his essay, had been one of the aims of a classical article on the unconscious by our next two authors, the analysts Serge Leclaire and Jean Laplanche.[58] One-time disciples of Jacques Lacan (from whom they each eventually took their distances), they may be associated with a shift of perspective on the subject of psychoanalysis and literature. Psychoanalysis was to be looked to not for exemplary solutions to the enigmas of literary criticism (as, say, Mauron or, with more skepticism, Starobinski may have thought) but, rather, as the locus *within the works of Freud* of textual enigmas of unprecedented richness. In this, they partake of a fundamental insight of Lacan, who, in a text aggressively titled *"Lituraterre,"* would write: "for if literary criticism might in effect be renewed, it would be because psychoanalysis is there for the texts to measure up to, the enigma lying on *its* side."[59]

Laplanche and Leclaire, whom Lacan called his two *L*'s or *ailes*, wings—Mallarmé again?—were the authors of two influential works on psychoanalysis published around 1970, each embodying a somewhat different relation between theory and fantasy. Leclaire's *Psychanalyser* was a high-theoretical speculation (by way of Frege's *Foundations of Arithmetic*, the grounding function of zero, and its assumed congruence with the Freudian motif of "castration") intent on engaging the virtually *meaningless* elements (or signifiers) of the unconscience as they surfaced in dream and symptom (as so many letters inscribed on the surface of the body erogenous).[60] Traces of this problematic are evident in *"Le Réel dans le texte,"* which ultimately dismisses the prospect of an other than trivial articulation of psychoanalysis and literature: "No text can bring into play what its very texture has been made to impede. . . ."[61] In Laplanche's *Life and Death in Psychoanalysis*, theory itself was revealed to be *subject* to the pressures of the unconscious.[62] It was a perspective rich with possibilities for the future of reading. Specifically, Laplanche demonstrated that for each of a series of crucial terms in Freud, two different concepts were at work. Moreover, if one strung together the first members of each conceptual doublet, one coherent interpretation emerged. If one strung together the second members, a second interpretation emerged. Thus, the whole of Freud figured as a polemical field of doubly inscribed terms in which two different interpretative schemes were doing battle, as it were, to invest a single terminological apparatus. Now, whereas the first scheme (gradualist, adaptive, and

continualist—the stuff of psychoanalytical ego psychology) existed in utter ignorance of the second (which was structural and discontinualist in perspective),
it quickly emerged that the second scheme mediated nothing so much as a
theory of the inevitability of the error entailed by the first. Freud's text, in sum,
emerged as a theory of irreducible blindness—repression—that was necessarily blind to its own functioning. It is that perspective, the fading of metalanguage, that is succinctly evoked in Laplanche's aptly titled essay, "*Interpréter
[avec] Freud*" ("Interpreting [with] Freud"), a text whose reference to the "almost kaleidoscopic" shifts in the structure of Freud's writings may recall the
kaleidoscopic properties of the Mallarmé corpus discussed above.[63]

We have reproduced a fragment of Laplanche's lectures on "castration" both
because they offer a superb example of the reversal-through-double-
inscription just evoked and because they signal a crucial break with Lacan,
who was inclined (as was Freud) to see in "castration" a bedrock of the unconscious.[64] For Laplanche, the fate of "castration" is played out in terms of the
twin valences of the term "anxiety." In a first sense, anxiety is nothing so much
as dammed up libido, a free-floating almost qualityless affect that, for lack of
an outlet, tends to overwhelm the subject. In a second sense, anxiety would
figure as a defense mechanism, a vaccinelike exposure to a real or fantasied
danger that would in turn mobilize the defenses of the subject. (In another
context, in order to dramatize the double inscription, I have referred to these
two versions of anxiety respectively as that of a toxin, and that of a tocsin.[65])
The second theory (of anxiety as a defense) is frequently referred to as more
sophisticated than the earlier abandoned theory, and that because the obvious
solution to the subject's predicament as originally construed (finding a suitable
sexual outlet) could only provoke smirks. And yet there is a glaring naiveté at
the heart of its sophistication, for Freud maintained that the prototype of the
dangers generative of anxiety was an actual threat of castration. The prospect,
even for fin-de-siècle Vienna, seems ludicrous. Now, just as there is a striking
naiveté at the center of the "sophisticated" theory, there is a surprising measure
of sophistication in the earlier "naive" theory. For one thing, the notion of a
free-floating psychical energy erupting in lieu of instinctual gratification or satisfaction appears structurally identical to the crucial emergence of the sexual
drive from the *instinct* it supplants, as described in *Three Essays on the Theory of
Sexuality*.[66] Second, Freud, in his "naive" theory, posits a defense mechanism
specific to the danger of being submerged by anxiety. That mechanism is phobia, the invention of a ludicrously unreal external danger as a decoy for all the
energy threatening to overwhelm and paralyze the subject from within. Of a
sudden, the sophistication of the "naive" theory becomes patent. A perfect example of that ludicrously unreal danger would be the threat of castration in the
second, "sophisticated" theory. In sum, the interplay between the sophisticated
theory with its central naiveté and the naive theory with its hidden, structural

sophistication takes on the contours of a chiasmus—and that figure, in turn, offers us nothing so much as the wherewithal to view "castration" as a phobic formation within Freud's own theory.

But if such is the case, it opens up the possibility of liberating analysis from the limitations of a narrow insistence on the absoluteness of sexual difference. Liberation indeed: May '68 was in the air, and there were few more characteristic critical gestures at the time than the abrupt positing of the limitations (or repressive aspects) of "castration," a theory of traumatic difference that had previously figured as emblem of the repressed par excellence. The brief texts we have assembled under the rubric "castration"—along with others I shall refer to—give a sense of the dimensions of the change. The first selection is Alexandre Kojève's curious meditation on the boytoys parading through Françoise Sagan's novels.[67] Kojève was, of course, one of the intellectual lights of the interwar years, the master of a famed Hegel seminar widely acknowledged to have been a model of Lacan's postwar seminar on Freud. Kojève's genius, as we have already indicated, lay in reading the nihilistic vision of Nietzsche's "last men" into the presumably triumphant end of history as envisaged by Hegel. One of the measures of that nihilism was that absolute waning of virility—call it castration—characterizing the increasingly Americanized Europe of the postwar years. Whence Kojève's text of 1956 on the "emasculated world" of modernity. It is a view fully in keeping with Lacan's perspective. With exquisite timing, Kojève would die of heart failure during the parodic end of history of May (in fact, early June) 1968.

Beyond the case of Kojève, it is tempting to define the much-debated distinction between structuralism and what has been called in this country "poststructuralism" in terms of a changed perspective vis-à-vis the category of "castration." Laplanche, whose expert dismantling of the concept we have summarized, had earlier been the author of a study of Hölderlin centered on the role played by the "absence of a lack" (*l'absence d'un défaut*), the "foreclosure" of the father's "castration" as the key genetic factor in the poet's psychosis.[68] Derrida, in a text marginally devoted to Michel Leiris, conflated his twin adversaries of logocentrism and phallocentrism.[69] In *Logique du sens* (*The Logic of Sense*), Gilles Deleuze had been intent on rescuing "the phallus as surface image" and "a new castration" from the threat of absorption by its degraded parodies.[70] A few years later, he joined Félix Guattari in a notorious attack on the pertinence of the category of castration: "We are far from done singing the litany of all we don't know about the unconscious; it is no less indifferent to castration than to the Oedipal, just as it knows nothing of parents, gods, law, and lack. . . ."[71] Under the rubric of the "shifting fate of a keystone concept: 'castration,'" we have also inscribed fragments of two bravura analyses of a famed Balzac novella, "Sarrasine." On the one hand, Roland Barthes's *S/Z* and its central affirmation: "Z is the inaugural letter of Zambinella, the initial of castration, in such manner that through that spelling error installed at the heart of his name, in the center of his body, Sarrasine contemplates in Zambinella his own castration."[72] On the other, Michel Serres's *L'Hermaphrodite: Sarrasine sculpteur*: Hermes encounters Aphrodite in the imperative to "exclude exclusion," the utter antithesis of Laplanche's *Hölderlin* with its lament over the "absence of a lack."[73] Finally, we have included pages from a classic of French feminism, an excerpt from Luce Irigaray's *Speculum de l'autre femme* (*Speculum of the Other Woman*) on the untenability of a female "castration complex," "the blind spot in a hoary dream of symmetry."[74]

The Mallarméan node with which we began has thus given way to a Freudo-Mallarméan node (which is just as often an anti-Freudo–Mallarméan node). Its ramifications are far-reaching indeed. Bachelard's shift from a "psychoanalytic" to a "phenomenological" model, the subject of one of our selections, is an offshoot. Althusser's effort to read Marx in congruence with Lacan's reading of Freud—the "specular" formations of ideology for narcissism, the "epistemological *coupure*, cut or rift" for "castration"—derives from it. (Indeed, Rancière's post-'68 critique of Althusser and the "epistemological *coupure*"— between ideology and science—was fully congruent with post-'68 critiques of "castration.") The list might be extended through other authors in our volume: Hélène Cixous on "male narcissism"; Philippe Sollers (whose idiosyncratic blend of philo-Semitism and anti-feminism has made him the French intelligentsia's exemplary "male narcissist") in the Freudo–Marxian eclecticism of his "Thèses générales"; Julia Kristeva, whose "semanalytic" efforts here take as their touchstone the Lacanian rereading of Freud's famous tag: *"Wo es war soll Ich werden"*; Serge Daney on voice in a Bresson film as object of desire; Georges Perec and Philippe Lejeune's discussion of the literary use to which that novelist's own psychoanalysis has been put in the autobiographical fiction *W*.

How, then, end this admittedly centripetal excursus?

Allusively.

Undecidably.

As though all the rest might (not) be literature.

NOTES

[1] The metaphor of text as "radioactive tracer" is borrowed from George Steiner's remarks on the vicissitudes of Homer in English, *No Passion Spent* (New Haven: Yale University Press, 1996), p. 93

[2] Mauron's books devoted entirely or in part to Mallarmé are *Mallarmé l'obscur* (Paris: Denoël, 1941); *Introduction à la psychanalyse de Mallarmé* (Neuchâtel: La Baconnière, 1950) [*Introduction to the Psychoanalysis of Mallarmé*, trans. Archibald Henderson, Jr., Will L. McLendon (Berkeley: University of California Press, 1963)]; *Des métaphores obsédantes au mythe personnel* (Paris: Corti, 1963); and *Mallarmé par lui-même* (Paris: Seuil, 1964).

[3] Among the others are E. Noulet, J. Scherer, and Mallarmé's biographer, H. Mondor.

[4] Claude Lévi-Strauss, *La Pensée sauvage* (Paris: Plon, 1962) [*The Savage Mind* (Chicago, University of Chicago Press, 1966)]: "Such logic works a bit in the manner of a kaleidoscope."

[5] Jean-Paul Sartre, *Mallarmé: la lucidité et sa face d'ombre* (Paris: Gallimard, 1986). [*Mallarmé, or the Poet of Nothingness*, trans. E. Sturm (University Park: Pennsylvania State Press, 1988)].

[6] For an insightful discussion of straying hands in Sartre, see D. Hollier, *"Etude de mains"* in *Politique de la prose: Sartre et l'an quarante* (Paris: Gallimard, 1982) [*The Politics of Prose: Essay on Sartre*, trans. Jeffrey Mehlman (Minneapolis: University of Minnesota Press, 1986)].

[7] *Les Mains sales,* Sartre's virtuoso dramatic exploitation of the metaphor of dirty hands, appeared in 1948.

[8] See S. B. Drury, "The Triumph of the Last Man," in *Alexandre Kojève: The Roots of Postmodern Politics* (New York: St. Martin's, 1994), pp. 79–87.

[9] Maurice Blanchot, *L'Espace littéraire* (Paris: Gallimard, 1955) [*The Space of Literature*, trans. A. Smock (Lincoln: University of Nebraska Press, 1982)].

[10] Ibid., p. 44.

[11] *Des Métaphores obsédantes au mythe personnel*, p. 234.

[12] See E. Kris, *Psychoanalytic Explorations in Art* (New York: International Universities Press, 1952).

[13] For an extended discussion of the stakes in that question, as posed by Freud, see Jean Laplanche, *Nouveaux fondements pour la psychanalyse: la séduction originaire* (Paris: P.U.F., 1987) [*New Foundations for Psychoanalysis*, trans. D. Macey (Oxford: Blackwell, 1989)].

[14] Jean-Pierre Richard, *L'Univers imaginaire de Mallarmé* (Paris: Seuil, 1961).

[15] Ibid., p. 14.

[16] Ibid., p. 18.

[17] Gaston Bachelard, *La Psychanalyse du feu* (Paris: Gallimard, 1938); an influential republication appeared in 1965 [*The Psychoanalysis of Fire*, trans. A. Ross (Boston: Beacon, 1964)].

[18] Richard, *L'Univers*, p. 22.

[19] Gérard Genette, *"Bonheur de Mallarmé?"* in *Figures* (Paris: Seuil, 1966), p. 94.

[20] *Des Métaphores*, pp. 45–46.

[21] Lacan's essays were collected in *Ecrits* (Paris: Seuil, 1966) [*Ecrits,* trans. A. Sheridan (New York: Norton, 1977)].

[22] Michel Foucault, "Le *Mallarmé* de J.-P. Richard," *Annales: Economies, sociétés, civilisations* (Sep.–Oct. 1964), pp. 996–1004.

[23] "Jean-Paul Sartre répond," *L'Arc* 30 (1966), pp. 87–96. In that interview, Sartre referred to Foucault's *The Order of Things* as "the last defense the bourgeoisie was able to erect against Marx."

[24] "Le *Mallarmé* de J.-P. Richard," p. 430.

[25] Foucault would elaborate the joint domain of power–knowledge (*pouvoir–savoir*) and its epistemologico-juridical formations in *Surveiller et punir: naissance de la prison* (Paris: Gallimard, 1975) [*Discipline and Punish: The Birth of the Prison*, trans. Alan Sheridan (New York: Vintage, 1973)] and *La Volonté de savoir* (Paris: Gallimard, 1976) [*The History of Sexuality*, vol. 1, trans. Robert Hurley (New York: Random House, 1978)].

[26] Martin Heidegger, *"Zur Seinsfrage"* (Frankfurt: Klostermann, 1956).

[27] Jacques Derrida, *"La Double séance,"* in *La Dissémination* (Paris: Seuil, 1972), pp. 199–317 [*Dissemination,* trans. Barbara Johnson (Chicago: University of Chicago Press, 1981)].

[28] Julien Gracq, *Lettrines* (Paris: Corti, 1967), p. 57: "One would have preferred it to be written in a more hierarchical language, one more mindful of the external signs of respect—like the splendid German language in which every noun explodes behind its capital."

[29] Raymond Picard, *Nouvelle Critique ou nouvelle imposture* (Paris: Pauvert, 1965) [*New Criticism or New Fraud?*, trans. F. Towne (Pullman: Washington State University Press, 1969)].

[30] "*Comment parler de la littérature,*" *Le Débat* 29 (March 1984).

[31] Antoine Compagnon, "Le Débat du *Débat,*" *Le Débat* 32 (Nov. 1984), p. 178.

[32] "*La Littérature entre son présent et son passé: un échange,*" *Le Débat* 79 (March-April 1994).

[33] "La Conversation," *Trois Institutions littéraires* (Paris: Gallimard, 1994), pp. 171, 132.

[34] Marc Fumaroli, *L'Age de l'éloquence: rhétorique et 'res literaria' de la Renaissance au seuil de l'époque classique* (Geneva: Droz, 1980), p. 30.

[35] Philippe Sollers, "*Littérature et Totalité,*" *Logiques* (Paris: Seuil, 1968), pp. 97–117.

[36] Marc Fumaroli, "*La littérature entre son présent et son passé,*" p. 24.

[37] In his *Theory of Heat* (1871), Maxwell wrote: "Now let us suppose that . . . a vessel is divided into two portions, A and B, by a division in which there is a small hole, and that a being, who can see the individual molecules, opens and closes this hole, so as to allow only the swifter molecules to pass from A to B, and only the slower ones to pass from B to A. He will thus, without expenditure of work, raise the temperature of B and lower that of A, in contradiction to the second law of thermodynamics." See as well Jeffrey Mehlman, "Mallarmé/Maxwell: Elements," *Romanic Review* 21.4 (Nov. 1980), pp. 374–80.

[38] Jean Hyppolite, "*Le 'Coup de dés' de Mallarmé et le message,*" *Figures de la pensée philosophique* (Paris: P.U.F., 1971), pp. 877–84. Due to space limitations, Hyppolite's essay has not been included in this collection.

[39] See, in particular, Michel Serres, *Feux et signaux de brume: Zola* (Paris: Grasset, 1975) and *La Naissance de la physique dans le texte de Lucrèce: fleuves et turbulences* (Paris: Minuit, 1977).

[40] Gilles Deleuze, *Nietzsche et la philosophie* (Paris: P.U.F., 1962), pp. 36–39 [*Nietzsche and Philosophy*, trans. Hugh Tomlinson (New York: Columbia University Press, 1983)].

[41] Ibid., p. 38.

[42] Jacques Rancière, *Mallarmé: la politique de la sirène* (Paris: Hachette, 1996).

[43] *Lire le Capital* (Paris: Maspero, 1973), vol. 3 [selections of the full work have been published in *Reading "Capital"*, trans. Ben Brewster (London: NLB, 1970)].

[44] Jacques Rancière, *La Leçon d'Althusser* (Paris: Gallimard, 1974).

[45] The perspective is compatible with that articulated by Foucault during the same years: *pouvoir* and *savoir* were said to be part and parcel of a single juridico-epistemological formation.

[46] Rancière, *Mallarmé*, p. 65.

[47] Ibid., p. 64.

[48] Charles Mauron, *L'Inconscient dans l'oeuvre et la vie de Racine* (Gap: Ophrys, 1957).

[49] See the selection from Nathalie Sarraute, *The Age of Suspicion* in Part IV of this volume.

[50] Roland Barthes, *Sur Racine* (Paris: Seuil, 1963), p. 9 [*Racine*, trans. Richard Howard (New York: Hill and Wang, 1964)].

[51] Picard, *Nouvelle critique*, p. 141: "*To surrealize*—and in the name of an utterly academic Surrealism—the whole of French literature in order to situate it in a perspective of the 'disordering of all the senses' is tantamount to putting a mustache on Mona Lisa or playing a Chopin funeral march as jazz. . . ."

[52] Roland Barthes, *Critique et vérité* (Paris: Seuil, 1966), p. 27 [*Criticism and Truth,* trans. K. P. Keuneman (Minneapolis: University of Minnesota Press, 1987)].

[53] Gérard Genette, "Psycholectures," *Figures* (Paris: Seuil, 1966), p. 134.

[54] Jean Laplanche, "*La Psychanalyse: mythes et théorie*," *Revue philosophique* 2 (1997), pp. 205–224.

[55] Ibid., p. 223.

[56] Its telling distinction between superimposition and comparison may be usefully confronted with the parallel structuralist distinction between "homologies" (between sets of relations) and "analogies" (between terms).

[57] Jean Starobinski, "*Psychanalyse et littérature*," in *La Relation critique* (Paris: Gallimard, 1970), p. 282.

[58] Jean Laplanche and Serge Leclaire, "*L'Inconscient, une étude psychanalytique*," *Les Temps modernes* 183, pp. 81–129.

[59] Jacques Lacan, "*Lituraterre*," *Littérature* 3 (1971), p. 5.

[60] Serge Leclaire, *Psychanalyser* (Paris: Seuil, 1968) [*Psychoanalyzing: On the Order of the Unconscious and the Practice of the Letter,* trans. P. Kamuf (Stanford: Stanford University Press, 1998)].

[61] Serge Leclaire, "*Le Réel dans le texte*," *Littérature* 3, (1971), p. 32.

[62] Jean Laplanche, *Vie et mort en psychanalyse* (Paris: Flammarion, 1970). See as well Jeffrey Mehlman's introduction to the English translation, *Life and Death in Psychoanalysis* (Baltimore: Johns Hopkins University Press, 1976).

[63] Jean Laplanche, "*Interpréter [avec] Freud*," *L'Arc* 34 (1968), pp. 37–46.

[64] See Freud, "Analysis Terminable and Interminable" *International Journal of Psychoanalysis*, 18 (1937); and Lacan, "*La Signification du phallus*," in *Ecrits* (Paris: Seuil, 1966), pp 685–95 ["The Signification of the Phallus," in *Ecrits*, trans. Alan Sheridan (New York: W. W. Norton 1977), pp. 281–91].

[65] Jeffrey Mehlman, *Revolution and Repetition: Marx/Hugo/Balzac* (Berkeley: University of California Press, 1977).

[66] See Laplanche, *Vie et mort*, ch. 1. The *drive* in Laplanche's energetic reading is said to be "propped" on the *instinct*. Its object is displaced, in the case of the prototypal case of orality, from milk to breast; its aim is metaphorized from ingestion to "incorporation." Later in Freud's thought, the very term "propping" (or "leaning on," *sich anlehnen*) will emerge *in repressed form* as part of Freud's jargon: "anaclisis" (*Anlehnung*) designates a form of "object choice."

[67] Alexandre Kojève, "*Le Dernier monde nouveau*," *Critique*, 60 (1956), pp. 702–708.

[68] Laplanche, *Hölderlin et la question du père* (Paris: P.U.F., 1961), p. 132.

[69] Jacques Derrida, "Tympan," *Marges—de la philosophie* (Paris: Minuit, 1972) [*Margins of Philosophy*, trans. Alan Bass (Chicago: University of Chicago Press, 1982)].

[70] Gilles Deleuze, *Logique du sens* (Paris: Minuit, 1969), pp. 236, 237 [*Logic of Sense*, trans. Mark Lester (New York: Columbia Univesity Press, 1990)].

[71] Gilles Deleuze and Félix Guattari, *Anti-Oedipe* (Paris: Minuit, 1972), p. 71 [*Anti-Oedipus: Capitalism and Schizophrenia*, trans. Robert Hurley, Mark Seem, Helen Lane (New York: Viking, 1977)].

[72] Roland Barthes, *S/Z* (Paris: Seuil, 1970), p. 113 [*S/Z*, trans. Richard Miller (New York: Hill and Wang, 1974)].

[73] Michel Serres, *L'Hermaphrodite: Sarrasine sculpteur* (Paris: Grasset, 1987), p. 87.

[74] Luce Irigaray, *Speculum de l'autre femme* (Paris: Minuit, 1974), pp. 99–102 [*Speculum of the Other Woman*, trans. Gillian Gill (Ithaca: Cornell University Press, 1985)].

PART III

The Central Case
of Mallarmé

JEAN-PAUL SARTRE

Requiem for a Poet: Mallarmé 1953

Sartre's pungent introduction to Mallarmé is a miniature existential psychoanalysis. As with Baudelaire and Genet, whom Sartre analyzed as well, Mallarmé's story is that of a rebellion—or will to negation—so absolute that it ends up negating itself: a "Stoic" challenge to reality, in the philosopher's Kojèvian formulation, culminates in a "skepticism" which undermines that very challenge. "Necessity" and "chance" play "master" and "slave" in an ultimately Hegelian reading of the poet's failure—to do more than intuit *the realm of freedom that Sartre's existentialism had staked out as the principal aspiration of genuine literature.*

Quite early in life, Mallarmé feels a rebellion welling up inside him which cannot find an outlet. Son and grandson of civil servants, brought up by a deplorable grandmother, he contests everything—family, society, Nature—even the pale and pitiable child whose reflection he glimpses in the mirror. The effectiveness of his defiance, however, is inversely proportional to its scope. To be sure, he must blow up the world. But how can he do so without soiling his hands? A bomb is just another object—like an Empire armchair, only a little nastier. How many intrigues and compromises are needed just to find the exact spot to plant it! Mallarmé was not and would never become an anarchist. He rejects any form of individual action. So desperate and absolute is his violence (and I say this without irony) that it turns into the impassive idea of violence. No, he will not blow up the world—he will merely place it within brackets. He opts for a terrorism of politeness. Always keeping an imperceptible distance from men, from things and from himself, his uppermost concern will be to express this distance in his poetry.

In his first poems, Mallarmé views the poetic act primarily as *recreation*. He needs to reassure himself that he is really where he ought to be. For him, writ-

Jean-Paul Sartre, "Requiem for a Poet: Mallarmé (1842–1898)," in Sartre, *Mallarmé, or the Poet of Nothingness*, trans. Ernest Sturm (University Park: Pennsylvania State University Press, 1988), from *Mallarmé: la Lucidité et sa face d'ombre* (Paris: Gallimard, 1986).

ing is a way of obliterating his detestable background. As Blanchot puts it, the
world of prose is self-contained; we shouldn't expect it to provide us with reasons to go beyond it. The reason the poet can isolate a poetic object in the world
is that he is governed by the imperatives of Poetry. To put it simply, he is engendered by it. Mallarmé always considered his "vocation" to be a categorical
imperative. What motivates him is neither the urgent character of his impressions nor the richness of the violence of his feelings. It is *a command*: "Your
writings will testify to the fact that you keep the Universe at a distance." Indeed, his first poems have no other subject than Poetry itself. It has been
pointed out that the Ideal constantly invoked in his (youthful) poems remains
an abstraction, simply negation in poetic dress. It will be his excuse: the resentment and hatred that make him flee from Being are covered up by the pretext
that his flight from Being is only a way of approaching the ideal.

But this would have entailed a belief in God; it is God who guarantees Poetry. In the preceding generation, poets had been minor prophets; God spoke
through their lips. But Mallarmé no longer believes in God. Yet when ruined
ideologies collapse, they don't collapse all at once; whole sections of the edifice
remain intact in people's minds. Even after killing God single-handedly, Mallarmé still sought divine approval. Poetry still had to remain transcendent,
even though he had eliminated the origin of all transcendence. With the death
of God, inspiration could only derive from corrupt sources. On *what* premise
could the necessity of poetry be established? Mallarmé could still hear the voice
of God, but in it he discerns the faint cries of Nature. So it was that one evening
he heard someone whispering in his room; was it the wind . . . or his ancestors? It is, of course, true that poems cannot draw inspiration in the prose of the
world; that a poem must have a prior existence; that before setting it down on
paper one can inwardly hear its song. But all this is the result of a mystification;
since the new poem striving to be born is in fact an old one seeking rebirth. It
turns out that the poems on our lips, which claim to arise from our heart, in fact
arise from our memory. Inspiration? No, mere recollection. Somewhere in the
future, Mallarmé catches a glimpse of a youthful figure of himself; beckoning
to him. He approaches it—it was his father. Time seems to be an illusion, the
future is nothing but the aberrant form in which the past appears to man. This
despair, which Mallarmé at that time called his "impotence"—for he tended to
reject any source of inspiration or any poetic theme other than the abstract and
formal concept of Poetry—drives him to postulate a full-fledged metaphysical
system, a vaguely Spinozist kind of analytical materialism. Nothing exists but
matter, the incessantly rippling waves of Being.

Waxing or waning, space is ever space.

From man's point of view, his own appearance transforms the eternal into the
temporal and the infinite into the contingent. Of course, *in itself,* an infinite and
eternal series of causes is all that could be; some all-knowing intelligence might

THE CENTRAL CASE OF MALLARMÉ

be able to comprehend its absolute necessity; but to a finite mode, the world appears to be an endless and absurd succession of chance encounters. If such is the case, then the reasons produced by our reason are just as mad as those coming from the heart. The principles guiding our thoughts as well as the categories of our actions are mirages: Man is an impossible dream. In this respect, the Poet's impotence symbolizes Man's impossibility. There is but one tragedy, ever the same, a tragedy resolved "immediately, in the very time it takes to disclose the unfolding of a dazzling defeat." In this tragedy:

> He casts the dice. . . . He who creates discovers he is once again matter, blocks, dice.

Once there *were* dice, now there *are* dice: once there *were* words, now there *are* words. And Man? A volatile illusion flitting over matter in movement. Mallarmé, a creature of pure matter, strives to produce an order superior to matter. His impotence is *theological*. For the poet, the death of God imposes the obligation to replace him. At this he fails. For Mallarmé, just as for Pascal, Man expresses himself in terms of drama and not in terms of essence. As "the latent lord who cannot become," he defines himself by his impossibility. "The insanity of the game of writing consists in assuming—solely by virtue of a doubt—some sort of obligation to re-create everything merely out of reminiscences." But "Nature simply exists; nothing can be added to it." During periods in which the way forward is blocked by the sheer bulk of a royal presence or by the complete triumph of a social class, poetic invention appears as pure reminiscence. You have arrived too late—everything has already been said. It would not be long before Ribot would turn this impotence into a theory by conflating our mental images with our memories. We can observe Mallarmé's pessimistic metaphysics: within matter—that shapeless infinity—there seems to be some deep-seated need to turn back on itself in order to know itself. To shed light on its obscure infinity, matter seems to produce those shreds of fire, those tatters of thought, called Man. But infinite dispersion takes hold of the Idea and scatters it. Man and contingency arise simultaneously and engender one another. Man is failure, "a stunted wolf in a pack of wolves." His greatness consists in living out his flawed nature until it finally explodes.

Hasn't the time come to explode? In Tournon, in Besançon, in Avignon, Mallarmé very seriously contemplated suicide. At first it seems to follow logically: if indeed Man is impossible, then this impossibility must be manifested by pushing it to the point of self-destruction. For once, matter couldn't be the cause of our action. Being engenders only Being. If, as the result of his own non-possibility, the Poet chooses Nonbeing, then his negation is the cause of Nothingness. Through Man's very disappearance a human order sets itself up against Being. Before Mallarmé, Flaubert had already tempted Saint Anthony in these words: "Do away with yourself. Do something which will make you God's equal! Think of it: He created you and now you shall use your courage and your freedom to destroy his handiwork." Isn't this what he always wanted? The suicide he is contemplating has the makings of a terrorist crime. Hadn't he said that suicide and crime were the only *supernatural* acts one could commit? Certain people seem to confuse their personal drama with that of humanity as a whole: this is what saves them. Mallarmé never doubts for an instant that, should he kill himself, the human race would perish with him. His suicide is thus a form of genocide; by his disappearing, Being would be restored in all its purity.

As contingency arises with Man, so will it disappear with him. "The infinite finally breaks loose from the family it has afflicted—ancient space—without chance. . . . This was to take place in the combinations of the Infinite when it confronts the Absolute. Necessary—extracts the Idea." Slowly, with each succeeding generation, the poetic idea brooded over the contradiction that renders it impossible. The death of God removed the last veil: it was the lot of this last offspring of the race to live out this contradiction in all its purity—and to die of it, thus writing the suitably poetic ending to human history. As sacrifice and genocide, man's affirmation as well as his negation, Mallarmé's suicide will reproduce the movement of the dice. Matter is once again matter.

If the crisis was not then and there resolved by his death, it was because of the "absolute lightning bolt" that came and rattled his windowpanes. From this searing experience of his imagined suicide, Mallarmé suddenly discovers his doctrine. If suicide is a successful solution, that is because it replaces the abstract and futile negation of all Being by an *act* of negation. To put it in Hegelian terms, by mediating on this absolute act, Mallarmé passes from "Stoicism," the purely formal affirmation of thought confronted with existence, to Skepticism, "the realization of that of which Stoicism is only the notion. . . . [In skepticism] thought achieves perfection, annihilating the being of the world with its *manifold determinations*; and the negativity of self-consciousness . . . becomes real negativity."

Mallarmé's first step was to back away in an attitude of universal condemnation and disgust. Driven to the top of his spiral, the heir "didn't dare budge" for fear of falling. But now he realizes that universal negation is tantamount to the absence of negation. Negation is an act; every act must take place in time and apply to a specific content. Suicide is an act because it effectively destroys a human being, and because it leaves the world haunted by an absence. If Being is dispersion, Man, in losing his being, achieves an incorruptible unity; better yet, his absence has an astringent effect on the being of the Universe—like Aristotelian forms, absence constricts things and imbues them with its secret unity. What the poem must reproduce is the very movement of the suicidal act. Since Man cannot create but still retains the capacity to destroy, since he affirms himself in the very act that annihilates him, the poem will thus be a labor of destruction. From the vantage point of death, Poetry will be, as Blanchot so nicely puts it, "that language, all of whose strength consists in not being, and all of whose glory consists in evoking, by its own absence, the absence of every-thing." Mallarmé can proudly write to Lefébure that Poetry has become *criti-cal*. Putting himself totally at risk, Mallarmé saw his essence as a man and a poet now disclosed in the light of death. He does not give up his *all-encompassing* defiance; he simply renders it effective. Soon he would be able to write that "poems are the only real bombs." He even reaches the point where he sometimes believes that he has in fact killed himself.

It is no accident that Mallarmé writes the word "Nothing" [*Rien*] on the first page of his complete works. Since the poem is both the suicide of Man and of Poetry . . . Being must ultimately reabsorb this death; the moment of Poet-ry's fulfillment must correspond to the moment of its annihilation. Thus, the truth these poems have come to embody is Nothingness.

> NOTHING . . .
> WILL HAVE TAKEN PLACE . . .
> BUT THE PLACE (ITSELF).

He is known for the extraordinary negative logic he invented: how, by means of his pen, a lace bedspread abolishes itself, lace curtains abolish each other, revealing only the absence of a bed: while the "vase, pure of any liquid" ago-nizes without ever consenting to exhale anything foretelling an invisible rose, or how a grave is burdened only with "the very absence of weighty wreaths."

> This virginal, fair and lively today

offers a perfect example of this inner annulment of the poem. Today, with its implied future, is pure illusion; the present is reduced to the past; a swan then remembers itself and, without hope, becomes frozen "in dreams of icy scorn"; the semblance of movement vanishes, leaving only the infinite, undifferenti-ated surface of the ice. The explosion of colors and shapes reveals to our senses a tangible symbol reminding us of Man's tragedy—that, in turn, dissolves into Nothingness. Such is the inner motion of these unprecedented poems, which are at once silent words and sham objects. In the final analysis, their very disap-pearance evokes the outlines of some "fleeting object whose absence was felt," and whose very beauty would offer a priori proof that *a lack of being* constitutes *a way of being.*

The proof is faulty. Mallarmé is lucid enough to realize that no particular experience could ever contradict the principles in whose name it was estab-lished. If chance appears at the outset, "no throw of the dice shall ever abolish it." "In an act involving chance, chance always realizes its own Idea by affirm-ing or negating itself."

In the poem, chance negates itself; poetry, born of chance and struggling against it, abolishes chance by abolishing itself, since what it symbolically abol-ishes is Man. In the last analysis, all this is mere "trickery." Mallarmé's irony arises from the fact that he is simultaneously aware of the utter futility of his

work and of its absolute necessity, and that, furthermore, he can discern this
pair of opposites which constantly engender and repel one another but can
never be synthesized: chance creating necessity, the illusion of Man—this part
of Nature gone mad—necessity creating chance, that which limits it and defines it *a contrario*, necessity destroying chance "word by word" in his verse,
chance in turn destroying necessity since words cannot be "fully employed,"
and then finally, necessity abolishing chance in the suicide of the Poem and
Poetry. In Mallarmé, there is an unhappy mystifier; for the benefit of his
friends and disciples he created and maintained the illusion of a grandiose
work in which the whole world would suddenly be dissolved. He claimed to be
preparing himself for it. But he knew perfectly well that it was impossible. It
was just that even his own life should seem to be subordinated to this absent
object—that is, the orphic explanation of the Earth (which is merely Poetry
itself); and I'm not so sure that he didn't conceive of his death as something that
would perpetuate this relationship to orphism as the poet's highest ambition,
and of his failure as the tragic impossibility of Man. A poet dead at the age of
twenty-five, killed by a sense of his own impotence—this wouldn't make any
headlines. But a fifty-six-year-old poet who dies just as he has finally acquired a
mastery that will allow him to embark on his magnum opus—this is the *very
embodiment of Man's tragedy*. Mallarmé's death is a memorable mystification.

But it is a mystification *by way of the truth:* For thirty years Mallarmé, the
"true histrion of himself," enacted to the world the one-character tragedy he
had so often dreamed of writing. He was the "latent lord who would never
become one, everyman's youthful shadow, hence a votary of myth," imposing
on the living "a subtle and faded eclipse through the disquieting and mournful
encroachment of his presence." According to the complex rules of this drama,
his poems *had* to fail in order to achieve perfection.

These had to do more than merely abolish language and the world, more
than even destroy themselves, they also had to be the fruitless outlines of an
impossible and unheard-of masterpiece that an untimely death prevented him
from undertaking. Everything *falls into place* if one considers these symbolic
suicides in the light of an accidental death and Being in the light of Nothingness. By an unforeseen about-face, this dreadful shipwreck imparts an absolute
necessity to each poem he created. Their most poignant meaning arises from
the fact that, while they fire our enthusiasm, their author attached no importance to them. He gave them a finishing touch when, on the eve of his death, he
pretended only to think about his future work, writing to his wife and daughter: "Believe me, it was to have been beautiful." True? Or false? But it is Man
himself, the very man Mallarmé aspires to be: Man everywhere dying from
the disintegration of atoms or from the cooling-down of the sun and mur-
muring—at the thought of a society he had wished to construct: "Believe me, it
was to be beautiful."

Hero, prophet, wizard, tragedian—it is fitting that this discreet and effemi-

nate man with little interest in women should die at the threshold of our century: he is its herald. More profoundly than Nietzsche, he experienced the
death of God. Long before Camus, he felt that suicide was the fundamental
issue facing Man. Later, others would take up his ceaseless struggle against
contingency without ever going beyond his lucidity, for his basic question was:
Can we ever find within determinism a way out of it? Can we reverse praxis
and rediscover our subjectivity by reducing both the universe and ourselves to
objectivity? He systematically applied to Art what was still merely a philosophical principle and later would become a political maxim: "Create and by
creating, create yourself." Shortly before the large-scale development of technology, he devised a technique of Poetry. At the very time that Taylor conceived of mobilizing men so as to render their work more efficient, he
mobilized language so as to assure the optimal yield from Words. What seems
to me even more touching was the metaphysical anguish he experienced so
fully, yet so modestly. Not a day went by that he wasn't tempted to kill himself,
and, if he went on living, it was only because of his daughter. But his reprieve
lent him a sort of enchanting and destructive irony. His "native illumination,"
consisted above all in the art of finding and establishing in his day-to-day existence, and even in his way of perception, "an erosive correspondence" to which
he submitted all objects of this world. He was a poet to the core, wholly committed to the critical self-destruction of Poetry; and yet, at the same time, he
remained removed from it. This sylph of cold ceilings contemplates himself: if
matter produces thought, then lucid thought about matter might just, perhaps,
escape determinism. In this way, even his poetry would be enclosed within
brackets. One day he received some drawings that pleased him: of all of them,
he was particularly attached to a picture of a sadly smiling old magus: "Because," he said, "he knows perfectly well that his art is an imposture. Yet he also
seems to be saying, *It might have been the truth."*

TRANSLATED BY ERNEST STURM

Mallarmé's Experience Proper *and* The Central Point
1952

This fragment from Blanchot's The Space of Literature (L'Espace lit-téraire) *speculates on Mallarmé's illustration of the Heideggerian proposition that poetry at its most intense is a will to identify with its own essence—whence the insistence on Mallarmé's fascination with the word* c'est. *But language in Blanchot's Mallarmé seems already to have embarked on the "deconstruction" of being we shall observe in our selection from Derrida. Whereas Sartre saw Mallarmé's "Igitur," meditating suicide, as a figure of the poet opting out of history, Blanchot offers that suicide as an allegory of a phenomenon intrinsic to language itself. Whereas Sartre affirmed that Mallarméan suicide had the mitigating virtue of being a willful "deed" or act, Blanchot posits death as a domain incompatible with intentionality: "it is not sure that death is an act." Finally, the work—*oeuvre*—all but dissolves in the passivity or listlessness of what Blanchot calls* désoeuvrement.*

MALLARMÉ'S EXPERIENCE PROPER

It seems that the specifically Mallarméan experience begins at the moment when he moves from consideration of the finished work, which is always one particular poem or another, or a certain picture, to the concern through which the work becomes the search for its origin and wants to identify itself with its origin—"horrid vision of a pure work." Here lies Mallarmé's profundity; here lies the concern which, for Mallarmé, "the sole act of writing" encompasses. What is the work? What is language in the work? When Mallarmé asks himself, "Does something like Literature exist?," this question is literature itself. It is literature when literature has become concern for its own essence. Such a

Maurice Blanchot, *The Space of Literature*, trans. Ann Smock (Lincoln: University of Nebraska Press, 1982), from *L'Espace littéraire* (Paris: Gallimard, 1955).

question cannot be relegated. What is the result of the fact that we have literature? What is implied about being if one states that "something like Literature exists"?

Mallarmé had the most profoundly tormented awareness of the particular nature of literary creation. The work of art reduces itself to being. That is its task—to be, to make present "those very words: *it is* . . . There lies all the mystery."[1] But, at the same time, it cannot be said that the work belongs to being, that it exists. On the contrary, what must be said is that it never exists in the manner of a thing or a being in general. What must be said, in answer to our question, is that literature does not exist or again that, if it takes place, it does so as something "not taking part in the form of any object that exists." Granted, language is present—"made evident"—in it: language is affirmed in literature with more authority than in any other form of human activity. But it is wholly realized in literature, which is to say that it has only the reality of the whole; it is all—and nothing else, always on the verge of passing from all to nothing. This passage is essential; it belongs to the essence of language because, precisely, nothing operates in words. Words, we know, have the power to make things disappear, to make them appear as things that have vanished. This appearance is only that of disappearance; this presence too returns to absence through that movement of wear and erosion which is the soul and the life of words, which draws light from their dimming, clarity from the dark. But words, having the power to make things "arise" at the heart of their absence— words that are masters of this absence—also have the power to disappear in it themselves, to absent themselves marvelously in the midst of the totality they realize, which they proclaim as they annihilate themselves therein, which they accomplish eternally by destroying themselves there endlessly. This act of self-destruction is in every respect similar to the ever so strange event of suicide which, precisely, gives to the supreme instant of *"Igitur"* all its truth.[2]

THE CENTRAL POINT

Such is the central point. Mallarmé always comes back to it as though he were returning to the intimacy of the risk to which the literary experience exposes us. This point is the one at which complete realization of language coincides with its disappearance. Everything is pronounced ("Nothing," as Mallarmé says, "will remain unproffered"); everything is word, yet the word is itself no longer anything but the appearance of what has disappeared—the imaginary, the incessant, and the interminable. This point is ambiguity itself.

On the one hand, in the work, it is what the work realizes, how it affirms itself, the place where the work must "allow no luminous evidence except of existing." In this sense, the central point is the presence of the work, and the work alone makes it present. But, at the same time, this point is "the presence of Midnight," the point anterior to all starting points, from which nothing ever begins, the empty profundity of being's inertia, that region without issue and without reserve, in which the work, through the artist, becomes the concern, the endless search for its origin.

Yes, the center, the concentration of ambiguity. It is very true that only the work—if we come toward this point through the movement and strength of the work—only the accomplishment of the work makes it possible. Let us look again at the poem: what could be more real, more evident? And language itself is "luminous evidence" within it. This evidence, however, shows nothing, rests upon nothing; it is the ungraspable in action. There are neither terms nor moments. Where we think we have words, "a virtual trail of fires" shoots through us—a swiftness, a scintillating exaltation. A reciprocity: for what is not is revealed in this flight; what there isn't is reflected in the pure grace of reflections that do not reflect anything. Then, "everything becomes suspense, fragmentary disposition with alternations and oppositions." Then, just as the tremor of the unreal turned into language gleams only to go out, simultaneously the unfamiliar presence is affirmed of real things turned into pure absence, pure fiction—a glorious realm where "willed and solitary celebrations" shine forth their splendor. One would like to say that the poem, like the pendulum that marks the time of time's abolition in "*Igitur*," oscillates marvelously between its presence as language and the absence of the things of the world. But this presence is itself oscillating in perpetuity: oscillation between the successive unreality of terms that terminate nothing, and the total realization of this movement—language, that is, become the whole of language, where the power of departing from and coming back to nothing, affirmed in each word and annulled in all, realizes itself as a whole, "total rhythm," "with which, silence."

In the poem, language is never real at any of the moments through which it passes, for in the poem language is affirmed in its totality. Yet in this totality, where it constitutes its own essence and where it is essential, it is also supremely unreal. It is the total realization of this unreality, an absolute fiction that says "being" when, having "worn away," "used up" all existing things, having suspended all possible beings, it comes up against an indelible, irreducible residue. What is left? "Those very words, *it is*." Those words sustain all others by letting themselves be hidden by all the others, and hidden thus, they are the presence of all words, language's entire possibility held in reserve. But when all words cease ("the instant they shimmer and die in a swift bloom upon some transparency like ether's"), "those very words, *it is*," present themselves, "lightning moment," "dazzling burst of light."

This lightning moment flashes from the work as the leaping brilliance of the work itself—its total presence all at once, it's "simultaneous vision." This moment is the one at which the work, in order to give being and existence to the "feint"—that "literature exists"—declares the exclusion of everything, but in this way, excludes itself, so that the moment at which "every reality dissolves" by the force of the poem is also the moment the poem dissolves and, instantly done, is instantly undone. This is in itself extremely ambiguous. But the ambiguity touches something more essential. For this moment, which is like the work of the work, which outside of any signification, any historical or esthetic affirmation, declares that the work is, depends on the work's undergoing, at this very same moment, the ordeal that always ruins the work in advance and always restores in it the unending lack of work, the vain superabundance of inertia.

TRANSLATED BY ANN SMOCK

NOTES

[1] A letter to Vielé-Griffin, 8 August 1891: ". . . There is nothing in this that I don't tell myself, less well, in the scattered whispering of my solitary conversations, but where you are the diviner, it is, yes, relative to those very words, *it is*; they are the subject of notes I have been working on, and they reign in the furthest reaches of my mind. There lies all the mystery: to establish the secret identities through a two-by-two which wears and erodes objects, in the name of a central purity."

[2] We refer the reader to another section of *The Space of Literature*, "The Work and Death's Space," the study specifically devoted to the "*Igitur*" experience. This experience can be discussed only when a more central point in literature's space has been reached. In his very important essay, "The Interior Distance", Georges Poulet shows that "*Igitur*" is "a perfect example of philosophic suicide." He suggests thereby that for Mallarmé, the poem depends upon a profound relation to death, and is possible only if death is *possible*: only if, through the sacrifice and strain to which the poet exposes himself, death becomes power and possibility in him, only if it is an act par excellence:

> Death is the only act possible. Cornered as we are between a true material world whose chance combinations take place in us regardless of us, and a false ideal world whose lie paralyzes and bewitches us, we have only one means of no longer being at the mercy either of nothingness or of chance. This unique means, this unique act, is death. Voluntary death. Through it we abolish ourselves, but through it we also found ourselves. . . . It is this act of voluntary death that Mallarmé committed. He committed it in *Igitur*.

We must, however, carry Poulet's remarks further. "*Igitur*" is an abandoned narrative that bears witness to a certitude the poet was unable to maintain. For it is not sure that death is an act; it could be that suicide was not possible. Can I take my own life? Do I have the power to die? *Un Coup de dés jamais n'abolira le hasard* is something like the answer in which this question dwells. And the "answer" intimates that the movement which, in the work, is the experience of death, the approach to it and its use, is not the movement of possibility — not even of nothingness's possibility — but, rather, a movement approaching the point at which the work is put to the test by impossibility.

CHARLES MAURON

Introduction to the
Psychoanalysis of Mallarmé
1950

*Charles Mauron's first volume on Mallarmé was written in collaboration
with the Bloomsbury critic Roger Fry. His last work on the poet was fully
in the orbit of the variety of psychoanalytic criticism he called "psychocritique." The selection below is a key transitional passage from his prepsycho-
analytic to his psychoanalytic periods. In it, we see his impassioned
elaboration of a network of associations traversing verse, letters, and prose
poems, and seeming to converge in the traumatic death of the poet's sister.
Note that it is not the gravity of the trauma but the sheer insistence of the
apparently unintended network—what Mallarmé may have meant by the
"shimmer below"—that Mauron uses to justify his recourse to psychoanalysis. (The two poems alluded to at the end of this selection, "Don du
poème" and "Sainte," are summarized on pp. 169–70.)*

My demonstration relates to what is, in my view, the most important event
in Mallarmé's life: the death of his sister.

MARIA

Maria died at thirteen, when Stéphane was fifteen. What is the significance
usually ascribed to this event? Neither Soula nor Thibaudet mentions it;[1] Mme
Emilie Noulet merely notes the fact in passing.[2] Dr. Mondor, who has furnished us with all the details known on this subject as on so many others, does
not use it as the basis of any psychological evaluation of Mallarmé.[3] As a matter
of fact, Maria's death does not even appear in the biographical chronology of

Charles Mauron, *Introduction to the Psychoanalysis of Mallarmé*, trans. Archibald
Henderson, Jr., and Will L. McLendon (Berkeley: University of California Press, 1963),
from *Introduction à la psychanalyse de Mallarmé* (Neuchâtel: La Baconnière, 1950).

the complete works.[4] By and large, everyone has agreed not to grant any importance to this "poor young phantom." This, in my opinion, is a grave misunderstanding of profoundly significant matters.

Mallarmé's work contains a single text that explicitly mentions Maria and her death. It is *"Plainte d'automne,"* at the opening of *Divagations.*

> Since Maria left me to inhabit another star — which, Orion, Altair, or you, green Venus? — I have always cherished solitude . . . , strangely, oddly, I have loved all that is summed up in this word: downfall [*chute*]. So, in the year, I prefer the last languid days of summer, which immediately precede autumn; in the daytime, I like to go for a walk when the sun is poised just before it vanishes, with rays of yellow copper on the gray walls, and red copper on the window panes . . . a barrel organ played languorously and melancholically under my window. It played in the great avenue of poplars, whose leaves appear dull to me even in spring ever since Maria passed there with candles, one last time. . . .

The reader will forgive the necessary excisions.

When he was about twenty, Mallarmé spoke of the death of his sister as having occurred unexpectedly five years before;[5] he saw it, at that time, as an event of some significance for his inner life. This is the fact. It is a rather surprising fact when we realize that Maria was but a child when she died. This is not to say that a brother cannot be affected for a considerable time by the death of a sister just reaching adolescence. But it does appear extraordinary, one must admit, for this brother, already grown, already a great poet, to give the death of this child sister as the source of his aesthetic tendencies. A hypothesis suggests itself: Mallarmé may have chosen this unhappy event, the most recent in his life, as a theme for the expression of a literary sadness. Against this interpretation, I will cite a second text, which is the letter written by Mallarmé to Cazalis on July 1, 1862;[6] Cazalis had just sent his friend a picture of Ettie Yapp, his beloved. Mallarmé replied:

> There is a touching phrase that illuminates your whole letter; it is, "Accept, my dear Mallarmé, this portrait of our sister." This is easy, since we are brothers, and yet it is very sweet. Yes, she will rank in all my dreams with the Chimènes, the Beatrices, the Juliets, the Réginas, and what is better, in my heart, alongside this poor young phantom who was my sister for thirteen years and who was the only person whom I adored, before I knew all of you: she will be my ideal in life as my sister is in death.

The date of this letter is very close to that of the *"Plainte d'automne."* I consider the sentence quoted as crucial. Indeed, the word "sister" might at first seem to be merely a natural way of putting it; literary exaltation prevails as he names off the great *amoureuses*; and then suddenly his true sister appears, from outside literature ("this poor young phantom, who was my sister for thirteen years") and in such circumstances that we cannot doubt the sincerity of the feeling. The end of the sentence is extraordinary: Maria has become an ideal dead girl

whom Ettie represents in life. I intend to develop the implications of this analogy between Ettie and Maria. In fact, I shall have to tie the first thread of this
network at once. But first I must emphasize the fact that any hypothesis of a
purely literary melancholy in "*Plainte d'automne*" is without foundation.

To repeat, around his twentieth year Mallarmé saw in Maria's death an important event of his inner life. He said so movingly and directly to his dearest
friend, confiding, indeed, that this young phantom was the only creature he
had loved till then. Without wishing to psychoanalyze, we may properly recall
that when his mother died, Mallarmé had been speedily committed to the care
of his grandparents, whom he loved only moderately, and soon had had to
divide his life between studies at boarding school and bourgeois family Sun-
days, with the result that Maria, in the absence of the remarried father, remained the only vital link that attached Stéphane to his mother and her
tenderness. Be that as it may, here now the child had become his "ideal in
death."

Let us return to Ettie. She did not marry Cazalis, despite his years of court-
ship; much later she married Maspéro, the Egyptologist, the companion of
Lefébure, who was, with Cazalis, Mallarmé's best friend.[7] After his wife's
death, Maspéro attended Mallarmé's receptions on the Rue de Rome. We are
thus working in a very narrow circle of human relationships. Ettie had died in
1877, and it is in all probability for Maspéro, who was left alone in the world,
that Mallarmé wrote the famous sonnet, "*Pour votre chère morte*." It is, then,
Ettie who says:

> *Sur les bois oubliés quand passe l'hiver sombre*
> *Tu te plains, ô captif solitaire du seuil,*
> *Que ce sépulcre à deux qui fera notre orgueil*
> *Hélas! du manque seul des lourds bouquets s'encombre.*

> [In woods forgotten when winter, somber, passes
> You lament, O solitary captive of the threshold,
> That this sepulcher for two which will be our pride
> Alas! with only the lack of heavy bouquets is encumbered.]

This poem is remarkable in the canon because it has an extraordinarily direct
and simple gravity. It delineates the lonely man, who, unable to share the "sepulcher for two," awaits, at midnight before the last embers of his fire, the visit
of the phantom that will seat itself in the now-empty armchair opposite him.

> *Qui veut souvent avoir la Visite ne doit*
> *Par trop de fleurs charger la pierre que mon doigt*
> *Soulève avec l'ennui d'une force défunte.*
> *Ame au si clair foyer tremblante de m'asseoir,*
> *Pour revivre il suffit qu'à tes lèvres j'emprunte*
> *Le souffle de mon nom murmuré tout un soir.*

[Who wishes often to receive the Visit must not
With too many flowers charge the stone that my finger
Raises with the listlessness of a force defunct.
Soul trembling to sit before the hearth so bright,
To live again it suffices that from your lips I borrow
The breath of my name murmured a whole evening.]

Despite the fact that Mallarmé was writing for Maspéro, he was also writing for himself and his dear dead sister. Ettie was linked with Maria, and we remember—if only vaguely—that the decor of this room, where a lonely man awaits a phantom's visit, often appears in the life of Mallarmé. It is the same decor, in fact, in which he worked out, from 1862 to 1866 (between the ages of twenty and twenty-four), all that part of his work in which obsessions, despairs, and funereal concerns came thick and fast. Let us note further that if the decor of the sonnet "*Pour votre chère morte*" repeats the decor of the Tournon evenings, the feeling differs. There is no anxiety in the 1877 poem: Mallarmé was thinking sadly of Ettie, and since the Ettie–Maria connection was a conscious one, as the letter to Cazalis proves, the anxiety that goes with an unconscious conflict was no longer present. Mallarmé was also thinking of the dead Maria with the sadness of any normal person. We have strong reason, then, to think that even at thirty-five Mallarmé still remembered the young phantom with an emotion that often opened up in him sources of the most genuine poetry. Can we, however, change these strong probabilities into at least a quasi-certainty? I believe we can.

The next text to be considered is that of the French exercise, a composition of his youth, which was published by Dr. Mondor in *Mallarmé plus intime* and was entitled "*Ce que disaient les trois cigognes.*" That Mallarmé should have preserved this composition among his papers is in itself remarkable enough. The explanation is not far to seek. The manuscript in fact carries, Dr. Mondor tells us, this note scrawled in the adult hand of the poet: "Story—on any topic—in the fourth or fifth year of the lycée." Now what is this subject freely chosen? One winter's night, in the middle of a forest ("In forgotten woods when winter, somber, passes"), a man is alone in his house, by the fireside, and he dreams of his dead young daughter. In the cemetery nearby, she leaves her grave, comes to visit her father, sits near him before the fire, dances, sings, and vanishes in the morning. The style is hardly childish, and some of the chief Mallarméan themes crowd into the story, as Dr. Mondor puts it in a single discreet statement: "This particular reading is especially for those whom the rose, the snow, the dawn, azure, lilies, winter griefs, dreamy songs, and an experimental vocabulary will set thinking."

It is natural to suppose that Mallarmé wrote "*Ce que disaient les trois cigognes*" after Maria's death, but we have no absolute proof that he did. Mallarmé places this composition "in the fourth or fifth year." He entered the fifth in October, 1857, after Maria's death in August. But since Dr. Mondor writes, "the date of the composition must not have been far from the date of the death of Maria Mallarmé, the schoolboy's sister," he evidently thinks there is a cause and effect relationship between the two events. The other hypothesis, that it was a coincidence, must not have deserved mention.

And how improbable such a coincidence would be! At twenty, Mallarmé saw his sister's death as the most important event of his inner life. At fifteen, he had described a survivor who was awaiting the visit of a dead girl. At thirty-five, he described the same survivor at the same fireside expecting the same visit. But at seventeen did he not exclaim, in *"Sa fosse est fermée."*

> *. . . n'était-ce pas assez pour ta faux déplorée,*
> *Dieu, d'avoir moissonné ma soeur, rose égarée . . .*
> *Hier! c'était ma soeur! aujourd hui mon amie!*

> [. . . was it not enough for your lamented scythe,
> God, to have reaped my sister, distracted rose . . .
> Yesterday! it was my sister! today my friend!]

All the evidence constrains us, then, to equate the young dead girl of the story with Maria. As for the Mallarméan themes listed above, which will play such a role in the melancholy poems of 1862–66, the same is true: they are not thrown together by chance; a central emotion evokes and arranges them. The subject of the story indicates quite clearly what this emotion is.

These convergences are significant in their own right. Numerous details will remove all doubt as to their true meaning. I will select only one. The finest lines of the sonnet of 1877 are perhaps

> *. . . la pierre que mon doigt*
> *Soulève avec l'ennui d'une force défunte.*

> [. . . the stone that my finger
> Raises with the listlessness of a force defunct.]

Now, the free composition of 1857 mentions "poor dead souls . . . sewn in their pale shroud, without being able to lift it with a finger. . . ." If the woods and the tomb under the snow, the flowers, the hearth, and the wait for the phantom did not supply enough convincing analogues, the strange and feeble finger lifting the shroud or the coffin stone would furnish us with unimpeachable evidence of a continuity that must, from now on, be given its due weight. The Mallarméan themes already evoked in the story of the fifteen-year-old student are interrelated; they are attached to the common center that a sorrowful event of the first importance creates in the poet's life and work. To give an explanation in depth of the one or the other, one must specify the role of this first emotional shock, then discover its echoes and symbols and follow the threads of the associations of ideas—in other words, study the complex network of emotions and expressions, of which his sister's death is, at least at first, the unique center. Whoever sets himself to this task gradually becomes convinced of the basic importance of Maria's death to Stéphane, and in the process arrives at a new way of seeing Mallarmé's work.

THE SHIMMER BELOW

The quasi-certainty that Maria's death played a crucial role in Mallarmé's life and work would be enough to prompt us to resort to psychoanalysis. Let us recall that Mallarmé lost his mother when he was five, the time of the normal Oedipal crisis. The two shocks were tied up with one another, the second reopening the first wound. One does not have to be a great psychologist to realize that a conjuncture of the sort can have profound and far-reaching emotional repercussions. A large number of neuroses originate in traumas experienced in infancy. We will return to that shortly. But there is another reason, purely literary, which by itself would have inclined us to a psychoanalytic study of Mallarmé. It is what I will call here, briefly, the "shimmer below." Simple acquaintance with Mallarmé's poems suggests the idea that there is a network of constant images, attracting and eliciting each other in such a way as to produce harmonies repeated from poem to poem. In *Mallarmé l'obscur* I studied several of these harmonies.[8] One of them, for instance, groups in various configurations the elements of a musician-angel; another shows extraordinary regularity in uniting images of hair, flames, sunset, triumph in love, and death. I recall this study purely to stress its experimental character. These lines of association are an incontestable fact and do not depend on any special theory. They suggest the idea of fixed obsessive points distinguishing the arabesque of the particular poem in a more or less ingenious or peculiar "obvious" [lisible] sense of the poem from a sort of constant architecture, which is probably subconscious and reveals itself, for our analysis, below the obvious level.

In order to be perfectly clear, let us take one example. The figure of the musician-angel in *Sainte* stands out. The angel itself, its wing, the ancient instruments, the raised finger, the feminine presence, and the silence in which an exquisite harmony is created are present and, I dare say, normally grouped. But consider *Don du poème*; the wing has become the dawn's; "angelic" is applied to the lamp; the feminine presence is that of a mother rocking her daughter; the ancient instruments would resound in her voice if she spoke; as for the lifted finger, it could press the breast for the newly born poem. The parts of the musician-angel are still present, then, but scattered. A new arabesque connects the fixed points. If one is satisfied with the arabesque itself, which I have called the "obvious" content of the poem, *Sainte* and *Don du poème* have nothing in common. But the subconscious web remains identical in the two cases. The result, which I have just illustrated by a single example, and which does not stem (let us repeat) from any a priori hypothesis, leads us quite naturally to think of psychoanalysis. It may be recalled that psychoanalysis to a certain extent assimilates written work to dreams, and sees dreams as superimposing what it calls a manifest content on a latent content. The manifest content is the dream as it appears to us, as we tell it upon awakening; the latent content is the deeper meaning, the inner significance of the symbolic rebus that first appeared. I shall not for the moment push that analogy any further, since all I intended to do was demonstrate that a comparative study of Mallarméan texts is bound to show the superimposing of two planes, two designs, and, presumably, two logics, since their surface pattern is found to change repeatedly while, by contrast, the underlying design remains constant.

TRANSLATED BY ARCHIBALD HENDERSON, JR.
AND WILL L. McLENDON

NOTES

[1] Camille Soula, *La Poésie et la pensée de Stéphane Mallarmé* (Paris: H. Champion, 1931). [Trans. note.]

[2] Albert Thibaudet, *La Poésie de Stéphane Mallarmé* (Paris: Gallimard, 1912), [Trans. note.]

[3] Emilie Noulet, *Etudes littéraires: l'hermétisme dans la poésie moderne* (Mexico City: Talleres Gráficos de la Editorial Cultura, 1944). [Trans. note.]

[4] A chronology given in such minute detail, however, that even the death of Canon Agricol Aubanel, uncle of the Provençal poet, is to be found in it. Maria Mallarmé died on August 31, 1857. The chronology gives for this same year: "July 25: death of Béranger. August 10: awarding of prizes at the Lycée de Sens. Stéphane Mallarmé, of Paris, boarding student: 4th place in French composition; 2nd place in Greek translation. October 5: Mallarmé returns to the Lycée de Sens as a boarder in the 4th year." Ed. Henri Mondor and G. Jean Aubry (Paris: Gallimard, 1945).

[5] *Plainte d'automne* was first published in 1864 (Mallarmé was twenty-two), at the same time as *Pauvre enfant pâle*, a prose poem that later becomes, in my opinion, the *Cantique de Saint-Jean.*

[6] Henri Cazalis (1840–1909) was a close friend of Mallarmé and published under the pseudonym Jean Lahor. He is said to have been a model for Proust's Legrandin.

[7] Eugénie Lefébure (1838–1908) was an early translator of Poe. Gaston Maspéro (1846–1916) was one of the most prolific Egyptologists of the nineteenth century.

[8] Charles Mauron, *Mallarmé l'obscur* (Paris: Denoël, 1941).

JEAN-PIERRE RICHARD

Mallarmé's Imaginative Universe
1961

Jean-Pierre Richard's capacious Univers imaginaire de Mallarmé *is,
with Jean Starobinski's study of Rousseau* Transparency and Obstruction
(La Transparence et l'obstacle), *one of the two masterpieces of French
thematic criticism. Significantly, both became targets for deconstruction in
important works by Derrida. In this fragment of Richard's introduction,
the critic appears eager to stave off an incipient conflict between "thematic"
and "structural" criticism. He invokes the "discontinuist" terms of the latter (syntax, structure, diacritical opposition) as favorably as the "con-
tinuist" terms of the former (empathy, expression, plenitude). Richard has
as "totalizing" a vision of the world of criticism as he does of Mallarmé's
oeuvre; and it may be suggested that in each case, despite his generosity of
vision (or perhaps because of it), the endeavor has proved ill-starred.*

My approach to Mallarmé's poetry is, I think, new: call it interrogative
and totalizing (*totalitaire*). My goal has been to understand Mallarmé
completely, to rejoin the spirit to the letter, the "content" to the
"form," and focus in a single beam all the illuminations emanating from his
incomparable oeuvre. In examining every aspect of a unique existential project
pursued by a unique consciousness, the goal has been to discover certain characteristic lines of development and parallel principles of organization. Criticism, in my view, can be both a hermeneutic and a combinatorial art. It
deciphers by bringing together. To that end, it proceeds not by prejudice but, in
the best of cases, by hypothesis. Rather than impose an immutable grid upon
the work, it approaches the object it seeks to comprehend with an open mind,
confident that the work, if properly presented, will reveal the virtual design
underlying its unity. In Mallarmé, for example, criticism will seek to link the
erotic to the poetic, to relate dramaturgy, philology, and aesthetics. It will expect the "*Contes indiens*" to continue the "*Sonnets funèbres*," see "*Hérodiade*" as
the sister of the "*Faune*," and imagine a direct route from "*Igitur*" to "*La*

Jean-Pierre Richard, *L'Univers imaginaire de Mallarmé* (Paris: Seuil, 1961).

Dernière mode." In short, criticism hopes to establish among the various individual works that make up Mallarmé's oeuvre, and among the various registers of that oeuvre—serious, tragic, metaphysical, precious, amorous, aesthetic, ideological, frivolous—a family resemblance that compels each element to illuminate the others.

This hope, I believe, is not peculiar to my own research. It is widely shared at present in the human sciences. More than that, it expresses the deepest wish of the person on whom it is focused, for it can be said that it was Mallarmé who has enabled us to understand Mallarmé, who has given us the key to understanding his own work. Indeed, as Claudel alerted us, that work contains a marvelous lesson in *method*: it encourages us to embark on a quest for signs and ciphers. Poetry, according to Mallarmé, must express the "mysterious meaning of the various aspects of existence."[1] Literary life consists in "reviving, inwardly, the presence of harmonies [*accords*] and meanings."[2] The most banal objects have meaning, and that meaning is associated with a "harmony," a correlation. Mallarmé wants to detect these abstract relationships—which he calls "motifs," "aspects," and "figures"—behind every perceptible event. In order to satisfy him, this network of relationships must cover the totality of the object under exploration. I will attempt to show the degree to which the idea of *structure* obsessed both his intelligence and his dreams. To understand an idea, a landscape, a book, or a woman—to see these things, as Mallarmé put it, in all their nakedness[3]—was to achieve, in the flash of an instant, a unified vision of their architecture. Ultimately, the celebrated orphic explanation of the world was supposed to establish a comprehensive set of relationships among objects of the most diverse kind: a global reorganization of all things was supposed to yield absolute intelligibility and transparency. This kind of understanding was not the exclusive privilege of Orpheus: it could be attempted in the most routine of circumstances. Listen, for example, to Mallarmé musing on the entrechats of a female *dancer*: "The only conceivable training for the imagination is this: during routine visits to some place of Dance, *without preconceived purpose, patiently* and *passively ask yourself,* at each step, each unusual position, each *pointe* and *taqueté, allongé* or *ballon, 'What could this possibly mean?'* or, better still, with inspiration, *read it.*"[4] No better method of reading can be imagined: for the dancer substitute Mallarmé himself, for the choreographic text the verbal figures of a poem, and you will have hit upon the most appropriate way into his world, one that keeps faith with his own teaching.

What I have done, then, is to take Mallarmé's great project of unifying the world through the book and, on a more modest level to be sure, attempted to apply it to its author. Heeding his lesson, I have taken his famous "*gouffre central d'une spirituelle impossibilité que rien soit exclusivement à tout*"[5]—the impossibility, so often demonstrated by Mallarmé, of grasping any detail without aiming through it to attain the whole of which it is a part—and placed it within his oeuvre itself. Since nothing there is insignificant, and everything relates to everything else, I have attempted to make the various segments of that work reflect one another, just as Mallarmé sought to do with "the words of the tribe," *les mots de la tribu*, in order to give them "a purer meaning" (*"un sens plus pur"*). In other words, I have treated the entire oeuvre as a single, vast poem that is its own echo. At various points the work of the critic might be compared—to borrow some Mallarméan metaphors—to spinning a spider's web, constructing a stained-glass window, or building a resonance chamber, or perhaps a cave whose walls force attention back upon an empty but illuminated, and possibly illuminating, center. I have tried to restore *initiative* to an oeuvre often frozen, perhaps by the fault of its author himself, in an overly abstract theoretical discourse or, conversely, sealed, seemingly lifeless, within the intimidating splendor of its hermeticism. Here, by *initiative*, I mean that pure power of commencement, of welling up, that Mallarmé himself so stubbornly sought in so many fields of experience.

This prospecting for essential structures and original themes will have taken place at the height of consciousness but not always at the level of the explicit. Nowadays we know that there are many modes and degrees of consciousness, not just the reflective. Consciousness also exists in prereflective or nonreflective states and manifests itself in sensation, feeling, and dreams. Think of Gaston Bachelard's imaginative consciousness. Or of Maurice Merleau-Ponty's perceptive consciousness (or aesthetic self-consciousness). Or of the consciousness of the Sartrian project, lived but not understood. Or of Jean Wahl's ontological sentimentality, or Gabriel Marcel's corporeal meditation, or, more generally, of phenomenological intentionality, psychoanalysis, gestalt psychology, and structuralist decodings. All of these are windows, of the most diverse sort, onto a realm in which meaning already exists but in a naive and implicit state, demanding of us only to be read in order to appear in a clear light. Accordingly, criticism is free to explore the underbrush, to follow half-covered tracks, to delve into the depths of the work in search of points of visibility and clarity. It is drawn to subterranean investigation. More than most other literary oeuvres, Mallarmé's poetry provides theoretical justification for this kind of research, because its surface is openly deceptive. Is not the famous "shimmering beneath the surface"[6] that Mallarmé identifies as the true "meaning" of his poem at once a visible brightness and a hidden light? If the true discourse is "that which is not said in discourse,"[7] we are bound by the poet himself to explore the silent margins of language, to blaze a trail into that infralanguage which for him constitutes the sole realm of true expression.

Mallarmé therefore allows us to explore the underpinnings of his work, or, in George Poulet's words, "its hidden aspect, the dark side of the moon"—in short, its mental interior. The meaning that the work asks us to allow to resonate within us cannot be reduced to a simple, linear discourse. To understand Mallarmé is not to look beyond the poem for a clear statement of a thesis supposedly disguised in the verse. On the contrary, it is to discover the raison d'être, the project implicit in its obscurity. The common assumption of all efforts to decipher the poems word by word is that each one is nothing but a cryptogram. If, however, the hermeticism of the poetry is to be usefully clarified by delving below the surface, then it seems to me that success is more likely to be achieved by searching for architectures than by attempting an interlinear translation. My ambition, in other words, has been to explain the syntax of Mallarmé's imagination, not to supply a dictionary. (J. Scherer has attempted something similar, but only in the realm of expression, where he sought to discern laws without discussing literal content.) Of course, there is a danger (to which I have no doubt succumbed) of confusing structural revelation with literal interpretation, thereby providing yet another "translation" of Mallarmé. This is a difficulty faced by all criticism directed toward apparently obscure texts. The hermeticism of such texts, whose apparent closure is in reality a profound form of expression, cannot be authentically opened up except in a second profundity, where what was dark becomes light. There is no point in trying to elucidate an obscure text by restoring a superficial legibility. Between the profound illumination of the depths and the simple light of the surface many misunderstandings are of course possible.

This risk had to be taken, however. In Mallarmé's work, therefore, I, too, tried to dip into the "the reviled shallow stream" ("*peu profond ruisseau calomnié*") which, beneath its surface ripples, carries the great unifying meanings. Here the amorous consciousness concocts its fantasies, the perceptive consciousness shapes its landscapes, and the aesthetic consciousness imagines its own transpositions. To my way of thinking, Mallarmé's poetry suffers from being approached too abstractly. Viewed naively, his work seems to me much more sensual in both intention and manner than is generally held. Isn't *ingenuousness* the cardinal Mallarméan value? "I think that in order to be truly man, nature thinking, *one must think with one's whole body,* which yields pregnant thoughts in unison with one another like the vibrations of violin strings in direct contact with their hollow wooden box," he wrote to his friend Lefébure on May 17, 1867.[8] What this *bois creux*, or hollow wood, became in Mallarmé's future oeuvre is quite clear: mandola, poem, book, and so on. Here, however, the essential point is that its emptiness remains in contact with the active fullness of a corporeal existence. Sound and resonant cavity are in direct, hence felicitous contact. The end of this letter is also worth citing. In it, Mallarmé, in the midst of a period of spiritual asceticism while simultaneously engaged in a series of extraordinary exercises in the decomposition of the psyche, celebrates the beauty of a full, pure voice and a song that knows itself to be in spontaneous harmony with the earth. The song in question is that of the cricket:

> Only yesterday, among the tender stalks of wheat, I heard that sacred voice of
> the ingenuous earth, already less decomposed than that of the bird, son of the
> trees immersed in the solar night, and which has about it something of the stars

and the moon, as well as a bit of death; but how much *purer*, especially, than the voice of a woman, who walked and sang before me, and whose voice seemed transparent to the thousand words that enveloped its resonance—and suffused with nothingness besides! All the earth's joy at not being decomposed into matter and spirit was in that cricket's unique sound.[9]

In this delightful reverie sensation quite simply delivers up its poetic content. Such lines confirm the truth of the sentence with which Marcel Raymond concluded his great book: "Poetry is not only . . . the quintessence of literature, it is above all a way of life, of existence, which can be cultivated but is first spontaneous."[10] Twenty-seven years after his paean to the cricket, Mallarmé himself again tells us that what he is looking for is "motifs that constitute a logic, with our very fiber."[11] This marvelous definition of poetry links its most obscure, most physiological elements to its clearest necessity.

My goal was to draw these same "motifs" from the "fibers" of the work, from its verbal tissue and imaginative substance. I looked for them in Mallarmé's favorite subjects (for example, mirrors, fire, gauze, creams, smoke, foam, clouds, clear water) and favorite forms (mountain passes, fountains, peninsulas, corollas, fingernails, passions in full flower or subsided), in the conditions to which his reveries invariably return (gushing, fluttering, reflexiveness, wavering, avowal, modesty), and in the essential attitudes that to my mind constitute his inner landscape. In short, I have tried to reconstruct his "atlases, herbariums, and rituals." In the pages that follow one will therefore find a comprehensive museum of the Mallarméan imagination, a museum of geology and botany as well as a bestiary and a feminary. Here one will discover a concrete phenomenology of Mallarmé's fetishes (fans, mirrors, dancers, chandeliers, tufts, folds, diamonds, butterflies), his favorite lights and sounds (effulgence, scintillation, radiance; tapping or sliding on the harp or violin, trumpet blast, muffled organ sound, contemplative sound of the mandola), obsessive rhythms, fundamental schemata (such as summoning up and evaporating, sealing up and gushing forth), concrete essences (fallen, wilted, spurted, summoned, evaporated), and various organs of expression (music, word, verse, poem, book) serving a single project.

No work can altogether turn its back on the world. Even to deny the world, the work has need of it. Escape is dependent on that which it would flee. Nothingness exists in us only when something is abolished. We must therefore resist the powerful vertigo of absence that Mallarmé's poetry seeks to create in us, a vertigo to which so many of his best commentators have succumbed, for the poetry itself remains intensely present, and it is this presence that we must begin by investigating. Dedicated to blankness though it may be, the poetry also needs a "drop, at bottom, of darkness implicit in the fact that something exists."[12] Things, bodies, forms, substances, humors, flavors—these will be, even for Mallarmé, the support and primary means of expression of the process whereby he invents himself. If that process is to be followed in minute detail, the invention must be caught at the moment of emergence, in the initial excitement of inception, while it is still mired in the sensuous clay from which it seeks to extricate itself, upon which it leaves the most accurate image of itself. For the object describes the spirit that possesses it; the outside reveals the inside. "I go in order to test my soul," Du Bos said, after Browning. And, in the same vein, Béguin liked to quote Novalis: "The path of mystery wends its way inward. Eternity, if it exists anywhere, exists within us, together with its worlds, the past and the future." I would add that this path first passes through an exterior, and that eternity can reveal itself in a body or a landscape. It is in the sensible world that the purest spirituality is put to the test and its quality determined.

So it is with Mallarmé: in its inception as well as its conclusion, his inner adventure insists on *proof*, which can come only from the sensible world. Reread, for example, the drafts of the famous *"Livre"*: these pages fairly clearly demonstrate that the most maniacal abstraction required dramatic embodiment, inscription in a human context, and proof of its value in the form of financial consequences. The idea of the work would reveal itself only in the meticulousness of a very concrete organization. Thus, even Mallarmé is someone for whom the external world exists, and it is no accident that he praised Gautier's notoriously "lucid" eye. What, indeed, is a poet, if not a man who, being gifted with a peculiar sensitivity to things and words, through them seeks certain metaphysical intuitions? Mallarmé himself says as much:

> A man may come . . . by some very simple and primitive means, to know, say, the symphonic equation peculiar to the seasons, the custom of sun and clouds; a remark or two of a similar order applies to those ardors, those storms that alter the heavens above our passions: if he has taken care to preserve from destruction, recreated by himself, a strict reverence for the twenty-four letters as they may have, by the miracle of infinity, been cast in some language, his own, as well as a sense for their symmetries, action, reflection, to the point of transfiguration into the supernatural term that is verse; then he will possess, this civilized denizen of Eden, the dearest of all goods, the basis of all felicity, a doctrine as well as a country.[13]

Above all he will possess the building blocks that all invention requires: sun, clouds, seasons—language constituting the simple and primitive sensuous material through which the poet must cause his reverie to pass.

Furthermore, that reverie, if sufficiently convincing, also sustains realities that might at first glance seem entirely alien to it: not sensible realities this time, but abstract and intelligible ones. For there is such a thing as a dreamworld (*onirisme*) of ideas. Despite what certain poets have believed, understanding is not the enemy of imagination. It is rather the culmination or the mask. Concepts live in us; they make sense first of all to the people who think them. The universality of a concept does not prevent it from forging a particular attachment to each individual's most intimate reality, whose stamp the concept then bears. Beneath its surface of luminous objectivity, it has, as Henri Michaux has written, an "inside," a "bearing," an "attitude"—in short, a way of being. Well known as a specialist in these obscure explorations, Michaux adds: "An idea is a *penchant*, a synesthetic obligingness."[14] As such, it aids and abets our most hidden moods and thereby acquires a physiology. What interests me in Mallarmé is not so much his ideology, which is often confused and contradictory, as the process by which flesh, blood, and reverie culminate in intelligent creations. There is now broad agreement in the human sciences that reason extends and develops the most obscure of experience. Since every system is rooted in personal experience, and since the drive for systematization itself originates in a deep-seated tendency (as is most definitely the case with Mallarmé), we have every right to consider a poet's most abstract theories as so many unavowed poems. "Content" and "form," "philosophy" and "style" can then be seen as stemming from the same instinct and subject to the same types of comprehension. Mallarmé encourages this line of inquiry, moreover, by never revealing his ideology in conceptual terms but, rather, allowing it to develop, within himself and before your eyes, in the form of figures and images. The idea does not become detached from the dream subtending it; it remains, for Mallarmé, musical, "sweet" (*suave*), "cheerful" (*rieuse*), and "proud" (*altière*),[15] at once succulent and transparent.

When approached this way, from its carnal side, and slowly unfolded to scrutiny, the Mallarméan oeuvre repays the effort required to penetrate it. Little by little, it exhibits the two essential qualities of a masterpiece—unity and simplicity. There is nothing accidental here, no mere decoration or padding, as one finds in so many lesser works. Nor are there contradictions that cannot be resolved by a subsequent application of intelligence. And whenever the poet hits on some lucky find, it is rare that the honesty of his imagination does not pursue it to its ultimate conclusion.

To this poetry, as intricate in its very essence as a spider's web and shaped by an imagination completely obsessed with associations and structures, we can therefore apply Mallarmé's own exquisite description of that other weblike reality: language. "Shaped by a pattern not at all random," it, too, "is put together in the same way as a marvelous piece of embroidery or lace: not a single thread or idea is wasted. If one disappears for a moment, it will reappear some time later, linked to another. Everything fits together in an ideal pattern, which may be simple or complex and which remains forever fixed in memory—no! in the instinct for harmony that we all possess, young and old alike."[16] The repetition of motifs, coupled with a certain austerity of sense data, guarantees that beneath the complexity of changes and modulations lies the rigor of thematic development. In his work, which he left incomplete and may have thought of as entirely occasional, Mallarmé hews throughout, with astonishing logic reminiscent of the logic of a dream, to a consistent line. Not even death could force him to waver from his pristine course: for us, it is as though the culmination of his endeavor in a final void, an apparent failure, placed it, in an unexpected and paradoxical way, in the only dimension in which it could truly achieve its end.

Someone may object that the emphasis here on logic is extreme, especially for a poet who, more than any other, acknowledged the sovereign power of chance both internally and externally. But it is also true that Mallarmé used all the resources at his disposal to tame this power of contingency and that he wrote precisely in order to vanquish it "word by word." Similarly, I believe that criticism can take on the task of vanquishing, step by step, the apparent disorder of Mallarmé's oeuvre. It will not succeed, however, by relating that disorder to another form of incoherence, that of the life in which the work is supposed to originate. Where does the writer most truly exist, if not in the concrete totality of his books? It is in the works that the writer confesses and creates himself, and it is therefore to the works that one must go first in search of him. With the greatest admiration, humility, and empathy the critic may therefore seek to elicit from both the work and the life, from the work—life complex, a unique design. This unity, which is often obscured by biographical accidents or the external pressures of history, is of a qualitative kind. It is equivalent to a certain identity of response to things and people. To know someone is to penetrate that identity. Listen once again to Mallarmé: speaking of Villiers, he was pleased to recall how his old friend remained eternally true to himself even in the most seemingly diverse activities: "whether in excursion or debate, he brought to this obscure pursuit the same biting, princely intelligence that he devoted to the search for the idea itself, the *special* and quite deluxe *organization* of the poet *binding as one*. . . . In the creature returned to its original state, instinct remains, *undivided* and *unfissured*, the chaste source of all the faculties."[17] And in conclusion he adds: "*The same everywhere*, or the only one, on *asphalt* and in his *cloud*."[18]

We no longer attribute such identity solely to the "organization" of genius. Rather, we recognize its existence in all human experience. Criticism is happy when it is able to grasp the *signs* of a great literary universe from within, as if in the moment of inception, when it is able to describe the *properties* or, if you will, the *mentality* of that universe. For there can be no doubt that, quite apart from the hazards of inspiration and crystallization, every important work has a style all its own; every important work affirms a distinctive attitude and reveals a unique manner of existence and expression. A man avows his being by the way in which he seeks to find it out. What the critic strives to reproduce within himself is this inimitable process of the masterpiece: he listens to its sonorities, caresses its texture, and falls in with its "tempo." The most tactile approach leads him to subscribe inwardly to the work. In the best of cases, his visceral sympathy with the quality of the work may allow him temporarily to make the structure of the work his own, to re-experience its law within himself.

*   *   *

Such an approach, however, raises certain problems of technique and method, which merit brief discussion. The first of these problems concerns the notion of *theme*, on which my entire project rests. What is a theme? Nothing, it seems, could be vaguer or more difficult to grasp. How does one fix a theme's contours? How does one identify its essence? Once again we turn to Mallarmé, who, in *Les Mots anglais*, a work concerned with language itself, defined the concept of *theme* in relation to that of *root*: "What is a root? A collection of letters, often consonants, in which we see certain words of a language as though dissected, reduced to bones and tendons and removed from their ordinary living state in such a way that we may discern a secret kinship among them: still more succinctly and faintly, one has a theme."[19] I am quite happy to accept this definition and apply it to realms other than philology: a theme would then be a concrete organizational principle, a fixed scheme or object, around which a world may have a tendency to establish and array itself. The essential element of a theme is the "secret kinship" of which Mallarmé speaks, the hidden identity that one must discover beneath the most varied appearances.

Themes are usually identified by the criterion of recurrence: the major themes of an oeuvre, the themes that constitute its invisible architecture and should therefore give us the key to its organization, are the themes most often developed, most frequently and obviously encountered. Repetition, here as elsewhere, indicates obsession. The critic who accepts this criterion is therefore inclined to look for key words, favorite images, and fetishized objects, which leads to analyses of statistical frequencies, to research of the sort exemplified in France by the work of Pierre Guiraud.[20] Though undoubtedly useful, this kind of work, in my view at least, cannot yield ultimate truths. To begin with, the extension of a theme frequently exceeds that of any related word: in Mallarmé, one obsessional theme has to do with the fracturing of unity, with fragmentation followed by reorganization of the scattered parts in some new unified whole. But no single French word encompasses a meaning of such complexity. There is another difficulty as well: any compilation of word frequencies assumes that the meaning of any given word remains fixed from one occurrence to the next. In fact, however, meanings vary from use to use: the sense of a word changes simultaneously in itself and in the context of the other words that surround it, support it, and breathe life into it. We now know that languages are *diacritical* realities: each element is less important than the *distance* that separates it from other elements. Thanks to these differences of quality and level, languages organize themselves into autonomous forms. Similarly, in thematics, definitions are relative; significance therefore exists only in a global, complex manner, in patterns that are incompatible with overly rigid categorizations. No statistical investigation or exhaustive cataloguing of themes can explain the intention behind them or their richness of meaning. Worse, the relief of the original system will be flattened out. Variations in meaning, and within a given meaning, differences of *stress* or *level* (that is, of the degree to which the given meaning is rooted in experience and has *resonance*), compel the critic to seek a more detailed and qualitative understanding. Each case must therefore be judged separately, on its own merits. Countless examples must be subjected to minute analysis in such a way as to allow us not only to recognize the centrality of a theme but also to gauge its value and appreciate the subtle ways in which it modifies its context. In the end, only a close, careful reading is capable of revealing the deep laws of vision and imagination.

Furthermore, frequency is not the only criterion that distinguishes the dominant themes of an oeuvre. Repetition is not always significant, or at any rate does not always signify what is essential. More important, perhaps, is a theme's strategic, or, if you prefer, *topological*, value. Major themes are those that occur at crucial points of inner space, at what Mallarmé would call "points of intersection," and which are therefore capable of imposing their organizing rules on very diverse realms of experience. In Mallarmé, for example, a certain crucial image of *nudity* dominates the erotic zone but also extends to the realms of pure thought, aesthetic reverie, and metaphysics. The same is true of such key figures as *fluttering*, *gushing*, and *radiance*. In order to bring out these themes, one needs only to superimpose different levels of experience, establish their comparative geography, and investigate the way in which they communicate so as to constitute a *single* experience. When we do this, the theme emerges as the transitive element that allows us to explore the inner expanse of the work in every direction, or, perhaps better, as the hinge element that allows the work to articulate itself as a significant volume. Thus, every thematic study is both cybernetic and systematic.

Within this active thematic system, individual tendencies tend to organize themselves as the parts of all living structures do: they combine to form versatile complexes governed by the law of isomorphism and the search for an optimal equilibrium. The idea of equilibrium, developed originally in the physical sciences, is also extremely important in sociology and psychology, as Claude Lévi-Strauss and Jean Piaget have shown.[21] It can be fruitfully employed, I believe, in the investigation of imaginative universes. Here one finds themes arranged in antithetical couples or, in more complex cases, in a series of feedback loops. In his reverie on ideas, for example, Mallarmé wavers, I think, between a desire for openness (the exploded idea, *vaporized* into a mere hint, or silence) and a need for closure (the idea *summoned up* and given a definite shape and outline). The closed and the open, the clear and the evanescent, the mediate and the immediate—these are a few of the imaginative pairs that I believe I have identified in the most diverse aspects of Mallarmé's experience. It then becomes important to notice how these oppositions are resolved, how their tension is reduced through the formation of new synthetic ideas or concrete forms in which satisfactory equilibria can be achieved. For instance, the opposition of the closed and the open culminates in certain benign figures within which the two contradictory needs can both be satisfied, either successively or simultaneously, such as the *fan*, the *book*, and the *dancer*. The essence will succeed in both summoning itself up and vaporizing itself in a synthetic phenomenon, *music*. At other times a static equilibrium will be achieved through the interaction of intricately intertwined forces, whose comprehensive balance ends in a euphoric state of "suspension." This, of course, was how Mallarmé himself imagined the internal reality of the poem and the ideal architecture of the objects that the poem was supposed to reorder within himself: cave, diamond, spider's web, rose window, kiosk, shell—all these are images reflecting the poet's desire that everything in nature should correlate with everything else and that perfect equality should reign among things. Mallarmé conceived of the mind as the keystone of this architecture, the absolute center through which everything else communicates, achieves balance, and is neutralized (or "annulled," as Mallarmé would add). Mallarmé's thematic structure itself thus provides us with the techniques for understanding it. What I have attempted to do, then, is to investigate the ways in which the poet's imaginative predilections managed to overcome their conflicts to achieve felicitous equilibria. To do this, one has only to reread his most beautiful poems, in which equilibrium is achieved spontaneously and effortlessly: here, what is usually called "felicity of expression" was perhaps simply a reflection of genuine happiness, that is, of a state in which an individual's most contradictory needs are satisfied all together, or even *by one another*, in a harmony achieved through association, balance, and fusion.

TRANSLATED BY ARTHUR GOLDHAMMER

NOTES

[1] *Propos sur la poésie,* ed. Henri Mondor (Monaco: Editions du Rocher, 1946), p. 134.

[2] *Oeuvres complètes* (Paris: Gallimard, 1945), p. 405.

[3] "Last night I was fortunate enough to see my Poem again in all its nakedness, and I want to attempt the work tonight." Mallarmé, *Correspondence* (Paris: Gallimard, 1959), p. 195.

[4] *Oeuvres complètes,* p. 507.

[5] Ibid., p. 333.

[6] Ibid., p. 382.

[7] Ibid., p. 386.

[8] *Correspondence,* p. 249.

[9] Ibid., p. 250.

[10] Marcel Raymond, *De Baudelaire au Surréalisme* (rev. ed. Paris: Corti, 1947), p. 358.

[11] "La Musique et les Lettres," *Oeuvres complètes,* p. 648. And later he would say to François Jammes ("*Dialogues*," p. 30): "You will play on our naked fiber."

[12] *L'Action restreinte, Oeuvres complètes,* p. 370.

[13] *Oeuvres complètes,* p. 646.

[14] Henri Michaux, "La Psilocybine," in *Les Lettres nouvelles* (25 Dec. 1959), p. 6.

[15] *Oeuvres complètes*, pp. 857, 1630.

[16] Ibid., pp. 857, 1650.

[17] "Villiers," ibid., p. 483.

[18] Ibid., p. 484.

[19] Ibid., p. 962.

[20] See Pierre Guiraud, *Index du vocabulaire du Symbolisme* (Paris: Klincksieck, 1953).

[21] See Claude Lévi-Strauss and Jean Piaget, *Logique et équilibre* (Paris: P.U.F., 1957).

GÉRARD GENETTE

Mallarmé's Happiness?
1962

Gérard Genette's critique of Richard on Mallarmé is at bottom a reminder of the fundamental incompatibility between Bachelardian phenomenology, Richard's principal inspiration, and the structuralism he claims to espouse as well. If, for Saussure, patron saint of structuralism, there are no positive terms in a structure, but only negative oppositions, the felicitous positivity of the sensuous intuitions around which Richard would organize his structure would be so many admissions of prestructuralist naiveté. In addition, Genette's comparison of Richard, in his inclusiveness, to Wagner, the Germanic bête noire *of the quintessentially French poet Mallarmé claimed to be, stands as a subtle but unmistakable accusation of literary insensitivity.*

"Baudelaire's failure has often been discussed; in these pages I hope to show a happy Baudelaire." Apart from the poet's name, this sentence from *Poésie et Profondeur* could be applied to any of Jean-Pierre Richard's critical essays, and in particular to his *Univers imaginaire de Mallarmé*,[1] whose central concern is to show us a happy Mallarmé.

Richard's fundamental critical principle is of course that the place to look for meaning and coherence in a work is at the level of sensations, substantive dreams, and avowed or unavowed preferences for certain elements or materials and for certain states of the external world—in other words, at the level of consciousness, deep yet open to material things, that Gaston Bachelard dubbed the "material imagination." To apply this method, which is in its own way a form of psychoanalysis, to the work of Mallarmé is to subject it to a severe test, because any psychoanalysis involves going from a manifest meaning to a latent content. And since the meaning of a poem by Mallarmé is rarely manifest, two hermeneutics, one literal and the other which Richard calls "structural," must be at once superimposed and differentiated.

The central thread of this "totalizing" (*totalitaire*) study, whose goal is noth-

---

Gérard Genette, "Bonheur de Mallarmé?" in *Figures* (Paris: Seuil, 1966).

ing less than to reconstruct the Mallarméan sensibility in its entirety, is the constant search, through and beyond all negative experience, for a happy connection with the sensible world. Although the Edenic immediacy of Mallarmé's childhood poems soon vanished, overwhelmed by the poet's obsession with imperfection and feelings of loneliness and impotence, he never gave up hope that this lost paradise might be regained, and Richard explores at length the web of sensory mediations by means of which the imagination strove to re-establish this contact: amorous reveries that reveal a subtle eroticism of the gaze, filtered through foliage, gauze, and make-up, and of desire, impelled by water and flame; nocturnal intimations of personal disaster, attenuated by rays of hope that permitted fragile moments of intimacy and illuminated the reflections of the specular consciousness; the resurrection, following the attempted suicide at Tournon, of the sensual world, symbolized by flowers, fireworks, fluttering fans, butterflies, and dancers in great profusion; the renewal of contact with other people, with the result that the former *sacred* power of azure was supplanted by the probative dialectical virtues of talk, the theater, and crowds; the reverie of ideas, the culmination of progressive alleviation of the weight of the material world which proceeds by stages from feather to cloud to foam to smoke to music to metaphor; images of light, which penetrated the Mallarméan gaze as it penetrated Impressionist painting, flooding, and thereby unifying, the sensual world with its diffuse splendor; and finally, the reverie of the Book, the culmination of utopian ideas about language which began with the word, invested with an illusory resemblance to the object; continued with verse, conceived as a "total word, new, foreign to the language" and endowed in turn with a power of analogy; and proceeded on to the poem, that medley of verbal mirrors and "structural" microcosm. More than a dream, this "Book" of glimpses and fragments summed up and subsumed everything else, for the World existed only to end up in it.

Yet no summary can so much as hint at the richness of this vast interior panorama, whose essence lies in its details. Some of Richard's analyses—of the erotics of foliage, for example, or the dynamics of fans, or the poetics of foam, lace, and fog—equal Bachelard's best pages on the material imagination. Crucial light is shed on the Mallarméan sensibility, and certain of the poet's unduly neglected works, such as *Les Mots anglais*, *Les Contes indiens*, and the columns from the fashion magazine *La Dernière mode*, take on their true importance. A certain image of Mallarmé, in all the subtle brilliance of his perceptible presence, is not fully available without the lenses that Richard's reading provides. "To dream of the flight of a bird as a symbol of the poetic act is not in itself especially original," Richard writes. "To imagine the sky as a ceiling that one can bump into requires nothing special in the way of imagination. But if the bird breaks a window, and if that window is also a tomb, a ceiling, and a page; and if that bird sheds feathers that first pluck the strings of a harp and then turn into plucked flowers, fallen stars, and foam; and if this bird-foam rends the transparency of the air even as it is shred to pieces; and if that transparency become birdsong erupts into a thousand droplets which then turn into waterspouts, flowers in full bloom, explosions of diamonds and stars, and rolled dice, then it is clear that the poet we are dealing with is none other than Mallarmé." Yes, it is clear, but one cannot help adding that only one critic is capable of introducing us in these terms to the spirit of Mallarmé, and this felicitous sentence proves that the critic we are dealing with is none other than Jean-Pierre Richard.

Nevertheless, this most valuable and enriching reading is also the occasion of a certain disappointment, which can be bluntly and no doubt too harshly expressed by saying that something is elusive in or missing from this account, namely, the poetry, or, more precisely, Mallarmé's *poetic labor*, and, furthermore, that a certain ambiguity prevails as to the relation between the work and everything else: reverie, eroticism, biographical contingencies, diaries, correspondence. Indeed, Richard's analysis, which from the outset declares itself to be an immanent reading, turns out to be doubly transcendent, or, if you prefer, doubly transitive with respect to the Mallarméan poetic object.

It is first of all vertically transitive, because in seeking to uncover the "underside" of the work it regularly shifts its attention from work to author. This is yet another instance of the psychologistic axiom that has governed nearly all criticism for more than a century, but modified (and perhaps aggravated) by two other axioms that constitute the legacy of Gaston Bachelard: the sensualist axiom, according to which what is fundamental (and therefore authentic) is sensual experience, and the eudemonic axiom, which posits a sort of instinct for sensual happiness as the basis of all imaginative activity. These three axioms are summed up quite well in this typically Richardian formulation: "Poetic happiness—often called felicity of expression—is perhaps nothing other than a reflection of happiness in life."[2] This is a hasty assertion, to put it mildly, and it is especially surprising to find it in a book about Mallarmé. Yet this certitude is the very soul of Richardian criticism. This epicurean prejudice is evident in a proliferation of euphoric epithets: here everything is *succulent, delicious, marvelous, beneficial, perfect; what pleasure* and *what joy* when everything thus *overwhelms* and *satisfies* us! Technique and abstraction then become but further pretexts for felicitous reverie. Mallarmé does not ponder literary forms, he *dreamily savors* a theme that no longer concerns the "tuft" or "fold" but the "word," the "verse," and the "book." He does not think but rather caresses ideas, savors concepts, intoxicates himself with argument. Thought cannot and should not appear except as the object that Richard calls "reverie of the idea," as if subsumed in the pure pleasure of its evocation. And if, by chance, a somewhat too rigid abstraction resists the effort to convert it to delectation ("Here . . . the links are too conceptual, which gives them a sometimes embarrassing rigidity or literalness"), the critic feels compelled to return as quickly as possible to the fundamental: "What pleasure, though, after these laborious decipherings, to discover in its naked state a reverie known to be essential."[3]

This systematic ascription of value to sensual and lived experience gives Richard a very peculiar view of the Mallarméan universe. In his work, one finds no trace of the will to absence and silence or ultimate exploitation of the destructive power of language that Maurice Blanchot so strongly emphasized. For Richard, Mallarmé's world is neither *vacant* nor silent. It teems with things and murmurs with pleasant sounds. Mallarmé cannot possibly be "seeking absence," much less finding it, since he can only be "expressing this rarefaction from the starting point of plenitude and pointing to the hollowing out of things by way of things truly present before us."[4] The phrase "truly present" flatly contradicts certain meditations on language which go back all the way to Mallarmé himself. And yet it would seem that the real evoked in its *"presque disparition vibratoire,"* its "almost shimmering disappearance," is not the same as the real of sensual presence. Even if it is true, moreover, that not all of Mallarmé's oeuvre can be reduced to the negative background of the *"Sonnet en x,"* it would seem difficult to neglect entirely the way in which that poem, as Mallarmé understood and wrote it, *contests* the objects it uses and must somehow *abolish* in order to constitute itself as a kind of verbal object. Mallarmé may well be, as Richard provocatively puts it, "the Chardin of our literature," but one has to read into this remark the fact that a painting by Chardin, whatever its material pretext, in the end represents only itself, and that painting, like poetry, begins where the real ends.

Are the objects, themes, and dimensions of poetry the same as those of sensual reverie? Can a poetic oeuvre, and especially the oeuvre of Mallarmé, be explained or even understood in terms of reverie? Does it *express* reverie? Even after reading Richard's book, one may continue to harbor doubts. It has been observed that the book is more convincing in its explanation of the prose of *Les Mots anglais* and *La Dernière mode*, which, as Richard points out, are indeed thinly disguised reveries, than it is of the poetry, in which the fantasies of the imagination are as it were transcended by the work of language. "The true condition of the true poet," Valéry said, "is as different as can be from the dream state," and this judgment is perhaps more apt of Mallarmé than of any other poet. After all, Bachelardian analysis is a method for exploring the dreams common to all mankind, and Bachelard himself saw reverie as a general category, which he occasionally illustrated with examples drawn from poets *among others*, including prose writers, philosophers, and even scientists diverted by the hallucinations of the imagination. To shift from this general category to a more individual focus is not without problems, and when Bachelard dwells on a particular author, such as Hoffmann in *The Psychoanalysis of Fire*, Poe in *L'Eau et les Rêves*, Nietzsche in *L'Air et les Songes*, or even Lautréamont, it is more as the representative of a type, an exemplary *complex*, than for that author's irreducible singularity. It is not even clear that the notion of psychic individuality makes much sense in this context. The study of an oeuvre as elaborate, self-contained, and intransitive as Mallarmé's poetry poses an even greater obstacle, insuperable perhaps by any psychology, no matter how open-ended and free-form (such as Richard's). Richard tells us all there is to know about Mallarmé's private dream world, which to some extent is still accessible to us. But all of Mallarmé's work strives to achieve an impersonal, autonomous language that is the opposite of *expression* and whose felicity perhaps owes nothing to any felicity of experience. Although Richard sifts that experience and digs into it in search of depths and breaks it up into as many elements as necessary in order to make those depths speak, one has the impression at times that no bottom can ever be reached. To say that there is some filiation, some deep relation, between a poet's reveries and his work is plausible. That this relation is one of seamless continuity, which makes it possible to pass easily from one to the other, is perhaps the utopia of thematic criticism. It is, nevertheless, a fruitful utopia, and one whose power to stimulate is far from being exhausted.

Thoroughly transitive, like all psychological criticism, Richardian criticism is also transitive in another, more specific sense, one that is already perceptible in *Littérature et Sensation, (Literature and Sensation)*, where one finds a horizontal transitivity. The studies in that book are linked in a subtle progression. The method is thematic, to be sure, but each theme, each variation, each figure is carried through a perpetual series of transitions indicated by the constant use of such connectives as *now*, *henceforth*, *accordingly*, and *next*. For example, the list of "ambiguous substances" in Mallarmé takes us from feather to lace, lace to cloud, and cloud to foam. Here, of course, it is the lightness or subtlety of matter that increases as the analysis proceeds, but one finds similar progressions in all of Richard's discussions, and, reading him, one would think that writers never settle on any one figure because they are always drawn to the next, which, though more satisfactory and complete than the one before, is nevertheless already threatened by yet another, until in the end every work dissolves into an endless series of modulations, a ceaseless chromaticism, like the infinite melodies of Wagnerian opera. For Richard, themes are always transitory. Not only is every theme a *bridge* between two other themes, but it is always deformed by the memory of its predecessor and the anticipation of its successor: "The carafe is therefore no longer an azure sky but not yet a lamp."[5] This constant, irresistible movement is one of the most effective charms of a critical oeuvre that is also, as hardly needs mentioning, a marvelous poetic and musical creation. But what a strange thematic study this is, which constantly devours its themes in order to ensure their continuity, and which, in so doing, also devours its own object or, at any rate, that which it takes to be the very ground in which it is rooted. "Criticism," Richard writes, "is fond of its subterranean explorations."[6] Here, then, we have the work of criticism as a series of burrows left by an indefatigable mole, burrows that forever threaten to undermine the work being studied.

Richard justifies this dangerous mobility with an observation that touches on an essential problem: "Criticism," he says,

> seems to me more like a journey than a stopping place. As it proceeds through various landscapes, it opens up, unfolds, and then conceals new perspectives. If insignificant fact-picking and excessive literalism are to be avoided, criticism must always move forward, generating new angles and perspectives as it goes. Like mountain-climbers in difficult stretches, it avoids falling only by keeping up its momentum. If it stood still, it would sink into paraphrase or gratuitousness.[7]

One cannot but approve the insistence on the fact that criticism ought not to content itself with merely identifying and classifying themes and that it must constantly seek to relate one theme to another. But a question remains: Is the relation between themes to be thought of as homogeneous and linear or as involving a system of discrete elements with a variety of functions? Richard often uses the terms *structure* and *network*, which would seem to favor the second hypothesis, but most of his analyses take the form of a continuous path, or, as he himself puts it, a "journey." Moreover, it is not always possible to decide whether this is to be thought of as an ideal journey, that is, as a series of motifs linked by their own power of association, or a real journey, which is to say, a journey imposed by the actual chronology of the work, there being always something of either miracle or artifice about the coincidence of these two orders.

There is a similar ambiguity, perhaps, in Richard's attitude toward structuralism. On the one hand, the stark intellectualism of structuralist thought is at odds with his profound taste for concreteness and experience: "Structure is of course an abstraction."[8] On the other hand, however, a highly intuitionistic interpretation of the notion of structure enables him to identify it with the more generous notion of *totality*: "As we have seen, the structural intuition cannot dwell on the use of a particular organizing form. It is not satisfied until it has embraced a totality of forms and objects."[9] This same interpretation also allows him to see his own book as a structuralist undertaking, since it is in fact a total intuition of Mallarmé's world. But can a structural analysis lay claim in advance to such a broad grasp? Structuralists do not seem to harbor such ambitions: Claude Lévi-Strauss, for example, denies that he is looking for *the* structure of a global society, instead claiming more cautiously that he is only seeing *structures* (note the plural) wherever they may be, without insisting that everything can be structured, much less that a structure can be totalizing. The best one can hope for is that it might be possible, at a second level, to establish metastructures or structures of structures, such as the relation (which may be one of opposition or symmetric reversal) between a kinship system and a linguistic system. Thus one might study (I mention the example for what it is worth) the structures of Mallarméan reverie, taken as a sort of inner discourse equipped with its own rhetoric, on the one hand, and, on the other, the structures of the poet's oeuvre. One might then ask what structural relations may exist between these two systems. But to do so would admittedly be an "abstract" undertaking. Ultimately, the basic premise, or prejudice, of structuralism is almost the opposite of the basic premise of Bachelardian analysis. It is that certain elementary functions of the most archaic forms of thinking are already highly abstract, and that the patterns and operations of the intellect are perhaps more "profound" and creative than the reveries of the sensual imagination; and, furthermore, that there exists a logic, indeed a mathematics, of the unconscious. One of Richard's noteworthy achievements is to have pointed out this embarrassing but perhaps fertile contradiction, which criticism, among other fields, is today obliged to measure and to *ponder*.

TRANSLATED BY ARTHUR GOLDHAMMER

NOTES

[1] Jean-Pierre Richard, *L'Univers imaginaire de Mallarmé* (Paris: Seuil, 1962).
[2] Ibid., p. 27.
[3] Ibid., p. 167.
[4] Ibid., p. 343.
[5] Ibid., p. 499.
[6] Ibid., p. 17.
[7] Ibid., p. 35.
[8] Ibid., p. 533.
[9] Ibid., p. 545.

MICHEL FOUCAULT

Richard's *Mallarmé*
1964

After Genette's critique of an all-too-Bachelardian Richard and Mauron's insistence that the thematic, *in its espousal of semantic plenitudes, would necessarily bypass the more uncanny aspects of whatever might be legitimately dubbed an "unconscious," Michel Foucault joined the fray with an unexpected defense of the seemingly rearguard Richard. It was a defense all the more unexpected in that Foucault was being described by Sartre (among others) as a structuralist. Here he takes his distance from that tendency, sends both Genette and Mauron (structuralist and psychoanalyst) packing, and affirms that Richard's achievement lay in delineating a third archival domain belonging to neither Mallarmé's "work" nor his "life" properly speaking. Here, then, is an early step toward the realm of "discourse"—entailing "neither a pure grammatical subject nor an opaque psychological one"—which Foucault would later make his own.*

B ecause this book is already two years old, it can no longer be read in isolation from its effects.[1] Already the reactions to the book can be interpreted as a unit, even if it is still too early to decipher what will come of them. A book becomes important not by virtue of what it stirs up but when language shifts around it, creating a void in which the book finds its home.

I will not criticize Richard's critics. I simply want to call attention to the space that has opened up around his text, to margins that, though seemingly filled with signs of polemic, in fact silently delineate the empty space in which his book is situated. When he is told that he could have written a more rigorous book had he employed a more explicitly psychoanalytic method,[2] or a more topical book had he chosen to interpret structural discontinuities,[3] his critics inadvertently reveal aspects of the work more prescient than their own objections. From outside they point to a new position, the position from which Rich-

Michel Foucault, "Le *Mallarmé* de J.-P. Richard," *Annales: Economies, sociétés, civilisations* 5 (Sept.–Oct. 1964).

ard, and Richard alone, began to speak, and which his language could not name because it originated there.

What exactly does Richard discuss? Mallarmé. But to say this is to be less than perfectly clear. As an analyst, Richard practices in a rather ambiguous domain, which includes poems, prose pieces, critical texts, remarks on fashion, English words and themes, fragments, projects, letters, and rough drafts. Its contours are vague, and it is hard to say exactly what it amounts to: Is it an opus together with outlines, early drafts, biographical material, and anecdotal sidelights? Or is it the silt of an unstanchable outpouring of language, which has to be treated as a work, fragmentary to be sure but virtually unique? Can one study, for itself and exclusively from within, this body of writing, which transcends the limits of any complete work but nevertheless gives us only the graphic component of Mallarmé?

Richard has been criticized for having been tempted by the metaphor of depth, for having hoped to catch a glimpse, beyond the shattered remnants of language, of a "shimmering beneath the surface"—in other words, of that which two hundred years of psychologism have taught us to regard as prior to language: something in the nature of soul, psyche, experience, life itself. As a result, Richard stands accused of continually shifting attention from the work to the man, and to that man's dreams, imagination, and oneiric relation to matter, space, and things—shifting attention, in other words, to the trajectory of Mallarmé's life (a matter partly of fate and partly of chance). But as everyone knows, literary analysis, having reached maturity, has freed itself from psychology.

Along with this goes a related criticism: Why did Richard systematically cut his analyses short, nip them in the bud, as it were? In order to demonstrate the consistency of Mallarmé's use of language, he relied on almost Freudian methods. But did he go far enough? Are the concepts of psychoanalysis still meaningful if they are applied only to relationships that exist within language itself, intralinguistic complexes? If, in discussing "*Igitur*," one introduces the depression that Mallarmé suffered at Tournon, the analysis is likely to remain tenuous and ungrounded so long as one refrains, out of respect for the purely literary dimension, from using such by now well-known categories as object loss, identification, and punishment by suicide. One simply cannot remain within this ambiguous realm, where what is at issue is no longer the work and not yet the psyche but only, in a rather Hegelian vein, experience, the spirit, or existence.

In the end, these two criticisms of Richard subsume all others: the ambiguity of an existential psychology, the constant equivocation between the work and the life, the gradual fusion or even bloating of structures in the temporal continuity of their metamorphoses, and the failure to choose between the standpoint of the signifier and that of the signified. All these ambiguities come together in the idea of a "theme" (which is at once a manifest linguistic complex, a persistent form of the imagination, and an unspoken existential obsession).

But Richard's "thematicism" is in no sense simply a name for, and dissimulation of, such vacillation. It is the methodological counterpart of a new object of literary analysis.

Until the nineteenth century one had at least a working idea, a reasonably clear and well-defined notion, of what a work of language (broadly defined) consisted of: an opus could include, in addition to published work, textual fragments, letters, and posthumous documents. These shared one common trait: they were composed of outer-directed language, language intended for at least some form of consumption, what one might call *circulating language*. In the nineteenth century, however, documentary conservation became absolute: with the creation of "archives" and "libraries," there came into being a reservoir of *stagnant language*, which exists only to be rediscovered for itself, in its raw form. This documentary mass of static language (consisting of stacks of drafts, fragments, and scribblings) is not just an addendum to the opus, a sort of ancillary material, a stammering satellite of the main body of the work destined only to shed additional light on what is said in the opus itself. It is not, in other words, a sort of involuntary exegesis. But neither is it an appendix to the author's biography, a key that will lay bare his secrets or reveal hidden connections between "the life and the work." In fact, what emerges with this stagnant language is a third object, irreducible to any other.

To be sure, critics and historians of literature have long since acquired the habit of relying on documentary evidence. In fact, this has been a moral obligation incumbent on literary investigators for years. A *moral* obligation, yes, but nothing more. By this I mean that if the nineteenth century made documentary conservation absolute, the twentieth century has yet to take full cognizance of two implications of that development: the need, first, for a comprehensive method for dealing with verbal documents and, second, for an awareness that stagnant language is a new object for our culture. Paradoxically, we have become familiar with such stagnant language over the past few decades, but no one has yet pointed out that it does not consist of fragments somehow more naive or primitive than the opus itself and is not simply a monument of the life or a place in which work and life come together. In other words, it does not fill the page that the old books traditionally left blank between the laudatory introduction or biographical preface and the first page of the *Complete Works*.

We are still not fully cognizant of this development or of the method that should flow from it.[4] Or, rather, I should say we were not fully cognizant of it until Richard published his book, for it seems to me that the originality of the work and the loneliness of Richard's difficult task are to be found precisely here. To criticize him on psychoanalytic grounds is facile, because his field of research is neither the work nor the life of Mallarmé but that mass of static, immobile, preserved language that is destined to be not consumed but illuminated, and that goes by the name of Mallarmé.

The hope, then, is that it will be possible to show that the 'Contes indiens' . . . continue the 'Sonnets funèbres,' see 'Hérodiade' as the sister of the 'Faune,' and imagine a direct route from 'Igitur' to 'La Dernière mode'." It is "to establish among the various individual works that make up Mallarmé's oeuvre, and among the various registers of that oeuvre—serious, tragic, metaphysical, precious, amorous, aesthetic, ideological, frivolous—a family resemblance that compels each element to illuminate the others." In other words, before settling on a method of analysis or interpretation, before opting for some form of "structuralism" or "psychoanalysis," before even announcing his choice (which is a mark of intellectual honesty but in no sense a foundational act), Richard explicitly took the crucial step of defining his object: a collection of words that is open, because any newly discovered text can be included in it, yet also closed in the absolute sense that it exists only as Mallarmé's language. In a practical sense, its extension is virtually unlimited. By contrast, its comprehension is as restricted as can be: it is limited to the Mallarméan sign.

Consequently, certain paths are marked out in advance, while all others are excluded. First, to oppose or even to distinguish between form and content is henceforth out of the question. Not because the source of their unity has at last been located but because the focal point of literary analysis has shifted: the problem now is to contrast *form* with *formlessness*, to study the history of a murmur. Rather than analyze the formal under its diurnal aspect, the face it turns toward meaning; rather than deal with its frontal function as signifier; we must consider its dark, nocturnal side, we must study the face it turns toward the undoing of form itself, toward the place from which it springs and into which it will ultimately vanish. Form is merely a mode in which nonform appears (the only such mode, perhaps, yet at best a momentary flash). One has to read Richard's very fine analysis of the Mallarméan tombstone.[6] The point is to build with fleeting, fragile, living words a stone that will stand forever upon what is no more. The tombstone, sculpting the words that it uses, will also kill them, thereby becoming form in two senses: it says (by virtue of its meaning) grave, but it is (by virtue of its words) monument. Yet it cannot express death without also expressing, fatally (because it is made of real words), resurrection in language: the black stone thus evaporates, its values are stood on their head. A marble that was dark beneath clear skies becomes at night a source of infinite light. Now it is the unsavory light of the streetlamp, now the "reviled shallow stream" (*"peu profond ruisseau calomnié"*). The tombstone as significant form disappears, the words that constituted it as a monument come undone, but with them also vanishes the hollow in which death was present. So that the grave becomes, or reverts to, language as murmur, a babble of fragile, perishable sounds. The tombstone was but the scintillating form of the formless, repeatedly disrupting the connection between the spoken word and death.

So it is unfair to criticize Richard for evading formal rigor by dealing with forms as malleable, wholly plastic entities. For his project is precisely to articulate the dissolution of form, its perpetual undoing. He discusses the interplay of form and formlessness, or, in other words, the crucial moment, so difficult to articulate, in which literature and murmur first come together and then split apart.

But who, then, is speaking in that mass of language audible only as a recurrent, sporadic murmur? Is it no one? Or is it the real Stéphane Mallarmé, of whose life, loves, anxieties, and historical existence there remain only the traces we read today? The answer to this question is important: equally impatient for that answer are the antipsychologists, who are quite right to think that biographies carry little weight, and the psychoanalysts, who know full well that once an interpretation is begun, its scope cannot be limited. So what line does Richard take? The Mallarmé to whom he refers in his analyses is neither the pure grammatical subject nor the thick psychological subject but he who says "I" in the works, letters, drafts, outlines, and confidences, hence he who, starting from afar and drawing successively closer to his still future or at any rate never-to-be completed work, takes its measure through a lingering haze of language. Hence, he is always transgressing the boundaries of his work, prowling its borders, moving in and across them only to be immediately repulsed—the guardian closer to the center than any other person, yet also more excluded. Conversely, it is also he who, in the tissue of the work itself, transcending it now in depth, discovers in and through it still future possibilities of language. So that he is himself the virtual unification of this necessarily fragmentary work, its one and only point of convergence. The Mallarmé whom Richard studies is therefore external to his work, but by virtue of an externality so radical and so pure that he is nothing other than the subject of that work, its only referent. He has no other content but it. His only relationship is with this solitary form. So that Mallarmé is also, in this layer of language, the crease that it describes within itself, that divides it inwardly as the very form of form itself.

To be sure, every point of Richard's analysis is threatened by two possible, and orthogonal, injunctions: on the one hand, to formalize, on the other, to psychologize. What emerges, however, from the unwavering straight line of his discourse is a new dimension of literary criticism. Before him this dimension was all but unknown (except perhaps to Jean Starobinski). One might contrast it with both the literary "I" and with psychological subjectivity by denoting it simply as the *speaking subject*. This of course poses (or proposes) challenges to logic, linguistics, and psychoanalysis. Yet all three of these disciplines are currently finding their way back to this very subject by different routes suggested by a variety of problems. The same speaking subject may also be a fundamental category of literary analysis.

In any case, this is what makes it possible to see an *image* as something other than a *metaphor* or a *fantasy* and to analyze it, perhaps for the first time, as *poetic thought*. Oddly enough, Richard has been criticized for sensualizing Mallarmé's intellectual experience and for treating in ecstatic terms what the poet experienced as the aridity and despair of the Idea, as if the succulence of pleasure might be the paradise, lost but forever sought, of the person whose work was early marked by the night of "*Igitur*." But reread Richard's analysis.[6] The story of Elbehnon ("I'll be none") is for him neither the transcription of a depressive crisis nor the philosophical equivalent of a libidinal suicide. In it, rather, he sees a situating or liberating of literary language around a central absence—a lacuna that is nothing other than the person who speaks: henceforth the poet's voice will traverse no lips; in the hollow of time, it will be the speech of Midnight. An extinguished candle.

That is why Richard cannot separate the experience of Mallarmé from two opposed yet related images, that of the cave and that of the diamond: the diamond, which to the enveloping world seems to sparkle though its heart is secretly dark, and the cave, a vast, murky void that echoes voices from its rocky circumference. These images are not just singular objects, however. They are themselves images of every other image: their configuration expresses the necessary relationship of thought to the visible. They show how speech, the moment it becomes pensive, is hollowed out at its core, plunging its origin, its subjective coherence, into the dark of night; it connects back up with itself only on the periphery of the perceptible, in the steady sparkle of a slowly rotating gem, or in the echo that lines the cavern's rocky walls with the sound of its voice. The Mallarméan imagination, as analyzed by Richard in terms of these two fundamental metaphors wherein all other images are contained, is therefore not the felicitous surface in which thought and the world connect; it is, rather, a dark volume that sparkles and resonates only around its edges. An image does not betoken the felicity of thought restored to its sensory paradise. In its very fragility it reveals thought plunged into darkness and thus capable of speaking only in a distant voice, which at the limit becomes the silence of things. That is why Richard's striking analyses of Mallarmé's images is so disturbing to contemporary tradition. He proceeds not from the metaphor to the impression or from sense data to the values they signify but, rather, from the named figure to the death of the poet who articulates himself therein (just as the radiance of the diamond points to its coal-black heart). The image can then be seen as the other side, the visible side, of death: when the speaker dies, his speech lingers on the surface of things, which signifies nothing but his passing. The thing perceived or felt becomes an image not when it functions as metaphor or conceals a memory but when it reveals that the person who has seen it and designated it and brought it into language is, forever and irreparably, absent. Richard's "sensualism," if one wants to use that word, has nothing in common with Bachelard's cosmological happiness. It is a "hollowed-out" sensualism, emptied of its center. For Richard, imagination is an act of thought that traverses its own death so as to greet itself in the self-alienation of language.

If the death or negation of the speaking subject is the power of which images are constituted, what makes them coherent? Neither the play of metaphor as in fantasy nor the metonymic proximity of the world. Images arrange and organize themselves in deep space. Richard has rightly perceived that this space should be linked not to either the world or the psyche but to the distance inherent in the power of language to name both death and that which is perceptible (*le sensible*). Mallarmé's words are by nature *wings* (the wing, unfolded, conceals the body of the bird; it reveals its own splendor but immediately whisks it away, carries it off into the depths of the sky, only to return ultimately in the form of faded, fallen plumage, absent the bird of which it is but the visible form). They are also *fans*, equivocal in their modesty (a fan hides the face, but not without revealing the secret that lay enfolded within, its power to hide necessarily dependent on display; conversely, when the fan closes on its ribs of pearl, it hides the enigmatic figures painted on its surface yet exposes to the light the decipherable face it was supposed to conceal). Hence the word, the true word, is pure: or, rather, it is the virginity of things themselves, plainly intact and vulnerable yet at the same time inaccessibly estranged, so remote as to make transgression impossible. The word that brings the image forth simultaneously expresses the death of the speaking subject and the distance of the spoken object.

Richard's book is also exemplary in its conduct of this kind of analysis: without resorting to alien concepts, he explores the still little-known area of literary criticism that one might call the *spatiality* of the work. Falling, separation, the pane of glass, the ray of light, the reflection—Richard does not interpret these as dimensions of an imaginary world reflected in poetry but as a deeper, less articulate kind of experience: that which falls, that which unfolds—these are both things and words, light and language. Richard has tried to reach that realm prior to all separation in which, at a throw of the dice, letters, syllables and sentences are scattered over the white page along with the aleatory shimmer of appearances.

If we wish to speak to literary works, we may avail ourselves at present of one of several modes of analysis: a logical (or metalinguistic) mode, a linguistic mode (defining and explaining the operation of signifying elements), a mythological mode (correlating elements of mythical narration), and a Freudian mode. In the past there were many others (such as the rhetorical and exegetic modes), and others will no doubt be developed in the future (perhaps someday a cybernetic mode). But the eclectic practice of turning from one to another of these modes of analysis will satisfy no one. And it is still too early to say whether literary analysis will soon discover a mode that subsumes all the others or a way of doing without any of them.

What mode did Richard employ? Did he in fact use any? If he truly sought to deal with Mallarmé as a cubic mass of language; if he truly attempted to explore a certain relationship with formlessness, seeking in it the voice of a subject absent from its own speech and of images that lay either beneath or at the limit of thought, and tracing a spatiality deeper than that of the world or of words; did he not thereby expose himself to a danger of arbitrariness? Did he not grant himself the freedom to follow his own whims and to rely without warrant on his own taste? Why reconstruct a Mallarmé of radiance, shimmering, and reflection at once persistent and tenuous, when one might equally well have chosen the Mallarmé of sunset, drama, or laughter—or of the bird driven from its nest?

In fact, Richard's analysis is tightly bound by a strict necessity. The secret of this seamless book is that in its final pages it doubles back on itself. The last chapter, "Forms and Means of Literature," is not the continuation of the first nine. It is in a sense the repetition, the mirror image, the microcosm, reproducing in miniature the pattern of what has gone before. All the figures previously analyzed by Richard (the wing, the fan, the tombstone, the cave, the radiant burst) are taken up again here, but with respect to the necessity of their origin. One discovers, for example, that for Mallarmé the word rooted in the nature of the thing signified, offering up its silent being in the play of its sonority, is nevertheless subject to the arbitrariness of language: it cannot name without simultaneously revealing and hiding. It is the figure closest to the thing but also its ineradicable distance. Thus, in itself, in the fiber of its being, prior to all the images to which it gives rise, the word itself is the flight of presence and the visible tombstone. By the same token, the word is not the diamond with its cosmological connotations inserted into the book as setting. Ultimately, the diamond form is only the internal doublet and derivative of the book itself, whose pages, words, and meanings combine, at each ceremonial reading, to set free an aleatory reflection, which is influenced by and interacts with other such reflections, and which reveals itself momentarily only by abolishing the others while at the same time holding them out as promise.

Thus, all of Richard's analyses are justified and made necessary by a law clearly revealed at the end of his work though formulated in fact throughout, running parallel to the text and bolstering it at every point. That law is not dictated by either the structure of language (with its rhetorical possibilities) or the sequence of life (with its psychological necessities). One might call it something like the naked experience of language, the relationship between the speaking subject and the very being of language. In Mallarmé, or, rather, in that chunk of language that we call "Mallarmé," that relationship took a historically unique form: this became the sovereign power that organized Mallarmé's words, syntax, poems, and (actual or unrealizable) books. Yet it can be found only in the concentrated and dilapidated language that is our only legacy, all that Mallarmé has left us. To that extent, Richard's "mode of analysis" is taken from Mallarmé himself: it is the relationship to the being of language that Mallarmé's works allow us to see, the same continuous relationship that made those sparkling words possible in the first place.

It is here, I think, that Richard's book reveals its deepest powers. Without invoking any externally defined anthropology, he has shown what the specific object of all critical discourse must be: the relation not of a man to a world or of an adult to his fantasies or his childhood or of a writer to a tongue, but of a speaking subject to that being—singular, difficult, complex, and profoundly ambiguous (because it denotes and gives being to all other beings, including itself)—we call language. Richard, by showing that this relation is not purely passive (as in conversation and everyday speech), and that a true literary work questions and disrupts the being of language, makes it possible to write criticism that is also history (what he does might strictly speaking be called "literary analysis"). His *Mallarmé* looks at the events of 1865–95 and shows what has become since then of the language with which every poet has to deal. Hence his more recent analyses (of Char, Saint-John Perse, Ponge, and Bonnefoy) occupy the space opened up by his *Mallarmé*: in these subsequent essays, he tests the continuity of his method and the unity of the history that Mallarmé inaugurated in the depths of language itself.[7]

TRANSLATED BY ARTHUR GOLDHAMMER

NOTES

[1] The book under consideration is Jean-Pierre Richard's *L'Univers imaginaire de Mallarmé* (Paris: Seuil, 1962).

[2] Charles Mauron, *Des Métaphores au mythe personnel: introduction á la psychocritique* (Paris: Corti, 1963).

[3] Gérard Genette, "Bonheur de Mallarmé?" *Tel quel* 10 (1962).

[4] The same problem exists in the field known as the history of ideas. The preservation of documents has given rise, in the sciences, philosophy, and literature, to a mass of ancillary texts, texts that are wrongly regarded as false sciences or quasi-philosophies or attenuated expressions of mere opinion, or even as foreshadowings or subsequent reflections of what would later become, or what had previously been, literature, philosophy, or science. In fact, here again, we are dealing with a new cultural object, which still awaits an appropriate definition and method and which cannot be dealt with by analogy as though it were some "quasi-genuine" form of the thing itself.

[5] *L'Univers*, 243–83.

[6] Ibid., 184–208.

[7] Jean-Pierre Richard, *Onze études sur le poésie moderne* (Paris: Seuil, 1964).

JACQUES DERRIDA

Mallarmé
1962

In "La Double séance," Derrida, wedging Mallarmé's "Mimique," the poetic evocation of a mime's performance, into the text of a Platonic dialogue, attempted to show that Mallarmé, properly read, offered the wherewithal to deconstruct Platonism—and exceed Richard's reading of the poet in the process. This selection, written for Gallimard's collective volume Tableau de la littérature française, *is entirely consistent with that longer piece. The "undecidable" is insistent in the term* hymen, *which means both marriage (or consummation) and membrane (or obstacle) impeding consummation. The theme of whiteness (snow, milk, swan, and so on) is tellingly dispersed by the whiteness of the page on which it is—over and again—inscribed. Derrida, in sum, presents Mallarmé as a breviary of deconstruction.*

> . . . I am inventing a language which must of necessity emerge
> from an utterly new poetics.
>
> —Mallarmé

Is there *a place* for Mallarmé in a "history of literature"? And first, to put it another way, does his text take place, its place, in some tableau of French literature? In a tableau? Of literature? French?

After nearly a century of reading, we are only just beginning to realize that something was concocted (*by* Mallarmé? in any case in connection with something that involved him, that seemingly passed *through* him) for the purpose of undoing historical categories and literary classifications, philosophies, and hermeneutics of every sort. We are just beginning to realize that the disruption of these categories will also have been the effect of what was, by Mallarmé, written.

In this connection it is no longer possible even to speak of an *event*, of the

From *Tableau de la littérature française* (Paris: Gallimard, 1962).

event of such a text. It is no longer possible to query its *meaning* without falling short of the mark, without falling back into a system of values that the text *practically* called into question—the question, first of all, of event (presence, singularity without possible repetition, temporality, historicity).

> Unique time in the world, because by virtue of an event, always, as I shall explain, there is no Present, not—a present does not exist . . . unless the crowd declares itself, unless—at all. He is ill-informed who would proclaim himself his own contemporary, deserting, usurping, with equal impudence, when a past ended while a future tarries or the two recombine in puzzlement in order to mask the difference.

The question also of meaning: Mallarmé was forever hunting significance wherever meaning evaporated, particularly in those twin alchemies, aesthetics and political economy.

> Everything is summed up in Aesthetics and Political Economy.

> In all only two avenues are open to mental research, two avenues in which our need bifurcates, the aesthetic on the one hand, and also political economy: with respect to this latter purpose, alchemy was, primarily, the glorious, premature, and beclouded precursor. All that was ever pure, as if devoid of meaning, before the apparition, now of the crowd, must be restored to the social realm. The worthless stone said to be the philosopher's dreams of gold: yet in finance it heralds the coming of credit, preceding capital or reducing it to the humility of money!

The purity of the sign can be *remarked* only at the point where the text, referring only to itself, designating its inscription and function while feigning unrequited reference to something other than itself, "loses everything, including meaning"—like specie stamped "legal tender."

If, moreover, Mallarmé marked a rupture, that rupture would still have the form of repetition. It would, for example, reveal the essence of past literature as such. One would have to discover, with the help of this text, in this text, the novel logic of this dual operation—which, moreover, could be attributed to Mallarmé only by invoking a naive and self-serving theory of signature, the very theory that Mallarmé, in defining what he meant by "operation," repeatedly dismissed. A text is made to obviate reference. To the thing itself, as we shall see, as well as to the author who therein inscribes nothing but his disappearance. Which is actively inscribed; it is not an accident of the text but its nature. It signs therein a permanent omission. The book is often described as a tomb.

> An ordering of the book of verse shines forth innate or everywhere, eliminates chance; so it is also necessary in order to omit the author . . .

> The right to accomplish anything exceptional or without vulgar entanglements must be paid for, by whomever, by his omission and one might say death as such.

The enigmatic *simulation* of rupture and repetition might be taken as a definition of *crisis*, the moment when simple *decision* ceases to be possible, when choice between opposing courses is suspended. Hence a crisis of criticism, which will always have wanted, through judgment, *to decide (krinein)* value and meaning, to discriminate between what is and what is not, between what has value and what does not, between what is true and what is false, what is beautiful and what is ugly, what is meaningful and its opposite. And also a crisis of rhetoric, which arms criticism with a whole hidden philosophy, a philosophy of *meaning*, of the *word*, of the *name*.

Was rhetoric ever interested in anything but the meaning of a text, its content? The substitutions that it defines are always of one pregnant sense for another. And even if one takes the place of the other, it is qua meaning that it becomes a theme for rhetoric, even if that meaning occupies the position of a signifier or, as one also says, a vehicle. But rhetoric does not deal as such with signifying forms (phonics, graphics) or syntactical effects, or at any rate deals with them only to the extent that they are controlled by semantics. If rhetoric and criticism are to see or do anything when they confront a text, that text must contain a *determinable* meaning.

Now, Mallarmé's text is organized throughout so that at crucial points its meaning remains *undecidable*. Consequently, the signifier will no longer allow itself to be passed over; it sits, resists, exists, and insists on being noticed. No longer is the work of writing to provide a transparent ether. Writing reminds us of its existence and forces us, since we can no longer simply pass through it en route to what it "means," to halt before it or work with it. It is a permanent reminder, perhaps best formulated in a passage of *Les Mots anglais*: "Reader, you have before your eyes this, a written text [*un écrit*]."

What holds decision in suspense is not the richness of meaning, not the inexhaustible resources of any word, but a certain play in syntax ("I am profoundly and scrupulously *syntaxier*"). The word *hymen* is inscribed in *"Mimique"* in a place that makes it impossible to decide whether it means the consummation of marriage or the veil of virginity. The syntax of the little French word *or* is sometimes calculated to prevent us from deciding whether it is a noun (meaning "gold"), a logical conjunction, or an adverb of time. Other, similar instances of syntactic play have been noted: *continue*, for example, can function as either a verb or adjective in the following context:

> Mais sans or soupirer que cette vive nue
> L'ignition du feu toujours intérieur
> Originellement la seule continue
> Dans le joyau de l'oeil véridique et rieur.

Elsewhere, moreover, *offre* acts as a verb and/or a noun, while *parjure* acts as verb and/or noun and/or adjective. The sign *and/or* (which, not coincidentally, encumbers many theoretical texts nowadays) points to the most striking effects of Mallarméan writing.

This is why the crisis in question does not pertain solely to Symbolism or to the period in which it flourished. Undecidability has ceased to depend on multiplicity of meaning, metaphorical richness, or a system of correspondences. Something has arisen here, something positive or negative as you will, in any case a certain angle of *view*, which blocks the polysemic horizon: the unity, the totality, the coalescence of meaning. For example, the sign *blanc* (white), with all that can to one degree or another be associated with it, is a vast reservoir of meaning (snow, cold, death, marble, and so on; swan, wing, fan, and so on; virginity, purity, hymen, and so on; page, canvas, veil, gauze, milk, semen, Milky Way, star, and so on). Omnipresent in Mallarmé's text, it exerts a sort of symbolic magnetism. And yet whiteness also marks, by way of the white page, the place where these "whites" are written. And above all the spacing between different meanings (that of white among others), *espacement de la lecture* (spaces in/of reading). The 'blanks' [*les blancs*] in fact take on importance". The white space has no determinate meaning; it is not simply subsumed by the plurivalence of all the other whites. Whether as addition to or subtraction from the polysemic series, whether as gain or loss of meaning, it folds the text back on itself, continually indicating its place ("where nothing will have taken place . . . but place"), the condition, the work, the rhythm. It will never be possible to decide whether "white" means something, or only, or also, the space of writing, the page *folding back* on itself. The use, also frequent, of the word *pli* (fold or crease, along with such variants as *pliage, ploiement, repli, reploiement,* and so on) has the same effect.

Aristotle, whose *Poetics* and *Rhetoric* inaugurated the traditional praise of metaphor (insofar as it enunciates identity or resemblance and makes it available to understanding), also said that not to signify a single thing was to signify nothing. Mallarmé's text not only breaks this rule, it foils the false transgression implicit in it, the symmetrical inversion, the polysemy that continues to *function as sign,* pointing to the law.

Is this, as has often been claimed, simply the power of words, of verbal alchemy? Is it not the case that the name, the act of naming, here achieves its ultimate effect, exhibiting a power granted to it by poetics, rhetoric, and philosophy from Aristotle to Hegel? Is not Mallarmé's theme the idealizing power of words to make the existence of an object appear or disappear simply by stating its name? Reread:

> I say: a flower! and beyond the oblivion to which my voice relegates any shape, as something beyond just calyxes, musically arises, idea itself and sweetly fragrant, what is missing from every bouquet.

Production and annihilation of the thing by the name; and above all creation, by the verse or the play of rhyme, of the name itself:

> The verse, which out of several syllables recreates a whole word, new, foreign to the language and seemingly incantatory, completes this isolation of speech.

And yet, in working on the unity of the word, the calm harmony of a vocable and a sense, Mallarmé also liberated its energy through disintegration. A word for him is no longer a component of language. The consequences of this are immense. Since I cannot explore these here, I will limit myself to a few examples.

Mallarmé knew that his "operation" on the word was also the dissection of a corpse: a decomposable corpse whose parts could be put to use *elsewhere*:

> To all kindred nature, close thereby to the organism in which life is vested, the Word presents itself, in its vowels and diphthongs, as a kind of flesh; and in its consonants as a delicate skeleton for dissection. Etc., etc., etc. If life feeds on its own past, or on a continual death, Science will rediscover this fact in language.

Already the identity of whole words is being swallowed up in a game that nevertheless seems to leave them intact. We are in a realm between homonym and synonym: in the lines that follow, *elle* (the female pronoun) refers to all *ailes* (wings, homonymous and *elle*), all birds, all dancers, all fans, not only when both are present in the rhyme

> *Car comme la mouette, aux flots qu'elle a rasés*
> *Jette un écho joyeux, une plume de l'aile,*
> *Elle donna partout un doux souvenir d'elle!*

but also when only one of the two summons the other in absentia

> *Une d'elles, avec un passé de ramages*
> *Sur ma robe blanche en l'ivoire fermé*
> *Au ciel d'oiseaux . . .*

or again

> *Quand s'isole pour le regard un signe de l'eparse beauté générale, fleur, onde, nuées et bijou, etc., si, chez nous, le moyen exclusif de le savoir consiste à en juxtaposer l'aspect à notre nudité spirituelle afin qu'elle la sente analogue et se l'adapte dans quelque confusion exquise d'elle avec cette forme envolée—rien qu'au travers du rite, là, énoncé de l'Idée, est-ce que ne paraît pas la danseuse . . .*

> [When a sign of the dispersed general beauty—flower, wave, clouds and jewel, etc.—sets itself apart for our regard, if our only way of knowing this consists in juxtaposing its aspect with our spiritual nakedness so that it might feel analogous and adapt thereto in some exquisite confusion of itself with that vanished form—by virtue simply of the rite, here, set forth by the Idea, does the dancer not appear . . .]

One could show that *aile* belongs to a series of rather masculine significations (phallic, associated with the shape of the feather), whereas *elle* propagates itself through a series of rather feminine significations. Below the level of the word, *L* stands between the two and sustains all the Mallarméan suspense:

> This letter might at times seem powerless to express by itself anything other than an appetition [*appétition*] not succeeded by any result . . .

The letter *i* gives rise to similar, equally calculated games, whether in graphic interplay of the line and dot or phonic interplay of sharp and drawn-out sounds. Thus the *fundamental I* enters into compounds of all sorts: with *l* for example, in *il* (he), or, conversely, in *lit* (bed) and *lis* (lily), both words that allow, as well, free passage between the verbal function and/or the nominal function (le *lit*/il *lit*, the bed/he reads; le *lis/lis!* le livre, the lily/read! the book). The lily (*lilium virginal*) is also the page. To cite one example, among many, concerning "that principal accessory of Villiers de l'Isle-Adam, a manuscript":

> *Livré au fait ignoble . . . plusieurs signes déjà lisibles . . . Il partagea l'existence des moins favorisés, à cause même de ce léger feuillet interposé entre le reste et lui! Alors je pense aux armes familiales et, notamment que ce papier, tenu comme un lis, eût bien abouti, en tant que légitime, immaculé, épanouissement, à cette main sur son "blason d'or."*

And quite near the hymen and the *la*, here, from "The Afternoon of a Faun," is the flower as an erect order:

> *Inerte, tout brûle dans l'heure fauve*
> *Sans marquer par quel art ensemble détala*
> *Trop d'hymen souhaité de qui cherche le la:*
> *Alors m'éveillerai-je à la ferveur première,*
> *Droit et seul, sous un flot antique de lumière,*
> *Lys! et l'un de vous tous pour l'ingénuité.*

Le lit, the bed, serves just as well to couch the written text as the dead body. *Le livre*, the book, is at the same time the site of the hymen and the figure of the sepulcher. The *porte sépulcrale* (gate of the sepulcher) is still close to a *fermoir héraldique* (heraldic clasp). In "*Hérodiade*," which includes a *lit vide*, an empty bed:

> *Elle a chanté parfois incohérente, signe*
> *Lamentable!*
> > *le lit aux pages de vélin,*
> *Tel, inutile et si claustral, n'est pas le lin!*
> *Qui des rêves par plis n'a plus le cher grimoire,*
> *Ni le dais sépulcral à la déserte moire,*
> *Le parfum des cheveux endormis. L'avait-il?*

The "*Prose pour des Esseintes*" again raises, not far from a *grimoire* (sorcerer's book) and a *livre de fer vêtu* (book clad in iron), among *cent iris, d'éternels parchemins,/avant qu'un sépulcre ne rie*, the *litige* (dispute) and the *tige de lis* (stem of the lily):

> *Oh! sache l'Esprit de litige,*
> *A cette heure où nous nous taisons,*
> *Que de lis multiples la tige*
> *Grandissait trop pour nos raisons.*

Bear in mind that these chains, infinitely more vast, more powerful, and more intertwined than I can give any inkling of here, are seemingly without support, always suspended. This is the Mallarméan doctrine of suggestion, of ambiguous allusion. This ambiguity, which allows the chains to float freely and uninterruptedly, also cuts them off, save by accident, from any meaning (signified theme) or reference (to things themselves or conscious or unconscious intentions of the author). Here lie countless potential pitfalls for criticism, and countless new methods and categories to invent.

So what we are left with is this: the "word," that is the parcels left over after its decomposition and reinscription, though never identifiable in their singular presence, refer in the end only to their own play, from which in truth they never emerge to point to something else. The *thing* is understood, in this extended *citation* from langue, as an "object effect" (*effet de chose*). Quite simply, the signifier (as we shall call it for the sake of convenience, since strictly speaking there is no longer any "sign" here), while never present for itself, stands out, in its place, by virtue of its potentialities and values. It could always be placed between inverted commas, for in the end is not what Mallarmé writes about the signifying power of the language in the form of *l'I*, *lit*, *lis*, and so on? This, among other things, is what might be called the *remark*. "Reader, you have before your eyes this, a written text."

L'absence éternelle de lit, like *le lis* absent from every bouquet, whatever the effects of its multiple meanings may be, also reminds us that *le lit*, the thing itself or the theme, is no more present in the text, no more indicated by it, than the word *lit* or *l'i* (the letter *i*) or the fragments in *enseveli*, abo*li*, and so on. If it were still possible to speak of subject here, the "subject" of the text would be this word, this letter, this syllable, and the text that they already form in the fabric of their relationships.

Mallarmé, moreover, is almost always writing about a text—this is the referent—and in some cases about an earlier version of his own text. Take the example of *or*: here is a striking demonstration of the use of homonym, of what Aristotle denounced as bad poetry, a rhetorical instrument of sophists. The first version *named* its referent, the event that was the text's pretext: the Panama scandal, the story of Ferdinand de Lesseps, and so on. To do so was still to confine these to the role of poetic occasions: "Apart from the verities that the poet can extract and keep as his secret, outside of conversation, meditating to produce them, transfigured, when the moment is ripe, nothing in this collapse of Panama interests me, for the glitter."

In the final version all that remains after extraction and condensation is the glitter of gold; the referent is erased: no proper name remains. One might assume that this was in order to clear the way for a poetic meditation on the general meaning of gold. And gold (*or*) is indeed, in some respects, the theme of this text, what one might call its "signified." On closer inspection, however, one sees that it is simply writing about the signifier, *or*, describing it, working with it. To be sure, the vein of gold is tapped to yield a whole thematic complex, a very rich one, but its primary purpose is to call attention to the signifier *or*: *l'or* as transformed from natural substance not only into monetary sign but also into a linguistic element, letters, syllable, and word. The act of naming, the direct relation to the thing, is thereby suspended. "This legal tender, a device of terrifying precision, clear to consciences, loses everything, including meaning." Thus begins a crisis in the analogous realms of political economy and language, or literary writing: *fantasmagoriques couchers du soleil*, phantasmagoric sunsets. All Mallarméan sunsets are moments of crisis, whose golden color is repeatedly recalled in the text by a sprinkling of golden touches, marked by the syllable *or* (deh*or*s, fantasmag*or*iques, trés*or*, h*or*izon, maj*or*e, h*or*s) until *l'effacement de l'or*. Which loses itself in the many *o*'s on this page, in an accumulation of zeroes that augment value only by referring it back to its own nothingness. "As a number swells and recedes toward the improbable, it inscribes ever more zeroes: signifying that its total is spiritually tantamount to nothing, almost." As for nothingness itself, nothing is settled.

This work on *or* is not limited to the page that bears this title. The sign *or* is remarked everywhere. In this triolet, for example: *Fasse le ciel qu'il nous signe, or / Bravos et louange sonore*. Here, *or* appears in proximity to *sonore*. Often Mallarmé places the noun *or* after the possessive pronoun *son — son or*. This is heard as *sonore*. It leaves *son* suspended between the possessive pronominal form and the substantive *son*, sound. It leaves *or* ringing between its nominal and descriptive values: *son or* (his/her gold), *son or* (golden sound, for in Mallarmé music and sunsets are basically golden), and *son or* (the vacuity of the phonic or graphic signifier *or*). Some examples will be useful. The first will also serve to bring out the interplay of *or* with *heure* (hour). One knows that *or* and *ores*, the logical conjunction and the adverb of time, both derive from the Latin *hora*, hour. *Encore* comes from *hanc horam*, which inflects all the *encores* and *alors* in Mallarmé in a certain way, at times suggesting an almost literal identity of *or* and *heure*: "*une éclipse, or, telle est l'heure*." "Igitur" dismantles or demonstrates this complicity of goldsmithing (*orfevrerie*) and horology (*horlogerie*). Consider:

Le Minuit:

Certainement subsiste une présence de Minuit. L'heure n'a pas disparu par un miroir, ne s'est pas enfouie en tentures, évoquant un ameublement par sa vacante sonorité. Je me rappelle que son or allait feindre en l'absence un joyau nul de rêverie, riche et inutile survivance, sinon que sur la complexité marine et stellaire d'une orfevrerie se lisait le hasard infini des conjonctions.

    Révélateur du Minuit, il n'a jamais alors indiqué pareille conjoncture, car voici l'unique heure. . . . J'étais l'heure qui doit me rendre pur . . .

[Midnight: Surely a presence of Midnight subsists. The time has not vanished through a looking-glass, has not wrapped itself in drapery, evoking a decor by its vacant sonority. I recall that its gold was going to simulate in absence a negative gem of daydreaming, a rich and useless survival, except that in the marine and stellar complexity of wrought gold the endless randomness of conjunction was legible.]

Le Sonnet en Yx:

Sur les crédences, au salon vide: nul ptyx,
Aboli bibelot d'inanité sonore,
Car le Maître est allé puiser des pleurs au Styx
Avec ce seul objet dont le Néant s'honore,
Mais proche la croisée au nord vacante, un or
Agonise selon peut-être le décor
Des licornes. . . .

[On the credenzas in the empty salon: no ptyx
Abolished bibelot of sonorous inanity,
For the Master has gone to draw tears from the Styx
With the one object with which Nothingness honors itself,
But near the crossing in the vacant north, a gold
Agonizes in accordance perhaps with the décor
Of unicorns . . .]

Mimique:

. . . un orchestre ne faisant avec son or, des frôlements de pensée et de soir, qu'en détailler la signification à l'égal d'une ode tue . . .

[. . . an orchestra with its gold, of rustling thought and night, merely detailing its meaning like a muffled ode . . .]

And the extraordinary syntax to which this word is subjected only complicates the semantic ambiguity (*or, telle est l'heure . . . ; Apitoyé, le perpétuel suspens d'une larme qui ne peut jamais toute se former ni choir (encore le lustre) scintille en mille regards, or, un ambigu sourire dénoue la lèvre . . . Or—le pliage est, vis-à-vis de la feuille imprimée grande, un indice . . .*) [Moved, the perpetual suspension of a tear, which can never altogether form itself or fall (again the chandelier) sparkles in a thousand eyes, gold, an ambiguous smile unseals the lip . . . Gold, the folding, compared with that of the broad, printed page, is a sign . . .].

Gold, the color of sunsets, moonrises (*ce lever de lune or*), and late afternoons, moments of critical ambiguity, also connotes the book-tomb, the clasp (*O fermoirs d'or des vieux missels! . . . à l'étincelle d'or du fermoir héraldique*).

Or: is this one word or several words? The linguist—and the philosopher—might say that since in each case the meaning and function are different, we ought to see a different word. Yet this diversity intersects with, and returns repeatedly to, a simulacrum of identity that must be accounted for. If what circulates in this way is not a family of synonyms, is it therefore merely a mask for a series of homonyms? But there is no name: the thing itself is (the) absent (thing); nothing is simply named; the noun is also a conjunction and an adverb.

Nor is it simply a word: the effect is often produced by a syllable into which the word has been dispersed. Neither homonymy nor synonymy, therefore.

The classical rhetorician also finds himself disarmed: none of the essentially semantic relations he is used to dealing with applies here. Neither metaphor (for there is no relation of resemblance among these *or*) nor metonymy (not only are these verbal entities not nouns, but no identity is stable enough in itself to give rise to relations of whole and part, cause and effect, and so on).

Why, moreover, should critical consideration of this *or* not play, at a distance, on its English homonym, or, rather, homogram, and with the disjunctive *versus* it expresses? One knows, and not just from biography, that Mallarmé's language was forever being shaped by English, with which it entered into regular exchanges, and that the problems implicit in these exchanges were explicitly raised in *"Les Mots anglais."* For this reason already, "Mallarmé" does not belong entirely to "French literature."

The historical shift thus effected, the inauguration and repetition of a *memorable crisis* ("Literature here is undergoing an exquisite, a fundamental, crisis"), reminiscent, in simulacrum, of the theological form of the great Book—how is one to incorporate this into a tableau?

The suggestion that Mallarmé's experiment should be compared to those of the great rhetoricians is a good one. Historically, he no doubt has more in common with them than with many of his "contemporaries," to say nothing of his "successors." But this is because he repudiated the rules of rhetoric, that is, the classical, philosophical, chastened self-representation the rhetorical tradition has given of itself since, say, Plato and Aristotle. His text transgresses the limits of that representation and gives a *practical* demonstration of its irrelevance. If, however, a rhetor is not one who submits his discourse to the rules of meaning, of philosophy, of philosophical dialectics, of truth—in short, not one of whom philosophical rhetoric approves because he accepts its rules of propriety—but, on the contrary, one whom Plato, in exasperation, sought to banish from the city as a sophist or antiphilospher, then Mallarmé was perhaps a very great rhetorician: a sophist, to be sure, but one who refused to be ensnared by the image that philosophy sought to impose on him by capturing him in a Platonic mirror while at the same time (and without contradiction) declaring him an outlaw. For Plato, like so many readers of Mallarmé, combined positive ignorance with professed admiration.

(No doubt, there should also have been some discussion here of Stéphane Mallarmé. Of his work, his thought, his unconscious, and his themes, of what in sum he apparently wanted to say, obstinately, about the play of necessity and chance, being and non-being, nature and literature, and other things of that sort. About influences sustained and exerted. About his life, to begin with, and his griefs and depressions, his teaching, his travels, Anatole and Méry, his friends, literary salons, and so forth. Until the final, and fatal, glottal spasm.)

TRANSLATED BY ARTHUR GOLDHAMMER

GILLES DELEUZE

Nietzsche and Mallarmé
1962

*If what has been called "literary theory" in this country can be character-
ized as the vicissitudes of a number of French readings of German-
language texts, Gilles Deleuze's* Nietzsche and Philosophy *figures as one
of the most important of those readings. In this selection from that book,
Deleuze warns—in direct contradiction to Derrida—that Mallarmé is
only* apparently *an ally in the grand Nietzschean enterprise of overturning
Platonism. From Deleuze's Nietzschean perspective, Mallarmé, the depressed English teacher from Sens, was no doubt as worrisome a prototype
as Kant, the philosopher "without a life" from Königsberg.*

NIETZSCHE AND MALLARMÉ

There are striking resemblances between Nietzsche and Mallarmé. Four main
similarities emerge, bringing the entire array of images into play:

First, to think is to send out a dice throw. Only a dice throw, on the basis of
chance, could affirm necessity and produce "the unique number which cannot
be another." We are dealing with a single dice throw, not with success in several
throws: only the combination victorious in one throw can guarantee the return
of the throw. The thrown dice are like the sea and the waves (but Nietzsche
would say: like earth and fire). The dice that fall are a constellation, their points
form the number "born of the stars." The table of the dicethrow is therefore
double, sea of chance and sky of necessity, midnight–midday. Midnight, the
hour when the dice are thrown . . .

Second, man does not know how to play. Even the higher man is unable to
cast the dice. The master is old, he does not know how to cast the dice on the
sea and in the sky. The old master is a "bridge," something that must be passed
over. A "childish shadow," feather or wing, is fixed on the cap of the adolescent,

---

Gilles Deleuze, *Nietzsche and Philosophy*, trans. Hugh Tomlinson (New York: Columbia University Press, 1983), from *Nietzsche et la philosophie* (Paris: P.U.F., 1962).

"of dainty stature, dark and standing in his sirenlike twisting," fit to revive the dicethrow. Is this the equivalent of Dionysus-child or even of the children of the blessed isles, the children of Zarathustra? Mallarmé presents child Igitur invoking his ancestors who are not men but Elohim, a race that was pure, that "stripped the absolute of its purity, in order to be it, and only left an idea of it, itself ending in necessity."

Third, not only is the throwing of the dice an unreasonable and irrational, absurd and superhuman act, but it constitutes the tragic attempt and the tragic thought par excellence. The Mallarméan idea of the theater, the celebrated correspondence and equations of "drama," "mystery," "hymn," and "hero" bear witness to a reflection that is comparable, at least apparently, to that of the *Birth of Tragedy*, if only by the powerful shadow of Wagner, as their common predecessor.

Fourth, the number-constellation is, or could be, the book, the work of art as outcome and justification of the world. (Nietzsche wrote of the aesthetic justification of existence: we see in the artist "how necessity and random play, oppositional tension and harmony, must pair to create a work of art"). Now, the fatal and sidereal number brings back the dice throw, so that the book is both unique and changing. The multiplicity of meanings and interpretations is explicitly affirmed by Mallarmé, but it is the correlate of another affirmation, that of the unity of the book or of the text "as incorruptible as the law." The book is the cycle and the law present in becoming.

Close as they are, these resemblances remain superficial. *For Mallarmé always understood necessity as the abolition of chance.* Mallarmé conceived the dicethrow in such a way that chance and necessity are opposite terms, the second of which must deny the first, and the first of which can only hold the second in check. The dicethrow only succeeds if chance is annulled; it fails because chance continues to exist in a certain way; "By the single fact that it is realised [human action] borrows its means from chance." This is why the number produced by the dice throw is still chance. It has often been noticed that Mallarmé's poem belongs to the old metaphysical thought of a duality of worlds; chance is like existence, which must be denied, necessity like the character of the pure idea or the eternal essence. So that the last hope of the dice throw is that it will find its intelligible model in the other world, a constellation accepting responsibility for it "on some vacant, higher surface" where chance does not exist. Finally, the constellation is less the product of the dice throw than of its passing to the limit or into another world. It matters little whether depreciation of life or exaltation of the intelligible prevails in Mallarmé. From a Nietzschean perspective, these two aspects are inseparable and constitute "nihilism" itself, that is to say, the way in which life is accused, judged, and condemned. Everything else flows from this, the race of Igitur is not the Overman but the emanation of another world. The dainty stature is not that of the children of the isles of the blessed but that of Hamlet, "bitter prince of reefs" of whom Mallarmé says elsewhere, "latent lord who cannot become one." Herodiade is not Ariadne but the frigid creature of *ressentiment* and bad conscience, the spirit that denies life, lost in her bitter reproaches to the Nourrice. The work of art in Mallarmé is "just," but its justice is not that of existence, it is still an accusatory justice that denies life, presupposes its failure and impotence. Even Mallarmé's atheism is a curious atheism, looking to the Mass for a model of the dreamed-of theater—the Mass, not the mystery of Dionysus . . . In fact, the eternal enterprise of life-depreciation has rarely been pushed so far in all directions. Mallarmé *does* discuss the dice throw, but the dice throw revised by nihilism, interpreted in the perspective of bad conscience and *ressentiment*. The dice throw is nothing when detached from innocence and the affirmation of chance. The dice throw is nothing if chance and necessity are *opposed* in it.

TRANSLATED BY HUGH TOMLINSON

JACQUES RANCIÈRE

The Hymn of Spiritual Hearts
1996

Jacques Rancière, who was perhaps the most insightful of Louis Althusser's collaborators in the structuralist project of Reading 'Capital,' *subsequently broke with his teacher on the understanding that Althusser's insistence in May 1968 on delaying political action until the requisite Theory of such action had been elaborated was more interested in the benefits of delay than in those of Theory. Rancière's study of Mallarmé appeared in 1996. In his implied opposition to the humanist Ludwig Feuerbach, his proletarian sympathies, and his belief that the time for the grand "shipwreck" (of Revolution) had not yet come, the Mallarmé he evokes in chiseled prose seems curiously aligned with the Althusserian Marx with whom he had broken some twenty years earlier.*

So, then: Nothing to do with art for art's sake, any more than with sinking into some night of language. But an aesthetic, in the sense not of a "theory of art" but of an idea of the configuration of the perceptible (*sensible*) which establishes a community. The Mallarméan *grimoire*, or sorcerer's book, is also a "book of the future":

> *Car j'installe, par la science,*
> *L'hymne des coeurs spirituels*
> *En l'oeuvre de ma patience*
> *Atlas, herbiers et rituels.*

> [For I incorporate, through science,
> the hymn of spiritual hearts
> in the work of my patience,
> atlases, herbariums, and rituals.]

A successor to the antiphonaries of old, the Mallarméan *grimoire* was not merely a game for "lonely celebrations." It was a book that chanted a hymn to the grandeur of a not yet existent crowd. Poetic hyperbole was the method of

Jacques Rancière, *Mallarmé: la politique de la sirène* (Paris: Hachette, 1996), pp. 53–67.

science itself. And it was inscribed in books of science, "atlases, herbariums, and rituals": maps of the heavens inscribed on fans, emblem books of floral calyxes designating the new figure of the Idea, and rituals to consecrate the common grandeur.

THE RELIGION OF THE CENTURY

Mallarmé was a man of his century. A century, as a measure of time, is no more real than a horizon line. It is an idea of a century. And the nineteenth century was the deployment of an idea that can be expressed in two ways. First, in terms of finishing off the previous century, the Enlightenment and the Revolution. "Finish off" had many meanings, delimited by two extremes: for some it meant to liquidate the century of unbelief and dereliction; for others, to complete a work that had only just begun, to continue, by building the new society, the work of those who had had time only to destroy the old order. What is more, these two opposed meanings could be drawn together in a common idea that summed up the second way of conceiving of the century's idea or task: that on the ruins of the old order the bonds of a new community must be forged. To that end, laws defining the relations of individuals to individuals and constitutions governing the interaction of representative institutions will never suffice. The representative regime had failed to live up to the promises of civic emancipation, just as the reign of gold had failed to live up to the promise of emancipating man's industrial powers. The two had come together to form a regime of selfishness, destructive of all communal bonds. Community had fallen short of its ideal. The idea of community is the idea of a bond. In the Latin of Romantic philology, the word for bond was *religio*. In order to complete the revolution, the community needs a new religion. At the dawn of the century, Hegel, Hölderlin, and Schelling had sketched an idea for one. This was to have been the "first systematic program of German idealism": to create for the people, on the basis of the new philosophy, which internalized and radicalized the political revolution, a new religion and mythology. The idea was abandoned in embryo, but in the rigors of speculative philosophy it was never forgotten. And Feuerbach, before Marx, deduced its consequences: it would be necessary to transcend the fraud of speculation and complete the task of founding a new religion of humanity, a religion that would restore to the bread and wine of everyday existence the human powers alienated in the form of divine attributes. But even as Hegel lay dying of cholera, the Saint-Simonians had already taken up a different trumpet to herald the century's spirit and task: the "new Christianity," the religion of rehabilitated matter, of the spirit made flesh in the scientific exactitude of railway lines establishing communication among men better than any form of language; in the spiritual community uniting the army of labor beneath a hierarchy of science and love; in the religious organization of industry, which would supplant the hierarchies of state and the maelstroms of revolution; and in that new temple, theater, which would replace the Church of old. Industry made religion, religion made industrial—these would establish the new hymn and the new theater in the place formerly occupied by that cold monster, the machinery of representative politics.

After the Saint-Simonians, the century continued to vacillate, sometimes opposing, sometimes commingling two ideas of religion's terrestrial future: there were some who hoped that man would take back God's attributes and transform them into the bread and wine of a new life delivered from all supra-terrestrial illusions, and there were others who hoped that new choirs would sing the praises of industry and progress to accompany the new forms of communication made possible by electricity and railroads. Where these two ideas came together, cities dreamed of civic religions and raised great edifices of glass and steel to house Industrial Expositions, to hold out to humanity the spectacle of a future in which man would at last be truly aware of his own nature. Mallarmé's poetry and aesthetics cannot be understood in isolation from these preoccupations of the century. But we need to determine exactly what role these secular concerns played in shaping the antecedents and forms of Mallarmé's "throw of the dice," his wager on the community's "religious" future.

TWO THESES ON DIVINITY

Mallarmé's idea of religion can be summed up in two key theses: one concerning mythology, the other Christianity. Set one after the other, these two theses constitute a history of the spirit, the third phase of which it is poetry's task to set down in writing. In regard to mythology, Mallarmé used and adapted to his own vision the anthropology of religion found in a book that he translated into French (in order to "eat," he tells us): George W. Cox's *Ancient Gods*. The thesis of the book is simple, not to say simplistic—that the gods and myths of the Greek pantheon were the personifications of natural phenomena. The proper names of the gods of Olympus and the heroes of the founding myths derived from common names borrowed from languages more ancient than Greek which had become unintelligible to the Greeks. Using these ancient words, earlier peoples had simply reported what they saw, episodes of the "tragedy of nature": the sun's dual evolution, both quotidian and annual, its death and rebirth. The names of the gods stand for the dawn and the dew and the power of the fiery star at its zenith, but above all for its perpetual descent into the kingdom of darkness and the miracle of its perpetual resurrection.

Was this simply anthropology according to the taste of the times, with linguistics lending dubious support to the rationalizations of the Enlightenment? Perhaps, but two key propositions are worth noting. First, that the gods originate not in astonishment and fear at the menace of natural phenomena but in the language that recounts those phenomena. From which it can be deduced that the true "purpose" of religion is to restore the power of language. Related to this is the second proposition, that the original object of religion was not so much the thunder that frightens, the drought that depresses, or the rain that refreshes and brings life but, rather, the coming and going of the light. When man first conceived names, he named not the benevolent and malevolent powers whose influence determined his supply of daily bread but the glorious powers that preside over his sojourn on earth. What mythology teaches us, in other words, is that the "religious" function is originally a function of the language of glorification.

With the coming of Christianity, however, the ancient idea of divinity, like the ancient idea of beauty, was deepened in ways that were tantamount to revolution. The banishment of the old gods led to a radicalization of the "glory" celebrated by language. The pomp of churches, the gold of their ciboria and monstrances, increased the apparent distance to the horizon on which the sun rose and set. The true content of glory was at last revealed, and its name was *absence*. The grandeur of the Christian religion lay in the fact that what it celebrated was the "real presence" of absence, the power of chimera. With its dark churches and golden ciboria, Christian ritual screened out the sunlight and the old "tragedy of nature," thereby revealing the intrinsic nature of the human animal. The human animal is chimerical. The "honor" of the human race is to "lend entrails to the fear that . . . metaphysical and claustral eternity inspires in itself" and to "exhale the pit with lusty howls over time."[1] The chimerical condition is the adventitious fold that absence for no apparent reason introduces into "claustral eternity," "space that remains identical to itself whether it grows or shrinks." Christianity in its purity reveals this distinctively human task of glorifying absence, which institutes "our communion or moves from one to all and all to one." Or, rather, it would reveal this task but for one unfortunate compromise: the "barbarous repast" of the body and blood of the Savior in the sacrament of the eucharist.[2] Mallarmé's "humanization" of religion thus ran counter to the century's dominant tendency. As summed up in Feuerbach's anthropology, this called for restoring to the daily bread and wine of family and community the honors that the illusory ceremony of the elevation had projected into the chimerical heaven of religion. Taking the diametrically opposite tack, Mallarmé sought to restore to the human sojourn the unique act of elevation of the chimera, the chalice containing the blood of neither god nor man: not the bread-flesh but the only thing that "illuminates" the life devoted to its acquisition, the kernel of wheat, or *gerbe juste initiale* (inchoate sheaf), that elevation of gold dust destined to fall to the sickle.[3] What was to succeed Christianity was not the religion of either the nurturing earth or the industrial corporation but the "religion" of artifice: the institution of artifacts and rituals capable of transferring to a community subject to the dominion of lusterless metallic gold and of the dark ballot box the pulverized gold of setting suns and agonizing nature, purified by the religion that, with its gold, celebrated the real presence of absence, otherwise known as its "mystery." Already the crowd has caught a preliminary glimpse of this religion of artifice in the still crude form of *feux d'artifice*, or fireworks, whose *gerbe multiple et illuminante* (radiant, multifarious spray) marks the annual cycle of the crowd's labors in public festivals.[4] But this same religion also presides over "intimate festivals"—the celebration of the residence furnished with *chimères tangibles*, tangible chimeras, such as bibelots, fabrics, books, and bouquets, which transpose the delicate and violent moments of the solar cycle—and the still more intimate festival of the book, which enfolds within its pages the play of the world.

THE POET AND THE WORKER

Mallarmé's politics come into the picture here, not unrelated, indeed precisely opposed, to the great Saint-Simonian dream of industrial religion. On a Sunday in June of 1832, as rumblings of republican riot echoed through Paris, a community of "apostles" in Ménilmontant staged a remarkable spectacle for the workers who came every Sunday to visit them: they began work on the temple of the new religion. To the accompaniment of the new choirs of king labor, Parisian bourgeois and working-class apostles, organized in platoons of diggers and barrow-pushers, solemnly dug up and hauled away earth from holes destined to become the foundation of the new temple.[5] Here was the perfect illustration of the "New Book," which would no longer be written in evanescent words and empty declarations on paper but inscribed in the very configuration of matter that was in the process of actually transforming thought on the ground. It makes no difference whether or not Mallarmé knew the story of this utopian Sunday. What does matter is that two of his prose pieces reproduce it exactly. "*Conflit*" and "*Confrontation*" both depict an identical scene in which men of the book are placed in relation to men with shovels[6]—identical except for the fact that Mallarmé demolishes any idea of a "new Christian" ceremonial, of a religious consecration of the labor of the ditch-digger made spiritual by men of the book in the role of barrow-pushers. Mercilessly, "the promenade prohibits work": the idle man on his morning stroll feels ill at ease when he has to share his hillside with the worker who, having risen much earlier, has already buried himself with his shovel deep in his hole; at noon the man of letters on vacation, his solitude protected by a fence, finds himself embroiled with the workman who has become accustomed to passing through the garden on his way from canteen to work; and in the evening the dreamer is bothered when his view is spoiled by "the strewing of the plague," railway workers collapsed in the open field, made sleepy by libations celebrating the end of work. Nothing direct comes of this confrontation, certainly nothing in the form of a hymn to labor, of consecration of the bread or transformation of the man of the book into a manual laborer or glorifier of work. Work is not and will not be glorious. The hole into which the workman has disappeared does not, and never will, stand for anything more than the futile effort of digging up earth here and transporting it there, only to repeat the same action in reverse: a pointless task whose only value is its universal equivalent, the everyday gold that can be exchanged for bread. Here we are confronted with the regular descent into a grave each day only to be reborn for the sake of mere survival. A cycle of production and reproduction, of birth in anonymous obscurity, in repetition aping the simple eternity in which there is no place to hide: in short, everything that is summed up in the word *proletarian*, everything that makes a mockery of any ritual consecration of labor.

Consecration, then, can only take place alongside. To imagine it, one has to begin with escape itself, with those Sunday libations whose intoxicating effects disrupt the regular alternation of working days and reparative nights. It is in this *other* hole hollowed out in the inexorable regularity of fate that consecration of human generations becomes possible. For these workers, in contrast to others more fortunate (some of whom may call themselves poets and trade joyfully on their pens) the daily bread wrested from a ditch is not enough. In the "shots" they quaff the day after payday, "they honorably reserve . . . a place for the sacred in life by calling a halt, stopping in expectation and committing temporary suicide." And they do so, of course, without consciousness of this "honor," "without attesting to what it is or illuminating the nature of this festival."[7] As for the golden chimera that supplements labor, food, and reproduction, they fail to see it symbolized, "magnified" in their proximity by the gold of the sun setting in a colonnade of trees.

When constellations shine above the sleeping ditch-diggers, the task of the poet-Hamlet becomes clear: to describe the "points of light" that restore to the slumbering honor of the herd the chimerical glory that it instinctively seeks. There was no populist tinge to this program. Mallarmé could lend his daughter and his couplets to the theatrical productions that his young cousins Paul and Victor Margueritte staged in a barn in Valvins, but he found himself unable to share the illusion of unity implicit in the "theater of the people." He thus derisively dismissed, in advance, what would become the program of Futurism and other avant-garde movements of the next century: "dilution, in electrifying and popular colors" of the "heavens' archaic other shore."[8] Hence, he shared neither populism's complacency nor the expectancy of Futurism. Whatever relations between the poet and the people might become in the future, for now they must be strictly separated: the poet's task must be removed from the normal cycle of day and night, from the ordinary exchange of labor for gold. Plato divided the human race into two groups: those upon whom the gods had conferred the gold of thought, and those doomed to labor in iron. In granting the former not only the symbolic gold but control of the city, he also denied them possession of material gold, that is, ownership of property or remuneration for their labor. The separation of the ditch-digger from the poet completed a similar divorce between real gold and symbolic gold. Here, however, Mallarmé registers an essential difference. For him, the composition of the soul was not determined by the gods' distribution of gold and iron. Revolutions were made for just that reason—so that anyone might be among the "elect," the first or the last willing to devote himself to the labor of the other gold, the symbolic gold, whose luster, rivaling the fires of the vanished sun in the honor of the chimerical race, will illuminate the festivals of the future. But this elect individual, who may be anyone, must observe a strict division of tasks and metals. If the poet is to prepare the "hymn of spiritual hearts," he must divorce his task from any traffic in monetary gain or social position. Not that he is to be rewarded, like the Platonic guardians or the "monks" of the English universities, by the labor of the men of iron. Like Mallarmé, he is to earn his daily bread by day so that he may freely devote his nights to his task as "preparer of rhythms."[9]

The solitude of the poet, and even the cloud with which he surrounds his verse, must be seen in this light. To assimilate these to the nihilist wish to situate the work within a "column of silence" hostile to the public space of democracy is therefore to miss its significance.[10] It would be much more accurate to relate Mallarmé's "limited action" to the Marxist idea that conditions must be ripe before a revolution can occur. The poet's isolation is strictly related to the "absence of present." The politics of the throw of the dice—and the ultimate meaning of the myth of the ship and the siren—must be understood to mean that conditions are not yet ripe for the union of poet and crowd in "the hymn of spiritual hearts." The "extraordinary hour" has not yet struck, and the "prodigious hall" or theater has yet to open. For the poem as for the community, it is madness to act as though the replacement of the reign of material gold by that of symbolic gold were already possible: "Gold at present strikes the race squarely on the head." The moment of celebrating its twilight has yet to arrive, a twilight of "sumptuousness akin to the vessel that goes down, surrenders, and celebrates sky and water with its blaze."[11] The poet who mistakes the Panama scandal or the collapse of some bank for the revolutionary dawn and celebrates it prematurely is like the reckless banker who squanders the gold of the future in the mediocrity of a routine bankruptcy. If the blaze of the great shipwreck is celebrated too soon, the Argonauts' vessel in the poem will be swallowed up by the abyss. The "epoch's tunnel" cannot be shortened in order to arrive sooner at the "central station," whose glass cupola might stand for that communal palace in which the "hymn of spiritual hearts" resounds. Such is the meaning of our little marine fable: the time of the great and glorious shipwreck has yet to come. It is rather the hour of the discreet siren, who refuses to silence in advance truths still sounded only as "scales, serious chords in prelude to the concert."[12] Better to "practice" those scales and chords while the "other crisis" is in gestation.

The injunction of solitude thus issued to both artist and work must therefore be understood in the proper light. It is precisely because of his solidarity with the worker, who daily buries himself in and is reborn from the common grave of work, that the poet must isolate himself in order to "sculpt his own tombstone" and fathom the "suicide" parodied by the Saturday night libations.[13] One must be careful not to misinterpret the assertion that the book "calls no reader to draw near" and "takes place all alone." This does not mean that the writer writes only for himself. It means that the book, in its material reality as a lonely volume whose pages simultaneously hide and reveal their treasure, is already the institution of a place. Hence, it is not for reasons of aesthetic elitism that the book defends, "against brutal space, the intimate, minutely folded delicacy of being in itself."[14] This reserved "delicacy" lies in the recesses that turn the "claustral eternity" of space into a world habitable by the human community. It is not for the purposes of any nihilistic ceremony that "the shrouded sense moves to arrange the pages in chorus."[15] The book that the poet's "suicide" sculpts into a tombstone is what sets the fate of man apart from the common grave, from the eternity of production and reproduction of life. The enshrouding of the choruses of the future in the book ends the Saint-Simonian illusion of a "new book." The act of writing takes place only on paper. But the same "tombstone" preserves the rhythms of the hymn for the festivals of the future, the *Thousand and One Nights* that a suddenly invented reading majority will devour with amazement."[16]

TRANSLATED BY ARTHUR GOLDHAMMER

NOTES

[1] Mallarmé, *Oeuvres complètes* (Paris: Gallimard, 1945), p. 56

[2] *"Catholicisme,"* in ibid., p. 391.

[3] Ibid., p. 394.

[4] *"La Cour,"* in ibid., p. 414, and *"Villiers de l'Isle Adam,"* in ibid., p. 499.

[5] See Jacques Rancière, *La Nuit des prolétaires* (Paris: Fayard, 1981).

[6] *"Conflit,"* in *Oeuvres complètes*, pp. 355–60; *"Confrontation,"* in ibid, pp. 409–412.

[7] *"Conflit,"* p. 359.

[8] *"Catholicisme,"* p. 394.

[9] *"Bucolique,"* in *Oeuvres complètes*, p. 401.

[10] Cf. Jean-Paul Sartre, *Mallarmé, la lucidité et sa face d'ombre* (Paris: Gallimard, 1986).

[11] *"Or,"* in *Oeuvres complètes*, p. 398.

[12] *"Solitude,"* in ibid, p. 408.

[13] *"Sur l'Évolution littéraire,"* in ibid., p. 869.

[14] *"Le genre ou les modernes,"* in ibid., p. 318.

[15] *"L'Action restreinte,"* in ibid., p. 372.

[16] *"Etalages,"* in ibid., p. 376.

PART IV
Novelties

New Novel

ALAIN ROBBE-GRILLET

A Future for the Novel
1956

While acknowledging the inertia of the novelistic community (readers and writers alike), Robbe-Grillet salutes a growing allergy to both psychological analysis and the concomitant metaphorics of depth in this programmatic text. Film, slated initially to illustrate *novelistic texts, begins to wreak havoc within the novel itself.*

It seems hardly reasonable at first glance to suppose that an entirely *new* literature might one day—now, for instance—be possible. The many attempts made these last thirty years to drag fiction out of its ruts have resulted, at best, in no more than isolated works. And—we are often told—none of these works, whatever its interest, has gained the adherence of a public comparable to that of the bourgeois novel. The only conception of the novel to have currency today is, in fact, that of Balzac.

Or that of Mme de La Fayette. Already sacrosanct in her day, psychological analysis constituted the basis of all prose: it governed the conception of the book, the description of its characters, the development of its plot. A "good" novel, ever since, has remained the study of a passion—or of a conflict of passions, or of an absence of passion—in a given milieu. Most of our contemporary novelists of the traditional sort—those, that is, who manage to gain the approval of their readers—could insert long passages from *The Princess of Clèves* or *Père Goriot* into their own books without awakening the suspicions of the enormous public which devours whatever they turn out. They would

Alain Robbe-Grillet, "A Future for the Novel," in *For a New Novel: Essays on Fiction*, trans. Richard Howard (New York: Grove, 1965), from *Pour un nouveau roman* (Paris: Minuit, 1963).

merely need to change a phrase here and there, simplify certain constructions, afford an occasional glimpse of their own "manner" by means of a word, a daring image, the rhythm of a sentence. . . . But all acknowledge, without seeing anything peculiar about it, that their preoccupations as writers date back several centuries.

What is so surprising about this, after all? The raw material—the French language—has undergone only very slight modifications for three hundred years; and if society has been gradually transformed, if industrial techniques have made considerable progress, our intellectual civilization has remained much the same. We live by essentially the same habits and the same prohibitions—moral, alimentary, religious, sexual, hygienic, and so on. And, of course, there is always the human "heart," which as everyone knows is eternal. There's nothing new under the sun, it's all been said before, we've come on the scene too late, and so on and so forth.

The risk of such rebuffs is merely increased if one dares claim that this new literature is not only possible in the future, but is already being written, and that it will represent—in its fulfillment—a revolution more complete than those which in the past produced such movements as Romanticism or Naturalism.

There is, of course, something ridiculous about such a promise as "Now things are going to be different!" How will they be different? In what direction will they change? And, especially, why are they going to change now?

The art of the novel, however, has fallen into such a state of stagnation—a lassitude acknowledged and discussed by the whole of critical opinion—that it is hard to imagine such an art can survive for long without some radical change. To many, the solution seems simple enough: such a change being impossible, the art of the novel is dying. This is far from certain. History will reveal, in a few decades, whether the various fits and starts which have been recorded are signs of a death agony or of a rebirth.

In any case, we must make no mistake as to the difficulties such a revolution will encounter. They are considerable. The entire caste system of our literary life (from publisher to the humblest reader, including bookseller and critic) has no choice but to oppose the unknown form that is attempting to establish itself. The minds best disposed to the idea of a necessary transformation, those most willing to countenance and even to welcome the values of experiment, remain, nonetheless, the heirs of a tradition. A new form will always seem more or less an absence of any form at all, since it is unconsciously judged by reference to the consecrated forms. In one of the most celebrated French reference works, we may read in the article on Schönberg: "Author of audacious works, written without regard for any rules whatever"! This brief judgment is to be found under the heading *Music*, evidently written by a specialist.

The stammering newborn work will always be regarded as a monster, even by those who find experiment fascinating. There will be some curiosity, of course, some gestures of interest, always some provision for the future. And some praise; though what is sincere will always be addressed to the vestiges of the familiar, to all those bonds from which the new work has not yet broken free and which desperately seek to imprison it in the past.

For, if the norms of the past serve to measure the present, they also serve to construct it. The writer himself, despite his desire for independence, is situated within an intellectual culture and a literature that can only be those of the past. It is impossible for him to escape altogether from this tradition of which he is the product. Sometimes the very elements he has tried hardest to oppose seem, on the contrary, to flourish more vigorously than ever in the very work by which he hoped to destroy them; and he will be congratulated, of course, with relief for having cultivated them so zealously.

Hence it will be the specialists in the novel (novelists or critics, or overassiduous readers) who have the hardest time dragging themselves out of its rut.

Even the least conditioned observer is unable to see the world around him through entirely unprejudiced eyes. Not, of course, that I have in mind the naive concern for objectivity which the analysts of the (subjective) soul find it so easy to smile at. Objectivity in the ordinary sense of the word—total impersonality of observation—is all too obviously an illusion. But *freedom* of observation should be possible, and yet it is not. At every moment, a continuous fringe of culture (psychology, ethics, metaphysics, and so on) is added to things, giving them a less alien aspect, one that is more comprehensible, more reassuring. Sometimes the camouflage is complete: a gesture vanishes from our mind, supplanted by the emotions that supposedly produced it, and we remember a landscape as *austere* or *calm* without being able to evoke a single outline, a single determining element. Even if we immediately think, "That's literary," we don't try to react against the thought. We accept the fact that what is *literary* (the word has become pejorative) functions like a grid or screen set with bits of different colored glass that fracture our field of vision into tiny assimilable facets.

And if something resists this systematic appropriation of the visual, if an element of the world breaks the glass, without finding any place in the interpretative screen, we can always make use of our convenient category of "the absurd" in order to absorb this awkward residue.

But the world is neither significant nor absurd. It *is*, quite simply. That, in any case, is the most remarkable thing about it. And suddenly the obviousness of this strikes us with irresistible force. All at once, the whole splendid construction collapses; opening our eyes unexpectedly, we have experienced, once too often, the shock of this stubborn reality we were pretending to have mastered. Around us, defying the noisy pack of our animistic or protective adjectives, things *are there*. Their surfaces are distinct and smooth, *intact*, neither suspiciously brilliant nor transparent. All our literature has not yet succeeded in eroding their smallest corner, in flattening their slightest curve.

The countless movie versions of novels that encumber our screens provide an occasion for repeating this curious experiment as often as we like. The cinema, another heir of the psychological and naturalistic tradition, generally has as its sole purpose the transposition of a story into images: it aims exclusively at imposing on the spectator, through the intermediary of some well-chosen scenes, the same meaning the written sentences communicated in their own fashion to the reader. But at any given moment the filmed narrative can drag us out of our interior comfort and into this proffered world with a violence not to be found in the corresponding text, whether novel or scenario.

Anyone can perceive the nature of the change that has occurred. In the initial novel, the objects and gestures forming the very fabric of the plot disappeared completely, leaving behind only their *significations*: the empty chair became only absence or expectation, the hand placed on a shoulder became a sign of friendliness, the bars on the window became only the impossibility of leaving. . . . But in the cinema, one *sees* the chair, the movement of the hand, the shape of the bars. What they signify remains obvious, but instead of monopolizing our attention, it becomes something added, even something in excess, because what affects us, what persists in our memory, what appears as essential and irreducible to vague intellectual concepts are the gestures themselves, the objects, the movements, and the outlines, to which the image has suddenly (and unintentionally) restored their *reality*.

It may seem peculiar that such fragments of crude reality, which the filmed narrative cannot help presenting, strike us so vividly, whereas identical scenes in real life do not suffice to free us of our blindness. As a matter of fact, it is as if the very conventions of the photographic medium (the two dimensions, the black-and-white images, the frame of the screen, the difference of scale between scenes) help free us from our own conventions. The slightly "unaccustomed" aspect of this reproduced world reveals, at the same time, the unaccustomed character of the world that surrounds us: it, too, is unaccustomed insofar as it refuses to conform to our habits of apprehension and to our classification.

Instead of this universe of "signification" (psychological, social, functional), we must try, then, to construct a world both more solid and more immediate. Let it be first of all by their *presence* that objects and gestures establish themselves, and let this presence continue to prevail over whatever explanatory theory may try to enclose them in a system of references, whether emotional, sociological, Freudian or metaphysical.

In this future universe of the novel, gestures and objects will be *there* before being *something*; and they will still be there afterward, hard, unalterable, eternally present, mocking their own "meaning," that meaning which vainly tries to reduce them to the role of precarious tools, of a temporary and shameful fabric woven exclusively—and deliberately—by the superior human truth expressed in it, only to cast out this awkward auxiliary into oblivion and darkness as soon as possible.

Henceforth, on the contrary, objects will gradually lose their instability and their secrets, will renounce their pseudo-mystery, that suspect inferiority which Roland Barthes has called "the romantic heart of things." No longer will objects be merely the vague reflection of the hero's vague soul, the image of his torments, the shadow of his desires. Or rather, if objects still afford a momentary prop to human passions, they will do so only provisionally, and will accept the tyranny of significations only in appearance—derisively, one might say—the better to show how alien they remain to man.

As for the novel's characters, they may themselves suggest many possible interpretations; they may, according to the preoccupations of each reader, accommodate all kinds of comment—psychological, psychiatric, religious, or political—yet their indifference to these "potentialities" will soon be apparent. Whereas the traditional hero is constantly solicited, caught up, destroyed by these interpretations of the author's, ceaselessly projected into an immaterial and unstable *elsewhere*, always more remote and blurred, the future hero will remain, on the contrary, *there*. It is the commentaries that will be left elsewhere; in the face of his irrefutable presence, they will seem useless, superfluous, even dishonest.

Exhibit X in any detective story gives us, paradoxically, a clear image of this situation. The evidence gathered by the inspectors—an object left at the scene of the crime, a movement captured in a photograph, a sentence overheard by a witness—seem chiefly, at first, to require an explanation, to exist only in relation to their role in a context which overpowers them. And already the theories begin to take shape: the presiding magistrate attempts to establish a logical and necessary link between things; it appears that everything will be resolved in a banal bundle of causes and consequences, intentions and coincidences. . . .

But the story begins to proliferate in a disturbing way: the witnesses contradict one another, the defendant offers several alibis, new evidence appears that had not been taken into account. . . . And we keep going back to the recorded evidence: the exact position of a piece of furniture, the shape and frequency of a fingerprint, the word scribbled in a message. We have the mounting sense that nothing else is *true*. Though they may conceal a mystery, or betray it, these elements which make a mockery of systems have only one serious, obvious quality, which is to *be there*.

The same is true of the world around us. We had thought to control it by assigning it a meaning, and the entire art of the novel, in particular, seemed dedicated to this enterprise. But this was merely an illusory simplification; and far from becoming clearer and closer because of it, the world has only, little by little, lost all its life. Since it is chiefly in its presence that the world's reality resides, our task is now to create a literature which takes that presence into account.

All this might seem very theoretical, very illusory, if something were not actually changing—changing totally, definitively—in our relations with the universe. Which is why we glimpse an answer to the old ironic question, "Why now?" There is today, in fact, a new element that separates us radically this time from Balzac as from Gide or from Mme de La Fayette: it is the destitution of the old myths of "depth."

We know that the whole literature of the novel was based on these myths, and on them alone. The writer's traditional role consisted in excavating Nature, in burrowing deeper and deeper to reach some ever-more intimate strata, in finally unearthing some fragment of a disconcerting secret. Having descended into the abyss of human passions, he would send to the seemingly tranquil world (the world on the surface) triumphant messages describing the mysteries he had actually touched with his own hands. And the sacred vertigo the reader suffered then, far from causing him anguish or nausea, reassured him as to his power of domination over the world. There were chasms, certainly, but thanks to such valiant speleologists, their depths could be sounded.

It is not surprising, given these conditions, that the literary phenomenon par excellence should have resided in the total and unique adjective, which attempted to unite all the inner qualities, the entire hidden soul of things. Thus, the word functioned as a trap in which the writer captured the universe in order to hand it over to society.

The revolution that has occurred is considerable: not only do we no longer consider the world as our own, our private property, designed according to our needs and readily domesticated, but we no longer even believe in its "depth." While essentialist conceptions of man met their destruction, the notion of "condition" henceforth replacing that of "nature," the *surface* of things has ceased to be for us the mask of their heart, a sentiment that led to every kind of metaphysical transcendence.

Thus, it is the entire literary language that must change, that is changing already. From day to day, we witness the growing repugnance felt by people of greater awareness for words of a visceral, analogical, or incantatory character. On the other hand, the visual or descriptive adjective, the word that contents itself with measuring, locating, limiting, defining, indicates a difficult but most likely direction for a new art of the novel.

TRANSLATED BY RICHARD HOWARD

ROLAND BARTHES

Literal Literature
1964

In an influential article on Robbe-Grillet's Voyeur, *Roland Barthes salutes the permanently "pre-suicidal" state to which literature has acceded in a resolutely unpsychoanalytic recasting of the Oedipus myth.*

We don't read a novel by Alain Robbe-Grillet the way—at once total and discontinuous—we "devour" a traditional novel, intellection leaping from paragraph to paragraph, from crisis to crisis, our eyes absorbing the typography only intermittently as if the act of reading, in its most material gesture, reproduced the very hierarchy of the classical universe, endowed with moments alternately pathetic and insignificant. No, in Robbe-Grillet, narrative itself imposes the necessity of an exhaustive ingestion of the material; the reader is subjected to a kind of relentless education, he has the sense of being held fast to the very continuity of objects and of actions. His capture results not from a rape or a fascination but from a gradual and inevitable investiture. The narrative's pressure is quite steady, appropriate to a literature of evidence.

This new quality of reading is linked, here, to the strictly optical nature of the novelistic substance. As we know, Robbe-Grillet's intention is to accord objects a narrative privilege hitherto granted only to human relations. Whence a profound renewal of the art of description, since in this "objective" universe substance is presented no longer as a function of the human heart (memory, instrumentality) but as an implacable space which man can frequent only by movement, never by use or subjection.

This is a great literary exploration, whose initial reconnaissance was made in *The Erasers. The Voyeur* constitutes a second stage, attained quite deliberately, for Robbe-Grillet gives the impression that his creation follows a methodically predetermined path; indeed, we may assume that his oeuvre will have a demonstration value and that, like every authentic literary act, this value

Roland Barthes, *Critical Essays*, trans. Richard Howard (Evanston: Northwestern University Press, 1972), from *Essais critiques* (Paris: Seuil, 1964).

will not be so much literature as the very institution of literature: certainly in the last fifty years, all significant writing possesses this same problematic virtue.

What is interesting about *The Voyeur* is the relation the author establishes between objects and story. In *The Erasers*, the objective world was sustained by elements of a murder mystery. In *The Voyeur*, there is no longer any such qualification of the story: *affabulation* tends to zero, to the point where it can scarcely be named, much less summarized (as the embarrassment of our critics testifies). Of course, I can say that on an unidentified island a traveling salesman strangles a shepherd girl and returns to the mainland. But am I quite certain about this murder? The act itself is narratively blanked out (a very visible hole in the middle of the narrative); the reader can only induce it from the murderer's patient effort to erase this void (so to speak), to fill it with a "natural" time. Which is to say that the extent of the objective world, the calm assiduity of reconstitution here close in upon an improbable event: the importance of antecedents and consequences, their prolix literality, their insistence upon being spoken, necessarily cast suspicion upon an act that suddenly, and contrary to the analytic vocation of the discourse, no longer has language for its immediate guarantee.

The act's blankness derives primarily, of course, from the objective nature of the description. A story (what we consider, precisely, "novelistic") is a typical product of our civilizations of the soul. Consider Ombredane's ethnological experiment: the film *Underwater Hunt* is shown to black students in the Congo and to Belgian students; the former offer a purely descriptive summary of what they have seen, precise, concrete, without *affabulation*; the latter, on the contrary, betray a great visual indigence, they have difficulty recalling details, they make up a story, seek certain literary effects, try to produce affective states. It is precisely this spontaneous birth of drama which Robbe-Grillet's optical system aborts at each moment; as with the Congolese, the precision of his spectacle absorbs all its potential interiority (a proof *a contrario*: it is our spiritualized critics who have desperately sought a story in *The Voyeur*—they realized that without a pathological or ethical argument the novel escaped that civilization of the soul which it is their responsibility to defend). There is, then, a conflict between the purely optical world of objects and the world of human interiority. By choosing the former, Robbe-Grillet cannot help being entranced by the annihilation of the anecdote.

There is, as a matter of fact, a tendentious destruction of story in *The Voyeur*. The plot recedes, diminishes, dies away under the weight of objects. Objects invest the story in a military sense, participate in it the better to devour it. It is remarkable that we do not know crime, nor motives, nor affects, nor even acts, but only isolated materials whose description, moreover, is denied any explicit intentionality. The story's data are neither psychological nor even pathological (at least in their narrative situation), they are reduced to certain objects gradually looming out of space and time without any avowed causal contiguity—a little girl (at least her archetype, for her name keeps changing), a piece of string, a stake, a pillar, some candy.

It is only the gradual coordination of these objects which delineates if not the crime itself then at least the place and moment of the crime. The materials are associated with each other by a kind of indifferent chance; but the repetition of certain constellations of objects (string, candy, cigarettes, the hand with pointed nails) creates the probability of a murderous application that would unite them all; and these associations of objects (as we might say, associations of ideas) gradually condition the reader to the existence of a probable plot, though without ever naming it, as if, in Robbe-Grillet's world, we had to shift from the order of objects to the order of events by a patient series of pure reflexes, scrupulously avoiding the mediation of a moral consciousness.

This purity can of course be only tendentious, and the whole of *The Voyeur* is created by an impossible resistance to anecdote. The objects figure as a kind of zero-theme of the plot. The novel keeps within that narrow and difficult zone in which anecdote (the crime) begins to go bad, to "intentionalize" the splendid stubbornness of objects in simply *being there*. Indeed, this silent inflection of a purely objective world toward interiority and pathology derives simply from a defect of space. If we recall that Robbe-Grillet's profound intention is to account for the whole of objective space, as if the novelist's hand closely followed his vision in an exhaustive apprehension of lines and surfaces, we realize that the return of certain objects, of certain fragments of space, privileged by their very repetition, constitutes in itself a flaw, what we might call an initial softening of the novelist's optical system, based essentially on contiguity and extension. We might then say that insofar as the repeated encounter with certain objects breaks the parallelism of vision and objects, there is a crime, that is, an event: the geometric flaw, the collapse of space, the eruption of a return is the breach by which a whole psychological, pathological, anecdotal order will threaten to invest the novel. It is precisely here, where the objects, by *representing* themselves, seem to deny their vocation as pure existences, that they invoke the anecdote and its retinue of implicit motives; repetition and conjunction strip them of their *Dasein*, of their *being-there*, in order to endow them with a *being-for-something*.

This mode of iteration is quite different from the thematics of classical authors. The repetition of a theme postulates a depth, the theme is a sign, the symptom of an internal coherence. In Robbe-Grillet, on the contrary, the constellations of objects are not expressive but creative; their purpose is not to reveal but to perform; they have a dynamic, not a heuristic role: before they appear, there exists nothing of what they will produce for the reader: they *make* the crime, they do not betray it: in a word, they are literal. Robbe-Grillet's novel remains, then, perfectly external to a psychoanalytic order: no question here of a world of compensation and justification, in which certain tendencies are expressed or counterexpressed by certain acts; the novel deliberately abolishes all past and all depth, it is a novel of extension, not of comprehension. The crime settles nothing (above all, satisfies no desire for a crime), never provides an answer, a solution, an outcome of crisis: this universe knows neither compression nor explosion, nothing but encounters, intersections of itineraries, returns of objects. And if we are tempted to read rape and murder in *The Voyeur* as acts deriving from a pathology, we are abusively inferring content from form: we are once again victims of that prejudice which makes us attribute to the novel an essence, that of the real, of *our* reality; we always conceive the imaginary as a symbol of the real, we want to see art as a litotes of nature. In Robbe-Grillet's case, how many critics have renounced the blinding literalness of the work in order to try to introduce into this universe whose implacable completeness is only too obvious, a dimension of soul, of evil, whereas Robbe-Grillet's technique is precisely a radical protest against the ineffable.

We might express this refusal of psychoanalysis in another way by saying that in Robbe-Grillet, the event is never *focused*. We need merely think of what in painting, in Rembrandt, for example, is a space visibly centered outside the canvas: this is more or less the world of rays and diffusions we meet in our novels of depth. In Robbe-Grillet, nothing of the kind: light is even and steady, it does not traverse, it displays, the act is not the spatial analogy of a secret source. Even if the narrative acknowledges one privileged moment (the blank page in the middle), it is not thereby concentric: the blank (the crime) is not the center of a fascination, it is merely the extreme point of a course, the limit from which the narrative will flow back toward its origin. This absence of focus undermines the pathology of the murder: the murder is developed according to rhetorical, not thematic means; it is revealed by topics, not by radiation.

We have just suggested that the crime was nothing more than a flaw of space and time (which are one and the same, since the site of the murder, the island, is never anything but the plan of a circuit). The murderer's entire effort is therefore (in the second part of the novel) to seal time back together, to regain a continuity which will be innocence (this is, of course, the very definition of an alibi, but here the resealing of time is not done in the presence of a detective or a policeman; it is done in the presence of a purely intellective consciousness, which seems to be struggling oneirically in the pangs of an incomplete intention). Similarly, in order for the crime to disappear, objects must lose their insistence on being grouped, constellated; they must be made to regain, retrospectively, a pure relation to contiguity. The desperate search for a seamless space (and as a matter of fact, it is only by its annihilation that we know about the crime) is identified with the very effacement of the crime, or more precisely, this effacement exists only as a kind of artificial glaze spread retroactively over the day. All at once, time assumes density, and we *know* that the crime exists. But it is then, just when time is overloaded with variations, that it assumes a new quality, the *natural*: the more *used* time is, the more plausible it appears: Mathias, the murderer, is obliged to pass his consciousness over the flaw of the crime unceasingly, like an insistent brush. Robbe-Grillet utilizes in these movements a special indirect style (in Latin, this style would employ a continuous subjective, which moreover would betray its user).

We are dealing, then, not so much with a voyeur as with a liar. Or, rather, the voyeuristic phase of the first part is succeeded by the mendacious phase of the second: the continuous exercise of the lie is the only psychological function we may grant Mathias, as if, in Robbe-Grillet's eyes, psychologism, causality, intentionality could broach the adequacy of objects only in the form of a crime, and in crime, in the form of an alibi. It is by scrupulously sealing his day together again with a thin coat of *nature* (a mixture of temporality and causality) that Mathias reveals his crime to us (and perhaps to himself?), for we never see Mathias except as a remaking consciousness. This is precisely the theme of Oedipus. The difference is that Oedipus acknowledges a crime that has already been before its discovery, his crime belongs to a magical economy of compensation (the Theban plague), whereas Mathias offers an isolated guilt, intellective and not moral, which is never involved in a general relation to the world (causality, psychology, society); if the crime is corruption, it is here only a corruption of time—and not of human interiority: it is designated not by its ravages, but by a vicious arrangement of duration.

Such, then, is the anecdote of *The Voyeur*: desocialized and demoralized, suspended on the surface of objects, arrested in an impossible movement toward its own abolition, for Robbe-Grillet's project is always to cause the novelistic universe to cohere by means of its objects and by them alone. As in those perilous exercises where the aerialist gradually eliminates parasitical points of support, *affabulation* is little by little reduced, rarefied. Ideally, it would be done away with altogether; and if it still exists in *The Voyeur*, it is rather as the locus of a possible story (*affabulation's* zero-degree, or what Claude Lévi-Strauss calls *mana*), in order to spare the reader the too-brutal effects of pure negativity.

Naturally, Robbe-Grillet's endeavor proceeds from a radical formalism. But in literature, this is an ambiguous reproach, for literature is by definition formal; there is no middle term between a writer's extinction and his aestheticism, and if we consider formal experiment harmful, it is writing and not experiment that we must forbid. One might say, on the contrary, that the formalization of the novel as Robbe-Grillet pursues it has value only if it is radical, that is, if the novelist has the courage to postulate tendentiously a novel without content, at least for as long as he seeks to raise the mortgages of bourgeois psychologism: a metaphysical or moral interpretation of *The Voyeur* is certainly possible (as our critics have proved), insofar as the zero-state of the anecdote liberates in an overconfident reader all kinds of metaphysical investitures; it is still possible to occupy the letter of the narrative by an implicit spirituality and to transform a literature of pure evidence into a literature of protest or outcry: by definition, the former is accessible to the latter. But for my part, I believe that this would be to strip *The Voyeur* of all interest. It is a book that can sustain itself only as an absolute exercise in negation, and as such it can take place in that very narrow zone, in that rare vertigo where literature unavailingly tries to destroy itself, and apprehends itself in one and the same movement, destroying and destroyed. Few works enter this mortal margin, but they are doubtless, today, the only ones that matter: in our present social circumstances, literature cannot be at once granted to the world and in advance of it, as is appropriate to any art of transcendence, except in a state of permanent presuicide; literature can exist only as the figure of its own problem, self-pursuing, self-scourging. Otherwise, whatever the generosity or the exactitude of its content, literature always ends by succumbing under the weight of a traditional form that compromises it insofar as it serves as an alibi for the alienated society which produces, consumes, and justifies it. *The Voyeur* cannot be separated from what is today the constitutively reactionary status of literature, but by trying to aseptacize the very form of narrative, it is perhaps preparing, without yet achieving, a deconditioning of the reader in relation to the essentialist art of the bourgeois novel. Such at least is the hypothesis this book allows us to propose.

TRANSLATED BY RICHARD HOWARD

NATHALIE SARRAUTE

The Age of Suspicion
1957

Nathalie Sarraute voices a general distrust (on the part of readers and nov-elists) of fictional characters. The new anti-Balzacian novel, she says, is learning how to free "the psychological" from its conventional support in characters. Even as photography freed painting from pictorial conventions, cinema is freeing fiction from its stock accoutrements.

Today, everybody is well aware, without being told, that *"la Bovary—c'est moi."* And since the important thing now, rather than to extend indefinitely the list of literary types, is to show the coexistence of contradictory emotions and to reproduce as closely as possible the wealth and complexity of the world of the psyche, the writer, in all honesty, writes about himself.

But that's not all. However strange it may seem, this same writer, who is awed by the reader's growing perspicacity and wariness, is himself becoming more and more wary of the reader.

For even the most experienced reader, if left to his own devices, tends to create types; he simply can't resist it.

He does it, in fact—in the same way as the novelist, once he has begun to relax—without even noticing that he is doing it, for the convenience of everyday life and as a result of long practice. Like Pavlov's dog, in whom the tinkle of a bell stimulates the secretion of saliva, he creates characters at the slightest possible suggestion. As in the game of "statues," each one he touches turns to stone. They merely serve to swell in his memory the vast collection of inanimate figures to which, day in, day out, he is constantly adding and which, since he first learned to read, has been regularly growing as a result of the countless novels he has absorbed.

But, as has already been demonstrated, the character as conceived in the old-style novel (along with the entire old-style mechanism that was used to

Nathalie Sarraute, *The Age of Suspicion* (New York: Braziller, 1963), from *L'Ere du soupçon*, 1957).

make him stand out) does not succeed in containing the psychological reality of today. Instead of revealing it—as used to be the case—he makes it disappear.

So that, as a result of an evolution similar to that in painting—albeit far less bold, less rapid, and interrupted by long pauses and retreats—the psychological element, like the pictorial element, is beginning to free itself imperceptibly from the object of which it was an integral part. It is tending to become self-sufficient and, insofar as possible, to do without exterior support. The novelist's entire experimental effort is concentrated on this one point, as is also the reader's entire effort of attention.

The reader, therefore, must be kept from trying to do two things at one time. And since what the characters gain in the way of facile vitality and plausibility is balanced by a loss of fundamental truth in the psychological states for which they serve as props, he must be kept from allowing his attention to wander or to be absorbed by the characters. For this, he must be deprived as much as possible of all indications which, in spite of himself, and as a result of a natural leaning, he seizes upon in order to create illusions.

This is why the character today is reduced to a shadow of his former self. Only reluctantly does the novelist endow him with attributes that could make him too easily distinguishable: his physical aspect, gestures, actions, sensations, everyday emotions, studied and understood for so long, which contribute to giving him, at the cost of so little effort, an appearance of life, and present such a convenient hold for the reader.[1] Even a name, which is an absolutely necessary feature of his accoutrement, is a source of embarrassment to the novelist. Gide avoids use of the patronymic for his characters, for the reason that it risks situating them at once in a world too similar to that of the reader, and his preference is given to unusual first names. Kafka's hero has for his entire name an initial only (that of Kafka himself); Joyce designates by the initials, H.C.E., for multiple interpretations, the protean hero of *Finnegans Wake*. And it would be most unfair to Faulkner's bold and very worthwhile experiments, which are so revealing of the problem of the present-day novelist, if we were to attribute to a perverse and childish desire to mystify the reader, the method used by him in *The Sound and the Fury*, which consists in giving the same forename to two different characters.[2] This first name, which he shunts back and forth from one character to the other, under the annoyed eye of the reader, like a lump of sugar under the nose of a dog, forces the reader to be constantly on the alert. Instead of letting himself be guided by the signposts with which everyday custom flatters his laziness and haste, he is obliged, in order to identify the characters, to recognize them at once, like the author himself, from the inside, and thanks to indications that are only revealed to him if, having renounced his love of comfort, he is willing to plunge into them as deeply as the author, whose vision he makes his own.

Indeed, the whole problem is here: to dispossess the reader and entice him, at all costs, into the author's territory. To achieve this, the device that consists in

referring to the leading character as "I" constitutes a means that is both effica-
cious and simple and, doubtless for this reason, is frequently employed.

Suddenly the reader is on the inside, exactly where the author is, at a depth
where nothing remains of the convenient landmarks with which he constructs
the characters. He is immersed and held under the surface until the end, in a
substance as anonymous as blood, a magma without name or contours. If he
succeeds in finding his way, it is thanks to stakes that the author has planted for
purposes of his own orientation. No reminiscences of the reader's world, no
conventional concern for cohesion or likelihood, distract his attention or curb
his effort. Like the author, the only barriers he encounters are those which are
either inherent to all experiments of this kind or peculiar to the author's vision.

As for the secondary characters, they are deprived of all autonomous existence and reduced to mere excrescences, quiddities, experiments, or dreams of
the "I," with whom the author identifies himself. At the same time, this "I," not
being the novelist, need not be concerned with creating a universe in which the
reader will feel too much at home, nor with giving the characters the proportions and dimensions required to confer upon them their rather dangerous "resemblance." His obsessed, maniacal, or visionary eye may seize upon them at
will, abandon them, stretch them in a single direction, compress, enlarge, flat-
ten, or reduce them to dust, to force them to yield the new reality he is striving
to find.

In the same way, the modern painter—and in this connection it might be
said that, since Impressionism, all pictures have been painted in the first
person—wrests the object from the universe of the spectator and deforms it in
order to isolate its pictorial content.

Thus, in a movement analogous to that of painting, the novel, which only a
stubborn adherence to obsolete techniques places in the position of a minor art,
pursues with means that are uniquely its own a path which can only be its own;
it leaves to the other arts—and, in particular, to the cinema—everything that
does not actually belong to it. In the same way that photography occupies and
fructifies the fields abandoned by painting, the cinema garners and perfects
what is left by the novel.

The reader, instead of demanding of the novel what every good novel has
more than often refused him, that is, light entertainment, can satisfy at the
cinema, without effort and without needless loss of time, his taste for "live"
characters and stories.

However, the cinema too would appear to be threatened. It too is infected by
the "suspicion" from which the novel suffers. Otherwise, how may we explain
the uneasiness which, after that of the novelist, is now being evidenced by certain "advanced" directors who, because they feel obliged to make films in the
first person, have introduced the eye of a witness and the voice of a narrator?

As for the novel, before it has even exhausted all the advantages offered by
the story told in the first person, or reached the end of the blind alley into which

all techniques necessarily lead, it has grown impatient and, in order to emerge from its present difficulties, is looking about for other ways out.

Suspicion, which is by way of destroying the character and the entire outmoded mechanism that guaranteed its force, is one of the morbid reactions by which an organism defends itself and seeks another equilibrium. It forces the novelist to fulfill what Arnold Toynbee, recalling Flaubert's teaching, has called "his deepest obligation: that of discovering what is new," and keeps him from committing "his most serious crime: that of repeating the discoveries of his predecessors."

TRANSLATED BY MARIA JOLAS

NOTES

[1] "Not once," Proust wrote in a letter to Robert Dreyfus, "does one of my characters shut a window, wash his hands, put on his overcoat, utter a phrase of introduction. If there is anything at all new about the book, this would be it . . ."

[2] Quentin is the first name of both the uncle and the niece; Caddy, that of the mother and the daughter.

PHILIPPE LEJEUNE

Reading Badly to Avoid Feeling Pain
1991

*As Philippe Lejeune describes, Georges Perec's "childhood memory," W,
broke new literary ground in 1975. The reader is invited to interweave two
separate sequences, presented in alternating chapters: the first, a fragmentary account of the half-forgotten, rather sad childhood of the narrator, a
Holocaust orphan in wartime France; the second, his childhood composition, a more aesthetically satisfying narrative about a Germanic Olympic
community, barbarously cruel in its cultivation of sports excellence, established in Tierra del Fuego. To work through the connections between the
two is presumably to participate in the psychoanalysis Perec was then undertaking. A rather different articulation between literature and psychoanalysis than the one Mauron undertook around Mallarmé's adolescent
composition, and one whose success is in part to be understood in terms of
the "Vichy syndrome," to borrow Henry Rousso's phrase, that gripped
France after the death of de Gaulle.*

In 1969 I was a subscriber to *La Quinzaine littéraire*. I had read Georges
Perec's *Les Choses* and *Un Homme qui dort* and was interested in him as a
writer. So I was curious when this serial fiction, *W*, so unusual for an austere journal like *La Quinzaine*, was announced. Very soon, however, I became
bored. I kept on reading for a few more chapters but thereafter seldom glanced
at Perec's tedious and bizarre text except to confirm that it was still stuck in the
same rut. Having just looked over my collection of back issues of the magazine,
I now understood how I could have been bored by a text that today seems so
overwhelming.

It was in early October 1969 that issue 80 of *La Quinzaine* announced that
publication of Perec's serial novel *W* would commence with the next issue,
promising "suspense, dreams, and humor." On the cover of issue 81, alongside
the notice of "the beginning of Georges Perec's serial novel," was a pistol—or,

From Philippe Lejeune, *La mémoire et l'oblique: Georges Perec autobiographe* (Paris:
P.O.L., 1991).

more precisely, a revolver, its hammer raised. Hence, there was reason to expect a mystery novel, an action adventure, a police thriller perhaps, and surely the solution of some crime. In any case, something pleasant—Rocambole, perhaps, or Arsène Lupin. Instead I found a text that was obviously a parody, impossible to read in a straightforward way, a strange remake, a son of Captain Grant who would probably visit Kafka's penal colony. I didn't get the connection with the pistol and couldn't see what the author was up to. And I doubted that he knew either, since the book seemed to bog down very quickly.

Several years later I find myself reading the same text. Now the chapters of W alternate with memories of childhood. The author seems to want the reader to respect this alternation. At the same time, however, the typography sharply distinguishes the two series of chapters, which are as different as oil and water. What is more, the constant back and forth from one set of chapters to the other every six or seven pages runs counter to all our habits of reading, disrupts the inertia that is an integral part of our reading pleasure, and necessitates tiring acrobatics. I wonder how many readers will be willing to play along. Most probably do what I do. Initially they try to play the game, then become discouraged and read the two series of chapters separately. Discouragement sets in at the beginning of part two. Indeed, in part one, what the reader is asked to do is rather easy: the relationship between the two texts is obvious, the connections as plain as the nose on your face. Two autodiegetic narrators recount a search for identity. In the second part, however, a prodigious gap suddenly opens up between the two series, as the narrator-character seems to vanish in the apparently heterodiegetic description of a nightmarish social system, while the childhood memories continue to unfold "as if everything were normal." If the reader is a good reader, instructed by what he learned from the back-and-forth of part one, he will continue to play the game. If so, he may then note a seemingly astonishing fact, the foreclosure of all discussion of the mother in the childhood memories of the second part (whereas the narrator of part one spoke of her a great deal, and we may assume that the child who takes refuge in Villard-de-Lans continues to think about her). The reader is likely to relate this foreclosure to the strange turn taken by the story.[1] But let us leave the good reader to his work, which will take him to the brink of the unbearable. The bad reader, insensitive to the pedagogical assistance that Perec provides, will read the two series separately. He will read the fictional chapters in sequence, and he will be struck, though not entirely surprised, by the shift that takes place in the space of a few chapters from Olympic sport to nightmare: the role of athletics in fascist regimes is well known. But his discomfort and disgust will be directed as much toward the story's narrator as toward the thing narrated.[2] The calm, cool scientific tone of the apparently impersonal, "unshockable" narrative voice is upsetting as it imperturbably describes an increasingly abject system, and precisely to the extent that one perceives the narrative to be talking about something that actually exists. But since the reader also knows that the author is inventing what he has the narrator describe (even if his invention is based, unfortunately, on well-known models), he is terrified by the author's weird indifference toward being drawn into the game. This painful impression becomes stronger still when one discovers that the drafts of the novel contain elaborately detailed descriptions of sadistic devices. For to imagine that W is inevitable is in a sense to become responsible for it: the virtual torturer is set to work within oneself, not without pain. The abject bond between victim and torturer is revived.

Now it is my turn to feel the need for silence. My role is to point out, not to fill, the gaps in the narrative. The thematic relationship between the two series of chapters is made explicit by Perec at the end: the adolescent fantasy of W is related to the extermination camps in which his mother very likely perished. This brief remark in extremis only confirms what the reader has already understood for some time. It also has another, ulterior function: to end the narrative by appearing to reveal its essence while in fact evading it. The essential thing is to know what function the child's drawings and stories had at age thirteen; and the meaning of the revelation he had in Venice in 1967, which revived his memory of the forgotten drawings—what was the meaning of the projected serial novel and its gradual evolution toward horror. If one reads the preliminary texts associated with this book, it becomes clear that Perec's original idea was to explain all these things. Later, however, he chose silence. In this respect *W ou le souvenir d'enfance* may be a psychoanalytic autobiography: a montage of symptoms, leaving the reader to face the problem of interpretation alone. It is clear that the gradual evolution in the description of W represents a kind of self-psychotherapy: pretending to develop the adolescent fiction by adopting its style, Perec in fact deciphers it by basing it more and more explicitly on its historical model, the Nazi camps. But he leaves us in the dark as to the purpose of this adolescent encoding and adult decoding, much as he eliminates from the fiction the deaf and dumb child who was none other than the object of the search. It is up to the reader to fathom this silence, which he will no doubt find unbearable, and to fill it with hypotheses. I alluded earlier to the perplexity I felt at Perec's maniacal insistence on constructing W down to the smallest detail, and the disturbing resemblance between these insanely intricate systems and the formal protocols that govern so much of his writing. I might also have reflected on the rather bewildering splitting of identity in the first part of the book. Or I might have described *W ou le souvenir d'enfance* as the visible portion of a vast work of mourning, whose submerged portion would no doubt touch on the tragic guilt that is the survivor's lot.

Discomfort with the content of the narrative, perplexity with the behavior of the narrator. Good readers will have the courage to accompany Perec all the way to the end of his journey toward an unbearable truth. Readers of the other kind (must we call them "bad" readers?) will prefer to think that the book is becoming "tedious," that it is "poorly constructed." They will skip chapters and jump to the end of the book in order to see if they have guessed correctly about W. Worst of all, they may feel relief upon discovering the historical reality of the Nazi camps, for this provides relief from the parable of W. If readers feel this, then they truly deserve to be called "bad."

In any case, bad readers will be punished for their sins. In reading the fictional narrative as a unit, they take white bread over crust. Except at the break between sections, the chapter transitions are smooth, and the writing in each chapter is consecutive and compact. This is not the case if one reads the childhood memory chapters in sequence: everything falls to pieces, or turns lumpy like a sauce that refuses to take. The chapter transitions seem arbitrary. Worst of all is the fragmentation, the hesitation, the perpetual stopping. Deliberate sabotage. Usually, the inherent discontinuity of childhood narratives is compensated by thematic structure and felicitous writing. With Perec, however, the reader has to be prepared for something else—otherwise he will be even more disappointed than I was when I discovered that the pistol on the cover of the magazine didn't indicate a murder mystery. What Perec writes isn't just different from the usual childhood narrative; it's the opposite. The whole childhood memory section seems to have been written to counter the expectations raised by the genre. On two occasions, "good" memories of childhood, maternal and educational, appear in the story as matters of regret. Lacking memories of this kind, the narrator seems bent on an opposite strategy. He refuses to embellish memory or to give it resonance through style. Intrusively present throughout is a hypercritical narrator, who points out errors, inaccuracies, and mystifications, who shreds the tinsel with which memories are bedecked and interrogates them harshly, under the harsh klieg lights of truth—Veritas as torturer. The records of these cruel interrogations are written in white. The reader is struck to discover that the critical impulse almost always stops on the threshold of what might be a form of reconstruction: interpretation. Nevertheless, *W ou le souvenir d'enfance* was written, in its final draft of 1974, "under analysis," and it grew out of the author's 1949 psychotherapy with Françoise Dolto. Total silence, an echo of which, if I may put it that way, can be found in *"Les Lieux d'une ruse"*: "I had to retrace my steps, revisit places with which I had broken all attachment. I have nothing to say about this subterranean world. I know that it existed and that its traces are now inscribed in me and in what I write."[2] What a temptation for a Freudian to look for the keys of memory, as Perec puts it in *W*, "the golden key given by the father." Perec abstains, and too bad for the reader who refuses to respect this. Too bad, also, for the "charming echoes of Oedipus and castration" and for the "little illustrated Oedipus."[3] Sometimes, however, as I shall show in a moment, Perec embarks on the path of interpretation: one has to live. But the general thrust is in the other direction. Rather than end (as in Stendhal) in revelation of the authentic, the discourse of doubt tends to obscure or dissolve it. I shall consider the two most spectacular instances of this strategy, which apparently seeks to represent memory as a blank.

In part one, the system of notes begun in chapters four and six is expanded to its most monstrous proportions in chapter eight. Distanced by self-quotation, the original text, the one that introduces the father and mother and is printed in bold type, is commented on in twenty-six notes greater in total length than the text itself. The signs marking the notes in the text are tiny and very hard to see unless one is looking for them. The notes themselves are set after the text, not as footnotes, and in the same typeface as the main text. The conscientious reader is forced into some painful acrobatics. In reading the original text, he missed the note markers. Now, for each note, he has to skip backward to identify the segment commented on, then return to the note, twenty-six times in all. I imagine that many readers end up reading the notes sequentially without referring back to the text, which is still fresh in their minds. At this point another type of acrobatics begins: the function of the notes in relation to the text varies considerably from note to note. Some correct the text, others criticize it, and still others expand on it in relation to a wide range of subjects. The notes take off in every direction, and the original text is left in shreds. Furthermore, the corrections do not give us a closer or more accurate view of the parents but plunge them even more deeply into ambiguity and uncertainty behind a new screen of language. When Perec begins to annotate the notes themselves, he points to the powerlessness of language to compensate for absence. This tragic insistence is the point of the book, but it can only be understood in conjunction with the "flood" of detail that spills over into the fictional chapters of the second part. The perpetually thwarted thrust of memory stands in contrast to the nightmarish smoothness of the fiction.

In the second part, Perec gives up on notes and opts instead for what might be called a "hyper-modalization" of discourse. He multiplies doubts and nuances: "I remember that . . . I think that . . . I now think that . . . today I know that . . . I can no longer remember if . . . it seems to me that . . . I believe that . . . I recall . . . perhaps . . . in any case . . . I do not think that . . . I think that." I know of no other narrative of childhood that piles up signs of doubt and subjectivity in such a monotonous way: it amounts to a sort of *basso continuo* that runs underneath all the childhood memories in part two. Any reader who reads these chapters sequentially will certainly come away bored. This is not Colette's *Sido* or Pagnol's *La Gloire de mon père*. Tragically, it is the opposite: an orphaned memory, clad in gray, which has taken vows of poverty and renounced the charms of literature. To be sure, Perec continues with his autobiographical orchestration: he sometimes connects the present to the past, notes where some things originate and how others remain constant, and alludes to various of his works. But all this is very discreet, so that the reader is quite surprised when in somewhat more insistent terms he seems to offer a rather discreet confidence about the emotional life of the adult ("From then on only strange women would come to you"). Most of the time, the writing, scrupulous and blank, avoids grandiloquence, damps down emotion, and keeps the tone muted.

Thus far I have been playing the part of the bad reader, who reads the two series separately. I confess that I was once this bad reader, although now I cannot read the book without suffering. Is there something surprising about the fact that two apparently negative reading experiences (of a labored fiction and gray souvenirs of childhood) together produce so powerful an effect? If "minus times minus" is to end up as "plus," the reader has to be willing to construct the place where the alternation of the two series acquires meaning; he must read *W* in a wrenching, allegorical way and experience, in the separation of the two sets of chapters, the foreclosure I spoke of earlier (since each set seems to ignore the other). As we shall see, Perec did not hit on this very effective structure immediately. It was the result of bold speculation on the mechanisms of reading. Other texts by Perec are based on similar calculations. Who would think that a reader would be willing to read a book consisting of 480 sentences all beginning with the same words? Yet this is what Perec did with *Je me souviens*. And the reader's memory, succumbing to the contagious effect of this method, expands on the text. Most of the autobiographical experiments of Perec that I commented on earlier (*L'Arbre*, *Lieux*, *Lieux ou j'ai dormi*) also relied on montage: Perec wants to squeeze meaning and feeling out of a system of juxtaposition by forcing the reader to assume responsibility for what ties the various parts of the system together. This doesn't always work: *La Boutique obscure* is less effective than *Je me souviens*. The right combination has to be found. In this respect, I see considerable similarity between Perec's work and that of Jean Eustache in film. One finds the same reserve, the same delicacy, the same elliptical strategy. One also finds the same desire to create emotion by using montages that require the collaboration of the reader or spectator yet leave him free to participate or not. Eustache's *La Rosière de Pessac* (1968–79) in some ways shares the same idea as *Lieux*. And his *Une Sale histoire* (1977) is a diptych: fiction and reality. One finds the same attentiveness to family history in Eustache's *Numéro zéro* (1971) as in Perec's *L'Arbre, histoire d'Esther et de ses frères*. Of course, there are also many differences. What makes the two men similar, however, is their desire to invent new autobiographical forms, not because they want to play around or "experiment" but because they want to say what the conventional forms no longer allow them to say, so as not to die in silence.

NOTES

[1] In part two, the mother is mentioned only twice: on p. 95 (in the conditional, the textbook image of the peaceful evening under suspension) and p. 162 ("How could I have known that I was supposed to go to Palestine? This was an actual plan that Aunt Esther and my grandmother came up with, probably because they were convinced that my mother would never come back"). None of the memories of the Villard-de-Lans period

involve the theme of the child's relationship to the mother (the news received or not received). Similarly, none of the memoires from the time of the Liberation and then the return to Paris in 1945 concerns the fate of the mother and the way in which the child learned or divined it. This silence in a narrative otherwise so minutely detailed is striking. The facts were related in part one (pp. 48–49 and 57) in such a way that the adult could reconstruct them. It remains to imagine how the child learned of them. Perec provides the reader with only one elliptical but distressing sign: the "walls of the ovens scraped by the fingernails of the gassing victims" (p. 213) can be related, in the fiction *W*, to the death of Caecilia, whose "bloody nails left deep grooves in the oaken door" (pp. 80–81). A glance at the early texts related to the novel confirms that this silence was intentional. In September 1970, Perec prepared a list of his childhood memories. All would eventually find their way into the book, except one, the last item in the list: "The 'it's a good thing that your mother is dead,' or something of that sort."

[2] *Penser/Classer* 71–72 (Paris: Hachette, 1985).

[3] *Penser/Classer* 67.

[4] The viewer of Claude Lanzmann's documentary film *Shoah* may feel something of the same attitude toward the director when he discusses matters of technique and organization with the people responsible for the genocide or with seeming cruelty presses survivors to finish telling stories they obviously find unbearable.

New Criticism

GÉRARD GENETTE

Structuralism and Literary Criticism
1966

In a lucid text rife with the fruit of a fresh reading of Claude Lévi-Strauss, the future founding co-editor of Poétique *speculates on the lessons of structuralism for literary criticism. Might the critic be to the novelist as the* bricoleur, *Lévi-Strauss's "tinkerer," is to the "engineer"? Might the "new rhetoric" called for by Francis Ponge now be in the offing? Genette lays out the structuralist case against Paul Ricoeur's hermeneutics and Georges Poulet's subjectivism, and he concludes by positing new, Borgesian perspectives for literary history.*

In a now-classic chapter of *The Savage Mind*, Claude Lévi-Strauss defines mythical thought as "a kind of intellectual tinkering or *bricolage*." The nature of bricolage is to make use of materials and tools that, unlike those of the engineer, for example, were not intended for the task in hand. The rule of bricolage is "always to make do with whatever is available" and to use in a new structure the remains of previous constructions, thus making the specific manufacture of materials and tools unnecessary, through a double operation of analysis (the extraction of various elements from various already-constituted wholes) and of synthesis (the forming of these heterogeneous elements into a new whole in which none of the reused elements will necessarily be used as originally intended).[1] It should be remembered that this typically "structuralist" operation, which makes up for a lack of production by means of an extreme ingenuity in the distribution of remnants, was discovered by an ethnologist attempting to account for the way myths are invented by so-called primitive

Gérard Genette, "Structuralism and Literary Criticism," in *Figures of Literary Discourse* (New York: Columbia University Press, 1982), from *Figures* (Paris: Seuil, 1966).

civilizations. But there is another intellectual activity, peculiar to more "developed" cultures, to which this analysis might be applied almost word for word: I mean criticism, more particularly literary criticism, which distinguishes itself formally from other kinds of criticism by the fact that it uses the same materials—writing—as the works with which it is concerned; art criticism or musical criticism are obviously not expressed in sound or in color, but literary criticism speaks the same language as its object: it is a metalanguage, "discourse upon a discourse."[2] It can therefore be a metaliterature, that is to say, " a literature of which literature itself is the imposed object."[3]

If in fact one isolates the more obvious functions of critical activity—the "critical" function in the literal sense of the term, which consists of judging and appreciating recent works with a view to helping the public make up its mind (a function linked to the institution of journalism), and the "scientific" function (linked, generally speaking, to the institution of the university), which consists of a positive study, solely with a view to knowledge, of the conditions of existence of literary works (the materiality of the text, sources, psychological or historical origins, and so on)—there is obviously a third, which is strictly literary. A book of criticism like Sainte-Beuve's *Port-Royal* or Maurice Blanchot's *The Space of Literature* is, among other things, a book, and its author is in his own way and at least to a certain extent what Roland Barthes calls an *écrivain* (a writer, in contradistinction to the mere *écrivant*, or someone who happens to write), that is to say, the author of a message that to some extent tends to be absorbed into spectacle. This "frustration" of meaning, which is frozen and constituted in an object of aesthetic consumption is no doubt the movement (or rather the *halt*) that constitutes all literature. The literary object *exists* only through it; on the other hand, it is dependent upon it alone and, depending on the circumstances, any text may or may not be literature, according to whether it is received (either) as spectacle or (else) as message: literary history is made up of these comings and goings, these fluctuations. That is, there is no literary object strictly speaking, but only a *literary function*, which can invest or abandon any object of writing in turn. Its partial, unstable, ambiguous literariness is not therefore a property of criticism: what distinguishes criticism from the other literary "genres" is its *secondary* character, and it is here that Lévi-Strauss' remarks on *bricolage* may find a somewhat unexpected application.

The instrumental universe of the *bricoleur*, says Lévi-Strauss, is a "closed" universe. Its repertoire, however extended, "remains limited." This limitation distinguishes the *bricoleur* from the engineer, who (in principle) can at any time obtain the tool specially adapted to a particular technical need. The engineer "questions the universe, while the *bricoleur* addresses himself to a collection of oddments left over from human endeavors, that is, only a subset of the culture."[4] One has only to replace in the last sentence the words "engineer" and *bricoleur* by "novelist" (for example) and "critic" respectively to define the literary status of criticism. The materials of the critical task are indeed those "oddments left over from human endeavors," which is what works of literature are once they have been reduced to themes, motifs, keywords, obsessive metaphors, quotations, index cards, and references. The initial work is a structure, like those primary wholes that the *bricoleur* dismantles in order to extract parts that may prove useful; the critic too breaks down a structure into its elements—one element per card—and the *bricoleur*'s motto, "it might always come in handy," is the very postulate that inspires the critic when he is making up his card index, literally or figuratively, of course. His next task is to build up a new structure while "rearranging these oddments." "*Critical* thought," one might say, paraphrasing Lévi-Strauss, "builds structured sets by means of a structured set, namely, *the work*. But it is not at the structural level that it makes use of it: it builds ideological castles out of the debris of what was once a *literary* discourse."

The distinction between the critic and the writer lies not only in the secondary and limited character of the critical material (literature) as opposed to the unlimited and primary character of the poetic or fictional material (the universe); this as it were quantitative inferiority, which derives from the fact that the critic always comes after the writer and has at his disposal only materials imposed by the previous choice of the writer, is perhaps aggravated, perhaps compensated by another difference:

> *The writer* works by means of concepts and *the critic* by means of signs. Within the opposition between nature and culture, there is only an imperceptible discrepancy between the sets employed by each. One way indeed in which signs can be opposed to concepts is that whereas concepts seem to be wholly transparent with respect to reality, signs allow and even require the interposing and incorporation of a certain amount of human culture into reality.

If the writer questions the universe, the critic questions literature, that is to say, the universe of signs. But what was a sign for the writer (the work) becomes meaning for the critic (since it is the object of the critical discourse), and in another way what was meaning for the writer (his view of the world) becomes a sign for the critic, as the theme and symbol of a certain literary nature. This, again, is what Lévi-Strauss says of mythical thought, which, as Franz Boas remarked, constantly creates new worlds, but by reversing means and ends: "signifieds change into signifiers, and vice versa." This constant interchange, this perpetual inversion of signs and meaning is a good description of the dual function of the critic's work, which is to produce meaning with the work of others, but also to produce his own work out of this meaning. If such a thing as "critical poetry" exists, therefore, it is in the sense in which Lévi-Strauss speaks of a "poetry of *bricolage*": just as the *bricoleur* "speaks through things," the critic speaks—in the full sense, that is to say, speaks up—through books, and we will paraphrase Lévi-Strauss once more by saying that "without ever completing his project he always puts something of himself into it."

In this sense, therefore, one can regard literary criticism as a "structuralist activity"; but it is not—as is quite clear—merely an implicit, unreflective structuralism. The question posed by the present orientation of such human sciences as linguistics or anthropology is whether criticism is being called upon to organize its structuralist vocation explicitly in a structural method. My aim here is simply to elucidate the meaning and scope of this question, suggesting the principal ways in which structuralism could reach the object of criticism, and offer itself to criticism as a fruitful method.

Literature being primarily a work of language, and structuralism, for its part, being preeminently a linguistic method, the most probable encounter should obviously take place on the terrain of linguistic material: sounds, forms, words, and sentences constitute the common object of the linguist and the philologist to such an extent that it was possible, in the early enthusiasm of the Russian Formalist movement, to define literature as a mere dialect, and to envisage its study as an annex of general dialectology.[5] Indeed, Russian Formalism, which is rightly regarded as one of the matrices of structural linguistics, was at first nothing more than a meeting of critics and linguists on the terrain of "poetic language." This assimilation of literature to a dialect raises objections that are too obvious for it to be taken literally. If literature *were* a dialect, it would be a translinguistic dialect effecting on all languages a number of transformations, different in their procedures but similar in their function, rather as the various forms of slang are parasitical in various ways on the various languages but are similar in their parasitical function; nothing of the kind can be proposed in the case of dialects. In particular, the difference between "literary language" and ordinary language resides not so much in the means as in the ends; apart from a few inflections, the writer uses the same language as other users, but he uses it neither in the same way nor with the same intention—identical material, displaced function: this status is exactly the reverse of that of a dialect. But, like other "excesses" committed by Formalism, this particular one had cathartic value: by temporarily ignoring content, the provisional reduction of literature's "literary being" to its linguistic being made it possible to revise certain traditional "verities" concerning the "truth" of literary discourse, and to study more closely the system of its conventions.[6] Literature had long enough been regarded as a message without a code for it to become necessary to regard it for a time as a code without a message.

Structuralist method as such is constituted at the very moment one rediscovers the message in the code, uncovered by an analysis of the immanent structures and not imposed from the outside by ideological prejudices. This moment was not to be long in coming,[7] for the existence of the sign, at every level, rests on the connection of form and meaning. Thus Roman Jakobson, in his study of Czech verse of 1923, discovered a relationship between the prosodic value of a phonic feature and its signifying value, each language tending

to give the greatest prosodic importance to the system of oppositions most rel-
evant on the semantic plane: stress or "dynamic accent" in Russian, length in
Greek, pitch or "musical accent" in Serbo-Croatian.[8] This passage from the
phonetic to the phonemic, that is to say, from the pure sound substance, dear to
early Formalist thinking, to the organization of this substance in a signifying
system (or at least one capable of signification) is of interest not only to the
study of metrics, since it was rightly seen as an anticipation of the phonological
method.[9] It represents rather well what the contribution of structuralism
might be to the study of literary morphology as a whole: poetics, stylistics, composition. Between pure Formalism, which reduces literary "forms" to a sound
material that is ultimately formless, because nonsignifying,[10] and traditional
realism, which accords to each form an autonomous, substantial "expressive
value," structural analysis must make it possible to uncover the connection that
exists between a system of forms and a system of meanings, by replacing the
search for term-by-term analogies with one for overall homologies.

A simplistic example might serve to clarify the matter: one of the traditional
unsolved problems of the theory of expressivity is the question of the "color" of
vowels, which was put into the forefront by Arthur Rimbaud's sonnet. The
advocates of phonic expressivity, such as Otto Jespersen or Maurice Gram-
mont, tried to attribute to each phoneme its own suggestive value, which, it
was thought, governed the makeup of certain words in all languages. Others
exposed the weakness of these hypotheses,[11] and, as far as the color of vowels
was concerned, the comparative tables drawn up by René Etiemble[12] show
quite clearly that the advocates of "colored sounds" agree on none of their attri-
butions.[13] Their adversaries naturally concluded from this that "colored
sounds" were a myth—and as a fact of *nature*, they may well be nothing more.
But the disparity of the individual tables does not destroy the authenticity of
each of them, and structuralism can suggest an explanation here that takes account both of the arbitrariness of each vowel-color and of the very widespread
sense of a vocalic chromaticism: it is true that no vowel evokes, naturally and in
isolation, a particular color; but it is also true that the distribution of colors in
the spectrum (which indeed is itself, as Gelb and Goldstein have shown, as
much a fact of language as of vision) can find its correspondence in the distribution of vowels in a given language.[14] Hence the idea of a table of concordance,
variable in its details but constant in its function: there is a spectrum of vowels
as there is a spectrum of colors; the two systems evoke and attract one another,
and the overall homology creates the illusion of a term-by-term analogy, which
each realizes in its own way by an act of symbolic motivation comparable to the
one analyzed by Lévi-Strauss in the case of totemism. Each individual motivation, objectively arbitrary but subjectively based, can be regarded, then, as the
index of a particular psychic configuration. The structural hypothesis, in this
case, gives back to the stylistics of the subject what it takes from the stylistics of
the object.

So structuralism is under no obligation to confine itself to "surface" analyses, quite the reverse: here as elsewhere, the horizon of its approach is the analysis of significations. "No doubt verse is primarily a recurrent 'figure of sound.' Primarily, always, but never uniquely. . . . Valéry's view of poetry as 'hesitation between the sound and the sense' is much more realistic and scientific than any bias of phonetic isolationism."[15] The importance attached by Jakobson, since his 1935 article on Pasternak, to the concepts of metaphor and metonymy, borrowed from the rhetoric of tropes, is characteristic of this orientation, especially if one remembers that one of the warhorses of early Formalism was a contempt for images, and the devaluation of tropes as marks of poetic language. Speaking of a poem by Pushkin, Jakobson himself was still insisting, in 1936, on the possibility of poetry without imagery.[16] In 1958 he took up this question with a very marked shift of emphasis: "Textbooks believe in the occurrence of poems devoid of imagery, but actually scarcity in lexical tropes is counterbalanced by gorgeous grammatical tropes and figures."[17] Tropes, as we know, are figures of signification, and in adopting metaphor and metonymy as poles of his typology of language and literature, Jakobson does not merely pay homage to ancient rhetoric—he places the categories of meaning at the heart of the structural method.

The structural study of "poetic language" and of the forms of literary expression in general cannot, in fact, reject the analysis of the relations between code and message. Jakobson's analysis, "Linguistics and Poetics," in which he refers at the same time to the technicians of communication and to poets like Gerard Manley Hopkins and Valéry or to critics like John Crowe Ransom and William Empson, shows this quite explicitly: "Ambiguity is an intrinsic, inalienable character of any self-focused message, briefly a corollary feature of poetry. Let us repeat with Empson: 'The machinations of ambiguity are among the very roots of poetry.'"[18] The ambition of structuralism is not confined to counting feet and to observing the repetitions of phonemes: it must also attack semantic phenomena which, as Mallarmé showed us, constitute the essence of poetic language and, more generally, the problems of literary semiology. In this respect, one of the newest and most fruitful directions now opening up for literary research ought to be the structural study of the "large units" of discourse, beyond the framework—which linguistics in the strict sense cannot cross—of the sentence. The Formalist Vladimir Propp was no doubt the first to deal (in regard to a series of Russian folktales) with texts of a particular scope,[19] made up of a large number of sentences, like statements capable in turn—and on an equal footing with the traditional units of linguistics—of an analysis that could distinguish in them, by a play of superimpositions and substitutions, variable elements and constant functions, and to rediscover in them the biaxial system, familiar to Saussurean linguistics, of syntagmatic relations (real connections of functions in the continuity of a text) and paradigmatic relations (virtual relations between similar or opposed functions, from one text to another, in the whole of the corpus considered). One would thus study systems from a much higher level of generality, such as narrative,[20] description, and the other major forms of literary expression. There would then be a linguistics of discourse which was a *translinguistics*, since the facts of language would be handled by it in great bulk, and often at one remove — to put it simply, a rhetoric, perhaps that "new rhetoric" which Francis Ponge once called for, and which we still lack.

The structural character of language at every level is sufficiently accepted by all today for the structuralist "approach" to literary expression to be adopted as it were without question. As soon as one abandons the level of linguistics (or that "bridge thrown between linguistics and literary history," as Leo Spitzer called studies of form and style) and approaches the domain traditionally reserved for criticism, that of "content," the legitimacy of the structural point of view raises very serious questions of principle. A priori, of course, structuralism as a method is based on the study of structures wherever they occur; but, to begin with, structures are not directly encountered objects — far from it; they are systems of latent relations, conceived rather than perceived, which analysis constructs as it uncovers them, and which it runs the risk of inventing while believing that it is discovering them. Furthermore, structuralism is not only a method; it is also what Ernst Cassirer calls a "general tendency of thought," or as others would say (more crudely) an ideology, the prejudice of which is precisely to value structures at the expense of substances, and which may therefore overestimate their explanatory value. Indeed, the question is not so much to know whether there is or is not a system of relations in a particular object of research, since such systems are everywhere, but to determine the relative importance of this system in relation to other elements of understanding: this importance measures the degree of validity of the structural method; but how are we to measure this importance, in turn, without recourse to this method? A circular argument.

Apparently, structuralism ought to be on its own ground whenever criticism abandons the search for the conditions of existence or the external determinations — psychological, social, or other — of the literary work in order to concentrate its attention on that work itself, regarded no longer as an effect, but as an absolute being. In this sense, structuralism is bound up with the general movement away from positivism, "historicizing history," and the "biographical illusion," a movement represented in various ways by the critical writings of a Proust, an Eliot, a Valéry, Russian Formalism, French "thematic criticism" or Anglo-American "New Criticism."[21] In a way, the notion of structural analysis can be regarded as a simple equivalent of what Americans call "close reading" and which would be called in Europe, following Spitzer, the "immanent study" of works. It is precisely in this sense that Spitzer, retracing in 1960 the evolution that had led him from the psychologism of his first

studies of style to a criticism free of any reference to the *Erlebnis*, "subordinat-
ing stylistic analysis to an explanation of the particular works as *poetic organ-
isms in themselves,* without recourse to the psychology of the author,"[22] called
this new attitude "structuralist." Any analysis that confines itself to a work
without considering its sources or motives would, therefore, be implicitly
structuralist, and the structural method ought to intervene in order to give to
this immanent study a sort of rationality of understanding which would replace the rationality of explanation abandoned with the search for causes. A
somewhat spatial determinism of structure would thus take over, but in a quite
modern spirit, from the temporal determinism of genesis, each unity being defined in terms of relations, instead of filiation.[23] "Thematic" analysis, then,
would tend spontaneously to culminate and to be tested in a structural synthesis in which the different themes are grouped in *networks*, in order to extract
their full meaning from their place and function in the system of the work.
This is the aim clearly expressed by Jean-Pierre Richard in his *L' Univers imaginaire de Mallarmé*, or by Jean Rousset when he writes: "There is a graspable
form only when there emerges a harmony or a relation, a line of force, an
obsessive figure, a texture of presences or echoes, a network of convergences; I
will call 'structures' those formal constants, those links that betray a mental
world and which each artist re-invents according to his own needs."[24]

   Structuralism, then, would appear to be a refuge for all immanent criticism
against the danger of fragmentation that threatens thematic analysis: the
means of reconstituting the unity of a work, its principle of coherence, what
Spitzer called its spiritual *etymon*. In fact, the question is no doubt more complex, for immanent criticism can adopt two very different and even antithetical
attitudes to a work, depending on whether it regards this work as an object or
as a subject. The opposition between these two attitudes is brought out with
great clarity by Georges Poulet in a text in which he declares himself to be an
advocate of the second:

> Like everybody else, I believe that the end of criticism is to arrive at an intimate
> knowledge of the reality criticized. Now, it seems to me that such intimacy is
> possible only insofar as critical thought *becomes* the thought criticized, insofar as
> it succeeds in refeeling, rethinking, re-imagining that thought from the inside.
> Nothing could be less objective than such a movement of the mind. Contrary to
> common belief, criticism must avoid attending to any *object* whatever (whether
> it be the person of the author, considered as someone else, or his work, consid-
> ered as a thing); for what must be obtained is a *subject*, that is to say, a spiritual
> activity that can only be understood if one puts oneself in its place and revives
> within us its role as subject.[25]

This intersubjective criticism, which is admirably illustrated in Poulet's own
work, is related to the type of understanding that Paul Ricoeur, following Wilhelm Dilthey and others (including Spitzer), calls *hermeneutics*. The meaning

of a work is not conceived through a series of intellectual operations; it is re-lived, "taken up again" as a message that is both old and forever renewed. Con-versely, it is clear that structural criticism is emerging from the objectivism condemned by Poulet, for structures are *experienced* neither by the creative con-sciousness nor by the critical consciousness. They are at the heart of the work, no doubt, but as its latent armature, as a principle of objective intelligibility, accessible only through analysis and substitutions to a sort of geometrical mind that is not consciousness. Structural criticism is untainted by any of the tran-scendent reductions of psychoanalysis, for example, or Marxist explanation; it exerts, in its own way, a sort of internal reduction, traversing the substance of the work in order to reach its bone-structure—certainly not a superficial ex-amination, but a sort of radioscopic penetration, and all the more external in that it is more penetrating.

There emerges, then, a limit rather comparable to the one Ricoeur fixed on structural mythology: wherever the hermeneutic resumption of meaning is possible and desirable, in the intuitive convergence of two consciousnesses, structural analysis would (partially at least) be illegitimate and irrelevant. One might then imagine a sort of division of the literary field into two domains, that of "living" literature, that is to say, capable of being experienced by the critical consciousness, which would have to be reserved for hermeneutic criticism, just as Ricoeur claims for hermeneutics the domain of the Judaic and Hellenic tra-ditions, with their inexhaustible and forever indefinitely present *surplus of meaning*; and that of a literature which is not exactly "dead" but in some sense distant and difficult to decipher: its lost meaning would be perceptible only to the operations of the structural intelligence, like that of "totemic" cultures, the exclusive domain of the ethnologists. There is nothing absurd in principle about such a division of labor, and it should be noted at the outset that it corre-sponds to the limitations of prudence that structualism imposes on itself, tack-ling primarily those areas that best lend themselves, and with the least "remainder," to the application of its method;[27] it should also be recognized that such a division would leave an immense and almost virgin field for struc-turalist research. Indeed, the sort of literature that has "lost" its meaning is much greater than the other, and not always of less interest. There is, as it were, a whole ethnographic domain of literature, the exploration of which would be of great interest to structuralism: literatures distant in time and place, chil-dren's and popular literature, including such recent forms as the melodrama or serialized fiction, which criticism has always ignored, not only out of academic prejudice but also because no intersubjective participation could animate it or guide it in its research; a structural criticism could treat it like anthropological material and study in great bulk and in terms of their recurrent functions, following the lines laid down by such folklore specialists as Propp and Skafty-mov. These works, like those of Lévi-Strauss on primitive mythologies, al-ready show how fruitful the structural method applied to texts of this kind can be, and how much it can reveal of the hitherto-unknown foundations of the canonical "literatures." Fantomas or Bluebeard may not speak to us as intimately as Swann or Hamlet; they might have as much to teach us. And certain officially consecrated works, which have in fact become largely alien to us, like those of Corneille, might speak better in that language of distance and strangeness than in that of the false proximity that we insist on imposing on them, often to no avail.

Here, perhaps, structuralism would begin to reconquer part of the terrain ceded to hermeneutics—for the true division between these two "methods" lies not in the object but in the critical position. To Ricoeur, who suggested to him the division described above, alleging that "one part of civilization, precisely the part which did not produce our own culture, lends itself to the structural method better than any other," Lévi-Strauss replied by asking: "Are we dealing with an intrinsic difference between two kinds of thought and civilization, or simply with the relative position of the observer, who cannot adopt the same perspectives vis-à-vis his own civilization as would seem normal to him vis-à-vis a different civilization?"[28] The inappropriateness that Ricoeur finds in the possible application of structuralism to the Judeo-Christian mythologies, a Melanesian philosopher would no doubt find in the structural analysis of his own mythical tradition, which he *interiorizes* just as a Christian interiorizes the biblical message; but, conversely, this Melanesian might find a structural analysis of the Bible quite appropriate. What Merleau-Ponty wrote of ethnology as a discipline can be applied to structuralism as a method: "It is not a specialty defined by a particular object, 'primitive societies.' It is a way of thinking, the way which imposes itself when the object is different, and requires us to transform ourselves. We also become the ethnologists of our own society if we set ourselves at a distance from it."[29]

Thus, the relation that binds structuralism and hermeneutics together might be not one of mechanical separation and exclusion but of complementarity: on the subject of the same work, hermeneutic criticism might speak the language of the resumption of meaning and of internal recreation, and structural criticism that of distant speech and intelligible reconstruction. They would thus bring out complementary significations, and their dialogue would be all the more fruitful, on condition that one could never speak these two languages at once.[30] In any case, literary criticism has no reason to refuse to listen to the new significations that structuralism can obtain from the works that are apparently closest and most familiar by "distancing" their speech;[31] for one of the most profound lessons of modern anthropology is that the distant is also close to us, by virtue of its very distance.

Moreover, the effort of psychological understanding initiated by nineteenth-century criticism and continued in our own time by the various kinds of thematic criticism has perhaps concerned itself too exclusively with the psychology of the authors, and not sufficiently with that of the public or the reader. We

know, for example, that one of the dangers of thematic analysis lies in the difficulty it often has in distinguishing between what is properly of concern to the
irreducible singularity of an individual creator and what more generally belongs to the taste, sensibility, or ideology of a period, or more generally still to
the permanent conventions and traditions of a genre or literary form. The
heart of this difficulty lies in a sense in the encounter between the original,
"deep" thematics of the creative individual and what ancient rhetoric called
topics, that is to say, the treasury of subjects and forms that constitute the com-
monwealth of tradition and culture. Personal thematics represents only a
choice made between the possibilities offered by the collective topics. It is
evident—to speak in a very schematic way—that the contribution of the topos
is greater in the so-called inferior, or as one ought rather to say *fundamental*,
genres, such as the folktale or the adventure novel, and the role of the creative
personality is sufficiently weakened in such works for critical investigation to
turn spontaneously, when dealing with them, to the tastes, requirements, and
needs that constitute what is commonly called the *expectations* of the public.
But we should also be aware of what the "great works"—and even the most
original of them—owe to these common dispositions. How can we appreciate,
for example, the particular quality of the Stendhalian novel without considering in its historical and transhistorical generality the common thematics of the
fictional imagination?[32] Spitzer recounts how the belated—and it would seem
somewhat ingenuous—discovery that he made of the importance of the traditional topos in classical literature was one of the events that helped to "discour-
age" him from psychoanalytic stylistics.[33] But the passage from what one might
call the psychologism of the author to an absolute antipsychologism may not be
as inevitable as it seems, for, conventional as it may be, the topos is not psychologically more arbitrary than the personal theme; it simply belongs to another,
collective psychology, for which contemporary anthropology has done something to prepare us and the literary implications of which deserve to be explored systematically. The fault of modern criticism is perhaps not so much its
psychologism as its overly individualistic conception of psychology.

Classical criticism—from Aristotle to La Harpe—was, in a sense, much
more attentive to these anthropological aspects of literature; it knew how to
measure, narrowly but precisely, the requirements of what it called *verisimilitude*, that is to say, the idea that the public has of the true or possible. The
distinctions between the genres, the notions of epic, tragic, heroic, comic, fictional, corresponded to certain broad categories of mental attitudes that predis-
pose the reader's imagination in one way or another and make him want or
expect particular types of situations and actions, of psychological, moral, and
aesthetic values. It cannot be said that the study of these broad diatheses that
divide up and inform the literary sensibility of mankind (and which Gilbert
Durand has rightly called *the anthropological structures of the imaginary*) has
been taken sufficiently seriously by literary criticism and theory. Gaston Bach-

elard gave us a typology of the "material" imagination: no doubt there also exists, for example, an imagination of behavior, situations, human relationships, a *dramatic* imagination, in the broad sense of the term, which strongly animates the production and consumption of theatrical and fictional work. The topics of this imagination, the structural laws of its functioning are obviously, and fundamentally, of importance to literary criticism: they will no doubt constitute one of the tasks of that vast axiomatics of literature that Valéry believed to be such an urgent necessity. The highest efficacity of literature rests on a subtle play between expectation and surprise "against which all the expectation in the world cannot prevail,"[34] between the "verisimilitude" expected and desired by the public and the unpredictability of creation. But does not the very unpredictability, the infinite shock of the great works, resound with all its force in the secret depths of verisimilitude? "The great poet," says Borges, "is not so much an inventor as a discoverer."

Valéry dreamed of a history of literature understood "not so much as a history of authors and of the accidents of their careers, or as that of their works, than as a History of the mind, insofar as it produces or consumes literature, and this history might even be written without the name of a single writer being mentioned." We know what echoes this idea has found in such authors as Borges or Maurice Blanchot, and Albert Thibaudet had already been pleased, by means of constant comparisons and transferences, to set up a Republic of Letters in which distinctions of person tended to be blurred.[35] This unified view of the literary field is a very profound utopia, and one that is not unreasonably attractive, since literature is not only a collection of autonomous works, which may "influence" one another by a series of fortuitous and isolated encounters; it is a coherent whole, a homogeneous space, within which works touch and penetrate one another; it is also, in turn, a part linked to other parts in the wider space of "culture," in which its own value is a function of the whole. Thus, it doubly belongs to a study of structure, internal and external.

We know that the acquisition of language by a child proceeds not by a simple extension of vocabulary but by a series of internal divisions, without modification of the overall acquisition: at each stage, the few words at its disposal are for the child the whole of language and it uses them to designate everything, with increasing precision, but without gaps. Similarly, for a man who has read only one book, this book is for him the whole of "literature," in the primary sense of the term; when he has read two, these two books will share his entire literary field, with no gap between them, and so on; it is precisely because it has no gaps to fill that a culture may *enrich itself*: it becomes deeper and more diversified, because it does not have to extend itself.

In a way, the "literature" of mankind as a whole (that is to say, the way in which written works are organized in men's minds) can be regarded as being constituted in accordance with a similar process—bearing in mind the crude simplification that is involved here: literary "production" is a *parole*, in the Saussurian sense, a series of partially autonomous and unpredictable individual acts; but the "consumption" of this literature by society is a *langue*, that is to say, a whole the parts of which, whatever their number and nature, tend to be ordered into a coherent system. Raymond Queneau makes the amusing remark that all literature is either an *Iliad* or an *Odyssey*. This dichotomy has not always been a metaphor, and one often finds in Plato the echo of a "literature" that was almost reduced to these two poems, and which was not regarded as incomplete for that reason. Ion knew and wished to know nothing other than Homer. "That seems to be enough for me," he says, for Homer speaks sufficiently well of all things, and the competence of the bard would be encyclopedic if poetry really proceeded from knowledge (it is this point, and not the universality of the work, that Plato challenges). Since then, literature has tended to subdivide rather than to extend, and for centuries the Homeric oeuvre has continued to be seen as the embryo and source of all literature. This myth is not devoid of truth, and the book-burner of Alexandria was not entirely wrong, from his point of view, to place the Koran alone in the scale against a whole library: whether it contains one book, two books, or several thousand, a library is a civilization that is always complete, because in men's minds it always forms a whole and a system.

Classical rhetoric was acutely aware of this system, which is formalized into the theory of genres. There was epic, tragedy, comedy, and so on—and all these genres shared without remainder the totality of the literary field. What was lacking in this theory was the temporal dimension, the idea that a system could evolve. Nicolas Boileau himself witnessed the death of the epic and the birth of the novel without being able to integrate these modifications into his *Ars poetica*. The nineteenth century discovered history, but it forgot the coherence of the whole; the individual history of works, and of authors, effaced the table of the genres. Ferdinand Brunetière alone attempted a synthesis, but we know that this marriage of Boileau and Charles Darwin was not a very happy one: the evolution of genres according to Brunetière is a matter of pure organicism, each genre being born, developing, and dying like a solitary species, without concern for its neighbor.

The structuralist idea, in this matter, is to follow literature in its overall evolution, while making synchronic cuts at various stages and comparing the tables one with another. Literary evolution then appears in all its richness, which derives from the fact that the system survives while constantly altering. Here, again, the Russian Formalists showed the way by paying special attention to the phenomena of structural dynamics, and by isolating the notion of *change of function*. Noting the presence or absence, in isolation, of a literary form or theme at a particular point in diachronic evolution is meaningless until the synchronic study has shown the function of this element in the system. An element can remain while changing function, or on the contrary disappear while leaving its function to another. "In this way the mechanism of literary evolution," says Boris Tomachevski, tracing the development of Formalist work on this point,

> became gradually more precise: it was presented not as a succession of forms, each replacing the other, but as a continual variation of the aesthetic function of literary methods. Each work finds itself oriented in relation to the literary milieu, and each element in relation to the whole work. An element that has a particular value in a certain period will completely change its function in another period. The grotesque forms, which were regarded in the period of Classicism as resources for the comic, became, in the Romantic period, one of the sources of tragedy. It is in this continual change of function that the true life of the elements of the literary work are to be found.[36]

In particular Viktor Shklovsky and Yuri Tynianov made a study, in relation to Russian literature, of those functional variations by which, for example, the same form can be transformed from a minor rank to that of a "canonical form," and which maintain a perpetual transference between popular literature and official literature, between academicism and the avant-garde, between poetry and prose, and so on. Inheritance, Shklovsky was fond of saying, usually passes from the uncle to the nephew, and evolution canonizes the junior branch. Thus Pushkin imported into great poetry the effects of eighteenth-century album verse, Nekrassov borrowed from journalism and vaudeville, Blok from gypsy songs, Dostoyevsky from the detective novel.[37]

In this sense, literary history becomes the history of a system: it is the evolution of the functions that is significant, not that of the elements, and knowledge of the synchronic relations necessarily precedes that of the processes. But, on the other hand, as Jakobson has remarked, the literary table of a period describes not only a present of creation, but also a present of culture, and therefore a certain image of the past, "not only the literary production of any given period, but also that part of the literary tradition which for the stage in question has remained vital or has been revived. . . . The selection of a new tendency from among the classics and their reinterpretation by a novel trend is a substantial problem for synchronic literary studies,"[38] and consequently for the structural history of literature, which is simply the placing in diachronic perspective of these successive synchronic tables: in the table of French classicism, Homer and Vergil have a place, Dante and Shakespeare do not. In our present literary landscape, the discovery (or invention) of the Baroque is more important than the Romantic inheritance, and our Shakespeare is not Voltaire's Shakespeare or Hugo's: he is a contemporary of Brecht and Claudel, as Cervantes is a contemporary of Kafka. A period is manifested as much by what it reads as by what it writes, and these two aspects of its "literature" act upon one another. As Borges puts it: "If it were given to me to read any page written today—this one for example—as one will read it in the year 2000, I would know the literature of the year 2000."[39]

To this history of the *internal divisions* of the literary field, with its already very rich program (one has only to think what a universal history of the opposition between prose and poetry would be like: a fundamental, elementary, constant, immutable opposition in its function, constantly renewed in its means), one should add that of the much wider division between literature and everything that is not literature; this would be, not literary history, but the history of the relations between literature and social life as a whole—the history of the *literary function*. The Russian Formalists insisted on the *differential* character of the literary fact. Literariness is also a function of nonliterariness, and no stable definition can be given of it: one is left simply with the awareness of limit. Everyone knows that the birth of the cinema altered the status of literature—by depriving it of certain of its functions, but also by giving it some of its own means. And this transformation is obviously no more than a beginning. How will literature survive the development of other media of communication? Already we no longer believe, as it was believed from Aristole to La Harpe, that art is an imitation of nature, and where the classics sought above all a fine resemblance, we seek, on the contrary, a radical originality and an absolute creation. The day when the Book ceases to be the principal vehicle of knowledge, will not literature have changed its meaning once again? Perhaps we are quite simply living through the last days of the Book. This continuing adventure ought to make us more attentive to certain episodes in the past: we cannot go on speaking of literature as if its existence were self-evident, as if its relation to the world and to men had never varied. We do not have, for example, a history of reading. Such a history would be an intellectual, social, and even physical history: if St. Augustine is to be believed,[40] his master Ambrose was the first man in Antiquity to read with his eyes, without speaking the text aloud. True history is made up of these great silent moments. And the value of the method may lie in its ability to find, beneath each silence, a question.

TRANSLATED BY ALAN SHERIDAN

NOTES

[1] Claude Lévi-Strauss, *La Pensée sauvage* (Paris: Plon, 1962), p. 26 [*The Savage Mind* (Chicago: University of Chicago Press, 1966), p. 17].

[2] Roland Barthes, *Essais critiques* (Paris: Seuil, 1964), p. 255 [*Critical Essays*, trans. Richard Howard (Evanston, Ill.: Northwestern University Press, 1972), p. 258].

[3] Paul Valéry, "Albert Thibaudet," *Nouvelle revue française* (July 1936), p. 6.

[4] Lévi-Strauss, *Savage Mind*, p. 19.

[5] Boris Tomachevski, "*La Nouvelle école d'histoire littéraire en Russie*," *Revue des études slaves* (1928), p. 231.

[6] "The object of literary study is not literature as a whole, but its literariness [*literaturnost*], that is to say, that which makes a work literary." This sentence written by Jakobson in 1921 was one of the watchwords of Russian Formalism.

[7] "In mythology, as in linguistics, formal analysis immediately raises the question of meaning." Claude Lévi-Strauss, *Anthropologie structurale* (Paris: Plon, 1958), p. 266 [*Structural Anthropology*, trans. Claire Jacobson and Brooke Grundfest Schoepf (New York: Basic Books, 1963), p. 241].

[8] Cf. Victor Erlich, *Russian Formalism* (2d. rev. ed., trans. The Hague: Mouton, 1965), p. 219.

[9] N.S. Trubetzkoy, *The Principles of Phonology* (1939), trans. C. A. M. Baltaxe (Berkeley: University of California Press, 1969), pp. 3–4.

[10] Cf. in particular the criticism by Boris Eichenbaum, Jakobson, and Tynianov of Sievers's methods of acoustic metrics, which tried to study the sounds of a poem as if it had been written in a totally unknown language. Erlich, *Russian Formalism*, p. 218.

[11] A synthesis of these criticisms is to be found in Paul Delbouille, *Poésie et sonorités* (Paris: Belles Lettres, 1961).

[12] René Etiemble, *Le Mythe de Rimbaud* (Paris: Gallimard, 1952), 2:81–104.

[13] "All colors have been attributed at least once to each of the vowels." Delbouille, *Poésie*, p. 248.

[14] See Adhemar Gelb and Kurt Goldstein, *Psychologische Analysen hirnpathologischer Falle* (Leipzig: Barth, 1920).

[15] Roman Jakobson, "Closing Statement: Linguistics and Poetics," in Thomas A. Sebeok, ed., *Style in Language* (Cambridge, Mass: MIT Press, 1960), p. 367.

[16] Erlich, *Russian Formalism*, p. 175.

[17] Jakobson, "Closing Statement," p. 375.

[18] Ibid., pp. 370–71.

[19] Vladimir Propp, *The Morphology of the Folktale* (1928), trans. L. Scott (Bloomington: Indiana University Press, 1958; 2d. rev. ed., Louis A. Wagner, ed., Austin: University of Texas Press, 1968).

[20] Claude Bremond, "*Le Message narratif*," *Communications* 4 (1964).

[21] One can, however, find a purely methodological state of structuralism, as it were, in authors who do not claim allegiance to this "philosophy." This applies to Georges Dumézil, who puts at the service of a typically historical investigation the analysis of the *functions* that unite the elements of Indo-European mythology, these functions being regarded as more significant than the elements themselves. It also applies to Charles Mauron, whose psychocriticism interprets not isolated themes but networks, the terms of which may vary without alteration to their structure. The study of systems does not necessarily *exclude* that of genesis or filiations: the minimum program of structuralism is that such a study should precede it and *govern* it.

[22] Leo Spitzer, "Les Etudes de style et les différents pays," in *Langue et littérature* (Paris: Belles Lettres, 1961).

[23] "Structural linguistics, like quantum mechanics, gains in morphic determinism what it loses in temporal determinism." Roman Jakobson, report presented to the VIIIth International Congress of Linguists, Oslo, 1957, published in *Proceedings of the VIIIth International Congress of Linguists* (Oslo, 1958).

[24] Jean Rousset, *Forme et signification* (Paris: Corti, 1961), p. xii.

[25] Georges Poulet, "*Réponse de,*" *Les Lettres nouvelles* (June 1959), pp. 10–13.

[26] Paul Ricoeur, "Structure et herméneutique," *Esprit* (Nov. 1963); "Structuralism and Hermeneutics," trans. Kathleen McLaughlin, in Ricoeur, *The Conflict of Interpretations*, Don Ihde, ed. (Evanston, Ill: Northwestern University Press, 1974).

[27] Cf. Claude Lévi-Strauss, *Esprit* (Nov. 1963), p. 632; "A Confrontation," *New Left Review* (July–Aug. 1970), pp. 62–61. [This is Lévi-Strauss's paraphrase of Ricoeur's remark. —*Ed.*]

[28] Lévi-Strauss, *Esprit*, p. 633; "A Confrontation," p. 61.

[29] Maurice Merleau-Ponty, *Signes* (Paris: Gallimard, 1960), p. 150 [*Signs*, trans. R. C. McCleary (Evanston, Ill: Northwestern University Press, 1964), p. 120].

[30] Lévi-Strauss suggests a relation of the same kind between history and ethnology: "Structures appear only to an observation practised from the outside. Conversely, this observation can never grasp the processes, which are not analytic objects, but only the particular way in which a temporality is experienced by a subject. . . . A historian can sometimes work as an ethnologist, and an ethnologist as a historian, but the methods themselves are complementary, in the sense the physicists give to this term; that is to say, one cannot, at one and the same time, rigorously define a stage A and a stage B (which is possible only from the outside and in structural terms), and reexperience empirically the passage from one to the other (which would be the only intelligible way of understanding it). Even the sciences of man have their relations of uncertainty." "*Les Limites de la notion de structure en ethnologie*," in R. Bastide, ed., *Sens et usage du mot structure* (The Hague: Mouton, 1962), pp. 44–45.

[31] A new signification is not necessarily a new *meaning*: it is a new connection between form and meaning. If literature is an art of significations, it is renewed, and with it criticism, by modifying this connection, either through the meaning or through the form. It thus happens that modern criticism is rediscovering in "themes" or "styles" what classical criticism had already found in "ideas" or "feelings." An old meaning comes back to us linked to a new form, and this "shift" displaces a whole work.

[32] It is in this light that I introduce the very fine book by Gilbert Durand, *Le Décor mythique de la Chartreuse de Parme* (Paris: Corti, 1961).

[33] Spitzer, "*Les études de style*," p. 27.

[34] Paul Valéry, *Oeuvres* (Paris: Gallimard, 1960), vol. 2, p. 560 ["Odds and Ends" in Valery, *Analects*, trans. Stuart Gilbert (Princeton: Princeton University Press, 1970), p. 113].

[35] Albert Thibaudet (1874–1936) was the author of an influential *Histoire de la Littérature Française de 1789 à nos jours* (Paris: Stock, 1936).

[36] Tomachevski, "*La Nouvelle école*," pp. 238–39.

[37] On the Formalist views of literary history, cf. Boris Eichenbaum, "The Theory of the Formal Method," and Jurij Tynianov, "On Literary Evolution" in *Readings in Russian Poetics*, ed. Ladislav Matejka and Krystyna Pomorska (Cambridge, Mass: MIT Press, 1970). See also Erlich, *Formalism*, pp. 254–55, and Nina Gourfinkel, "*Les Nouvelles methodes d'histoire litteraire en Russie*," *Le Monde slave* (Feb. 1929).

[38] Jakobson, "Closing Statement," p. 352.

[39] Jorge Luis Borges, *Other Inquisitions*, trans. Ruth L. C. Simms (New York: Simon and Schuster, 1965).

[40] St. Augustine, *Confessions*, bk. VI, trans. quoted by Borges, *Other Inquisitions*, pp. 117–18.

Poetics
1972

Tzvetan Todorov, co-founder and co-editor of Poétique, *made his initial mark on the critical scene in 1966 with a memorable anthology of Russian Formalist texts. In the wake of two major exercises in poetics—whose pretexts were* Les Liaisons dangereuses *and* The Decameron—*he offers, in this selection from the* Encyclopedic Dictionary of the Sciences of Language, *a succinct evocation of the most suggestive aspects of poetics.*

The term "poetics," as transmitted to us by tradition, designates, first, any internal theory of literature. Second, it applies to the choice made by an author among all the literary possibilities (on the order of thematics, composition, style, and so on): a critic may speak of "Hugo's poetics" in this sense. Third, it refers to the normative codes constructed by a literary school, a set of practical rules whose use is obligatory. Only the first use of the term will concern us here.

Poetics thus understood proposes to elaborate categories that allow us to grasp simultaneously the unity and the variety of literary works. The individual work will illustrate these categories; its status will be that of example, not of ultimate end. For example, poetics will be called upon to elaborate a theory of description that will bring to light not only what all descriptions have in common but also what permits them to remain different; but it will not be asked to account for particular descriptions in a given text. Poetics will then be capable of defining a conjunction of categories of which we know of no instance *at the moment*. In this sense, the object of poetics is constituted more by potential works than by existing ones.

This primary option defines the scientific ambition of poetics: the object of a science is not the particular fact but the laws that allow us to account for it. Unlike the known attempts to establish what is (in such cases) improperly

From Oswald Ducrot and Tzvetan Todorov, *Encyclopedic Dictionary of the Sciences of Language*, trans. Catherine Porter (Baltimore: Johns Hopkins Univ. Press, 1979), from *Dictionnaire encyclopédique des sciences du langage* (Paris: Seuil, 1972).

called a science of literature, poetics does not propose as its task the "correct" interpretation of the works of the past; rather, it proposes the elaboration of instruments permitting the analysis of these works. Its object is not the set of existing literary works but literary discourse itself as the generative principle of an infinite number of texts. Poetics is thus a theoretical discipline nourished and fertilized by empirical research but not constituted by it.

Among its major tasks, poetics must first supply an answer to the question, "What is literature?" In other words, it must try to reduce this sociological phenomenon that has been called literature to an internal and theoretical entity (or else demonstrate the lack of such an entity); or, to take another approach, it must define literary discourse with respect to other types of discourse and thus give itself an object of knowledge that is the product of a theoretical undertaking and, consequently, at a certain distance from observable facts. The answer to this first question will be at once a starting point and a final goal; everything in the work of the poetician must contribute to this elucidation, which by definition can never be complete.

Second, poetics must supply instruments for the description of a literary text; that is, it must be able to distinguish levels of meaning, to identify the units that constitute them, and to describe the relationships in which the units participate. With the assistance of these primary categories, we can begin to study certain more or less stable configurations. We can undertake, in other words, the study of types, or genres; we can also study the laws of succession, that is, of literary history.

The goals and objects of poetics must be distinguished from those of neighboring disciplines: (1) Reading assigns itself the task of describing the system of a particular text. It uses the instruments elaborated by poetics, but it is more than the simple application of these instruments; its goal—which is different from that of poetics—is to bring to light the meaning of a particular text, insofar as the meaning cannot be exhausted by the categories of poetics. (2) The object of linguistics is the language itself, the object of poetics, a discourse; nevertheless, both often depend on the same concepts. Each is inscribed within the framework of semiotics, whose object is all signifying systems. (3) The acquisitions of poetics may provide a contribution to anthropological or psychological research. The problems of aesthetic value in particular, intimately linked as they are to the whole of cultural evolution, arise in the anthropological framework.

TRANSLATED BY CATHERINE PORTER

JULIA KRISTEVA

Prolegomena to the Concept of "Text"
1969

In this essay, Julia Kristeva reveals her program for "dynamizing structuralism" by distinguishing between the "phenotext," the text-phenomenon given to perception and whose inner logic structuralists had made it their business to analyze, and the "genotext," the complex movement of signification (or "semiosis") whose deceptively placid end-product is the phenotext itself. In this way, Kristeva opens the text up to history and subjectivity, a perspective she would develop in a context indebted to Mikhail Bakhtin (whose notion of dialogism is implicit in Kristeva's "intertextuality") and Ferdinand de Saussure (whose odd meditations on embedded Anagrams *informs her notion of poetic "paragrams").*

Reaching beyond the "work" and the "book"—or, in other words, beyond the complete, finished message—so-called literary work today deals with *texts*: meaningful products whose epistemological complexity harkens back, after a lengthy detour, to the sacred hymns of Antiquity. If these products are to be understood and incorporated into the *discourse* currently influencing the social, a theory is needed, a theory that will have to be elaborated as a linguistic analysis of the text as *self-producing signifier.*

Here, *analysis* is to be taken in its etymological sense (αναλυσιζ), meaning a *dissolution* of the concepts and operations that currently represent meaning, an *emancipation* based on the contemporary discursive apparatus for dealing with the signifier (psychoanalysis, philosophy, and so on) and aimed at *detaching* oneself from it in order to seek *resolution* in an uninterrupted *death* (or eclipse of the tangible surface).

This theory must first circumscribe the concept of its "object," the *text*, by distinguishing it from the totality of so-called literary and poetic discourses. Having pinpointed the specific nature of the text in this manner, the theory may then go on to a critical examination of the set of discourses currently classified as "literary," "scientific," "religious," "political," and so on.

From Julia Kristeva, *Semiotike: Recherches pour une sémanalyse* (Paris: Seuil, 1969).

A *text* will then be a certain type of signifying production occupying a precise place in history and amenable to study by an appropriate science, which will need to be specified in detail.

Now, since a text is a practice in and on the signifier, texts can be found in various forms in various types of "literary," "philosophical," "religious," and "political" discourse and writing. It will accordingly be necessary to discover the textual axis within the spoken and written totality, as well as to pinpoint the "textual" particularity in each effect of language.

Since a text is produced in language, it is inconceivable apart from the linguistic material itself, and as such it falls within the purview of a theory of signification, which we shall call *semanalysis*, in order to distinguish it, first of all, from semiotics and, furthermore, in order to emphasize the fact that the study of signifying practices is not to be confined by the "sign," which is rather to be decomposed in such a way as to open up a new space within it, a space of invertible and combinatorial *sites*—specifically, the space of *significance*.

Semanalysis, then, is the theory of textual signification which looks upon the *sign* as a specular element responsible for representing the engendering—the process of germination—that takes place within it while, at the same time, enclosing it and defining its laws. In other words, semanalysis, though mindful of the fact that a text exhibits a system of signs, opens up another scene within that system: a scene hidden behind the screen of structure, and which is significance *as an operation of which structure is merely a displaced by-product*. While avoiding the deceptive notion that it might be possible to abandon the terrain of the *sign* which makes it possible, semanalysis rejects any obligation to adopt a single point of view, the central point of view of a structure to be *described*, assuming instead the possibility of combinatorial views restoring the production to be *engendered*. Taking *langue* in the Saussurean sense—that is, as opposed to *parole*—as its basis, semanalysis avoids both psychological thematicism and aestheticizing idealism, the two approaches currently vying for the monopoly of what has been called *écriture* (Derrida). Semanalysis is linguistics, yet it has nothing whatsoever to do with the descriptive approach that takes a "corpus" as a repository of informational content allowing communication to take place between sender and recipient. Note that the linguistics based on these theoretical principles, which currently dominate the process of technocratization of the so-called "human" sciences, is crudely substantialist and "thingish"—that is, in more precise terms, phenomenological. It works with a linguistic "corpus" like a surface structured by distinct signifying entities which signifies a certain phenomenon: a message based on a code. What we call *semanalysis* cannot be conceived in these terms. "A body is where it acts" (Leibniz). A text is not a linguistic *phenomenon*, that is, it is not a structured meaning exhibited within a linguistic corpus seen as a flat structure. It is its *engendering*: an engendering inscribed in a linguistic "phenomenon," the *phenotext* comprising the printed text but legible only when one *vertically* retraces the genesis: first, of its linguistic categories, and second, of the topology of the signifying act. Significance will therefore be that engendering which can be doubly apprehended: first, engendering of the fabric of the language; second, engendering of the "I" that places itself in a position to present the significance in question. What opens up within this vertical dimension is the (linguistic) operation of generation of the phenotext. We call this operation a *genotext*, thus splitting the notion of text into phenotext and genotext (surface and depth, signified structure and signifying productivity).

The generative zone thus created yields an object of knowledge which "is not governed by the principles of Euclidean localization" and has no "substantial specificity" (Bachelard). The text is therefore a "dynamized object." The discourse that deals with it, semanalysis, aims to discover what types of dynamized objects present themselves as significant.

If the work of signifying always takes place on the dividing line between phenotext and genotext, the specificity of the text stems from the fact that it is a translation of the genotext into the phenotext, which can be identified in reading by opening the phenotext to the genotext. In other words—and here I will venture a preliminary operational definition that will be filled out and made more precise in what follows—to analyze a signifying production as textual comes down to showing how the process whereby the signifying system is generated is manifested in the phenotext. The term "textual" may be applied to any signifying practice that accomplishes, at all levels of the phenotext (in its signifier and signified alike) the *process whereby the signifying system that it asserts is generated*. More concisely, a practice is textual if it exemplifies the Freudian precept, "*Wo es war, soll Ich werden*," Where id was, there shall ego be.

TRANSLATED BY ARTHUR GOLDHAMMER

PHILIPPE SOLLERS

General Theses
1971

This programmatic statement, issued in expanded form at the Cluny Collo-
quium on Literatures and Ideologies *held in April 1970, conveys a sense*
of the extraordinary theoretical analogism characterizing the vanguard
journal Tel quel *during its years of greatest influence. The journal had*
been founded by Sollers and friends in 1960 as an alternative to the political
posturing of Sartre's Les Temps modernes *on the left and the "mannered*
capers" of the "young hussards" on the right. It began under the patronage
of Francis Ponge as an affirmation of literature's right to attend solely to
itself, but a mere ten years later, literature was being dismissed as an ideo-
logical "effect." Ponge had been supplanted by the dissident Surrealists Ba-
taille and Artaud, and the journal that had earlier claimed one would do
far better by "representing" the world than by "contesting" it was now—
under the banners of Marx and Freud, but more specifically of Derrida,
Kristeva, Lacan, and Althusser—challenging the very model of represen-
tation.

Concerning the ongoing research of an avant-garde literary group, we wish to state the following fundamental theses:

1. The dominant bourgeois ideology is forever trying to accredit the idea that we are experiencing a "crisis of civilization," whereas we believe that what is needed is an in-depth analysis of the repercussions of a worldwide crisis in the capitalist mode of production. Ideologically, the extent of this crisis can be grasped through the study of "modes of sig-nification" (including, among others, "literature").

2. In our view, the theoretical foundation for such an analysis is provided first and foremost by historical materialism and dialectical materialism, plus the unconscious since Freud. The intellectual accessories available

Philippe Sollers, *"Thèses générales"* in *Tel quel*, 44 (Paris: Seuil, 1971).

to us for the study of this field will include: first and foremost, an experimental practice ("avant-garde literature" in its specific historicity over the past century in Western civilization), plus the various emerging sciences of language: linguistics, semiotics. At the *intersection* of this practice and these sciences, and under the *scrutiny* of psychoanalysis and Marxism—Leninism, new operational concepts are being developed: writing [*écriture*], the text.

3. Writing and the text are for us *integrators* of the effect formerly known as "literary," an ideological effect whose only content, as Medvedev has written, consists of "emerging ideologies, the living process of the formation of the ideological horizon." We must evaluate the relationship between this productive and critical integration and the sciences, as well as its consequences for a new type of philosophical practice.

4. The research that we are conducting cannot be characterized as either "formalist" or "sociological." It is neither a mechanistic analysis of the direct expressivity of social and economic determinations nor a limited deciphering of linguistic components. Within material modes of production, themselves produced by transformations which they in turn transform through dialectical feedback, writing and the text are not merely ideological or merely formal. They are not reducible to any type of subjective "emanation" ("creative psychology," and so on). Their function is to bring out the materiality of the symbolic stakes in a given phase of history, and, in particular, the scene of philosophical and political conflicts, according to a specific, relatively autonomous, indirect mode.

5. In the Surrealist movement one finds these multiple stakes in a concentrated form. There can be no doubt that this movement effected a change in "point of view" with respect to art and literature. Today, the important point is to note that it did so by (mis)construing all of our crucial cultural issues.

   a. Divorce between the bourgeois conception of literature and a linguistic practice at odds with the rhetorical code (example: Lautréamont, Mallarmé).

   b. Emergence of the unconscious as a basis of "framing" the problems of language (but Surrealism soon drifted toward Carl Jung and missed its connection with Freud).

   c. Consideration of Eastern cultures (which the Surrealists did not develop beyond the stage of a project obscured by various mystifications, a project most explicitly pursued by Antonin Artaud).

d. Revolutionary activity: Surrealism attempted to define itself in relation to Marxism but remained attached to utopian socialism (Fourier), confused the materialist dialectic with the Hegelian dialectic,
subordinated politics to ethics, and tried to reconcile materialism
with idealism, leading straight to spiritualism.

All of the preceding points were subject to a "fantastic synthesis" in Surrealism, whereas one must show instead that their differences were functional. On
the *outer* edge of Surrealism we inscribe the names of Artaud and Georges
Bataille: by this we mean that their practices—organic experimentation with
written thought (Artaud), attempt to define a heterogeneous anthropology
(Bataille)—are *unthinkable* within Surrealist ideology.

6. We define the ideological effect known as "literature" as a derivative of
philosophy invested in and by verbal representation, which dominates
it; as a dramatization of philosophy for the purpose of enticing and
enmeshing social subjects; and as a philosophical "laboration" undergoing transformation within historical materialism. Under the feudal
mode of production, it can be said that "literature" provided a mythical
coherence based on symbols, while under the capitalist mode of production it functions as narrative appropriation regulated by the sign.
What needs to be conceptualized now is the transition to another (socialist) mode of production. This crisis and this transition can be
grasped, under the pressure of Freud's discovery, in three types of conceptual intervention: the problem of the *signifier* in Lacan (signifying
what "represents the subject for another signifier") leading to the possibility of psychoanalysis as science or theory of the subject of science; the
problem of *writing* in Derrida, which leads to a critique of all the concepts of metaphysics subject to the domination of Logos, hence to a
reinterpretation of the whole history of philosophy, as well as a general
theory of modes of notation in history; and finally, the foundation,
based on transformation of the formalist and linguistic contribution, of
a dialectical theory of *signifying practices* as *semanalysis* (Kristeva).

7. "Until now," Engels wrote in *The Dialectics of Nature*, "natural science
and even philosophy have completely neglected the influence of man's
activity on thought. On the one hand they know only nature, on the
other, thought." We believe that the time has come for a writing about
natural science and thought, for the "theater of the scientific age" called
for by Bertolt Brecht—a theater of knowledge in language and in the
writing of language. "The writer needs the teachings of science more
and more. Slowly, his art has begun to develop a science, or at any rate
a technology which, in relation to the technology of previous generations, stands roughly as chemistry stands to alchemy."

8. If the repressed of philosophy, as Althusser has shown, is indeed politics, the repressed of literature might be philosophy. In fact, literature lives off of philosophy, and does so in a complex, not merely passive way, since it fills in, as performance, where philosophy cannot assume its proper role (or at least what was taken as such until philosophy "ended" with Hegel): namely, to serve self-consciously as a locus for effective utterance (*énonciation effective*). Literature restores an "imaginary" dimension to philosophy, a dimension with which philosophy, preoccupied with conceptualizing the symbolic field displaced by science, cannot concern itself. "Literature" might then function as the repressed of a repressed, as a negation to the second degree, which, if doubly subverted by a theory of the unconscious and of writing linked to politics, would give rise to a key strategic weapon, making it possible to attack the process whereby language is produced and materially transformed in history.

9. A new practice of writing, dissolving the effects of "literature" and criticizing their transitory formations, can on the other hand consolidate that new form of "philosophical praxis," Marxism, and provide it, without subordination (as was the case in the couple philosophy/literature, which, still under the domination of idealism, itself opposed science and politics), not with a *derivative* but with a *productive reprise*. Here, then, as Lacan foresaw in *La Science et la Vérité*, is where the revolutionary, the writer, and the analyst come together.

10. Vladimir Mayakovsky already said: "The myth of apolitical art must be smashed to smithereens." In the process of rejecting spiritualism and idealism, which are associated with the *subject* of literature, and their accomplice, formalism, in order to establish a dialectical materialist practice of writing, we are not saying that the ideological struggle must be *directly* political. But the political task, marked by a constant need to take a position in history and the class struggle, will be fulfilled at its specific level if writing becomes aware of itself in its function as "universal connection" and in its materialist practice of contradictions and the struggle of opposites; if it bases itself on the sciences of nature, language, history, and the unconscious; and if it knows, as Lenin wrote, that "only socialism will free science from its bourgeois chains."

11. Engels said that Hegel had written a "dialectical poem": the text that we have in mind for the future should be a historical and dialectical materialist text of the ideological praxis of Marxism as it transforms (through the unconscious itself) the foundations of our thinking. Here we are referring to very concrete consequences: in chemistry, as is well known, an innovation in writing, the use of a *dash* to indicate a chemi-

cal bond in formulae of what is known as atomic notation, had tremen-
dous influence. The text introduces a significant, "intramolecular"
notation of this type into the order of discourse. The text will be to
typical classical literature what chemistry was to alchemy.

At this level such a practice can be understood simultaneously as an analysis of
the foreclosure of the subject in the discourse of science: that is why we have
said that the text "knew" psychosis. Consequently, we are saying that the text is
developing an innovative form of knowledge that must inevitably take the
form of a questioning and renewal of all other forms of knowledge.

TRANSLATED BY ARTHUR GOLDHAMMER

PART V

Psychoanalysis and Literature

Contours

CHARLES MAURON

Methodological Postface to
Psychocriticism of the Comic Genre
1963

The key element in this methodological appendix is the insistence on the difference between the comparison and the superimposition of texts. Comparison establishes similarities; superimposition, rooted in Francis Galton's photographic experiments, attends solely to "enigmatic coincidences." The "enigma" lies in the fact that appreciation of such repetitions is inseparable from an awareness of the difference mediating them. As such, they are sheer manifestations of the uncanny. Note the distance traveled since our selection from Charles Mauron on Mallarmé, where the sole "superimposition" mentioned is between manifest and latent contents of a dream.

Psychocriticism aims to increase our understanding of literary texts by first identifying and then studying relations whose source, because it cannot be traced to an author's conscious will or accounted for by chance, can therefore plausibly be sought in his unconscious personality. Despite their obsessive character, these relations will have gone largely unnoticed: superimposition of texts can bring them to light. When psychocriticism is applied to a genre, the foregoing description must be modified in two ways. First, obsessive features will in general already have been isolated and brought to light by their recurrence in various works, yet conscious imitation may seem inadequate as an explanation. Second, only generic features of the unconscious personality, or at any rate features common to a very large number of individuals in a particular culture, can be considered.

Charles Mauron, *Psychocritique du genre comique* (Paris: José Corti, 1963).

In any event, psychocriticism is intentionally incomplete: it does not claim to replace other critical disciplines but can be practiced in combination with them. The psychocritical method involves the following steps:

1. By superimposing a writer's texts as Francis Galton superimposes photographs,[1] one attempts to discover obsessive and presumably involuntary patterns of association or sets of images.

2. One then studies the writer's work in order to figure out how the patterns, images, or—to use a more general term—structures revealed in step one are repeated and transformed. In practice, these structures loosely define dramatic figures and situations. Because these structures range from characteristic associations of ideas to imaginative fantasies, thematic analysis must be combined with analysis of dreams and their metamorphoses. What generally emerges from this is a personal "myth."

3. The personal myth and its avatars are interpreted as an expression of the unconscious personality and its evolution.

4. The results thus achieved through study of the work are checked against the known facts of the writer's life.

In the present study, certain changes will be required because the method is to be applied not to a single author but to a genre. Stylistic features of the texts will be blurred. Mythical figures and situations will become, if not archetypes in Jung's sense, then at least the shared property of large social groups. Finally, collective reality will replace individual reality.

The principles of psychocriticism have much in common with Ernst Kris and Leopold Bellak's account of the creative function (as an oscillation between psychic levels).[2] Aesthetically, psychocriticism takes a broad view, according to which creativity depends on three main factors: unconscious imaginative fantasy, the contents of consciousness, and style, or, to put it in more picturesque terms, the keyboard on which the writer plays. In this perspective, the work of art exists in language as an object of communion between self and nonself, compensating for the solitude of the individual.

TRANSLATED BY ARTHUR GOLDHAMMER

NOTES

[1] In order to uncover unconscious processes, psychoanalysis in the strict sense makes use of the technique of free association, which is not applicable to literature. In psychocriticism, free association is replaced by the superimposition of texts. Care should be taken not to confuse superimposition with comparison. In comparison a distinct view is maintained of each juxtaposed text. By contrast, superimposition blurs each text in order to focus atten-

tion exclusively on the enigmatic coincidences among them. On this key point, see my introduction to *Des Métaphores obsédantes au mythe personnel* (from *Obsessive Metaphors to Personal Myth*).

[2] See Ernst Kris, *Psychoanalytic Explorations in Art* (New York: International Universities Press, 1952).

JEAN STAROBINSKI

Psychoanalysis and
Literary Understanding
1970

The eminent thematic critic speaks to what most interests him in psycho-
analysis. At a time when the structuralists—Leclaire and Laplanche, both
in the orbit of Lacan—began suggesting that what was latent *was not a*
meaning concealed behind *the manifest content, but an unperceived orga-*
nization of *the manifest content, Starobinski opted for a more phenomeno-*
logical solution: what was latent was rather a meaning implicit in *the*
manifest content. In a celebrated article on the unconscious, Jean
Laplanche and Serge Leclaire, with specific reference to the work of
Georges Politzer, had characterized the phenomenological interpretation of
the unconscious as fundamentally obfuscatory.

Therein lies the central difficulty: psychoanalytic discourse, which was supposed to be scientific discourse about man's affective life, cannot avoid becoming an expressive dramaturgy, constantly in danger of being carried away by the intrinsic inventiveness of its own rhetoric. One thing no doubt compensates for another. Ever since Freud, psychoanalysis has faced two complementary dangers: that of accentuating its rationalist, objective side at the price of narrowing its focus and stifling its inventiveness; and that of letting its figurative rhetoric run away with itself, transforming the discipline into a literature of speculation that readily bends the malleable language of metaphor to its own purpose. Freud, always careful to avoid both the scientific dryness and the garrulous inventiveness of some of his followers and to engage in constant dialogue with his patients, maintained his mythology midway between the expressive language of poetry and the highly conventionalized quantitative language of science.

Jean Starobinski, "*Psychoanalysis and Literary Understanding,*" trans. Arthur Goldham-mer, *The Living Eye* (Cambridge: Harvard University Press, 1989), from *La Relation critique* (Paris: Gallimard, 1970).

*   *   *

These ambiguities account for Freud's appeal both to critics interested in doing scientific criticism and to writers (Surrealists) eager to liberate man's deepest language. The reservations I have just expressed, which prevent me from confronting literary works purely and simply as a psychoanalyst, do not prevent me from recognizing the value of the psychoanalytic contribution or from acknowledging my debt to psychoanalysis—in which I find, especially in the work of Freud, a lesson in exegetical technique.

In both the therapeutic relation with a patient and the examination of a literary work, there must be an initial phase, a phase of experience. In vigilant neutrality, the gaze goes out to meet the reality presented to it without undue haste to identify definitive structures, for the danger is great that it would simply impose its own. As far as possible, one refrains from interpreting and simply takes in data useful for later interpretation. With the literary work, everything is present from the first, and nothing can be added. By contrast, in treating an analysand, the psychoanalyst can approach the subject again and again, seek new associations, overcome resistances. Evident as these differences are, literary criticism can benefit from adhering to the psychoanalytic principle of "free-floating attention"—a sort of vigilance in suspense, a watchful benevolence. Little by little certain themes, certain similarities, will stand out. Attention is drawn to what the work passes over in silence, as well as to the quality of its intonation, its rhythms, its verbal energy and organization. Structures, connections, and "networks" (Charles Mauron) begin to take shape as if of their own accord, as the work develops a complex presence whose organic structure must be identified.

Psychoanalysis casts the old problem of the relation between the life and the work in a new light. It forbids us to settle for biography that is nothing more than a collection of anecdotes. A man's "inner" history is the history of his relation with the world and with others. For psychoanalysis, it is the history of the successive stages of desire. Biography thus becomes the history of those actions through which the developing individual (body and consciousness) creates himself by seeking what he lacks. At this level, a continuity is established between work and life, because the work, sustained by the individual who produces it, is itself an act of desire, a revealed intention. Since life and work are no longer incommensurable realities, psychoanalysis confronts us with a significant entity, an expansive, continuous melody that is at once life and work, destiny and expression: the life takes on the value of expression, and the work takes on the value of destiny. To explain the work in terms of the life becomes inconceivable since everything is work and at the same time everything is life.

Even so, psychoanalysis itself advises against completely eliminating the boundary between life and work, for in the work desire lives a singular life: an indirect life, in which reality is transposed into image and image into reality. Even if we do not entirely accept the facile theory of compensation, it is still true that desire detaches itself from the world in order to become desire of the work and to a certain extent desire of desire, desire of itself. Each work serves a different function with respect to its author and in its indirect relation with the world. Psychoanalysis encourages us to search for the work's vital function, that is, what in the work the writer wished to reveal or hide or protect or simply chance.

We should, to be sure, be suspicious of a psychoanalysis that would be satisfied to show us the antecedents of the work, a world of memory filled with details of the past. Such an approach would decipher symbols in a regressive direction, working back from the present to the antecedent, from the literary expression to the underlying desire, as if the literary were a mask to be torn away. That kind of psychoanalytic criticism simply follows the artist's path in reverse. It thinks it has explained the work when in reality all it has done is to reveal certain of its necessary preconditions. Only by nullifying Baudelaire's work through such regressive analysis can one speak, as René Laforgue has done, of "Baudelaire's failure." Such a method limits itself to seeking the previous instrumental and material cause of the work while neglecting the final cause—its actual *project*, to use a word much in fashion. As a result, one loses sight of the work and becomes caught up in a "background" world. One hypothetically reconstructs the author's prior experience and early wishes. Mistaking the shadow for the substance, one is all too likely to overlook the fact that work is itself part of experience, and often the only part of the author's experience to which we have access. Of course it is good, when we are granted access to it, to know the inner history that precedes the work, which can be useful in deciphering the work's purpose. But great literary works are so clear about their purpose, about their intentional axis, that it is enough to read them with an eye to the meanings with which they are replete, even when the author hesitates between several competing versions. Their meaning lies ahead of them because it lies entirely within them.

Meaning abounds; one must know how to gather it in. Psychoanalysis deserves credit for pointing out that in psychic life nothing is accidental, and that a perspicacious observer can make rich sense of accidents that someone less observant would very likely dismiss as meaningless. Symbols emerge and hitherto unsuspected connections become obvious.

The famous distinction that Freud makes in the *Interpretation of Dreams* between latent and manifest content is, I think, unlikely to be fruitful in literature if interpreted as a distinction between the hidden and the apparent. If we reject the manifest meaning of a work of art in favor of a supposed latent meaning, we must perforce deal with what is no more than a conjectural prehistory or subhistory. The analyst must settle for using biographical incidents to reconstruct a coherent (perhaps too coherent) sequence of desires, fixations, repressions, and sublimations. He speaks in place of the work. He deprives the work of its reality and regards it as a screen, bestowing the force of reality upon what is actually no more than a tissue of hypotheses. Rather than latent it is better to say *implicit*: what is present *in* the work, not *behind* it, but which we were unable to decipher at first glance. The latent content is evidence that needs to be made evident. This is what Maurice Merleau-Ponty had in mind when he wrote: "Phenomenology and psychoanalysis are not parallel. Far better than that: both are directed toward the same latency." In criticism, the convergent operation of phenomenology and psychoanalysis might be called stylistics. Even if Freud is right that the symbol is what dissimulates or disguises an underlying desire, it is also what reveals or designates desire. It is not clear why the symbol must be dispelled (as if it were an intervening screen) in order to let us enter a region prior to or beyond the work of literature. Let us grant the symbol the right to live a life of its own. By so doing, we give ourselves a chance of providing a truly complete interpretation: the work would not cease to represent a current experience, the text would retain its legitimacy, and the critical gaze could investigate the forms that reveal themselves in the pages of the book. To be sure, the work includes in its meaning the writer's past and personal history. But it is a transcended history, a history that we must not forget is directed toward the work, a history that is intertwined with the work itself, a past become inseparable from its implicit or explicit representation in the vital present of a work wherein a future is already being invented. Understood in these terms, the work is dependent on both a past destiny and an imagined future. To choose the past alone (say, childhood) as the only explanatory dimension is to make the work a consequence, when for the writer it is very often a way of anticipating his own future. Far from being constituted solely under the influence of an original experience or prior passion, the work must be seen as an original act in itself, a point of discontinuity, in which an individual, throwing off the shackles of the past, undertakes to invent with his past a fabulous future, a timeless construct.

TRANSLATED BY ARTHUR GOLDHAMMER

SERGE LECLAIRE

The Real in the Text
1971

Serge Leclaire, at the time a faithful disciple of Lacan, offers a pessimistic assessment of the relations between literature and psychoanalysis. Literature would exist in order to conceal the traumatic potential of the (Lacanian) real. Of Lacan's tripartite typology—imaginary, symbolic, real— the last term is the most difficult to define. If the imaginary is Lacan's term for the narcissistic and the symbolic for the (structural) unconscious, the "real" is perhaps best characterized as the symbolic (unconscious) when it takes on the disruptive force of a kick in the teeth. But it is just that kick that literature would serve to buffer—which would put the literary and psychoanalytic projects at loggerheads with each other.

The work of the psychoanalyst is defined by one imperative: *to unmask the real.* His goal is to reveal the inconceivable place in which anxiety unfolds, to shine light into the crack in which ecstasy hides. It is in this locus of the impossible that the psychoanalyst locates the object as nameless index of the real.

Of course, *the real* has to be clearly distinguished from *reality*: the real designates the constitutive defect of the structural dimension, whereas reality consists of constructions apt to contain or even conceal real lack. It also needs to be pointed out that the object should be conceived, on the basis of psychoanalytic practice, as something firm yet impossible to grasp (*un terme insaisissable*), like the object of a partial drive, described by Freud as different from the concrete object that satisfies a need, or again, like the paradoxical small-o object (the little other, purely heterogeneous to the signifier) conceptualized by Jacques Lacan.

If questioned about textual matters, the psychoanalyst will inevitably refer to the text that is given to him to read, namely, the unconscious. The metaphor of a text is of course used deliberately by Freud to describe the unconscious, both as a system of representations and a locus of the psychic apparatus, upon

Serge Leclaire, "Le réel dans le texte in *Littérature,* 3 (1971).

which "unconscious memory traces" are inscribed and arranged in accordance with a logic that might be called the logic of desire.

Before offering a few psychoanalytic observations on the relation of the text to the real, and therefore to the object, it will be useful to consider briefly the nature of the text that consists of unconscious memory traces. *What is written is the indelible real of a libidinal event,* an event that is necessarily "traumatic" on account of the violence it does to the literal (or signifying) "lawful order": pain and pleasure always occur as instantaneous destruction of the literal (signifying) network that invariably underlies all order. One has to imagine a "mystic writing pad" capturing as it occurs the mark (or, perhaps better, the breach or gash) left by the intrusion that constitutes the libidinal event: no blank sheet could possibly be large enough or permanent enough. The recording (inscription) of the unconscious memory trace forces us to think rigorously about the nature of the text and, to begin with, to give up any notion of a substrate on which a mark might be imprinted. What psychoanalysis requires, through the deciphering of the unconscious text, is that the letter of that text *derive its status as referent from its relation to a libidinal event,* that is, a disruption of order, rather than from the fact of being unalterably engraved in bronze. In short, the text is not inscribed on any "substrate."

What psychoanalysis identifies as the memory of a pleasurable experience is nothing more than the referent constituted by a sort of negative recording of violence inflicted on "lawful order." A new "disorder" (libidinal experience) can then occur in relation to this unconscious memory trace, and pleasure can be experienced again. Clearly, then, it is the system of traces and its violent (violating) relationship to literal (signifying) order that constitutes both the text and its surface, the trace and its "substrate."

Note in passing that the unconscious text is intrinsically constitutive of the "erogenous body," which Freud conceived of as a collection of sites capable of receiving sexual excitement. The erogenous body, a set of sites in which order takes the form of a conflict between order and disorder (or an antinomy between the life instinct and the death instinct), is a *double* as strange and disturbing as it is familiar: any pertinent approach to the concept of body must provide a correct place for the unconscious text, the erogenous or libidinal corpus or "double" traditionally known as the soul, or η ψυχη.

The psychoanalyst can legitimately ask what the relation is between the activity of writing and the process constitutive of the unconscious, which is the recording or inscription of unconscious memory traces. The evocation of the strictly indelible character of the unconscious memory trace comes from consideration of the concern with permanence that lies at the root of every text, and it is reasonable to think that a letter marked on paper always tends to re-present the indelible breach that constitutes the inscription of a letter in the unconscious corpus.

From the standpoint that the psychoanalyst necessarily adopts, the activity

of writing can thus be seen as an attempt to re-produce or re-present the unconscious text—an attempt whose obligatory failure establishes the rules intrinsic
to the practice of writing.

To see this more clearly, let us now look at the place of the real in the unconscious text and at what becomes of it when literary re-presentation is attempted.

The logic of the unconscious text is defined in relation to the real. In other
words, the cause of desire functions under the opaque aspect of the object as a
major premise, regulating the order of the letters and guaranteeing in every set
the di(s)order, the absolute heterogeneity that the object is with respect to the
letter (the Lacanian signifier). It maintains, within the unconscious corpus, the
real of the breach, or, to put it another way, the possibility of a castration that is
not mere semblance. Accordingly, in the best-known of the formations of the
unconscious, fantasy, a placeholder for the *object* (child, penis, or breast) is
combined with a *verb* (to beat, breach, or devour) to constitute a text which
imperatively governs the libidinal activity of the subject. Upon analysis, it turns
out, substitutions, displacements, and reversals are possible with respect to each
of these terms. But no matter what placeholders emerge for the objects, no
work can reduce the crucial place they occupy, that of the object as nameless
index of the real. No subjective splitting (in other words, no subjective position)
can be conceived solely in terms of literal (signifying) play if the object is not
placed, as in the structure of the fantasy, within the very breach that constitutes
the subject.

What, then, does this imply for the real, and consequently for the object in
any attempt at literary re-presentation? As we know, there is no place. Precisely because *the letter written on paper* attempts (unconsciously) to re-produce
the rupture of unconscious inscription, it *actually accomplishes an erasure, a su-
ture of the breach.* The act of writing a single word or even a single letter in itself
implies that one is contributing to the defense and exaltation of the "lawful
order" *that does not wish to know anything about the unacceptable real* (for Freud,
it is the incompatible, the *Unverträglich*, that is subject to the primal repression
that constitutes the Unconscious). Under the cover of wishing to re-present the
breach, the written letter even constitutes a sort of rehabilitation of the fault, of
that referent of the unconscious text whereby di(s)order is assured of the power
to perpetuate itself and the libidinal order is assured of survival (and the pleasure of repetition). More precisely, the letter written on paper insidiously tends
to substitute itself for the object and to reintegrate the absolutely other, or the
real (lack, anxiety, jouissance), in a literary order in which the quasi-fetishized
materiality of the text takes the place and function assumed by the real-object
(the object as unnameable index of the real) in the reference text constituted by
the unconscious corpus.

Thus, the text takes charge of the real just as a spider's web takes charge of
the space that it organizes and in which it unfurls its trap. The writing of a

single letter is an action that resolves the relationship to the object in its own way by effacing its seal with its nameless breach in which the real resides. No text can open up what its very texture is designed to fill. No artifice of writing can truly divest itself of the intrinsic function of the text, which is to cloak. Make no mistake: these words are not meant to imply that the text is a super-structure. What I am saying is that every text is, in its very structure, the veiling of a defect and that by itself a text can do no more than reveal semblances of lack. The "true" or "good" text is one whose author has resigned himself to the strictures inherent in writing. The text is thereby relieved not only of artifices destined to reproduce some rupture or breach but also of overlays intended to affirm its coherence. It is valuable for the rigor of its structure, which neither denies nor veils its cloaking function. Its beauty would then resemble the delicacy of a web, whose troubling aura of the real would remain to *dé-lire* (to un-read, in delirium).

No doubt it is enough to know that the literary text thereby settles its score with the real and takes charge of the object by transposing it paradoxically as letter in order to unravel the tangled rules of writing, the "laws" of the literary text. I am even inclined to think that the efforts of our best contemporary scribes would be greatly clarified if they could only take full account of what they already know: that writing is first of all an impossible attempt to master the unconscious text. But perhaps it is in the very impossibility of what he attempts that the writer truly discovers the real.

TRANSLATED BY ARTHUR GOLDHAMMER

Interpreting [with] Freud
1968

Jean Laplanche's exemplary readings of Freud are based on the proposition that Freud's work at its most theoretical was subject to the same unconscious pressures as the very dreams and symptoms it purported to comprehend. Lacan's maxim that "there is no metalanguage" or discourse through which we can hope to distance ourselves from that aspect of language which alienates us applies even to Freud's theory of repression: in the course of its consolidation, his theory was itself necessarily subject to the forces of repression. Whereas Alan Sokal and Jean Bricmont, for instance, have recently polemicized on the subject of French misappropriations of scientific discourse, Laplanche suggests in this selection—and, in Life and Death in Psychoanalysis, *demonstrates—that the way in which Freud's biology and physics are wrong, the very structure of his error, is crucial to an understanding of the way in which he is psychoanalytically right.*

I f I characterize my approach to the Freudian text as "psychoanalytic" and "interpretative," it is not in the sense that Ernest Jones, taking his inspiration from Freud himself, uses these words in his biography. The model Freud proposed in various places for the psychoanalytic study of thought, for a "psychography" of artists, philosophers, and so forth, should not be taken as the last word of psychoanalysis on the matter.[1] Caught between the reduction of thought to purely subjective conditions deriving from the contingencies of an individual history and the merely rational critique of that thought, Freud never managed to do more than strike a shrewd compromise: psychoanalysis, he says, can point out the weak points in a theory, but it is up to rational criticism, to internal criticism, to demonstrate the weaknesses uncovered by another discipline.

As applied to philosophers, and by Jones to Freud himself, this method clearly overlooks a crucial aspect of Freud's discovery: like the neurotic with

Jean Laplanche, *La révolution copernicienne inachevée* (Paris: Aubier, 1991), originally in *L'Arc*, 1968, 34.

respect to his symptoms but even more so, the thinker with respect to certain errors of his reasoning "must in some sense be right." A psychoanalytic psychography that consistently took this maxim seriously could not base its explanations solely on the contingent or aberrant; it would have to point toward some desire, whose forms and sources would define a fragment of a more general combinatorial system.[2]

Nevertheless, any attempt to psychoanalyze a thinker and his work would remain open to one fundamental objection: the psychoanalytic method can only be applied in a therapeutic context. Even if we wish to ignore this objection (as Freud did in the case of Judge Schreber, for example), it must be granted that, in the case of Freud, the available biographical information is incredibly thin and shockingly fragmentary and censored (above all by the author himself).

These objections carry considerable weight, but primarily as grounds for not attempting a psychoanalytic psychography of Freud. The project whose possibility we are considering here is of a different nature: it is to transpose, mutatis mutandis, the Freudian method of analysis from an individual and his desire to the *exigencies* of a theory, to that which, in the discursive sphere, is *most akin* to desire. And just as my earlier discussion of interpretation in psychoanalytic therapy was rather fragmentary, my remarks here will be limited to a few observations about method.

As employed by the psychoanalyst, the dismantling of thought and expression, the treatment of "insignificant" material on a footing of equality with repeated declarations of principle, of part with whole, and so on are sound methodological principles because they attack the secondary elaborations and dodges of rational understanding from the rear, thereby revealing alternative networks of meaning. What one might call the "principle of egalitarian analysis" culminates in renewed respect for literalness. Although literalness of reasoning is obviously not to be neglected, it has to be contrasted with, and counterbalanced by, notional literalness. In joint work with J.-B. Pontalis, he and I were able to show how dissection of Freud's theories revealed not an amorphous mass of material but the rigor of Freud's approach to the formulation and use of concepts.[3]

To traverse the work in every direction, without omitting anything and without granting priority to any aspect a priori, was for us perhaps the equivalent of the fundamental rule of therapy. Once this rule was formulated and applied, various unconscious mechanisms and processes first uncovered in the psychoanalytic interpretation of neuroses and dreams could also be seen in Freud's work.

As we have seen, an *absurd detail* may stamp an entire dream with the *symbol of negation*. In the history of Freudian thought, this unconscious process can be seen at work more than once. For example, when Freud in 1895 introduced the concepts of *bound energy* and *free energy*, which eventually became fundamental parts of his doctrine, he claimed merely to be adopting a distinction first made by Josef Breuer between two sorts of cerebral energy—tonic or quiescent energy and kinetic energy. When one looks at Freud's procedure, however, three things stand out: first, Freud thought it worthwhile to use terms different from those introduced by Breuer; second, the terms that Freud used were in fact borrowed from the physics of Hermann von Helmholtz, where they had a very precise meaning with which Freud and Breuer himself were both familiar; and third, the Freudian usage of those terms is aberrant and even absurd with respect to Helmholtz's usage, since Freud's free energy corresponds, broadly speaking, to Helmholtz's bound energy and vice versa. For us, this is a sign that a displacement has taken place, that an inversion needs to be corrected: what Freud unconsciously sought to mark in this way with the sign of criticism was Breuer's theory, which he always explicitly professed to accept.

A striking example of *forgetfulness, in the sense of repression,* can be found in Freud's theory of the origins of sexuality, or the sexual drive. After giving, in *Three Essays on Sexuality*, a remarkable description of the way in which sexuality grows out of *all* forms of human activity (a description punctuated by such terms as autoeroticism, "propping" ["anaclisis"], polymorphous perversity, and so on), Freud later turned to his theory of the "id," which seemingly restored the sexual drive to a place in the natural and biological order. The psychoanalyst, faced with such an extraordinary instance of forgetfulness (which Freud's successors would perpetuate), cannot resist subjecting it to interpretation, from which it emerges that this forgetfulness was the product, the intellectual avatar, of a fundamental repression: namely, the repression whereby the sex drive, stripped of its infantile and intersubjective origins, was ultimately attributed to the subject as a fact of nature, leading, after a series of complex and random detours, to a quasi-instinctual regulation of the individual's sexual activity.

Equivalences or permutations of signifier and signified or of object and expression, apparent confusion of the sphere of reality and causality with that of metaphor—all this is to be corrected, analyzed, and interpreted. For example, when we are told that the "ego is not only a surface but the projection of a surface," it serves no purpose to criticize the crude confusion between, on the one hand, the spatial psychic apparatus on whose surface the ego is presumed to be located and, on the other hand, the real process of projection (in both the geometrical and neurological senses), whose addition to the spatial model was apparently justified by some remarkably jejune arguments. One has to reach the point of understanding that there are complex relationships—tightly interlocking networks—linking the metaphors consciously proposed by Freud, the unconscious metaphors revealed by interpretation of his thought, and the type of reified metaphors (such as identifications) that psychoanalysis has found to be a fundamental feature of human existence.

Two things should by now be clear: first, that an interpretation of this type should be significantly removed from the manifest content, and second, that it should cast a suspicious eye on any aspect of Freudian doctrine that smacks of "egological" re-elaboration. Does it follow that the use of a critical methodology based on a "flattening" of the signifiers in the work implies total rejection of all perspective, historical as well as architectonic? Here I must beg the reader's indulgence, because I can do no more than touch on this complex issue.

In an interpretive approach inspired by the Freudian discovery, perhaps the notion of history (history of a theory) should be explored at a different level: just as historians have moved from *le problème* to *la problématique*, perhaps we should move from *l'histoire* to *l'historique*. This *historique* is in no sense simpler than history proper; it is not some sort of *geometrical* concept that can account for the transition from one "system state" to another.[5] Indeed, it is more complex, unfolding on several levels at once. But before discussing its principles, it is worth pausing to examine the multiple functions of contradiction and to describe the role and crucial significance of the repetitive agency of desire.

Architectonic? The term carries with it so many connotations of system, aesthetic order, and harmony that the analyst will inevitably greet it warily. In many contexts he will prefer the term *structure*, which, though fashionable at the moment and therefore subject to many ambiguous uses, has recently been defined in very clear terms by Jean Pouillon.[6] Freudian psychoanalysis brings its own special accent to this definition, an accent associated with its method: structure cannot be identified with form or system insofar as the latter imply, among other things, an equilibrium among parts whose relative importance depends in an almost volumetric sense on what proportion of the total space they occupy. As we have seen, one result of Freudian interpretation is to devalue considerations of order, subordination of part to whole, and so on, by showing, for example, how a tiny detail of the manifest system can, at the level of the unconscious, serve as a counterweight to considerable quantities of "energy." For Freud (speaking of both his work and his object), structure is a binary or ternary equilibrium among elements that can, over the course of time, find themselves totally displaced and invested with a very different function while retaining their original name and, apparently, their original nature in the manifest text. Consider the pleasure principle. Freud's occasional efforts to state what it means are fairly clumsy. Indeed, the term is all but impossible to grasp until one recognizes certain structural disruptions, certain almost kaleidoscopic shifts in investment, which lead to what appears to be a paradox: the pleasure principle, which in the early stages of Freud's work was related to the sexual drive, was later linked to the death instinct and ultimately presented as the regulator of *Eros*, a constructive force yielding a very different synthesis from that which was described in 1905 as *sexuality*.

A structural history of Freudian thought may be possible, but only if its method is thoroughly Freudian. This means living with the work and its difficulties and fully accepting the need for a prior "reductive" analysis. Can one criticize such a history if it leads to a relatively static view, if, that is, its result is to demonstrate, beneath the mutations of Freudian theory, the permanence of an exigency, of a discovery that has perhaps yet to find adequate *scientific* formulation?

TRANSLATED BY ARTHUR GOLDHAMMER

NOTES

[1] Sigmund Freud, "The Claims of Psychoanalysis to Scientific Interest," *Standard Edition* of the *Complelete Psychological works of Sigmund Freud*, vol. 13, (London: Hogarth Press, 1953) pp. 179–182.

[2] See my *Hölderlin et la question du père* (Paris: P.U.F., 1961).

[3] J. Laplanche and J.-B. Pontalis, *Vocabulaire de la psychanalyse* (Paris: P.U.F., 1967).

[4] *Three Essays on the Theory of Sexuality,* in *Standard Edition* of the *Complete Psychological Works of Sigmund Freud*, vol 7.

[5] Paul Ricoeur, "Une interprétation philosophique de Freud," *La Nef*, 31 (July-October 1967). See Paul Ricoeur, *La Nef*, p. 115.

[6] See *Les Temps modernes* 246 (Nov. 1966).

Shifting Fate of a Keystone Concept: "Castration"

One significant source of structuralism, as we have noted, was Ferdinand de Saussure's affirmation that in language there are no positive terms but only differences ("negative oppositions"). For Freud, the castration complex, the child's fantastical effort to accommodate sexual difference (rather than deny it), was the "bedrock" of the unconscious. In structuralism's imperialist phase, efforts were made to articulate linguistic difference (à la Saussure) with sexual difference (à la Freud)—as though the castration complex managed to embody the structuralist lesson traumatically, indeed apocalyptically, in the flesh. One could no more attain psychical—or structuralist—maturity without coming to terms with the castration complex than Althusser's Marx could accede to his maturity without submission to the blade of a coupure épistémologique. *(Indeed, the case can be made that one "cut" was a discursive borrowing from the other.) Before long, however, it appeared that the investment in (castratory) difference was less threateningly liberating, as structuralism would have it, than merely inhibitory in its conventionality. The working through of that insight marks the transition from structuralism to post-structuralism, a prospect that this section is intended to illustrate.*

ALEXANDRE KOJÈVE

The Latest New World
1956

The archness of style, cultural pessimism, and extravagance of allusion in Alexandre Kojève's essay on the boytoys parading through Françoise Sa-

---

A review of two novels by Françoise Sagan, *Bonjour tristesse* (1954) and *Un certain sourire* (1956). "Le Dernier monde nouveau," *Critique*, 60 (1956), pp. 387–397.

*gan's novels serve as a reminder that Kojève's extraordinarily influential
prewar seminar on Hegel served as an inspiration for Lacan's legendary
seminar on Freud. The allusions: if, as Hegel saw, history came to an effective end with Napoleon's victory at Jena; if, as the dandy Beau Brummel
saw, there could be no purpose in wearing a uniform (since there were no
battles left to win); if, as Sade saw, the bedroom was the only suitable place
left for the exercise of violence; then, despite the protestations of Hemingway and his ilk, emasculation—effective castration—was the modern
condition par excellence, and Sagan the exemplary novelist of the new dispensation.*

A new sort of world has been born to literature.[1] I for one, find it perfectly natural that this blessed event should have taken place in Paris,
and that the child, being purely literary, should have been born to an
unwed mother.

To be sure, this new world itself was not born yesterday. Although investigation of paternity is no longer prohibited by law, in this case the father's identity is far from clear, there being no shortage of men who might claim this
heavy responsibility. A German, himself a man of genius, discreetly insinuated
that it might well have been the Great Corsican, and this while the putative
father was still alive. I myself have lately come to the firm conviction that the
last conqueror was indeed responsible for what he surely took to be the honor
and pleasure of conceiving our new world. The German who made this allega-
tion clearly anticipated how the child whose birth he heralded would turn out.
Yet despite this visionary's infatuation with reason (*Vernunft*), many people
with plenty of common sense still refuse to take even his visions seriously, to say
nothing of the still more worrisome visions of some of his disciples.

In England, however, one contemporary seems to have had an equally clear
insight into the matter. In any event, he certainly noticed that because of his
Franco-Italian rival's exploits, only a man dressed in civilian garb (and obviously in the color of mourning) could henceforth aspire to the honor (which
some consider futile) of virile heroism (if only in haberdashery). This pacific
genius died unknown, however, a martyr to his sensational discovery (which
had an unforgettable impact on society in the narrow sense), and without leaving any literary remains; his hagiographers never revealed to the uninitiated
the true meaning of his lugubrious witness (the material relics of which are still
preserved in a French convent).

Last but not least, there was in France once upon a time a marquis, impris-
oned by the Tyrant but liberated by the People, who also understood that in the
new world of freedom everything must henceforth be committed in private:
crimes, in particular, of necessity conceived as (nobly gratuitous) acts of egalitarian and fraternal Liberty. At first, however, the popular Liberators took this

Liberated Man for nothing more than a libertine. Even today, his few elite readers are taxed with a lack of seriousness by the many who cannot be accused of a shortage of that commodity. So he, too, never divulged the Secret.

In fact, I decided to write and even publish this text because I am keen at last to reveal the mystery so jealously guarded by those in the know (assuming that any others remain). I dedicate these pages to those who may read them, and therefore, most certainly, to Mademoiselle Sagan, into whose hands some vigilant Argus will doubtless deliver them.

Had this young lady not written her first two books with such care, the world in question might never have been "born to literature." Before this French girl took up her pen, no writer wished to discuss it, at least not in fine language. To be sure, a great modern American writer, a specialist in the analysis of manly behavior, did consider the problem of this world, emasculated by its still-unidentified father. Having grown a beard (long since turned white) probably in order to muster up the courage for his heroic struggle with despair, this well-known writer searched the world over for the last human male, or rather for the truly male last man, and claimed to have found him in the Caribbean Sea in the person of an old fisherman, admittedly half dead. The only worthy adversary he could find for him was, as it happens, a fish—a heroic and powerful adversary to be sure, but still a fish (of a different species, incidentally, from the fish that served as a model for one of the symbols of a well-known religion).[2] But this quite recent natural history of the modern Anglo-Saxon remained quite as esoteric as the already venerable Germanic apocalypse of Universal History.

Thus, it was a very young Frenchwoman who claimed the (literary) glory of revealing to her worldwide readership (comprising both men and women) the nature of the world in which that glory was reaped, in a manner honorable to be sure but perhaps a bit "unconscious" (in the philosophical sense) or "naive" (in Schiller's sense, that is, as opposed to "sentimental").

To put it in a nutshell, the world she describes is a new world because it is completely and utterly devoid of men (in the sense of Malraux, Montherlant, and Hemingway, to mention only these three classics, leaving Homer and the rest in peace). A world without men as seen by a young woman, to be sure.[3] But a world that differs in every respect from that already-musty one in which another young woman (not from Paris) saw as it were nothing but the flannel trousers worn almost exclusively in that bygone era by those regarded as true men. By contrast, in the new world laid bare for us by the young woman to whom this world has laid itself bare, men (not in the ambiguous sense of the equivocal English word but in the precise, strict anatomical and physiological sense)—in this new world, I reiterate (with manly humiliation), those who do duty for men have an annoying tendency to display themselves either stark naked (albeit requisitely muscled) or partially clad to young women by no means amazed at the sight. In my day (for me the good old days, as the days about which one speaks with a certain regret have been in every age)—in my day, I repeat (with manly pride), nudity, even total nudity, was limited to pretty girls (in art and literature at any rate). As it was also in the more distant past. God knows, moreover, that it was no easy thing to undress a manly man in times of yore. It took four or five people to relieve a refulgent knight of his shining armor, and until quite recently the help of a strapping youth was not superfluous when it came to extracting an illustrious officer from his polished boots. Since then things have no doubt much improved. Already in my day the uncomplicated and comfortable if effeminate Indian pajama had conquered the free Western world thanks to the British conquerors of the servile Orient. As a literary theme, however, this occi-oriental garment (initially reserved exclusively for men and, on mama's orders, kept strictly off-limits to well-bred young ladies) played no role except in the music hall. It would indeed be difficult to imagine a serious (masculine) author of the time describing the pajamas of a (literary) hero, a soldier, say, on the blood-stained soil of revolutionary Spain, who is called upon to initiate (in a sleeping bag, let us imagine for the sake of concreteness) a young woman into the mysteries of pure love, a young woman whose purity (in the moral sense) has remained intact despite repeated rape at the hands of a dozen (reactionary) males. Of course, in our new world (where pure young ladies happily no longer need to be raped in order to become fit for proper, or, if you prefer, pure and simple lovemaking), the young lady who evokes this world for us describes nothing in detail except her own pajamas, whose immaculate purity is maternally looked after by the second man of her choosing. But it is hard to say why today's lady writers shouldn't describe equally well, and with equal fraternal concern, the pajamas worn by the ex-virile partners in the seemingly masculine loves of their novels' heroines. For those heroines already "detail," with supremely masculine indifference (which, as they themselves confess with touching humility, still seems "marvelous" to them), the virile forms that reveal themselves when a future conquest parades by on the street, or rather on the sidewalk of the Promenade des Anglais—one of those conquests whose "torso" they will embrace when the matter comes to a conclusion in bed (though such a torso, even if it belonged to the Apollo Belvedere, will in certain respects never rival that of a Venus of the Capitol or for that matter elsewhere).

That all of this is profoundly humiliating for those of us who, by Mendelian happenstance, were born with male bodies, none of us can honestly deny (unless he has completely forgotten the nonsexual sense of the generic name he bears). Although in that case it takes a certain courage not to deny and oppose but to conform and accept. But to go from there to expressing indignation, such as some still claim to be capable of . . . Or to treat these new young ladies as "Amazons" with barbs of that refined irony that has so advantageously replaced the outmoded bronze of the heroic legends of ancient Greece, lately revived by certain sophisticated modern thinkers . . . [4] Let them tell us, rather, what quail are to be eaten where rare birds are no longer to be found. In any case, I should not like to think that anyone intends to advise these so-called Amazons (who, incidentally, have shown no hostility toward any husbands, including their own) to divide themselves, if only for laughs, into two groups, one of which would imitate the role of those with whom they can no longer do battle for want of combatants.

For millennia, men "took" girls. Then it became fashionable for girls to "give" themselves. But is it the girls' fault if, in the new world, in which male heroism does not exist, they can no longer be either "given" or "taken" but must, like it or not, allow themselves to be done unto? Isn't it in any case preferable that, under these conditions, they do so with the best grace and will in the world in which we are all now obliged to live, at least until death calls? What good would it do to dispatch these gracious but willing "Amazons" to convents (as some people apparently would like to do, though they would never dare say so out loud) or to other professional healers of presumably bruised souls (as is sometimes suggested on the false pretext that the girls in question are not "truly happy," even if those who offer the suggestion never volunteer to bear the quite exorbitant cost of the moral improvement they advocate)? Even if we assume that these girls were so far restored to "normality" that they were henceforth completely "happy" to behave as "genuine ladies," would they then find the genuine men they would need in a world where the acme of male power is now to be found in the peaceful if arduous (though duly motorized) labor of the fecund husband?

To conclude with one final observation, let me say that for me Cécile and Dominique (a name to be read as feminine), as well as Françoise herself, are young ladies no different from any other. By this I mean no different from all the other young ladies of all times and all places who have been blessed with extraordinary intelligence and with what is vulgarly (or nobly?) known as guts (even if not all were blessed with the precocious and brilliant literary talent that at least one has demonstrated). What the three aforementioned young ladies have that is new (and humiliating for us, who are still men, at least from a certain point of view) is this: that, thanks to the third, the first two have begun to live not in the world about which young ladies dream almost as much as young gentlemen but in that strange new world that is ours, which differs from all previous worlds by the fact that there are virtually no genuine wars or true revolutions, and in which, therefore, one will soon be unable to die a glorious death anywhere but in a (public or private) bed, unless one is willing, sword in hand, to face wild animals (ruminant and uncastrated) or climb peaks above twenty-five thousand feet in height. But there are very few such peaks, and what few there are will soon be abandoned owing to total dissipation of the virile interest they still arouse, or else equipped with safety-engineered cable lifts or helicopter pads, which we all hope will soon serve only peaceful purposes so that they may be used by people of all ages and either gender. As for the wild animals that are currently used to actualize the virtual virility of certain authentic human males (primarily Iberian), there is considerable risk that a segment of the public (not at all "naive" but quite "sentimental," to quote once more the great poet of *Sturm und Drang*) that refuses (even in the once-aristocratic fatherland of the last civilian dandies) to tolerate the (painless) execution of an authentic killer will soon cry out for an end to the suffering (so cruelly and humiliatingly) inflicted on poor vegetarian beasts that have caused no one any harm.

So, now that heavenly peace has at last been restored to earth, the ancient deities (male and female alike) who laughed so hard when Achilles fought his battles but who in more recent times have nearly died of thirst may also have to content themselves with a smile and a glass of the whiskey known to us as scotch, which people everywhere sip peacefully and water down with cubes of ice—as even the most epicurean of sages would willingly allow.

TRANSLATED BY ARTHUR GOLDHAMMER

NOTES

[1] See Robert Paris in *Les Temps modernes* 125 (June 1956), p. 1903.

[2] To grant in this way exclusive honor to fish and fishermen would be unjust to unemasculated bovines and their valiant adversaries, had the latter not been the subject of an earlier book by the author in question, who has devoted the better part of his literary work, not to mention his life, to bloody battles between (male) mammals, and who turned to cold-blooded animals only once his own (virile) decline had set in.

[3] The author wishes to make it clear that "seen" here modifies "world" and not "men." To take it otherwise would be to distort his innermost thought beyond recognition.

[4] Again, the author wishes to make clear that "revived" here refers to ancient Greece, lest anyone think that it refer to the famous poetic "bronze," which could be manufactured today quite readily and even used as it was used (at a time when no one could make anything better, at least in the way of metal) by those legendary heroes whose virility no one would have dared to contest (whether during their lifetimes or after their glorious deaths). Such a misconstruction would expose me to the risk (surely grave for any author) of misinterpretation, not to say total misunderstanding.

JEAN LAPLANCHE

Lecture of 20 May 1975
1975

Laplanche's first book, Hölderlin et la question du père ([1961] Hölderlin and the Question of the Father)*, was a study of Friedrich Hölderlin's
psychosis, which was attributed to his "foreclosure" of the phallic "signifier" and, concomitantly, of the castration complex. Hölderlin, Laplanche
concluded, suffered from the "absence of a lack." Years later, in this lecture
at the University of Paris dating from 1975, he took his distance from
Lacan, who had forged the concept of psychical "foreclosure," by demonstrating the full complexity of the "migration" of such terms as "anxiety,"
"phobia," and "castration" in Freud. Might the castration complex figure
nothing so much as a phobic formation within Freud's discourse? (The
point is further elaborated in the editor's introduction, pp. 181–182).*

I will of course not try to draw any final conclusions today, but I do want to
complete our exploration of one avenue that we started down earlier. We
began by considering initiation rituals and moved on to symptoms, in particular phobic symptoms. These are interesting because, like all symptoms (and
perhaps more clearly than most), they reveal the double meaning of symbolization: phobic symptoms not only symbolize a representation, hence a representative content, but also fix or bind affect, specifically the affect of anxiety. We
have also looked at a curious shift in the place occupied by phobia in Freud's
theory, a shift that is of more than anecdotal interest. Initially, phobias were
classified along with obsessional neuroses. Later, they were associated with actual neuroses. And still later, from the time of little Hans onward, in all Freudian and psychoanalytic theory, they were again linked to the psychoneuroses,
this time in the group of hysterias. This, as we observed earlier, was not strictly
a nosographic problem; rather, it reflected differing views regarding the relation of affect to representation, the theory of a major affect, namely, anxiety,
and finally, the ultimate significance of the symptom with respect to what one
might call either the external-internal interaction (*jeu*) or that between the real

Jean Laplanche, *Problématiques*, vol. 2 (Paris: Presses Universitaires de France, 1980).

and its symbolization. To sum up what we have said thus far, initially the theory was that a phobia was the displacement of a particular affect (anxiety) from a repressed, deleted (*barré*) representation to another, present representation. The anxiety was therefore misplaced, and the problem was to look beyond the displacement for what the subject was really frightened of, the initial "trauma." In this perspective, the symptom was what Freud called a *mnemic symbol*, examples of which can be found in the "Project for a Scientific Psychology." The second stage, the transition to actual neuroses, was no less important. Here an anxiety was conceptualized as an unsymbolized, extrapsychical stimulus that bypassed the psyche. This theory is not as outmoded and discredited as one might think: even today, one entire school of French psychoanalysis still relies on a theory of this type to justify its notion of psychosomatic symptoms as bypassing the mechanisms of psychic fantasy. The third stage, in which phobia was once again subsumed under the head of psychic phenomenon, this time as a form of hysteria, is discussed in detail in my discussion of Freud's metapsychology. Two salient points are to be noted. First, there is of course the treatment of the phobic symptom once again as a psychic neurosis. The phobic object is a symbol which has a "meaning." It can be interpreted, that is, related to other representations. In the analysis of little Hans, Freud is unyielding in his effort to achieve precisely such a reduction of the object of anxiety, in Hans's case a horse. Not only does he say that the horse in question is the father (or the mother, the difference being of no importance here), but he also tries to give an interpretation that brings all the details together through a series of representations: the horse in the case of little Hans is not just any horse but a horse of a certain color, with a particular type of bit in its mouth, which behaves in a certain way, falls down, moves its legs, bites, and so on. Hence at this stage the phobic symptom symbolizes another representation. At the same time, however, this third theory of the phobic symptom retains the best part of the theory of actual neuroses: specifically, it focuses on the crucial moment when the affect, cut off from the repressed primary representation, seeks to express itself on its own. And when it manifests itself in this way, cut off from its representation, it simultaneously loses the qualitative property of being this or that affect and becomes pure "quantity," or the aggression of the drive in its naked state, in the form of anxiety. In this new theory, the emphasis is on the moment of desymbolized affect which falls between two contrasting moments in which the affect is bound to representations. Note, moreover, that in this theory, there is not just displacement from one representation to another. The representation has changed, to be sure, but the affect has also metamorphosed to the point where it is unrecognizable—from love of the father to fear of the horse.

I turn now to the final phase (of Freud's thought, at any rate), the period of *The Problem of Anxiety*. I have already discussed this text in previous years. It is an ambiguous work, in which one finds both the worst of Freud, in certain formulations, and the best, in the concrete analyses. It is a work well worth delving into with an open mind and considerable "indulgence" for some of its parts, in view of the evident richness of others. Although phobia is one of the text's major themes, Freud does not claim to have arrived at a conclusive interpretation. At one point he lets slip that he is ashamed that, after so many years, psychoanalysis is still unable to shed much light on the metapsychology of what is apparently the simplest of all neuroses. Indeed, the subject of phobia itself is approached from several different angles in the text, and these different approaches are not easy to integrate. Rather than attempt to achieve a synthesis, we will work toward an interpretation. The clinical references (well after the publication of the case histories) are mainly to the phobia of little Hans and to childhood fear of wolves in the so-called Wolfman case. One line of thought in *The Problem of Anxiety* seems to me a step backward from the position taken in the meta-psychological essays, namely, that which takes off from the idea that what accounts for anxiety is "actual danger." In the metapsychological essays, danger was indeed present, but that danger was internal: it was the drive itself that was dangerous, the love of the father that was intolerable and had to be repressed and was therefore transformed into anxiety. In other words, in keeping with Freud's early theory, what one saw was a veritable transformation of sexual desire into anxiety, the two being seen as different faces of a single process. In the later line of thought, the one I am criticizing, things are different: they are in a sense much more rationalized and "behavioralized." The idea of a *love dangerous in itself* for the most part disappears. In one of the developments of the phobia theme, it does reappear as such, but the dominant inspiration is still the idea that the drive is not dangerous in itself but only in virtue of its consequences, of the *external sanctions* it may incur. The prototype of this punishment is obviously "castration"—prototype in the sense that, for Freud, the whole problem of symbolization and its attendant dangers hinges on castration. *Prototype*: the word means both an original position—and we have seen that this original position was even conceived as protohistorical—and a central position, in the sense that castration is seen as a kind of focal point, both the target and fulfillment of every threat. Not only "prior" threats but even threats "subsequent" to the so-called historical time of the castration complex; and "primary" threats such as separation, weaning, and separation from the feces in defecation as well as (what one might call) "adult" threats such as banishment, loss of social consensus, moral guilt, and anxiety about death. Since the emphasis here is on so-called real danger (danger that presumably follows satisfaction of the drive rather than danger inherent in the drive), anxiety, Freud tells us, is associated not with the repressed but with the forces of repression: "It is anxiety that produces repression, not as I formerly thought repression that produces anxiety." This brief remark is all I will say here about the change in Freud's perspective concerning the "theory of anxiety" (a theme that I developed at greater length in previous lectures, which are now available in published form).[1]

What can be said about symbolization in relation to the two aspects just noted, namely, the symbolization of representation and the symbolization of anxiety? With respect to representation, the horse does indeed symbolize, crudely speaking, the father, or, more precisely, the danger of castration by the father. This danger is conceived as an external threat, which is real in the sense that the threat of castration is real, actually made by the father or one of his substitutes, and, furthermore (this is where the castration complex "gels," as it were), the danger is confirmed by actual perception of the anatomical difference between the sexes. How is the danger of castration symbolized? It is replaced, Freud tells us, by another equally real danger.

> I formerly treated phobia as a projection, in that it replaces the internal danger of the drive by an external perceptual danger. [This is an explicit allusion to the metapsychological essays.] The advantage of making such a substitution is that one can defend oneself against the external danger by fleeing it or avoiding it, whereas flight is pointless if the danger comes from within [this point is in fact developed in the metapsychological essays: once the anxiety-provoking animal is placed in a specific location in the streets of Vienna, certain quite concrete steps can be taken to confine the anxiety to a particular time and place]. This observation is not incorrect, but it does not go to the heart of the matter, since the demand of the drive is not in itself a danger. On the contrary, it is a danger only because it entails a true external danger, the threat of castration. Hence in the case of phobia, we are basically dealing with the substitution of one external danger for another external danger.

Note the clear abandonment here (though happily contradicted a few pages later) of the notion of a primary internal danger of aggression by the drive which constantly threatens to transform itself into anxiety and which needs to be symbolized. In the passage we are commenting on, there is no further symbolization of anxiety. Anxiety has become *fear through and through*, in the sense that it is associated with a real danger and is dealt with through a whole strategy that seeks to inhibit it, arrest its development, and make use of it in small quantities. This is the so-called theory of anxiety as signal. The anxiety signal, we are told, is what triggers defense mechanisms and is even what is *used* as a trigger: the ego uses anxiety as a sort of "yellow light" that prevents a greater danger from arising. Rather than something that needs to be symbolized, anxiety now finds itself on the side of the signifier—not, to be sure, on the side of that which symbolizes but at least on the side of that which marks, which signals danger. Of course, this is only one line of Freud's thinking, and it is summarized very schematically. Reread chapter four of *The Problem of Anxiety* and you will note other lines of thought. In particular, you will see how different affects contribute to the symptom and to the anxiety that is inextricably associated with it; how anxiety is fueled, despite what Freud would have us believe, not just by actual fear but also by all the affects associated with the Oedipal complex: not just fear of the father but also love for the mother and perhaps, above all, homosexual love for the father; and fueled in particular by the regressive form of that love, the regressive oral form in which *to be loved* becomes *to be devoured*. In the perspective of "real danger," to be devoured should appear as a punishment. But Freud cites a clinical example that challenges this theory of the punishment of gratification by demonstrating that there are *pleasurable* anxieties and dangers. This is the case—unfortunately summarized in just a few lines—with a third phobia that Freud had occasion to analyze, the case he refers to as the Gingerbread Man.

> Since [analyzing Hans and my "Russian," the "Wolfman"], I have found a third case, a young American, who admittedly did not suffer from an animal phobia but who, for that very reason, is helpful in understanding the other cases. He became sexually excited upon being read a fantastic child's tale about an Arab chieftain who pursues an "edible" person (the Gingerbread Man) in order to eat him. He identified with this edible person, and it was easy to see that the Arab chieftain was a substitute for the father. This was the first fantasy this young man used to abet his autoerotic activity. [Freud here digresses to discuss various matters of general import.] Note that the image of being devoured by the father is part of a fund of archaic material typical of childhood, and analogies from mythology (Kronos) and animal life are universally known.

What I want to emphasize here is that the anxiety is once again associated with the drive and not with the punishment of the drive. Or, at any rate, we can say that punishment and drive are one and the same. The amalgam that Freud tried to make with behavioral psychology and the conditioned reflex—"if you seek sexual pleasure, you will be castrated"—the sort of rational psychology that he attempted to introduce in *The Problem of Anxiety*, here breaks down completely. In this case the anxiety is described as a substitute for love, literally as its other face. Why does the subject cling to his symptom in this context? Not just because his symptom is a first line of defense against anxiety: the symptom is loved because of the anxiety it triggers, because this anxiety itself is associated with the drive, with pleasure.

In *The Problem of Anxiety*, the problem of symbolization is treated in the context of regression (that is why it is such a rich subject) and in terms of a series of different levels of symbolization. The pretext or occasion for this was Otto Rank's theory of birth trauma, which raised the question of the origin of different types of anxiety. Rank's contribution was to pursue to the full the hypothesis that anxiety is basically neonatal, a consequence of the trauma of birth. In his book on the subject, Rank offers curiously little description of this supposed anxiety of birth. He is less interested than Freud in any actual description of what happens at birth or, more generally, in the psychology of the neonate or infant. Yet he asserts that all subsequent anxieties, including that of castration, are forms of camouflage. As is so often the case in psychoanalysis, there is reason to wonder about the connection between a term such as *camouflage* or *defense* and elaboration or symbolization. Here, Freud, in his discussion of Rank, demonstrates his superiority by showing how one anxiety situation leads to another (rather than saying that one camouflages another and insisting that all must be traced back to their least common denominator, which is always the primordial separation); he shows how these situations become progressively richer, and how affect and representation become increasingly independent of each other. In effect, at birth (which Rank presents as the basic anxiety situation) affect and danger are inseparable. In fact, this situation is not experienced as a situation—it is a situation without representative content. In the series of separations that succeed the anxiety of birth, the first separations of child and mother are crucial (this is true for both Freud and Rank, and I have also called attention to this): fear of the dark, anxiety of abandonment, stranger anxiety. Freud dwells on this subject at length, not only in this text but also in the *Introduction to Psychoanalysis*. Pursuing Freud's and Rank's analyses to the end, one finds that the anxiety of absence is in all cases the anxiety of *being abandoned to the mounting pressure of the drive* without recourse to the one object that can relieve that pressure, which is symbolized by the "breast." If one completes this analysis by reading the analysis that Freud gives of depression in *Mourning and Melancholia*, it becomes clear that this anxiety of loss (which is already, and essentially, the anxiety of being left alone with one's drive) is always correlated with the horror of being abandoned in the presence of a hidden face of the object. Here I am alluding to what Freud calls the "shadow of the object," which, in loss, falls upon the self, or again to what Melanie Klein calls the "bad object." In other words, in the anxiety of loss there is splitting, and there is also internalization of the bad object to which the infant is abandoned as if to an uncontrollable stimulus, hence a source of anxiety.

The Problem of Anxiety describes a series of symbolizations of this loss or anxiety, culminating in the situation known as "castration," starting rather cleverly from a point that supposedly reveals a seemingly tangible origin to the problem of the symbol, because at this starting point symbol and symbolized, affect and representation, are coalesced as one. More elegant still, there is also the inverse situation, because birth, the primary situation, which is experienced without being posited, either unsymbolized or implicitly symbolized, is explicitly posited as such but by the other—on the side of the mother. Here the child is seen as a separate individual, at once object and symbol, the culmination of a whole series of symbols. We find this series of symbols and partial objects not only in *The Problem of Anxiety* but also in another text in which it is introduced in a schematic form that deserves consideration: "On the Transpositions of the Drives, in Particular in Anal Eroticism." Here, Freud is led to the conclusion that the subject, and more precisely the female subject, "slides along the chain of symbolic equivalents (breast, penis, child, etc.)." By contrast, *The Problem of Anxiety* stresses discontinuity rather than sliding from one symbol to another.

In a schema like the one I discussed last time, of the "neurological" type—that of the *Project for a Scientific Psychology*—if one can describe chains of representations, affect (which circulates from one representation to another) is ultimately no more than a postulate, a symbolized thing incapable of knowing itself, a sort of "X." In a schema of this type, one can ultimately denote the affect by an "X" and never assign any value to that X. By contrast, in *Anxiety*, Freud insists, as clinical experience obliges us to insist, that symbolization is distinguished as much by its failures as by its successes. Consequently, the moments of desymbolization in the transition from one symbol to another are absolutely essential and impossible to miss: the moment after a symbol is lost and before another is found is the moment of anxiety, of that "free-floating anxiety" which Freud sought to identify even in the history of a neurotic symptom.

Apart from those moments of anxiety which mark the transition from one symbolization to another, what we see in this case of phobia, in contrast to what one finds in the symptoms of hysteria, is the persistence of anxiety in the symptom itself. Whereas a hysterical symptom theoretically leads to a "good result," in that the anxiety that briefly reveals itself is soon completely fixated, in the phobic symptom the persistence of a certain free-floating, unsymbolized anxiety indicates that the psychic mechanism has to some degree failed. What would a successful symbolization be like? Obviously this is a new field of inquiry. Freud sometimes gives the impression that a successful symbolization is one that leaves no room for anxiety to appear, no crack through which it can enter. This again calls to mind what one contemporary school of psychoanalysis, accentuating this line of thinking in Freud, portrays as the ultimate symbolization, namely, castration and its logic. This logic is absolutely rigorous in character, all-encompassing, and universal. It is theoretically flawless—and yet it fails because the unconscious evades it. If the all too perfect dilemma of castration is "either phallic or castrated," implying the possibility of taking up *one* of these positions, the unconscious, generally in neurosis, issues the following verdict or oracle: "Whether you are phallic or castrated, you will in any case be castrated." In Freud's thinking the logic of the castration complex was intended to be the logic of *a phase*, hence transitional, not definitive: it is characteristic of *infantile* genital organization, which is supposed to be supplanted by adult genital organization, in which the opposition phallic–castrated gives way to masculine–feminine. Ineluctably, however, in the thought of both Freud and later analysts such as Lacan, this phase has tended to become the ultimate form of all psychic organization: what has become the ω of the system was to have been only the ψ.

Was it in order to block this ineluctable tendency that some civilizations have been unwilling to accept the castration complex as such but have sought as it were to re-inforce it, to further mark the mark, to symbolize the castration that wants to see itself as "symbolic castration?" Earlier we discussed the fundamental interest of the symbolism of initiation rituals. In more than one respect they inaugurate something new with respect to the castration complex. First, they introduce a new dimension, that of explicit recognition by the other, recognition of belonging to either a group or an age cohort but in any case a verbalized and socialized recognition. Second, they reinforce the mark of castration by inscribing it on the body, and in some cases they even call for periodic renewal of that mark, for example by reopening the wound made at the time of initiation. We also saw that these rituals introduce a much more ambiguous symbolism than Freud was initially willing to acknowledge, a symbolism that is ambivalent or even bisexual. And finally (are we here perhaps getting into what Freud had in mind when he spoke of the masculine–feminine pair as replacing the phallic–castrated pair?), in contrast to the logic of castrative symbolism, which recognizes only one opposition—either a symbol is present or it is absent—these rituals seem to acknowledge and inscribe two symbols: obviously a masculine symbol, but also a positive feminine symbol. This, at any rate, is what is suggested by the ritual of subincision, with its slit and bleeding. Despite appearances, despite the wound that to the psychoanalyst inevitably suggests simple mutilation, these symbols cannot be reduced to mere subtraction: they also involve the creation of an opening (we also saw this in our discussion of the cave paintings described by André Leroi-Gourhan). They introduce a logic that is more the logic of the mark than the logic of difference. They presage a certain turning away from what has been called *Unterschied* (difference, plus–minus, minus being simply the negative of plus) and toward *Verschiedenheit*, or diversity. Or, in any case, if there is difference, that difference is symbolized by a pair of elements that are both positive rather than by presence–absence.

I have ended this year's course with these lectures on symbols in initiation rites and symbols at work in phobic symptoms. Perhaps in coming years we will turn our attention to other aspects of these issues, such as sublimation and symbolization in therapy, in relation to a further question, namely, Is there such a thing as "successful" symbolization?

NOTE

[1] Jean Laplanche, *Problématiques de l'angoisse* (Paris: P.U.F., 1980).

GILLES DELEUZE AND FÉLIX GUATTARI

Anti-Oedipus
1972

In the Logic of Sense *(Logique du sens [1969]), an influential effort to
rehabilitate the category of the superficial (which would no longer mean of
little depth but of vast extension), Gilles Deleuze was careful to make room
for an "adsorptive" reading of "castration," a "surface phenomenon" to be
distinguished from the "devouring-absorptive" castration of the depths and
the "privative" variant of the heights. In his collaborative effort of 1972
with Félix Guattari,* Anti-Oedipus, *however, "castration" was rejected
wholesale as part and parcel of the "ideology of lack." An exemplary work
of post–May '68 enthusiasm: Bisexuality, yes! Castration, no!*

Such is the case with castration, and its relationship to Oedipus in both
instances. Castration is at once the common lot—that is, the prevalent
and transcendent Phallus, and the exclusive distribution that presents itself in girls as desire for the penis, and in boys as fear of losing it or refusal of a
passive attitude. This something in common must lay the foundation for the
exclusive use of the disjunctions of the unconscious—and teach us resignation.
Resignation to Oedipus, to castration: for girls, renunciation of their desire for
the penis; for boys, renunciation of male protest—in short, "assumption of
one's sex."[3] This something in common, the great Phallus, the Lack with two
nonsuperimposable sides, is purely mythical; it is like the One in negative theology, it introduces lack into desire and causes exclusive series to emanate, to
which it attributes a goal, an origin, and a path of resignation.

The contrary should be said: neither is there anything in common between
the two sexes, nor do they cease communicating with each other in a transverse
mode where each subject possesses both of them, but with the two of them
partitioned off, and where each subject communicates with *one sex or the other
in another subject.* Such is the law of partial objects. Nothing is lacking, nothing

Gilles Deleuze and Félix Guattari, *Anti-Oedipus: Capitalism and Schizophrenia*, trans.
Robert Hurley, Mark Seem, and Helen R. Lane (Minneapolis: University of Minnesota
Press, 1983); from *L'Anti-Oedipe* (Paris: Minuit, 1972).

can be defined as a lack; nor are the disjunctions in the unconscious ever exclusive but, rather, the object of a properly inclusive use that we must analyze. Freud had a concept at his disposal for stating this contrary notion—the concept of bisexuality; and it was not by chance that he was never able or never wanted to give this concept the analytical position and extension it required. Without even going that far, a lively controversy developed when certain analysts, following Melanie Klein, tried to define the unconscious forces of the female sexual organ by positive characteristics in terms of partial objects and flows. This slight shift—which did not suppress mythical castration but made it depend secondarily on the organ, instead of the organ's depending on it— met with great opposition from Freud. He maintained that the organ, from the viewpoint of the unconscious, could not be understood except by proceeding from a lack or a primal deprivation, and not the opposite.

Here we have a properly analytical fallacy (which will be found again, to a considerable degree, in the theory of the signifier) that consists in passing from the detachable partial object to the position of a complete object as the thing detached (phallus). This passage implies a subject, defined as a fixed ego of one sex or the other, who necessarily experiences as a lack his subordination to the tyrannical complete object. This is perhaps no longer the case when the partial object is posited for itself on the body without organs, with—as its sole subject—not an "ego," but the drive that forms the desiring-machine along with it, and that enters into relationships of connection, disjunction, and conjunction with other partial objects, at the core of the corresponding multiplicity whose every element can only be defined *positively*. We must speak of "castration" in the same way we speak of oedipalization, whose crowning moment it is: castration designates the operation by which psychoanalysis castrates the unconscious, injects castration into the unconscious. Castration as a practical operation on the unconscious is achieved when the thousand breaks-flows of desiring-machines—all positive, all productive—are projected into the same mythical space, the unary stroke of the signifier.

We have not finished chanting the litany of the ignorances of the unconscious; it knows nothing of castration or Oedipus, just as it knows nothing of parents, gods, the law, lack. The Women's Liberation movements are correct in saying: We are not castrated, so you get fucked. And far from being able to get by with anything like the wretched maneuver wherein men answer that this itself is proof that women are castrated—or even console women by saying that men are castrated, too, all the while rejoicing that they are castrated the other way, on the side that is not superimposable—it should be recognized that Women's Liberation movements contain, in a more or less ambiguous state, what belongs to all requirements of liberation: the force of the unconscious itself, the investment by desire of the social field, the disinvestment of repressive structures. Nor are we going to say that the question is not that of knowing if women are castrated, but only if the unconscious "believes it," since all the ambiguity lies there. What does belief applied to the unconscious signify? What is an unconscious that no longer does anything but "believe" rather than produce? What are the operations, the artifices that inject the unconscious with "beliefs" that are not even irrational but, on the contrary, only too reasonable and consistent with the established order?

TRANSLATED BY ROBERT HURLEY ET AL.

NOTES

1 "A child is being beaten," S.E. vol. 17.

2 Ibid.,

3 Sigmund Freud, "Analysis Terminable and Interminable" (1937), in *Standard Edition of the Complete Psychological Works of Sigmund Freud*, ed. James Strachey (New York: Macmillan, 1964), vol. 23, pp. 250–52: "The two corresponding themes are in the female, an *envy for the penis*—a positive striving to possess a male genital—and, in the male, a struggle against his passive or feminine attitude to another male. . . . At no other point . . . does one suffer more from an oppressive feeling that one has been 'preaching to the winds,' than when one is trying to persuade a woman to abandon her wish for a penis on the ground of its being unrealizable or when one is seeking to convince a man that a passive attitude to men does not always signify castration and that it is indispensable in many relationships in life. The rebellious overcompensation of the male produces one of the strongest transference-resistances. He refuses to subject himself to a father-substitute, or to feel indebted to him for anything, and consequently he refuses to accept his recovery from the doctor."

ROLAND BARTHES

S/Z

1970

At the core of Balzac's novella Sarrasine *is a nightmare of exposure. Egged on by the fellow members of her theatrical troupe, the glorious* castrato *Zambinella allows the French sculptor Sarrasine, who believes him to be a woman, to pursue him amorously—until Sarrasine is undone by the final devastating revelation. Roland Barthes, in a famously detailed analysis, centered his reading on a version of Freud's castration complex: a male is undone, branded with the mark of Zambinella, by his discovery that the "woman" of his dreams is in fact castrated.*

*S*arraSine: customary French onomastics would lead us to expect *Sarra-Zine*: on its way to the subject's patronymic, the Z has encountered some pitfall. Z is the letter of mutilation: phonetically, Z stings like a chastising lash, an avenging insect; graphically, cast slantwise by the hand across the blank regularity of the page, amid the curves of the alphabet, like an oblique and illicit blade, it cuts, slashes, or, as we say in French, *zebras*; from a Balzacian viewpoint, this Z (which appears in Balzac's name) is the letter of deviation (see the story *Z. Marcas*); finally, here, Z is the first letter of La Zambinella, the initial of castration, so that by this orthographical error committed in the middle of his name, in the center of his body, Sarrasine receives the Zambinellan Z in its true sense—the wound of deficiency. Further, S and Z are in a relation of graphological inversion: the same letter seen from the other side of the mirror: Sarrasine contemplates in La Zambinella his own castration. Hence the slash (/) confronting the S of SarraSine and the Z of Zambinella has a panic function: it is the slash of censure, the surface of the mirror, the wall of hallucination, the verge of antithesis, the abstraction of limit, the obliquity of the signifier, the index of the paradigm, hence of meaning.

TRANSLATED BY RICHARD MILLER

Roland Barthes, *S/Z*, trans. Richard Miller (New York: Hill and Wang, 1974), from *S/Z* (Paris: Seuil, 1970).

MICHEL SERRES

The Hermaphrodite
1987

In Michel Serres's very different reading of Sarrasine, *significantly titled*
The Hermaphrodite, *the key encounter is not between male and (castrated) "female" but between music, in its supreme fluidity, and sculpture.
Serres's gods in this selection, however, are not Nietzsche's Apollo and
Dionysos but Hermes (god of exchange) and Aphrodite: Hermes + Aphrodite = Hermaphrodite. If reality is to be thought of thermodynamically, as
a chaotic superabundance spiraling entropically toward the dead fixity of
stone, then the sculptor's encounter with the musician is anything but an
encounter with* lack.

*Several allusions in Serres's elliptical text call for comment. The refer-
ence to a moral* macédoine *or salad is borrowed from Balzac's narrator. On
an icy night, he finds himself observing a party from a windowsill, his one
foot frozen, the other tapping the rhythm being danced—in effect, sculpture and music in the flesh.* Enantiomorphics *is the science of symmetrical,
noncongruent objects (such as the narrator's body as just evoked). The final
paragraph in this selection is a critique of Barthes's* S/Z, *the spinning
wheels of whose "combination lock" are given the lie by the downward
spiral of Serres's entropic vision.*

Why did God create the world, when he might have remained content with his infinite goodness alone? The answer is staggering: no
one creates out of want, only out of excess. The creator is superabundant. The Lanty family, for example, exhibits superabundance of many
kinds: of talent, wealth, style, and charm. The novella, unable to exclude, aspires to an agglutinating mix in order to achieve saturation, or supersaturation,
the prerequisite of productivity. For some strange reason, people nowadays
tend to believe that invention depends on deficiency, flaw, or folly, whereas
actually it requires plenitude, excess, or surplus. God created the world because

Michel Serres, *L'Hermaphrodite: Sarrasine sculpteur* (Paris: Flammarion, 1987).

he was superabundant, Balzac his books because he possessed super powers: fertility comes with happiness. The *novella* seeks the positive, the plus sign.

And finds, at times, the *macédoine* of morality. One would think that moralists, disgusted by disparity, would hate hodgepodge. And that critics, being disgusted by what neither distinguishes nor differentiates itself, would dislike mixes of every description. Yet salad recipes preclude proscription: start with carrots and add all the radishes you like, and artichoke hearts if you please— superabundance has no limit. Using turnips does not rule out adding cabbage. Coming from the kitchen, watch the judge grimace, see his bile rise. Here there is supersaturation, which has no central law. No sauce binds it, no principle will coagulate it. But neither will anything make it turn, change color, or go flat. Making a salad typifies the process of universal addition, of inclusion without dominance.

Mixing of this kind is fundamental to a deep, an algorithmic idea of the universal. From the Greeks on down, our thought has been shaped by an abstract, theoretical mathematics, deduced from first principles and sculpted into an axiomatic pyramid by the principle of noncontradiction. Such is the first rigorous sense of *Logos*. And since the days of the biblical prophets our thought has been shaped by the principle of Solomon as revised by the Gospel according to John: nothing new under the sun; in the beginning was the Light of the Word—*logos* in a second luminous sense, it, too, sculpted by exclusion. Another, more supple form of mathematics or logos, more viscous and concrete, more utilitarian and pragmatic, was driven out by the Greek miracle and the light of the solitary sun and relegated to the margins for three millennia, revived only on rare occasions, in certain works and in timid forms, by the Arabs, during the Renaissance, by Leibniz, and in the nineteenth century. This repressed formalism, algorithmic in nature, has returned and triumphed in the age of the computer, where it has occupied the fortress and now threatens even the abstract mathematics that originated with the Greeks. When it comes to light, it prefers speed, whereas the Greeks taught us to prefer clarity. It corresponds to the philosophy of mixed bodies. And it marks the end of the Greek era and the beginning of a new world. I shall soon come back to these forms of thought.

An algorithm is like a recipe for salad. *Sarrasine* seeks a superabundance for creation which the dominant philosophy cannot provide. As usual in such cases, it blindly searches for a common bond that eludes it only by our lights, which exclude all other solutions. Start with antithesis and you will end with castration. Start with left–right enantiomorphy or the superimposition of images, start with symmetry, and you will create the hermaphrodite, the very type of inclusion. How long did Hermes search for Aphrodite? Gratified at having found her.

To achieve this joy in superabundance, this superpotent and creative excess, with an eye to such inclusion, one must first preclude proscription or moderate the phallic law, shave the mountaintops and carefully fill in the valleys between qualities, whittle down the grandiose but useless column that stands in the crossroads. One must imagine Hermes gentle, gracious, and calm.

Then the paternal image turns a bit somber: ugly, short, pockmarked, as boring as a banker, the count seems profound only by virtue of what he quotes. Talk to him about animals and he answers you with proper nouns and phrases learned from books. Worry about the solution to some problem and he'll answer you with more questions, piling up footnotes and reciting Wellington and Metternich, the generals and strategists of real or theoretical armies. You will have recognized the critic and his terrifying phallic knowledge, the glittering society of the ugly, short, and pockmarked who translate in their own way the creations of the poets, of Lord Byron and all the other superabundant creators, dividing them, cutting them up—only phallic law castrates—destroying. Stop quoting, stop judging, give up criticism, make things up. To that end, plunge into Aphrodite, risen one day from the petulant sea, or from the contradiction-free mixture of qualities.

Le Chef-d'oeuvre inconnu conjures up Aphrodite as the precondition of the work, born of the palette, sprung from the nautical noise; *Sarrasine* ressurects Hermaphrodite as champion of inclusion and condition of the work, born of the additive plenitude of meaning. *Sarrasine*, or the superabundant androgyne: one has to imagine Hermes fulfilled.

But not satisfied by the sophisticated form of shredding that chops a text up into lines, words, and letters and reduces it to the coded sequence readable from or hidden behind the old combination lock, whose wheels, each turning independently of the others, were marked with numbers. The number of sequences that can be produced this way is enormous, tending toward infinity. What is more, the text presumably reveals or hides itself in this multiplicity like a pin in a stack of needles: every word in the text appears in the dictionary as a number on its wheel. This leads to the notion of a plurality of meanings, an idea that left the generation before ours reeling with dizziness, no doubt owing to its ignorance of combinatorics, the basic science of coding. This horn of plenty, spewing forth its infinite variety of meanings, reflects a basic misconception, what might jocularly be called the sophism of the combination lock. The difference between what can be said and what is said is the difference between a huge number and a very small one. As the text proceeds, the wheels are no longer free to turn: its sense converges to one.

When I refer to fullness of meaning, it is not the multiplicity suggested by this misleading calculation that I have in mind.

TRANSLATED BY ARTHUR GOLDHAMMER

LUCE IRIGARAY

The Speculum of the Other Woman
1974

In the promotion of the theoretical fiction (of female "castration") invented by Freud's young patient Little Hans to "bedrock" status, the principal losers, to be sure, were women. Balzac's Zambinella, that is, might be a false or defective female, but from the classical Freudian perspective, the feminine condition itself was defective. Structuralism began with Claude Lévi-Strauss' vision of society in terms of the exchange of words, goods, and women— "Lévi-Strauss, or l'Ecole des femmes," in Catherine Clément's Molièresque phrase. Might structuralism's affinity for the castration complex have misogynistic roots? In this selection from Speculum of the Other Woman, *a breviary of post-structuralist feminism, Luce Irigaray examines the blind spot in Freud's "hoary dream of symmetry."*

'What happens with the girl is almost the *opposite*. The castration complex prepares for the Oedipus complex instead of destroying it; the girl is driven out of her attachment to her mother through the influence of her envy for the penis, and she enters the Oedipus situation as though into a haven of refuge. In the absence of fear of castration, the chief motive is lacking which leads boys to surmount the Oedipus complex. Girls remain in it for an indeterminate length of time; they demolish it late, and even so, incompletely.'[1]

Why interpret the little girl's development and especially its relationship to the Oedipus complex as the opposite—or "almost," more or less the opposite—of the boy's? As the opposite, the other side, reverse, of the masculine Oedipal situation? Or its negative? Especially in the photographic sense.[2] Especially in the specular sense.[3] It seems that the same gaze, the same "mirror," the same specula(riza)tion is being used, that an attempt is being made to work out an *a contrario* representation of the process under discussion.

Luce Irigaray, *Speculum of the Other Woman*, trans. Gillian C. Gill (Ithaca, N.Y.: Cornell University Press, 1985), from *Speculum de l'autre femme* (Paris: Minuit, 1974).

Does "opposite" mean "placed over against something on the other or far-ther side of an intervening line; contrary in position"? Or does it mean "op-posed," "hostile," or "harmful to," contrary like Mary in the rhyme or as as the dictionary develops the meaning?

This decisive moment in sexual structuring is then supposedly produced in the little girl's case as the "opposite" of the (so-called) masculine economy. Or so Freud would wish, for he thinks of sexual difference from within the realm of the same, and attributes all the properties (and improprieties) of the dictio-nary definition listed above to the sex "opposite" his own.

So "the castration complex [in the girl] prepares for the Oedipus complex in-stead of destroying it." Yet the female Oedipus complex cannot be thought of as the "same" complex as the boy's. It already assumes that the first cathexes, the first "tropisms" have been abandoned, rejected, and "hated." It assumes a break in contact with the original object, a turning-away from the desire for origin. According to Freud, at any rate. And these operations are the result of the "castration complex" which, for the girl, is not a complex in the same way as for the boy since it is simply a matter (as it were!) of taking note of a "fact" or a *"biological destiny"*; "the accomplished fact of castration." This "castration" that Freud accounts for in terms of "nature," "anatomy," could equally well be in-terpreted as the prohibition that enjoins woman—at least in this history— from ever imagining, fancying, re-presenting, symbolizing, and so on (and none of these words is adequate, as all are borrowed from a discourse that aids and abets that prohibition) her own relationship to beginning. The "fact of castration" has to be understood as a definitive prohibition against establishing one's own economy of the desire for origin. Hence, the hole, the lack, the fault, the "castration" that greets the little girl as she enters as a subject into represen-tative systems. This is the indispensable assumption governing her appearance upon the scene of "presence," where neither her libido nor her sex/organs have any right to any "truth" except the truth that casts her as "less than," other side, backside, of the representation thereby perpetuated.

In fact this desire for re-presentation, for re-presenting oneself, and for rep-resenting oneself in desire is in some ways *taken away from woman at the outset* as a result of the radical devalorization of her "beginning" that she is inculcated with, subjected to—and to which she subjects herself: is she not born of a cas-trated mother who could only give birth to a castrated child, even though she prefers (to herself) those who bear the penis? This shameful beginning must therefore be forgotten, "repressed"—but can one speak at this stage of repres-sion when the processes that make it possible have not yet come into being, and may, for this very reason, never come into being? Even if woman is sexually repressed, this does not imply that she actively achieved this repression[4]—in order to defer to a valid representation of origin. Therefore the girl shuns or is cast out of a *primary metaphorization* of her desire as a woman, and she becomes inscribed into the phallic metaphors of the small male. And if she is no male, because she sees — he says, they say — that she doesn't have one, she will strive to become him, to mimic him, to seduce him in order to get one: "The girl is driven out of her attachment to her mother through the influence of her envy for the penis and she enters the Oedipus situation as though into a haven of refuge." Like a skiff moored to a bollard that keeps it from venturing out to sea again. "In the absence of fear of castration the chief motive is lacking which leads boys to surmount the Oedipus complex." The girl indeed, has nothing more to fear since she has *nothing* to lose. Since she has no representation of what she might fear to lose. Since what she might, potentially, lose, has no value. She will therefore fear not the loss of her castrated sex organ but only the loss of *the love of her owner*: "In her, far more than in the boy, these changes seem to be the result of upbringing and of intimidation from outside that threaten her with a loss of love."[5] And the superego "cannot attain the *strength* and *independence* which give it its cultural significance."[6]

TRANSLATED BY GILLIAN C. GILL

NOTES

[1] Freud, "Femininity," *SE*, vol. 22, p. 129.

[2] Cf. "A Note on the Unconscious in Psychoanalysis," in *Standard Edition of the Complete Psychological Works of Sigmund Freud*, ed. James Strauhey (New York: Macmillan, 1964), vol. 12, p. 264, where Freud further explains that "some of these negatives which have held good in examination are admitted to the 'positive process' ending in the picture." But woman is never admitted, except as that mirage of man called "femininity."

[3] "They are, these women, a product of our temperament, an image inversely projected, a negative of our sensibility." Proust, *Within a Budding Grove*, trans. C. K. Scott Moncrieff (New York: Random House, 1981), vol. 2, p. 955.

[4] The same barrier that separates the "subject" from the "woman" is that which keeps the conscious and unconscious apart. Which is another way of perceiving the strength of the "virginity taboo," and of the censorship of the female "libido."

[5] "The Dissolution of the Oedipus Complex," *SE*, vol. 19, p. 178.

[6] "Femininity," p. 129.

PART VI

Literature/Theory/Science

GASTON BACHELARD

The Poetics of Space
1957

As an epistemologist, Gaston Bachelard undertook to dismantle a variety of misleadingly gratifying intuitions about the world—to "cure," in his words, the mind of its "felicities." The title The Psychoanalysis of Fire *is exemplary in this regard. At the same time, though, he was entranced by the very reveries he would undermine—those* philia *of the mind he regarded as no less deleterious than its* phobia. *"Sublimation" was the psychoanalytic category that allowed him to savor—as poetry—the very illusions he would challenge. In this selection, which marks Bachelard's transition from "psychoanalysis" to "phenomenology," poetry achieves an additional measure of autonomy in relation to its impure origins: sublimation remains a category ultimately inadequate to the pure pleasures of poetry. Bachelard's poet is happy in the precise sense that Jean-Pierre Richard's Mallarmé would soon be, much to the displeasure of Gérard Genette. Significantly, this farewell to psychoanalysis and welcome to phenomenology invokes Jung at a strategic juncture.*

The phenomenological situation with regard to psychoanalytical investigation will perhaps be more precisely stated if, in connection with poetic images, we are able to isolate a sphere of *pure sublimation*; of a sublimation that sublimates nothing, is relieved of the burden of passion and freed from the pressure of desire. By thus giving to the poetic image at its peak an absolute of sublimation, I place heavy stakes on a simple nuance. It seems to me, however, that poetry gives abundant proof of this absolute sublimation, as will be seen frequently in the course of this work. When psychologists and psychoanalysts are furnished this proof, they cease to see anything in the poetic image but a simple game, a short-lived, totally vain game. Images, in particular, have no significance for them—neither from the standpoint of the passions nor from that of psychology or psychoanalysis. It does not occur to them that

Gaston Bachelard, *The Poetics of Space*, trans. Maria Jolas (New York: Orion, 1964), from *La Poétique de l'espace* (Paris: Quadrige, 1957).

the significance of such images is precisely a poetic significance. But poetry is there with its countless surging images, images through which the creative imagination comes to live in its own domain.

For a phenomenologist, the attempt to attribute antecedents to an image, when we are in the very existence of the image, is a sign of inveterate psychologism. On the contrary, let us take the poetic image in its being. For the poetic consciousness is so wholly absorbed by the image afloat on the language, above customary language; the language it speaks with the poetic image is so new that correlations between past and present can no longer be usefully considered.

The examples I shall give of breaks in significance, sensation and sentiment will oblige the reader to grant me that the poetic image is under the sign of a new being.

This new being is happy man.

Happy in speech, therefore unhappy in reality, will be the psychoanalyst's immediate objection. Sublimation, for him, is nothing but a vertical compensation, a flight upward, exactly in the same way that compensation is a lateral flight. And right away, the psychoanalyst will abandon ontological investigation of the image to dig into the past of a man. He sees and points out the poet's secret sufferings. He explains the flower by the fertilizer.

The phenomenologist does not go that far. For him, the image is there, the word speaks, the word of the poet speaks to him. There is no need to have lived through the poet's sufferings in order to seize the felicity of speech offered by the poet—a felicity that dominates tragedy itself. Sublimation in poetry towers above the psychology of the mundanely unhappy soul. For it is a fact that poetry possesses a felicity of its own, however great the tragedy it may be called upon to illustrate.

Pure sublimation, as I see it, poses a serious problem of method for, needless to say, the phenomenologist cannot disregard the deep psychological reality of the processes of sublimation which have been so lengthily examined by psychoanalysis. His task is that of proceeding phenomenologically to images which have not been experienced, which life does not prepare, but which the poet creates; of living what has not been lived, and being receptive to an openness of language. There exist a few poems, such as certain poems by Pierre-Jean Jouve, in which experiences of this kind may be found. Indeed, I know of no oeuvre that has been nourished on psychoanalytical meditation more than Jouve's. However, here and there, his poetry passes through flames of such intensity that we no longer need live at its original source. He himself has said: "Poetry constantly surpasses its origins, and because it suffers more deeply in ecstasy or in sorrow, it retains greater freedom."[1] Or again: "The further I advanced in time, the more the plunge was controlled, removed from the contributory cause, directed toward the pure form of language."[2] I cannot say whether or not Jouve would agree to consider the causes divulged by psychoanalysis as "contributory." But in the region of "the pure form of language," the psychoanalyst's causes do not allow us to predict the poetic image in its newness. They are, at the very most, opportunities for liberation. And in the poetic age in which we live, it is in this that poetry is specifically "surprising." Its images are therefore unpredictable. Most literary critics are insufficiently aware of this un-predictability, which is precisely what upsets the plans of the usual psychologi-cal explanations. But the poet states clearly: "Poetry, especially in its present endeavors, [can] only correspond to attentive thought that is enamored of something unknown, and essentially receptive to becoming."[3] Later: "Conse-quently, a new definition of a poet is in view, which is: he who knows, that is to say, who transcends, and names what he knows." Lastly: "There is no poetry without absolute creation."[4]

Such poetry is rare.[5] The great mass of poetry is more mixed with passion, more psychologized. Here, however, rarity and exception do not confirm the rule but contradict it and set up a new regime. Without the region of absolute sublimation—however restrained and elevated it may be, and even though it may seem to lie beyond the reach of psychologists or psychoanalysts, who, after all, have no reason to examine pure poetry—poetry's exact polarity cannot be revealed.

We may hesitate in determining the exact level of disruption, we may also remain for a long time in a domain of the confusing passions that *perturb* po-etry. Moreover, the height at which we encounter pure sublimation is doubtless not the same for all souls. But at least the necessity of separating a sublimation examined by a psychoanalyst from one examined by a phenomenologist of po-etry is a necessity of method. A psychoanalyst can, of course, study the human character of poets but, as a result of his own sojourn in the region of the pas-sions, he is not prepared to study poetic images in their exalting reality. Carl Jung said this, in fact, very clearly: by persisting in the habits of judgment in-herent in psychoanalysis, "interest is diverted from the work of art and loses itself in the inextricable chaos of psychological antecedents; the poet becomes a 'clinical case,' an example, to which is given a certain number in the *psycho-pathia sexualis*. Thus the psychoanalysis of a work of art moves away from its object and carries the discussion into a domain of general human interest, which is not in the least peculiar to the artist and, particularly, has no impor-tance for his art."[6]

Merely with a view to summarizing this discussion, I should like to make a polemical remark, although indulging in polemics is not one of my habits.

A Roman said to a shoemaker who had directed his gaze too high: *Ne sutor ultra crepidam* (Cobbler not beyond thy shoe!)

Every time there is a question of pure sublimation, when the very being of poetry must be determined, shouldn't the phenomenologist say to the psycho-analyst: *Ne psuchor ultra uterum* (psychiatrist not beyond thy womb!)

TRANSLATED BY MARIA JOLAS

NOTES

[1] Pierre-Jean Jouve, *"En Miroir,"* in *Mercure de France*, p. 109. André Chédid has also written: "A poem remains free. We shall never enclose its fate in our own." The poet knows well that "his breath will carry him farther than his desire." (*Terre et poésie,* G.L.M. §§ 14 and 25.

[2] Jouve, *"En Miroir,"* p. 112.

[3] Ibid., p. 1700

[4] Ibid., p. 100

[5] Ibid., p. 9: *"La poésie est rare."*

[6] Carl G. Jung "On the Relation of Analytical Psychology to the Poetic Art," in *Contributions to Analytical Psychology*, trans. by H. G. Baynes and Cary F. Baynes (New York: Harcourt, Brace, 1928).

MICHEL SERRES

From Math to Myth
1961

In a 1961 essay introducing the several volumes of his Hermès *series, Michel Serres situates his work at the interface between Bachelard's episte- mology and his criticism. The former would already be protostructuralist and as such an example of the "new classicism" that structuralism prom- ised. The latter would take the "romantic" investment in myths and under- lying meanings to its elemental limit. The new task would be to open up the world of cultural meanings and myths to the new formalist dispensation, granting Bachelard's epistemology the decisive victory over his criticism which it had never quite achieved.*

We have a vague idea that the cultural horizon is changing before our very eyes. We no longer dream quite the same dreams as our imme- diate predecessors did. We no longer think or write as they did. The twentieth century is making its second revolution, which consists, if I may put it this way, of culturally digesting the first. And this digestion has not been without discomfort. This century has witnessed a number of profound up- heavals in our scientific thinking: revolutions have already occurred, while oth- ers, we dimly sense, are soon to follow. The theoretical universe has shifted abruptly, while the world of practice and technology, held back by inertia, have followed at a slower pace. We no longer live in the world as we did just a short while ago. It seems clear that these changes must eventually have some impact on our view of culture. People have therefore been pondering them with new urgency. Their thinking has been characterized in one respect by the *critical* use of the notion of structure, imported from science. If, however, one feels not so much urgency as anxiety at the widespread use of this notion and the consid- erable nonsense to which it has given rise (this is one source of the indigestion to which I alluded a moment ago), one may wish to supply a normative, cathar- tic, and purgative definition. The idea of structure is by no means the mysteri- ous key that, as some people seem to think, can open all doors, it is a clear,

Michel Serres, *Hermès* (Paris: Editions de Minuit, 1968).

distinct, and illuminating principle of method and nothing more. It should therefore be possible to clarify matters quickly.

Again, the place to start is with Gaston Bachelard, one of the few thinkers capable of describing a pure form *while at the same time* interpreting the profound cultural implications of its content. In his work, however, he clearly differentiates these two projects and keeps them in polemical tension with each other, as if the joy of one brought deliverance from the pleasures of the other (and vice versa). It is as if the work of bringing form into the world remained unfinished, preliminary, and approximate (the word "open" has been applied to Bachelard's philosophy for this reason): his epistemology is more impressionistic than systematic, while his literary criticism is more symbolist and archetypal than formalist. Now, it so happens that the contemporary idea of criticism can easily be characterized as Bachelardian incompleteness to the nth degree. Classicism, we may fairly say, exists wherever cultures are excluded for the sake of reason, wherever meaning is ignored for the sake of truth (to the point where some, such as Pascal, would rather hold reason in contempt than admit that cultural content has any rational significance whatsoever). Romanticism, by generalizing the classical idea of truth and embracing the notion of meaning, attempted to incorporate, and promote, cultural content as such. In this way, it inaugurated the project that still occupies us today, that of comprehending the pluralism of meaning, of decoding languages other than the language of pure reason.

To succeed at this, romanticism was obliged painstakingly to construct a method, as rationalism had done in its search for truth. Now, for the sake of brevity, I shall skip the preliminaries and state, as one may do with some confidence, that the methodological truth of romanticism is the technique of *symbolic analysis*. If the classical problem is the problem of truth, whose field is reason, the romantic problem is the problem of meaning, whose field is the history of human attitudes. Hence, the methodological horizon of the former is order (deductions, themes, conditions, and so on), whereas the methodological horizon of the latter is the symbol. To be faithful to the ideal of order, it is necessary and sufficient that there exist a model in which order is ideal, perfectly realized. The rigorous sciences provided such a model. Mathematical order, the order of the exact sciences, was the archetype of the classical method, an archetype—or eminent model—which that method attempted to mimic. When the range of questioning is broadened, however, and the obscurity of meaning has to be dealt with as such, the reference archetype is ill-adapted to its role. The realm of meaning does not mimic any archetype of rigor or order, any model sprung fully armed from the brow of pure reason. *Hence, an archetype had to be chosen from the domain of meaning itself, and the full essence of the cultural content under analysis had to be projected onto this model.* Because an ideal model could not be invoked as a normative index, a concrete model had to be constructed within the field of analysis itself, and the content of that model rather than its order became the primary referent. Content was therefore seen not as an imitation of an ideal model but as a *repetition, content for content*, of a universal and concrete symbol. In those days, symbols descended from heaven to earth—but not entirely, for they descended only from the empyrean of ideas to the land or history of *myth*.[1] In this sense, the analytic technique of Hegel, Nietzsche, and Freud was symbolic and archetypal: the essential question was *where* to choose the archetype, from what symbolic universe it ought to be taken. Broadly speaking, nineteenth-century symbolic analysis took its models from *mythical history*: thus Apollo, Dionysus, Ariadne, Zarathustra, Electra, Oedipus, and so on *eminently represent (or symbolize) the totality of the essence of a significant cultural content*.[2] The meaning of this content is understood and internalized when one succeeds in showing that it duplicates or repeats the archetype, realizes it anew, carries it over from myth into history, from the eternal to the evolving. Content and symbol correspond in meaning, and this correspondence engenders history or the eternal return, so that the technique of symbolic analysis is linked to the conception of history. Conversely, historical typologies are engendered by the choice of a set of archetypes. Now we can understand the significance of symbolic analysis: it is the projection of a compact meaning onto a unique, concise archetype situated at the earliest possible (that is, most archaic) point of historical origin. The selected set of models then becomes mythical history itself, because myth is not only symbol but *ultimate origin*. From classicism to romanticism, the notion of model went from clear to obscure (or, in the problem domain, from the true to the significant), from normative to symbolic, from *transcendent* to *original*.[3] Where man was concerned, the domain of reference shifted from the rational to the totality of signifying functions.

This rapid analysis has identified notions that until quite recently were of central concern: the problem of meaning and signs, symbolism and language, archetypes and history, comprehension of obscure cultural content, fascination with the original and originary, and so on. Note, in particular, *the variety of models used*. The thinkers of the past were unaware of a truth which is as clear to us as a thousand suns, that as their problems varied so did their frame of reference: the symbolic analysis of romanticism was not a methodological miracle created out of nothing but one of a series of variations. If truth is the problem, mathematics is the only ultimate arbiter; if the empirical is at issue, then the arbiter must be mechanics, physics, or natural philosophy; and if it is cultural significance that concerns us, finally, we have nothing to work with but the set of archetypes lodged in the immemorial memory of humankind. The nature and function of the model thus vary, but what interests us is the variation itself.

The reader, I hope, will forgive the brevity of these remarks. Let us return now to Bachelard. *His literary criticism was still a moment in this series of variations,* but *the last moment*. In this sense, he was the last symbolic analyst, the last "romantic" critic. This is so for a very simple reason: it was he who introduced the last possible variation in the choice of reference archetypes. In his work, earth, fire, air, and water *replace* Apollo and Oedipus; the elements replace the heroes of myth as archetypes. True, Bachelard does on occasion write about Empedocles or Ophelia, but only in a derivative sense: Empedocles is merely a species belonging to the genus fire, Ophelia to the genus water. *The typology stemming from mythic history is subordinated to that stemming from a mythified natural history,*[4] the novel domain from which Bachelard chose his archetypes. With dazzling insight he demonstrated (by way of a chiasmus) that these formed the basis of both the perspicuous models of science (this was the result of Bachelard's psychoanalysis of objective knowledge) and the symbolic archetypes of culture (as one sees from his psychoanalysis of the signifying material imagination).[5] No further variation is possible for two reasons: first, because Bachelard drew his archetypes from the last myth of the last science (he was thus the last romantic), and second, because he brought together, in bold conjunction, clarity of form and density of content (he was therefore the first neoclassic).[6] He changed symbols, in other words, but remained a symbolist in the great tradition of the nineteenth century.

Just as that century gave rise to archetypes, our own century, having become formalist, has been trying to create structures. In the past, a model was taken to be the realization of an essence; now it is taken to be a paradigm (that is, the exemplary realization of a structure). In the one case, the model is primary, in the other, secondary. On the one hand, it is the reference that explains or, rather, stimulates understanding; on the other hand, it is the very object of explanation itself. In order to make the transition from symbolism to formalism—that is, from the model as the end of method to the model as problem, we must first be sure that no further variation in choice of symbolic archetype is possible. Before choosing to drain all symbols of meaning and focusing instead on formal structure, we need to make sure that the world of symbols has been exhaustively explored. That is why I say that Bachelard was the last symbolist: the domain from which he chose his archetypes was *all of nature,* which nothing could conceivably *extend.* What is more, he looked to the *original of nature,* which nothing could possibly *precede.* He was therefore the last "psychoanalyst," for he wrote a generalized psychoanalysis (impervious to further generalization) in which the corporal unconscious was supplanted by the natural unconscious, in which the mythical history of the world supplanted and dominated the mythical history of man—a physioanalysis, in other words. Since, moreover, this physioanalysis subsumed everything that went before—psychoanalysis, socioanalysis, and so on—nothing remained for Bachelard's successors but to become—or to revert to being, but in a new way—*logoanalysts.* Contemporary structuralist methods can therefore be fairly characterized as a form of *logoanalysis.*

Accordingly, all methodological and critical questions now revolve around the notion of *meaning*, and even, I dare say, around the quantification of meaning. Take any form whatsoever to which one wishes to assign a methodological function. Suppose we fill it with meaning and charge it with significance, be it material, historical, human, or existential, to the very last detail. This form then becomes an archetype, which is to say, the referent of a symbolic analysis: the language of meaning has no terms other than archetypes. Ideograms are its only means of expression. We do not know how to speak it in letters whose content and possible relations are undefined. We know only how to design synthetic tableaus and hypercharged images. Therefore, the more symbolic a form becomes, the more difficult it is to conceive of it in formal terms. An archetype—be it a god, hero, or element—is supercharged with significance to the maximum possible degree (in this respect, Oedipus—a proper name that has become a common noun—is an ideogram which makes it possible to speak the language without language of the unconscious). Symbolic analysis cannot help but see the archetype as the totality of a fully achieved essence. An archetype is a form saturated with meaning. Bachelard, in my view, put his finger on certain supersaturated archetypes (with a *maximum maximorum* of significant content), archetypes that were mythically or symbolically primary and without possible predecessors in a realm of myth chosen to be without analog. With him, variation ended: symbolic analysis was perfected, that is, terminated. This marked the end of the romantic ideal: it closed out the range of imaginable symbols and filled out the roster of archetypes. What was left was a form of analysis or criticism that was the inverse of symbolic analysis: its method was to *empty form of the totality of its meaning,* of all its possible meanings, that is, to conceive of form in formal terms, shifting from the ideographic writing of symbolic analysis to the abstract language of structural analysis. Surprisingly, however, it turned out that by draining form of meaning one gains a better handle on the problems of meaning.

This was truly the end of an era. We no longer map constellations in the sky which tell man who he is as through a glass darkly. Bachelard was the last to do so. After him a new age began—but what new age? What dawn obliterated those symbolic constellations, the Minotaur, Argo, the Swan, and the Great Bear?

Let us return to Bachelard. He spent his life describing the new scientific spirit and the new criticism. In addition, he attempted to establish a new equilibrium between those two efforts, which because of him have been forever since inseparable. That lesson cannot be forgotten: historically, it was of the utmost importance, because it marked the beginning of a *new classicism*, in which reason no longer turned its back on cultural content. It sought to understand such content not through the mediation of symbolic archetypes but directly, with its own devices, and attempted to disclose the structural rigor of cultural accumulation. That is why I have called it *logoanalysis.*

With Bachelard gone, science has been proceeding along one path and cultural analysis along another, but *their future is henceforth linked*. Furthermore, although these paths, when examined closely, turn out not to be Bachelardian (which would have pleased him), the conjunction of the formal and the cultural remains, a conjunction that he obscurely indicated or, if you prefer, achieved in practice. Now that he is gone, a *New New Scientific Spirit* remains to be written, a work that would take account of the continuing revolution in what has been rather inaptly called "modern mathematics" along with advances in the other exact sciences. This has yet to be done. A *New New Criticism* is also needed, and that is even now being written. It is being written with misgivings for the simple reason that the epistemology just alluded to does not yet exist. Hence this new classicism—a classicism of the finesses of geometry and the geometries of finesse, a classicism that seeks to finish what Bachelard left incomplete, seeks to reunite reason with meaning without recourse to the obscurity of symbolism and to decipher the subtle grammar of cultural content—has run into difficulty in laying its foundations for want of a clear and distinct perception, a precise evaluation, of the methodological notion of a form to be brought out and isolated—in short, a structure.

In order to maintain clarity and precision, it is enough to avoid distortion and ambiguity when *importing* the idea of structure from the realm of scientific theory to that of cultural criticism. In algebra, for instance, there is nothing at all ambiguous about the idea of structure. When that idea was introduced into anthropology by Claude Lévi-Strauss or into the history of religion by Georges Dumézil, there was no twisting of words or obscurity. Their analyses are authentically structural. This is less apparent in the work of Martial Gueroult, however, where the idea of structure plays a broader and less methodological role, except in his studies of Descartes, where one can in fact isolate a structure.

Let us pause for a moment to consider what I mean by "importation." Given a clear and precise methodological concept that has been shown to be successful in a specific subject area (and methods can and should be judged only by their fruits), workers in other areas of science, criticism, and so forth vie with one another to try it out in their respective fields. This was true in the past of the methodological concept of symbols. Symbolic analysis was developed by what I earlier referred to, in broad terms, as romantic criticism, but it also turned up in many other areas of nineteenth-century thought, including mathematics (symbolic calculus), physics (physical modeling), and economics. In *L'Oeil et l'esprit*, Merleau-Ponty had an intuition of this type of methodological transfer, but he limited its generality by attributing it to fashion and citing only the relatively insignificant example of the concept of gradient. In fact, fashion comes into play only as the effect of a certain *law of entropy* following a series of importations. At a certain point in this series, the rigorous sense of the concept is partially or totally lost, after which it is discussed only as hearsay, much as a child will try out words it hears being used by grown-ups. In order to overcome this gradual clouding of meaning, this noise, it is enough to trace the informational chain resulting from the importation back to its source, that is, to the point where the conceptual content is most truthful. That point is not fixed in advance. There is no single point from which all truth is imported. That was the classical idea, which was based on the pre-eminence of one science. Clearly, in an age of epistemological pluralism, it is no longer the case. Insofar as the notion of structure is concerned, the point of origination is, as we have seen, algebra. This is not to say that the mathematicians were the first to use it, only that they were the first to give it the *precise, codified meaning* that has brought innovation to contemporary methodology. Indeed, as early as the seventeenth century, the term was used in its Latin sense as a synonym for construction or architecture. Leibniz, for example, speaks of the "structure" of animals and plants to refer to their general plan of organization or layout, to the architectural scheme of their constitution. Structure, then, was the way in which something was constructed, the spatial arrangement of its members and organs. When we forget the new meaning of the term, we very quickly fall back into this earlier usage. According to Gueroult, for example, technological analysis of systems uses the term structure in this sense, in the general case. More abstractly, the word has been used (by late-nineteenth-century economists, for example) to refer to all laws governing the organization of a given phenomenon. And again it is easy to fall back into this usage if one forgets the sense derived from algebra. And there are even more discreditable uses of the term, discreditable because they are quite vague and without substance. Indeed, the spatial extension of this fashionable term is directly proportional to the imprecision of its meaning. It is clearly risky to import the notion of structure as it was understood in the seventeenth century into fields other than biology. In fact, only highly formalized concepts can be freely imported. That is why the new concept of structure is quite freely importable.

Because it is formal, we have abandoned symbolic analysis. Symbols and archetypes refer to a meaning; they are the key to a method only because they define a precise semantic field. Psychoanalytic typology is a gallery of symbols, each of which refers to a clinical picture definable by elements of meaning. The same is true of the typologies of Nietzsche, Kierkegaard, Bachelard, and so on. Here, the singular becomes model by way of semantic filling, through supersaturation of meaning. To symbolize is to establish precise correspondences between a particular sign and a semantic content. To formalize is completely different.

If classical mathematics was generally symbolic (in that a given sign had a specific meaning), modern mathematics is formal. In a formal system, one is not concerned with meaning in any way; one never refers either explicitly or implicitly to a significant content. One studies only a set of well-formed (undefined) objects, where the rules stating what a well-formed object is are set forth in advance. On the one hand, there can be no symbol where there is no underlying semantics. A symbolic analysis is an economy of thought in which the (complex) order of meaning is replaced by the (clear, simple, rapid) order of the sign, but the *true* order, that which underlies the entire analysis, is the order of meaning. Symbolic order states nothing new but makes interpretation possible. On the other hand, a group of formal notions has no underlying semantics. A symbolic analysis consists in *translating* meaning content into signs, coding and decoding a language. Formal analysis consists in forging a language defined by its own rules: only after this is done does the possibility exist of translating that language into contents or models. The first approach starts with meaning, whereas the second discovers (or produces) it.

That said, the notion of structure is a *formal* notion. Here is a definition, in which I underscore points that are often misinterpreted: *a structure is an operational set of undefined meaning* (whereas an archetype is a concrete set of overdetermined meaning) *consisting of an arbitrary number of elements, whose content is unspecified, and a finite number of relations, whose nature is not specified,* but whose functions are defined, as are certain results with respect of the elements. If one specifies some definite content for the elements along with the nature of the relations between them, one obtains a model (or paradigm) of the structure: *the structure is thus the formal analogon of all the concrete models that it organizes.* Rather than symbolize a content, a model "realizes" a structure. The term structure has this clear and distinct definition and no other. The nonsense to which it has given rise can only be compared to the distortion that results as a message circulates among the players in a game of "telephone."

In view of this definition, given any cultural content whatsoever, be it God, table, or washbasin, an *analysis is structural if (and only if)* it exhibits the content as a model in the sense given above. Structural analysis thus gives rise to a new methodological spirit, a profound revolution in regard to the question of meaning. Instead of the one-to-one relationship between symbol and symbolized (meaningful content to meaningful content) that one finds in romantic analysis, structuralist criticism proposes a one-to-many relationship between a structure (pure, formal, and devoid of meaning) and its models, each of which is uniquely meaningful. This yields a new capacity to classify and create typologies. Instead of engendering families grouped around archetypes by similarity of meaning, one engenders families of models with distinct significant content but sharing a common structural analogon of form. This is the operational invariant that organizes them when all content has been abstracted away. Once the structure (of abstract elements and relations) has been isolated, it is possible to discover every conceivable model: in other words, it is possible to *construct an existent cultural entity by filling a form with meaning.* Meaning ceases to be that which is given in obscure terms needing to be deciphered. It is rather that which one adds to a structure to create a model. Symbolic analysis, which sits as it were below meaning, is crushed by it. In contrast, structural analysis sits above meaning, which it *dominates, constructs,* and *produces.* That is why its typology is indifferent to meaning, unlike the typology produced by symbolic analysis, which was conditioned by it.[7]

To free oneself from meaning in order to dominate it, rather than accept it and seek to discover its native language; to engender an existent entity from a formal analogon; to deduce the purely formal consequences of a given structure and identify its possible models at each stage in the process—a structural analysis is all of these things. There can be no doubt that the method has applications outside mathematics. There is no fundamental reason why it cannot be imported into problem areas in which, prior to Bachelard, symbolic analysis triumphed—historical, literary, and philosophical criticism.

The novelty of this method lies in the fact that the analyst, for the first time since the classical era, places his trust in *abstraction* in the broad sense. In this respect, it is possible to speak of a *new classicism.* Previously, it seemed impossible to understand a cultural element without thrusting it into a series of supersaturated constellations of myth, which in some obscure way comprised an essence, a meaning, a singular existence, a history, and an origin. If we wished to understand languages other than that of reason, there seemed no choice but to collect the stammerings of those languages in a compact form whose mythic hyperexistence was supposed to ensure its longevity. Mythical symbols were immemorial souvenirs of all languages in their nascent state. Structural analysis reveals that reason is deeply implicated in formations that do not appear to be in any immediate sense its offspring. That is why I have proposed the term *logoanalysis,* by which I mean demonstrating the structural rigor within a cultural accumulation, identifying patterns discoverable by pure reason and underlying the mythologies that used to be seen as the substrate of the cultural— these are the primary goals of logoanalysis. Its objective is to discover the rational (structural) schemata it assumes exist beneath the layers of myth that once provided the archetypes on which symbolic analysis thrived. Classicism placed its trust in what might be called regional reason, whereas the new criticism places its trust in the idea of a *generalized reason* that subsumes the realm of meaning in the manner set forth above.

In this there is more than a method; there is also a promise, the promise of an astonishing reconciliation which seems to be taking place without having been consciously sought in the history of ideas. To begin with, this new way of thinking has a unifying power in a world of endless pluralism and regional complexity. But that is not all: even more important is the subtle way in which reason has been gaining ground in an area where it had been largely surpassed for more than a century (largely here is used in the sense of extension). Reason has regained in depth what it had lost in breadth.

The present era may thus reconcile truth with meaning. It also holds out hope of success in an endeavor that once seemed hopeless: understanding the Greek miracle of mathematics and the amazing outpouring of Greek mythology. It was right to give the figures of that other, Dionysiac world thick, compact, and obscure meanings, projections of the human soul, of its feelings and its fate: at stake was nothing less than man's reality and destiny, his happiness and misfortune, conceived in universal terms. But apart from being symbols from the past, might those figures, saturated as they are with meaning and causality, not also be meaningful models of transparent structures from the realm of knowledge, intellect, and science? Perhaps it is not senseless to look into what might be paradigmatic about mythical symbols or what patterns might lurk in parables. Perhaps, in other words, it is not senseless to aim for a new interpretation of cultural accumulation in terms of pure cognitive order. And, indeed, it *is* not senseless if one recognizes the formal rigor of the new methods and the supple complexity of the new critical tools. The twin strands of Bachelard's legacy might then lead to a dual truth, and the unity of the Hellenic miracle might at last be understood. The logoanalytic method of the new classicism points toward a new relationship between the indeterminacy of the abstract and the proliferation of significant content in human culture.

TRANSLATED BY ARTHUR GOLDHAMMER

NOTES

1 Where one sees the pure turn into the mythical, which is both universal and singular.

2 Symbolic analysis thus invites us to *understand* history (in the broad sense) in terms of its mythological archetypes. If one were to measure the distance between these symbols and their historical meaning, one would discover that the more precise and refined the symbolic analysis, the smaller the distance: ultimately one arrives at the technique of Georges Dumézil, for whom a certain history *is* the myth itself.

3 These overly general remarks obviously call for certain caveats. In the classical era, for example, a philosopher such as Leibniz was already moving from truth to meaning, clear to obscure, normative to symbolic, and transcendent to original. In his work, we therefore find a *classical method*, a *symbolic method*, and—already!—cultural content (literature, history, philology, and so on). He preserves the ideal of clarity and distinction but wants to embrace the obscure as such.

4 This history is even more fundamental than that which speaks of the inception of gods and heroes.

5 This surprising connection explains, in an unexpected way, why Bachelard, unlike Baudelaire, never wrote about artificial dreams, why he never wrote books entitled *Hashish and Dreams*, *Betel and Dreams*. The reason is that opium, belladonna, and mescaline are substances belonging to a nonmythical, nonarchetypal chemistry. A false (and original) alchemy is the counterpart of true dreams even as a true (and current) chemistry finds its counterpart in false images: a phenomenon that may be observed in Sartre. Thus the Socrates of *The Birth of Tragedy* can not be the historical Socrates: symbolic analysis requires a mythical Socrates in order to dwell within its truth. The result can be generalized. *Might the soul's truth be the mind's falsehood and vice versa?* This would help explain the secret link, in Romantic philosophy, between the symbolic method and irrationalism. Or, to defuse the paradox a bit, what is true for man lies in what is marginal for reason (that limit, understood temporally, is origin, and, understood logically, is obscurity).

6 There is a third reason: *no myth has precedence over the myth of the elements*. There is no myth of an origin this side of it. As is recounted by Hesiod or Aristophanes. Thus the

origin of the constitution of the world precedes the origin of history. There is no comprehensive myth this side of it. Every mythology is subordinate to a cosmogony.

[7] This is essential: a structural analysis is successful and fruitful when it manages to *reconstruct* a cultural element on the basis of a form. The understanding afforded by symbolic
analysis was in the order of a *recognition*: one rediscovers Electra or Dionysus here or
there, thus recognizing it. The understanding afforded by a structural analysis ought to
stem from a *reconstitution*. From which it follows that if I am able to reconstitute a cultural element, I will no longer be fascinated by a myth of origins but will effect a genesis.
It is on this basis (among others) that one may recognize an analysis as being authentically structural: it will have succeeded in reconstituting its object as a model.

MICHEL FOUCAULT

Trapping One's Own Culture
1972

The mercurial Michel Foucault, whom we last encountered defending Jean-Pierre Richard (against Gérard Genette) from being tarred with a Bachelardian brush, here praises Bachelard in terms—the summoning of minor figures out of the archives with major results—that are not without recalling the specific talents of Foucault himself.

W hat strikes me particularly about Bachelard is that in some sense he is playing against his own culture, with his own culture. In traditional teaching—and not only in teaching, but in the received culture—there are a certain number of established values, certain things that must be said and other things that must not be said, certain works that are praiseworthy and others that can be ignored. There are the great and the not so great, the hierarchy, the whole heavenly host with its Thrones and Dominions, Angels and Archangels. It's all very hierarchical. Well, Bachelard encourages you to let go of that whole system of values, and he makes you let go of it while reading all of it and setting each part against the others.

He reminds me, if you will, of a skillful chess player who knows how to capture major pieces with his pawns. Bachelard does not hesitate to challenge Descartes with a minor philosopher or even a—well, frankly, a bizarre and rather deluded eighteenth-century scientist. He doesn't hesitate to subject the greatest of poets to scrutiny alongside some minor figure whose work he stumbled on one day in a secondhand bookshop. And in doing so, his goal is not to reconstruct the great, all-encompassing culture of the West or Europe or France. It is not to show that a single great spirit is all-pervasive and everywhere the same. On the contrary, one has the sense that he is out to trap his culture in its own crevices, to trip it up on its out-of-the-way excursions and explorations, its gaffes and sour notes.

TRANSLATED BY ARTHUR GOLDHAMMER

Michel Foucault, "Piéger sa propre culture," in *Dits et Ecrits*, II (Paris: Gallimard, 1994), p. 382.

PART VII

Changing Times—
and Spaces

GAËTAN PICON

Literature Twenty Years Later
1976

*First published in 1949 and updated on the occasion of each of its many
reprintings, Gaëtan Picon's popular and influential survey of postwar
French literature encountered problems, after 1968, that went far beyond
the routine tune-up required to correct the parallax effect induced by a
moving object. The matter was not that the object was moving too fast, nor
even that it underwent radical changes. Rather, the object was lost: it no
longer appeared on the screen.*

*The post–'68 French cultural landscape didn't fit a mold custom-made
for the literature of 1945. As suggested by the Alexandre Dumas-like the
title Picon gave to the introduction to this last edition—the time of the
literary Musketeers (Sartre, Camus, Malraux) had passed. What began in
1949 as a survey of contemporary literature ended up, in 1976, with a contemporary culture from which literature (at least literature as usual) was
absent.*

*Picon's feeling of estrangement came not from some radical novelty of
the literary works produced during the last decades but, rather, from the
increasingly marginal relevance of the works themselves in the literary
field. The substance of literature had changed. The study of individual authors or works has been discarded for questions such as: What is an author?
What is a work? It was no longer a question of knowing what's happening
in the field but of what was happening to it.*

Written in 1948 and previously revised in 1957, *Panorama of the New
French Literature* needed still further revisions if it was not to dis-
appoint the reader of 1976, for over the past decade things have
changed even more dramatically. Nevertheless, I did not want to make revisions so drastic as to turn it into a different book. I have preserved its value
system, because its values are still my values. I have also stayed with the same

Gaëtan Picon, "La Littérature vingt ans après," *Panorama de la nouvelle littérature
française* (rev. ed., Paris: Gallimard, 1976), pp. 7–13.

basic premise, which was that the book should focus on change and innovation at the expense of tradition. Indeed, I have gone even further in this direction, eliminating anything that might look like list-making, a procedure obviously doomed to failure, in favor of detailed analysis of major works and significant trends, even where those works were more interesting for what they set out to do than for what they achieved. Yet I have also preserved here and there a passage that I would no longer dream of writing today. And I have let stand a preface that I surely would not now write in the same tone. I made these choices because I felt that it would be useful if this history retained its historical character: although this new edition is a work that can be consulted in 1976, it is also a specimen of a state of mind that in 1948, was not its author's alone. In its essentials my state of mind has not changed, but that of the time has changed drastically, so that two poles now stand in stark opposition: on the one hand, values to which I remain attached, on the other the spirit of the present moment, which I acknowledge but do not always espouse.

There is, however, a good deal that might be said about this change of climate, the rupture it has produced, and the way in which it is nevertheless linked to the climate in which this book was originally conceived. At first glance, in fact, it might seem that the present marks a continuity with or consecration of the past, rather than a rupture. Is not much of what I saw and set down many years ago now widely accepted? Is not the official image of contemporary literature as now conceived by cultural institutions, universities, and the media broadly similar to that which I championed without the support of those authorities in the 1949 edition? If André Malraux, Jean-Paul Sartre, and Albert Camus were already famous names, neither Raymond Queneau nor Jean Genet nor Michel Leiris nor Georges Bataille nor Antonin Artaud nor Julien Gracq nor any of the poets I discussed, except Paul Eluard and Louis Aragon, then enjoyed the unquestioned prominence they have since achieved. I say this without excessive vanity on my part: I was, of course, expressing views I shared with others, including my elders from the *Cahiers de la Pléiade* and my friends from *Fontaine* and *Confluences*. But we were a long way from being heeded by everyone. Not only were all the writers I just mentioned excluded from university syllabi (a defensible choice, given that distance does have its virtues), but the press and other media whose duty is to be up to the minute were generally also wary of them, but for rare exceptions. My discussion of René Char earned me the derision of *Le Canard enchaîné*, and *Le Monde*, with a few ironic sentences, dismissed my book as a monument of extravagance.

Today, this central current of modernity, and particularly poetic modernity, no longer meets with opposition, at least not openly. The most recent and most daring work immediately becomes fodder for doctoral dissertations, and the literary pages of *Le Monde*, while not hostile to the Ancients, are largely open to the Moderns. It takes some courage to fly in the face of received opinion, and those who do so are occasionally greeted with sympathy of a sort. To be sure, newspaper reviews and literary programs on radio and television often settle for the comfortably traditional or downright mediocre. By design, they discuss only what they believe the public is capable of understanding. The rest of literature goes unexamined or even unmentioned. This other literature suffers from a bad "image," and the media do nothing to attract unlikely "consumers." But for a few heartening exceptions, however, incomprehension is no longer regarded as sufficient grounds for condemnation. Never again will a Claude Farrère deprive a Paul Claudel of a seat in the Académie Française. Indeed, the Académie would gladly admit all the writers featured in this book—if only they would permit it.

But as literary modernity has triumphed, modernity has ceased to be invested in literature. The literary modernists have achieved recognition just as the things that in my view made them what they are are being vilified and "demystified." Literature, understood not as a source of pleasure (this was never enough to define it) but as a complex game that engaged the sensibility, the intellect, and all the other dimensions of humanity—a game that everyone plays differently, some poorly and clumsily, others in unexpected, disruptive ways—literature, in other words, as a series of works that owe their place in our historical memory to the brio with which they participated in this game, has come under suspicion and been repudiated. It is almost totally absent from bookstore windows on the Boulevard Saint-Michel (how surprised an aficionado of the "just published" would be if he were to return to the Latin Quarter after an absence of twenty years!), and if it lingers still in the shops of Saint-Germain-des-Prés and the Place Victor-Hugo, it does so with a rather impudent and guilty air, like the tins of caviar in the window of Fauchon. Not that literature is not the subject of countless works, and still widely produced. But, clearly, most of the people who study it and deal with it of late are not of the same blood type as their predecessors. Literature nowadays is the business of "scientists" interested not in such palpable qualities of the work as its historical context, impact on our sensibility, humor, tone, and authorial ideology but in structures that lie beyond the immediate consciousness of both reader and writer, in the combinatorics of an impersonal language, in the general tropes that are applied in specific ways in the work, or in the accidents that lead writing in directions that it knows not and does not wish to go, the writer's "intention" being a form of "mystification." Literature is of interest only to the extent that it lends itself to the illumination of linguistics, psychoanalysis, and sociology, that is, to the extent that it can be integrated into the human sciences.

Obviously the project of establishing a science of literature need not be contested as such; it should be allowed to run its course. One may doubt that structuralism is the final form of science. And one may doubt that science is justified in dismissing the postulate that in some areas some things may be unknowable. Nevertheless, opting for knowledge is just one option, and the person who chooses that option thereby distances himself from the warmth of lived experience, even if he is abundantly familiar with that warmth, and even if he rediscovers it in moments like the one that Claude Lévi-Strauss evokes with such moving modesty in the final lines of his impressive conclusion to *Mythologiques*, when the subject at last emerges from anonymous thought and allows himself to dream.[1] Living is not thinking, and while Lévi-Strauss is right to say that relying solely on what an author thinks and says about his work does not get us very far toward understanding it, neither does science take us very far into creation, and for the same reason. The author of *Mythologiques*, who complains in the pages just alluded to of being bored by today's ever-more self-conscious literature (for which he bears a certain responsibility), might well agree. The myth of Orpheus alerted us to this danger long ago.

How did the mystique of the Marquis de Sade and Georges Bataille get mixed up in recent years with the prestige attached to the work of men like Ferdinand de Saussure and Claude Lévi-Strauss? How did the portrait of Che Guevara come to be displayed in bookstores on the Boulevard Saint-Michel alongside the works of Roman Jakobson—or, even more astonishing, of Antonin Artaud, who set no great store by social revolution? How did literature come to be valued *simultaneously* for its amenability to logical-mathematical formalization and its promise of new forms of excitement, of violence and subversion? It is not enough to say (although it is true) that we are dealing here with apples and oranges: indeed, these apples and these oranges coexist in the same display windows and on the same course syllabi and *together* constitute the very selective, very limited culture of today's young intellectuals. Though surely associated with different temperaments, rigor and ardor have the same enemy, namely, literature, to the extent that it is precisely and intentionally what it appears to be: a realm not of knowledge but of sensibility and intuition, a place for mimicking action and existence, not for experiencing them, an instrument for simulating knowledge and life. If both the rigorous and the ardent are drawn to literature today, it is because they hope either to dissolve it in the acid of scientific formulae or explode it in the incandescence of life; it is to witness, if not in fact hasten, the death of literature.

I am reminded of André Breton's first meeting with Paul Valéry, when Breton, asked what he expected of literature, answered that he hoped it would induce states similar to those produced by certain expressions of Rimbaud, such as *Mais que salubre est le vent* (How salubrious the wind is.) How clearly the boundary between what was and what is stands out in this light! Because Breton wanted poetry to produce an effect, to induce a certain "exalted" mental state, he was and is recognized as a precursor of one of the contemporary attitudes toward literature I am describing. But because for him this exalted mental state involved words, because he dwelt on those words and did not discard them after use (or subject them to scientific decoding), and, furthermore, because he was keen to meet Valéry, who had himself known Mallarmé, who, though unable to meet Baudelaire, had at least visited Mistral and Leconte de Lisle, and so on, and, finally, because he, Breton, was prepared to insert himself into this chain (even if he eventually broke more than one of its links), he now finds himself eclipsed by Artaud—something that would have been unimaginable thirty years ago.

It sometimes seems that "values," if widely accepted, lose some of their luster—a heavy price to pay. Indeed, it was Breton himself who insisted that Surrealism go into hiding. Comprehension is sometimes said to be inversely proportional to extension; the depth of floodwaters diminishes as those waters spread; and so on. But these analogies and metaphors are not very convincing. Does communication destroy values? Is disappearance enough to revive them? It is truer to say that the resistance to the communication of values collapses only when the internal resistance to their expression also breaks down. Widespread acceptance is a sign that labor has come to an end. Clarity dawns upon a work (or an idea or a life or an era) only when it has fully emerged from obscurity, that is, from existence. If what we once loved seems now to stand on shaky ground, it would be absurd, sacrilegious, to believe that it never made sense, that we were mystified. A certain use of literature is obviously intimately related to a certain civilization of individual consciousness and to the individual as an "irretrievable" nexus of emotions, illusions, and experiences. But if the human sciences denounce the arbitrary, deceptive garrulousness of the *cogito*, whose narrowness and docility are now rejected in favor of a vital insistence on the absolute, the attack comes at a moment when the *cogito* can no longer defend itself because its incomparable and miraculous journey is now over. Exposed to the light of day, laid out in the open, the *cogito* is but a shadow of its former self; but to have seen it in the glory of its true chiaroscuro—that was something else.

Literary passion, as we have known it, extends from the present to the past: it exists only when inflamed by some work in progress. If so many young minds feel no passion for literature, if they take it only as an object for scientific analysis, perhaps that is because there are few works now in progress that are capable of eliciting passionate response. This book attests to a time when it was still possible to feel passion for works in progress, works whose last word had yet to be written; it has no other justification. To love is to prefer. To my mind, the essential experience of my generation will have been the experience of *choice*, and not just artistic choice. For just as we had to reject the repetitiousness and pretentiousness of "art" in favor of more innovative approaches, we also had to reject a radical absence of freedom in favor of freedom that to us seemed real, limited and "mystified" though it may have been. For or against the October Revolution, the Spanish Republic, the democracies, for or against the writers of the *N.R.F.*, the Surrealist Revolution, Cubism, and abstraction: our entire lives will have been a series of choices. This experience has given our consciousness its unity; our successors have not followed in our footsteps, which explains why, in such a short time, so vast a gulf has opened up between us. I, for one, do not believe in clean slates, and I do not believe that in the name of the higher principles of knowledge and action one can lump together all the works of the past, each one canceling out the next, any more than one can lump together all societies in the name of one society from which all alienation will have been banished. To be sure, works of literature and art are mere illusions, opinions. And yet at a particular time and place it is given to some of them to touch all the fibers of our being in such an uncanny way that we may come to prefer the impure, ambiguous game of literature, which never gets to the bottom of anything, to other forms of commitment, which may be clear and productive but remain unilateral. Today, this preference is on the wane, but it was passionate in the recent past, which this book reflects, and we may perhaps rediscover this passion when we become aware, ultimately, of a thirst, a hunger not truly satisfied.

TRANSLATED BY ARTHUR GOLDHAMMER

NOTE

[1] Between 1966 and 1971, Lévi-Strauss published the four volume series of his *Mythologiques* (*The Raw and the Cooked*, *From Honey to Ashes*, *The Origin of Table Manners*, *The Naked Man*).

MAURICE BLANCHOT

Proposal for *Revue Internationale* 1961

Maurice Blanchot's tentative program for a transnational—mostly East and West European—journal never saw the light of day, in part due to the international crisis that led to the construction of the Berlin wall in August 1961. The journal was to be edited by a committee comprised of intellectuals from different countries, and every issue of the review would have been published simultaneously in the language of each country represented on its board.

The project was rooted in the feeling that the world was undergoing a series of radical if difficult to pinpoint historical changes (decolonization being one of them) and—as far as writers were concerned—the sense that linguistic and literary utterances were undergoing a momentous and multifarious process of what Gilles Deleuze and Félix Guattari have since called "deterritorialization." Blanchot encapsulates the latter sentiment by referring to Yuri Gagarin, the Soviet cosmonaut he oddly credits with the utterance of the "first words spoken in space." The journal—the first review of literature in the age of cosmic utterance—had indeed the ambition of becoming a sort of literary station (a communicating vessel launched in literary space).

A literary text, Blanchot often claimed, is a translation without an original; literature is originally "translated from . . ."—even if it be from silence. Thus, each of the national editions of the journal would have been both an original and a translation. Similarly, at the level of the content, the journal would account for the fact that contemporary events themselves no longer originate on the linear narratives of national histories; nothing happens that is not, from its very inception, already refracted in the prism of international space. We have entered the time of the "rhizomatic" event (to borrow another concept from Deleuze and Guattari). For this reason, the word "international" in the title is central to the project: the time of the

Maurice Blanchot, from "*Textes préparatoires pour une* 'Revue internationale'," [1961] *Lignes* 11 (Sept. 1990), pp. 179–91.

revue française, *be it* nouvelle *or even—as Paulhan revived it in 1953—* nouvelle nouvelle, *is over.*

Among its many utopian dimensions, halfway between Surrealism and some aspects of the group experiments of May '68, this project reflects a strong communitarian inspiration; the journal is envisioned as a literary form per se. It was as if, to play on the title of Blanchot's just published Le Livre à venir, *the journal was the book to come, both the book of the future and the future of the book, the site for the invention of a plural authorship, of a radically new type of writing agency that would relegate the single-author, traditional book to obsolescence.*

The following five fragments by Maurice Blanchot are part of a series of twelve texts (including contributions by Hans Magnus Enzensberger, Leszek Kolakowski, Louis-René des Forêts, two by Dionys Mascolo, and one each by Elio Vittorini and Francesco Leonetti) prepared in the planning stages of the Revue internationale. *None of these texts were intended for publication. All were for "internal use." They are reproduced here as written.*

I

1. The gravity of the project: We are all aware that we are coming to the end of a period of extremely rapid change, to what might be called a change of epoch. I am not just alluding here to the possibility of upheaval in specific places (in France, a regime in constant danger of being overwhelmed by forces it has unleashed; more globally, the issue of Berlin, among others). What I have in mind is far more serious: namely, the fact that today all issues are international, and even minor international issues have become intractable because they merely reflect a state of tension that basically precludes any return to the traditional idea of peace and makes even war—good old conventional war— seem like a relaxation of tension (thus making military solutions tempting).

In such a time of extremes, the idea of creating a new review that would simply be more interesting or better than its competitors would be pathetic. Hence, we must constantly emphasize what is essential in our project: the challenge is to come up with an adequate response to the enigma of these changing times.

2. This crucial focus on the essence of the project can be achieved by adhering to certain basic principles:

a. The project, being international in scope, is essentially collective. This means that we seek not common ground on which all of us can stand but new possibilities, which we hope to discover by pooling our efforts, questions, and resources and, above all, by transcending, internally, the limits of our individual thinking.

All editorial decisions should therefore be unreservedly collegial, and each of us should participate fully in the editorial process, not simply by assenting to joint decisions but by truly rolling up our sleeves, contributing time and ideas, and thinking about how we can achieve our collective goals. If we are not totally dedicated to this joint effort, it would be better not to begin at all. It may turn out, moreover, that a collective editorial board is not practically feasible. In that case, we should give up the experiment; but we must first try it, and if the idea proves to be utopian, then we should be willing to fail as utopians.

b. This review should not be a review, that is, a panorama of the cultural, literary, and political activities of the day. It should focus on a very limited number of topics. In other words, we should not give the impression that we are interested in, and curious about, everything. Or, to put it another way, we should be interested only in the totality, in subjects where everything is at stake; our interest, our passion, should always be focused on the whole. But we should also ask ourselves whether things "outside" the totality are not of fundamental interest as well.

c. Accordingly, this review will not be a cultural review: our interest in literature, for example, is not a cultural interest. When we write, we do not write to enrich the general culture. What matters to us is a search for the truth or, rather, a certain just demand, perhaps for justice, for which literary expression, owing to its central interest and unique relationship to language, is essential.

d. In practical terms, this means that each issue should be organized around the lead article and that great importance should be attached to tone, style, and form; less important material (such as reader's reports, and so on) should be excluded.

II

1. A review can be the expression of a doctrine that is already formulated or of a group that is already in existence (Surrealism). Or it may help to shape latent tendencies whose contours remain vague. Or, finally, it may be a collective, creative effort to go beyond what exists, to search in new directions. Participants may find the mere existence of the review an incentive to pursue their own thinking a little further than they might otherwise have, or to take a slightly different tack. Each participant assumes responsibility for statements he did not write, for a quest that is no longer solely his own, and for knowledge that does not originate with himself. A collective review makes such things possible. The editors of such a review occupy a status intermediate between author and reader. Hence, a great deal of joint preparation is required. And

since unanimity is neither possible nor desirable, discussion and dialogue should be carried on within the pages of the review itself.

2. The need for dialogue and discussion is even greater in the project currently under discussion, for this is to be, in a fundamental sense, an international review: not just multinational or universal in the abstract sense that boils all issues down to a vague and empty uniformity, but truly international, in the sense of being a joint consideration of literary, philosophical, political, and social issues as they occur in specific linguistic and national contexts. This assumes that each participant is willing to give up the exclusive right to define and examine his own issues and to recognize that these are also issues for everyone else, hence amenable to joint scrutiny. The review should therefore be not just a place for intellectual exchange but also a space for questions, discussion, and dialogue.

3. Nevertheless, everyone involved must agree from the outset to certain basic principles:

Concerning the *political outlook:* On the one hand, we must question everything. We must ask fundamental questions about the age, and we must try to restore the full strength and dignity of the word *question* by being willing to question even the value of *questioning.*

In questioning everything, however, we must avoid being merely frivolous or skeptical on the grounds that history offers no assurances, no definite answers. For example, whatever individual attitudes we may take toward Marxism, the fact remains that we are in intimate contact with Marxism and are, in a sense, dependent on it, if only as an object of criticism. The necessity, *at some point,* to envision all problems as if they were purely political problems while *at the same time* regarding them as not purely political but as raising other issues as well comes from Marxism and leads us to posit Marxism dialectically without thereby being condemned to repeat the Marxist dialectic.

4. The requirements of literature and the arts: literature and the arts may very well be subjected to (for example) a Marxist form of critique. This is completely acceptable and even necessary, provided that the critique is new and eschews tired commonplaces. But we must also grant that literature, currently at any rate, constitutes not only a distinctive form of experience but a fundamental one, which questions everything, including itself and the dialectic. For while it is true that the dialectic can and should embrace literature and incorporate it as part of its process, it is also true that the literary mode of expression eludes the dialectic and is not subordinate to it. Literature represents a distinctive kind of power, a kind of power perhaps not predicated upon possibility (and the dialectic has to do only with that which is possible): art is endless challenge, challenge to itself and challenge to other forms of power, in the sense not of mere anarchy but of an unfettered search for the distinctive form of power that art and literature represent (power without power).

Stated very briefly and schematically, literature can thus be viewed as:

- affirmation of works: the movement toward the work is essentially enigmatic;

- a search for itself, an experience that should not be limited in anyway or subjected to dogmatic restrictions, since it is a creative form of protest, satisfying itself through the force of creation alone;

- a search for a way of searching in which something other than literature might be at stake. (Literature, even so-called pure literature, is *more* than literature. Why? More in what sense? Why doesn't literature seek to fulfill itself through the indispensable illusion of being more than just literature, as the assertion of an extraliterary truth?)

5. This suggests that there is an irreducible difference or even a clash between political responsibility, which is at once global and concrete (accepting Marxism as definitive of truth and the dialectic as a method of discovering it), and literary responsibility (which is a response to a demand that can take shape only in and through literature).

This clash need not be resolved at the outset. It is a given; it exists as a problem, not a frivolous problem but one to be wrestled with, and all the more difficult to resolve owing to the fact that each of its discordant terms engages us absolutely, as in a sense does the disparity between them.

6. Glimmers of a solution do exist, however: one of the tasks of the review should be to look into them.

III

There should be no division between the critical and anthological sections of the review, because general critical knowledge should seem as essential as the literary pieces and selections; the latter can play an implicit critical role (though they must never be used as mere illustration), and vice versa.

Intellectual Developments
I think that an important role should be played by a column or essay prepared jointly by the members of each national editorial board with the help of information provided by foreign editorial boards, the purpose of which will be to give some idea of recent intellectual developments. Implicitly or explicitly, this column should respond, in a very free-form fashion, to needs of various kinds. First, it should serve as a sort of critical news service by providing a rundown of books published in other countries: in France, it should feature primarily books translated from Italian, German, and English, with the French portion curtailed or incorporated into the text for comparative purposes (since the weekly magazines and other reviews already cover French output). Second, the column should also, perhaps primarily, focus on a particular intellectual event, be

it philsosphical or poetic or sociological (I have in mind discussion of such things as publishing trends, journal articles, and so on).

Of course, the column may also deal with the other arts. However, when it comes to music, painting, and so on, I think it is more important to publish occasional in-depth studies of issues that may or may not be related to contemporary developments.

There should also be critical reviews of French and foreign books that seem worthy of individual consideration, apart from the survey of current developments. In the context of the "course of events column," works are treated as part of what's happening, as harbingers of things to come. In the criticism section, however, they are treated simply as themselves.

World Developments

A similar column, different in style but also quite free in form, should be reserved for *short* texts of critical interest contributing to a dialogue on political changes and other current world developments. Today, for example, one might want to include reflections by *writers* on Yuri Gagarin's adventure in space: what does it mean, what about Khrushchev's use of the word "fatherland," the first words spoken in space, and so on?

I V

Memorandum on "The Course of Events"

For the sake of our friends abroad, we need a precise summary of the points we have agreed on concerning the *purpose* and *structure* of "The Course of Events." Again, two points bear emphasizing:

1. The purpose of the review is to lay the groundwork that will enable the writer to *express* the "world" and everything that takes place in the world, but as a writer and in a writer's perspective, the writer's only responsibility being to tell the truth as writer. This type of responsibility is quite different from (though no less essential than) the responsibility that had such a powerful impact on the relationship between literature and public life after 1945, a responsibility to which the simplistic label "Sartrian commitment" has been attached. It follows from this that the review can take only an indirect and not a direct interest in political reality. The search for the "indirect" is one of our major tasks, where of course the term "indirect" refers to criticism that is not simply allusive or elliptical but more radical, in the sense of aiming to uncover the hidden significance of the "root" (for example, the *Spiegel* affair interests us not because it led to a government crisis or because it exposed government meddling in the courts but for the many other things it revealed: the myth of military secrecy, the need to tell the *whole* truth regardless of the consequences, writers' claims to authority and responsibility, and so on).[1]

2. The meaning of the title "The Course of Events" should be made clear by the *structure* and *form* of the column.

    a. The text of the column should be dispersed throughout each issue, which should begin and end with sections of it. Since the column will be interrupted wherever another type of text is inserted, it should be identified by some distinctive characteristic. We therefore propose that each text that is part of this column should be *numbered*. The series of numbers will then indicate that each segment is to be regarded as part of a "series" of related texts. In this way the column will be seen to possess "disrupted continuity."

    b. The column should be a place for experimenting with the *short form* (as the term is understood in contemporary music). By this we mean not only that each text should be brief (from one-half to three or four pages in length) but also that it should be regarded as a *fragment*, not necessarily containing its entire meaning in itself but rather being open to a broader meaning as yet unstated, perhaps even acknowledging the inevitability of a certain essential *discontinuity*. Within this very difficult experimental framework of the "short form," each writer will deal with whatever seems important to him in what is happening (or not happening): poetic, philosophical, and political issues raised by contemporary intellectual, scientific, and other developments, whether invisible to most observers or obvious to all, and taken both from books and daily life.

    c. The structure of this column should be such that it can accommodate, in addition to these "fragments" or commentaries, other texts printed in a different typeface and serving as a sort of *signpost*: for example quotations (such as Aby Warburg, *Der liebe Gott steckt im Detail*, or Theaetetus, "Via a thousand routes and without moving a step, always return to the same point"); aphorisms (of thought rather than style); and, above all, "news items" written in a very sober style and intended to provide not information but meaning—a sort of ephemeris consisting of those rare phenomena that describe the "course of events."

We take upon ourselves the responsibility of choosing which events to include, and because any such choice inevitably reflects a particular view of the world, our choice itself will carry meaning (for example, the *Spiegel* affair counts as an event but the recent French elections do not; the censoring of certain books in France would also count, but literary prizes would not). Each editorial board should therefore prepare a series of "short news items" to be discussed and agreed upon at our meetings. This will be an important function, since we will be taking it upon ourselves to counter overt, official history with the rudiments of a truer, more secret history, and since we will in effect be using stark actuality as commentary and even reinforcing its starkness by drafting these items in a rather blunt (and consciously tendentious) style. To achieve our goal, we will need the active cooperation of our correspondents in the Eastern bloc and English- and Spanish-speaking countries.

THE COURSE OF EVENTS

On Translation

1. The translator will in a sense be the real writer of the review. Hence, the problem of translation should be raised in the very first issues. The danger is that the translator will unify disparate texts all too readily. Languages are never contemporary: how is this difference of historical level to be maintained in translation? There is also the problem of dialects: German literary language, and especially poetic language, is often dialectal, and in my view the problem of translating dialect has never been satisfactorily resolved. (Italian, too, is not as unified as French.) Leyris, Bonnefoy.[2] For the latter, the bad French translations of Shakespeare reflect an implicit metaphysical opposition.

2. Translation as an original form of literary activity. The translator is the secret master of linguistic difference: his task is not to abolish that difference but to use it, to alter his own tongue in such a way as to awaken it to what differences exist in the original. The translator is nostalgic: he senses in his own tongue the lack of possibilities of expression implicit in the source. French, for example, is rich by virtue of what it does not possess.

3. The example of Hölderlin, a man fascinated by the power of translation. His translations of *Antigone* and *Oedipus* are works on the edge of madness, deliberately intended not to bring the Greek text into German or to take the German language back to the Greek sources but to unify the two powers, West and East, in the simplicity of a pure, all-embracing tongue. Ultimately, translation is madness. (Perhaps Laplanche . . .).

The review will consist of fragments, not articles (the essay in search of a form). To simplify, one can say that there are four kinds of fragments: the fragment that is simply a dialectical moment of a larger whole; the concentrated, obscurely violent aphoristic form, which is already a fragment of a complex sort (etymologically, aphorism is the same as horizon, a horizon that sets a limit rather than opening the way to something beyond); the fragment linked to the mobility of the quest, to the peripatetic thought that fulfills itself in distinct statements, statements insistent upon their distinctness (Nietzsche); and the literature of the fragment, which sets itself apart from the whole, either because it believes that the whole has already been achieved (all literature is eschatological literature) or because, beyond those forms of language which express the whole (the voices of knowledge, labor, and salvation), it senses another form of language, which frees thought from being merely directed toward unity, in other words, a form of language which insists on an essential discontinuity. In this sense, all literature, however brief or infinite, is fragment if it points to a linguistic space in which the purpose and function of each moment is to render all other moments indeterminate, or else—and this is the other side of the coin—in which what is at stake is some affirmation incapable of being reduced to a unifying process.

(Of course the question of the fragment can also be approached in other ways, but I think it is essential, especially for this project. It is always the question of the review as form, as a quest for its proper form.)

This is a reflection on our projects: we are always talking about themes and questions, but are we sure that the "world" can be thematized? There may well be a profoundly athematic attitude, which we glimpse, for instance, when we refuse to talk about someone who is close to us, when we refuse to transform that person into a theme, an object of reflection, because we are willing only to speak to him, not about him. This accounts for the aversion we may feel to becoming issue-hunters and, even more, to forcing other writers to look upon the world as nothing more than a source of issues for the review. There is surely an element of violence in such an attitude, and even if one can feel justified in doing such violence to oneself, it cannot be imposed on others as the one true method.

Further thoughts. The "issues" in which the review is interested will differ: as to subject or theme; as to treatment of those themes; as to the way in which different texts may be assembled into a whole; but also as to the form or essence of the issues. What do I mean by difference of form or essence? There are, for example, questions that originate in an insignificant, barely noticed fact, which is then shown to have some important implication (transition from the implicit to the explicit). As a result, the implication threatens to overwhelm the fact. Thus, it seems to me that it is an essential feature of *the quotidian* that it eludes our grasp, evades us, and thus escapes into insignificance. It is uneventful; it has no subject. Therein lies its depth. In this sense the quotidian, too, may resist thematization. Other kinds of issues: some that are already widely discussed and accepted as important (for example, de-Stalinization). What shall we do about them? Should we refuse to take an interest in them as such? Should we approach them only indirectly, from an angle, in terms of some minor aspect, or should we dismiss them? Determination to cut things down to size. And finally, there are ultimate questions, questions that are not asked, that always remain off-limits, questions that one distorts by recasting them in some specific context. This is where new forms of questioning are developing in secret, as it were, as if there were forms of questioning that permit too many questions to be asked, more than the process of questioning has the power to sustain. The need to question may exceed the power to ask questions. Perhaps only solitary questioning, of the sort that expresses itself in literature as a literary work, can sustain such a need, the need to keep on questioning precisely where there are no more questions to be asked.

· The Conquest of space: reflection on "place." When "man" became "spaceman," what for a moment seemed crucial was the overcoming of the limits of place: in principle, one man existed where there was no horizon, in the absoluteness of an almost homogeneous space. This newly acquired freedom from place (however illusory it may have been), with its implicit alleviation of the human condition, continued and provisionally completed the work of technology, shaking sedentary civilizations, destroying human particularisms, and taking man beyond the utopia of childhood (if childhood is characterized by a desire to return to "place").

But no sooner had Gagarin seemingly transcended "place" than Khrushchev saluted him on behalf of earth, his "fatherland." Thus, the statesman saw the cosmonaut not as someone who challenged the very idea of "place" but as someone who honored "place" with his prestige.

a. The relation to the Outside was modified not radically but phenomenologically. Speech as sole relation with the former "place": the cosmonaut was obliged to speak, and to speak constantly. Technology is dangerous, to be sure, but not as dangerous as *genii loci*. There may perhaps be something to be said against the paganism in which anti-Christian thought deliberately takes refuge: Heideggerian paganism, the poetic paganism of *roots*. Truth is nomadic.

Boulez and Mallarmé, *Pli selon pli*. Boulez's lecture at Donaueschingen, in which he demonstrated the incompatibilities of music-poetry. It is on the basis of these incompatibilities that contact is possible. And Boulez believes that he has found the point of contact in architectonic, rhythmic verbal structures and their musical equivalents. All the difficulty lies in the word equivalents. This calls Ludwig Wittgenstein's problem to mind: each language has a structure about which one can say nothing in the language itself, but which can be treated in another language, which in turn has a structure that can be dealt with only in another language, and so on.

2. New treatment of the text in contemporary music.

3. The very difficult question of the relation between "modern" literature and the "modern" arts also arises. Is there any relation between them less superficial than the usual association of Einstein, Picasso, Joyce, and Schönberg?

· The myth of the scientist. Whenever Teilhard de Chardin ventures to make a controversial claim, he inevitably states that he is confining himself to the realm of scientific observation, and he does so, moreover, not in a presumptuous way but in all naiveté: "Speaking as a scientist . . ." When Charon repeats Chardin's view that there can be no "corpuscles" unless there is a psyche, he presents this hypothesis (already proposed by Nietzsche) as a *scientific discovery*. When does a scientist cease to be a scientist? Can one call cosmological models and unified theories scientific?

· Questions that can be taken from books: Claude Lévi-Strauss's *The Savage Mind*, Régine Pernoud's book about the bourgeoisie,[3] Jacques Ellul's book on propaganda, the book by Gilbert Durand on the anthropological structures of the imaginary, Frantz Fanon on violence.

· In the novel, the divine point of view conveniently replaced by the view of the police, who see and know everything (Chesterton, Orwell, Corrado Alvaro, Graham Greene, the new novel, Ollier, Robbe-Grillet, Uwe Johnson). Nowadays one tends to see not an enigma of the private soul but an enigma of public space. When everything is revealed, something still eludes our grasp.

· Has the possibility of total destruction changed the meaning of violence? What is the revolutionary significance of violence, in view of the constant danger that it may turn into total destruction? Is this question at the root of de-Stalinization?

· Study de-Stalinization from the standpoint of language. What changes has it brought about in political language? Some new terms have appeared: cult of personality, peaceful coexistence, Khrushchev's more concrete language. But has Soviet official language changed?

· The role of radio in Germany, with respect to the possibilities and temptations it offers to the German writer, the situation there being quite different from that in France and no doubt Italy as well. England, America?

· The decline of the myth of the unknown soldier, despite its persistence. The unknown soldier was the antihero, the obscure, unnoticed ghost who lived on in national memory as the "forgotten one." The memorial of nonmemory, the apotheosis of the nameless.

· Reflections on the idea and form of what is referred to as a "review." Several notes: a short historical study (perhaps there is something to be learned from the evolution of this form of publication in the various countries where it has a history); the Surrealist review, which was one of the movement's authentic creations; critique of all reviews. A collective publication but without real collective structure, or else a dog-

matic review, a doctrinal tool and weapon of combat, the organ of a
party or school but not a form of research. Periodical publication is
purely arbitrary. How is the spirit of idleness and freedom from worries about time to be introduced into a periodical? How can literary
texts, resistant to incorporation into any whole, any form of unity, be
arranged in the unit known as a review? Etc.

· Critical texts: the position of Ernst Bloch in contemporary German
thought. An unpublished text by Bloch.

· Cultural isolation in France and Italy.

· The structure of French publishing . . .

TRANSLATED BY ARTHUR GOLDHAMMER

NOTES

1 In October 1962, governmental action against the magazine *Der Spiegel*, accused of di-
vulging state secrets, launched a political crisis that was to turn into the most severe of
West Germany's history.

2 Pierre Leyris and poet Yves Bonnefoy were among the most active French translators of
English literary classics at the time.

3 Blanchot refers to a series of recent titles: Claude Lévi-Strauss, *La pensée sauvage* (Paris:
Plon, 1962), Régine Pernoud, *Histoire de la France bourgeoise*, 2 vols. (Paris: Seuil, 1960–
62), Jacques Ellul, *Propaganda*, translated by Konrad Kellen and Jean Lerner (New York:
Knopf, 1965), Gilbert Durand, *Les structures anthropologiques de l'imaginaire* (Paris:
Corti), Frantz Fanon, *Les damnés de la terre* (preface by Sartre) (Paris: Maspéro, 1961).

SITUATIONIST INTERNATIONAL

All the King's Men
1963

Communism, Marxist philosophers used to say, is the end of philosophy; it is philosophy (so to speak) "totaled," both destroyed and realized, both nowhere and everywhere: philosophy, overcome as a separate instance (books, libraries, academic departments, and so on), has become the world itself.

It might be said of the Situationists—who were rightly referred to as the first explosive aesthetic politics since Dada and Surrealism—that, halfway between the revolutionary committee ("these kinds of soviets or communication councils") *and the avant-garde chapel, they went pretty far in the poetic (aesthetic) hijacking of the Marxian philosophical apocalypse: Revolution is poetry, rather than philosophy, realized. Life must stop being elsewhere.*

The main target of Guy Debord's and the Situationists' interventions is the "society of spectacle," the ultimate state of serialized separation between individuals induced by the extension of the social division of labor, beyond the workplace, into the domain of "unspecialized" social and personal time. It imposes the consumer/producer division even on the cultural field. Culture has become the main engine for implementing and reproducing the social program of separation.

The Situationalists' first journal was called Potlatch *(1954–57). The reference to those legendary Northwest Indian ceremonies of collective challenge and destruction is by itself an indication that poetry would be realized (as opposed to reified) when, having overcome the discipline of the history of poetry, it would enter the undisciplined poetry of history. Poetry, an event in communication, occurs when the work is consumed (squandered, wasted away) on the altar of communality: communication understood in terms not of exchange value, but of use value, no longer a matter of transmitting a representation (from poet to cultivated poetophile) but of destroying separation (between producer and consumer, fused in the heat of*

Situationist International, "All the King's Men," from *Situationist International Anthology*, ed. and trans. Ken Knabb (Berkeley: Bureau of Public Secrets, 1981), p. 68–75, from *Internationale Situationiste* 8 (Jan. 1963).

the insurrectional collective moment). Poetry plus revolution "totals" commodity. Poetry realized is thus, at the same time, consummate poetry and poetry consummated, poetry as the unstoppable virus of the nonconsumable that threatens to deprogram (détourner) *all the marketing strategies of serialized consumerism.*

The problem of language is at the heart of all struggles between the forces striving to abolish present alienation and those striving to maintain it; it is inseparable from the entire terrain of those struggles. We live within language as within polluted air. In spite of what humorists think, words do not play. Nor do they make love, as Breton thought, except in dreams. Words *work*—on behalf of the dominant organization of life. And yet they are not completely automatized; unfortunately for the theoreticians of information, words are not in themselves "informationist"; they embody forces that can upset the most careful calculations. Words coexist with power in a relationship analogous to that which proletarians (in the modern as well as the classic sense of the term) have with power. Employed *almost* constantly, exploited full time for every sense and nonsense that can be squeezed out of them, they still remain in some sense fundamentally strange and foreign.

Power presents only the falsified, official sense of words; in a manner of speaking, it forces them to carry a pass, determines their place in the production process (where some of them conspicuously work overtime) and gives them their paycheck. Regarding the use of words, Lewis Carroll's Humpty Dumpty quite correctly observes, "The question is which is to be master— that's all." And he, a socially responsible employer in this respect, states that he pays overtime to those he employs excessively. We should also understand the phenomenon of the *insubordination of words*, their desertion, their open resistance, which is manifested in all modern writing (from Baudelaire to the Dadaists and Joyce), as a symptom of the general revolutionary crisis of the society.

Under the control of power, language always designates something other than authentic experience. It is precisely for this reason that a total contestation is possible. The organization of language has fallen into such confusion that the communication imposed by power is exposing itself as an imposture and a dupery. An embryonic cybernetic power is vainly trying to put language under the control of the machines it controls, in such a way that information would henceforth be the only possible communication. Even on this terrain, resistances are being manifested; electronic music could be seen as an attempt (obviously limited and ambiguous) to reverse the domination relation by diverting machines to the profit of language. But real opposition is much more general, much more radical. It denounces all unilateral "communication," whether in the old form of art or in the modern form of informationism. It calls for a communication that undermines all separate power. Wherever there is communication, there is no state.

Power lives off stolen goods. It creates nothing, it recuperates. If it created the meaning of words, there would be no poetry but only useful "information." Opposition would not be able to express itself in language; any refusal would be outside it, would be purely lettristic. What is poetry if not the revolutionary moment of language, inseparable as such from the revolutionary moments of history and from the history of personal life?

Power's stranglehold over language is similar to its stranglehold over the totality. Only a language that has been deprived of all immediate reference to the totality can serve as the basis for information. Information is the poetry of power, the counterpoetry of law and order, the mediated falsification of what exists. Conversely, poetry must be understood as immediate communication within reality and as real alteration of this reality. It is nothing other than liberated language, language recovering its richness, language that breaks its rigid significations and simultaneously embraces words, music, cries, gestures, painting, mathematics, facts, acts. Poetry thus depends on the greatest wealth of possibilities in living *and changing* life at a given stage of socioeconomic structure. Needless to say, this relationship of poetry to its material base is not a unilateral subordination, but an interaction.

Rediscovering poetry may become indistinguishable from reinventing revolution, as has been demonstrated by certain phases of the Mexican, Cuban, and Congolese revolutions. Outside the revolutionary periods when the masses become poets in action, the small circles of poetic adventure could be considered the only places where the totality of revolution subsists, as an unrealized but close-at-hand potentiality, like the shadow of an absent personage. What we are calling poetic adventure is difficult, dangerous and *never guaranteed* (it is, in fact, the aggregate of behaviors that are *almost impossible* in a given epoch). We can only be sure about what is no longer the poetic adventure of an era—its false, officially tolerated poetry. Thus, whereas Surrealism in the heyday of its assault against the oppressive order of culture and daily life could rightly define its arsenal as "poetry without poems if necessary," it is now a matter for the Situationist International of a poetry *necessarily* without poems. What we say about poetry has nothing to do with the retarded reactionaries of some neoversification, even one based on the least ancient of formal modernisms. Realizing poetry means nothing less than simultaneously and inseparably creating events and their language.

All in-group languages—those of informal groupings of young people; those which present avant-garde currents develop for their internal use as they grope to define themselves; those which in previous eras were conveyed by way of objective poetic production, such as *trobar clus* and *dolce stil nuovo*[1]—all these aim at and achieve a certain direct, transparent communication, mutual recognition, accord. But such attempts have been the work of small groups, isolated in various ways. The events and festivals they have created have had to remain within the most narrow limits. One of the problems of revolution is that of federating these kinds of soviets or *communication councils* in order to initiate a direct communication everywhere that will no longer have to resort to the enemy's communication network (that is, to the language of power) and will thus be able to transform the world according to its desire.

It is a matter not of putting poetry at the service of revolution but, rather, of putting revolution at the service of poetry. It is only in this way that the revolution does not betray its own project. We will not repeat the mistake of the Surrealists, who put themselves at the service of the revolution right when it had ceased to exist. Bound to the memory of a partial and rapidly crushed revolution, Surrealism rapidly became a reformism of the spectacle, a critique of a certain form of the reigning spectacle which was carried out from within the dominant organization of that spectacle. The Surrealists seem to have overlooked the fact that every internal improvement or modernization of the spectacle is translated by power into its own encoded language, to which it alone holds the key.

Every revolution has been born in poetry, has first of all been made with the force of poetry. This is a phenomenon that continues to escape theorists of revolution — indeed, it cannot be understood if one still clings to the old conception of revolution or of poetry — but has generally been sensed by counter-revolutionaries. Poetry, whenever it appears, frightens them; they do their best to get rid of it by means of every kind of exorcism, from auto-da-fé to pure stylistic research. The moment of real poetry, which has "all the time in the world before it," invariably wants to reorient the entire world and the entire future to its own ends. As long as it lasts its demands admit of no compromises. It brings back into play all the unsettled debts of history. Fourier and Pancho Villa, Lautréamont and the *dinamiteros* of the Asturias — whose successors are not inventing new forms of strikes — the sailors of Kronstadt and Kiel, and all those in the world who, with us or without us, are preparing to fight for a long revolution are equally the emissaries of new poetry.

Poetry is becoming more and more clearly the empty space, the antimatter, of consumer society, since it is not consumable (in terms of the modern criteria for a consumable object: an object, that is, of equivalent value for each of a mass of isolated passive consumers). Poetry is nothing when it is quoted, it can only be *detoured*, brought back into play. Otherwise, the study of the poetry of the past is nothing but an academic exercise. The history of poetry is only a way of running away from the poetry of history, if we understand by that phrase not the spectacular history of the rulers but, rather, the history of everyday life and its possible liberation; the history of each individual life and its realization.

We must leave no question as to the role of the "conservers" of old poetry, those who increase its dissemination while the state, for quite different reasons, eliminates illiteracy. These people are only a particular type of museum curator. A mass of poetry is naturally preserved in the world, but nowhere are there the places, the moments, or the people to revive it, communicate it, use it. And there never can be except by way of *détournement*, because the understanding of past poetry has changed through the loss as well as the acquisition of knowledge; and because any time that past poetry can be effectively rediscovered, its being placed in the context of particular events gives it a largely new meaning. But, above all, a situation in which poetry is possible must not restore any poetic failure of the past (such failure being the inverted remains of the history of poetry, transformed into success and poetic monument). Such a situation naturally moves toward the communication of, and the possible sovereignty of, *its own poetry*.

At the same time that poetic archaeology restores selections of past poetry, which are recited by specialists on LPs for the neoilliterate public created by the modern spectacle, the informationists are endeavoring to do away with all the "redundancies" of freedom in order to *simply transmit orders*. The theorists of automation are explicitly aiming at producing an automatic theoretical thought by clamping down on and eliminating the variables in life as well as in language. But bones keep turning up in their cheese! Translating machines, for example, which are beginning to ensure the planetary standardization of information along with the informationist revision of previous culture, are victims of their own preestablished programming, which inevitably misses any new meaning taken on by a word, as well as its past dialectical ambivalences. Thus, the life of language—which is bound up with every advance of theoretical comprehension ("Ideas improve; the meaning of words participates in the improvement")—is expelled from the machinist field of official information. But this also means that free thought can organize itself with a secrecy beyond the reach of informationist police techniques. The quest for unambiguous signals and instantaneous binary classification is so clearly linked with existing power that it calls for a similar critique. Even in their most delirious formulations, the informationist theorists are no more than clumsy precursors of the future they have chosen, which is the same brave new world that the dominant forces of the present society are working toward—the reinforcement of the cybernetic state. They are the vassals of all the lords of the technocratic feudalism that is now constituting itself. There is no innocence in their buffoonery; they are the king's jesters.

The choice between informationism and poetry no longer has anything to do with the poetry of the past, just as no variant of what the classical revolutionary movement has become can anymore, anywhere, be considered as part of a real alternative to the prevailing organization of life. The same judgment leads us to announce the total disappearance of poetry in the old forms in which it was produced and consumed, and to announce its return in effective and unexpected forms. Our era no longer has to *write out poetic orders;* it has to carry them out.

TRANSLATED BY KEN KNABB

NOTE

[1] *Trobar clus*: the hermetic poetics of early Provençal troubadours. *Dolce stil nuovo*: the thirteenth-century Italian school of amorous poetry (Dante, Cavalcanti).

MARGUERITE DURAS

20 May 1968: Description of the Birth of Students–Writers Action Committee 1968

In Paris, the student uprising of May '68 was marked by the proliferation of small, ephemeral, mostly self-authorizing groups. The Students–Writers Action Committee lasted four months, from May to September 1968.

*This text is a sort of internal report from one of its members, retelling the circumstances that gave the committee a sense of identity, after a majority of its initial members seceded to create a Writers Union (*Union des Écrivains*) — separating "writers from writers," as Duras says. Indeed, this secession originated from two diverging views of literature and, more specifically, from two diverging views of the relationship between literature and representation.*

The secessionists were self-proclaimed writers who, as individual producers of cultural goods, wanted their professional interests, their rights, and their names to be defended against publishers, the media, capitalism, and so on by a stronger union. Those who remained couldn't have cared less: they didn't join a revolutionary situation with royalties in mind. Following Maurice Blanchot's definition of literature as a type of writing that doesn't bestow any rights (beyond the right to death), they saw the committee as an opportunity to break with literature as usual.

The committee, far from representing individual writers (or representing writers as individuals), developed into an agency for the collective appropriation of individual texts, erasing any individual markers left on the speech acts it authorized. Its workings, inspired by a kind of literary ultrabolshevism, put in place what Duras describes as a quasi-sacrificial process — a revolutionary version of the death of the author. In this regard,

Marguerite Duras, "20 May 1968: Description of the Birth of Students–Writers Action Committee," in *Green Eyes*, trans. Carol Berko (New York: Columbia University Press, 1990), pp. 53–62, from "20 Mai 1968: Texte politique sur la naissance du comité étudiants–écrivains," in *Les Yeux verts* (Paris: Cahiers du cinéma, 1987), pp. 71–82.

the most significant detail of the piece is probably the absence of any proper names. Following this logic to the letter, Duras didn't even sign it when she first published it in Le Nouvel observateur.

Only once are there sixty of us. It's the 20th of May at the Sorbonne, in a room of the Philosophy Library. The matter at hand is the Constituent Assembly of the Students–Writers Action Committee. Fifteen are famous: writers, journalists, television commentators. Forty others, not writers, journalists, students, sociologists, sociologists.

Some resolutions pass by unanimous vote. A boycott of the ORTF [*Office de Radio et Télévision Française*] in particular.

There are numerous speeches. The ones most listened to are those of the television commentators. Most of the others are inaudible. Two presidents succeed each other. It proves useless to elect a third.

Several times it is proclaimed that "everyone must speak." In fact, six or seven manage to do so, including the television commentators and students. The students because they severely criticize the undesirable development of the assembly. The commentators because they are talking about Television.

No matter. Projects are outlined, often in detail. Committees are appointed. An administration is set up. A headquarters will be guaranteed.

The goodwill gushes, imposing its good intentions.

The subcommittees will never meet. Those who come forward in stunning spontaneity—to guarantee the headquarters and the administration—will return, some only very rarely, others never. No headquarters, no administration will be guaranteed.

Those who are the most voluble will be the least constant. For the most part they will be seen only once, this one time. The next day, the first drain occurs.

Out of sixty, twenty-five return. Not a single television commentator. Some sociologists, still. Writers too, not as famous as the day before. Students, yes. For the journalists, it's over.

The language is not as lofty. The discourse digresses.

An average is set in the course of several days: fifteen to twenty come every evening to the meeting of the Students–Writers Committee. They are not always the same ones. Except for three or four.

These make up the resources of the Students–Writers Action Committee. Starting from their concrete incumbency, at the agreed place, at the agreed time, the committee is constructed.

At the end of three days—the committee then emigrates to Censier [a branch of the University of Paris]—a second drain occurs. A certain number of writers, as a group, leave the committee, take over the Literary Society and, behind closed doors, found the Literary Union, which will take the writer firmly in hand, in the strictest sense of the word, and will at last ponder the writer's status, role, interests, and, still behind closed doors, the writer's wound: language.

This departure, the main one, separates writers from writers.

Although theoretical — out of about thirty, three or four would come to the committee — this departure plunges certain committee members into bewilderment for several hours. Except for the three or four and, soon, a few others.

For two weeks more, the same average as there was at the Sorbonne is set.

Around the three or four, who are now seven or eight, different comings and goings numerically keep the committee going every evening.

Two or three students come irregularly, as critics. Always very carefully listened to during this period. Then, less and less.

Sometimes someone comes whom we've never seen before; comes back eight days running, then never again.

Sometimes someone comes whom we've never seen before, and keeps coming back.

Sometimes someone comes whom we've never seen before — where does he think he's come? — reads the newspaper, and disappears forever.

Sometimes someone comes whom we've already seen, or seen again.

Sometimes someone comes whom we've never seen before, comes back a few days later, then at intervals less and less far apart, then, suddenly, stays.

Often it's a matter of a single visit. Someone comes, looks, sometimes listens, and disappears. Sometimes someone comes, offers a poem in manuscript or reads a poem. Takes off again for Switzerland. For Montreuil.

A month goes by. And already the absences are noticed: the committee is set.

In general, the same reasons make some flee and other stay.

The main reason is the composition of the committee. It is impervious to all analysis. Chance, at the intersections of streets, would accomplish almost the same thing. The newcomers, unable to label the "milieu" into which they've chanced and no more able to explain "why" these people are gathered together, flee.

The other reason — the effects of which are felt even sooner — is the very business of the committee.

Every day, for several hours, with a relentlessness that could pass for lunacy, the committee collectively develops texts. As a rule, the newcomer doesn't resist this more than twice.

Unconcerned with people leaving, the committee, tirelessly, continues its text development.

Two out of three times, the newspapers neglect these texts or put them in belatedly, as filler. What does the committee care. It goes on.

It's the hell of collective development that determines the daily selection — once Massa's gang is gone.

Endurance varies according to a mysterious criterion. Here one can therefore proceed only by empirical analysis. This is what can be said: not holding

out against this hell are the writers who one might have thought—
beforehand—wouldn't hold out. Holding out are those who one might have
thought—beforehand—would hold out.

The difference in the beginning, between those who stay and those who flee
quickly becomes a new difference, getting bigger all the time, between those
who have stayed and those who have fled.

Those who stay and those who flee use the same word to name the senseless
rehashing of the sessions as well as the uncommon endurance needed to hold
out.

—It's IMPOSSIBLE, each group says.

To repudiate a text is also to develop that text.

Such-or-such text that, if it were read somewhere else would bring agreement, is rejected here. The first impulse is to refuse, to refuse the text submitted
for judgment. The training for approval is such that once freedom is given
rein, the first thing it does is to REFUSE.

Naturally, it's the work of an INDIVIDUAL that is submitted to criticism
and collective development. Otherwise, collective development is illusory. Still
otherwise, meaningless.

At first reading: distrust is at its peak. Right away, the text is put on trial to
bring out—again and always—the irreducible isolation of the thought process. Its author, unrecognized, is objectively punished precisely for his irresponsibility. The "fruit of his womb" is massacred.

At second reading: distrust yields. Third reading. Fifth reading. Behold, the
INDIVIDUAL having served his sentence, the community gets down to
work.

Put through the mill, tossed out, ridiculed, repudiated, GONE, a text comes
back to life. And often in a form scarcely different from its initial one.

Thus, with just a grammatical change, this text becomes COMMUNAL. It
has gone through the tunnel. Comes out. Takes wing.

—I'm bored here, a writer declares.

We don't see him again. But his leaving is embarrassing. Though predictable, his impatience redefines him in our eyes. We realize afterward, on reading what he has written, that in fact all he has done is to move safe and sound
from the old to the new.

The texts coming out of the Students–Writers Committee are almost always models of precision. Yes. They bear no trace of the enormous difficulty of
their birth.

This difficulty is experienced as the main attraction of the business of collective development. It defines collective development at its very core.

It is the effect of each one's resistance to the activity of the group. Of each
one's bad faith in the face of the objectivity of the group. Of each one's subjectivity in the face of the objectivity of the group. It is as old as the world.

The difficulty of each one in SURVIVING is similar in kind to this general difficulty. Here each one's difficulty is something that is shared. It becomes the difficulty of each and every one to make their survival a communal affair.

The committee is IMPOSSIBLE TO LIVE WITH. This is the way it is made. The galley has been scudding ahead for four months. *We* are in the engine room. Every kind of sabotage—at night—has been tried. To no effect.

Nothing holds us together but refusal. Delinquents of class society, but alive, unclassifiable but unbreakable, we refuse. We push our refusal to the point of refusing to be assimilated into the political groups that claim to refuse what we refuse. We refuse the refusal programmed by the institutions of the opposition. We refuse that our refusal, tied up and packaged, bear a trademark. And that its vital wellspring dry up, and that its course be turned back.

The Students–Writers Committee has no militant organizational or party policy. None would have been able to hold out.

If the request is made—and it regularly is—to clearly state *just once* the ideas of each individual, this request is always rejected by the majority. There follows the relief of having escaped some danger. We say that we refuse to be divided by theory, the poison of the clear idea. We don't go so far as to say what would seem to be the truth: what we have built in common is less the stock of ideas we have acquired than the distrust we have for them.

Our refusal also covers the refusal to be divided by idiosyncrasies.

From the first day, our wariness was founded not only on the score of ideas but on one's private life, on a reference to individuality. And that happened naturally. Only insult takes its inspiration from "information," from the private trait.

—You who have. You who are.

Only insult, the better to hit home, resorts to the regressive value of having something on someone.

As a rule, all the committee members have the familiar instinct for keeping silent about their reasons for being there instead of somewhere else.

Furthermore, only a slow psychoanalytic exploration could probably clarify—and feebly—the ins and outs of these reasons. The common denominator—and this for all Action Committees—would be *unbridled refusal*, whether conscious or not.

Everyone, through constant effort, preserves the FUNDAMENTAL COMMON OPACITY in which the committee is immersed.

Often we don't do anything. We say:

I shall point out to you that we're not doing anything.

Habit.

The problem is somewhere else.

It's precisely in these periods when nothing is going on that the committee *exists* in the most incontestable way. Why would one be compelled to do something? And risk his secret coming to the surface of his life, *to exist*.

Every day we are caught in the personal paradox of being drawn back to this hellish assemblage AMONG A THOUSAND POSSIBLE ALTERNA-TIVES, like this very one we would have chosen.

This assemblage has the effect on each and every one of us of an ATTRAC-TIVE REPULSION. We are constantly poised between the movement of rejecting it and that of coming back to it. It offers and denies itself at the same time. Its form is in process.

What is it all about? Maybe about something else entirely? Maybe.

We are the anticell. Around us there are only others like us, other action committees. No orders. No suggested model, no militants. Or else we refuse. Or else we swallow the poison. We function. We connect. No authoritative language here, no "line." Here, we don't *classify* anyone from the beginning. Here, we have disorder.

Lacking suitable references, let's continue by analogy: the committee has the inconsistency of dreams. It has the importance of dreams. Like the dream, it is striking. And it is an everyday affair.

One can dream of a love without an object. The bond that connects us is chance.

For anyone coming from the outside, the apparent absence of some sort of affinity among its members *already* makes it resemble a society, but *still* a particular kind of society: COMICAL, OF CRAZIES.

— You are crazy, repeatedly comes out of the mouth of people who observe us.

We do not respond.

— You show a political unrealism that is beyond all limits.

Again habit. Unreality is still the crime. We will have to wait a hundred years.

We have held out against the last barricades, against the elections, against the summer, against the students dispersing, against their coming back, against the closing of the faculties, against their reopening, against the violent quarrels, against the worst insults. For two months no one has deserted us.

These proofs seem to us sufficient. We are eternal.

We are the prehistory of the future. We are that effort. That precondition for the latter to become possible. We are at the beginning of the TRANSI-TION. We are that effort.

We must never have had a profoundly alienating social existence. Otherwise we would not have held out. The ones who fled—in a word as in a thousand—were already firmly ensconced in the system. They can always say the contrary. To no avail.

No one is ever satisfied with the way the sessions develop. As a rule, it is said that problems of detail take too much time. But what kind of general problems ought to replace them is only rarely defined.

A remarkable consequence of our endurance begins to be felt. Every meeting becomes a prelude to the next one. In such a way that the newcomer has a hard time, presently, in following what we are saying, in understanding *what is happening* at the moment, and what is the *object* of our concerns. Our sessions, even spread out over time, no longer circumscribe our connection. The connection extends beyond them. We become incomprehensible to those who haven't joined us in time. They get things wrong.

—It's deplorable, *you are wasting time*. This is just the moment when you have to sign the texts, use your names.

Habit. The inner work that is done here is not counted in the evaluation. We are progressing, together, toward a rigorous freedom.

Those who flee with no regrets leave us, let's admit it, *already* with no regrets, on our side.

This recruitment, starting with each one's intention to be interchangeable, this enhancement of depersonalization, seems to us to be the only revolutionary stance. It goes with the enhancement of the person separated from his persona.

We have decided, as a majority, to publish a bulletin that will, we hope, reflect the experience.

We don't know if the committee will hold out against this test.

N.B.: The above text was rejected by the Students–Writers Action Committee. It was judged too "personal," "literary," "malicious," "false." The breaking up of the Students–Writers Action Committee originated in this rejection. L'Observateur— several years ago—published a part of it as well as passages by Maurice Blanchot and by Dionys Mascolo which were also supposed to appear in the Bulletin of the Committee. Those two signatures alone were mentioned, mine was omitted.

TRANSLATED BY CAROL BERKO

ROLAND BARTHES

Writing the Event
1968

In the academic year 1966–67, Roland Barthes devoted his seminar at the Ecole des Hautes Etudes to the structural analysis of historical discourse. What, he asked, distinguishes a page written by a historian from one written by a novelist? Valéry used to say that the ultimate message of a page of literature is I am a page of literature. *Similarly, according to Barthes, the ultimate signified of a page of historiography would be:* this is real, this happened for real, I am not inventing—*in other words,* I am not a page of literature. *One recognizes a page of history because it displays the signs of reality, exactly the same way the other bears the signs of literature. These discrete markers, the catalysts of what Barthes called a "reality effect," allow the reader to orient himself and recognize he is reading a historiographical narrative and not a fictional one. But reality, here, owes nothing to the referent; it is semiologically and rhetorically induced; produced, as a signified, independently from any type of actual, factual, extratextual support or documentation. Generated by a series of signals indicating* this happened, *it is thus a signified that tries to pass for a referent.*

While Barthes was meditating on this ultimate structuralist dereferentialization of discourse, a totally different type of reality effect was erupting in the streets of Paris. History shifted sides and unexpectedly broke in on the other flank of discourse; ignoring the arcane distinctions between referent and signifier, it took the floor and started speaking.

When May '68 broke out, what is often referred to as a linguistic turn was itself taking a turn (revolution in the revolution) away from Saussurian structural analysis and toward the performative.[1] In many regards, the events of May served as a background for a series of wild and festive experiments (travaux pratiques) in applied linguistics, a storming of the codes, a revolution of the politics of language as well as the language of politics.

Roland Barthes, "Writing the Event" in *The Rustle of Language*, trans. Richard Howard (New York: Hill and Wang), pp. 149–54, from "L'Ecriture de l'événement", in *Le Bruissement de la langue* (Paris: Seuil, 1984), pp. 175–81. First published in *Communications* 12 (Nov. 1968).

To describe the event implies that the event has been written. How can an event be written? What can it mean to say "writing the event"? The event of May '68 seems to have been written in three fashions, three writings, whose polygraphic conjunction forms, perhaps, its historical originality.

I. SPEECH

Every national shock produces a sudden flowering of written commentary (press, books). This is not what I want to speak of here. The spoken words of May '68 had original aspects, which must be emphasized.

1. Radiophonic speech (that of the "peripheral" stations) clung to the event, as it was occurring, in a breathless, dramatic fashion, imposing the notion that knowledge of present reality is no longer the business of print but of the spoken word. "Hot" history, history in the course of being made, is an auditive history,[1] and hearing becomes again what it was in the Middle Ages: not only the first of the senses (ahead of touch and sight), but the sense that establishes knowledge (as, for Luther, it established the Christian faith). Nor is this all. The (reporter's) informative word was so closely involved with the event, with the very opacity of its present, as to become its immediate and consubstantial meaning, its way of acceding to an instantaneous intelligibility; this means that in terms of Western culture, where nothing can be perceived without meaning, it was the event itself. The age-old distance between act and discourse, event and testimony, was reduced; a new dimension of history appeared, immediately linked to its discourse, whereas all historical "science" had the task to acknowledge this distance, in order to govern it. Not only did radiophonic speech inform the participants as to the very extension of their action (a few yards away from them), so that the transistor became the bodily appendage, the auditory prosthesis, the new science-fiction organ of certain demonstrators, but even, by the compression of time, by the immediate resonance of the act, it inflected, modified the event; in short, wrote it—fusion of the sign and its hearing, reversibility of writing and reading which is sought elsewhere, by that revolution in writing which modernity is attempting to achieve.

2. The relations of force between the different groups and parties engaged in the crisis were essentially *spoken*, in the sense that the tactical or dialectical displacement of these relations during the days of May occurred *through* and *by* (confusion of the means and of the cause which marks language) the communiqué, the press conference, the declaration, the speech. Not only did the crisis have its language, but in fact the crisis *was* language: it is speech that, in a sense, molded history, made it exist like a network of traces, an operative writing, displacing (it is only stale prejudice that considers speech an illusory activity,

noisy and futile, and set in opposition to actions); the "spoken" nature of the crisis is all the more visible in that it has had, strictly speaking, no murderous, irremediable effect (speech is what can be "corrected"; its rigorous antonym, to the point of defining it, can only be death).[2]

3. The students' speech so completely overflowed, pouring out everywhere, written everywhere, that one might define superficially—but also, perhaps, essentially—the university revolt as a *Taking of Speech* (as we say *Taking of the Bastille*). It seems, in retrospect, that the student was a being frustrated of speech; frustrated but not deprived—by class origin, by vague cultural practice, the student has the use of language; language is not unknown to him, he is not (or is no longer) afraid of it; the problem was to assume its power, its active use. Hence, by a paradox that is only apparent, just when the students' speech made its claims solely in terms of content, it actually involved a profoundly ludic aspect; the student had begun to wield speech as an activity, a free labor, and not, despite appearances, as a simple instrument. This activity took different forms, which correspond perhaps to phases of the student movement throughout the crisis.

  a. "Wild" speech, based on "invention," consequently encountering quite naturally the "finds" of form, rhetorical shortcuts, the delights of formula, in short *felicity of expression*; very close to writing, this discourse (which affected public opinion intensely) logically assumed the form of *inscription*; its natural dimension was the wall, fundamental site of collective writing.

  b. "Missionary" speech, conceived in a purely instrumental fashion, intended to transport "elsewhere" (to factory gates, to beaches, into the street, and so on) the stereotypes of political culture.

  c. "Functionalist" speech, conveying the reform projects, assigning to the university a social function, here political, there economic, and thereby rediscovering some of the watchwords of a previous technocracy ("adaptation of teaching to society's needs," "collectivization of research," primacy of the "result," prestige of the "interdisciplinary," "autonomy," "participation," and so on).

"Wild" speech was quite rapidly eliminated, embalmed in the harmless folds of (Surrealist) "literature" and the illusions of "spontaneity"; as writing, it could only be useless (until it became intolerable) to any form of power, whether possessed or claimed; the other two kinds remain mixed: a mixture that rather nicely reproduces the political ambiguity of the student movement itself, threatened, in its historical and social situation, by the dream of a "social technocracy."

2. Symbol

There was no lack of symbols in this crisis, as was often remarked; they were produced and consumed with great energy; and, above all, a striking phenomenon, they were *sustained* by a general, shared willingness. The paradigm of the three flags (red/black/tricolor), with its pertinent associations of terms (red and black against tricolor, red and tricolor against black), was "spoken" (flags raised, brandished, taken down, invoked, and so on) by everyone, or just about: a fine agreement, if not as to the symbols, at least as to the symbolic system itself (which, *as such,* should be the final target of a Western revolution). The same symbolic fate for the barricade: itself the symbol of revolutionary Paris, and itself a significant site of an entire network of other symbols. Complete emblem, the barricade made it possible to irritate and unmask other symbols; that of property, for example, henceforth lodged, for the French, in the fact that it appeared much more in the car than in the house. Other symbols were mobilized: monument (Bourse, Odéon), demonstration, occupation, garment, and of course language, in its most coded (symbolic, ritual[3]) aspects. This inventory of symbols should be made; not so much because it is likely to produce a very eloquent list (this is improbable, despite or because of the "spontaneity" that presided over their liberation), but because the symbolic system under which an event functions is closely linked to the degree of this event's integration within the society of which it is both the expression and the violation: a symbolic field is not only a junction (or an antagonism) of symbols; it is also formed by a homogeneous set of rules, a commonly acknowledged recourse to these rules. A kind of almost unanimous adherence to one and the same symbolic discourse seems to have finally marked partisans and adversaries of the contestation: almost all played the same symbolic game.[4]

3. Violence

Violence, which in modern mythology is linked, as if it followed quite naturally, with spontaneity and effectiveness—violence, symbolized here concretely, then verbally, by "the street," site of released speech, of free contact, counterintellectual space, opposition of the immediate to the possible ruses of all mediation—violence is a writing: it is (a Derridian theme) the trace in its profoundest gesture. Writing (if we no longer identify it with style or with literature) is itself violent. It is, in fact, the violence of writing that separates it from speech, reveals the force of inscription in it, the weight of an irreversible trace. Indeed, this writing of violence (an eminently collective writing) possesses a code; however one decides to account for it, tactical or psychoanalytic, violence implies a language of violence, that is, of signs (operations or drives) repeated, combined into figures (actions or complexes), in short, a system. Let us take advantage of this to repeat that the presence (or the postulation) of a code does not intellectualize the event (contrary to what anti-intellectualist mythology constantly states): the intelligible is not the intellectual.

Such, at first glance, are the orientations that a description of the traces which constitute the event might take. Yet such a description risks being inert if we do not attach it, from the start, to two postulates whose bearing is still polemical.

The first consists in rigorously separating, according to Derrida's proposition, the concepts of speech and of writing. Speech is not only what is actually spoken but also what is transcribed (or rather transliterated) from oral expression, and it can very well be printed (or mimeographed); linked to the body, to the person, to the will-to-seize, it is the very voice of any "revendication," but not necessarily of the revolution. Writing is integrally "what is to be invented," the dizzying break with the old symbolic system, the mutation of a whole range of language. Which is to say, on the one hand, that writing (as we understand it here, which has nothing to do with "style" or even literature) is not at all a bourgeois phenomenon (what this class elaborated was, in fact, printed speech), and, on the other, that the present event can only furnish marginal fragments of writing, which as we saw were not necessarily printed; we will regard as suspect any eviction of writing, any systematic primacy of speech, because, whatever the revolutionary alibi, both tend to *preserve* the old symbolic system and refuse to link its revolution to that of society.

The second postulate consists in not expecting written description to afford a "decoding." Considering the event from the viewpoint of whatever symbolic mutation it can imply means, first of all, breaking as much as possible (this is not easy, it requires the sort of continuous labor begun in various quarters, it must be recalled, some years ago) with the system of meaning which the event, if it seeks to be revolutionary, must call into question. The critical aspect of the old system is *interpretation*, that is, the operation by which one assigns to a set of confused or even contradictory appearances a unitary structure, a deep meaning, a "veritable" explanation. Hence, interpretation must gradually give way to a new discourse, whose goal is not the revelation of a unique and "true" structure but the establishment of an interplay of multiple structures: an establishment itself *written*, that is, uncoupled from the truth of speech, more precisely, it is the relations which organize these concomitant structures, subject to still unknown rules, which must constitute the object of a new theory.

TRANSLATED BY RICHARD HOWARD

INTRODUCTORY NOTE

[1] Barthes, "Recherches sur le discours de l'histoire (1966–1967)" in *Oeuvres complètes* (Paris: Seuil, 1994) vol. 2, p. 452.

NOTES

[1] One recalls streets filled with motionless people seeing nothing, looking at nothing, their eyes down, but their ears glued to transistor radios, thus representing a new human anatomy.

[2] The insistence with which it was repeated, on either side, that, whatever happens, *afterward* can no longer be like *before* doubtless translates, negatively, the fear (or the hope) that in fact *afterward* would become *before*: the event being speech, it can, mythically, cross itself out.

[3] For instance: lexicon of revolutionary work ("committees," "commissions," "motions," "points of order," and so on), rituals of communication (second-person-singular forms, first names, and so on).

[4] The most important aspect of this inventory would ultimately be to discover how each group played or did not play the symbolic game: rejection of the (red or black) flag, refusal of the barricade, and on.

HÉLÈNE CIXOUS

The Laugh of the Medusa
1975

The Homeric episode of Ulysses' encounter with the Sirens carried a mes-
sage in favor of sublimation: it sent a warning against the perils incurred by
the soul during its earthly voyage, exposed as it is to being diverted by the
sensual temptations represented by the Sirens and, in so doing, forgetting its
higher destination in the service of the Muses. Thus, the narrative promotes
the classical ideal of a culture conceived as the safekeeping (under the pro-
tection of the Muses) of a soul separated from a body prone to the Sirens'
seduction.

Cixous completely rewrites the episode—"for the Sirens," she writes,
"were men." In her version, the distinction between Muses and Sirens has
become irrelevant: the Sirens are now the voice of logocentrism and, as
such, preach the gospel of disembodiment—phallic and phonic—trying to
convince the (male or female) traveller that s/he should write not with his
or her body but with his or her soul, that s/he should renounce his or her
body in order to write.

For, she argues, the very first victim of the logocentric sublimation is the
body. Homer's (female) Sirens were (falsely) liberating. Cixous's (male)
ones are truly repressive. If Ulysses were to cede to Homer's Sirens, he
would risk losing his soul. If Cixous's Ulysses were to succumb to her Sirens,
he or she would risk losing his or her body. "Feminine writing" is intended
to defeat them. The phrase, indeed, emphasizes an essential affinity between
writing, body, and femininity: writing, when associated with a body con-
ceived as a subversive, multicentered, signifying disseminator, produces a
"femininity effect."

Hélène Cixous, "The Laugh of the Medusa," trans. Keith Cohen and Paula Cohen, in
Elaine Marks and Isabelle de Courtivron, eds., *New French Feminisms* (New York:
Schocken, 1981), pp. 245–51, from "Le Rire de la méduse," *L'Arc* 1975, pp. 39–54.

I mean it when I speak of male writing. I maintain unequivocally that there is such a thing as *marked* writing; that, until now, far more extensively and repressively than is ever suspected or admitted, writing has been run by a libidinal and cultural—hence political, typically masculine—economy; that this is a locus where the repression of women has been perpetuated, over and over, more or less consciously, and in a manner that's frightening since it's often hidden or adorned with mystifying charms of fiction; that this locus has grossly exaggerated all the signs of sexual opposition (and not sexual difference), where woman has never *her* turn to speak—this being all the more serious and unpardonable in that writing is precisely *the very possibility of change*, the space that can serve as a springboard for subversive thought, the precursory movement of a transformation of social and cultural structures.

Nearly the entire history of writing is confounded with the history of reason, of which it is at once the effect, the support, and one of the privileged alibis. It has been one with the phallocentric tradition. It is indeed that same self-admiring, self-stimulating, self-congratulatory phallocentrism.

With some exceptions, for there have been failures—and if it weren't for them, I wouldn't be writing (I-woman, escapee)—in that enormous machine that has been operating and turning out its "truth" for centuries. There have been poets who would go to any lengths to slip something by at odds with tradition—men capable of loving love and hence capable of loving others and of wanting them, of imagining the woman who would hold out against oppression and constitute herself as a superb, equal, hence "impossible" subject, untenable in a real social framework. Such a woman the poet could desire only by breaking the codes that negate her. Her appearance would necessarily bring on, if not revolution—for the bastion was supposed to be immutable—at least harrowing explosions. At times, it is in the fissure caused by an earthquake, through that radical mutation of things brought on by a material upheaval when every structure is for a moment thrown off balance and an ephemeral wilderness sweeps order away, that the poet slips something by, for a brief span, of woman. Thus did Heinrich von Kleist expend himself in his yearning for the existence of sister-lovers, maternal daughters, mother-sisters, who never hung their heads in shame. Once the palace of magistrates is restored, it's time to pay—immediate bloody death to the uncontrollable elements.

But only the poets—not the novelists, allies of representationalism. Because poetry involves gaining strength through the unconscious and because the unconscious, that other limitless country, is the place where the repressed manages to survive: women, or as E.T.A. Hoffmann would say, *fairies*.

She must write her self, because this is the invention of a *new insurgent* writing that, when the moment of her liberation has come, will allow her to carry out the indispensable ruptures and transformations in her history, first at two levels that cannot be separated.

First: individually. By writing her self, woman will return to the body that has been more than confiscated from her, has been turned into the uncanny stranger on display—the ailing or dead figure, which so often turns out to be the nasty companion, the cause and location of inhibitions. Censor the body and you censor breath and speech at the same time.

Write your self. Your body must be heard. Only then will the immense resources of the unconscious spring forth. Our oil will spread, throughout the world, without dollars—black or gold—nonassessed values that will change the rules of the old game.

To write. An act that will not only "realize" the decensored relation of woman to her sexuality, to her womanly being, giving her access to her native strength; it will give her back her goods, her pleasures, her organs, her immense bodily territories which have been kept under seal; it will tear her away from the superegoized structure in which she has always occupied the place reserved for the guilty (guilty of everything, guilty at every turn: for having desires, for not having any; for being frigid, for being "too hot"; for not being both at once; for being too motherly and not enough; for having children and for not having any; for nursing and for not nursing . . .)—tear her away by means of this quest, this analysis and illumination, this emancipation of the marvelous text of her self that she must urgently learn to speak. A woman without a body, dumb, blind, can't possibly be a good fighter. She is reduced to being the servant of the militant male, his shadow. We must kill the false woman who is preventing the live one from breathing. Inscribe the breath of the whole woman.

Second: An act that will also be marked by women's *seizing* the occasion to *speak*, hence her shattering entry into history, which has always been based on *her suppression*. To write and thus to forge for herself the antilogos weapon. To become *at will* the taker and initiator, for her own right, in every symbolic system, in every political process.

It is time for women to start scoring their feats in written and oral language.

Every woman has known the torment of getting up to speak. Her heart racing, at times entirely lost for words, ground and language slipping away—that's how daring a feat, how great a transgression it is for a woman to speak—even just open her mouth—in public. A double distress, for even if she transgresses, her words fall almost always upon the deaf male ear, which hears in language only that which speaks in the masculine.

It is by writing, from and toward women, and by taking up the challenge of speech, which has been governed by the phallus, that women will confirm women in a place other than that which is reserved in and by the symbolic—that is, in a place other than silence. Women should break out of the snare of silence. They shouldn't be conned into accepting a domain that is the margin or the harem.

Listen to a woman speak at a public gathering (if she hasn't painfully lost her wind). She doesn't "speak," she throws her trembling body forward; she lets go of herself, she flies; all of her passes into her voice, and it's with her body that she vitally supports the "logic" of her speech. Her flesh speaks true. She lays herself bare. In fact, she physically materializes what she's thinking; she signifies it with her body. In a certain way she *inscribes* what she's saying, because she doesn't deny her drives the intractable and impassioned part they have in speaking. Her speech, even when "theoretical" or political, is never simple or linear or "objectified," generalized: she draws her story into history.

There is not that scission, that division made by the common man between the logic of oral speech and the logic of the text, bound as he is by his antiquated relation—servile, calculating—to mastery. From which proceeds the niggardly lip service that engages only the tiniest part of the body, plus the mask.

In women's speech, as in their writing, that element which never stops resonating, which, once we've been permeated by it, profoundly and imperceptibly touched by it, retains the power of moving us—that element is the song: first music from the first voice of love which is alive in every woman. Why this privileged relationship with the voice? Because no woman stockpiles as many defenses for countering the drives as does a man. You don't build walls around yourself, you don't forego pleasure as "wisely" as he. Even if phallic mystification has generally contaminated good relationships, a woman is never far from "mother" (I mean outside her role functions: the "mother" as non-name and as source of goods). There is always within her at least a little of that good mother's milk. She writes in white ink.

Woman for women. There always remains in woman that force which produces/is produced by the other—in particular, the other woman. *In* her, matrix, cradler; herself giver as her mother and child; she is her own sister-daughter. You might object, "What about she who is the hysterical offspring of a bad mother?" Everything will be changed once woman gives woman to the other woman. There is hidden and always ready in woman the source; the locus for the other. The mother, too, is a metaphor. It is necessary and sufficient that the best of herself be given to woman by another woman for her to be able to love herself and return in love the body that was "born" to her. Touch me, caress me, you the living no-name, give me my self as myself. The relation to the "mother," in terms of intense pleasure and violence, is curtailed no more than the relation to childhood (the child that she was, that she is, that she makes, remakes, undoes, there at the point where, the same, she mothers herself). Text: my body—shot through with streams of song; I don't mean the overbearing, clutchy "mother" but, rather, what touches you, the equivoice that affects you, fills your breast with an urge to come to language and launches your force; the rhythm that laughs you; the intimate recipient who makes all metaphors possible and desirable; body (body? bodies?), no more describable than god, the soul, or the Other; that part of you that leaves a space between yourself and urges you to inscribe in language your woman's style. In women there is always more or less of the mother who makes everything all right, who nourishes, and who stands up against separation; a force that will not be cut off but will knock the wind out of the codes. We will rethink womankind beginning with every form and every period of her body. The Americans remind us, "We are all Lesbians"; that is, don't denigrate woman, don't make of her what men have made of you.

Because the "economy" of her drives is prodigious, she cannot fail, in seizing the occasion to speak, to transform directly and indirectly *all* systems of exchange based on masculine thrift. Her libido will produce far more radical effects of political and social change than some might like to think.

Because she arrives, vibrant, over and again, we are at the beginning of a new history, or rather of a process of becoming in which several histories intersect with one another. As subject for history, woman always occurs simultaneously in several places. Woman un-thinks, expends (*dé-pense*) the unifying, regulating history that homogenizes and channels forces, herding contradictions into a single battlefield. In woman, personal history blends together with the history of all women, as well as national and world history. As a militant, she is an integral part of all liberations. She must be farsighted, not limited to a blow-by-blow interaction. She foresees that her liberation will do more than modify power relations or toss the ball over to the other camp; she will bring about a mutation in human relations, in thought, in all praxis: hers is not simply a class struggle, which she carries forward into a much vaster movement. Not that in order to be a woman-in-struggle(s) you have to leave the class struggle or repudiate it; but you have to split it open, spread it out, push it forward, fill it with the fundamental struggle so as to prevent the class struggle, or any other struggle for the liberation of a class or people, from operating as a form of repression, pretext for postponing the inevitable, the staggering alteration in power relations and in the production of individualities. This alteration is already upon us—in the United States, for example, where millions of night crawlers are in the process of undermining the family and disintegrating the whole of American sociality.

The new history is coming; it's not a dream, though it does extend beyond men's imagination, and for good reason. It's going to deprive them of their conceptual orthopedics, beginning with the destruction of their enticement machine.

It is impossible to *define* a feminine practice of writing, and this is an impossibility that will remain, for this practice can never be theorized, enclosed, coded—which doesn't mean that it doesn't exist. But it will always surpass the discourse that regulates the phallocentric system; it does and will take place in areas other than those subordinated to philosophico-theoretical domination. It will be conceived of only by subjects who are breakers of automatisms, by peripheral figures that no authority can ever subjugate.

Hence the necessity to affirm the flourishes of this writing, to give form to its movement, its near and distant byways. Bear in mind to begin with, first, that sexual opposition, which has always worked for man's profit to the point of reducing writing, too, to his laws, is only a historico-cultural limit. There is, there will be more and more rapidly pervasive now, a fiction that produces irreducible effects of femininity. Second, that it is through ignorance that most readers, critics, and writers of both sexes hesitate to admit or deny outright the possibility or the pertinence of a distinction between feminine and masculine writing. It will usually be said, thus disposing of sexual difference: either that all writing, to the extent that it materializes, is feminine; or, inversely—but it comes to the same thing—that the act of writing is equivalent to masculine masturbation (and so the woman who writes cuts herself out a paper penis); or that writing is bisexual, hence neuter, which again does away with differentiation. To admit that writing is precisely working (in) the in-between, inspecting the process of the same and of the other without which nothing can live, undoing the work of death—to admit this is first to want the two, as well as both, the ensemble of the one and the other, not fixed in sequences of struggle and expulsion or some other form of death but infinitely dynamized by an incessant process of exchange from one subject to another. A process of different subjects knowing one another and beginning one another anew only from the living boundaries of the other: a multiple and inexhaustible course with millions of encounters and transformations of the same into the other and into the in-between, from which woman takes her forms (and man, in his turn, but that's his other history).

In saying "bisexual, hence neuter," I am referring to the classic conception of bisexuality, which, squashed under the emblem of castration fear and along with the fantasy of a "total" being (though composed of two halves), would do away with the difference experienced as an operation incurring loss, as the mark of dreaded sectility.

To this self-effacing, merger-type bisexuality, which would conjure away castration (the writer who puts up his sign: "bisexual written here, come and see," when the odds are good that it's neither one nor the other), I oppose the *other bisexuality* on which every subject not enclosed in the false theater of phallocentric representationalism has founded his/her erotic universe. Bisexuality: that is, each one's location in self (*repérage en soi*) of the presence—variously manifest and insistent according to each person, male or female—of both sexes, nonexclusion either of the difference or of one sex, and, from this "self-permission," multiplication of the effects of the inscription of desire, over all parts of my body and the other body.

Now, it happens that at present, for historico-cultural reasons, it is women who are opening up to and benefitting from this vatic bisexuality which doesn't annul differences but stirs them up, pursues them, increases their number. In a certain way, "woman is bisexual"; man—it's a secret to no one—being poised to keep glorious phallic monosexuality in view. By virtue of affirming the primacy of the phallus and of bringing it into play, phallocratic ideology has claimed more than one victim. As a woman, I've been clouded over by the great shadow of the scepter and been told: idolize it, that which you cannot brandish. But at the same time, man has been handed that grotesque and scarcely enviable destiny (just imagine) of being reduced to a single idol with clay balls. And consumed, as Freud and his followers note, by a fear of being a woman! For, if psychoanalysis was constituted from woman, to repress femininity (and not so successful a repression at that—men have made it clear), its account of masculine sexuality is now hardly refutable; as with all the "human" sciences, it reproduces the masculine view, of which it is one of the effects.

Here we encounter the inevitable man-with-rock, standing erect in his old Freudian realm, in the way that, to take the figure back to the point where linguistics is conceptualizing it "anew," Lacan preserves it in the sanctuary of the phallos (ϕ) "sheltered" from *castration's lack*! Their "symbolic" exists, it holds power—we, the sowers of disorder, know it only too well. But we are in no way obliged to deposit our lives in their banks of lack, to consider the constitution of the subject in terms of a drama manglingly restaged, to re-instate again and again the religion of the father. Because we don't want that. We don't fawn around the supreme hole. We have no womanly reason to pledge allegiance to the negative. The feminine (as the poets suspected) affirms: ". . . And yes," says Molly, carrying *Ulysses* off beyond any book and toward the new writing, "I said yes, I will Yes."

The Dark Continent is neither dark nor unexplorable. It is still unexplored only because we've been made to believe that it was too dark to be explorable. And because they want to make us believe that what interests us is the white continent, with its monuments to Lack. And we believed. They riveted us between two horrifying myths: between the Medusa and the abyss. That would be enough to set half the world laughing, except that it's still going on. For the phallologocentric sublation (*la relève*) is with us, and it's militant, regenerating the old patterns, anchored in the dogma of castration. They haven't changed a thing: they've theorized their desire for reality! Let the priests tremble, we're going to show them our sexts!

Too bad for them if they fall apart upon discovering that women aren't men, or that the mother doesn't have one. But isn't this fear convenient for them? Wouldn't the worst be, isn't the worst, in truth, that women aren't castrated, that they have only to stop listening to the Sirens (for the Sirens were men) for history to change its meaning? You only have to look at the Medusa straight on to see her. And she's not deadly. She's beautiful and she's laughing.

Men say that there are two unrepresentable things: death and the feminine sex. That's because they need femininity to be associated with death; it's the jitters that give them a hard-on! For themselves! They need to be afraid of us. Look at the trembling Perseuses moving backward toward us, clad in apotropes. What lovely backs! Not another minute to lose. Let's get out of here.

Let's hurry: the continent is not impenetrably dark. I've been there often. I was overjoyed one day to run into Jean Genet. It was in *Pompes funèbres*. He had come there led by his Jean. There are some men (all too few) who aren't afraid of femininity.

Almost everything is yet to be written by women about femininity: about their sexuality, that is, its infinite and mobile complexity, about their eroticization, sudden turn-ons of a certain minuscule-immense area of their bodies; not about destiny, but about the adventure of such-and-such a drive, about trips, crossings, trudges, abrupt and gradual awakenings, discoveries of a zone at one time timorous and soon to be forthright. A woman's body, with its thousand and one thresholds of ardor—once, by smashing yokes and censors, she lets it articulate the profusion of meanings that run through it in every direction— will make the old single-grooved mother tongue reverberate with more than one language.

We've been turned away from our bodies, shamefully taught to ignore them, to strike them with that stupid sexual modesty; we've been made victims of the old fool's game—each one will love the other sex. I'll give you your body and you'll give me mine. But who are the men who give women the body that women blindly yield to them? Why so few texts? Because so few women have as yet won back their body. Women must write through their bodies, they must invent the impregnable language that will wreck partitions, classes, and rhetorics, regulations and codes, they must submerge, cut through, get beyond the ultimate reserve-discourse, including the one that laughs at the very idea of pronouncing the word "silence," the one that, aiming for the impossible, stops short before the word "impossible" and writes it as "the end."

Such is the strength of women that, sweeping away syntax, breaking that famous thread (just a tiny little thread, they say) which acts for men as a surrogate umbilical cord, assuring them—otherwise they couldn't come—that the old lady is always right behind them, watching them play phallus, women will go right up to the impossible.

When the "repressed" of their culture and their society returns, it's an explosive, *utterly* destructive, staggering return, with a force never yet unleashed and equal to the most forbidding of suppressions. For when the Phallic period comes to an end, women will have been either annihilated or borne up to the highest and most violent incandescence. Muffled throughout their history, they have lived in dreams, in bodies (though muted), in silences, in aphonic revolts.

And with such force in their fragility; a fragility, a vulnerability, equal to their incomparable intensity. Fortunately, they haven't sublimated; they've saved their skin, their energy. They haven't worked at liquidating the impasse of lives without futures. They have furiously inhabited these sumptuous bodies: admirable hysterics who made Freud succumb to many voluptuous moments impossible to confess, bombarding his Mosaic statue with their carnal and passionate body words, haunting him with their inaudible and thundering denunciations, dazzling, more than naked underneath the seven veils of modesty. Those who, with a single word of the body, have inscribed the vertiginous immensity of a history sprung like an arrow from the whole history of men and from biblio-capitalist society, are the women, the supplicants of yesterday, who come as forebears of the new women, after whom no intersubjective relation will ever be the same. You, Dora, you the indomitable, the poetic body, you are the true "mistress" of the Signifier. Before long, your efficacity will be seen at work when your speech is no longer suppressed, its point turned in against your breast, but written out over against the other.

In body. — More so than men who are coaxed toward social success, toward sublimation, women are body. More body, hence more writing. For a long time it has been in body that women have responded to persecution, to the familial-conjugal enterprise of domestication, to the repeated attempts at castrating them. Those who have turned their tongues 10,000 times seven times before not speaking are either dead from it or more familiar with their tongues and their mouths than anyone else. Now, I-woman am going to blow up the Law: an explosion henceforth possible and ineluctable; let it be done, right now, *in* language.

Let us not be trapped by an analysis still encumbered with the old automatisms. It's not to be feared that language conceals an invincible adversary, because it's the language of men and their grammar. We mustn't leave them a single place that's any more theirs alone than we are.

If woman has always functioned "within" the discourse of man, a signifier that has always referred back to the opposite signifier that annihilates its specific energy and diminishes or stifles its very different sounds, it is time for her to dislocate this "within," to explode it, turn it around, and seize it; to make it hers, containing it, taking it in her own mouth, biting that tongue with her very own teeth to invent for herself a language to get inside of. And you'll see with what ease she will spring forth from that "within" — the "within" where once she so drowsily crouched — to overflow at the lips she will cover with foam.

Nor is the point to appropriate their instruments, their concepts, their places, or to begrudge them their position of mastery. Just because there's a risk of identification doesn't mean that we'll succumb. Let's leave it to the worriers, to masculine anxiety and its obsession with how to dominate the way things work — knowing "how it works" in order to "make it work." For us the point is not to take possession in order to internalize or manipulate, but rather to dash through and to "fly" (*voler*).

Flying is woman's gesture—flying in language and making it fly. We have all learned the art of flying and its numerous techniques; for centuries we've been able to possess anything only by flying; we've lived in flight, stealing away, finding, when desired, narrow passageways, hidden crossovers. It's no accident that *voler* has a double meaning, that it plays on each of them and thus throws off the agents of sense. It's no accident: women take after birds and robbers just as robbers take after women and birds. They (*elles*) go by, fly the coop, take pleasure in jumbling the order of space, in disorienting it, in changing around the furniture, dislocating things and values, breaking them all up, emptying structures, and turning propriety upside down.

What woman hasn't flown/stolen? Who hasn't felt, dreamt, performed the gesture that jams sociality? Who hasn't crumbled, held up to ridicule, the bar of separation? Who hasn't inscribed with her body the differential, punctured the system of couples and opposition? Who, by some act of transgression, hasn't overthrown successiveness, connection, the wall of circumfusion?

A feminine text cannot fail to be more than subversive. It is volcanic; as it is written it brings about an upheaval of the old property crust, carrier of masculine investments; there's no other way. There's no room for her if she's not a he. If she's a her-she, it's in order to smash everything, to shatter the framework of institutions, to blow up the law, to break up the "truth" with laughter.

For once she blazes *her* trail in the symbolic, she cannot fail to make of it the chaosmos of the "personal"—in her pronouns, her nouns, and her clique of referents. And for good reason. There will have been the long history of gynocide. This is known by the colonized peoples of yesterday, the workers, the nations, the species off whose backs the history of men has made its gold; those who have known the ignominy of persecution derive from it an obstinate future desire for grandeur; those who are locked up know better than their jailers the taste of free air. Thanks to their history, women today know (how to do and want) what men will be able to conceive of only much later. I say woman overturns the "personal," for if, by means of laws, lies, blackmail, and marriage, her right to herself has been extorted at the same time as her name, she has been able, through the very movement of mortal alienation, to see more closely the inanity of "propriety," the reductive stinginess of the masculine-conjugal subjective economy, which she doubly resists. On the one hand, she has constituted herself necessarily as that "person" capable of losing a part of herself without losing her integrity. But secretly, silently, deep down inside, she grows and multiplies, for, on the other hand, she knows far more about living and about the relation between the economy of the drives and the management of the ego than any man. Unlike man, who holds so dearly to his title and his titles, his pouches of value, his cap, crown, and everything connected with his head, woman couldn't care less about the fear of decapitation (or castration), adventuring, without the masculine temerity, into anonymity, which she can merge with, without annihilating herself—because she's a giver.

I shall have a great deal to say about the whole deceptive problematic of the gift. Woman is obviously not that woman Nietzsche dreamed of who gives only in order to.[1] Who could ever think of the gift as a gift-take-takes? Who else but man, precisely the one who would like to take everything?

If there is a "propriety of woman," it is paradoxically her capacity to depropriate unselfishly, body without end, without appendage, without principal "parts." If she is a whole, it's a whole composed of parts that are wholes, not simple partial objects but a moving, limitlessly changing ensemble, a cosmos tirelessly traversed by Eros, an immense astral space not organized around any one sun that's any more of a star than the others.

This doesn't mean that she's an undifferentiated magma, but that she doesn't lord it over her body or her desire. Though masculine sexuality gravitates around the penis, engendering that centralized body (in political anatomy) under the dictatorship of its parts, woman does not bring about the same regionalization that serves the couple head/genitals and is inscribed only within boundaries. Her libido is cosmic, just as her unconscious is worldwide. Her writing can only keep going, without ever inscribing or discerning contours, daring to make the vertiginous crossings of the other(s) ephemeral and passionate sojourns in him, her, them, whom she inhabits long enough to look at from the point closest to their unconscious from the moment they awaken, to love them at the point closest to their drives; and then further, impregnated through and through with these brief, identificatory embraces, she goes and passes into infinity. She alone dares and wishes to know from within, where she, the outcast, has never ceased to hear the resonance of fore-language. She lets the other language speak—the language of 1,000 tongues which knows neither enclosure nor death. To life she refuses nothing. Her language does not contain, it carries; it does not hold back, it makes possible. When id is ambiguously uttered—the wonder of being several—she doesn't defend herself against these unknown women whom she's surprised at becoming, but derives pleasure from this gift of alterability. I am spacious, singing flesh, on which is grafted no one knows which I, more or less human, but alive because of transformation.

Write! and your self-seeking text will know itself better than flesh and blood, rising, insurrectionary dough kneading itself, with sonorous, perfumed ingredients, a lively combination of flying colors, leaves, and rivers plunging into the sea we feed. "Ah, there's her sea," he will say as he holds out to me a basin full of water from the little phallic mother from whom he's inseparable. But look, our seas are what we make of them, full of fish or not, opaque or transparent, red or black, high or smooth, narrow or bankless; and we are ourselves sea, sand, coral, seaweed, beaches, tides, swimmers, children, waves . . . More or less wavily sea, earth, sky—what matter would rebuff us? We know how to speak them all.

Heterogeneous, yes. For her joyous benefits she is erogenous; she is the erotogeneity of the heterogeneous; airborne swimmer, in flight, she does not cling to herself; she is dispersible, prodigious, stunning, desirous and capable of others, of the other woman that she will be, of the other woman she isn't, of him, of you.

TRANSLATED BY KEITH COHEN AND PAULA COHEN

NOTE

[1] Reread Jacques Derrida's text, "Le Style de la femme," in *Nietzsche aujourd'hui* (Paris: Union Générale d'Editions, 1973), where the philosopher can be seen operating an *Aufhebung* of all philosophy in its systematic reducing of woman to the place of seduction: she appears as the one who is taken for; the bait in person, all veils unfurled, the one who doesn't give but who gives only in order to (take).

MONIQUE WITTIG

The Mark of Gender
1985

*Even though Wittig and Cixous both attack the myth of the neutrality of
language, they do it from two opposite points of view. Cixous wants women
to speak as others, Wittig would like them not to be cornered in a position of
otherness. She campaigns for a way out of otherness, for the right for
woman not to speak with a difference. While Cixous's feminine writing
aims at subverting a phallocentric tradition that "contains" the feminine,
repressing and confining it to silence, Wittig (who forcefully opposes the
concept of feminine writing altogether) wants to subvert the rules of a
heterosexual language which forces sex (femininity) upon certain individuals on the grounds that they are female—a language that forces a female
speaker, every time she speaks to do so as a woman, to be feminine in the text
("to appear in language under her proper physical form"). While, for Cixous, the dominant form of language condemns woman to speak as a man,
for Witting it obliges her, willingly or not, to speak as a woman.*

*Using Emile Benveniste's landmark analysis of personal pronouns
"L'Homme dans la langue" (Man within Language) as a starting point,
Wittig thus develops the utopia of a language free of these marks of gender.
Personal pronouns—that is, first and second person—that inscribe the
protagonists of the speech act (both the speaker and the addressee) in the
message are not gendered (both sexes use "I" and "you" identically); thus
the pronouns themselves are the abstract markers of a nongendered subjectivity. But they are also the switches that turn on the process of generalized
linguistic gendering (possessive and relative pronouns, participles, and so
on). Wittig's literary utopia is geared toward the invention of a language
that wouldn't release these switches; that would eradicate the marks of gender by circumventing the rules of grammatical agreement, a formal con-
straint that, in its own guise, is not unlike that of Georges Perec's decision to
write a whole novel,* La Disparition, *without once using the letter* e.

Monique Wittig, "The Mark of Gender," in *The Straight Mind* (Boston: Beacon, 1992),
pp. 76–89.

I

The mark of gender, according to grammarians, concerns nouns. They talk about it in terms of function. If they question its meaning, they may joke about it, calling gender a "fictive sex." It is thus that English when compared to French has the reputation of being almost genderless, while French passes for a very gendered language. It is true that, strictly speaking, English does not apply the mark of gender to inanimate objects, to things or nonhuman beings. But as far as the categories of the person are concerned, both languages are bearers of gender to the same extent. Both indeed give way to a primitive ontological concept that enforces in language a division of beings into sexes. The "fictive sex" of nouns or their neuter gender are only accidental developments of this first principle and as such they are relatively harmless.

The manifestation of gender that is identical in English and in French takes place in the dimension of the person. It does not concern only grammarians, although it is a lexical manifestation. As an ontological concept that deals with the nature of Being, along with a whole nebula of other primitive concepts belonging to the same line of thought, gender seems to belong primarily to philosophy. Its raison d'être is never questioned in grammar, whose role is to describe forms and functions, not to find a justification for them. It is no longer questioned in philosophy, though, because it belongs to that body of self-evident concepts without which philosophers believe they cannot develop a line of reasoning, and which for them go without saying, for they exist prior to any thought, any social order, in nature. So they call gender the lexical delegation of "natural beings," their symbol. Being aware that the notion of gender is not as innocuous as it appears, American feminists use gender as a sociological category, making clear that there is nothing natural about this notion, as sexes have been artificially constructed into political categories—categories of oppression. They have extrapolated the term *gender* from grammar and they tend to superimpose it on the notion of sex. And they are right insofar as gender is the linguistic index of the political opposition between the sexes and of the domination of women. In the same way as sex, man and woman, gender, as a concept, is instrumental in the political discourse of the social contract as heterosexual.

In modern theory, even in the assumptions of disciplines exclusively concerned with language, one remains within the classical division of the concrete world on the one hand, and the abstract one on the other. Physical or social reality and language are disconnected. Abstraction, symbols, signs do not belong to the real. There is on one side the real, the referent, and on the other side language. It is as though the relation to language were a relation of function only and not one of transformation. There is sometimes a confusion between signified and referent, so that they are even used indifferently in certain critical works. Or there is a reduction of the signified to a series of messages, with relays of the referent remaining the only support of the meaning. Among linguists, the Russian Mikhail Bakhtin, a contemporary of the Russian Formalists whose work has at last been translated, is the only one who seems to me to have a strictly materialist approach to language. In sociolinguistics, there are several developments in this direction, mostly among feminists.

I say that even abstract philosophical categories act upon the real as social. Language casts sheaves of reality upon the social body, stamping it and violently shaping it. For example, the bodies of social actors are fashioned by abstract language as well as by nonabstract language. For there is a plasticity of the real to language: language has a plastic action upon the real. According to Sande Zeig, social gestures are the result of this phenomenon.

About gender, then, it is not only important to dislodge from grammar and linguistics a sociological category that does not speak its name. It is also very important to consider how gender works in language, how gender works upon language, before considering how it works from there upon its users.

Gender takes place in a category of language that is totally unlike any other and which is called the personal pronoun. Personal pronouns are the only linguistic instances that designate the locutors in discourse and their different and successive situations in relationship to that discourse. As such, they are also the pathways and the means of entrance into language. And it is in this sense — that they represent persons — that they interest us here. It is without justification of any kind, without questioning, that personal pronouns somehow engineer gender all through language, taking it along with them quite naturally, so to speak, in any kind of talk, parley, or philosophical treatise. And although they are instrumental in activating the notion of gender, they pass unnoticed. Not being gender-marked themselves in their subjective form (except in one case), they can support the notion of gender while they seem to fulfill another function. In principle, pronouns mark the opposition of gender only in the third person and are not gender bearers, per se, in the other persons. Thus, it is as though gender does not affect them, is not part of their structure, but only a detail in their associated forms. But, in reality, as soon as there is a locutor in discourse, as soon as there is an "I," gender manifests itself. There is a kind of suspension of the grammatical form. A direct interpellation of the locutor occurs. The locutor is called upon in person. The locutor intervenes, in the order of the pronouns, without mediation, in *its proper sex* — that is, when the locutor is a sociological woman. One knows that, in French, with *je* ("I"), one must mark the gender as soon as one uses it in relation to past participles and adjectives. In English, where the same kind of obligation does not exist, a locutor, when a sociological woman, must in one way or another, that is, with a certain number of clauses, make her sex public. For gender is the enforcement of sex in language, working in the same way as the declaration of sex in civil status. Gender is not confined within the third person, and the mention of sex in language is not a treatment reserved for the third person. Sex, under the

name of gender, permeates the whole body of language and forces every locutor, if she belongs to the oppressed sex, to proclaim it in her speech, that is, to
appear in language under her proper physical form and not under the abstract
form, which every male locutor has the unquestioned right to use. The abstract
form, the general, the universal, this is what the so-called masculine gender
means, for the class of men have appropriated the universal for themselves.
One must understand that men are not born with a faculty for the universal
and that women are not reduced at birth to the particular. The universal has
been, and is continually, at every moment, appropriated by men. It does not
happen by magic, it must be done. It is an act, a criminal act, perpetrated by one
class against another. It is an act carried out at the level of concepts, philosophy,
politics. And gender by enforcing upon women a particular category represents a measure of domination. Gender is very harmful to women in the exercise of language. But there is more: gender is ontologically a total impossibility.
For when one becomes a locutor, when one says "I" and, in so doing, reappro-
priates language as a whole, proceeding from oneself alone, with the tremen-
dous power to use all language, it is then and there, according to linguists and
philosophers, that the supreme act of subjectivity, the advent of subjectivity
into consciousness, occurs. It is when starting to speak that one becomes "I."
This act—the becoming of *the* subject through the exercise of language and
through locution—in order to be real, implies that the locutor be an absolute
subject. For a relative subject is inconceivable, a relative subject could not speak
at all. I mean that in spite of the harsh law of gender and its enforcement upon
women, no woman can say "I" without being for herself a total subject—that
is, ungendered, universal, whole. Or, failing this, she is condemned to what I
call parrot speech (slaves echoing their masters' talk). Language as a whole
gives everyone the same power of becoming an absolute subject through its
exercise. But gender, an element of language, works upon this ontological fact
to annul it as far as women are concerned and corresponds to a constant attempt to strip them of the most precious thing for a human being—subjectivity. Gender is an ontological impossibility because it tries to accomplish the
division of Being. But Being as being is not divided. God or Man as being are
One and whole. So what is this divided Being introduced into language
through gender? It is an impossible Being, it is a Being that does not exist, an
ontological joke, a conceptual maneuver to wrest from women what belongs to
them by right: conceiving of oneself as a total subject through the exercise of
language. The result of the imposition of gender, acting as a denial at the very
moment when one speaks, is to deprive women of the authority of speech, and
to force them to make their entrance in a crablike way, particularizing themselves and apologizing profusely. The result is to deny them any claim to the
abstract, philosophical, political discourses that give shape to the social body.
Gender, then, must be destroyed. The possibility of its destruction is given
through the very exercise of language. For each time I say "I," I reorganize the

world from my point of view and through abstraction I lay claim to universality. This fact holds true for every locutor.

II

To destroy the categories of sex in politics and in philosophy, to destroy gender in language (at least to modify its use) is therefore part of my work in writing, as a writer. An important part, since a modification as central as this cannot happen without a transformation of language as a whole. It concerns (touches) words whose meanings and forms are close to, and associated with, gender. But it also concerns (touches) words whose meanings and forms are the furthest away. For once the dimension of the person, around which all others are organized, is brought into play, nothing is left intact. Words, their disposition, their arrangement, their relation to each other, the whole nebula of their constellations shift, are displaced, engulfed or reoriented, put sideways. And when they reappear, the structural change in language makes them look different. They are hit in their meaning and also in their form. Their music sounds different, their coloration is affected. For what is really in question here is a structural change in language, in its nerves, its framing. But language does not allow itself to be worked upon without parallel work in philosophy and politics, as well as in economics, because, as women are marked in language by gender, they are marked in society as sex. I said that personal pronouns engineer gender through language, and personal pronouns are, if I may say so, the subject matter of each one of my books—except for *Le Brouillon pour un dictionnaire des amantes* (Lesbian Peoples: Material for a Dictionary), written with Sande Zeig. They are the motors for which functioning parts had to be designed, and as such they create the necessity of the form.

The project of *The Opoponax*, my first book, was to work on the subject, the speaking subject, the subject of discourse—subjectivity, generally speaking. I wanted to restore an undivided "I," to universalize the point of view of a group condemned to being particular, relegated in language to a subhuman category. I chose childhood as an element of form open to history (it is what a narrative theme is for me), the formation of the ego around language. A massive effort was needed to break the spell of the captured subject. I needed a strong device, something that would immediately be beyond sexes, that the division by sexes would be powerless against, and that could not be coopted. There is in French, as there is in English, a munificent pronoun that is called the "indefinite," which means that it is not marked by gender, a pronoun that you are taught in school to systematically avoid. It is *on* in French—*one* in English. Indeed it is so systematically taught that it should not be used that the translator of *The Opoponax* managed never to use it in English. One must say in the translator's favor that it sounds and looks very heavy in English, but no less so in French.

With this pronoun, that is neither gendered nor numbered, I could locate

the characters outside of the social division by sexes and annul it for the duration of the book. In French, the masculine form—so the grammarians say—
used when a past participle or an adjective is associated with the subject *on*, is in
fact neuter. This incidental question of the neuter is in fact very interesting, for
even when it is about terms like *l'homme*, like *Man*, grammarians do not speak
of neuter in the same sense as they do for *Good* or *Evil*, but they speak of masculine gender. For they have appropriated *l'homme*, *homo*, whose first meaning
is not *male* but *mankind*. For *homo sum*. Man as male is only a derivative and
second meaning. To come back to *one*, *on*, here is a subject pronoun which is
very tractable and accommodating since it can be bent in several directions at
the same time. First, as already mentioned, it is indefinite as far as gender is
concerned. It can represent a certain number of people successively or all at
once—everybody, we, they, I, you, people, a small or a large number of
persons—and still stay singular. It lends itself to all kinds of substitutions
of persons. In the case of *The Opoponax*, it was a delegate of a whole class of
people, of everybody, of a few persons, of I (the "I" of the main character, the
"I" of the narrator, and the "I" of the reader). *One*, *on* has been for me the key to
the undisturbed use of language, as it is in childhood when words are magic,
when words are set bright and colorful in the kaleidoscope of the world, with
its many revolutions in the consciousness as one shakes it. *One*, *on* has been the
pathway to the description of the apprenticeship, through words, of everything
important to consciousness, apprenticeship in writing being the first, even before the apprenticeship in the use of speech. *One*, *on*, lends itself to the unique
experience of all locutors who, when saying I, can reappropriate the whole language and reorganize the world from their point of view. I did not hide the
female characters under male patronyms to make them look more universal,
and nevertheless, if I believe what Claude Simon wrote, the attempt at universalization succeeded. He wrote, speaking about what happened to the main
character in *The Opoponax*, a little girl: "I see, I breathe, I chew, I feel through
her eyes, her mouth, her hands, her skin. . . . I become childhood."

Before speaking of the pronoun which is the axis of *Les Guérillères*, I would
like to recall what Marx and Engels said in *The German Ideology* about class
interests. They said that each new class that fights for power must, to reach its
goal, represent its interest as the common interest of all the members of the
society, and that in the philosophical domain this class must give the form of
universality to its thought, to present it as the only reasonable one, the only
universally valid one.

As for *Les Guérillères*, there is a personal pronoun used very little in French
which does not exist in English—the collective plural *elles* (*they* in English)—
while *ils* (*they*) often stands for the general: *they say*, meaning *people say*. This
general *ils* does not include *elles*, no more, I suspect, than *they* includes any *she*
in its assumption. One could say that it is a pity that in English there is not even
a hypothetical plural feminine pronoun to try to make up for the absence of *she*

in the general *they*. But what is the good of it, since when it exists it is not used. The rare times that it is, *elles* never stands for the general and is never the bearer of a universal point of view. An *elles* therefore that would be able to support a universal point of view would be a novelty in literature or elsewhere. In *Les Guérillères*, I try to universalize the point of view of *elles*. The goal of this approach is not to feminize the world but to make the categories of sex obsolete in language. I, therefore, set up *elles* in the text as the absolute subject of the world. To succeed textually, I needed to adopt some very draconian measures, such as to eliminate, at last in the first two parts, *he*, or *they-he*. I wanted to produce a shock for the reader entering a text in which *elles* by its unique presence constitutes an assault, yes, even for female readers. Here again the adoption of a pronoun as my subject matter dictated the form of the book. Although the theme of the text was total war, led by *elles* on *ils*, in order for this new person to take effect, two thirds of the text had to be totally inhabited, haunted, by *elles*. Word by word, *elles* establishes itself as a sovereign subject. Only then could *il(s)*, *they-he*, appear, reduced and truncated out of language. This *elles* in order to become real also imposed an epic form, where it is not only the complete subject of the world but its conqueror. Another consequence derived from the sovereign presence of *elles* was that the chronological beginning of the narrative—that is, the total war—found itself in the third part of the book, and the textual beginning was in fact the end of the narrative. From their comes the circular form of the book, its *gesta*, which the geometrical form of a circle indicates as a modus operandi. In English, the translator, lacking the lexical equivalent of *elles*, found himself compelled to make a change, which for me destroys the effect of the attempt. When *elles* is turned into *the women* the process of universalization is destroyed. All of a sudden, *elles* stopped being *mankind*. When one says "the women," one connotes a number of individual women, thus transforming the point of view entirely, by particularizing what I intended as a universal. Not only was my undertaking with the collective pronoun *elles* lost, but another word was introduced, the word *women* appearing obsessively throughout the text, and it is one of those gender-marked words mentioned earlier which I never use in French. For me it is the equivalent of *slave*, and, in fact, I have actively opposed its use whenever possible. To patch it up with the use of a *y* or an *i* (as in *womyn* or *wimmin*) does not alter the political reality of the word. If one tries to imagine *nogger* or *niggir*, instead of *nigger*, one may realize the futility of the attempt. It is not that there is no solution to translating *elles*. There is a solution, although it was difficult for me to find at the time. I am aware that the question is a grammatical one, therefore a textual one, and not a question of translation. The solution for the English translation then is to reappropriate the collective pronoun *they*, which rightfully belongs to the feminine as well as to the masculine gender. *They* is not only a collective pronoun but it also immediately develops a degree of universality which is not immediate with *elles*. Indeed, to obtain it with *elles*, one must produce a work of transformation that involves a whole pageant of other words and that touches the imagination. *They* does not partake of the naturalistic, hysterical bent that accompanies the feminine gender. *They* helps to go beyond the categories of sex. But *they* can be effective in my design only when it stands by itself, like its French counterpart. Only with the use of *they* will the text regain its strength and strangeness. The fact that the book begins with the end and that the end is the chronological beginning will be textually justified by the unexpected identity of *they*. In the third part, the war section, *they* cannot be shared by the category to be eliminated from the general. In a new version the masculine gender must be more systematically particularized than it is in the actual form of the book. The masculine must not appear under *they* but only under *man*, *he*, *his*, in analogy with what has been done for so long to the feminine gender (*woman*, *she*, *her*). It seems to me that the English solution will take us even a step further in making the categories of sex obsolete in language.

Talking about the key pronoun of *The Lesbian Body* (*Le Corps lesbien*) is a very difficult task for me, and sometimes I have considered this text a reverie about the beautiful analysis of the pronouns *je* and *tu* by the linguist Emile Benveniste. The bar in the *j/e* of *The Lesbian Body* is a sign of excess. A sign that helps to imagine an excess of I, an "I" exalted. "I" has become so powerful in *The Lesbian Body* that it can attack the order of heterosexuality in texts and assault the so-called love, the heroes of love, and lesbianize them, lesbianize the symbols, lesbianize the gods and the goddesses, lesbianize the men and the women. This "I" can be destroyed in the attempt and resuscitated. Nothing resists this "I" (or this *tu*, which is its same, its love), which spreads itself in the whole world of the book, like a lava flow that nothing can stop.

To understand my undertaking in this text, one must go back to *The Opoponax*, in which the only appearance of the narrator comes with a *je*, "I," located at the end of the book in a small sentence untranslated in English, a verse of Maurice Scève, in *La Délie*: "*Tant je l'aimais qu'en elle encore je vis*" ("I loved her so that in her I live still"). This sentence is the key to the text and pours its ultimate light upon the whole of it, demystifying the meaning of the opoponax and establishing a lesbian subject as the absolute subject while lesbian love is the absolute love. *On*, the opoponax, and the *je*, "I" of the end have narrow links. They function by relays. First *on* completely coincides with the character Catherine Legrand as well as with the others. Then the opoponax appears as a talisman, a sesame to the opening of the world, as a word that compels both words and world to make sense, as a metaphor for the lesbian subject. After the repeated assertions of Catherine Legrand that I *am the opoponax*, the narrator can at the end of the book take the relay and affirm in her name: "I loved her so that in her I live still." The chain of permutations from the *on* to the *je*, "I," of *The Opoponax* has created a context for the "I" in *The Lesbian Body*. This understanding both global and particular, both universal and unique, brought from within a perspective given in homosexuality, is the object of some extraordinary pages by Proust.

To close my discussion of the notion of gender in language, I will say that it is a mark unique of its kind, the unique lexical symbol that refers to an oppressed group. No other has left its trace within language to such a degree that to eradicate it would not only modify language at the lexical level but would upset the structure itself and its functioning. Furthermore, it would change the relations of words at the metaphorical level far beyond the very few concepts and notions that are touched upon by this transformation. It would change the coloration of words in relation to each other and their tonality. It is a transformation that would affect the conceptual-philosophical level and the political one as well as the poetic one.

LÉOPOLD SÉDAR SENGHOR

The Teaching of Leo Frobenius
1973

Around the time that Africa in the 1930's was gaining artistic and cultural respectability in the circles of avant-garde artists and connoisseurs, the work of German anthropologist Leo Frobenius provided black students (from Africa or the Caribbean) who were launching Negritude in Paris with an alternative to the alienating models of assimilation (the myth of "Français à part entière," of fully fledged French black nationals). Against the prevailing identification of precolonial Africa with a continent of sparse barbaric tribes, Frobenius's works promoted a vision of an ancient, precolonial, pan-African civilization (an African worldview) whose heritage— though mainly aesthetic—could proudly withstand comparison with other, more technically aggressive, more utilitarian civilizations, in terms of age and existential value.

Negritude reconnected the black diaspora with an Africa still untainted by slavery and colonialism, and restored a sense of African authenticity: it provided black intellectuals with cultural models that spare them the parody of European canons. It helped them discover that, in the antiimperialist fight, they had intellectual weapons of their own, giving them what Senghor calls "independence of mind." It allowed them to retrieve, in French, the system of black signifieds.

Here, then, is an anthology of the work of the great German anthropologist Leo Frobenius, in honor of the hundredth anniversary of his birth. It is fitting that this honor should come now, in the second half of the twentieth century, which among other things is notable for the African nations' debut on the international stage. For no one did more than Frobenius to reveal Africa to the world and Africans to themselves.

I can think of no more fitting introduction for this anthology than to mention some of the lessons we have learned from Frobenius's work, and especially

Léopold Sédar Senghor, "Les Leçons de Leo Frobenius" in *Négritude et civilisation de l'univers (Liberté III)* (Paris: Seuil, 1973), pp. 398–404.

from his two fundamental books, both of which have been translated into French: *Histoire de la civilisation africaine* and *Le Destin des civilisations.*[1] When I say "we," I mean the handful of black students in the Latin Quarter in the 1930s who, along with Aimé Césaire of the Antilles and Léon Damas of Guiana, launched the Negritude movement.

I still own the copy of *Histoire de la civilisation africaine* in which Césaire inscribed the date "December 1936" on page three, just after the title page. A year earlier, while teaching high school in Tours and working on a doctoral thesis on "Verbal Forms in the Languages of the Senegalo–Guinean Group," a work cut short when I "entered politics," I had begun taking courses at the Institut d'Ethnologie and the Ecole Pratique des Hautes Etudes in Paris. I was therefore intimately familiar with the thinking of the leading Africanists, especially the anthropologists and linguists. Yet my discovery of Frobenius struck me as a bolt out of the blue. It suddenly illuminated the whole prehistory and history of Africa to its innermost core. Our minds and hearts are still stamped with the mark of the master, like the tattoos applied in initiation rites in the sacred forest.

Chapter Two of the first book of *Histoire*, "What Africa Means to Us," is one that we learned by heart. It is a chapter filled with lapidary formulations such as this: "The idea of the 'barbarian Negro' is a European invention, the repercussions of which dominated Europe until the beginning of this century."

Leo Frobenius did more than any other scholar to clarify for us the meaning of words like *emotion, art, myth*, and *Eurafrica*.

Take *emotion*. Previously, our teachers, trained in the rationalist mold (not so much the rationalism of Descartes, which was less hegemonic than is sometimes thought, as the "scientific" rationalism of the nineteenth century), had taught us to be wary of emotion and to allow ourselves to be guided by discursive reason alone. For when we "went up," as we used to say, from our backwoods to Paris, our goal was of course not only to seize the arms of the colonizers but also, dialectically, to challenge the efficacy of those arms and discover the secret with which to forge weapons of our own.

But we also asked another question: Had our ancestors left us *their* weapons, the *values* of *their* civilization? The priest who headed my school in Dakar denied that they had left us anything. But already the French capital had felt the blast of Louis Armstrong's trumpet as a sort of condemnation; Josephine Baker's hips had shaken the city's walls; and the "fetishes" of the Trocadéro Museum had led to a "Negro Revolution" in the School of Paris. Still, we labored over our dissertations at the Lycée Louis-le-Grand and the Sorbonne, where to the astonishment of our professors we invoked "black values," we lacked not just "deep insight" but a philosophical justification. It was Leo Frobenius who gave us both the insight and the justification just as, our studies over, we were preparing to embark on lives of political activism armed with the word and the idea of Negritude. It was Frobenius who helped us give meaning to that word, a meaning at once solid and humane.

From his *Histoire* we learned that "man, more than any other living organism, is equipped to 'receive reality'. . . . The ability to receive reality is the
faculty of being *moved* by the essence of phenomena—not by facts, but by the
reality that dictates those facts, or, in other words, by the essence of the facts."[2]
In countless passages of this and other works, Frobenius contrasts the *real* with
the *factual*, the *sense* with the *sign*. The "essence of the facts" is therefore their
meaning, which we perceive symbolically in the perceptible qualities of the
objects and individuals that subtend those facts. This accounts for the primary
importance that Frobenius attaches to intuitive reason. "In civilization," he
writes, "that is, in feeling, sensibility is thought. . . . What we call civilization
is often the expression of the soul, the language of the soul, at least when dealing with men, whose thought is still primarily *intuitive*."[3] More than anyone
else, including Henri Bergson, it was Frobenius who rehabilitated intuitive
reason in our eyes and restored it to its place of primacy. After reading him we
turned back to the philosophers and found that the Greeks, too, granted primacy to intuitive reason, and that even Descartes looked upon "feeling" as an
aspect of reason.

Moreover, it is in feeling, or emotion, that *art* originates. If this idea is now
universally accepted, this was not the case at the beginning of the century.
"There is no need to explain," Frobenius says in *Histoire*, "that art is the meaning of life and that when we delve into styles of life we also learn about the
essence of life."[4] This means that art is first of all perception of the essence of
life, of that spiritual energy in the Other which causes emotion. Being *moved*,
man begins to "play" the Other—be it animal, vegetable, celestial body, or
what have you; he brings the Other to life. He does this first by dancing, then
by sculpting, painting, and singing. The "essence of life" is represented by the
internal structures, external forms, and behavior of the Other—in short, by
rhythm. The other's impact on the self, together with the self's reaction to that
impact, accounts for the differences of style not only among artists but also—
and this is what interests us here—among peoples.

Each people possesses its own distinctive *paideuma*, that is, its own distinctive way of being moved, of being "struck." But the artist—dancer, sculptor, or
poet—is not content with bringing the Other to life. He *re-creates* the Other so
as to animate that life and experience it more fully. He does this by means of
rhythm, whereby he creates a superior reality, a reality truer, or more real, than
factual reality.[5]

Which brings us to *myth*. As the dictionary says, myth is a "fabulous narrative, often popular in origin, which dramatically portrays beings that symbolically embody forces of nature or aspects of the human condition."[6] At this point
we need to back up a bit to consider Frobenius's famous distinction between
the *understanding* and the *soul*. "At issue," he points out, "is the limitation of the
human perceptive faculty, which is in part intellectual and conditioned by the
senses and in part *paideumatic* . . . and conditioned by feeling. Corresponding, perhaps, to this distinction between the two most important types of or-

gans by means of which we relate to life is a division of the environment into a *realm of factual phenomena* and a *realm of real phenomena*."[7] Take, for instance, young boys being initiated into a civilization defined by the Bull. Among other things, their initiation will involve a ceremony in which, struck by the essential reality of the Bull, they will begin to dance, perhaps wearing the mask of the Man-Bull-Moon, as I have witnessed in the Ivory Coast. This is the phase of art, which follows the phase of emotion. In the sacred forest, the boys experience these two ancient epochs. And they also experience a third epoch: the time of myth. They are told how the king, through his dynasty, is descended from the Sacred Bull, himself the offspring of the god or goddess Moon. As Frobenius writes, "man first experiences civilization and myth; only later does he become capable of expressing them."[8]

Myth, then, is first of all a narrative, a series of coherent images by means of which one tells a story. But this story needs to be revealed to the boys undergoing initiation, *ex-plicated* or unfolded. The story contains its own *meaning*, in the form of symbolic images that previously existed only as dance, sculpture, or painting, because in the obscure but expressive force of emotion and rhythm they were sufficient unto themselves. Frobenius, completing the teaching of the masters of the initiation ceremony, taught us to see our myths not only as works of art but as expressions of the values of the civilization of Negritude, or *Negerheit*, which when all is said and done is simply a *Neger sein*, as my friend Janheinz Jahn has put it. Hence the title of the third part of *Histoire*: "Poetry."

Emotion and *intuitive reason*, *art* and *poetry*, *image* and *myth*: these and other synonymous words and notions crop up in connection with the Negro, and their study is pertinent. The first two terms may be compared with such German words as *Einfühlung*, *Gefühl*, *Wesenheit*, and *Weltanschauung*, for which equivalents can be found in African Negro languages and which express certain fundamental values of the German *Seele*, or *Germanness*. Africa has always exerted a fascination on Germans, who have felt a *Sehnsucht nach Afrika*. For proof of this one has only to glance at the list of great German Africanists compiled by Booker W. Sadji, the son of the Senegalese writer, who is a professor of German: Heinrich Barth, Adolf Overweg, Friedrich Hornemann, Edward Vogel, Gerhard Rohlfs, Gustav Nachtigal, Robert Flegel, and Franz Thorbecke.[9] And this list is by no means exhaustive. One should also mention such anthropologists and linguists as Sigismund Koelle, Diedrich Westermann, and August Klingenheben.

Nevertheless, it was not until Frobenius came along that the affinities between the "Ethiopian," or African Negro, soul and the German soul were revealed, the effect of which was to destroy certain tenacious prejudices dating back to the seventeenth and eighteenth centuries. One of those prejudices was that, like humanity itself, each ethnos develops in a single, linear fashion from the stone age to the age of steam, electricity, and the atom. In *Destin*, an early version of "ethnic characterology," Frobenius tells us that, like individuals, ethnoi are diverse or even opposed, like the Hamites and Ethiopians, with respect to their feelings and ideas, myths and ideologies, customs and institutions; that each ethnos, because of its *paideuma*, or soul, reacts to the environment in a unique way and develops autonomously; and finally, that although Germans and "Ethiopians" are at different stages of development, they belong to the same spiritual family. And he concludes: "The West created English realism and French rationalism, the East, German mysticism. . . . There is total harmony with the corresponding African civilizations: *sense of the fact in the French, English, and Hamitic civilizations, sense of the real in the German and Ethiopian civilizations.*"[10] This judgment is now confirmed by ethnic characterologists, who assign the Germans to the "introverted" ethnotype and Negroes to the "fluctuating" ethnotype, both characterized essentially by energy and depth of feeling.

The consequences of this discovery are easily imagined, as is the additional confidence it gave us in ourselves. For paradoxically, our French professors had taught us to respect the German genius, whether restricted within the narrow confines of a principality or expanded to the dimensions of the globe (or even the universe), for its wealth of contrasts, not to say contradictions, for its vigorous logic and visionary mysticism, angelic gentleness and brutal force, its poets and musicians and its engineers.

In this way Frobenius helped us to emerge from the ghetto to which we had confined ourselves in the first phase of Negritude and to seek a "conciliatory accord." Only then could we hope to fulfill our destiny by way of what Jacques Maritain called "integral humanism."

Now that the African nations have joined the international community as members of the United Nations and the old colonial regimes have been abolished nearly everywhere on the continent, the association between the Africans states and the European Economic Community is developing around the idea of "Eurafrica." We took this idea from Frobenius, and nothing has been more fruitful in working toward the Civilization of the Universal. By *Eurafrica* the German anthropologist meant a civilization that developed around the Mediterranean and probably flourished in the late Paleolithic and Neolithic periods, as described in book five of *Histoire*, entitled "The Earliest Art of the Image." He returned to this subject in *Destin*: "The soil of Africa also yielded abundant evidence of Paleolithic civilizations, especially in mountainous regions. Several scholars believe that the Cheleans come from Africa, as well as the Capsians who in the neo-Paleolithic period dominated Spain all the way to the frontiers of Franco–Cantabrian civilization. This is a fact of the utmost importance for 'primitive history,' and especially for its second neo-Paleolithic period. In Europe, all these civilizations vanished at around the time the glaciers receded in the middle of the Neolithic period (five thousand years before the birth of Christ). They were absorbed or snuffed out."[11]

Advances in prehistorical studies have by now made us familiar with the concept of Eurafrica. Since the time of Abbé Breuil and Father Teilhard de Chardin, moreover, almost every year has yielded additional evidence that it was in Africa that man first emerged from the animal state. And the last Congress of African Prehistorians, which met in the capital of Ethiopia in 1971, moved the date of that emergence back by some 5,500,000 years.

Here, too, Frobenius was a precursor: whether the question was the emergence of man or the emergence of art, he was always in the vanguard. In his words: "At the beginning of this chapter, we asked whether the sculptures in bone, stone, and ivory of the first civilization of the middle epoch of the Stone Age, sculptures found in Europe and not in Africa, were not transpositions into the hard materials favored by the northern style of artifacts originally created in other materials by equatorial precivilizations as developed in the advanced epoch of the Stone Age and transformed in the south, for example in the Capsian."[12]

Of course, the status of Africanism has evolved since the time of Frobenius, and great discoveries have been made. There has been real progress. We no longer carry his books like the Bible or the Koran when we travel. Nevertheless, his two magisterial works are still in my library, and I consult them often. For if we have achieved a political independence that seems more nominal than real, we are still under the economic domination of Euramerica, and its ideologies, though antagonistic to one another, besiege Negritude.

For decades I have been saying that independence of mind is a sine qua non of all other forms of independence, and this Leo Frobenius helped us to achieve. For that reason he remains our Teacher.

TRANSLATED BY ARTHUR GOLDHAMMER.

NOTES

[1] Leo Frobenius, *Histoire de la civilisation africaine*, trans. Dr. H. Bach and D. Ermont (Paris: Gallimard, 1933), and *Le Destin des civilisations*, trans. N. Guterman (Paris: Gallimard, 1940).

[2] *Histoire*, p. 25.

[3] *Destin*, p. 114.

[4] *Histoire*, p. 39.

[5] See the chapter entitled "*Le Réel dans la civilisation*" in *Destin*.

[6] *Petit Robert* (Paris: L. Robert, 1984), s.v. "Mythe".

[7] *Histoire*.

[8] Ibid., p. 109.

[9] Cf. Booker W. Sadji, "Négritude et Germanité," a speech for the annual school prize award ceremonies in Dakar Senegal, 1972.

[10] *Destin*, p. 131.

[11] Ibid., pp., 64, 65.

[12] *Histoire*.

EDOUARD GLISSANT

Poetic Intention
1997

In What Is Literature? *Sartre wrote: "Since words are transparent and since the gaze looks through them, it would be absurd to slip in among them some panes of rough glass."[1] Sartre's resistance to poetry, a mode of writing he describes as a sort of linguistic cataract, follows from his intolerance toward every type of writing that would interfere with language's transparency.*

The Negritude movement, however, forced Sartre to go beyond this politics of prose. He radically revised his initial position in "Black Orpheus," the introduction he wrote for Senghor's 1949 landmark anthology of black Francophone poets. "It is necessarily through a poetic experience," he wrote, "that the black man, in his present condition, must first become conscious of himself."[2] In Sartre's worldview, prose is the tool for the liberation of the white industrial proletariat, poetry the tool for the liberation of the black pre-industrial, mostly rural, non-European proletariat.

The very opacity of the signifier, an effect of the colonial situation, endows it with a specifically linguistic revolutionary dimension. "In the nineteenth century," Sartre continues,

> *most ethnic minorities passionately endeavored to resuscitate their national languages while struggling for their independence. . . . [However], when the Negro declares in French that he rejects French culture, he accepts with one hand what he rejects with the other; he sets up the enemy's thinking-apparatus in himself, like a crusher. This would not matter: except that this syntax and vocabulary—forged thousand of miles away in another epoch to answer other needs and to designate other objects—are unsuitable to furnish him with the means of speaking about himself, his own anxieties, his own hopes."[3]*

Negritude's early dream of retrieving the African worldview (the African signified, Black Orpheus's Eurydice) stumbles here on the linguistic obstacle (the white signifier experienced as a linguistic prosthesis). What

Edouard Glissant, from *L'Intention poétique* (Paris: Gallimard, 1997), vol. 2, pp. 41–50.

kind of independence of mind is available when one doesn't own the tools
for one's linguistic independence? The second generation of Francophone
writers, especially those from the Caribbean Islands, sensitive to the impli-
cations of this complex linguistic situation and therefore more future-
oriented, stopped focusing primarily on reaccessing a past African
authenticity. "As for our names," as Aimé Césaire has it in his Tragedy of
King Christophe, *"since we cannot lift them from the past, let's do it from*
the future."⁴ And, more recently, Edouard Glissant, in a slightly less affir-
mative mode: "My nation and its language remain to be built."⁵

I do not contend that the only pure and innocent communities are those
once inhabited by the people whom I today claim as ancestors but from
whom I am descended only in the most distant and roundabout way (the
circumstances are obscure). I am reluctant always to sanctify what I find
strange and mysterious. What is perfectly plain, however, is that in those ancestral lands myth never insisted quite so stubbornly on cultivating but a single
dark fruit: the individual clinging to his unfathomable freedom. And society in
its bloody struggles was never so ferociously intent on perpetuating the very
root of that fruit, namely, private property.

I see, moreover, that in my country *the title* to my land belongs to others: yet
another obscure circumstance, which at once mocks and merges with the poetics of being. I see that this land, in which so many nameless people marked by
the history of others (by denial and oblivion) never sleep—that this land, thus
fertilized by a people's blood, not only does not belong to that people (which
lives in it yet outside it) but is made a laughingstock by this record of unjust
ownership. It must be granted, moreover, that in our familiar history we have
merely allowed things to take their course, to degenerate from elite to elite. We
have learned to anticipate, to accumulate (wretchedly), to desire. So there we
are, neither better nor worse in the clash of interests. And late to boot in the
realm of technology, on which the West prides itself. Perhaps not even enhanced by our ridiculous desires. Yet I proclaim that our destiny, our function
in the world, is different, and that beyond this wish, this cry, this passion, we
must make a careful, minute inventory of all that has been taken from us. We
must seriously prepare for the moment when wisdom will be at liberty in our
land (at last the property of all).

And if I listen to the voice of the West, to the greatest political leaders, the
most profound dogmatic thinkers, the wisest creators, I *hear* silence whenever
the future sharing of the various abysses in man is broached. In this respect we
are all novices in the new injunction. And I am not forgetting that throughout
Western history the very possibility of any such relationship has been flatly denied (as if to rule it out, cast doubt on it, reject it in advance). Here, only the

poets were heeding the world, fertilizing the ground in advance. And we know how long it takes for their voices to be heard.

Only poets.

And people ask: What do you do, if not speak the language of the West? And what do you discuss, if not precisely what you reject? But I do not reject; I establish correlations. And if I answer that, like those who do not think of themselves as French, who do not feel French, yet who use the French language, I too have to sort out my relation to that tongue, they tell me that I am more French than I think. Once again, they have the right to reveal to me what I am. (I, for my part, refrain from raising the acknowledged past, the decisive act, or the intransigent mob.) Of course, if I protest in this way, they ask why I have to work with language, weigh concepts, and declaim Homer and Dante? They would rather I be more "authentic," indeed, more savage. Then they would grant my difference. But my difference lies in the use I make of the concept, not in the refusal (or impossibility) of abstraction. It lies in my passionate commerce with the language, not my ignorance of it. The Philosopher spoke of the unconscious germ of the conscious maturity of Civilizations. Perhaps, in the modern world, with its smattering of half-baked knowledge, its tons of accumulated menace, we are all living (relative to the obligation to change ourselves—without exchanging ourselves—with the other) with both our conscious germ and our unconscious maturity. Germ: knowledge given by birth, growth that sees itself growing. Maturity: tool, weapon, relevance, moment, freedom. To be sure, we possess neither absolute awareness of, nor total power over, the how or the when: we are unraveling the fabric in which the world ensnares us. But we are conscious of consciousness: the germ is known and felt.

All "voluntarist" literature (which by its very nature is soon to be transcended) is today preparing our minds for maturity, arming our style (*langage*) with knowledge.

What, then, is style? My chosen cry? Not only that but also *the absence* that thrills to the sound of that cry.

For if you stuff this or that down my throat in order to persuade me that I
    must surrender
I shall wail about the man who one night climbed the acacia-covered hill,
chased, from jungle to forest and forest to woods, over the sea and across
    bridges, to this bluff,
and who knew, as it were, only the slope, the incline, the swinging bridge, the
    lurching abyss, the swaying of the bluff
and who, his toes thrust through the night into the mud, was the first to climb
    into the thick gloom,
there to utter a cry that was immediately lost in the immensity of that
    minuscule space

swallowed up, snuffed out, eaten away in the workshops and cane fields, in
    the violated splendor of the Single Season (the cry),
daily whittled down at each crossroads in the humiliation of the conquest in
    which the other ensnared us,
drained of so many suspected talents
(when the slaves' breath invariably turned sour in the cavern of cane)
the shout from the highest bluff, unheeded by the world,
engulfed by the wave of sticky sweetness that entraps man.
And it is around this absence this silence this inwardness that I weave
the language in my breast, which thus begins with a lack.
And my language, whether stiff and obscure or alive or tense, is this lack
first of all, but it is also the will to transform my cry into speech hurled at the
    sea.

(What is the importance of the language one uses when it is the quality of the
cry, of the utterance, that measures the depth of the implant? Whatever tongue
is authorized, therein thou shalt build thy language.)

    Indeed, being no longer chooses itself in the solitary resonance of a language.
For some Frenchmen, the word *sun* may have taken on a new meaning with
Louis XIV, just as for some Englishmen the word *sea* resonated differently
after Trafalgar, yet I remain alien to this slow process of maturation, which
eventually contaminates the users of any tongue. Until recently, in other words,
every nation used to ripen to perfection in the unique, often exclusive, invariably aggressive projection of its tongue. But I am not an heir to that uniqueness;
I need not even react against it. The Académie's efforts to purify French are no
concern of mine (they neither satisfy me nor outrage me nor make me smile).
In contrast (not to say, in defiance of grammar, *in revenge*), what does excite me
is my encounter with the law of language. For the ties of my communities to
the cultural entity which that law used to represent were, when all is said and
done, ties of alienation. I have no need to prove loyalty or continuity, only to
nudge things in my direction: this is my way of recognizing the law.
    In the past, the Swiss, Belgians, and Canadians were regarded as exceptions
on account of their multilingualism. Indeed, this exceptional status may have
been responsible for certain peculiarities, certain forms of cultural inhibition.
This distinctiveness still serves as a pretext for internal conflicts in these countries. To be multilingual at a time when every language used to assert its solitary genius (often in opposition to other languages as unified nation faced
unified nation) was not without danger or traumatic consequences. Today,
however, a nation is no longer "consubstantial" with a—*its*—language. Multilingualism is the natural condition of part of the world. Some African children
voluntarily study two (or even three) languages in school, and now that the
time when the imposition of a language created complexes, feelings of rootless-

ness, and cultural sterility is past, this new condition is inaugurating a new era of expression.

In the past, one developed and perhaps classified different styles within a framework sublimated (or "made exclusive") by a single language, but soon it will be *natural* to speak more than one language. Style (or choice of expression) will flow effortlessly through one language after another, not because some mechanism of vocabulary requires it (for otherwise style would be reduced to a kind of Esperanto) but for good reason. Hence, any analysis of style will have to take account not only of the languages involved but also of the ontological dimension of their interaction. Yes, to describe a style will be to describe a general attitude toward words, but it will also be to explore the source (in the individual or community) of an elocutory symbiosis signifying one aspect of the speaker's relationship to the totality of the world.

Language will then cease to be simply an obstacle to, or fulfillment of, individual expression. It will also involve, inevitably in contradictory fashion, possession (*détention*) and interaction (*relation*). Poetic style will be approached not merely in terms of its difference from customary speech but as a stylized language within language (that is, a novel combination of several languages harmoniously reconciled by the poetic style in question).

Furthermore, because style has been valued in Western history as a positive accomplishment, a triumphant achievement within the norms of a specific language, in the future it will very likely encourage a conscious and fruitful nostalgia in languages in which that achievement is not understood, just as many of us who know no German once daydreamed over Hölderlin's *Rhine*, struggling with the aid of various translations to penetrate to the heart of the text. This lack, this consciousness of a lack, will have to be taken into account if certain modern styles (which will quickly become ancient styles) are to be appreciated. The conventions and rules formulated by linguists are already out of date with respect to the vagabond languages and dialects by means of which different (collective) individuals manifest their presence to the world. Linguistics will have to shift from static analysis to dynamic description if it wants to capture the phenomenon. Otherwise it will simply corroborate an anachronism and lend its support to the most obtuse academic compromises.

Hence it makes no sense nowadays to try to purify a language by banishing all foreign words. Surely it is more profitable to acknowledge the fact that all languages both give and receive (because all nations both give and receive in their relations with other nations) and to work toward transforming historical or accidental compounds into genuine composites. These efforts cannot be regulated by a suspect authority. On the contrary, a certain suspicion of linguistic rhetoric may signify, deep down, a disarray on the part of those who refuse to share either the world or words. The silence of words may reveal the silence of the world in an individual or group. The era of languages proud of their purity must end: the adventure of plural styles (of the poetics of a world first diffracted and then reconstituted) is beginning.

The road descends to the bank, held in the embrace of light and dark greens which catch the gaze on either side and narrow its focus. Here and there one sees flashes, sparks that though motionless seem to move, of red flowers. No tree, no outline is visible. Only green, illuminated by the fragile wind of red flowers. A single spirit.

(When I say *tree*, and when I think *tree*, I never envision the single tree, the trunk, the mast of sap which, juxtaposed to others, constitutes that light-cleaved mass, the forest. In Europe, the forest delighted me: I used to visit the woods at Hesdin as if visiting a simplified world, in which avenues and vistas held promise of thicker, denser realms. Here, however, the tree is spirit, Wholeness, teeming density. If, in my clumsy way, I attempted to draw a tree, I would set down an expanse of vegetation, whose indeterminate growth would be ended only by the heaven of the page. The unique is swallowed up in the Whole.)

Hence, I remember few of the names that distinguish these plants. I hesitate to classify trees, birds, and flowers. What stands out against the mass is significant: (sugar cane); the cheesemaker who at midnight leaves the realm of vegetation and enters the circle of ancestral powers; the *acoma* and *courbaril*, as stunted and ravaged as the runaway slaves over whom they once watched; the *arum* and *balisier*, splendid yet sullied by their touristic uses; the poppies of the windowboxes; and a few others that are also, like these, part of our history. For the rest, let us leave the spirit its undivided force. What is that red flower? Simply the flower, wind-blown on the heights of the Whole.

Today, human truths are rarely encapsulated in brilliant, compact utterances. They are to be gauged, rather, by the repetition, the arduous, perpetually renewed task of formulating a theory of the obvious (almost the banal), whose lessons are repeatedly rejected. Brilliance lies in the art of capturing the obscure in its revealed light; accumulation is the art of consecrating the obvious on the altar of its duration, at last made visible. Brilliance is one's own; accumulation is everyone's. Brilliance crystallizes the absolute and unrealizable wish for the Other; accumulation leads to relative, perfectible knowledge of relatedness.

The poetics of duration, by its opposition to, and encompassing of, the brilliance of the moment, permits, at the level of expression (where the poem is no longer the sole, the aristocratic reservoir, the unique conduit of poetic knowledge), a reordering of the deeply buried imperatives of relatedness. It suspends the imperiousness of language, and by stages, layer by obscure layer, reveals how each being is related through suffering to the world drama. Or rather, it does not reveal; it slowly, ponderously unveils. It makes it possible to root each community's unique, particular, luminous principle in the patience of its rapidly illuminated relationship with the Other. It arms with knowledge those who have neither knowledge nor power in the world, establishing that greatness is not the exclusive possession of power but tangent to a kind of lucidity, a vocation that culminates in desire of, appeal to, realization of the Other. Brilliance, though ardent and rich, is snuffed out by failure to recognize the world as relation. You are not you unless you actively, consciously accept me. Otherwise you eat away at yourself; you sterilize yourself. This, for the time being, is the unregulated law of the universe. History, before transcending itself, strives to link up all Histories. As time runs out, this is what it wants, for now. Every community arms itself by receiving when it has the power to give. We shall experience absolute joy when, having connected to the multiplicity which everywhere longs for equality, we are all liberated from want, misfortune, backwardness, solitude, injustice, madness, and the unconscious—of the Other.

I build my style out of rock. To be sure, I write, according to a scribe whose name I have forgotten, like a schoolteacher (*instituteur*) from Fort-de-France (or perhaps Fort-Lamy). But it is literally my style which *institutes* me. I abuse the blessed parenthesis: (this is how I breathe). But never mind that. There is a more occult influence: in the unsuitability of this style to those who ought to have been the first to harken to it. This is because I am confronted with two necessities: to encompass the (devastated) historical wasteland that has swallowed up our voice, and to hurl that voice into the here and now, into the history to be made with others. Anxiety and obscurity are the result. Given its intention, this style is not today accessible to those who ought to be the first to hear it. Yet they hear no style of their own. Their natural speech is muffled by poverty. In the best of cases, when poverty is escaped, their borrowed speech is subject to the derision of someone else's linguistic usage. The freedom of a community should not be limited to rejecting a language; it might in some cases be enhanced by taking the imposed language and using it to construct a style, to create. Fetishistic respect for the imposed language contributes to sterilizing the creative capacity of the community. Oppressive power seeks to perpetuate this respect. It accomplishes this by creating a group of semiliterates whose role in this respect is fatal. "Creolism" is both enrichment of the language and victory over the phony men of letters. My nation and its language remain to be built—in time, in depth, in knowledge, in taste. World drama. Working alone, a few of us push the word as far as it can go. Trembling with the enormous privilege of our limited knowledge. We call out to the future nation, and already we cannot breathe without it. For it is not merely a state, it is a poetics of being. We are suffocating. We cry out for those who have no voice, but it is their language which sustains us in our efforts. They die; they are *truly* suffocating. We despise the literate bards. When our people finally find their voice, our voices will be secure. Isolated in our tiny land, we are running dry, but we are also (we, the land, the voiceless people, the voice of the sea) the call, the fire, the force, the prayer of the world. How are we to relate to the Other when we do not (yet) possess any (learned) opacity to oppose him, to propose to him? Language, still a novice here, incorporates these possibilities.

The world's tragic joy: its obscure workings will determine the fate of unconscious maturity. Therefore grant those who have no voice the right "deliberately" to forge for themselves a language, until such time as they can express themselves comfortably. The imperative is to admit the durability of every style. What is needed, both by communities steeped in history and by communities devoid of everything, is not a language of communication (abstract, bloodless, and "universal" in the familiar sense) but a way for mutually liberated opacities to communicate (regularly if possible) about their differences, their styles.

TRANSLATED BY ARTHUR GOLDHAMMER

NOTES

[1] Jean-Paul Sartre, "What Is Literature?", in *"What is Literature?" and Other Essays*, trans. Bernard Frechtman (Cambridge, Mass.: Harvard University Press, 1988) p. 39.

[2] "Black Orpheus" [1948], Ibid., p. 293.

[3] Ibid., p. 301.

[4] Aimé Césaire, *La tragédie du roi Christophe* (Paris: Présence africaine, 1963), p. 39.

[5] Edouard Glissant, *L'intention poétique (Poétique II)* (Paris: Gallimard, 1997), p. 6.

'ABDELLATÎF LA'BÎ

Prologue to the Review *Souffles* 1966

In the aftermath of independence, intellectuals from the former French colonies found themselves at a difficult crossroads. An independent nation, it seemed, must have a literature the same way it does a national football team, an anthem, a flag. But how does one create a literature from scratch? And for whom? Edouard Glissant, for example, after dedicating his writing to a nation that had yet to be built and to find its language, confesses to "the unsuitability of this style for those who ought to have been the first to harken to it"[1]

For writers from North Africa, it was a question not simply of style but of languages; it was not so much a matter of anticipating a future language as a question of the postcolonial future of the language in which they were writing, the language in which they became independent and they accessed independence.

Hence the paradox most of them had to face of a national literature aimed at a nonnational readership: most Maghrebian literature, writes La'bî, is "one long open letter to the West." This, however, is not simply a transitional phenomenon; it goes beyond the aftereffects of colonial "acculturation." La'bî talks about a generation of writers for whom, having "discovered their literary vocation by way of French," French remains the linguistic and cultural medium within which they were called into writing—"came into writing," Cixous would have said.

French is at once the language of the former colonizer and the language of literature, suggesting that the much debated question of national literature might not be the real issue. The alternative, here, might not be between one or two literatures, written in one or two languages, French or Arabic, but between two cultural spaces, one in which literature remains a structuring reference and the other where it does not. For cultures born in the postcolonial space might have to skip the literary stage; they are born,

'Abdellatîf La'bî, "Prologue de la revue *Souffles*" [1966] in Abdelkebir Khatibi, *Le Roman maghrébin* (Paris: Maspero, 1968), pp. 142–46.

postliterate. Who needs writers, one might ask, in a space where there is no reader?

The poets who have contributed to this manifesto issue of the review *Souffles* are all well aware of the fact that to publish a text of this kind is to stake out a position at a time when the problems of our national culture have reached a point of extreme tension.

The current situation is not, as one might expect, a period of great creativity. The cultural agitation that certain individuals and organizations want to characterize as a crisis brought on by the growth of our national literature is in fact merely a symptom of stagnation, indeed of a certain misunderstanding of the deeper significance of literary work.

Petrified contemplation of the past, paralysis of form and content, virtually shameless imitation and borrowing, inflation of fake talent—this is our daily bread, made of adulterated flour and shoveled into our mouths by newspapers, magazines, and a small but greedy band of publishers.

Besides being prostituted in various ways, literature has become an aristocratic affectation, a badge of honor, and a source of power for the intelligentsia and the wheeler-dealers.

What is going on here is not even close to a quarrel between Ancients and Moderns. In fact, the literature that plagues us today is astonishingly eclectic, full of allusions and borrowings. An objective critic might well come here to study literary trends extinct elsewhere but somehow kept alive here. And since the tourist brochures speak of a "land of contrasts," it is interesting to note that we have something to offer every sensibility, every nostalgic taste: residues of classical medieval poetry, the oriental poetry of exile, Western Romanticism, early twentieth–century Symbolism, and Social Realism, to say nothing of the detritus of undigested Existentialism.

"Representatives" of "Moroccan literature" carry all this baggage with them to international meetings, and writers' congresses are held here. Readers are simultaneously bewildered and disgusted by it all. Their dissatisfaction finds justification in the fact that their problems are reflected in the foreign literatures graciously placed at their disposal by various "missions." Our national literature suffers, we are often told, from a kind of "complex" because what is currently being written is incapable of "touching" the reader or gaining his approval or eliciting any type of reflection, any response not conditioned by social and political indoctrination.

In a very different vein, North African literature written in French, once a source of considerable hope, is going nowhere at present and to many observers seems already to have become a part of history. Yet it cries out today for critical scrutiny.

Two of its most brilliant representatives have already delivered moving, if premature, funeral orations.[1] After analyzing the situation of the colonized writer, his linguistic difficulties, and his lack of genuine readers, both came to the conclusion that this literature was "doomed to die young."

Other writers have been reluctant to accept this depressingly fatalistic view. Nevertheless, after subjecting themselves to lucid self-criticism, writers on both sides of the issues seem to agree on one paradoxical fact—that this suicidal literature continues, in spite of everything, to make progress, though more slowly than in the past.

A glance at recent publications is enough to show that those who announced the imminent death of this literature were perhaps a little too hasty. To say this is obviously not to minimize the problems that French North African literature must face, including the very basic question of its status. These are delicate matters, which must be approached with care and subtlety. In fact, the situation of the writers of the previous generation (Kateb Yacine, Mohammed Dib, Mouloud Feraoun, Mouloud Mammeri, Albert Memmi, and even Driss Chraïbi) turns out to be closely related to the colonial problem in its linguistic, cultural, and sociological implications. From the colorful, pacifist autobiographies of the 1950s to the insistently militant works of the Algerian War period, we find that despite the diverse talents and creative power of these writers, all their work can be encompassed within the category of "acculturation." It stands as an excellent illustration of this particular relationship of colonized to colonizer in the cultural domain. Thus, although it is true that North Africans do appear in these works and that indigenous writers did speak out against abuses, this literature was almost always a one-way street. It was written for readers in the "metropolis" and destined for foreign consumption. It was a foreign audience that one hoped to move or whose solidarity one hoped to enlist; it was to a foreign audience that one had to demonstrate that the fellah of Kabylia and the worker of Oran were not all that different from the peasant of Brittany or the longshoreman of Marseilles. Today, one has the impression that all this literature was one long open letter to the West, a sort of compilation of the grievances of the Maghreb. To be sure, the usefulness of this lengthy deposition no longer needs demonstrating. The works of these North African writers shocked progressives in France and elsewhere and helped to raise their consciousness. In this sense, these works were revolutionary.

Not to be unduly rigid ourselves, we should, moreover, make an exception for the two or three writers whose work, even if it shared these common concerns initially, cannot be confined within any such straitjacket.

Surely, it is no secret that this literature is of only limited concern to us now. In any case, it does not respond to our current need for a literature capable of facing up to the realities of the present, to new issues that have sown disarray and triggered instinctive rebellion.

Obviously the situation had to deteriorate, or, if you prefer, ripen, to a certain point before the texts in this issue could be written.

The poets who cry out in these pages have not been exempt from the distress suffered by their elders, but they have been obliged to evaluate with a cold eye the limits of their heritage, which they do not view as an unmixed blessing. They hope to demonstrate that they are not so much carrying on an old tradition as starting a new one.

In conditions of peace, amid the chorus of insults heaped on underdevelopment, and while enduring the humiliations of the present, they have witnessed the mutations of a society that has all too often been mistaken for a test bed or a storehouse of legends. And they have served not only as witnesses but also as actors in the vanguard. Despite the kaleidoscope of styles, their voices join to sound a forceful alarm.

Certain assumptions remain to be overcome, certain contradictions to be patched up or transcended, but old complexes have been swept away, and new currents have begun to flow.

Given where things now stand, we can already guess what charges that will be leveled against us, in particular owing to the language in which we have chosen to express ourselves.

Without wishing to get bogged down in a morass of irrelevant issues, we want to anticipate this charge by responding in advance that four of the poets represented here discovered their literary vocation by way of French. In this there is nothing dramatic or paradoxical. In today's world, it is an all too common situation. The only thing that matters is that the poet should achieve congruence between his written language and his inner world, his intimate emotional dialect. Some never achieve this. Others, even though they write in the language of their nation, never delve below the surface, either of themselves or of the reality they wish to abstract and interrogate.

Linguistic displacement notwithstanding, each poet in this collection succeeds in conveying his deepest feelings by employing a language that has been passed through the filter of his own history, mythology, and anger—in other words, a language filtered by the poet's personality.

Another problem remains, however—that of the audience for this poetry. The point has of course been made (though oddly enough never taken seriously) that if these works have any place or role to play in our national literature, they can always be translated. Furthermore, the question of an audience for all of our literature is not as simple as some people believe. In Morocco, the number of people capable of reading a work of literature, let alone of appreciating, interpreting, or criticizing it, is minuscule. Illiteracy on the one hand and superficial cultivation on the other combine to limit the potential readership to a ridiculously small number.

This paradoxical situation is a consequence of the present state of Morrocan society. It cannot be remedied by argument or magic. Given this state of affairs, why give up trying? Why should we allow silence to be reinstated, more oppressive and devastating than ever? To begin with, a poet's language is "his own," the language that he creates and develops within the chaos of language itself, shaped by the way in which he rearranges the various worlds and tendencies that coexist within him.

Why despair of this situation as a handicap when we need to use all available means to catch up with the present and respond to the urgent needs of the moment?

The next generation may resolve the problem, but that generation will bear the stamp of a new world, a world that will no longer be ours but toward which we are working in full awareness of what we are doing.

TRANSLATED BY ARTHUR GOLDHAMMER

INTRODUCTORY NOTE

[1] Edouard Glissant, *L'intention poétique (Poétique II)* (Paris: Gallimard, 1997), p. 6.

NOTE

[1] See Malek Haddad, *Les zéros tournent en rond* (Paris: Maspero, 1961), and Albert Memmi, *Portrait du colonisé* (Paris: Buchet-Chastel, 1957).

ASSIA DJEBAR

The White of Algeria
1993

Assia Djebar recounts a thirty-year long war of languages that followed in the wake of the Algerian war of independence, a war of languages as a result of which she found herself trapped between at least two increasingly conflicting allegiances.

Assia Djebar is generally referred to as an "Algerian writer" or novelist or film maker; it is not insignificant that in these pages she refers to herself "as a writer and an Algerian." The very concept of an Algerian writer has become the hostage of what, initially experienced as a war of languages, ends up accounting for the crumbling of the dream of an independent Algerian literature which had been nurtured during the war of independence. The initial tension between the French and Arabic languages grew into a more radical conflict between two diverging cultural spaces, one of them excluding literature. In today's Algeria, she feels, literature itself is doomed to be a foreign language, as illustrated by the quantity of "Algerian writers" who are not even translated in Arabic.

"Arabization"—the "war against the French language"—might even be a pretext, one senses, as suspicion increases against "that minority of writers who express themselves in French." For French isn't excluded from the "language of science and technology." And the Algerian media are invaded by "American series dubbed in French." Moreover, French literature isn't the only victim: Djebar mentions Kafka and other writers. As if she were pulled into the French cultural orbit not so much because she writes in French, but because of what she writes. Literature as such—a certain idea of literature—might thus look suspicious to postcolonial cultures. Thus the question, at least in part, might be whether or not postcolonial cultures aren't those whose formation skips the literary stage, cultures that start in a context where literature is obsolete: as though having no literary past deprived them of a future.

Assia Djebar, "The White of Algeria," trans. Andrew Benson, in *Another Look, Another Woman: Retranslations of French Feminism*, Lynne Huffer, ed., *Yale French Studies* 87 (1995), pp. 141–48, from *"Le Blanc de l'Algérie"* (Strasbourg: Carrefour des littératures européennes: 1993).

Algeria today . . . in the wake of a series of murders of writers and intellectuals that was triggered, it seems, in response to increased repression—the only policy anyone can find to brandish against a religious fundamentalism set on taking power whatever the cost; in the face of these convulsions which are plunging my country into a war that dares not speak its name and that again could be euphemistically referred to as "events";[1] in this return of violence and its anesthetizing vocabulary, what is this "white" (the whiteness of dust, light without sun, dilution, and so on) and why bring it up here?

Rather than simply inscribing my comments in the wake of those made on this tragedy by sociologists, historians, political scientists, and even pamphleteers, I can find no other way to express *my own* unease as a writer and an Algerian than by referring to this color, or rather, this noncolor. Kandinsky said that "white, on our soul, acts like absolute silence." Here, by means of this reference to abstract painting, I am setting off a discourse that is, in such circumstances, somewhat off-center.

Irreversibly, the edges of the chasm are gaping, pulling into the abyss not only some of the boldest intellectuals, but, according to the luck of a bloody lottery, some of the meekest as well. Indeed, the violence so unleashed, in its blind acceleration certainly accentuates the vanity of the spoken word, but also its necessity. Any word that would not primarily be one of passion, and that, groping about in the dark for the limits of its reach, could remain aware of its own fragility and even of its inanity comes too late. But beneath the leaden sky where it unfurls, let such a word come out of its hiding place to set traps and ambush all ambiguities; to wit, the fact that the media takeover of any intellectual resistance (one remembers before 1992 the media transforming a few fanatics of God [*fous de Dieu*] into a spectacle) only ended up in a thickening white noise, the blank zone of the projectors, widening the desert (here I am only referring to Algerian intellectuals on the verge of the dizzying abyss and not, of course, to the solidarity, in France and elsewhere, which is trying to organize itself).

For I am haunted, personally—in the calm before the storm—by the long and abiding state of morbidity in which Algerian culture has lingered: discourse secreting and fomenting the latent brew of discord—not because of the emptiness of political speech that wasted little time in degenerating into a mere bandying of words and the recital of socio-economic findings trapped within their own science. No!

It has often seemed to me that, in an Algeria that has increasingly become culturally fragmented (and where the traditional sexual segregation has tightened all the screws), words have, of necessity, lost their edge even before they could sharpen themselves by their own flickering light.

And yet, I am moved only by that need for words with which to confront this imminent disaster. Writing and its urgency.

Writing about an Algeria teetering on the brink and for which some people are already preparing the white shroud.

I lived in Algeria as a university academic for much of the thirty years of independence; as such, I tried to fight, like my peers, and before long, to little avail, against the setting-up of an educational system whose absurdity—no, worse than that, whose imbecility—in the sense of inherent and irremediable weakness—sent so many young people headlong into a distressing cultural underdevelopment, one that fed itself, true, on a hunger for social justice that was being simultaneously sharpened and frustrated. Their numbers have been growing because of an unbridled population boom deliberately encouraged by the state.

Now that the three knocks have already sounded on the stage of this drama (or this tragedy), it would be useless to indict a policy that preached from on high a massive cut-rate Arabization backed by elites more often than not graduated from the Sorbonne, and not just any Oriental universities or medieval "*zaouias*." And all the while, such a policy claimed a desire for modernity, when it only meant technology!

Long before the Islamic fundamentalist danger flared up, fanned by all these winds of popular dissent, long before it turned oppressive, some dissident intellectuals had denounced the pseudopopulism of a self-congratulatory authoritarianism that was using the wealth from our nationalized oil to shore up its self-serving image.

My intention, more limited in scope, is to throw light on the cultural, there to focus on the fatal point where the inevitable failure anchored itself.

Throughout the 1960s, Algeria polished up its official image as a representative of international third-world politics, while in its own market towns and villages, in every lower-class district (already mired in the twin sicknesses of unrest and poverty), everything relating to communication—or the word—was progressively sealed off. Inexorably, the poison seeped in—what I do not flinch from calling a "war between languages."

Algerian literature—from Apuleius in the second century to Kateb Yacine and Mouloud Mammeri, our contemporaries departed in such untimely fashion—has always inscribed a linguistic triangle:

A first language of rock and soil, let us say, sprung from the original language, the Lybico–Berber that for a while lost its written form, except among the Touaregs.[2]

A second language, that of the prestigious outside, of the Mediterranean or Eastern or Western heritage, reserved, it is true, for literate minorities: in the past, for a long time, it was an Arabic kept in the shadow of official French; a

French now marginalized when it is used to creative ends, but valued at school only as a "language of science and technology."

The third partner in this *"ménage à trois,"* the most visible, dominant, public language, the language of power—that of diatribes but also, in written form, the medium of scribes, lawyers, and notaries. This role has been filled by different languages throughout our history: Latin until Augustine; Classical Arabic in the Middle Ages; Turkish, which, during the "Kingdom of Algiers," took over administrative and military usage. Then, after 1830, French entered the stage, dressed in a colonial uniform; now, the so-called "modern" Arabic taught to the young under the pompous ahistorical term of "national language." (To be logical, our "national language"—or that of a reborn postcolonial Algerian State—was Turkish for three centuries, and Arabic only for the last three decades. This Arabic may be "classical" but it is limited and soulless. The Nation, though, like all nations, enriches its language with the swelling of its verve and sap, in bad times as in good.)

As for the "war between languages" mentioned above, I came to experience it personally only gradually at the university. At first, I underestimated its quasi-neurotic symptoms: that certain academics, spouting a grotesquely pompous jargon of scholastic Arabic, devoid of any real thought, as soothing and meaningless as Church Latin, should suddenly decide, long after the war of independence, to become born-again aggressive nationalists, waging war against the French language, and, if need be, against the "West"; there was a comedy of human stupidity, which sooner or later, it seemed to me, would inspire an Algerian Flaubert or Gogol.

To sum up, this drive for institutionalized mediocrity worked on two fronts: for example, promoting the "national language" in the media meant, first, authoritatively restricting the living space of other languages, cutting off programs in French and Berber from television and radio, like so many limbs. The second tier of discordance in this sterilizing monolingualism, the diglossia of Arabic (that vertical variability of structure that could give school children a precious mental agility), was handled the worst by far when compared with other Arab educational systems, undoubtedly because of a massive importation of Middle Eastern teachers, and, above all, because of a ban on the popular culture that feeds on a dialect suffused with the iridescence of regional variations, a dialect subtle in its innate power to convey contention, irony, and dreams.

Thus, denying a whole people their genius went hand in hand with being suspicious of that minority of writers who express themselves in French and who, against the odds, or, for lack of better, in exile, managed to continue to produce.

Jacques Berque, who recently declared that "Islamic fundamentalism" wants to claim modernity while rejecting substructures, says of Algeria and its linguistic choices that it is living a situation that has never existed in any of the twenty other Arab countries, those which also had to face diglossia, with the presence of one or two second languages. He concludes that Algeria has been good at turning a potential source of superiority into a major problem!

Following the—prestigious—example of Georges Bataille who, on the day war was declared in 1939, began his work *Le Coupable* ("I am beginning because of the events but shall not speak about them . . ."), perhaps it is time for the few writers occupied with questions of "Algerianity" (*algérianité*) to tackle texts they may feel constrained to write, no longer in memory of a colonial past in which their childhood took place, but in the light of the present threats on the land of their ancestors, even if they have left it behind.

I use the word "Algerianity," a far broader notion than the "Algerian identity" recorded on official papers; just as in the past it included Camus and Roblès alongside Ferraoun and Kateb, it would now link Derrida and Mohammed Dib, or Hélène Cixous and myself.

Writing Algeria as territory. The desert of writing, "that which, from the indefinite white which starts out, reconstitutes the margin," in the words of André Dubouchet, speaking in 1986 in Hölderlin's house in Tübingen.

And what of the white of Algeria, "out of tune, out of sorts [*désaccordée*]; as if by the snow"? I am counting back to it.

I appear to have lingered over the ruins of deliquescent knowledge, whose pathetic failure ought to have acted much earlier as a warning of an explosion, that of October 1988. Six hundred young corpses in the sun—the future bled white—were not entitled to the least liturgical mourning in any of the three languages, or in a symphony of all three together: where was poetry to be found, then? Where, its summits? Where, its abysses? Aphasia was no longer condemnation but a mask pulled over a decomposing face . . .

Kateb Yacine, whom I saw in Brussels one month later, was quiet, determined to be quiet. When he made up his mind, a bit later, to return to exile to write, to write of his rage no doubt, he was struck down by leukemia, the white disease.

The "opening" that followed on the political front allowed a multiparty system and, it was hoped, democracy: it turned out to be fragile and fit only for buffoons. Then, after the murder of the head of state, with everyone watching live, one Monday in June of 1992, things accelerated in a chain reaction.

Two weeks before Tahar Djaout was murdered,[3] when I was paying public homage in Paris to Mohammed Dib, I expressed my anguish over the deadlock in which the noncommunicable—the white blankness, as it were, of Algerian misfortune—plunged first and foremost our writers into an abyss:

> The proud ally of the wind, you say
> The bird traveler, yes, that land of Algeria,
> The proud ally, barefoot in the sand, hair like brushwood

and stomach rounded, Algeria of the shadows
She fed those angel faces arising in full sunlight, over there
She kohled their cold eyes with a dancing anger
Rouged their cheeks with solitary boredom
Reddened their mouths with screaming silence
Thirty years on, words come full circle in a heavy sky
and return to their source
They explode, sedition of space:
"events," state of siege, riot police, outlaw
and the victims of chance, wide-eyed, and tears
It all comes back—but in a pitiful inversion.

In fact, during the bloody days of October, the insomnia that plagued me in the middle of Algiers, with its curfew, where tanks threaded through the streets, led me to begin a text called "Deserted Algiers," never finished; my anger, when I reread the translucent poetry written by Dib (appealing for a "beyond-powerlessness") found, thanks to the silence of that friendship, a sort of outlet.

I realized that the desert could seize our words from within.

Algeria left untranslated: the outstanding works of the most important "national" writers (Kateb, Dib, Ferraoun, Mammeri) translated almost throughout the world, were left untranslated into the "national language" for thirty years! All they were reluctantly allowed was the academic readership at universities, but confined to the "foreign languages" department! From time to time, they were anthologized in some dreary secondary-school readers.

More serious still: the treasures of oral literature in the delicate dialects—the living breath of the Algerian people over centuries—were equally excluded; a few were, sometimes, transcribed. One never tired of harking back to yesteryear's manly struggle, but no attention was paid to the treasures expressing courtly love, or nostalgia, jewels that ran the gamut from deeply felt mysticism to voluptuous and tender beauty. Living Algerian Arabic, a language for doves and poets, but not for the new civil servants.

As for Berber, it was banned very early on at universities (if you wanted to study it, you had to go to Naples or Aix!) and persecuted even in primary schools, fueling the fire of discontent leading to the Kabyle crisis in 1980.[4]

Each language, then, was confined to its area, regional or social—condemned to a ghetto—while in between them lay a no-man's-land. Wan whiteness crept in, like a lonely wind or frost.

The worst occurred during the mid-1980s. The tap controlling the consumption of live images was opened fully (nonpictures for the most part), allowing in French television or, more accurately, American series dubbed into French. At the same time, a decision was made to end—under the pretext of saving money—the circulation of any press which expressed opinions from elsewhere, thereby starving researchers and real readers—a minority, it's true—to whom books were as vital as food and drink. In universities, a stop was put to the teaching of the main European languages—apart from French and English—putting a whole section of the Algerian memory out of reach—all that lies in Spanish, Italian, and Turkish archives.

This means that a whole treasure has been put out of bounds, including *Nedjma* and *The Stranger*, but also *Nausea*, Kafka's *Letter to His Father*, and *Dr. Zhivago,* because they have not been translated into the "national language": blacklisted—rather, whitelisted or whitewashed in the dirty white of tacit, lazy censorship. In fact, I think it is really the brighter-than-white shine of the ring around the bull's eye. These works, which might have sparked interest in young minds, had to be kept out of reach. So that they do not fly off and reach the point of no return: the inquisitive, questioning reader who, in their mirror, would have felt less deprived.

Between creator and reader, whether in French, Arabic, or Berber, stretched the inner border of a "new" Algeria, that is, one fragmented, sealed off from any thought nurtured somewhere else and drained of the sap of its scorned roots. Held in that tight grip, Algeria was unmoored and delivered, wide-open, to the peddlers, to all kinds of "media" of all persuasions, as well as the warped zealot.

In this "unsaid" of the cultural desert, you could begin to hear, underground, the barely audible crackle of the current fissure.

The white of silence and that of the page waiting in vain for an original text and its translated double, at the risk of being somewhat betrayed.

The white of writing, in an untranslated Algeria? For the time being, Algeria, writingless, despite all the actions of writing, despite its angers and groans, alas, for the time being, a bloody but writing-less country.

How can we mourn our friends, our colleagues, without beforehand saying out loud why yesterday's funeral took place, the funeral of the Algerian dream? The white of dawn—between the colonial night and the rising day? "White square on a white background," like a Malevich painting, exclaiming, at the turn of the century: "But this desert is brimming with an objective sensitivity that pervades everything!"

In the brilliance of that desert, in the retreat of writing in search of a language outside languages, endeavoring to scrub out, in ourselves, all the furies of collective self-devouring, to find that place "from within-among words" (*en dedans de la parole*) that remains our one and only fertile homeland.

TRANSLATED BY ANDREW BENSON

NOTES

[1] The euphemism used by the French government and media reporting on a national liberation struggle (1954–62) they did not want to dignify with the name of "war." Djebar uses the allusion sarcastically, as does Dib in the poem she includes later.—TRANS.

[2] Traced as far back as 1200 B.C., when they tangled with the Egyptian pharaohs, the Berbers are part of the motley grouping of original people along the Mediterranean shores. (The Arab invaders from the East did not settle in earnest until the eighth century A.D.) They shared a linguistic base and a common writing system with the Semito-Phoenicians, leaving some stone monuments inscribed with these "Lybico–Berber" characters.

Although varieties of the Berber language have survived and are thriving in North Africa in oral form, the written version had all but disappeared in the twentieth century, kept barely alive in the transcription system of the Nomadic Touaregs of the Sahara, who may now number well over a million.

[3] Born in 1954, and trained as a mathematician, he was one of the younger generation of Algerian intellectuals. Of probable Kabyle ancestry, he was murdered by Fundamentalist sympathizers on 26 May 1992. He had published poems and novels in France. His last publications were *Les Vigiles* (Seuil, 1991) and *L'Exproprié* (Majault, 1991). His short and gifted life qualified him for almost all of the unforgivable sins on the FIS list: writer, journalist of avowed secular bent, trained and published in the West, and with homosexual leanings. His paper *Algérie Actualité* had published excerpts of Djebar's last and controversial historical meditation on the life of the Prophet, *Loin de Médine*.

[4] A probable reference to the strikes and street riots in the city of Azazga, in Greater Kabylia, triggered around the visit and subsequently banned public lecture on Kabyle language and culture by Mouloud Mammeri. — TRANS.

PART VIII
The Sound Track

MARC FUMAROLI

On Conversation
1992

Marc Fumaroli has no sympathy for the hieratic cult of writing that is the common denominator of most modernist and postmodern theories of litera-ture. Nor does he have any sympathy for a literary space to which only those adepts who have taken a vow of silence are admitted, citizens of the austere Republic of Kamchatkian letters to which the best nineteenth-century French critic, Sainte-Beuve, had already confined Baudelaire and his un-speakable Les Fleurs du mal. *The game of the desert island (even when this island is Valery Larbaud's "Kerguelen") is the wrong approach for lit-erature: books are not stones, and the melancholy solitude of an Egyptian obelisk exiled to the middle of a Parisian square is a fate that no one should wish for them. Moreover, it goes against the genuine grain of French litera-ture, which from early on demonstrated a healthy contempt for those satur-nine writers and scholars who are so proud to have left their voices in the cloakroom. "In the beginning," Fumaroli declares in another work, "French 'literary' religion was not a religion of the book."[1] In one way or another, most of Fumaroli's contributions to recent French literary debates have sought to rehabilitate the spoken word and the places where it is spo-ken; and they have been devoted not to literature as such but to French literature, a "kingdom," as he writes elsewhere, that "subordinates writing to speech."[2] Intent on reversing a century long anticonversational French literary prejudice, Fumaroli thus sides with Sainte-Beuve against Proust's "deconstructions" as well as Mallarmé's "funereal atheology."[3]*

For books are not, contrary to Proust's saying, the children of silence; they are born in and from conversation, fueled and refined by it, and they feed it in return. The idea of a divorce between speech and writing is coun-terintuitive for understanding French literature's genuinely social and so-ciable inspiration, a literature that traditionally interlaces the performance of conversation (in the salons) and its representation (in memoirs, private letters, even in novels); far from excluding each other, speech and writing,

Marc Fumaroli, "De la Conversation," in *Trois institutions littéraires* (Paris: Gallimard, 1994), pp. 113–20.

*closely interwoven, imitate each other, play with each other, compete with
each other. Conversation and literature are, in fact, each other's favorite
subjects. One talks about literature and writes about conversation. French
literature at its best is the registrar of the festival of prose improvisations
that were staged in the Parisian Salons, of the soft theatricality that conversation brings to social life.*

> The history of conversation . . . strikes me as impossible, like the
> history of anything that is essentially relational and fleeting, of any-
> ting essentially dependent on impressions.
>
> —Sainte-Beuve

To propose, even in the form of an improvised talk, a history of conversation might seem as nonsensical as to attempt a history of tears, fare-
wells, or first encounters. *Scripta manent, verba volant* (Writing
remains, words fly). Is conversation nothing more than ephemeral and pointless banter, a bourgeois parlor game? In France, a fierce prejudice has taken
hold of both word and thing. In recent years, a swarm of metaphysical co-
leoptera have laid waste to the one and the other, all the while emitting chatter
and chirps in the midst of which one can make out such words and phrases as
"incommunicability," "absurd," "suspicion," and "language as trap, screen, or
prison." Sociology has followed close behind, and then linguistics: on the ruins
of conversation, communication has been enthroned. Nevertheless, this latest
plague on Egypt (prophesied by writers from *La Peste* to *La Jalousie*) has not
destroyed either the natural French taste for talk or the old article of faith of
the national religion according to which *il n'est bon bec que de Paris* (Villon).[1]
This ancient French pride, this delighted confidence in the *genius loci*, which is
thought to favor not only the oral and social but also the literary and philosophical aspects of the common tongue, has both illustrious ancient antecen-
dents and weighty modern exponents. People spoke and engaged in dialogue,
both oral and written, in Athens and elsewhere before Plato. But conversation
existed only in Athens, where theater was born, and was not truly raised to the
level of art—atticism—until Athenian conversation was dramatized in written form in the dialogues of Plato. While it is true that the word *conversation*,
from the Latin, did not come into common use in French until the sixteenth
century, that which it served at that time to designate had been biding its time,
so to speak, in Greek texts since the end of Antiquity. It was revived in modern
Europe, and first of all in Italy, only after the dialogues of Plato and his Latin
emulator Cicero were rediscovered in Venice and Florence.

How, in a few words, to characterize the singular form of oral collaboration which the Platonic dialogues stylized and imitated in writing? The talk involved free men, who gathered in places not connected with political activity (usually homes of friends but sometimes outdoors in the countryside around Athens or on the city's streets). These men were drawn to one another by a natural inclination to talk, as if they looked upon conversation as the most exciting of all games, the supreme game, worthy of the gods. Of course, the fact that Socrates, the feared ironist, was a frequent participant in these games raised them to the highest pitch of passion and difficulty. Ultimately, though, Socrates being Socrates because he is always himself, at home in all circumstances, the games in which he served as referee differed according to the character of his interlocutors: in each case, the subject of the conversation is different. No subsequent writer would ever succeed in representing the meandering, shifting quality, the varying tonalities—in a word, the music—of conversation as naturally as Plato, whose touch is as delicate as it is direct. The history of literary dialogue in prose was like that of printing, photography, and film: no sooner was it invented than it achieved perfection. This perfection is all the more miraculous in that these dialogues, conceived for the purpose of teaching philosophy at the Academy, initially introduce the reader to conversations that are uneven in quality, by turns pedestrian and lively, but that suddenly and without warning rise to dizzying heights, posing the most difficult questions the human mind can raise: about happiness, truth, the good life, poetry, art, music, theology, and cosmology. From its inception, conversation, a higher form of relaxation among free men, was also presented as the most subtle of pedagogical methods and, despite its apparent discontinuity, the most encyclopedic of forms. Of course, it is Socrates' irony that acts as yeast, transforming a pleasant exchange of opinions into a breathless struggle between two or more combatants yielding remarkable, at times blinding, insights. Yet even this yeast would be nothing without a good dough, human nature in all the diversity and singularity of its representatives, in all the reality of its psychological and social types, perfectly blended to provide a delicious and subtle feast of speeches, emotions, and thoughts. Socrates, who through these dialogues became the immortal master of the Academy, reveals not only the philosophical vocation of conversation but also its roots in human nature, ignorant yet avid for knowledge. Already in the naive and elemental happiness of the game, the refreshing exchange of words among free men, the weight of nature, society, politics, and economics begins to rise from the earth. A space opens up. With the addition of a teacher, that space widens into a veritable runway from which thought can take off. Out of the diversity of his interlocutors, their divergences and disagreements, Socrates makes a rose window that reveals something of the inaccessible unity of truth, and with that revelation comes felicity of a kind that no worldly pleasure or possession can equal.

Indeed, the Platonic dialogue (contemporary with the comedy of Aristophanes and the tragedy of Sophocles) is not the origin of the history of conversation; it is the center, the source. Conversation begins when Socrates and his animated company of Athenians come together, and ends when they part. People in all times and places have known how to argue, chat, exchange words, gossip, lecture, and negotiate—but, since Plato, to converse has meant to abandon these barbarous forms of discourse for the naturalness of human speech, to bathe once more in the Attic light. In this way, without effort, we glimpse sparks, at least, of the great blaze of the Socratic spirit and experience the philosophical ascent that is achieved at home, when a number of people gather for the purpose of contemplation, in the hope of moving a little closer to unity, truth, and happiness.

Was France, or more precisely Paris, the Athens of the Moderns, hence on occasion their Academy as well? Immanuel Kant suggested as much in his *Anthropology* (1798):

> The form of well-being that seems most fully in accord with human nature is that provided by a good meal in good company (and if possible with a variety of dining companions). Chesterfield says that these must be no fewer in number than the Graces nor greater than the Muses. . . . The French nation is distinguished by its taste for conversation, in which it is the model for all others. It is a courteous nation, especially toward visiting foreigners, even though courtly manners are now out of fashion. The Frenchman communicates his thoughts not out of self-interest but rather because good taste insists on it. Since good taste is concerned primarily with commerce with women in high society, the conversation of women has become the lingua franca of this milieu. Such an inclination has an indisputable effect on the willingness of people to render services and be helpful to others and eventually instills the principles of a universal philanthropy. This renders a whole people amiable.[2]

Was France thus chosen to enjoy the supreme happiness of the free man, conversation, the banquet in pleasant company? If Paris was another Athens, it certainly was not Plato's Academy. Kant borrows Thucydides' judgment of the Athenians to condemn the French:

> The other side of the coin is a vitality not sufficiently kept in check by mature principles. Lucid reason coexists with a frivolity that does not allow certain forms to endure merely because they are venerable or were once a source of extreme delight, however satisfactory they may have proved in the interim. There is also a contagious spirit of freedom which infects reason itself and, when it comes to the relation of people to state, generates enthusiasm capable of shaking things to their foundation and bursting all bonds. Without departing much from reality, merely by exaggerating the traits of the French and baldly setting them down in no particular order, one would quickly assemble the ingredients of an arresting caricature.[3]

Without Socrates, with the sophists in charge of the game, conversation is but a shadow of its former self, exemplifying that perpetual adolescence of the spirit for which Joubert criticized Voltaire: there is enough detachment for playfulness and pleasure but not enough spiritual maturity to understand the value of the durable institutions (the Platonic Academy survived for almost a thousand years) necessary to transform elite sociability into philosophical perseverance and contemporary customs into traditions.

Less profound but better known is the testimony of Mme de Staël, the quintessentially French outsider, whose remarks are also more flattering to French self-esteem than Kant's. In the wake of the tragedies of 1792 to 1794, those remarks went a long way toward reassuring France of its sociable vocation and setting it back on the path of conversation:

> It is, I think, generally acknowledged that wit and the taste for conversation are more widely shared in Paris than in any other city in the world and that what is called homesickness, that vague longing for the place of one's birth which has nothing to do with the friends whom one has left behind, is intimately associated with the pleasure of talk, which nowhere equals what the French recall experiencing at home. Volney recounts that during the Revolution, French émigrés set out to clear land and build a colony in America. From time to time, however, they dropped everything and went, as they put it, "to chat in town," and that town, New Orleans, was six hundred leagues from where they lived. People of all classes in France feel the need to talk. Here, speech is not simply what it is elsewhere, a means of communicating one's ideas, feelings, and affairs; it is also an instrument that one delights in playing and that enlivens the spirit, as music does for some nations and strong liquor for others.[4]

After thirty years of existentialism, the new novel, and the "class struggle," thirty years in which frivolity and fashion stoked the flames of terror, we are greeted from abroad by works on "the civilization of manners" (Norbert Elias), "the pragmatics of discourse" (Erving Goffman), and "the optimal conditions of oral cooperation" (Grice). Unconnected with these scholarly works, *Babette's Feast*, a Danish film based on a short story by Karen Blixen, had the same effect on today's French audiences as Mme de Staël's chapter "On the Spirit of Conversation" had on readers during the First Empire: it reminded them of old pleasures. The film shows how the guests at a Danish banquet come alive in conversation over a dinner lovingly prepared for them by a woman from Paris. She is an exiled *communarde*: though a victim of the French political tragedy, she has nevertheless sustained the faith in humanity and kindness that good food, good wine, and good conversation foster in France in spite of everything. Babette was also one of the great cooks of France during the sumptuous Second Empire. To thank her guests, she has ordered from France, and prepared with all of her still intact talent, everything that her homeland has to offer by way of pleasuring the palate, stimulating conversation, and suspending disagreement: a beautiful table, great wines, and gastronomic delights. Conversation is inseparable from its commodities; it revels in luxury. For one blessed evening, the iceberg of puritanical silence melts in the heat of this great convivial ritual. Men and women, villagers and dignitaries, experience for the first time the ecstasy of the gourmet and the joy of hearty conversation. For a few eventful hours the serious and anxious people portrayed by Dreyer and Bergman subscribe to the French gospel of Brillat-Savarin and Rabelais.

TRANSLATED BY ARTHUR GOLDHAMMER

INTRODUCTORY NOTES

[1] Marc Fumaroli, *La Diplomatie de l'esprit: De Montaigne à La Fontaine* (Paris: Hermann, 1994), p. 306.

[2] Marc Fumaroli, "Le génie de la langue française," in *Trois Institutions littéraires* (Paris: Gallimard, 1994) p. 271.

[3] Fumaroli, *La Diplomatie*, p. 320.

NOTES

[1] This saying comes from the following stanza of François Villon:

> *Prince, aux dames parisiennes,*
> *De beau parler donnez le prix;*
> *Quoi qu'on dise d'Italiennes,*
> *Il n'est bon bec que de Paris.*

> [Prince, award the prize for good conversation
>   to the women of Paris.
> Whatever they say about Italian women,
> all good mouths come from Paris.]

[2] Immanuel Kant, *Anthropology from a Pragmatic Point of View*, trans. Victor Dowdell (Carbondale: Southern Illinois University Press, 1978), pp. 186, 228 (translation amended).

[3] Ibid., pp. 228–29 (translation amended).

[4] Germaine de Staël, *De l'Allemagne* I, ch. xi ("De l'esprit de conversation").

BERNARD DORT

The Text of a Textless Theater
1995

Just after the end of World War II, Jean Vilar, the leader of a new genera-
tion of French stage directors, declared his pleasure at the fact that no sig-
nificant French writer showed any interest in writing for the stage (this
was before Sartre's and Camus's, box office successes, not to mention
Samuel Beckett's and Eugène Ionesco's). Vilar saw this as a very encourag-
ing sign for theater: between author and director, book and stage, text and
performance, the divorce—initially filed for by Antonin Artaud—had
been finalized. Theater was on its own, had gained its cultural autonomy:
no longer was it a literary subfield. In the future, its great names would be
not playwrights but directors, and people would go to the theater not to
hear a play but to see a staging.

Along with Roland Barthes, Bernard Dort was a founding member of
the journal Théâtre populaire *(1954); since then, he became one of the*
most attentive analysts of the life of the theater in Europe. In this text, he
offers a tableau of recent trends in stage direction that is not nearly as clear-
cut as Vilar's prophecy would have had it. The author may have been up-
staged; but it does not follow that theater has been totally or irreversibly
liberated from texts, or that it has become the arena for multimedia impro-
visations. On the contrary: the very scarcity of contemporary playwrights
gives more weight to the classical repertoire. And, more significantly, the
past decades have seen stage directors show an increasing interest in and
respect for texts as such. This is an evolution exemplified by the new mean-
ing in French of the word dramaturge: *it no longer refers to the author of*
a play but, semantically contaminated (via Brecht) by its German sibling,
to the literary adviser or consultant. This person's mediation has become
essential in the "interpretative" process that leads to the performance of
texts destined, whether intended or not, for the stage.

Bernard Dort, "Le Texte d'un théâtre sans texte" in *Le Spectateur en dialogue* (Paris:
P.O.L., 1995), pp. 257–69.

Subtext and Supertext

Performance is not simply external to the text. The choice is not a simple either/or: either faithfully reproduce what is written or else do violence to the integrity of the text. Indeed, the influence of the stage can be felt in the very structure of the dramatic narrative. Without performance, the text would remain incomplete, perhaps even incomprehensible. A play is not a statement that emanates from a single source, the author. It is shaped by other mouths, those of the characters, who, to complicate matters still further, do not exist prior to the text. It is the text, in conjunction with the stage directions, which makes the characters what they are. Hence, the dramatic text is by definition fragmentary and composite. The spoken text consists of as many textual layers as there are characters: Tartuffe does not speak as Dorine speaks. The result is a superimposition of styles which do not define a single common style unless the action requires it. Nor is the diction of each character uniform. It varies depending on the person to whom the character is speaking: Don Juan does not speak to Sganarelle as he speaks to Don Luis. Finally, the spoken text never exhausts the whole range of things that a character might conceivably say. It always leaves room for a *subtext*. The subtext gives the text proper its meaning and form. And, of course, in modern acting technique, from Stanislavsky on, the subtext takes on enormous importance. Some authors even make the subtext explicit: think of what Brecht does in the gutter scene (the reuniting of Grusha and Simon) in *The Caucasian Chalk Circle*: "Listen to what he (or she) thought but did not say." And the singer gives voice to what Grusha and Simon cannot say to each other. Whether explicit or not, however, the subtext must be perceptible: the text could not be performed without it. Conversely, every text also depends on a *supertext*: the social and ideological conditions under which the play was conceived and written. Nothing could be more obvious. For instance, when Marivaux's characters allude to the money they expect to make as a result of some relationship or engagement, they often specify the precise amount: in *Les Fausses Confidences* Araminte is a young widow with "an income upward of fifty thousand *livres*," the count promises Marton "a thousand *écus*" if he succeeds in marrying Araminte, and the thirty-five-year-old woman whom Monsieur Rémy intends for Dorante has "an income of at least fifteen thousand *livres*." In Marivaux's day, these figures immediately revealed the magnitude of what was at stake. Today, the typical spectator finds them meaningless. According to Deloffre's edition of Marivaux's plays, fifty thousand *livres* was the equivalent of about \$80,000 in 1968, and a thousand *écus* amounted to "roughly \$6,000"—no trifle. The woman on whom Dorante has set his sights is no middle-class housewife: Araminte is a wealthy woman. If he marries her, Dorante will have access to luxury, opportunity, and perhaps even power. Many such pecuniary indications could be cited, but ideological references also abound: the spoken text constantly alludes to the social context, and since it originates with a person immersed in that context and was addressed to a contemporary audience, there was no need to make the context explicit. Unless we are familiar with it, however, or it is somehow recreated for us, the text remains incomplete, possibly even incomprehensible. Once again, the performance must create (or re-create) the conditions under which the text can be understood. The performance must supplement the text with subtexts and supertexts, without which it may well remain beyond our grasp.

THE REVIVAL OF THE STAGE

Now, it so happens that the greatest theatrical texts, the ones that have been interpreted on stage most frequently and in the most diverse manner, are also the ones that seem most problematic to read, that are complex to the point of being almost incoherent and rich to the point of being chaotic. A self-contained text, which expressly answers all the questions it raises, is unlikely to be performed over and over again. Plays that are really polemics in disguise rarely survive. By contrast, a more open-ended text, which answers questions only by raising new ones and capitalizes on its open-endedness, is more likely to endure. The reason for this difference is that plays of the latter type trust in and require performance to flesh them out.

The relation between text and performance is therefore never simple or one-sided. The text gives rise to the performance: the script contains the seed of theatricality. It anticipates its performance and in some cases even suggests changes in the "model" of representation. But the performance also produces the text: performance completes the script and temporarily fixes its meaning. Sometimes performance even engenders the text (Molière and Shakespeare were both actors). Some of the greatest works in the classical repertory seem to have stemmed not so much from the dramatic writing as from the stagecraft of their period. In any case, stagecraft and its hazards appear to have entered into the writing process itself. (In French, interestingly enough, it used to be more common to speak of "composing" a play than of "writing" one: *on compose une pièce, on écrit un roman*.) Listen to Brecht musing about Shakespeare: "Shakespeare's plays are extraordinarily alive. It almost seems as if the published version were based on the lines actually spoken by the actors, including all the improvisations and corrections made in rehearsal." As for *Hamlet*, Brecht adds that

> the leading man in Shakespeare's Globe Theater was a stocky fellow who was always short of breath. So for a period of time all of Shakespeare's heroes were stocky, short-winded fellows—Macbeth and Lear alike. It was for this actor, and no doubt with his help, that the action was made more interior. And the pace was quickened. The play became much more interesting as a result. Once the script (based on a play by one Thomas Kyd) had been adapted and reworked on stage to the end of the third act, it seems as if the company had difficulty figuring

out how to get the indecisive Hamlet character into the frenetic bloodbath that
had made the earlier play a success. The fourth act contains several scenes that
help to solve this problem. Perhaps the actor used them all, or perhaps he kept
only one, whereas the others found their way into the published script. All are
inspired solutions to a problem of stagecraft.[1]

To be sure, Brecht was neither a philologist nor a historian of the theater. His
account of the genesis of the *Hamlet* text is largely fanciful—yet his fantasy is a
good description of how a dramatic text evolves from performance. It also suggests the extent to which the multiple meanings of this particular text may be
related to this type of practice.

Of course, there are also plays that were written far from any stage, quite
deaf to the exigencies of performance. Their number is small. The most "literary" of dramatic authors often worked closely with actors: the plays of Jean
Giraudoux, for instance, are indelibly associated with the name of Louis Jou-
vet. Nevertheless, there are texts that, though not written for the stage (indeed,
one might even say that they were written *against* the stage—opposition being
a form of recognition), eventually found their way to the stage and helped
bring about profound changes in the nature of performance. I am thinking of
what Goethe, commenting on Kleist's *Der Zerbrochene Krug* (*The Broken Jug*),
called the "invisible theater": "If [Kleist] were able, with the same natural
manner and skill, to resolve a truly dramatic problem and cause an action to
unfold before our eyes and senses as he here allows an already completed action
to reveal itself little by little, it would be a wonderful gift to German theater."
This remark applies to some of the most important dramatic oeuvres of the
early nineteenth century: those of Heinrich von Kleist, Alfred de Musset, and
Georg Büchner especially. Not only were these authors unable to see their
plays performed in their lifetime, but they deliberately chose to write in opposition to the theater as it then existed. Their plays seemed to be addressed not to
spectators but to readers. They defied contemporary rules of stagecraft and
seemed to be written for the "theater of the armchair." Many theorists of the
time noted the peculiarity of such writing and wondered about its significance.
August Wilhelm Schlegel, for example, remarked "that there are dramatic
works which their authors did not intend to appear on stage, and which would
have little effect if produced but which can be read with admiration." Hegel
pointed out that "there is today, especially in Germany, a general tendency to
look upon the composition of a play with performance regarded as a minor
detail. . . . Hence, most of our modern dramas are never performed, for the
simple reason that they are not dramatic." This he blamed on a certain "contempt for the audience," for the "German author wants above all to express his
personality without asking whether what he wants to say will or will not please
the audience." For Hegel, the stage was the proof of the text. He even held this
proof to be valid for all times and places: speaking of the Greek tragedies, he

noted that "while we rarely see them performed nowadays," they "still satisfy us because they were adapted to the stage in their own time."[2]

In a sense, the invisible theater of the early nineteenth century reversed the burden of this proof. Plays not performed when written avenged themselves later on. Those playwrights who enjoyed success with their contemporaries, such as Eugène Scribe in France and August von Kotzebue in Germany, have all but vanished from today's repertory. (Curiously, these once-glorious reputations did not decline everywhere at the same rate: for instance, Scribe's *Verre d'eau* remained in the German repertory much longer than in the French.) In the meantime, playwrights whose works were formerly deemed impossible to perform have replaced these once-popular authors to become classics of the twentieth-century theater (not always in their original form, however: think of the many stage versions of Musset's *Lorenzaccio*). What happened in the interim was that the conception of the theater, hence of the dramaturgic "model," changed. In the nineteenth century, the notion of a "well-crafted play" reflected the dominant theatrical form: the Italian stage, still more or less governed by the laws of perspective and the need to create an illusion of reality. Wit this kind of staging, there was no place for plays such as Kleist's *Kätchen von Heilbronn* or Musset's *Lorenzaccio*. With technological advances and, above all, the advent of a new conception of scenic space, however, the stage was totally transformed, thereby creating a place for the invisible theater. More than that, the invisible theater was now seen as having anticipated this transformation. Once an exception, almost an aberration, it became the rule. Thus, the text served as a "touchstone" for the theater.

Woyzeck is a case apart. As is well known, Büchner never completed the play. Several manuscripts survived. All were difficult to decipher, and there were discrepancies among them. The uncompleted text, the uncertain reading of many passages, and the absence of any commentary or statement of intention on Büchner's part make this one of the most problematic texts in Western dramatic literature. Written in 1837, *Woyzeck* had to wait more than forty years before finally being published in 1879 in a faulty edition whose very title, *Wozzeck*, was a mistake. The first performance did not come until 1913. At that point the play's prodigious career began (and much work was done to establish its text). The work became a model for expressionist and postexpressionist dramaturgy: from Ernst Toller to Brecht, playwrights repeatedly rewrote *Woyzeck*. The play also became a favorite of "experimental" directors: from Max Reinhardt (1921) to Karge and Langhoff (1980), not a single great director (including, in France, Roger Blin in 1951, Vincent-Jourdheuil at the Théâtre d'Espérance in 1973, and, more recently, Jean-Louis Houdin in 1981 and Jacques Lassalle in 1984) failed to test his talents against Büchner's enigmatic text. Unfinished, repetitious, and incomplete, *Woyzeck* can be seen as the modern dramatic text par excellence: a play that asks a great deal of its staging and depends on performance to fill in or expose its lacunae and condensations.

Written in ignorance or defiance of the theatrical practice of its time, the play anticipated modern practice. When Antonin Artaud mentioned *Woyzeck* as one of the first works to be included in the repertory of his Theater of Cruelty, he was no doubt contradicting his own stated desire "to banish old master-pieces"—but he also anticipated the new alliance of text and staging that might well be taken as characteristic of today's theater, notwithstanding the false opposition often drawn between text and direction or between a theater of text and a "theatrical theater."

An Einsteinian Revolution

Did the advent of stage directing change nothing in the theater? Was the "Co-pernican revolution" (the replacement of the written text by the stage as the center of gravity of theatrical activity) merely an illusion? To make such a claim would be to deny the obvious. But if we are to measure the extent of the change and have some chance of grasping what is going on between text and performance, we must stop thinking of the two as impervious to each other.

As we have seen, the alleged primacy of the written text masked the fact that the text was in a sense shaped in advance by the stage. The classical text in-cluded stage directions for its performance. It anticipated the staging. More often than not it was referred to as a script rather than a text. A *script* is a text that has internalized the laws of performance. In a similar way, an opera li-bretto does not exist independently of the music to which it will be set. Most of the great opera composers, from Mozart to Verdi, to say nothing of Wagner, were actively involved in the composition of libretti. It was not until Claude Debussy (with Maeterlinck's *Pelléas et Mélisande*) and Alban Berg (with Büch-ner's *Wozzeck* [*sic*]) that composers attempted to set unaltered dramatic texts to music. However, unlike the libretto, which generally serves only to produce a score, a play is not exhausted by a single production. Although it may be shaped by a particular type of stagecraft, it can be adapted to other types of perfor-mance, provided that the text is sufficiently rich and open-ended. One might summarize this situation by saying that what was a play, with all the rigidity of dramatic structure that the word implies, becomes a text: a text for the theater, capable of new configurations on stage.

This is where the change lies. Today's theater will not tolerate any dominant form. It proposes no fixed model. Once singular, it has become plural. This is not simply a matter of architecture or stagecraft (in the sense attached to the term before it replaced "scenery"—this shift in thinking and terminology is significant). It is also a matter of audience: it makes a difference whether one is staging a performance for a few dozen informed theatergoers or for thousands of people whose only knowledge of the theater is through television. The social characteristics of the audience also matter: one is not likely to put on the same show for urban slum-dwellers as for rural youths or sophisticated intellectuals.

In short, the theater has not just traded text for performance and shifted its center of gravity. There is no more center. Or, rather, there are many centers, each with different norms.

TRANSLATED BY ARTHUR GOLDHAMMER

NOTES

[1] Bertold Brecht, *Ecrits sur le théâtre*, vol. 1, trans. J. Tailleur et al. (Paris: L'Arche, 1972).

[2] G. W. F. Hegel, *Esthétique*, vol. 3, pt. 2, trans. S. Jankélévitch (Paris: Aubier-Montaigne, 1944).

SERGE DANEY

The Organ and the Vacuum Cleaner
1983

While postwar theater was trying, following Artaud, to rid itself of the tute-
lage of authors and of the literary myth of authorship, French film directors
and critics did the opposite: they did everything they could to reinforce cin-
ema's association with literature and to adjust the literary model of author-
ship to the complexity and specificity of film production. "French cinema,"
writes Serge Daney, "is unique, resembles no other. . . . This French
specificity is encapsulated in one single word: it is a cinema of authors, with
all the literary richness that is connoted by this word: author."¹ This liter-
ariness, however, in no way implies any particular or subservient respect for
literary works as such. It does not refer to a tradition of adapting literary
classics for the screen (compared to the Anglophone film, French cinema
does relatively little of that); rather, it refers to the fact that French film-
makers claim for themselves the same privileged status of authorship that
writers used to enjoy. At the very moment the author, deconstructed, was
being evacuated from the literary space, cinema seems to have offered him a
refuge.

In French cinephilia, the cult of authorship has almost always been as-
sociated with the privileging of a series of phonocentric features. Both Serge
Daney and Michel Chion (among many others) have argued that French
cinema is immediately recognizable for its soundtrack, for the special way it
sounds *French: beyond any consideration of language or accent, images*
seem less to speak than to rustle, to be haunted by speech. French critics
have always indulged in describing what they perceive as an anxious rela-
tionship with a particularly fragile umbilical soundtrack. French cinema,
Chion writes, is one of the few "where voice does not go without saying";²
voice is never taken for granted. Hence the uneasiness he senses, when
comparing the various dubbings of Fellini's Casanova, *in the French*
soundtrack—an uneasiness that betrays the anxiety of a cinema threatened
"to no longer be the master of its own voice."³

Serge Daney, "L'Orgue et l'aspirateur," in *La Rampe: Cahier critique 1970–82* (Paris:
Cahiers du Cinéma/Gallimard, 1983), pp. 138–48.

Daney served as managing editor of Cahiers du cinéma *for many years. After André Bazin, he was the most brilliant, incisive, theoretically provocative of French film critics. Practicing cinema as a daily addiction, he was the voice of the culture of cinephilia. The following analysis of the disjunctive synthesis between the sound and the visual components of film, of the dialectic between the voices of the actors and the sound of the image is based on the soundtrack of a scene from Robert Bresson's* Le Diable probablement.

I would like to describe the sound setup (*dispositif sonore*) in a scene close to the beginning of Robert Bresson's 1977 film *Le Diable probablement (The Devil Probably)*. The scene in question is the one in which Charles and his friends enter a church (we have already seen them hooted out of a political rally) and immediately find themselves involved in a rather lugubrious debate, whose subject, we quickly discover, is postconcilial Catholicism. How can I describe this scene (or fragment of a scene: Bresson's films have long since dispensed with scenes) *from the standpoint of sound*?

· Nothing prepares for it. At no point does the viewer anticipate where things are going. We are quickly (all too quickly for those who did not like the film) plunged into the middle of a debate, which, because it is reduced to this middle, is immediately denaturalized.

· There are no sides in the debate; everyone is against everyone else. It might be better to call it a *round of speeches* rather than a debate, and those speeches are delivered in an irritatingly toneless, zombielike manner. Or perhaps one should call it a series of questions without pause for response or reply.

· Everyone speaks, but each person utters only a single sentence. Each sentence is punctuated by a loud, sustained organ note. The vehemence lacking in the words seems to have been shifted to these impromptu interruptions. In a previous quick shot, we caught a glimpse of the organist as he sat down at his instrument and lifted the cover of the keyboard.

· In addition to these two sounds, that of the organ above and the discussion below, each oblivious of the other, there is a third sound, of a vacuum cleaner being run over a red carpet.

What holds this fragment together? Where is the thread, the logic? Not in the presumed psychology of the characters (Charles has supposedly decided to join this debate) or in the dramatization of the scene (in which he is supposed to have had a hand). It lies elsewhere, namely, in the fact that from the moment Charles and his friends enter the church, they are caught up in a random, heterogeneous system of sounds, a montage consisting of the debate, the organ, and the vacuum cleaner, which literally *disposes* of them. This Bressonian heterology consists of three terms: the high (organ), the low (debate), and a third term that destroys the opposition between high and low, namely, the trivial (vacuum cleaner). All the newcomers can do is add their own sounds to the ambient sound configuration, or, rather, chaos, which is the true "subject" of the film. Or perhaps, as we are told in Godard's 1976 *Ici et ailleurs* (*Here and Elsewhere*), sound is always *too loud*.

There is something paradoxical about *Le Diable probablement*. Never before has Bresson seemed so concerned with being topical, yet at the same time he has never been more vehemently, radically insistent on his contempt for *all* discourse. Not only because talk and speechifying inevitably lead to theater (bombast, pathos), thereby transforming "models" into actors, histrionic performers, but also because all discourse, insofar as it aims at triviality (or worse, edification) presupposes an *emitter*, and for Bresson the human emitter is ridiculously inadequate as a sonic system (*dispositif sonore*).

There is a sonic hierarchy, in which speech and speechifiers occupy the bottom rung. Charles encounters several of the latter in the course of his (elegant) calvary, from the bookseller who "preaches destruction" in a crypt to the ineffable Dr. Mime, the great psychoanalyst. If the speechifiers are (irrevocably) condemned, it is because they are reasoners without resonance. Their talk is dull, colorless, and stilted. Their attitude toward money is similar: think of the checkbook with which the bookseller wants to buy the prostitute, or the stack of banknotes and checks that we glimpse in Dr. Mime's half-open drawer. In paper money there is something solidified, turdlike, and soundless, something we can grasp more fully if we look again at the "inspired" scene in the film, the one that shows the second visit to the church. When Valentin follows Charles into the church "conditionally" (he is under the influence of drugs), it is under the sign of sacrilege (Valentin breaks open the poorbox) and simulacrum (Charles plays Monteverdi on a record player) that the simultaneous clinking of coins and tinkle of music set up the metaphor *voice/gold*.

Yet another reasoner is Michel, the ecologist. He is a well-known Bressonian figure: the "best friend" who makes edifying speeches and is usually sexually desired (but not loved) by the heroine, a situation of which he takes advantage (think of Jacques, the friend of the *Pickpocket*). In *Le Diable probablement*, Michel is working on a militant film about ecology which we see him showing to (or perhaps in collaboration with) a group of friends. Some critics have poked fun at this scene, which they see as an indication that a senile Bresson is willing to do anything to make his supposed portrait of youth credible. But the scene is anything but simple. The film without a film is silent, and Michel and his friends "speak" the commentary as it is projected. As to the commentary (*commentaire*), there is no better example of what Pascal Bonitzer has termed the *comment-taire* (how to silence): the young people read it, mouth the words, mumble their way through the text. What we see is nothing less than the fabrication of a voice-over narrative.

There is a disturbing quality in the alternation, in the film within the film, between oftentimes violent images (the washing of the oil tanker, the red slime, the slaughter of a baby seal) and the moving hands of the commentators, who hold electric lamps that pick out the words on paper that are to be read or recited—posted over the images, as it were. The fabrication of a voice-over: it is quite bold of Bresson to film these well-dressed youths, who, as they watch images that illustrate their own cause, can respond only with words that have *already* ceased to resonate and begun to stagnate. Enough has already been said in the *Cahiers* about the dubious facility of the voice "over" (the rationale for the quotation marks will become clear in a moment) that one cannot fail to be struck by what is going on before our very eyes: the separation of the silent violence of the images from the blasé commentary, the distancing of the silent visual cry from the voice keeping "out of sight" in obscurity.

Here we confront the inability of human discourse (and of the human voice) to *bear* the violence of the world. Bresson's pessimism is hardly new: in *Le Diable*, it is simply more naked. Clearly, the problem is not what Charles is looking for (his quest) or what he thinks (his convictions). It does not matter whether or not he opposes the ecological crusade or the macrobiotic diet. Indeed, the debate over ideas invariably takes off against a deafening background of sound (the shouts in the crypt, the trees being cut down); the decibel level is high. The sound is always too loud. And if Michel is discredited in Charles's eyes, it is not because the cutting of the trees (to which he consents) contradicts his ecological convictions but because the horrible sound that the falling trees make makes all debate *pointless in advance, because it is inaudible.*

So much for Bresson's "materialism": so far as discourse is concerned, it is the ear, not the brain, that decides. The voice is only a noise, one of the softest kinds of noise. And what Charles wants is not to be convinced (for he is certain of his superiority) or to convince (since he is prepared to say virtually anything in order to have the last word) but to be vanquished. And in the Bressonian logic of sonic bodies (*corps sonores*) he can be vanquished only by a noise louder than all the rest: a gunshot into the water and then into the back of the neck.

At the risk of disappointing, therefore, the question of whether Charles is a symbol of present-day youth as seen by Bresson has to be set aside. Bresson is not at last, in old age, turning his attention to young people; youth has always been the only subject that interests him. The Bressonian "model" is never more then thirty years old. It is better to study Charles as one sonic body among others—the chosen one.

At bottom, Charles cares about only one thing: having the last word—not, however, in the manner of the glib talker who wins arguments intellectually but more in the manner of a parrot. Amid the bedlam produced by machines out of control, he has the last word only because he never has the first. He is best compared to the nymph Echo, who, according to Ovid, "cannot speak first, / cannot keep silent when spoken to, / and repeats the last words of the last voice she hears."

A poor transmitter–receiver, the Bressonian hero-nymph can stand up to the overwhelming volume of sound only by being, like the twice-empty church, a mere conduit, a resonance chamber. In Charles's sham tirade against Dr. Mime, all he can do is read, in the thick voice of an exasperated snob, a list of the "horrors" of modern civilization that he has torn from a magazine. He can only repeat. Living—up to the moment when he buys the right to die from the silent Valentin—is merely a matter of allowing the world, whose sound is too loud for him, to resonate within, without speaking for himself or even opening his mouth; he is an accompanist of the world's din. His is an old-fashioned form of resistance, known to schoolchildren the world over: he hums with his mouth closed. In this there is, of course, religious nostalgia: in the Middle Ages, the term *neume* was applied to musical phrases emitted in a single breath (*uno pneumate*)—without opening the mouth, because if one did open it, who knows what might enter in? *Le diable probablement*—probably the devil.

Thus, we must digress a moment to consider the voice. In Lacanian terms, it is a question of an object "a", and one of its partial objects is the mouth. But the voice is not produced exclusively in the mouth. It always originates deeper down. *The voice involves the entire body.*

What distinguishes the cinematic voice is that it can have a visual double, a shadow that seems to prey on it. It never seems easier to grasp or more tangible than *at the moment* when it is emitted, when it leaves the body through purposefully twisted lips. This mentonymy is crucial: what is *seen* (the moving lips, the open mouth, the tongue and teeth) justifies the belief in the reality of what is *heard* at the same time.

There is no other way of assigning a body to a voice than by way of such a visual stand-in: it is the image that ascribes reality to what remains invisible by definition. Silent film lived off this emtonymy (no smoke without fire, no moving lips without voice) resolved into metaphor (the interpolated title took the place of the voice). As Anne-Marie Miéville says in Godard's 1978 *Comment ça va (How are things going)*, the eyes are in command. We blame the discrepancy between image and sound when a film is poorly synchronized or dubbed. But to appreciate the full import of such complaints, one has to ask if we are capable of recognizing a poorly synchronized foot or back. Obviously, this question comes from Bresson, who was one of the first to take the fragmentary bodies of his "models" as the ghost of the voice, its visual stand-in, as it were.

"Dubbing is crude and naive," he writes in *Notes sur le cinématographe.* "Unreal voices, inconsistent with the movement of the lips. Out of sync with the lungs and the heart. Coming 'from the wrong mouths.'" Bresson is one film-maker (Jacques Tati is another) who has always insisted on a certain realism of sound. In this respect, he was deeply influential on the most innovative New Wave filmmakers. Note, however, that he mentions not only the mouth and lips but also the lungs and heart. Although he insisted on realism, he never made a fetish of directly recorded sound; rather, he stubbornly insisted on me-ticulous postsynchronization of carefully mixed and orchestrated tracks. Why? Precisely because he *drew a distinction between the voice and the mouth*. If one looks at the mouth, it is easy (and takes no effort) to see that something is being said. But the voice involves the whole body, including the heart and lungs, which cannot be seen.

In order to pursue this theme farther, one needs to be wary of such terms as "voice-over" and the like, which are altogether too dependent on the visual and, as such, surreptitiously extend the hegemony of the eye, with the inevi-table consequence that the ear is mutilated: film, we are told, is primarily im-ages, which "strike the eye" and "orient vision." The advent of direct sound recording in televised news reports, ethnographic documentaries, and propa-ganda films, together with the wild enthusiasm for the essential immediacy of the audiovisual (Jean Rouch and Jean-Marie Straub, quickly copied but poorly understood), led people to pattern sonic space after visual space, which served to guarantee its veracity, to authenticate it. In fact, however, the two spaces are heterogeneous. A more precise description of each is required, along with ter-minology for specifying their interaction.

To begin with, there is always a danger of importing what is primarily a vocabulary of technical terms. One saw this in the phrase "images and sounds," which became so overused after Godard introduced it that it lost all specific meaning. For whom does a film consist of images and sounds? For the person who makes it and the person who deconstructs it, the technician and the semi-ologist, but not for the person who *watches* it. Just when talking about "images and sounds" became the last word in materialism (although for Godard it was already the "and" that was interesting), people began to notice that this termi-nology made it impossible to discuss the place of the spectator, the system of which he was a part, or his desire. The problem had to be approached from a different angle—in terms of the gaze (which is neither the eye nor the image) and the voice (which is neither the mouth nor the ear nor the sound). And also in terms of drives (the "scopic" drive: to look is not the same as to see, to listen is not the same as to hear).

In terms of images, the distinction between on-screen and off-screen occur-rences, while no doubt useful for writing a screenplay or critically analyzing a film, is not subtle enough for a theory of *missing objects* because there are differ-ent types of off-screen events. Some objects are permanently missing (either because they are unrepresentable—for instance, to take the standard example, the camera that cannot film itself filming the scene—or taboo, such as the prophet Muhammad), while others are temporarily out of sight, hence subject to the familiar alternation of presence and absence, or *Fort Da*, to use the Freudian metaphor. The possibility of eternal return is greeted by the spectator with either horror or relief. These are not the same, even if they happen off-screen.

The same on-screen/off-screen distinction that is already of dubious value in discussing the visual is altogether too crude for analyzing voices. Broadly speaking, the term *voice-over* refers to the voices of off-screen speakers. But this really depends on a distinction between sound that is synchronized and sound that is not: the voice is reduced to its visual stand-in, which is itself reduced to the configuration and shape of the lips. The voice-over is then identified with an absence in the image. I favor the opposite approach: voices should be related to their effects *in* or *on* the image.

I will use the term *voice-over* narrowly to describe an off-screen voice that always runs parallel to the sequence of images and never intersects with it. For example, in a documentary about sardines, the voice-over can say whatever it likes (whether it describes sardines or slanders them makes no difference); it remains without measurable impact on the fish. This voice, superimposed on the image after the fact and linked to it by editing, is a purely metalanguistic phenomenon. It is addressed (both as statement and delivery) solely to the viewer, with whom it enters into an alliance or contract that ignores the image. Because the image serves only as the pretext for the wedding of commentary and viewer, the image is left in an enigmatic state of abandonment, of frantic disinheritance, which gives it a certain form of presence, of obtuse significance (Barthes's third meaning), which (with a certain element of perversity) can be enjoyed incognito, as it were. To see this, mute the sound on your television and look at the images *left to themselves*. Voice-over of this kind can be *coercive*. If, speaking of sardines, I say that "these grotesque animals, driven by a suicidal compulsion, hasten toward the fisherman's nets and end their lives in the most ridiculous way imaginable," this statement will contaminate not the sardines but the gaze of the spectator, who is obliged to make what sense he can of it despite the obvious disparity between what he sees and what he hears. The voice-over narrative, which coerces the image, intimidates the gaze, and creates a double-bind, is one of the primary modes of *propaganda* in film.

This is the level at which a director like Godard operates: one might call it the "voice-over degree zero." In his 1976 *Leçons de choses* (the second part of *Six fois deux*, *Six Times Two*), the sudden intrusion of a shot of a marketplace (an intrusion that is as violent as it is sudden, since like all of Godard's images it is totally unpredictable) is immediately baptized "fire" by the soundtrack. This is justified in part by a play on words (*flambée des prix* is French for "skyrocketing prices," hence the connection to the image of the marketplace, but *flambée* also means "blaze," hence the connection to the soundtrack), in part as a response to the intrusiveness of the image and the enunciation of the word, retroactively re-marking the violence. One sees the same thing in *Ici et Ailleurs* with the sequence on "how to organize an assembly line." With each new image, Godard's voice hollowly repeats the words: "Well, this way . . . like this . . . but also like that." In relation to the "one-by-one" sequence of images the voice plays the same role as quotation marks in a text: it highlights but also distances.

The voice-over is focal point of all power, all arbitrariness, all omission. In this respect, there is little difference between Marguerite Duras's 1975 *India Song*, the documentary about sardines, a Situationist film, and the Chinese propaganda film on which it is based: the contract with the viewer (seduction, pedagogy, demagogy) depends on coercion of the image. The potential here for the exercise of power is unlimited. The only way to escape from this vicious circle is for the voice-over to take a risk, and to do so *as voice*: either by multiplication (not one voice but many voices, not one certitude but many enigmas) or, even more, by singularization. And the way to escape from the politics of the *auteurs* is through a "politics of voices, inimitable voices (Godard, Duras, and, for some time now, Bresson). Radio takes its revenge on film, Dziga Vertov on Sergei Eisenstein, the simple voice on the constructed dialogue, and the feminine on the masculine.

By contrast, I will use the term, "in voice" to refer to a voice that participates in the image, merges with it, and has material impact on it by way of a visual stand-in. If my commentary on sardines has the effect of leaving the poor fish stranded in their mere presence as sardines, my voice has a totally different effect if, in the course of a live report, I ask someone a question. Even if that question is spoken off-camera, my voice intrudes upon the image, affecting my interlocutor's face and body and triggering a furtive or perhaps overt reaction, a response. The viewer can measure the violence of my statement by the disturbance it causes in the person who receives it, as one might catch a bullet or a ball (or other small-"a" objects), to one side or head on. This is the technique used by Joris Ivens and Marceline Loridan in their 1976 *Comment Yukong déplaça les montagnes* (How Yukong Moved the Mountain). It is also the technique of horror films and of the "subjective" films of Robert Montgomery. One also sees it in the now somewhat outmoded technique of having a voice put familiar questions to the characters in a film, who halt their action long enough to respond. Think, for example, of Sacha Guitry's paternalistic attitude toward his "creations," or of the complicity between the narrator and characters in films from Salah Abou Sefi's *Entre ciel et terre* to Louis Berlanga's *Bienvenue, Mr. Marshall* (Welcome, Mr. Marshall).

The "in" voice is the focal point of a different but just as redoubtable form of power. What is presented as the emergence of truth may well be merely the production of discomfort in the guinea pig forced to answer questions as the viewer looks on. There are at least two other kinds of voices: those spoken "within" the image, either through a mouth ("out voice") or through an entire body ("through voice").

The "out" voice is basically the voice as it emerges from a mouth. It is projected, dropped, thrown away: one of various objects expelled from the body (along with the gaze, blood, vomit, sperm, and so on). With the out voice we touch on the nature of the cinematographic image itself: though flat, it gives the illusion of depth. Both the voice-over and the in voice emanate from an imaginary space (whose position varies with the type of projection equipment, configuration of the theater, placement of loudspeakers, and location of the spectator). By contrast, the "out" voice emanates from an illusory space, a decoy. It emerges from the *filmed* body, which is a body of a problematic sort, a false surface and a false depth. It is a container with a false bottom, with no bottom at all, which expels (and therefore makes visible) objects as generously as Buster Keaton's taxis can disgorge regiments. This filmed body is made in the image of the barracks in *Cops* or of the church in *Seven Chances*.

The out voice is a form of pornography in the sense that it fetishizes the *moment* of emergence from the lips (stars' lips, or, in *X.27*, Marlene foregoing lipstick before the firing squad). Similarly, porno films are entirely centered on the spectacle of the orgasm seen from the male side, that is, *the most visible side*. The out voice gives rise to a "material theater" since it is central to every religious metaphor (passage from inside to outside *with* metamorphosis). To grasp the moment of emission of the voice is to grasp the moment when the object *o* separates from the partial object. Pornographic cinema is a denial of this separation, which threatens to reduce the object *a* to unproductive expenditure (waste) and the partial object to its status as orgasm (meat). It attempts to sustain as long as possible the fetish of an orgasm that can only be followed by another orgasm and so on, ad infinitum—the constant obligation of the visible, "the transparent sphere of seminal emission," as Pascal Bruckner and Alain Finkielkraut nicely phase it. There is a pornography of the voice comparable in every way to the pornography of sex (abusive use of interviews, mouths of political leaders, and so on). Clever writers have woven stories around this theme (such as Daniel Schmid's *L'Ombre des anges* [*Angels' Shadow*], in which a prostitute is paid to listen, and *Le Sexe qui parle*, in which a woman's vagina *expresses* its insatiable appetite).

Finally, a "through voice" is a voice that originates within the image but does not emanate from the mouth. Certain types of shot, involving characters filmed from behind, from the side, or in three-quarter view or from behind a piece of furniture, screen, another person, or an obstacle of some sort, cause the voice to be separated from the mouth. The status of the through voice is ambiguous and enigmatic, because its visual stand-in is the body in all its opacity, the expressive body, in whole or in part. It is well known that for reasons of economy, poor filmmakers often film speaking characters from behind rather than in front. Of course, the backs in question are not "real." For Bresson (and

Straub) the whole problem is to shift the effect of frontal filming to some other part of the body, to something round and smooth. Modern filmmaking (since Bresson, in fact) has featured a large number of bodies filmed from behind (sometimes in seductive and provocative ways). Direct *and* indirect, here *and* not here. The latest (and not the least mysterious) of these back shots is of Anne-Marie Miéville in *Comment ça va*.

I will conclude with a word on the famous "Bressonian voice," which both exasperated and enchanted a generation or two of filmgoers. The timbre of the voice has been attributed to Bresson's outspoken hatred of the theater. A smaller number of critics has seen it as Bresson's unavowed homage to a class (the *grande bourgeoisie*) whose children he fetishizes but at the cost of transforming them into young, déclassé aristocrats caught up in Dostoyevskian plots. Both of these views are correct. But one can also say that the Bressonian voice is a voice that requires the *minimum* possible opening of the mouth, that limits, or reserves, the spectacle of emission as much as possible.

In *Le Diable probablement* there is indeed a radical disjunction of voice and mouth. On the one hand, the voice involves the entire body, instruments, and machines (the organ blows, the vacuum cleaner breathes). Bresson's slogan might be: Don't look to see *where the voice is coming from*, don't look for the visible origin of what you hear. To that end, after showing how voices are reduced to noise, he shows how noises begin to constitute voices (all of which Charles hears, except that he is not Joan of Arc, and to him the voices say nothing). On the other hand, he sees the mouth in terms of its function as orifice, or hole, and of the pleasure of its possessor—the mouth as an instrument of the devil's pleasure.

TRANSLATED BY ARTHUR GOLDHAMMER

INTRODUCTORY NOTES

[1] Serge Daney, "Le cru et le cuit (Etat du cinéma français)" (1980), *La Rampe: Cahier critique 1970–82* (Paris: Cahier du cinéma/Gallimard, 1983), p. 157.
[2] Michel Chion, *La Voix au cinéma* (Paris: Cahier du Cinéma, 1993), p. 35.
[3] Ibid., p. 85.

PART IX
Commitment Redux

JACQUES DERRIDA

On the Need to Keep the Word
Commitment
1996

These pages reproduce two of the eight endnotes that conclude the letter Jacques Derrida sent to Claude Lanzmann, in lieu of a full-fledged article, for the special issue of Les Temps modernes *commemorating the fiftieth anniversary of Sartre's journal. Since the core of this letter is a reading of the manifestos in which Sartre first outlined and defended the theoretical foundations of his program of literary commitment, it offers a timely closure for this anthology, which opened with Sartre's 1945 "Presentation" of* Les Temps modernes.

Most of deconstruction's first moves, in France, were both directly and indirectly targeted against the then-dominant ideological and philosophical platform represented by Les Temps modernes. *Thus, Derrida's contribution to this issue was an event in itself—as was the fact that he was not merely invited to contribute to the anniversary issue but his contribution was the issue's lead piece.*

This is the first text that Derrida entirely devotes to a close reading of Sartre; it is also the first, since his May '68 essay "The Ends of Man," in which he takes issue with Sartre by name. Derrida's distance vis à vis Sartre hasn't disappeared; it is even palpable in the way the piece is written, not as a "real" article but as the epistolary outline, the draft of a possible article, of what he would say if he had time to truly write it. His reservations are numerous, and some momentous. It is less a homage than a reacquaintance. Whatever the importance of these reservations, though, they cannot overshadow the fact that in 1996, for reasons of timeliness—a sense of the enduring timeliness of commitment, and of the commitment to timeliness, which might bear Sartre's signature—Derrida thought it time to put an end to what might have looked like a ban on Sartre.

From Jacques Derrida, " 'Il Courait mort: Salut, Salut' ", *Les Temps modernes* (March–April 1996), pp. 40–45.

Note 5. Imperative need to keep the word "commitment," a fine word, still brand-new (pledge, wager and language, "situation," infinite responsibility, critical freedom with respect to all apparatuses, and so on), while perhaps inflecting it in a somewhat different sense: toward where we find ourselves looking to find ourselves—"we," today. Keep or reactivate the forms of that "commitment" by changing its content and strategies. Which is what's going on now, what people are looking for at *T.M.* (*Les Temps modernes*), though in a "style" that often remains foreign to me (but why? it would take books to explain it—unless those books are already available, ready to be read as basically a collection of possible quotations: this isn't what you do to mark an anniversary, any more than you explain to your hosts at an anniversary party the meaning of an anniversary as social code or all the possibilities of aporia that lurk in the discourse of invitation or the experience of hospitality).

For many intellectuals nowadays, the "in" thing is to turn up one's nose at the word and the concept "commitment." Idiotic and suspect. But when I reread certain postwar definitions of "commitment," I often have the feeling that they could *literally* be offered as the most just watchwords to today's "intellectuals." With certain conditions, to be sure. Take any number of passages from the "Presentation," and analyze or isolate certain "blocks." I for one (and no doubt many others today) would be prepared to subscribe to, to inherit, what is stated below concerning infinite responsibility in singularity ("singular and absolute project," "singularity of our era," and so on), but I would also be suspicious of, or want to "date," the reference to "metaphysical choice," the eternalist cliché, and the humanist rhetorical tranquillity which were perhaps the price to be paid for the strategy of a "contemporary review" of the "times" in the wake of the Spanish Civil War, the Occupation, and the Resistance. I would therefore assert the right (in the name of another time, my own, which has pondered other questions and done other work) to understand and, of course, approve statements such as the one below (but one could easily multiply examples at will), and I want to reserve the right to continue to savor it while paring away certain portions with a severe but anxious hand:

> when adversaries clash on the subject of disarming the FFI or the help to be given the Spanish Republicans, it is that metaphysical choice, that singular and absolute project which is at stake. Thus, by taking part in the singularity of our era, we ultimately make contact with the eternal, and it is our task as writers to allow the eternal values implicit in such social or political debate to be perceived.

If there were more space, I would develop two points.

1. If I am embarrassed by the word "eternity" and find it "dated," it is not because I wish to replace it with a historicist logic of the ephemeral. Elsewhere, I have tried to develop arguments about "sur-viving," "survival," spectrality,

and messianicity, which can no longer be contained within these oppositions. As for "metaphysical choice," here again it would take too long to explain or justify my reservations.

2. This brings us, perhaps, to one of the questions, and therefore one of the tasks, that remain before us: Did the history of *Les Temps modernes* follow to the letter the program of this "Presentation," for instance, the passage I just quoted? Did not the journal itself, over the course of half a century, make its own "selection," a selection that will have been its history, its life, and its "times"? No doubt the answer, up to a certain point, is "yes, and no," and there can be no uniform response. One would have to reread everything!

Or, to take another example, how can one not subscribe today to the journal's refusal to become an organic instrument of organic intellectuals (it saw itself solely as an "instrument of inquiry" and stated that "we have no political or social program")? How can one not subscribe to such a statement concerning the political independence of the committed intellectual and even his independence with respect to politics and indeed the political ("concerning the political and social events to come, our journal will take a position in each case. It will not do so *politically*—that is, in the service of a particular party")? The italics are Sartre's. But how can one avoid wanting to change the wording of the passage that immediately follows: "it will attempt to sort out the conception of man which inspires each one of the conflicting theses, and will give its opinion in conformity with the conception it maintains"?

By the same token, to take another example, I think I understand and to a certain extent approve of what Sartre "means" in this context when he attacks "writing so as not to say anything." But I would be tempted to place many conditions on what "not saying anything" might mean. And on the need to respect, in a sense, the *possibility* (one can speak in order "just to speak," "to say nothing," or "just to talk to somebody else," to attest to the possibility of speaking). And I would want to say something about the responsibility to say something in order to put speech and writing and language to the test, to measure them against themselves, that is, against the other, and in the name of what is still called "thought" or "poetry" or "literature" (to say nothing of the awesome question of "meaning" and its limits). What philosophy of language, what practice of literature, what concepts of language, poetry, and literature, what philosophy and what concepts *tout court* are implicit in this ban on "speaking so as not to anything"? And how is this to be reconciled with the subsequent conclusion, where my agreement comes to an abrupt end, right in the middle of a sentence, at the customs station, as it were, right on the border marked by the brief word "and," beyond which I cannot go. I mark the "and" in question with a double underscore:

> I recall, in fact, that in "committed literature," *commitment* must in no way lead
> to a forgetting of *literature*, <u>and</u> that our concern must be to serve literature by

infusing it with new blood, even as we serve the collectivity by attempting to give it the literature it deserves.

Note 6. *Short imaginary interview in response to one of those surveys* . . .

"—It seems clear, sir, from what you've said, that despite your eloquently phrased admiration and frequent expressions of gratitude, you are unwilling to follow Sartre and his *direct heirs* at *T.M.* What might be the reasons for this? Can you give a name to what it is that evidently causes you to hold back, despite the fact that you emphatically and convincingly describe yourself as friendly and sympathetic?

—Uh, literature—but I've explained myself on this point elsewhere . . .

—Really? Only that? Sartre's literature?

—Almost all of it (except perhaps *La Nausée*), but above all literature and the experience of language *for* Sartre. His academic models and his rhetoric. As if he had passed right by everything that matters to me. Yet he is the one who, whatever he may have said about them, introduced me to Bataille and Blanchot and Ponge and other writers nearly fifty years ago. For which I feel enormous gratitude. And then I'm not forgetting that *T.M. also* published excellent literary and poetic texts that had nothing Sartrian about them.

—And what else? The psychoanalysis?

—Uh, yes, and the philosophy—his textbook examples and his rhetoric, I've discussed these things elsewhere. But it was Sartre, whatever he may have said about them, who introduced me to Hegel, and Husserl, and Heidegger and thus to many others nearly fifty years ago. For which I feel immense gratitude. . . . And then I'm not forgetting that *T.M. also* published philosophical texts that had nothing Sartrian about them. . . ."

TRANSLATED BY ARTHUR GOLDHAMMER

PIERRE BOURDIEU

Commitment and Autonomy
1992

In What Is Literature? *Sartre enjoined writers to leave the ivory tower.* "*To be sure, the book is the noblest, the most ancient of forms; to be sure, we will always return to it. But there is a* literary *art of radio, film, editorial work, and reporting. There is no need to popularize.*" *He continued,* "*It is improper for us to stoop in order to please. . . . I do not think that we shall ever have the full use of the 'mass media,' but it would be a fine thing to begin conquering it for our successors*"[1]

Pierre Bourdieu, who can be counted, at least in the purely generational sense of the word, as one of those successors, doesn't look at the legacy of Sartre's program with the gratitude Sartre anticipated: improper or not, some stooping occurred, encouraged by the desire to break away from the ivory tower, and its effects have been infinitely more damaging than Sartre's triumphalist optimism could have imagined. It officialized the reign of the heteronomous intellectual (the equivalent, for a society regulated by the media and the market, of the Marxian organic intellectual), whose omnipotent servility has ruled the autonomous intellectual out of the cultural field. In the following pages, which form the conclusion of a book devoted to the nineteenth-century genesis of this field, Bourdieu foregrounds the threat of being dismantled the field is now facing, a century after its implementation: any claim to autonomy in the field of cultural production is contested by the growing interpenetration between culture (arts and science as well) and the market.

This is a call to arms, a call addressed to cultural producers to retake control and ownership of their instruments of production and circulation. Retreat is no longer possible: Bourdieu no longer believes (as Julien Gracq still did in the late 1940s) in the accessibility of the ivory tower. The only way out is a way ahead: cultural producers must reclaim the ownership of

Pierre Bourdieu, "For a Corporatism of the Universal," in *The Rules of Art: Genesis and Structure of the Literary Field*, trans. Susan Emanuel (Stanford: Stanford University Press, 1995), pp. 340–48, from "Pour un corporatisme de l'universel," in *Les Règles de l'art: Genèse et structure du champ littéraire* (Paris: Seuil, 1992), pp. 461–72.

their instruments of production and circulation. This means not to turn off the TV, or to decline appearing on it, but only to address it on one's own terms—as Bourdieu himself did in 1996 when he devoted broadcasts to virulent denunciations of the media's grip on culture and politics. It was a solution, by the way, that is not radically different from the one Sartre advocated in 1946.

Intellectuals are paradoxical beings who cannot be thought of as such as long as they are apprehended through the obligatory alternative between autonomy and commitment, between pure culture and politics. This is because intellectuals are constituted, historically, in and through their overcoming of that opposition: writers, artists and scholars asserted themselves for the first time as intellectuals, at the time of the Dreyfus Affair, when they intervened in political life *as intellectuals,* meaning with a specific authority founded on their belonging to the relatively autonomous world of art, science, and literature, and on all the values associated with that autonomy—disinterestedness, expertise, and so on.

Intellectuals are two-dimensional figures who do not exist and subsist as such unless (and only unless) they are invested with a specific authority, conferred by the autonomous intellectual world (meaning independent from religious, political or economic power) whose specific laws they respect, and unless (and only unless) they engage this specific authority in political struggles. Far from there existing, as is customarily believed, an antinomy between the search for autonomy (which characterizes the art, science, or literature we call "pure") and the search for political efficacy, it is by increasing their autonomy (and thereby, among other things, their freedom to criticize the prevailing powers) that intellectuals can increase the effectiveness of a political action whose ends and means have their origin in the specific logic of the fields of cultural production.

In order to be in a position to define what the major directions of a collective action by intellectuals might be, it is necessary and sufficient to repudiate the tired alternative between pure art and engaged art which we all have in our minds, and which periodically arises in literary debates. But it is formidably difficult to banish the forms of thought we apply to ourselves when we take ourselves as objects of thought. This is why, before stating these directions and in order to be able to do so, we must try to make as explicit as possible the unconscious deposited in each intellectual by the very history of which intellectuals are the products. Against the genesis amnesia, which is the basis of all forms of the transcendental illusion, there is no more effective antidote than the reconstruction of the forgotten or repressed history perpetuated in these apparently ahistorical forms of thought structuring our perception of the world and of ourselves.

This is an extraordinarily repetitive history, since its constant change disguises a pendulum swing between two possible attitudes toward politics, either commitment or retreat (at least this was so until this opposition was overcome with Zola and the Dreyfusards). The "engagement" of "philosophes" which Voltaire in 1765, in the article in the *Philosophical Dictionary* called "The man of letters," contrasts with the scholastic obscurantism of decadent universities and academies, "where things are only half said," has a successor in the participation by "men of letters" in the French Revolution—even though, as Robert Darnton has shown, "literary bohemia" seized the opportunity of the revolutionary "disorders" to take revenge on the most consecrated of the followers of the philosophes.

In the postrevolutionary period of restoration, "men of letters," being held responsible not only for the current of revolutionary ideas—through the role of *opinion-makers* conferred on them by the proliferation of newspapers in the first phase of the revolution—but also for the excesses of the Terror, are regarded with mistrust and even contempt by the young generation of the 1820s; they are mistrusted most especially by the Romantics who, in the first phase of the movement, challenge and reject the pretension of the "philosophe" to intervene in political life and to propose a rational vision of historical evolution. But, once the autonomy of the intellectual field finds itself threatened by the reactionary politics of the Restoration, the Romantic poets, led to assert their desire for autonomy in a rehabilitation of feeling and religious sensibility against Reason and the criticism of dogma, hasten to claim, as do Michelet and Saint-Simon, freedom for the writer and the scholar, and to assume in fact the prophetic function which was that of the eighteenth-century philosopher.

But in a new swing of the pendulum, the populist Romanticism which seems to have carried away virtually all the writers in the period before the 1848 Revolution does not survive the failure of the movement and the installation of the Second Empire: the collapse of illusions which I will expressly call "forty-eighter" (to evoke the analogy with the illusions of 1968, whose collapse still haunts our present day) leads to that extraordinary disenchantment, so vigorously evoked by Flaubert in *Sentimental Education*, which provides a favorable terrain for a new assertion of intellectuals' autonomy, this time radically elitist. The defenders of art for art's sake, like Flaubert and Théophile Gautier, assert the autonomy of the artist by opposing "social art" and the "literary bohemia" just as much as they oppose a bourgeois art subordinated in matters of art (and also the art of living) to the norms of the bourgeois clientele. They oppose this newborn power which is the cultural industry by refusing the servitude of "industrial literature" (except as an alimentary substitute for a private income, as with Gautier and Nerval). Not admitting any other judgment than that of their peers, they assert the closing in on itself of the literary field, but also the writer's renunciation of leaving his ivory tower to exercise any form of power whatsoever (thereby making a break with the poet as visionary [*vates*] like Hugo or the prophet-scholar like Michelet).

By an apparent paradox, it is only at the end of the century, at a time when the literary field, the artistic field, and the scientific field arrive at autonomy that the most autonomous agents of these autonomous fields intervene in the political field as intellectuals—and not as cultural producers converted into politicians, like Guizot or Lamartine—that is, with an authority founded on the autonomy of the field and all the values associated with it: ethical purity, specific expertise, and so on. In a concrete fashion, intrinsically artistic or scientific autonomy is asserted in political acts like Zola's *J'accuse* and the petitions designed to support it. These interventions of a new kind tend to maximize the two dimensions constitutive of the identity of the intellectual who is invented through them—"purity" and "engagement"—giving birth to a *politics of purity* that is the perfect antithesis of the reason of state. They imply in effect the assertion of the right to transgress the most sacred values of the collectivity— patriotic values, for example, with the support given to Zola's defamatory article against the army, or much later, during the Algerian war, the call for support for the enemy—in the name of values transcending those of citizenship or, if you will, in the name of a particular form of ethical and scientific universalism which can serve as foundation not only for a sort of moral magisterium but also for a collective mobilization to fight to promote these values.

It would suffice to add to this overview of the major stages in the genesis of the figure of the intellectual some indications of the cultural policy of the 1848 Republic or that of the Commune in order to have an almost complete picture of the possible relations between cultural producers and power such as they might be observed either in the history of a single country, or in the political space of European states today. History carries an important lesson: we are in a game in which all the moves made today, wherever, have already been made— from the rejection of politics and the return to the religious, to the resistance to actions by a political power hostile to intellectual things, via the revolt against the grip of the media, or the disabused abandonment of revolutionary utopias.

But the fact of finding oneself thus at "endgame" does not necessarily lead to disenchantment. It is clear in effect that the intellectual (or, better, the autonomous fields that make the intellectual possible) is not instituted once and for all with Zola, and that the holders of cultural capital may always "regress," as a result of a disintegration of that unstable combination which defines the intellectual, toward one or another of apparently exclusive positions, either toward the role of "pure" writer, artist or scholar, or toward the role of political actor, journalist, politician, expert. Moreover, contrary to what the naively Hegelian vision of intellectual history might have us believe, the claim of autonomy inscribed in the very existence of the field of cultural production must reckon with obstacles and powers that are ceaselessly renewed, whether we are dealing with external powers such as those of the Church, the state and great economic enterprises, or internal powers, and in particular those which accompany control of the specific instruments of production and distribution (press, publishing, radio, television).

This is one of the reasons—along with the differences in national histories—why the *variations* among countries in the state of relations now and in the past between the intellectual field and political power mask the *constants*, which are nevertheless more substantial and are the real foundation of the possible unity of intellectuals of all countries. The same *intention of autonomy* can in effect be expressed in opposite stances (secular in one case, religious in another) according to the structure and the history of the powers against which it must assert itself. Intellectuals of different countries must be fully conscious of this mechanism if they want to avoid letting themselves be divided by conjunctural and epiphenomenal oppositions that stem from the fact that the same will to emancipation runs up against different obstacles. Here I could take the example of the most visible French philosophers and German philosophers [including Michel Foucault and Jürgen Habermas] who, since they pit the same concern for autonomy against contrasting historical traditions, seem to oppose each other with apparently inverse relations regarding truth and reason. But I could equally well take the example of an issue like public opinion polls, which some in the West take as particularly subtle instruments of domination, whereas to others, in the countries of Eastern Europe, they appear as the conquest of liberty.

In order to understand and master the oppositions that are in danger of dividing them, intellectuals of different European countries can only overcome the oppositions that threaten to divide them if they have a vivid awareness of the structures and the national histories of the powers they must stand up to in order to exist as intellectuals. They must, for example, know how to recognize in the statements of any one of their foreign colleagues (in particular when these statements seem disconcerting or shocking) the effects of historical and geographical distance from the experience of political despotism such as Nazism or Stalinism, or from ambiguous political movements like the student revolts of 1968, or, where internal powers are concerned, the effects of the present and past experience of intellectual worlds very unequally subject to open or latent censorship by politics or economics, the university or the academy, and so on.

When we speak as intellectuals, that is, with the ambition to be universal, it is always, at any moment, the historical unconscious inscribed in the experience of a singular intellectual field which speaks through our mouths. I think that we only have a chance of achieving real communication when we objectify and master the various kinds of historical unconscious separating us, meaning the specific histories of intellectual universes which have produced our categories of perception and thought.

I want to come now to an exposition of the particular reasons why it is espe-

cially urgent today that intellectuals mobilize and create a veritable *Internationale of intellectuals* committed to defending the autonomy of the universes of
cultural production or, to parody a language now out of fashion, *the ownership
by cultural producers of their instruments of production and circulation* (and hence
of evaluation and consecration). I do not think I am succumbing to an apoca-
lyptic vision of the state of the field of cultural production by saying that this
autonomy is very severely threatened or, more precisely, that a threat of a totally new sort today hangs over its functioning; and that artists, writers, and
scholars are more and more completely excluded from public debate, both because they are less inclined to intervene in it and because the possibility of an
effective intervention is less and less frequently offered to them.

The threats to autonomy result from the increasing interpenetration between
the world of art and the world of money. I am thinking of new forms of sponsorship, of new alliances being established between certain economic enterprises (often the most modernizing, as in Germany, with Daimler-Benz and
the banks) and cultural producers; I am thinking, too, of the more and more
frequent recourse of university research to sponsorship, and of the creation of
educational institutions directly subordinated to business (as with the *Tech-
nologiezentren* in Germany or the business schools in France). But the grip or
empire of the economy over artistic or scientific research is also exercised inside
the field itself, through the control of the means of cultural production and
distribution, and even of the instances of consecration. Producers attached to
the major cultural bureaucracies (newspapers, radio, television) are increasingly forced to accept and adopt norms and constraints linked to the requirements of the market and, especially, to pressure exerted more or less strongly
and directly by advertisers; and they tend more or less unconsciously to constitute as a universal measure of intellectual accomplishment those forms of intellectual activity to which they are condemned by their conditions of work (I am
thinking, for example, of *fast writing* and *fast reading*, which are often the rule
in journalistic production and criticism). One could ask whether the division
into two markets characteristic of the fields of cultural production since the
middle of the nineteenth century, with on one side the narrow field of producers for producers, and on the other side the field of mass production and "industrial literature," is not now threatening to disappear, since the logic of
commercial production tends more and more to assert itself over avant-garde
production (notably, in the case of literature, through the constraints of the
book market).

It would be necessary to analyze the new forms of stranglehold and dependence, like the ones introduced by sponsorship, and against which the "beneficiaries" have not yet developed appropriate systems of defense, since they are
not fully aware of all their effects; it would also be necessary to analyze the
constraints imposed by state sponsorship—even though it seems to escape the
direct pressures of the market—whether through the recognition it grants

spontaneously to those who recognize it because they need it in order to obtain a form of recognition they cannot get by their work alone, or whether, more subtly, through the mechanism of commissions and committees—places of negative co-optation which often result in a thorough standardization of the avant-garde, either scientific or artistic.

The exclusion from public debate of artists, writers, and scholars is the result of the conjoined impact of several factors: some grow out of the internal evolution of cultural production—like the increasingly narrow specialization that leads researchers to give up the wider ambitions of the intellectual in earlier days—whereas others are the result of the increasingly strong grip of a technocracy that, with the often-unconscious complicity of journalists (themselves caught in the game of competition), puts citizens on extended intellectual vacation by favoring "organized irresponsibility," in the words of Ulrich Beck; it finds an immediate ally in a technocracy of communication—more and more present, via the media, in the universe of cultural production. One would have to develop, for example, the analysis of the production and reproduction of technocratic power or, better, *epistemocratic* power, in order to understand the almost unconditional delegation, founded on the social authority of educational institutions, which the great majority of citizens grant, on the most vital issues, to the "state nobility" (the best example being the almost unlimited confidence which those who have been called "nucleocrats" enjoy, notably in France).

With less and less to communicate (in fact and by right) the greater their success, measured by the size of the audience they address, those who control access to the instruments of communication tend to spread the emptiness of media droning inside the apparatuses of communication, and tend increasingly to impose superficial and artificial problems born of simple competition for the biggest audience on to the political field as well as the fields of cultural production. The deepest forces of inertia of the social world—not to mention economic powers that, especially through advertising, exercise a direct hold on the written and spoken press—can thus impose a domination all the more visible in that it is accomplished only via complex networks of reciprocal dependence, like the *censorship* exercised through the intersection between mutual controls of competition on the one hand, and the interiorized controls of self-censorship on the other.

These new masters of thoughtless thought monopolize public debate to the detriment of professionals of politics (parliamentary legislators, trade union leaders, and so on); and also to the detriment of intellectuals, who are subject, even within their own universe, to sorts of *specific power plays* such as surveys aiming to produce manipulated classifications, or the "top-ten" lists newspapers publish on anniversary occasions, and so forth, or even publicity campaigns aiming to discredit productions destined for the narrow (and long-term) market at the expense of the products of wide circulation and short cycle which new producers launch on to the market.

It has been shown that the successful political demonstration is the one that manages to make itself visible in the papers and especially on television, and hence to impress upon journalists (who may contribute to its success) the idea that it is successful—with the most sophisticated forms of demonstration being conceived and produced, sometimes with the help of communications advisers, with an eye on the journalists who must take notice of them.[1] In the same way, an ever-larger part of cultural production—when it is not coming from people who, since they work in the media, are guaranteed the support of the media—is predefined, down to date of appearance, title, format and size, content, and style—to catch the attention of journalists who will make it exist by speaking about it.

Commercial literature has not just come into existence recently; nor is it new that the necessities of commerce make themselves felt at the heart of the cultural field. But the grip of the holders of power over the instruments of circulation—and of consecration—has undoubtedly never been as wide and as deep as it is today—and the boundary has never been as blurred between the experimental work and the *best-seller*. This blurring of boundaries to which so-called "media-oriented" producers are spontaneously inclined (as shown by the fact that the journalistic lists of hits always juxtapose the most autonomous and the most heteronomous producers) constitutes the worst threat to the autonomy of cultural production. The heteronomous producer, whom the Italians magnificently call *tuttologo*, is the Trojan horse by means of which all forms of social stranglehold—that of the market, of fashion, of the state, of politics, of journalism—are imported into the field of cultural production. The basis on which one can condemn these *doxosophes*, as Plato called them, is implicit in the idea that the specific force of the intellectual, even in politics, can rely only on the autonomy conferred by the capacity to respond to the internal requirements of the field. Zhdanovism, which flourishes among mediocre or failed writers and artists, is only one piece of evidence among others that heteronomy arrives in a field through the producers who are the least capable of succeeding according to the norms it imposes.

The anarchic order reigning in an intellectual field that has achieved a high degree of autonomy is always fragile and threatened, to the extent that it constitutes a challenge to the laws of the ordinary economic world and to the rules of common sense. It is dangerous for it to depend on just the heroism of a few. It is not virtue that can found a free intellectual order: it is a free intellectual order that can found intellectual virtue.

The paradoxical and apparently contradictory nature of the intellectual means that any political action aiming to reinforce the political efficacy of intellectuals' enterprises is fated to give itself an apparently contradictory slogan. On the one hand, the aim is to reinforce autonomy, notably by reinforcing the separation from heteronomous producers and by fighting to guarantee cultural producers the economic and social conditions of autonomy in relation to all forms of power, not excluding those of state bureaucracies (and, first of all, in respect to the publication and evaluation of the products of intellectual activity). On the other hand, it must tear cultural producers away from the temptation to remain in their ivory tower, and encourage them to fight, if only to guarantee themselves the power over the instruments of production and consecration and, by involving themselves in their own times, to assert the values associated with their autonomy.

This fight must be *collective* because the effectiveness of the powers exercised over them results in large part from the fact that those intellectuals who confront them are dispersed and in competition with each other—and also because efforts at mobilization will always be suspect, and doomed to failure, so long as they can be suspected of being used as part of struggles for leadership by an intellectual or a group of intellectuals. Cultural producers will not find again a place of their own in the social world unless, sacrificing once and for all the myth of the "organic intellectual" (without falling into the complementary mythology of the mandarin withdrawn from everything), they agree to work collectively for the defense of their own interests. This should lead them to assert themselves as an international power of criticism and watchfulness, or even of proposals, in the face of the technocrats, or—with an ambition both more lofty and more realistic, and hence limited to their own sphere—to get involved in rational action to defend the economic and social conditions of the autonomy of these socially privileged universes in which the material and intellectual instruments of what we call Reason are produced and reproduced. This *Realpolitik of reason* will undoubtedly be suspected of corporatism. But it will be part of its task to prove, by the ends to which it puts the sorely won means of its autonomy, that it is a corporatism of the universal.

TRANSLATED BY SUSAN EMANUEL

INTRODUCTORY NOTE

[1] Jean-Paul Sartre, "What Is Literature?", in *"What Is Literature?" and Other Essays*, translated by Bernard Frechtman (Cambridge, Mass.: Harvard University Press, 1988), pp. 216, 217, 218.

NOTE

[1] P. Champagne, *Faire l'opinion: Le nouveau jeu politique* (Paris: Minuit, 1990).